THE

BOOK OF ENOCH

TRANSLATED FROM

PROFESSOR DILLMANN'S ETHIOPIC TEXT

EMENDED AND REVISED IN ACCORDANCE WITH HITHERTO UNCOLLATED ETHIOPIC MSS. AND WITH THE GIZEH AND OTHER GREEK AND LATIN FRAGMENTS WHICH ARE HERE PUBLISHED IN FULL

EDITED

WITH INTRODUCTION, NOTES, APPENDICES, AND INDICES

BY

R. H. CHARLES, M.A.

TRINITY COLLEGE, DUBLIN, AND EXETER COLLEGE, OXFORD

1893

ISBN 978-1-60386-424-4

PREFACE

It is unnecessary to apologize for the appearance of this book, as some such work has long been a desideratum to scholars. A knowledge of Enoch is indispensable to New Testament students.

It would be best perhaps, at the outset, to mention briefly the features in which this edition differs from previous editions of Enoch.

I. First, the Translation is made, in the main, from a British Museum MS. which is incomparably better than those on which Professor Dillmann's Ethiopic text is based. But as this MS., which I designate G, is still unpublished, I have followed Dillmann's text, and, in every instance in which I have deviated from it in deference to G or other British Museum MSS., I have given in my Critical Notes the Ethiopic reading adopted, and that as a rule as it stands in the MS. followed, though it may be vicious alike in orthography and syntax. These instances are in all about six hundred. It will be remarked that on p. 4 they are said to be three hundred and twenty-two. The explanation of this discrepancy is to be found in the fact that the bulk of this book was already in type when the Gizeh MS. was published by M. Bouriant, and that I have allowed the Introduction to remain as it already stood before the publication of this Greek fragment. But as the examination of this fragment speedily made it clear that I had under-estimated the value of these new Ethiopic

MSS., I was obliged to follow their authority in three hundred additional instances against Dillmann's text. However, as I could introduce only a limited number of these new readings into the Critical Notes already in type, the reader will not unfrequently have to consult Appendix C for the text followed in the Translation in the earlier chapters. In addition to the new readings incorporated in the Translation, a number of others are proposed in Appendices C, D, and E. These are preceded by the readings they are intended to displace, and are always printed in italics. I might add that the Gizeh fragment, which, through the kindness of the Delegates of the Press, is added on pp. 326–370, will be found to be free from the serious blemishes of M. Bouriant's edition.

To the kindness of the Rev. M. R. James, King's College, Cambridge, I owe the Latin fragment in Appendix E. This fragment was lately discovered by Mr. James in the British Museum. It will be seen that it helps to emend the Ethiopic text in a few points.

II. Of late years the criticism of Enoch has reached certain assured results. From these duly given and substantiated a fresh departure in criticism is made. The so-called *Grundschrift* is shown to proceed from at least four different authors. The book thus becomes intelligible, and much light is thereby thrown on the internal history, and thought-developement of the Jews in the two centuries preceding the Christian era. The present writer is convinced that until this plurality of authorship is recognized, no true or adequate interpretation of Enoch is possible. In the book of Enoch we have a typical example of the Oriental method of editing. Less important books were constantly rescued from oblivion by incorporation in larger books. Plagiarism and literary property were ideas alike foreign to the Palestinian consciousness of the time. As the name of David attracted different collections of the Psalms, and the name of Solomon successive collections of proverbs, so the name of Enoch attracted various treatments of celestial and terrestrial phenomena as well as of the problem of the suffering righteous.

III. The history of important conceptions which appear frequently in Enoch, such as that of Hades, the Resurrection, the Messiah, &c., is traced but briefly, as the present writer hopes to issue later an independent work on the Eschatology of pre-Christian Apocryphal and Apocalyptic literature.

IV. An attempt is made to give some account of the influence of Enoch on subsequent literature, especially that of the New Testament.

The Slavonic Enoch, which is mentioned occasionally in the following pages, I hope to publish shortly. This Apocryph, which is critically revised and translated by my friend Mr. Morfill, the Reader in Russian and the other Slavonic Languages, will be furnished with an Introduction and Notes.

The many changes introduced into the text when already in type, as well as the incorporation of much fresh material, have made, I fear, the presence of occasional errors inevitable. I shall be grateful for any corrections.

My best thanks are due to Dr. Sanday, to whom I am under manifold obligations, and in connexion with whose Seminar this work was primarily undertaken; to Dr. Neubauer, whom I have consulted with advantage in season and out of season: to Professor Margoliouth, for his courteous and ever-ready help in questions affecting the Ethiopic text: and finally and chiefly to my wife, whose constant sympathy and unwearied labour in the verification of references and the formation of indices have materially lightened the burthen of my work.

R. H. CHARLES.

APRIL, 1893

CONTENTS

PAGE

party reflected in the books of Enoch (p. 30). The varying conceptions of the Messiah in these books corresponding to the historical events of the times (pp. 30, 31). The teaching of the Similitudes stands in clear contrast with xci–civ (p. 32). Part V (p. 32), the Book of Celestial Physics lxxii–lxxviii, lxxxii, lxxix; date uncertain. Part VI (pp. 32, 33), Noachian and other interpolations; incorporated in the main before the Christian era. § 11. The Influence of Enoch on Jewish Literature—the *Book of Jubilees*, the *Apocalypse of Baruch*, *IV. Ezra*, *Testaments of the Twelve Patriarchs* (pp. 33–38). The Influence of Enoch on Patristic Literature—the *Epistle of Barnabas*, *Justin Martyr*, *Irenaeus*, *Athenagoras*, *Tertullian*, *Clemens Alex.*, *Origen*, *Anatolius*, *Hilary*, *Chrysostom*, *Jerome*, *Augustine*, *Apostolic Constitutions*, *Syncellus* (pp. 38–41). Influence of Enoch on the New Testament—the General Epistles, *Book of Revelation*, *Pauline Epistles*, *Epistle to the Hebrews*, *Acts of the Apostles*, *Gospels* (pp. 41–49). On New Testament doctrine of the Messianic Kingdom, the Messiah, Sheol and the Resurrection, Demonology (pp. 50–53).

THE BOOK OF ENOCH.—SPECIAL INTRODUCTIONS, TRANSLATION, CRITICAL AND EXEGETICAL NOTES 55–308

SECTION I (chapters i–xxxvi) 55–105

INTRODUCTION.—A. *Critical Structure.* B. *Relation of this Section to* (*a*) lxxii–lxxxii; (*b*) lxxxiii–xc; (*c*) xci–civ. C. *Its Date.* D. *The Problem and its Solution* . 55–57

TRANSLATION AND CRITICAL AND EXEGETICAL NOTES . 57–105

SECTION II.—THE SIMILITUDES (chapters xxxvii–lxxi) . . 106–186

INTRODUCTION.—A. *Critical Structure.* B. *Relation of* xxxvii–lxxi *to the rest of the book.* C. *Date.* D. *The Problem and its Solution* 106–109

TRANSLATION AND CRITICAL AND EXEGETICAL NOTES . 110–186

SECTION III.—THE BOOK OF CELESTIAL PHYSICS (chapters lxxii–lxxxii) 187–219

INTRODUCTION.—A. *Its Critical Structure and Object.* B. *Its Independence of* i–xxxvi. C. *Its Calendar and the Knowledge therein implied* 187–191

TRANSLATION AND CRITICAL AND EXEGETICAL NOTES . 191–219

SECTION IV.—THE DREAM-VISIONS (chapters lxxxiii–xc) . 220–259

INTRODUCTION.—A. *Critical Structure.* B. *Relation of this Section to* (*a*) i–xxxvi; (*b*) xci–civ. C. *The Date.* D. *The Problem and its Solution* 220–223

TRANSLATION AND CRITICAL AND EXEGETICAL NOTES . 223–259

CONTRACTIONS

Dln.	= Dillmann.
A, B, C, &c.	refer to Ethiopic MSS. See p. 2.
Syn. Gk.	= the Greek fragments preserved in Syncellus.
Giz. Gk.	= the Gizeh Greek fragment.

The remaining contractions are for the most part familiar.

ERRATA

Page 5, line 10 from top, *for* B.C. *read* A.D.
„ 38, „ 13 „ *for* three times and twice *read* twice and once
„ 38, „ 17, 18 „ *erase* Ep. Barn. xvi. 6. Cf. En. xci. 13.
„ 66, „ 8 „ *for* eyebrows *read* eyelids
„ 66, „ 21 „ *for* Gk. τὸ στίλβειν *read* Giz. Gk. στίβεις
„ 70, „ 16 „ *for* which *read* of those who
„ 71, „ 24 „ *for* ሰኑፍሳት *read* ሰንፍሳት
„ 73, *erase* Crit. Note on x. 7.
„ 74, „ 25 „ *for* ኵሎሙ *read* ዙሎሙ
„ 76, „ 4 from bottom, *for* Papius *read* Papias
„ 80, „ 6 from top, *remove comma after* forth
„ 81, „ 6 „ *for* the walls of the house *read* its walls
„ 81, „ 23 „ *for* thereon *read* (thereon)
„ 84, last line, *for* Gk. *read* Syn. Gk.
„ 92, line 21 from top, *for* ወኪ *read* ወእ
„ 98, „ 16 „ *for* ኵ (*twice*) *read* ዙ (*twice*)
„ 98, „ 18 „ *for* „ „ *read* „ „
„ 99, „ 17 „ *for* then *read* there
„ 101, „ 14 „ *for* then *read* and thence
„ 101, „ 23 „ *for* then *read* there
„ 104, „ 16 „ *for* one of these blows *read* they blow
„ 105, „ 15 „ *for* ኵ *read* ዙ
„ 116, „ 22 „ *before* The original *add* Are beautifully resplendent.
„ 120, „ 19 „ *for* Fanuel *read* Rufael
„ 120, „ 19 „ *for* ፋኑኤል *read* ሩፋኤል. (In this instance the reading of G M is corrupt.)
„ 121, „ 21 „ *for* G M *read* G
„ 124, „ 29–30 „ *for* Taken over into the Interpolations *read* from whence it was borrowed: cf. also
„ 180, „ 29 „ *for* ገጸው *read* ጸገው
„ 248, *erase* exegetical note on xc. 3.
„ 286, last line, *for* land *read* law

GENERAL INTRODUCTION

§ 1. Short Account of the Book.

In Gen. v. 24 it is said of Enoch that he walked with God. This expression was taken in later times to mean not only that he led a godly life, but also that he was the recipient of superhuman knowledge. It was not unnatural, therefore, that an Apocalyptic literature began to circulate under his name in the centuries when such literature was rife. In the present book, translated from the Ethiopic, we have large fragments of such a literature, proceeding from a variety of authors. Additional portions of this literature may be discovered in the coming years. Only recently two Slavonic MSS., which belong to this literature, but are quite independent of the present book, have been printed in Russia.

The present book from the Ethiopic belongs to the second and first centuries B.C. All the writers of the New Testament were familiar with it, and were more or less influenced by it in thought and diction[1]. It is quoted as a genuine production of Enoch by S. Jude, and as Scripture by S. Barnabas. The authors of the Book of Jubilees, the Apocalypse of Baruch and IV Ezra, laid it under contribution. With the earlier Fathers and Apologists it had all the weight of a canonical book, but towards the close of the third and the beginning of the fourth centuries it began to be discredited, and finally fell under the ban of the

[1] For a full account of its influence on earlier Jewish and Christian literature, see the closing Chapter of this Introduction.

Church. Almost the latest reference to it in the Early Church is made by George Syncellus in his Chronography about 800 A.D., who has preserved for us some long passages in Greek. The book was then lost sight of till 1773, when an Ethiopic version of it was found in Abyssinia by Bruce. This traveller brought home three copies of it, two old MSS. and a transcript from one of them. From one of these Laurence made the first modern translation of Enoch in 1821.

§ 2. The Ethiopic MSS.

There are seventeen MSS. of this book in Europe. Of these one is in Paris, a transcript of B in the Bodleian. Another is in the Vatican Library, but of this MS. I know nothing further. The remaining fifteen are designated by the letters A B C D, &c. Of these Laurence based his text on A, and Dln. on A B C D E. For a description of these five MSS. see Dln.'s *Liber Henoch, Aethiopice, Annotat.* pp. 1, 2.

Of the remaining MSS., all of which are in the British Museum, two were obtained by purchase, F, L in 1861 and 1862, and the rest fell into the hands of the expedition against King Theodore at Magdala.

These MSS. with their Nos. in the British Museum Catalogue are as follows:

F. Add. 24185	19th cent.	Divided into 106 chs.
G. Orient. 485	Beginning of 16th cent.	Without usual division and numbering of chs.
G[1]. „	„	Consists only of xcvii. 6b–cviii. 10. See Crit. Note on xci. 6.
H. Orient. 484	18th cent.	Divided into 108 chs.
I. „ 486	„	Chs. i–lx. 12a wanting.
K. „ 490	„	Divided into 107 chs.
L. Add. 24990	„	
M. Orient. 491	„	Without usual numbering and division into chs.
N. „ 492	„	Divided into 87 chs.
O. „ 499	„	Divided into 106 chs.

I collated these MSS. with Dln.'s Ethiopic text on more than three hundred passages. The result of this test was so favourable to G and G^1 that I made a complete collation of these MSS. and have given the bulk of their variants in my critical notes.

The superiority of G to all other MSS. will be evident from the following seventeen passages. In these I have adopted a different text from Dln. in accordance with the Ethiopic MSS. which were supported by the independent testimony of the Greek of S. Jude 15, of the Greek fragments of Enoch in G. Syncellus, and of the Greek fragment of Enoch published by Mai in Patrum Nova Bibliotheca, vol. ii. These passages and the MSS. that support the reading adopted are—

Enoch i.	9	G M	supported by S. Jude 15.		
vi.	3	G M	„	Greek of Syncellus.	
	5	G M	„	„	„
viii.	3	G K M	„	„	„
ix.	4	G M	„	„	„
	8	G M	„	„	„
x.	3	G M	„	„	„
	10	G M	„	„	„
	10	G K M	„	„	„
	11	F G H L	„	„	„
xv.	8	G	„	„	„
	11	G	„	„	„
	12	M	„	„	„
xvi.	1	E N	„	„	„
		A E F G H K L M N O		„	„
lxxxix.	42	G	„	„	fragment of Mai.
	45	D	„	„	„

For the evidence of the above MSS. on these passages see Crit. Notes in loc. It will be remarked that G agrees fourteen times out of the seventeen with the Gk., and M eleven times, K three times, E F H L N twice, and A D O once each. Hence it would appear that the five MSS. A B C D E on which Dln.'s text is founded and in a somewhat less degree F H I K L N O rest on a recension which did not affect G at all and was probably subsequent to it and only partially affected M. This probable conclusion becomes a certainty when we examine the rest of the book. The following list of passages in which we have departed from Dln.'s text, in deference to the better readings of the British Museum MSS., shows that G represents an ancient unrevised text, and that G^1 M are nearly related to G; but that all the rest belong more or less closely to another type of text, of which we may regard Dln.'s text as a partially adequate representation. This latter type of text gives an inferior meaning, frequently when opposed to G alone, and nearly always when opposed to GM, G G^1, or G G^1M, or these supported by one, two, or more of the other MSS. Thus I have followed against Dln.

G alone	102	times.
G with one or more of CDEFHKLNO	7	"
G M	126	"
G M with one or more of ABCDEFHIKLNO	38	"
G G^1	12	"
G G^1 with EN and ILO	2	"
G G^1 M	19	"
G^1 M	2	"
M alone or with Greek or with other MSS.	11	"
D with Greek	1	"
E N with Greek	1	"
F I	1	"
	322	

Thus in 322 instances I have followed the above MSS. against Dln. In every instance, however, I have also given Dln.'s text with its translation that the reader may form his own judgment.

Before passing from this subject I will give a few passages to show how weakly at times Dln.'s text is supported even by inferior MSS. See Crit. Notes on xxxix. 7 where G M and seven other MSS. are against him; liii. 7 where G M and nine other MSS.; lxvii. 3 where G M and eight other MSS.; lxvii. 13 where G M and all MSS. but B C; xc. 18 where

G M and nine MSS.; xc. 19 where G M and eight MSS.; xciii. 10 where G M and seven MSS.

I will adduce one more point under this head. On xcviii. 2 all MSS. but G G^1 M agree in giving a vox nulla. The agreement of these later MSS. in presenting a counterfeit word points either to a recension or to the same ancestry.

§ 3. Greek Version.

Only fragments of this version have come down to us preserved in the chronography of George Syncellus (about 800 B.C.). These are vi–ix. 4; viii. 4–x. 14; xv. 8–xvi. 1; and in a Vatican MS. (Cod. Gr. 1809) published by Mai in the Patrum Nova Bibliotheca, vol. ii. Only lxxxix. 42–49 is found in this MS. I have printed these fragments in parallel columns with the translation from the Ethiopic.

The Greek version has, no doubt, undergone corruption in the process of transmission; yet in many respects it presents a more faithful text than the Ethiopic. This we might infer to some extent from what has gone before, and the following instances where it undoubtedly preserves the truer reading will more than confirm this view:—vi. 6; viii. 1; ix. 6, 10; x. 14; xv. 11; lxxxix. 45, 48. In these instances we have followed the Greek version against all the Ethiopic MSS. The Greek version is by no means free from corruptions.

As the Greek fragment which has lately been discovered at Cairo has not yet been published, I have not been able to avail myself of it.

§ 4. Emendations.

The text presented by the best MSS. is still far from perfect, and contains many primitive errors. Some of these have been emended successfully by Dln. and Hallévi. I have introduced into the text emendations of Dln. in the following passages:—lvi. 7; lxii. 2; xc. 38; and emendations of Hallévi in lxvii. 13; lxxvii. 1–3; ci. 4, 9; and emendations of my own in xvi. 1; xli. 9; xlvi. 2; lx. 6, 19, 24; lxiii. 7;

lxxvi. 6, 10; xc. 20, 21. For the reasons see Crit. Notes in loc.

There are still many passages which are undoubtedly corrupt. On many of them I have given suggestions of Hallévi and of my own. See Crit. Notes on lxv. 10; lxix. 1, 13, &c.

§ 5. Editions of the Ethiopic Text.

Laurence, *Libri Enoch Versio Aethiopica*, Oxoniae, 1838. Dillmann, *Liber Henoch, Aethiopice, ad quinque codicum fidem editus, cum variis lectionibus.* Lipsiae, 1851. For an account of the MSS. see pp. 2–5.

§ 6. Translations.

Four translations with introductions and commentary have already appeared. The latter two of them we shall criticise shortly.

Laurence, *The Book of Enoch, an apocryphal production, now first translated from an Ethiopic MS. in the Bodleian Library*, Oxford, 1821.

Hoffmann (A. G.), *Das Buch Henoch in vollständiger Übersetzung mit fortlaufendem Commentar, ausführlicher Einleitung und erläuternden Excursen*, 2 vols. Jena, 1833–38.

Dillmann, *Das Buch Henoch übersetzt und erklärt*, Leipzig, 1853. This splendid edition at once displaced the two that preceded it, corrected their many ungrammatical renderings, and furnished an almost perfect translation of a text based on five MSS. So much however has been done in the criticism of Enoch since 1853 that the need of a new edition is imperative alike in respect of the text, translation, interpretation, and criticism of the book. For a criticism of the Ethiopic text of Dln. see pp. 3–4. As for the translation some of the renderings are grammatically impossible. See, for instance, Crit. Notes on xv. 11; lxi. 10; lxxxix. 7; xcix. 16; cvi. 13. Many other inaccuracies in the translation are silently corrected in his Lexicon. For some of these see Crit. Notes on viii. 1;

xxxvii. 2, 5; xxxviii. 2; xli. 5; lxxxiii. 5; lxxxv. 2; xcix. 5. Further he has omitted to translate the opening words of xxxvii. 1 and a clause in xci. 6. As for the interpretation of the book, this has been pressed and strained in order to support the critical views which Dln. then held but which he has long since abandoned. His critical views indeed have undergone many changes, but these undoubtedly are in the right direction.

In his edition of 1853 Dln. insisted that the book proceeded from one author with the exception of certain historical additions, vi–xvi; xci. 12–17; xciii; cvi–vii, and of certain Noachic interpolations, liv. 7–lv. 2; lx; lxv–lxix. 25; and also cf. xx; lxx; lxxv. 5; lxxxii. 9–20; cviii.

In 1860 in Herzog's *R. E.*, Ed. 1, vol. xii. 308–310, and in 1871 in Schenkel's (*Bibel-Lex.*) iii. 10–13, he recognised the separate authorship of xxxvii–lxxi and asserted with Ewald its priority to the rest of the book.

In 1883 in Herzog's *R. E.*, Ed. 2, vol. xii. 350–352 he abandons his original standpoint so far as to describe the book of Enoch as a mere 'combination of the Enoch and Noah writings,' and concedes that xxxvii–lxxi are later than the rest of the book. His final analysis is as follows. (1) i–xxxvi; lxxii–cv, with the exception of certain interpolations, form the ground-work and were composed in the time of J. Hyrcanus. (2) xxxvii–lxxi together probably with xvii–xix were written at latest before 64 B.C. (3) The Noachic fragments vi. 3–8; viii. 1–3; ix. 7; x. 1, 11; xx; xxxix. 1, 2[a]; liv. 7–lv. 2; lx; lxv–lxix. 25; cvi–cvii. (4) cviii.

Yet despite every defect, Dln.'s edition will always maintain a unique position in the Enoch literature.

SCHODDE. *The Book of Enoch translated with Introduction and Notes*, Andover, 1882. The introduction is interesting and the account of the bibliography though incomplete is helpful, but the arrangement of the text and notes in this edition is most inconvenient. The translation is made from Dln.'s Ethiopic text. But the work as a whole is unsatisfactory. All Dln.'s slips and inaccuracies, with one or two exceptions, are perpetuated, even those which have been corrected in his Lexicon, and to these Dr. Schodde has added a goodly number of his own. At times he translates directly from the German instead of the Ethiopic. As for instance in xxxvi. 3 he translates ምዕራብ wrongly 'every evening' instead of 'to the west.' The explanation of this strange mistake is found in Dln.'s rendering 'gegen Abend,' which may be translated either way. Again in lxii. 4 he gives the extraordinary rendering 'when the son enters the mouth of the mother,' instead of the obvious translation 'enters the mouth of the womb.' Here again Dln.'s 'Wann sein Sohn in den Muttermund tritt,' explains Dr. Schodde's error. It is possible that this error should be set down to an imperfect knowledge of English, such as he displays in xxi. 3 where the words 'tied together to it' represent some stars as tied to a void! whereas the literal translation is 'bound together in it'; or in xxv. 5 where he renders 'it will be planted towards the north' instead of 'it will be transplanted to the north.'

At other times Dr. Schodde confounds words that in the Ethiopic closely resemble each other, as in xxvii. 2 'here will be their judgment' instead of 'here will be the place of their punishment'; in xxxii. 3 'of attractive beauty' instead of 'of goodly fragrance'; in lxxxix. 18 'abode' instead of 'assembly.' Again in lxxiii. 8 he comments rightly in the notes on the waxing moon, but his translation wrongly refers to the waning moon. On the other hand the notes on the astronomical Chs. are often misleading and unintelligible: cf. lxxii. 3, 35: lxxiv. 6; lxxv. 1. A more thorough study of Dln.'s commentary would have saved him from such misconceptions.

It will be sufficient to point to one or two more mistranslations in this book.

xix. 1 'On the day when the great judgment . . . shall be consummated,' instead of 'on the day of the great judgment . . . till they are consummated.'

lxxiv. 14 'To the sum of these are added sixty-two days,' instead of 'an addition is made to the sixty-two days.'

lxxvi. 10 'After these northerly winds from the seventh portal,' instead of 'After these are the north winds: from the seventh portal,' &c.

In the face of such a list as the above, and it is by no means exhaustive, it is hard to congratulate Dr. Schodde, and yet we are grateful to him for the good service he has rendered in introducing the knowledge of Enoch to the Western world.

I should add that Dr. Schodde's analysis of Enoch is:—

i. The groundwork i–xxxvi; lxxii–cv, before the death of Judas Maccabee.

ii. The Similitudes xxxvii–lxxi, between 37–4 B.C.

iii. Noachic interpolations liv. 7–lv. 2; lx; lxv–lxix. 25; cvi–cvii.

He thinks it probable that xx; lxx; lxxv. 5; lxxxii. 9–20; xciii. 11–14 are also interpolations.

§ 7. Critical Inquiries.

I had intended to give a critical history of all the work done on Enoch since 1850, and had collected almost sufficient materials for that purpose, when I found that my space would not permit of such a large addition to the book. I shall therefore content myself with enumerating these inquiries and adding occasional notes.

Lücke, *Einleitung in die Offenbarung des Johannes* (2nd Ed. 1852), pp. 89–144: 1071–1073. Lücke regards the book as consisting of two parts; the first embraces 1–xxxv; lxxi–cv, written at the beginning of the Maccabaean revolt (p. 142), or according to his later view in the reign of J. Hyrcanus (p. 1072); the second consists of the Similitudes and was written in the early years of Herod the Great (p. 142). lix. 7–14 and lxiv–lxvii. 1 are interpolations of an uncertain date. In his first edition Lücke maintained the Christian authorship of the whole book.

Hofmann (J. Chr. K.), 'Ueber die Entstehungszeit des

Buch Henoch (*Zeitschr. D. M. G.* vi. 1852, pp. 87–91); *Schriftbeweis* (2nd Ed.), i. 420–23; *Die heil. Schrift N.T.'s zusammenhängend untersucht*, vii. 2, p. 205 sqq. Hofmann regards Enoch as the work of a Christian writer of the second century A. D. His chief contribution to the understanding of Enoch is his correct interpretation of the seventy shepherds in lxxxix–xc.

Dillmann. See above under editions; also *Zeitschr. D. M. G.*, 1861, pp. 126–131. This is a criticism of Volkmar's theory.

Jellinek, *Zeitschr. D. M. G.*, 1853, p. 249.

Gildemeister, *Zeitschr. D. M. G.*, 1855, pp. 621–624, gives the Greek fragment of Enoch from the Codex Vaticanus (Cod. Gr. 1809) and discusses the relative merits of the Greek and Ethiopic versions.

Ewald, *Abhandlung über des äthiopischen Buches Henokh Entstehung, Sinn und Zusammensetzung*, 1855; *History of Israel*, v. 345–349 (transl. from the Germ.). It was the merit of Ewald first to discern that Enoch was composed of several originally independent books. It is, in fact, as he declares, 'the precipitate of a literature once very active which revolved . . . round Enoch' *Hist.* (v. 349). Though this view was at once assailed by Köstlin and nearly every other critic since, its truth can no longer be denied, and Holtzmann's declaration that 'the so-called groundwork (i. e. i–xxxvii; lxxii–cv) is composed of a whole series of sections, some of Pharisaic and others of Essene origin' (*Theol. Literaturzeitung*, 1890, p. 497), is a notable sign of the return to Ewald's view. But though future criticism must confirm Ewald's general judgment of the book, it will just as surely reject his detailed analysis of its parts. His scheme is—

(1) Book I, xxxvii–lxxi (with the exception of certain interpolations), circ. 144 B. C.

(2) Book II, i–xvi; lxxxi. 1–4; lxxxiv; xci–cv, circ. 135 B.C.

(3) Book III, xx–xxxvi; lxxii–xc; cvi–cvii, circ. 128 B. C.; cviii later.

(4) Book IV, the Noah book. vi. 3–8; viii. 1–3; ix. 7; x. 1–3, 11, 22[b]; xvii–xix; liv. 7–lv. 2; lx. 1–10, 24, 25; lxiv–lxix. 16. Somewhat later than the former.

(5) Finally the editing, compressing, and enlarging of the former books into one vol.

WEISSE, *Die Evangelien-Frage*, 1856, pp. 214–224. Weisse agrees with Hofmann and Philippi in maintaining a Christian authorship of the book, but his advocacy of this view springs from the dogmatic principle that the entire idea of Christianity was in its pure originality derived from the self-consciousness of Christ.

KÖSTLIN, 'Ueber die Entstehung des Buchs Henoch' (*Theol. Jahrb.*, 1856, pp. 240–279; 370–386). Köstlin, as we have already remarked, contended against Ewald that the book of Enoch did not arise through the editing of independent works, but that by far the larger part of Enoch was the work of one author which through subsequent accretions became the present book. Though this view must be speedily abandoned, it must be confessed that the Articles in which it is advocated are masterly performances, and possess a permanent value for the student of Enoch.

HILGENFELD, *Die jüdische Apokalyptik*, 1857, pp. 91–184. This work like that of Köstlin is of lasting worth and indispensable in the study of Enoch. We cannot, however, say so much for the conclusions arrived at. Many of these are, in fact, demonstrably wrong. According to Hilgenfeld, the groundwork consists of i–xvi; xx–xxxvi; lxxii–cv written not later than 98 B. C. The later additions, i. e. xvii–xix; xxxvii–lxxi; cvi–cviii are the work of a Christian Gnostic about the time between Saturninus and Marcion. There are no Noachic interpolations.

There is no occasion to enter on the, for the most part, barren polemic between Hilgenfeld and Volkmar on the interpretation and date of Enoch, to which we owe the following writings of Hilgenfeld:—'Die jüdische Apokalyptik und die neuesten Forschungen' (*Zeitschr. f. wissenschaftl. Theol.*, iii. 1860, pp. 319–334: 'Die Entstehungszeit des ursprünglichen Buchs Henoch' (*Z. f. w. Theol.*, iv. 1861, pp. 212–222): 'Noch ein Wort über das Buch Henoch.' (*Z. f. w. Theol.*, v. 1862, pp. 216–221). In *Z. f. w. Theol.*, xv. 1872, pp. 584–587, there is a rejoinder to Gebhardt (see below).

VOLKMAR, 'Beiträge zur Erklärung des Buches Henoch.' (*Zeitschr. D. M. G.*, xiv. 1860, pp. 87–134, 296): 'Einige Bemerkungen über Apokalyptik' (*Zeitschr. f. w. Theol.*, iv. 1861, pp. 111–136: 'Ueber die katholischen Briefe und Henoch,' iv. 1861, pp. 422–436; v. 1862, pp. 46–75. As Hilgenfeld reckoned the periods of the seventy shepherds at seven years each, starting from 588 B.C., and thus arrived at 98 B.C., Volkmar started from the same anterior limit and reckoned each period at ten years. He thus found the entire rule of the shepherds to last 700 years or, through certain refinements, peculiarly Volkmarian, 720 years, and so arrived at the year of Barcochab's rebellion 132 A.D.—a year which has exercised a strange fascination over him and has been fatal to his reputation as a critic. Thus Enoch was written 132 B.C. It was the work of a disciple of Akiba, and was designed to announce the final victory of Barcochab. Volkmar restated his theory in an essay: Eine Neutestamentliche Entdeckung, Zürich, 1862. His views have received more attention than they deserved through the rejoinders of Hilgenfeld, Dillmann, Langen, Sieffert, Gebhardt, Drummond, and Stanton.

GEIGER, *Jüdische Zeitschr. f. Wissensch. und Leben*, 1864–65, pp. 196–204. This article deals mainly with the calendar in Enoch. I have adopted one of his suggestions in x. 4.

LANGEN, *Das Judenthum in Palästina*, 1866, pp. 35–64. Langen regards Enoch as an early but highly composite work put together in its present form about 160 B.C. (pp. 36, 64), and emanating from orthodox and patriotic Judaism as a protest against heathen religion and philosophy.

SIEFFERT, *De apocryphi libri Henochi origine et argumento*,

Regimonti, 1867. Sieffert (p. 3) takes the groundwork to be i–xvi; xx–xxxvi; lxxii–lxxxii; xci–cv, written by a Chasid in the age of Simon the Maccabee (p. 11–13): lxxxiii–xc is a later addition about the year 108 B.C., and xvii–xix; xxxvii–lxxi; cvi–cviii are of Essene origin and composed before 64 B.C. (pp. 27–29).

HOLTZMANN, *Geschichte des Volkes Israel,* 1867, vol. ii, pp. 201, 202.

HALLÉVI, 'Recherches sur la langue de la rédaction primitive du livre d'Énoch' (*Journal Asiatique,* 1867, pp. 352–395). This most interesting essay proves beyond doubt that Enoch was originally written in Hebrew. Unhappily the writer has lost much time over passages which better MSS. show to be mere corruptions of the text. There are many errors in the Ethiopic part of this essay, but these are most likely due to the press. I have given the most probable of Hallévi's suggestions in my Critical Notes, and have adopted several of them in my translation.

PHILIPPI, *Das Buch Henoch, sein Zeitalter und sein Verhältniss zum Judasbriefe,* Stuttg. 1868. This writer agrees with Hofmann, Weisse and Volkmar, in regarding the book as post-Christian. He thinks it was written in Greek by one author, a Christian, about 100 A.D. It is notable that all the four writers, who assign a post-Christian origin to the book, have done for dogmatic reasons.

WITTICHEN, *Die Idee des Menschen,* 1868, pp. 63–71; *Die Idee des Reiches Gottes,* 1872, pp. 118–133, 145–150.

These books I have not been able to see.

GEBHARDT, 'Die 70 Hirten des Buches Henoch und ihre Deutungen mit besonderer Rücksicht auf die Barkochba-Hypothese' (Merx' *Archiv für wissenschaftl. Erforschung des A. T.* 1872, vol. ii. Heft ii. pp. 163–246). In this most trenchant criticism of the different explanations of chs. lxxxix–xc the writer carefully refrains from advancing any theory of his own. Nay more, he holds it impossible with our present text to arrive at a true interpretation of the author's meaning. But this writer's despair of a true interpretation is overhasty and his condemnation of the text is unwarrantable.

ANGER, *Vorlesungen über die Geschichte der Messianischen Idee,* 1873, pp. 83–84.

VERNES, *Histoire des Idées Messianiques,* 1874, pp. 66–117; 264–271. These sections are composed mainly of a French translation of Dln.'s German version. Vernes thinks that the earliest part of Enoch was written in Aramaic by a contemporary of J. Hyrcanus; and that the Similitudes spring from a Christian and Gnostic circle about the close of the first century A. D. (pp. 264 sqq.).

KUENEN, *Religion of Israel,* 1874–1875, iii. 265, 266 (translated from the Dutch Edition of 1869–70).

TIDEMAN, 'De Apocalypse van Henoch et het Essenisme,' (*Theol. Tijdschrift,* 1875, pp. 261–296). Tideman regards the book as proceeding from different authors living at different periods. His analysis is as follows:—

(1) The oldest book: i–xvi; xx–xxxvi; lxxii–lxxxii; xciii; xci. 12–19; xcii; xciv–cv from the hand of a Pharisee in the early times of the Maccabees 153–135 B. C.

(2) The second book: lxxxiii–xci. 10 from an Essene writer who added it to the older book 134–106 B. C.

(3) The Apocalypse of Noah: xvii–xix; xli. 3–9; xliii. 1, 2; xliv; liv. 7–lv. 2; lix–lx; lxv–lxix. 25; lxx; cvi–cvii, from an author versed in Jewish Gnosticism 80 A. D.

(4) The Similitudes (with the exception of the Noachic interpolations) written by a Christian in the days of Domitian or Trajan when the Christians were persecuted and the Romans were at war with the Parthians 90–100 A. D.

(5) Ch. cviii by the final editor of the book, a Christian Gnostic of the type of Saturninus, 125 A. D.

Christian interpolations are found in xc. 38; cv.

Tideman thinks that we have in the Similitudes a combination of the thought that the Messiah is to be a man in the clouds (Daniel), and of the doctrine that he was to proceed from the community. En. xc. 37, 38.

DRUMMOND, *The Jewish Messiah*, 1877, pp. 17–73. Drummond gives a concise and able review of the work of former critics on Enoch. He rightly approves and further enforces Hofmann's interpretation of the seventy shepherds as angels. He agrees with the limits assigned by Tideman to the oldest book in Enoch; but concludes, against Hilgenfeld and Tideman, that the Similitudes could not *entirely* be the work of a Christian; for if they were such, there would undoubtedly have been some reference to the crucified and risen Christ such as we find in Test. xii. Patriarch. Levi, 4. The difficulties of the case are met, he believes, by supposing that a Christian Apocalypse has been worked into the tissue of an earlier Jewish production, and that all the Messiah passages are due to the former. His chief arguments are: (i) the title 'son of a woman' could not have been applied by a pre-Christian Jew to a supernatural Messiah; (ii) a consistent text is possible by an omission of the Messiah passages, a text also which answers to the title placed at the beginning of each Similitude; (iii) the closing ch. lxxi confirms this view where in the description of a Theophany there is no mention of the Messiah and the title 'Son of Man' is applied to Enoch; (iv) the Book of Jubilees though using Enoch extensively does not cite the Messiah passages.

This theory is as untenable as that of Hilgenfeld and Tideman. As for (i) the title in question is not found in the oldest MS.; (ii) in itself will have no weight if we bear in mind the want of logical sequence and the frequent redundancy characteristic of Semitic writings generally and of Jewish apocalypses in particular. Moreover in no instance that I am aware of does any superscription in Enoch give an exact account of the Chs. it introduces. (iii) This argument not only fails to testify against the genuineness of the Messiah passages but also furnishes one of the strongest proofs of their being original constituents of the text. It is first to be observed that lxxi must be regarded as an interpolation on quite other grounds (see notes in loc.). In the next place what significance are we to attach to the appearance of the title 'The Son of Man' in the interpolations and as applied there to Enoch, lx. 10; lxxi. 14? We can only understand this by studying the method of the interpolator. In the Noachic interpolations we find that the interpolator seeks to adapt his additions to their new contexts by incorporating technical terms from these contexts. Thus the following technical terms and phrases among others are taken over into his interpolations; 'Lord of Spirits,' see xxxvii. 2 (note); 'Head of Days,' xlvi. 1 (note); 'Angels of Punishment,' lvi. 1 (note); 'Those who dwell on the Earth,' xxxvii. 5 (note); but either through ignorance or of set purpose the technical phrases are misused. At the same time the presence of many such misused technical terms in the interpolation over against the technical terms in their adjoining contexts is demonstrative evidence as to the genuineness of the latter. Every copy or caricature presupposes an original. And this is exactly what we find in connexion with the title, 'The Son of Man.' It is found repeatedly throughout the Similitudes in the technical sense of a supernatural Messiah and Judge of the World, and accordingly it would be surprising in the extreme if it escaped the fate of the other technical designations. But the interpolator has not disappointed us; the inevitable 'caricature' appears in lx. 10 and lxxi. 14, and therein we have the best evidence we could desire for the genuineness of the technical designation in the Similitudes.

The Similitudes, therefore, are neither of Christian authorship as Hilgenfeld supposes nor of Jewish authorship worked over by a Christian. All evidence internal and external will, as we shall see presently, prove not only that they are Jewish but also pre-Christian. (iv) It would be most unreasonable to expect the Book of Jubilees to quote or refer to the Messiah passages, seeing that throughout it there is not even the faintest allusion to a Messiah.

HAUSRATH, *Neutestamentliche Zeitgeschichte*, Erster Theil, 3rd ed., 1879, pp. 185–189; 191–193. The oldest book, i–xxxvi; lxxii–cv, is referred to the time of J. Hyrcanus. The Similitudes, with the exception of the Noachic interpolations, were probably composed in the reign of Herod the Great. Hausrath thinks that the Messiah-passages may have won somewhat of a Christian colouring in the process of translation from Hebrew to Greek and Greek to Ethiopic by Christian hands.

LIPSIUS, art. 'Enoch' in Smith and Wace's *Dictionary of Christian Biography*, vol. ii. 1880, pp. 124–128. (1) The oldest book dealt with celestial physics, xvii–xix; xxi–xxxvi; lxxii–lxxix; lxxxii, in which Enoch appears as a teacher of such higher wisdom. This however is an unhappy synthesis; for the demonic doctrine of xvii–xix connects it peculiarly with the Noachic interpolations, while its Greek colouring as strongly disconnects it with the ultra-Jewish lxxii–lxxix; lxxxii. (2) In the second book i–xvi; lxxx–lxxxi; lxxxiii–cv which never existed independently but only as an expansion of the former, Enoch is represented as a preacher of righteousness. This book belongs to the reign of J. Hyrcanus. (3) The Similitudes written under the later Maccabeans or the Herods. (4) Noachic interpolations liv. 7–lv. 2; lx. 7–25; lxv–lxviii. 1 and probably x. 1–3; 22^b; xli. 2–9; xliii–xliv; lix; lxix. 2, 3; cvi–cvii. Other interpolations and additions xx; cviii.

This article forms a valuable contribution to the criticism of Enoch, and I welcome it all the more gladly as I arrived at many of its results before I was acquainted with it.

WESTCOTT, *Introduction to the Study of the Gospels*, 1881, 6th ed., pp. 99–109; *Gospel of St. John*, 1882, p. 34. In the former work this writer recognises the probability of the different sections of the book as proceeding from different authors, yet he essays the impossible task of moulding their conflicting features into one consistent whole. In the latter work Dr. Westcott asserts that the title in Enoch is 'A Son of Man'; but wrongly; for it is as definitely 'The Son of Man' as the language and sense can make it. The being so named, further, is superhuman, and not merely human as Dr. Westcott states.

SCHODDE. See above (pp. 7–8).

WIESELER, 'Ueber die Form des jüdischen Jahres um die Zeit Jesu' (*Beiträge zur richtigen Würdigung der Evangelien*, 1869). We have here an interesting and valuable discussion of the Calendar in Enoch.

'Zur Abfassungszeit des Buchs Henoch' (*Zeitschr. D.M.G.*, 1882, pp. 185–193). Wieseler assigns the Similitudes no less than the rest of the book to the reign of J. Hyrcanus.

SCHÜRER, *A History of the Jewish People in the Time of Jesus Christ* (translated from the second and Revised Ed. of the German), vol. iii. div. ii. pp. 54–73, 1886. This is a most judicious statement of the results already attained by criticism. In accordance with these Schürer divides the book into three parts: (1) 'the original writing' i–xxxvi; lxxii–cv, written in the reign of J. Hyrcanus; (2) the Similitudes written in the time of Herod the Great; (3) the Noachian Fragments, liv. 7–lv. 2; lx; lxv–lxix. 25, and probably cvi–cvii. cviii is a later addition. He is careful, however, to remind us that the 'original writing is composed of very heterogeneous elements.' While he rightly dismisses as idle all attempts to introduce chronological exactness into the interpretation of the seventy Shepherds, he thinks there can be no doubt as to where the different periods are intended to begin and end. It was Schürer who was the first to recognise the validity of Hoffmann's interpretation of the Shepherds and to give it currency. This article concludes with a very full list of patristic passages referring to Enoch and with an excellent bibliography of the literature.

STANTON, *The Jewish and the Christian Messiah*, 1886, pp.

44–64, 139–140, 142, 153, 170–175, 286, 305, 311–315, 332, 335, 347.

The analysis of the book given in Schürer is adopted also here. Dr. Stanton agrees likewise with the generality of critics in assigning the first part, i. e. i–xxxvi; lxxii–cv, to the reign of J. Hyrcanus. The Similitudes must, he thinks, be ascribed to a Jewish Christian or to a Jew influenced by Christian ideas. The fragments of a lost Apocalypse of Noah are probably xxxix. 1, 2[a]; liv. 7–lv. 2; lx; lxv–lxix. 25. It is to be hoped that the author of this admirable book will add to our indebtedness, and give to the book of Enoch the fuller and profounder treatment it deserves.

REUSS, *Gesch. der heil. Schriften A. T.'s* §§ 498–500.

HOLTZMANN, *Einleitung in das N. T.*, 1886, 109, 110.

PFLEIDERER, *Das Urchristenthum*, 1887, pp. 310–318. This writer accepts the traditional view with regard to the ground-work, and approves of Drummond's theory as to the origin of the Messiah-passages in the Similitudes. This theory he seeks further to substantiate, but without success.

BALDENSPERGER, *Das Selbstbewusstsein Jesu*, 1888, pp. 7–16. This writer assents to the traditional view and date of the ground-work. The Similitudes he assigns to the years immediately following on the death of Herod the Great. He believes there are many references to the Romans in the Similitudes, and that Augustus and Herod are designed under the phrase 'the kings and the mighty.'

SALMON, *Introduction to the N. T.*, 4th ed., 1889, pp. 527, 528.

PETER, *Le Livre d'Henoch. Ses Idées Messianiques et son Eschatologie*, Genève, 1890. This is an interesting little treatise, but by no means free from blemishes. The Similitudes are pre-Christian, and the traditional view and date of the ground-work are here reproduced.

DEANE, *The Pseudepigrapha*, 1891, pp. 49–94. This is a

praiseworthy attempt to popularise a knowledge of these works. The writer assigns the traditional ground-work to the years 153–130 B.C., and regards the Similitudes as written a few years later. Many of this writer's statements on the theology and influence of Enoch are to be taken with extreme caution.

THOMSON, *Books that influenced our Lord and His Apostles*, 1891, pp. 95, 103, 108, 225–248, 389–411. Mr. Thomson's analysis is as follows:—

(1) Book of the Similitudes and the Book of the Weeks, xxxvii–lxxi; xci. 12–xcix, written about the year 210 B.C.

(2) Noachic Fragments, lx; lxv–lxix. 24.

(3) Book of the Fall of the Angels and of the Luminaries, i–xxxvi; lxxii–xci. 11; c–cvii, written not later than 160 B.C.

(4) cviii. Mr. Thomson's chief ground for regarding xxxvii–lxxi as the oldest section is derived from the presence of the Noachic interpolations. As he believes that these interpolations are confined to this section, he infers that xxxvii–lxxi is therefore the oldest and that i–xxxvi; lxxii–xci were not yet in existence. Even if Mr. Thomson were right in his facts, quite another conclusion would be possible. But this writer's premises are without foundation. Interpolations are found in every section in Enoch and numerously in the sections which Mr. Thomson regards as free from them. It cannot be said that this book contributes much to the better interpretation of Enoch, and this is all the more to be deplored as its author obviously possesses abundant ability for the task.

CHEYNE, *Origin of the Psalter*, 1891, pp. 22, 375, 412–414, 423–424, 448–449, and about fifty references besides. 'Possible Zoroastrian Influences on the Religion of Israel, *Expository Times*, 1891, p. 207. Dr. Cheyne accepts provisionally the traditional division of Enoch into the ground-work, Similitudes and Noachic fragments, and regards the Similitudes as pre-Christian. He deals mainly with the dogmatic teaching of the book and its place in the development of Jewish religious thought, and points to the Essene and Zoroastrian elements which have found a place in it.

De Faye, *Les apocalypses juives*, Paris, 1892, pp. 28–33, 205–216.

§ 8. From a Hebrew Original through the Medium of a Greek Translation.

Laurence and Hoffmann believed on various grounds that the original was written in Hebrew. Jellinek (*Zeitschr. D.M.G.*, 1853, p. 249) argues for the same conclusion from Hebrew fragments of Enoch which are preserved in various Jewish writings. Dln. (*Buch Henoch*, Einleit. li–liii) holds the same view and urges in support of it the accurate knowledge shown by the book of the localities round Jerusalem, the intimate acquaintance of its writers with the Old Testament, and that not through the medium of the LXX but directly with the Hebrew, the frequent etymologies resting only on a Hebrew basis and the Hebraistic style, which is so all pervading that there is not a single expression in the book which does not readily admit of retranslation into Hebrew.

The evidence furnished by Dln. is quite sufficient to establish a Hebrew original. And his conclusion has been further and finally confirmed by Hallévi. This scholar has retranslated the entire book into Hebrew, and in the *Journal Asiatique*, Avril–Mai, 1867, pp. 352–395, has proved his thesis to demonstration. There is much that is far-fetched and more ingenious than true in this able article, yet none the less its author has established his contention. As proofs of a Hebrew original he adduces (1) frequent paronomastic expressions possible only in Hebrew (see Crit. Note on vi. 6); (2) Hebrew etymologies of proper names; (3) unintelligible expressions rendered clear by reproduction in Hebrew.

This Hebrew original was first translated into Greek. Portions of this translation still exist (see pp. 62–75, 83–85). It was from this Greek translation that the Ethiopic version was made. Ethiopic did not exist as a literary language before 350 (see Nöldeke 'Semitic Languages,' *Encyc. Brit.*, 9th ed., vol. xxi. 654). The translation of the Bible into Ethiopic was made between 350 and 600, and it is probable that the book of Enoch was not made much earlier than the later date.

The Place of Composition.—There is no room for doubt as to the Palestinian origin of the book. The various authors are at home in Palestine and accurately acquainted with the various localities close to Jerusalem, the valleys, brooks, and other natural features in its immediate neighbourhood. To them further Jerusalem is the city of the elect, the centre of the coming Messianic kingdom, and Gehenna is the destined habitation of the apostate. Greek elements have no doubt found an entrance in certain fragments of the book, but as a rule there is a deliberate and sustained opposition rendered to all Hellenistic ideas and influences. The whole tone and exegesis of the book are Palestinian in character.

§ 9. The Object of Apocalyptic Literature.

The object of Apocalyptic literature in general was to solve the difficulties connected with the righteousness of God and the suffering condition of his righteous servants on earth. The righteousness of God postulated according to the Law the temporal prosperity of the righteous, and postulated this temporal prosperity of necessity; for as yet there was no promise of life or recompense beyond the grave. But in the experience of God's servants this connexion of righteousness and temporal reward was so often found to fail that the Psalmists at times go so far as to complain that the best things of this life are bestowed on the wicked. The difficulties thus arising from this conflict between promise and experience might be shortly resolved into two, which deal respectively with the position of the righteous as a community, and the position of the righteous man as an individual. The Old Testament prophets had concerned themselves chiefly with the former and pointed in the main to the restoration of Israel as a nation and to Israel's ultimate possession of the earth as a reward of their righteousness. But later with the growing claims of the individual, and the acknowledgment of these in the religious and intellectual life, the latter problem pressed itself irresistibly on the notice of religious thinkers, and made it impossible for any conception of the divine rule and righteousness to gain acceptance, which did not render adequate satisfaction to the claims of the righteous individual. It was to this difficulty in particular that Apocalyptic addressed itself, though it did not ignore the former. It strove to show that alike in respect of the nation and of the individual the righteousness of God would be fully vindicated. In order to justify their contention Apocalyptic writers sketched in outline the history of the world and of mankind, the origin of evil and its course, and the final consummation of all things, and thus in fact presented a Semitic philosophy of religion. The righteous as a nation should yet possess the earth: even in this world the faithful community should attain to all its rights either in an eternal or in a temporary Messianic kingdom. So Apocalyptic taught universally and thus enforced the teaching of prophecy. As for the destiny of the individual, and here lay the chief interest and service of Apocalyptic, this was finally to be determined according to his works. For though the righteous individual might perish amid the disorders of the world, his death could not fall out without God's knowledge, and though cut off here apparently as a sinner, he would not fail to attain through the resurrection the recompense that was his due in the Messianic kingdom or in heaven itself. The conceptions as to this risen life, its duration and character, vary with each writer.

With this short introduction we will now proceed to consider the different writings in this book, their respective characteristics and dates, and the various accounts they offer of the future lot of the righteous community and of the righteous individual.

§ 10. THE DIFFERENT ELEMENTS IN THE BOOK OF ENOCH, WITH THEIR RESPECTIVE CHARACTERISTICS AND DATES.

The book of Enoch is a fragmentary survival of an entire literature that once circulated under his name. To this fact the plurality of books assigned to Enoch from the first may in some degree point: as for instance the expression 'books' in civ. 12: Book of Jubilees iv; vii; Test. XII. Patriarch. Jud. 18; Origen *c. Celsum* v. 54; *in Num. Homil.* xxviii. 2 (Ed. Lommatsch); Aug. *De Civ. Dei* xv. 23; and G. Syncellus, p. 20 (Ed. Dindorf.) 'the first book.'

This presumption becomes a matter of demonstration on the following grounds. The references to Enoch's writings in the Book of Jubilees and in the Test. XII. Patriarch. cannot in many instances be traced to the existing book of Enoch. The last passage attributed by Syncellus to Enoch has no corresponding part in the Ethiopic. Portions of the Ethiopic version are manifestly lost, as, for instance, the close of the first Similitude. And finally two Slavonic MSS. have been recently published in Russia which belong to this literature and yet differ from the Ethiopic Enoch throughout in diction and matter.

This preliminary conclusion is finally confirmed on internal grounds. All critics are agreed in ascribing the Similitudes xxxvii–lxxi to a different authorship from the rest. For the main grounds for this conclusion see pp. 106–107. Criticism is further agreed as to the presence of a large body of interpolations. But the interpolations are far more numerous than has hitherto been observed, and the discrimination and due appreciation of these are indispensable to the understanding of the book. They are found throughout the book, and are as follows:—

vi. 3–8; viii. 1–3; ix. 7; x. 1–3, 11; xvii–xx. See notes in loc.

xxxix. 1, 2[a]; xli. 3–8; xliii–xliv; liv. 7–lv. 2; lvi. 5–lvii. 3[a]; lix–lx; lxv–lxix. 25. See notes on liv. 7.

l. See notes in loc.

lxxi. See notes in loc.

lxxx–lxxxi. See notes in loc.

xc. 15; xci. 11; xciii. 11–14; xcvi. 2; cv–cvii. See notes in loc.

The bulk of these belong to a lost Apocalypse of Noah (mentioned in the Book of Jubilees x; xxi), i.e. vi. 3–8; viii. 1–3; ix. 7; x. 1–3, 11; xvii–xx; xxxix. 1, 2[a]; xli. 3–8; xliii–xliv; liv. 7–lv. 2; lix–lx; lxv–lxix. 25; cvi–cvii. We might refer l, lvi. 5–lvii. 3[a]; lxxi; lxxx–lxxxi; xciii. 11–14 to the same source, but only indirectly in their present form, as they appear to be of the nature of a mosaic. We can hardly be wrong in ascribing them largely to the authorship of the editor who brought all the writings into one whole. cv may be due to the same editor. cviii is undoubtedly a later addition.

Disregarding the closing chapter we find that there are thus three distinct elements in the book:—

(*a*) The so-called ground-work i–xxxvi; lxxii–civ.

(*β*) The Similitudes xxxvii—lxx.

(*γ*) The Noachian and other interpolations, as given above.

The question now arises: are we justified in regarding i–xxxvi, lxxii–civ as proceeding from the same author? This question is discussed at length in the Special Introductions to sections i–xxxvi; lxxii–lxxxii; lxxxiii–xc; and xci–civ, and it is there shown that these four sections are distinct writings as to authorship, system of thought, and date. We will not resume here the grounds for this conclusion, but will sketch briefly the various independent writings contained in the book of Enoch, with their respective characteristics and dates.

Part I, consisting of chs. i–xxxvi, written at latest before

170 B.C. and mainly from the prophetic standpoint of such chs. as Is. lxv–lxvi. This is, undoubtedly, the oldest part of the book, being anterior to lxxii–lxxxii; lxxxiii–xc; and xci–civ (see Special Introductions). It is laid under contribution by the authors of these sections. As lxxxiii–xc was written not later than 161 B.C. i–xxxvi must be some years earlier, and further, as there is not the faintest allusion to the persecutions and massacres of Antiochus Epiphanes, we are probably safe in fixing on 170 B.C. as the latest limit possible for its composition. This book i.e. i–xxxvi is noteworthy as being most probably the first to mention the resurrection of the righteous and the wicked: to describe Sheol according to the conception accepted later in the New Testament as opposed to that of the Old Testament: and to represent Gehenna as a final place of punishment. In other respects the writer of i–xxxvi has not advanced much beyond the Old Testament prophetic view of the Messianic kingdom. This kingdom, he holds, is to be ushered in by the resurrection of the righteous and the wicked (with the exception of one class of the latter) followed immediately by the final judgment. The wicked angels, demons, and men were to be punished according to their deserts, and the righteous to become members of the eternal Messianic kingdom. The scene of the kingdom was to be the earth purged from all violence and sin. Peace, and happiness, and prosperity were to prevail everywhere. Sin should never again appear on the earth, and after a life crowned with all good things, and blessed with patriarchal years and numberless offspring, the righteous were at length to die in peace, as in Is. lxv–lxvi.

It is manifest here that the writer apprehended neither the thought of the immortality of the soul, which was pressing itself on the notice of Judaism from the side of the Greek, nor the doctrine of the resurrection of the righteous to an eternal blessedness which was seeking recognition from the side of Zoroastrianism.

Part II, consisting of lxxxiii–xc, written between 166–161

B.C., and mainly from the same standpoint as Daniel. The grounds for discriminating this section from the rest are given at length in the Special Introductions to those sections. We find there that the writer of lxxxiii–xc has made use of i–xxxvi. He is moreover of an ascetic turn of mind. These visions came to him before he was married, the implication being that he has no such supernatural experiences after marriage. But as visions are inferior to actual waking intercourse with the angels, such as Enoch enjoyed in i–xxxvi, it is clear even on this single ground that these two parts are from different authors.

The writer of lxxxiii–xc has advanced considerably beyond the naive and sensuous views of the kingdom presented in i–xxxvi. His conceptions are more spiritual. He writes a few years later than the last chapters of Daniel, and like the latter has risen to the conception of an everlasting blessedness. He may be indebted to this writer for the fourfold division of the seventy angel reigns among the four great world powers to which, in succession, Israel was subject, and the phrase 'glorious land' (lxxxix. 40, cf. Dan. xi. 16, 41) may be drawn from the same source. His eschatological views are developed at greater length than those of Daniel, but he follows in some respects prophetic rather than apocalyptic ideas. In Daniel the final crisis is sudden and unmediated, but in lxxxiii–xc it is ushered in through the warlike efforts of the Chasids led by Judas Maccabaeus. In this strife the heathen enemies of Israel are destroyed. Then ensue the judgment and condemnation of the fallen watchers, the faithless angel shepherds, and the apostate Jews.

The judgment appears to be followed by the resurrection of righteous Israelites only: if this is so, then this book diverges from the teaching of Daniel xii. 1, 2 and the earlier book of Enoch i–xxxvi. The righteous Jews are all assembled in the New Jerusalem established by God Himself, and their ranks are swelled by those Gentiles who had hitherto been neutral, but are now converted to the worship of Israel's God. At the close of all appears the Messiah. This is the earliest reference to the Messiah in non-canonical literature. But he has no rôle to play: he has not as yet vindicated for himself a real place in the Apocalyptic doctrine of the last things.

This Messianic kingdom lasts on earth for ever, and its members enjoy everlasting blessedness.

Part III, consisting of xci–civ, and written between 134–94 B.C., or possibly 104–94 B.C. For a detailed criticism of this writing and its relations see Special Introduction to this part.

As we pass from lxxxiii–xc to xci–civ we feel we are entering into a world of new conceptions. In all previous Apocalyptic writings, the resurrection and the final judgment have been the prelude to an everlasting Messianic kingdom; but here we encounter quite a new schema of the last things. These great events are relegated to the close of the Messianic kingdom, and not till then in fact do the righteous enter on their reward. In this writer we have a fusion of prophetic and apocalyptic ideas, but a fusion which, without doing actual violence to either, gives expression to both in a profounder and more comprehensive system. As we see in such Apocalyptic writings as the Apócalypse of Baruch, iv Ezra and Revelation, that an adequate fulfilment is given to the promise that the righteous should inherit the earth through the establishment of a temporary Messianic kingdom: so in xci–civ the Messianic kingdom, in which the righteous possess the earth in peace, lasts from the eighth to the close of the tenth week. In this kingdom no place is found for a personal Messiah: the righteous, with God's help, vindicate their just cause and destroy their oppressors. On the close of this kingdom follow the final judgment and the risen spiritual life of blessedness in a new heaven. From such a view of the future it is obvious that for the writer the centre of interest has passed from the material world to the spiritual, and the Messianic kingdom is no longer the goal of the hopes of the righteous. Their faith finds its satisfaction only in a blessed immortality in heaven itself. The righteous, it is true, who are living on the advent of the Messianic kingdom will indeed be recompensed with all good things, but the departed righteous will not rise thereto, but will find their reward in the everlasting spiritual bliss that is the inheritance of all the faithful after the final judgment. In the meantime they are at rest, guarded as the apple of an eye by the angels of God, and will in due time, on the close of the Messianic kingdom, attain to the resurrection. This resurrection of the righteous appears not to be of the body but of the soul only, as we find in a later book, the Psalms of Solomon, or in the still later Book of Jubilees. As for the wicked they will descend into the pain of Sheol and abide there everlastingly. Here Sheol appears as Hell for possibly the first time.

The writer of this section lived towards the close of the second century B.C. He was a Pharisee strongly opposed to all hellenizing tendencies, but apparently influenced by kindred Zoroastrian ideas. His chief denunciations are directed against the Sadducees. These oppress the righteous, and the rulers who are in league with them connive at their oppression. The persecution which the righteous undergo is severe, but far removed from the murderous oppression of which they were the victims from 95 B.C. onwards. We may therefore regard this book as written before that date, and after the breach between J. Hyrcanus and the Pharisees, i.e. between 134 and 95 B.C.; or if we may take c. 2 to be an allusion to Aristobulus' murder of his brother, between 104–95 B.C.

Part IV.—The Similitudes, consisting of xxxvii–lxx and written between 94–79 B.C. or 70–64 B.C. For full account see pp. 106–109.

The Similitudes introduce us to the events and aspirations of a time not far removed in years from the period we have just been considering but very remote in character. The sufferings of the righteous mourned over in xci–civ are of slight consequence compared with their afflictions of this later date. Their plaint is no longer now of the greed and avarice of the rich; of their superstitions and idolatries, their hellenistic tendencies and apostasies. For their grief they have now graver and more abundant reason. Their blood is now crying to heaven for vengeance. Their foes, moreover, are not as in xci–civ the Sadducees secretly backed by the rulers of the nation, but the rulers themselves are now their foremost and declared oppressors, and take the chief part in their destruction. These rulers are the Maccabean princes, and not the Herods; for as yet there is no reference to Rome, though we know that Rome interposed authoritatively in the affairs of Palestine about 64 B.C. The widespread influence of the book on the writers of the New Testament (see pp. 41–53) witnesses in the same direction, and is inexplicable on any date subsequent to the time of the Maccabees. The date of the Similitudes therefore must be later than 95 and before 64 B.C., or more precisely between 95–80 B.C. or 70–64 B.C. For the fuller treatment of this subject see pp. 107–108, and the notes referred to there.

The varying relations in which the Maccabees stand to the Chasid or Pharisaic party are faithfully reflected in the books of Enoch. In lxxxiii–xc the Maccabees are the leaders of the righteous, and their efforts form the prelude to the Messianic kingdom. In xci–civ they are no longer regarded as the chiefs and friends of the Chasids, and yet they have not become their open foes. They are, however, the secret abettors of their Sadducean oppressors. But when we turn to the Similitudes the scene is wholly changed. The Maccabeans are now the open and declared enemies of the Pharisees and add to their other guilt the slaying of the righteous.

It is still more instructive to observe the conceptions regarding the Messiah to which the writers of these books were led by the events of their times. In lxxxiii–xc we have the Messiah coming forth from the bosom of the community. He is a man only, but yet a glorified man and superior to the community from which he springs. So far as he is a man only, he may be regarded as the prophetic Messiah as opposed to the Apocalyptic Messiah of the Similitudes: and yet he is not truly the prophetic Messiah; for he has absolutely no function to perform, and he does not appear till the world's history is finally closed. Accordingly his presence here must be accounted for purely through literary reminiscence, and the hope of the Messiah must be regarded as practically dead at this period. The writer felt no need of such a personality so long as the nation had such a chief as Judas Maccabaeus. It was very different fifty years or more later, when the fondest enthusiasts could no longer look to the Asmonaeans for any help or stay in the time of their distress. Accordingly the writer of xci–civ refers only once to the recreant chiefs of the nation as secret upholders of the enemies of the righteous, and directs the thoughts of his readers no longer to a religious monarchy but to a religious commonwealth or restored theocracy established by the righteous themselves, and owning no head but God alone. This Messianic kingdom, further, which was without a Messiah, was to have only a temporary continuance, and heaven was to be the true and final abode of the righteous. Once more, as we turn to a somewhat later book, we find in the Similitudes that the irremediable degradation and open hostility of the Maccabees have caused the hopes and aspirations of religious thinkers to take various directions. Of these some returned to a fresh study of the Old Testament, and revived, as in the Psalms of Solomon, the expectation of a prophetic Messiah, sprung from the house and lineage of David. Others followed the bold and original thinker of this period, who, starting from a suggestive phrase in Daniel, conceived the Messiah as the supernatural Son of Man, who, possessing divine prerogatives, should destroy the wicked, and justify the righteous, and vindicate a transformed heaven and earth as their habitation for everlasting. For a full account of the Messiah of the Similitudes we must refer the reader to the notes on xlvi. 3, and xxxviii. 2.

The teaching of the Similitudes stands throughout in clear contrast to that of xci–civ. Whilst in the latter there is no Messiah, in the former the conception of the Messiah plays a more important role than had ever yet been assigned to him. In the former, again, there seems to be only a resurrection of the righteous; in the latter a resurrection of all Israelites. In the former the Messianic kingdom was only temporary; in the latter it was of everlasting continuance. In the former the final judgment was held at the close of the Messianic kingdom; in the latter at its beginning. In the former there was a resurrection of the spirit only, in the latter of the body also.

Part V.—The Book of Celestial Physics consisting of lxxii–lxxviii; lxxxii; lxxix. There are no materials at hand for fixing the date of this section. In the Special Introduction to this part we have shown at some length that it is an independent writing, and distinct originally from all the other constituents of the book. A close examination of this section leads manifestly to the excision of lxxx–lxxxi, and to the restoration of lxxxii to its original position before lxxix. The object of the writer is a quasi-scientific one. His aim is to justify the Hebrew calendar against the heathen calendars, and particularly the Greek, and to insist on the value of the moon as an infallible divider of time till the new Creation. The only blessing pronounced by him is for those who sin not as the sinners in the reckoning of their days (lxxxii. 4). The interpolator of lxxx–lxxxi was a man of quite a different type. His sympathies were wholly moral and religious. There is an order of nature, it is true, but this order is continually thrown into disorder by the sin of men, and the moon thus becomes a misleader of men (lxxx. 4). Accordingly we are not surprised to find that the blessing pronounced by this writer is on the man against whom there is no record of unrighteousness (lxxxi. 4).

Part. VI.—The Noachian and other interpolations. These have been enumerated above (p. 25). So far as we may trust to internal evidence, it would appear that nearly all these interpolations were added by the editor who put the different books together, and sought by means of his additions from an existing Apocalypse of Noah, and possibly from elsewhere, to give a complete account of the different great world judgments. When this editing took place we cannot determine definitely, but we may with safety conclude that it was before the beginning of the Christian era. The contents of these interpolations—which deal with a vast variety of subjects, such as the books of Noah, the deluge, the evil wrought by the Satans and the fallen angels, the secrets of celestial phenomena, and other cabbalistic lore—do not admit of being shortly summarised.

§ XI. The Influence of Enoch on Jewish and Patristic Literature and on the New Testament in Phraseology, Ideas, and Doctrine.

The book of Enoch exercised a very important influence on the Christian and Jewish literature of the first three centuries A. D. The first notice of a book of Enoch appears to be due to a Jewish or Samaritan Hellenist (so Schürer). This notice, which has come down to us successively through Alexander Polyhistor and Eusebius, asserts that Enoch was the founder of Astrology: cf. Euseb. *Praep. Evang.* ix. 17. 8 (Gaisford) *τοῦτον εὑρηκέναι πρῶτον τὴν ἀστρολογίαν.*

The Influence of Enoch on Jewish Literature.

Excluding for the present the consideration of the New Testament and of Christian testimonies generally, the book of Enoch was probably used by the author of the Assumption of Moses written about the Christian Era. Cp. iv. 8—Tristes et gementes quia non poterint referre immolationes Domino patrum suorum with En. lxxxix. 73: and x. 3, 4—Exiet de habitatione sancta sua with Enoch i. 4, 'will come forth from

His dwelling': and x. 4—Tremebit terra, *usque ad fines suas* concutietur, et alti montes humiliabuntur et concutientur with En. i. 5, 6, 'unto the ends of the earth—the high mountains will be shaken and—made low.'

In the *Book of Jubilees*, written before 70 A.D., Enoch is largely drawn upon: cp. Book of Jubilees—

CH. I. 'I have *forsaken* them because of all the evil they have wrought—in *forsaking* the covenant' with En. lxxxix. 51, 54.

'Until I descend and dwell with them' with En. xxv. 3; lxxvii. 1.

'From the day of the new creation,' &c. with En. lxxii. 1.

II. In this chapter the ideas of En. lx. 16–21 are further developed and a presiding spirit is assigned to every natural phenomenon.

III. In this chapter there is the first mention of the 'heavenly tables'—a phrase borrowed from Enoch. See for full treatment of this phrase xlvii. 3 (note).

IV. 'Jared: for in his days the angels of the Lord descended on the earth.' Cf. En. vi. 6; cvi. 13.

'He took himself a wife and her name was Edna.' Cf. En. lxxxv. 3.

'He was with the angels of God six years of this jubilee.' Cf. En. xii. 1. This refers to Enoch's temporary sojourning with the angels.

'They (i.e. the angels) showed him (i.e. Enoch) everything in earth and heaven—and he wrote it all down.' Cf. En. xxi–xxxvi; lxxii–lxxxii.

'He testified to the watchers,' &c., En. xii–xiv. 7.

'We conducted him (i.e. Enoch) into the Garden of Eden.' This refers to Enoch's final translation. Cf. En. lxx.

'There he writes down,' En. xii. 4. 'The Scribe.' Cf. xv. 1; xcii. 1.

V. 'He (i.e. God) bade us bind them (i.e. the fallen watchers) in the depths of the earth.' Cf. En. x. 4–12.

The account as to the destruction of the children of the watchers depends directly on En. x. 12; xii. 6.

The account of the heavenly 'seven water torrents' and 'the fountains of the great deep' are derived from En. lxxxix. 2–7.

VI. Compare the account of the year of 364 days with its implicit polemic against En. lxxiv. 10, 12; lxxv. 2; lxxxii. 4, 6, 11.

VII. Compare the three classes of grants here described with En. vii; lxxxix. 6: the constant prohibitions against the eating of blood (cf. also xxi) with En. vii. 5; xcviii. 11: 'Enoch, the seventh in his generation' with En. xciii. 3.

VIII. 'Mount Zion, the centre of the navel of the earth' with En. xxvi. 1, 2.

X. Compare the doctrine of this chapter and of xxi regarding the demons, the children of the watchers with En. xv. 12–xvi (notes).

These demons are subject to Satan. Cf. En. liv. 6.

XI. The worship of idols and of demons (also in i and xxii). Cf. En. xix. 1; xcix. 7.

XVI. 'Plant of righteousness' (also in xxi), a phrase used of Israel. Cf. En. x. 16 (note).

XXI. Compare the list of evergreen trees given here with En. iii.

XXIII. The life of the righteous though it extend to a thousand years is still finite. Cf. En. v. 7 (note). There is no resurrection of the body—apparently the teaching of En. xci–civ.

The *Apocalypse of Baruch*, written not long after 70 A.D., has many affinities with Enoch both in diction and in thought, and is manifestly dependent on it.

Apoc. Bar. xiii. 8, 'Judicium enim est excelsi qui non respicit personas.'	En. lxiii. 8, 'His judgments have no respect of persons.'
xxiv. 1, 'Aperientur libri in quibus scripta sunt peccata omnium qui peccaverunt.'	En. xc. 20, 'He took the sealed books and opened them.'
xxix. 4, A later form of the myth of Behemoth and Leviathan which is found first in En. lx. 7–9.	En. lx. 7–9.

xxix. 5, 'Terra dabit fructus suos unum in decem millia.'	En. x. 19, 'Each measure will bear ten thousand.'
xxxv. 2, 'O oculi mei estote scatebrae et palpebrae oculorum meorum fons lacrimarum.'	En. xcv. 1, 'Oh that mine eyes were a cloud of water that I might weep over you and shed my tears as a water cloud.'
li. 3, 'Qui plantaverunt in corde suo radicem sapientiae' (cf. lix. 7).	En. x. 16, 'The plant of righteousness.'
li. 10, 'Assimilabuntur angelis et aequabuntur stellis.'	En. civ. 6, 4, 'Have great joy as the angels—shine as the stars.' Cf. lxix. 11.
liv. 2, 'Cui nihil difficile est.'	En. lxxxiv. 3, 'Nothing is too hard for thee.'
lvi. 6, 'Cum (Adam) transgressus esset, mors, quae non erat tempore ejus, fuit.'	En. lxix. 11, 'Man was created exactly like the angels—and death could not have taken hold of him.'
lvi. 10–3, 'Etiam angelis fuit periculum. Adhuc enim illo tempore, quo creatus fuit, erat eis libertas; et descenderunt ex iis et commisti sunt cum mulieribus. Et tunc illi qui sic operati sunt, in vinculis cruciati sunt.'	En. vi–x.
lix. 2, 'Lex aeterna.'	En. xcix. 2, 'The eternal law.'

The dependence of this book on Enoch is still more evident if we may regard it as proceeding from one author; for it reproduces in the main the conceptions of En. xci–civ save that it expects a Messiah. Thus in this Apocalypse of Baruch the Messianic Kingdom is only of temporary duration. The Messiah reigns till sin is at an end lxxiv. 2, 3. During his reign the earth yields 10,000 fold, and there are no premature deaths. At the close of this period the Messiah returns to heaven and the resurrection ensues l–li. 6. The righteous are then transformed and made like the angels li. 5, 10.

The author of *IV. Ezra*, writing between 81–96 A. D., has made a not infrequent use of Enoch, and this mainly of the Similitudes.

4 *Ezra* vi. 49–52 takes up and develops further the myth found in En. lx. 7–9.	En. lx. 7–9.
vii. 32, 33, 'Et terra reddet qui in ea dormiunt, et pulvis qui in eo silentio habitant, et promptuaria reddent quae eis commendatae sunt animae. Et revelabitur Altissimus super sedem judicii.'	En. li. 1, 3, 'And the earth will give back those that are treasured up within it, and Sheol also will give back that which it has received, and hell will give back that which it owes . . . And the Elect One will sit on My throne.'
4 *Ezra* [vi. 2] 'Et dicet tunc Altissimus contra illos populos resuscitatos: respicite et videte quem abnegastis, aut quem non coluistis aut cujus praecepta rejecistis.'	En. lxii. 1, 'Thus the Lord commanded . . . those who dwelt on the earth and said: "Open your eyes and lift up your horns if ye are able to recognise the Elect One."' En. lx. 6, 'Who have not served the righteous law and who deny the righteous judgment and who take His name in vain.'
[vi. 1] 'Revelabitur furnus gehennae, et ex adverso ejus iterum paradisus jucunditatum.'	En. xlviii. 9, 10; xxvii. 3.
[vi. 49] 'Ut renoves creaturam tuam.'	En. lxxii. 1.
[vi. 60, 68] A development of	En. c. 5.
vii. 55 'Super stellas fulgebunt facies eorum.'	En. civ. 2, 'Ye will shine as the stars of heaven.'
'. . . nostrae autem facies super tenebras nigrae.'	En. lxii. 10, 'Darkness will be piled upon their faces.'

In the *Testaments of the Twelve Patriarchs* there are nine direct references to Enoch. Of these Lev. 10, 14 are probably references to En. lxxxix. 50; xci. 6, 7; Dan. 5 to En.

lxxi. 15 whereas Sim. 5; Lev. 16; Jud. 18; Zeb. 3; Napht. 4; Benj. 9 cannot be traced directly to any passage in the Ethiopic Enoch. Reub. v and Napht. 3, though Enoch is not directly mentioned, may be referred to En. vi–ix. 2.

From the second century onwards all knowledge of the book of Enoch vanishes from Jewish literature with the exception of a few references that are given by Jellinek in the *Zeitschr. D. M. G.*, 1853, p. 249.

The Influence of Enoch on Patristic Literature.

Still adjourning the consideration of the New Testament we find a large body of Christian testimonies. The *Epistle of Barnabas*, written not many years after 70 A. D., cites Enoch three times and twice as Scripture: iv. 3—*τὸ τέλειον σκάνδαλον ἤγγικεν περὶ οὗ γέγραπται, ὡς Ἐνὼχ λέγει*: xvi. 4—*λέγει γὰρ ἡ γραφή· καὶ ἔσται ἐπ' ἐσχάτων τῶν ἡμερῶν καὶ παραδώσει κύριος τὰ πρόβατα τῆς νομῆς καὶ τὴν μάνδραν καὶ τὸν πύργον αὐτῶν εἰς καταφθοράν.* Cf. En. lxxxix. 56, 66. Ep. Barn. xvi. 6. Cf. En. xci. 13.

In the second century *Justin Martyr*, *Apol.* ii. 5 (quoted in note on ix. 8, 9): cp. also i. 5. Enoch is not mentioned in these passages but is used.

Irenaeus, iv. 16. 2 (quoted in note on xiv. 7).

Athenagoras (about 170 A. D.) in his *πρεσβεία* x regards Enoch, though he does not name him, as a true prophet: *ἴστε δὲ μηδὲν ἡμᾶς ἀμάρτυρον λέγειν, ἃ δὲ τοῖς προφήταις ἐκπεφώνηται, μηνύειν. ἐκεῖνοι μέν, εἰς ἐπιθυμίαν πεσόντες, παρθένων . . . ἐκ μὲν οὖν τῶν περὶ τὰς παρθένους ἐχόντων οἱ καλούμενοι ἐγεννήθησαν γιγάντες κ.τ.λ.*

Tertullian, writing between 197 and 223, regards Enoch as Scripture, *Apol.* xxii (quoted in note on xv. 8, 9); *De Cultu Feminarum*, i. 2 (quoted on viii. 1).

I. 3: Scio scripturam Enoch, quae hunc ordinem angelis dedit, non recipi a quibusdam, quia nec in armarium Judaicum admittitur. Opinor, non putaverunt illam ante cataclysmum editam post eum casum orbis omnium rerum abolitorem salvam esse potuisse. But Tertullian proceeds to show that this was possible: cum Enoch filio suo Matusalae nihil aliud mandaverit quam ut notitiam eorum posteris suis traderet. He then pronounces the singular critical canon: Cum Enoch eadem scriptura etiam de domino praedicarit, a nobis quidem nihil omnino rejiciendum est, quod pertineat ad nos . . . A Judaeis potest jam videri propterea rejecta, sicut et cetera fere quae Christum sonant . . . Eo accedit quod Enoch apud Judam apostolum testimonium possidet. II. 10 (quoted on viii. 1). *De Idol.* iv (quoted on xix. 1). Cf. also *De Idol.* ix; *De Virg. Veland.* vii: Si enim propter angelos, scilicet quos legimus a deo et caelo excidisse ob concupiscentiam feminarum, &c. *De Idol.* xv: Haec igitur ab initio praevidens spiritus sanctus etiam ostia in superstitionem ventura praececinit per antiquissimum propheten Enoch.

Clemens Alex. Eclogae Prophet. Ed. Dindorf, iii. 456 (quoted on xix. 3); iii. 474 (quoted on viii. 2. 3); *Strom.* iii. 9 (quoted on xvi. 3).

Origen (185–254) does not regard Enoch as inspired, and yet he does not wholly reject it. Cf. *Contra Celsum*, v. 52. Celsus argues that other *ἄγγελοι* descended to the earth before Christ: *ἐλθεῖν γὰρ καὶ ἄλλους λέγουσι πολλάκις καὶ ὁμοῦ γε ἑξήκοντα ἢ ἑβδομήκοντα· οὓς δὴ γενέσθαι κακοὺς καὶ κολάζεσθαι δεσμοῖς ὑποβληθέντας ἐν γῇ· ὅθεν καὶ τὰς θερμὰς πηγὰς εἶναι τὰ ἐκείνων δάκρυα.* In a lengthy rejoinder Origen remarks, v. 54: *ἐν ταῖς ἐκκλησίαις οὐ πάνυ φέρεται ὡς θεῖα τὰ ἐπιγεγραμμένα τοῦ Ἐνὼχ βιβλία.* That Origen was undecided as to the value to be attached to Enoch is clearer from the following passages. *In Joannem*, vi. 25 (Lommatsch. i. 241): *ὡς ἐν τῷ Ἐνὼχ γέγραπται, εἴ τῳ φίλον παραδέχεσθαι ὡς ἅγιον τὸ βιβλίον.* *In Num. Homil.* xxviii. 2 (Lommatsch. x. 366): De quibus quidem nominibus plurima in libellis, qui appellantur Enoch, secreta continentur, et arcana: sed quia libelli ipsi non videntur apud Hebraeos in auctoritate haberi, interim nunc ea, quae ibi nominantur ad exemplum vocare differamus. *De Princip.* i. 3. 3 (Lommatsch. xxi. 73): Sed et in Enoch libro his similia describuntur; iv. 35 (Lommatsch. xxi. 476) (quoted on xix. 3).

Anatolius appointed Bishop of Laodicea in 269. Quoted in Euseb. *Hist. Eccl.* vii. 32. 19: *τοῦ δὲ τὸν πρῶτον παρ' Ἑβραίοις μῆνα περὶ ἰσημερίαν εἶναι, παραστατικὰ καὶ τὰ ἐν τῷ Ἐνὼχ μαθήματα.*

Thenceforward the book fails to secure a single favourable notice. *Hilary*, who died 368 A.D., writes in his *Comment. in Ps.* cxxxii. 3: Fertur id de quo etiam nescio cuius liber extat, quod angeli concupiscentes filias hominum, cum de caelo descenderent, in hunc montem Hermon maxime convenerant excelsum. Chrysostom (346–407) does not indeed mention Enoch, but declares that the story of the angels and the daughters of men rests on a false exegesis, *Homil. in Gen.* vi. 1 and is a blasphemous fable.

Jerome (346–420) regards Enoch as apocryphal. *De Viris Illustr.* iv: Judas frater Jacobi parvam, quae de septem catholicis est, epistolam reliquit. Et quia de libro Enoch, qui apocryphus est, in ea assumit testimonia a plerisque rejicitur: tamen auctoritatem vetustate jam et usu meruit et inter sanctas computatur. *Comment. on Ps.* cxxxii. 3: Legimus in quodam libro apocrypho, eo tempore, quo descendebant filii dei ad filias hominum, descendisse illos in montem Hermon, et ibi iniisse pactum quomodo venirent ad filias hominum et sibi eas sociarent. Manifestissimus liber est et inter apocryphos computatur. *Comment. on Epist. ad Titum*, i. 12: Qui autem putant totum librum debere sequi eum, qui libri parte usus sit, videntur mihi et apocryphum Enochi, de quo Apostolus Judas in Epistola sua testimonium posuit, inter ecclesiae scripturas recipere.

Augustine (354–429) pronounces strongly against Enoch. *De Civ. Dei*, xv. 23. 4: Scripsisse quidem nonnulla divina Enoch illum septimum ab Adam, negare non possumus, cum hoc in Epistola canonica Judas Apostolus dicat. Sed non frustra non sunt in eo canone Scripturarum . . . Unde illa quae sub ejus nomine proferuntur et continent istas de gigantibus fabulas, quod non habuerint homines patres, recte a prudentibus judicantur non ipsius esse credenda. Cp. also *De Civ. Dei*, xviii. 38.

Enoch is finally condemned in explicit terms in *Constit. Apostol.* vi. 16: *καὶ ἐν τοῖς παλαιοῖς δέ τινες συνέγραψαν βιβλία ἀπόκρυφα Μωσέως καὶ Ἐνὼχ καὶ Ἀδάμ, Ἠσαΐου τε καὶ Δαβὶδ καὶ Ἠλία καὶ τῶν τριῶν πατριαρχῶν, φθοροποιὰ καὶ τῆς ἀληθείας ἐχθρά· τοιαῦτα καὶ νῦν ἐπενόησαν οἱ δυσώνυμοι, διαβάλλοντες δημιουργίαν, γάμον, πρόνοιαν, τεκνογονίαν, νόμον, προφήτας.*

Under the ban of such authorities the book of Enoch gradually passed out of circulation and knowledge in the Western Church, and with the exception of vi–ix. 4; viii. 4–x. 14; xv. 8–xvi. 1 and another fragment which are preserved by *Syncellus* in his *Chronography*, pp. 20–23; 42–47 (Ed. Dind. 1829) it was lost to western Christendom till the present century. Syncellus adds that the book of Enoch runs counter in some respects to the tradition of the Church, and is untrustworthy through the interpolations of Jews and heretics: *καὶ ταῦτα μὲν ἐκ τοῦ πρώτου βιβλίου Ἐνὼχ περὶ τῶν ἐγρηγόρων, εἰ καὶ μὴ τελείως χρὴ προσέχειν ἀποκρύφοις μάλιστα τοὺς ἁπλουστέρους, διά τε τὸ περιττά τινα καὶ ἀτριβῆ τῆς ἐκκλησιαστικῆς παραδόσεως ἔχειν καὶ διὰ τὸ νενοθεῦσθαι αὐτὰ ὑπὸ Ἰουδαίων καὶ αἱρετικῶν.* (Ed. Dindorf, pp. 47, 48.)

The Influence of Enoch on the New Testament.

The influence of Enoch on the New Testament has been greater than that of all the other apocryphal and pseudepigraphal books taken together. The evidence for this conclusion may for the sake of convenience be arranged under two heads. (A) A series of passages of the New Testament which either in phraseology or idea directly depend on or are illustrative of passages in Enoch. (B) Doctrines in Enoch which had an undoubted share in moulding the corresponding New Testament doctrines.

(A) We will begin with the General Epistles. I quote from the Revised Version when a more accurate rendering is desirable.

(*a*) *S. Jude* 4. Denying our only Master and Lord.	En. xlviii. 10. 'Denied the Lord of spirits and His anointed.' Cf. xxxviii. 2; xli. 2; lvii. 8.
6. 'The angels which kept not,' &c.	En. x. 5, 6, 12, 13.
13. 'Wandering stars.'	En. xviii. 15.
14. 'The seventh from Adam.'	En. lx. 8. 'The seventh from Adam.'
14, 15. A direct quotation from	En. i. 9; v. 4; xxvii. 2.
1 *S. Peter* iii. 19, 20.	En. x. 4. 5, 12, 13.
iv. 17. 'Judgment to begin at the house of God.'	En. i. 7. 'Judgment . . . over all the righteous.'
2 *S. Peter* ii. 4. (Observe how appropriately ταρταρώσας is used in connection with the fallen angels: Tartarus was originally the place of punishment of the Titans.	En. x. 4–6, 12, 13.
iii. 13. 'A new heaven and a new earth.'	En. xlv. 4, 5; lxxii. 1; xci. 16.
1 *S. John* ii. 1. 'Jesus Christ the righteous.'	En. xxxviii. 2. 'The Righteous One.'
ii. 8. 'The darkness is past and the true light,' &c.	En. lviii. 5. 'It has become bright as the sun upon earth, and the darkness is past.'
i. 7. 'Walk in the light.'	En. xcii. 4. 'The righteous . . . will walk in eternal light.'

[The contrast between light and darkness in S. John's Epistles repeatedly enforced in Enoch. See xxxviii. 4 (note).]

iii. 2. 'We shall be like Him.'	En. xc. 37, 38.
S. James i. 8. 'Double-minded man.'	En. xci. 4. 'A double heart.' See note.
v. 1–6. Woes against the rich.	En. xciv. 8–11 with parallel passages.

(*b*) *Book of Revelation.*—The writer or writers of this book are steeped in Jewish apocalyptic literature.

Rev. i. 4. 'Seven spirits which are before His throne.' Cf. iv. 5; viii. 2.	En. xc. 21. 'Seven first white ones.' Cf. Tobit xii. 15.
ii. 7. 'To him that overcometh will I give to eat of the tree of life': also xxii. 2, 14, 19 'the right to the tree of life.'	En. xxv. 4, 5. Only the elect in the Messianic kingdom are allowed to eat of the tree of life.
iii. 5. 'Clothed in white raiment.'	En. xc. 31. 'Clothed in white.'
10. 'Them that dwell upon the earth.'	En. xxxvii. 5. 'Those that dwell on the earth.'

[This phrase has always a bad sense in Revelation with the exception of xiv. 6. Cf. vi. 10; viii. 13; xi. 10; xiii. 8, 14; xvii. 8, and that in this respect Revelation follows the use of this phrase in the Noachic interpolations, see En. xxxvii. 5 (note).]

iii. 12. 'The New Jerusalem.'	En. xc. 29.
20. 'I will come unto him and sup with him.'	En. lxii. 14. '(The righteous) will eat, and lie down, and rise up with that Son of man.'
21. 'Sit with Me on My throne.' Cf. xx. 4.	En. cviii. 12. 'I will seat each on the throne of his honour.'
iv. 6. 'Round about the throne were four living creatures.'	En. xl. 2. 'On the four sides of the Lord of Spirits I saw four presences.'
v. 11.	En. xiv. 22; xl. 1; lxxi. 8.
vi. 10. 'How long, O Master, the holy and true, dost thou not judge and avenge our blood on them that dwell on the earth?'	En. xlvii. 2. 'The prayer of the righteous that it (i.e. the shedding of their blood) may not be in vain before the Lord of Spirits, that judgment may be done unto them, and that they may not have to suffer for ever.' Cf. xcvii. 3–5; xcix. 3, 16; civ. 3: also xxii. 5–7 where the souls of the righteous in Hades pray for vengeance.
vi. 15, 16. Compare the fear of 'the kings of the earth,	En. lxii. 3, 5. 'The kings, and the mighty, and the exalted

and the princes, and the chief captains, and the rich, and the strong' when they see 'the face of him that sitteth on the throne.'	. . . will be terrified . . . and pain will seize them when they see that Son of Man sitting on the throne of His glory.'
Rev. vii. 1. The four angels of the winds.	En. lxix. 22. 'The spirits of the winds.'
15. 'He that sitteth on the throne shall dwell among them.'	En. xlv. 4. 'I will cause Thine Elect to dwell among them.'
17. 'Shall guide them unto fountains of waters of life.'	En. xlviii. 1.
viii. 3, 4. Angel with golden censer of incense offers it with the prayers of the saints before God. In v. 8 the elders do so also.	This intercession of the angels is found frequently in Enoch, ix. 1–3, 10, 11; xv. 2; xl. 7; xlvii. 2; xcix. 3.
ix. 1. 'I saw a star from heaven fallen unto the earth.'	En. lxxxvi. 1. 'And I saw . . . and behold a star fell from heaven.'
20. 'Repented not of the works of their hands that they should not worship demons, and the idols of gold, and of silver, and of brass, and of stone, and of wood.'	En. xcix. 7. 'Others will make graven images of gold, and silver, and wood, and clay, and others will worship impure spirits and demons.'
xii. 10. 'The accuser of our brethren is cast down.'	En. xl. 7.
xiii. 14. 'Deceiveth them that dwell on the earth.'	En. liv. 6. 'Leading astray those that dwell on the earth.' Cf. lxvii. 7.
xiv. 9, 10. The worshippers of the beast are to be 'tormented with fire and brimstone in the presence of the holy angels, and in the presence of the lamb.'	En. xlviii. 8, 9. The unrighteous burn 'in the presence of the righteous.'
10. 'Holy angels.'	En. passim.
20. 'Blood came out of the winepress even unto the horses' bridles.'	En. c. 3. 'The horses will walk up to the breast in the blood of sinners.'

Rev. xvi. 5. 'Angel of the waters.'	En. lx. 16. 'Spirit of the sea.'
xx. 12. 'And the books were opened' and 'another book was opened which is the book of life.'	En. xc. 20. 'The books were opened.' En. xlvii. 3. 'The books of the living.'
13. 'The sea gave up the dead which were in it, and death and Hades gave up the dead which were in them.'	En. li. 1. 'The earth also will give back those that are treasured up within it, and Sheol also will give back that which it has received, and hell will give back that which it owes.' Cf. lxi. 5.

xx. 11–15. The last judgment is held after the temporary Messianic kingdom (xx. 4, 5), just as in En. xci–civ. There is however no resurrection in the temporary Messianic kingdom of Enoch as there is in Revelation.

15. 'Cast into the lake of fire.'	En. xc. 26. 'Cast into that fiery abyss.'

xxi. 1, 2. We have here a new heaven and a new earth, and a new Jerusalem coming down from heaven: yet in xxii. 14, 15 all classes of sinners are said to be without the gates of the city. But if there were a new earth, this would be impossible. This contradiction may have arisen from combining the divergent Messianic conceptions which appear in Enoch. Cf. xlv. 4, 5; xc. 29.

(*c*) We shall next deal with the *Epistles of S. Paul.* This Apostle, as we know, borrowed both phraseology and ideas from many quarters: from the Greek poets; from the apocryphal writings, as the Book of Wisdom; from the lost Revelation of Elias—1 Cor. ii. 9 according to Origen, and Eph. v. 14 according to Epiphanius. We shall find that he was well acquainted with and used the Book of Enoch.

Rom. viii. 38. 'Neither angels, nor principalities, nor powers.'	En. lxi. 10. 'Angels of power and angels of principalities.'
ix. 5. 'God blessed for ever.'	En. lxxvii. 1. 'He that is blessed for ever.'
1 *Cor.* vi. 11. 'Justified in the name of the Lord Jesus.'	En. xlviii. 7. 'Saved in his (i. e. the Messiah's) name.'

xi. 10. Tertullian, *C. Marc.* v. 8; *de Virg. Veland.* 7, explains this verse through a reference to the bad angels spoken of in Enoch who would be incited to wantonness by unveiled women.

2 *Cor.* iv. 6. 'To give the light of the knowledge of the glory of God in the face of Jesus Christ.'	En. xxxviii. 4. 'The light of the Lord of Spirits is seen on the face of the holy.'
xi. 31. 'He who is blessed for ever.'	En. lxxvii. 1. 'He who is blessed for ever.'
Gal. i. 4. 'This present evil world.'	En. xlviii. 7. 'This world of unrighteousness.'
Eph. i. 21. 'Above all principality and power.'	En. lxi. 10. 'The angels of power and the angels of principalities.'
9. 'According to His good pleasure.'	En. xlix. 4. 'According to His good pleasure.'
v. 8. 'Children of light.'	En. cviii. 11. 'The generation of light.'
Phil. ii. 10. 'At the name of Jesus every knee should bow.'	En. xlviii. 5. 'Will fall down and bow the knee before Him' (i. e. the Messiah).
Col. i. 16. 'Principalities and powers.'	En. lxi. 10. 'The angels of power and the angels of principalities.'
ii. 3. 'In whom are hid all the treasures of wisdom and knowledge.'	En. xlvi. 3. 'The Son of man . . . who reveals all the treasures of that which is hidden.'
1 *Thess.* v. 3. 'Then sudden destruction cometh upon them as upon a woman with child.'	En. lxii. 4. 'Then shall pain come upon them as on a woman in travail.'

Both these passages refer to the sudden appearing of the Messiah.

v. 5. 'Sons of light.'	En. cviii. 11. 'The generation of light.'
2 *Thess.* i. 7. 'The angels of His power.'	En. lxi. 10. 'The angels of power.'
1 *Tim.* i. 9. 'Law is not made for a righteous man but for the lawless,' &c.	En. xciii. 4. 'He will make a law for sinners.'

1 *Tim.* i. 15. 'Worthy of all acceptation' (cf. iv. 9).	En. xciv. 1. 'Worthy of acceptation.'
v. 21. 'The elect angels.'	En. xxxix. 1. 'Elect and holy children of the high heaven.'
vi. 15. 'King of Kings and Lord of Lords.'	En. ix. 4. 'Lord of Lords . . . King of Kings.'
16. Dwelling in, the light which no man can approach unto, whom no man hath seen.'	En. xiv. 21. 'None of the angels could enter (there) and no man could behold the form of the face of the Honoured and Glorious One.'

(*d*) *Epistle to the Hebrews.* This Epistle was probably written by Barnabas. As we have seen above (p. 38) this writer cites Enoch as Scripture in the Epistle which goes by his name.

Hebrews iv. 13. 'There is no creature that is not manifest in His sight: but all things are naked and laid open before the eyes of Him with whom we have to do.'	En. ix. 5. 'All things are naked and open in Thy sight, and Thou seest all things and nothing can hide itself from Thee.'
xi. 5. 'Enoch was translated . . . for before his translation he had this testimony that he pleased God.'	The parallel passage must, it seems, depend on the Enoch book where Enoch is always accounted an example of righteousness and therefore translated. Cf. xv. 1; lxxi. 14, &c. In Ecclus. xliv. 16 Enoch is translated indeed, but is cited as an example of repentance. Philo, *De Abrahamo*, speaks of the former evil life of Enoch.
xi. 10. 'The city which hath foundations whose builder and maker is God' (cf. xiii. 14).	En. xc. 29. 'Where God Himself builds the New Jerusalem.'
xii. 9. 'Father of spirits.'	'Lord of spirits,' passim in Similitudes.
22. 'The heavenly Jerusalem.'	En. xc. 29.

(*e*) *Acts of the Apostles.*

iii. 14. 'The Righteous One,' i. e. Christ. Cf. also vii. 52; xxii. 14.	En. xxxviii. 2. 'The Righteous One' (i. e. the Messiah).
iv. 12. 'There is none other name under heaven . . . whereby we must be saved.'	En. xlviii. 7. 'Saved in His (i. e. the Messiah's) name.'
x. 4. 'Thy prayers . . . are gone up for a memorial before God.'	En. xcix. 3. 'Raise your prayers as a memorial . . . before the Most High.'
xvii. 31. 'He will judge the world in righteousness by the man whom He hath ordained.'	En. xli. 9. 'He will appoint a judge for them all, and He will judge them all before Him.'

(*f*) *The Gospels.*

S. John ii. 16. The temple is called 'God's house,' but owing to sin of Israel 'your house,' i. e. merely house of Israel. Cf. S. Luke xiii. 35 and parallels.	En. lxxxix. 54. Temple = house of the Lord of the sheep. En. lxxxix. 56. But owing to sin of Israel it is said 'He forsook that their house.'
v. 22. 'He hath committed all judgment unto the Son.'	En. lxix. 27. 'The sum of judgment was committed unto Him, the Son of Man.'
27. 'He gave him authority to execute judgment because he is the Son of Man.'	
xii. 36. 'Sons of light.'	En. cviii. 11. 'The generation of light.'
xiv. 2. 'Many mansions.'	En. xxxix. 4. 'Mansions of the righteous.' Cf. xxxix. 7; xlviii. 1, &c.
S. Luke i. 52. 'He hath put down princes from their thrones.'	En. xlvi. 5. 'He will put down the kings from their thrones.'
ix. 35. 'This is My Son, the Elect One.' So Greek ὁ ἐκλελεγμένος.	En. xl. 5. 'The Elect One,' i. e. the Messiah. Cf. xlv. 3–5; xlix. 2, 4, &c.
xiii. 35. See on S. John ii. 16.	
xvi. 8. 'Sons of the light.'	En. cviii. 11. 'The generation of light.'

S. Luke xvi. 9. 'Mammon of unrighteousness.'	En. lxiii. 10. 'Mammon of unrighteousness.'
xviii. 7. 'Shall not God avenge His Elect which cry to Him day and night, and He is long-suffering over them.' Cf. 2 Pet. iii. 9; Ecclus. xxxii. 18.	En. xlvii. 1, 2. See Translation. This verse of S. Luke suggests another rendering of Enoch. 'The prayer of the righteous . . . that judgment may be executed on them and that He may be no more long-suffering over them.'
xxi. 28. 'Your redemption draweth nigh.'	En. li. 2. 'The day of their redemption has drawn nigh.'
xxiii. 35. 'The Christ of God, the Elect One,' ὁ ἐκλεκτός.	En. xl. 5. 'The Elect One.'
S. Matthew v. 22, 29, 30; x. 28 where Gehenna is the place of final punishment.	En. xxvii. 2; xc. 26, 27 where Gehenna first definitely appears as hell.
xix. 28. 'When the Son of Man shall sit on the throne of His glory.'	En. lxii. 5. 'When they see that Son of Man sitting on the throne of His glory.'
'Ye also shall sit on twelve thrones.'	En. cviii. 12. 'I will seat each on the throne of his honour.'
xix. 29. 'Inherit eternal life.'	En. xl. 9.
xxi. 13; xxiii. 38. See S. John ii. 16.	En. lxxxix. 56. En. lxxxix. 54.
xxv. 41. 'Prepared for the devil and his angels.'	En. liv. 5. 'Chains . . . prepared for the hosts of Azazel.'
xxvi. 24. 'It had been good for that man if he had not been born.'	En. xxxviii. 2. 'It had been good for them if they had not been born.'
xxviii. 18. 'All authority hath been given to Me in heaven and on earth.'	En. lxii. 6. '(The Son of man) who rules over all.'
S. Mark xi. 17. See S. John ii. 6.	En. lxxxix. 54.

(B) Doctrines in Enoch which had an undoubted share in moulding the corresponding New Testament doctrines, or are at all events necessary to the comprehension of the latter.

(*a*) The nature of the Messianic kingdom and of the future life.

(*b*) The Messiah.

(*c*) Sheol and the Resurrection.

(*d*) Demonology.

(*a*) THE KINGDOM. We shall only deal with one incident coming under this head; it is found in the three Synoptists: S. Matt. xxii. 23–33; S. Mark xii. 18–27; S. Luke xx. 27–36. This incident can only be rightly understood from Enoch. When the Sadducees said, 'Whose wife shall she be of them? for the seven had her to wife,' they are arguing from the sensuous conception of the Messianic kingdom—and this was no doubt the popular one—given in En. i–xxxvi, according to which its members, including the risen righteous, were to enjoy every good thing of earth and have each a thousand children. The Sadducees thought thereby to place this young prophet on the horns of a dilemma, and oblige Him to confess either that there was no resurrection of the dead, or else that polygamy or polyandry would be practised in the coming kingdom. But the dilemma proves invalid: and the conception of the future life portrayed in our Lord's reply tallies almost exactly in thought, and partially in word, with that described in En. xci–civ, according to which there is to be a resurrection indeed, but a resurrection of the spirit, and the risen righteous are to rejoice 'as the angels of heaven' (En. civ. 4; S. Matt. xxii. 30; S. Mark xii. 25), 'being companions of the heavenly hosts' (En. civ. 6).

(*b*) THE MESSIAH. The Messiah is referred to in xc. 37, 38. He is represented as the head of the Messianic community out of which He proceeds, but He has no special rôle to fulfil and His presence in that description seems due merely to literary reminiscence. This Messiah-reference exercised no influence on New Testament conceptions. But with regard to the Messiah described in the Similitudes the case is very different. Four titles applied for the first time in literature to the personal Messiah in the Similitudes are afterwards reproduced in the New Testament. These are 'Christ' or 'the Anointed One,' 'the Righteous One,' 'the Elect One,' and 'the Son of Man.'

'*Christ*' or '*the Anointed One.*' This title, found repeatedly in earlier writings but always in reference to actual contemporary kings or priests, is now for the first time—see xlviii. 10; lii. 4—applied to the ideal Messianic king that is to come. It is associated here with supernatural attributes. A few years later in another writing, the Psalms of Solomon (xvii. 36; xviii. 6, 8), it possesses quite a different connotation. In those Psalms the Messiah, though endowed with divine gifts, is a man and nothing more, and springs from the house of David.

'*The Righteous One.*' This title, which occurs in Acts iii. 14; vii. 52; xxii. 14 (cp. 1 S. John ii. 1), first appears in Enoch as a Messianic designation; see En. xxxviii. 2; liii. 6. Righteousness is one of the leading characteristics of the Messiah, xlvi. 3.

'*The Elect One.*' This title likewise appearing first in Enoch, xl. 5; xlv. 3-4; xlix. 2, 4; li. 3, 5, &c., passes over into the New Testament, S. Luke ix. 35; xxiii. 35, 'The Christ, the Elect One.' In the Old Testament we find 'Mine Elect,' Is. xlii. 1, but not 'the Elect One.'

'*The Son of Man.*' This definite title (see notes on xlvi. 2, 3) is found in the Book of Enoch for the first time in Jewish literature, and is, historically, the source of the New Testament designation, and contributes to it some of its most characteristic contents. For an account of the relations between the Enochic and New Testament uses of this title, we must refer to the Appendix on 'The Son of Man' at the close of the book.

(*c*) Sheol. If we except the Psalms we have in Enoch the first instances in which this word is found in its New Testament signification. For the history of this word and its meanings, see note on lxii. 10.

It is further interesting to note that the writer of xci–civ delivers himself of a sustained polemic in cii. 4–civ. 9 against the Old Testament doctrine of Sheol, and the fact that this writer in xci. 4 borrows Ecclus. i. 25 makes it probable that the immediate book he had in view is Ecclesiasticus, which enforces dogmatically and repeatedly the Old Testament doctrine of Sheol.

THE RESURRECTION. This doctrine, which is first taught beyond possibility of doubt in Dan. xii, though a true exegesis will find many intimations of the doctrine in earlier books, was made a common-place of Jewish theology by the book of Enoch. For the various forms this doctrine assumed, see note on li. 1.

(*d*) THE DEMONOLOGY of Enoch reappears for the most part in the New Testament.

(*a*) The angels which kept not their first estate, S. Jude 6; 2 S. Pet. ii. 4, are the angelic watchers who fell from lusting after the daughters of men, and whose fall and punishment are recounted in En. vi–xvi. They have always been imprisoned in darkness from the time of their fall.

(β) Demons. These are, according to Enoch xvi. 1, the spirits which went forth from the souls of the giants who were the children of the fallen angels and the daughters of men. These demons were to work moral ruin on the earth without hindrance till the final judgment as disembodied spirits.

So in the New Testament. The demons are disembodied spirits, S. Matt. xii. 43–45; S. Luke xi. 24–26. They are not punished till the final judgment: S. Matt. viii. 29, 'Art Thou come hither to torment us *before the time*?' They are subject to Satan, S. Matt. xii. 24–28.

(γ) Satan appears in Enoch as the ruler of a counter kingdom of evil, yet a kingdom subject to the Lord of Spirits. He led astray the angels and made them his subjects, liv. 6; lxix. 5.

A Satan also led astray Eve, lxix. 6. The Satans (as in Job) can still appear in heaven, xl. 7. The functions of the Satans are threefold: they tempted to evil, lxix. 4, 6; they accused the fallen, xl. 7; they punished the condemned as angels of punishment, liii. 3; lvi. 1.

So in the New Testament there is the counter-kingdom of sin, S. Matt. xii. 26; S. Luke xi. 18; 'if Satan cast out Satan, how shall his kingdom stand?' Satan led astray the angels, Rev. xii. 4, and led astray man, 2 Cor. xi. 3. The demons are subjects of Satan, S. Matt. xii. 24–28. The functions of Satan are tempting, S. Matt. iv. 1–12; S. Luke xxii. 31; accusing, Rev. xii. 10; punishing, 1 Cor. v. 5, where impenitent sinners are delivered over to Satan for punishment.

THE BOOK OF ENOCH

SECTION I.

(CHAPTERS I—XXXVI.)

INTRODUCTION.

A. *Critical Structure.* B. *Relation of this Section to* (*a*) lxxii–lxxxii; (*b*) lxxxiii–xc; (*c*) xci–civ. C. *Its Date.* D. *The Problem and its Solution.*

A. Critical Structure. For the relation of this Section to the rest of his book, see General Introduction (p. 26). This Section is at once incomplete and composite. To determine its original form is perfectly hopeless; it has suffered from all the evils incident to tradition and unscrupulous interpolation. It is impossible to regard it as a complete work in itself, and its leading ideas preclude our finding its original complement in the other Sections of the book. It is composite in character, not to speak of extensive interpolations (i.e. xvii–xix). There are two distinct world-conceptions present. In xii–xvi the transcendence of God is pictured in an extreme degree. He dwells in heaven in a crystal palace of fire, into which not even an angel may enter, xiv. 9–23; whereas in i–xi, xx–xxxvi, the *old Hebrew standpoint* is fairly preserved. God will come down to judge on Sinai, i. 4; the Messianic kingdom will be established on earth, and all sin will vanish, x. 17–22; the chambers of blessing in heaven will be opened, xi. 1; Jerusalem will be the centre of the Messianic kingdom, xxv. 5; and God Himself will come down to visit the earth with blessing, and will sit on His throne on earth, xxv. 3; men will enjoy patriarchal lives, and die in happy old age, v. 9; x. 17; xxv. 6.

There are many interpolations: vi. 3–8; viii. 1–3; ix. 7; x. 1–3; xvii–xix. The peculiarity attaching to these interpolations is that no attempt is made to assimilate them to their new contexts. Generally they stand in glaring contradiction with them.

B. (*a*) **Relation of i–xxxvi to lxxii–lxxxii.** These two sections come from different authors; see Special Introd. to lxxii–lxxxii. (*b*) **Relation of i–xxxvi to lxxxiii–xc.** These two Sections are of distinct authorship. The former is the older, and was known to the author of the latter; see Special Introd. to lxxxiii–xc. (*c*) **Relation of i–xxxvi to xci–civ.** These two Sections are likewise independent; but the author of the latter was acquainted with i–xxxvi or some form of it; see Special Introd. to xci–civ.

C. Its Date. As i–xxxvi is anterior to lxxxiii–xc, the oldest of the remaining Sections of the book, and as that Section must have been written before 161 B.C., we have thus the latest possible date of the composition of i–xxxvi. But it is highly probable, that it was written much earlier, earlier in fact than the persecution under Antiochus; for to the horrors of that persecution, which impressed themselves so strongly on the author of Daniel, and of En. lxxxiii–xc there is not the faintest allusion in i–xxxvi.

D. The Problem and its Solution. The author essays to justify the ways of God. The righteous will not always suffer, and the wicked will not always prosper, i. 1. The limits thereto are set by death, xxii, and by great world judgments. But the cure of the world's corruption can only be understood by apprehending its cause, and this cause is to be traced to the lust of the fallen Watchers for the daughters of men. Original sin stands not in the following of Adam—whose sin seems limited in its effects to himself, xxxii. 6—but in the evil engendered through the Watchers, ix. 6, 9, 10; x. 8. Hence the Watchers, their companions and children were destroyed, x. 4–10, 12; and their condemnation and confinement form the prelude to the first world judgment, of which the Deluge forms the completion, x. 1–3. But though only the righteous survived the Deluge, sin still prevailed in the world through the demons—the spirits which had gone forth from the slaughtered children of the Watchers and the daughters of men, and all manner of corruption was wrought through them, xvi. 1, as they escape punishment till the final judgment. But the recompense of character is not withheld till the last judgment; there is a foretaste of the final doom immediately after death, xxii. In the second and last judgment on Sinai, i. 4, the Watchers, the demons, and godless, x. 12; xvi. 1, and all classes of Israel, with one exception, receive their final award, i. 9. To make this possible, this judgment is preceded by a General Resurrection of Israel, xxii. A final end is now made of sin on the earth, and the earth cleansed, x. 15, 16, 20–22; the wicked are cast into Gehenna, and their punishment is a spectacle for the righteous to behold, xxvii. 2; the Messianic kingdom is established, with Jerusalem and Palestine as its centre, xxv. 5—there is no Messiah, and God abides with men, xxv. 3; all the Gentiles will become righteous and worship God, x. 21; the righteous are allowed to eat of the tree of life, xxv. 4–6, and thereby enjoy patriarchal lives, v. 9; xxv. 6, begetting 1000 children, x. 17, and enjoying unlimited material blessings, v. 7, x. 18, 19; xi. 2.

As to what becomes of the righteous, after the second death, there is no hint in this fragmentary Section. There is much celestial, terrestrial, and subterrestrial geography in xvii–xix, xxi–xxxvi.

TRANSLATION.

I. 1. The words of the blessing of Enoch, wherewith he blessed the elect and righteous, who will be living in the day of tribulation, when all the wicked and godless are to be removed. 2. And Enoch answered and spake—(Enoch) a righteous man, whose eyes were opened by God, that he might see a vision of the Holy One in the heavens, which the angels showed me, and from them I heard everything and I understood what I saw, but not for this generation, but for the remote generations which are for to come. 3. Concerning

I. 2. **God.** I have rendered **እግዚአብሔር** by 'God,' and **እግዚእ** by 'Lord.' The former word is at times a rendering of ὁ κύριος, and at times of ὁ θεός in the LXX. It occurs ten times in Enoch. **አምላክ**=ὁ θεός is found nine times. **Vision of the Holy One.** So BG **ቅዱስ** and the Giz. Gk. Other MSS. 'holy vision.'

I. 1. **The elect and righteous.** This designation is found also in xxxviii. 2, 3, 4; xxxix. 6, 7; xlviii. 1; lviii. 1, 2; lxi. 13; lxii. 12, 13, 15; lxx. 3. 2. **The Holy One.** For this and similar designations of God see v. 3. The change from the third to the first person in this verse, is of frequent occurrence in this book: cf. xii. 1–3; xxxvii. 1, 2; lxx. 1–3; lxxi. 5; xcii. 1.

the elect I spake, and uttered a parable concerning them: the Holy and Great One will come forth from His dwelling, the God of the world. 4. And going from thence He will tread on Mount Sinai and appear with His hosts, and in the strength of His might appear from heaven. 5. And everyone will be smitten with fear, and the watchers will quake, and great fear and trembling will seize them unto the ends of the earth. 6. And the high mountains will be shaken, and the high hills will be made low, and will melt like wax before the flame. 7. And the earth will be rent and all that is upon the earth will perish, and there will be a judgment upon everything and upon all the righteous. 8. But to the righteous He will give peace and will protect

---

3. **Uttered a parable concerning them: the Holy One.** So G omitting the **ዘ** in Dln.'s text, and the Giz. Gk. *ἀνέλαβον τὴν παραβολήν μου.* Dln., misled by the **ዘ** and taking **ምስለ** as a preposition, translates: 'conversed concerning them with the Holy One.' 7. **The earth will be rent.** So G **ትሠጠቅ** and the Giz. Gk. *διασχισθήσεται.* Other MSS. **ትሠጠም** 'will sink

---

In xci–civ these changes are confusing. **3. The elect.** This designation belongs mainly to the Similitudes. It is found in i. 8; v. 7; xxv. 5; xl. 5; xli. 2; xlviii. 1, 9; li. 5; lvi. 6, 8; lviii. 3; lxi. 4, 12; lxii. 7, 8, 11; xciii. 2. **Holy and Great One.** This title is found elsewhere in x. 1; xiv. 1; xxv. 3; lxxxiv. 1; xcii. 2; xcvii. 6; xcviii. 6; civ. 9. God is designated simply as 'the Holy One,' xciii. 11, and as 'the Great One,' xiv. 2; ciii. 4; civ. 1 (twice). **Come forth from His dwelling.** Cf. Mic. i. 3; Is. xxvi. 21. Assumptio Moyseos x. 3. **God of the world.** Cf. lviii. 4; lxxxi. 10; lxxxii. 7; lxxxiv. 2; also xii. 3; lxxxi. 3. **4.** Sinai, whence the Law was given, will likewise be the place of future judgment. Cf. Deut. xxxiii. 2; Ps. lxviii. 17. **5. Watchers.** This name belongs to the fallen angels here and in x. 9, 15; xii. 2, 4; xiii. 10; xiv. 1, 3; xv. 2; xvi. 1, 2; xci. 15. In xx. 1; xxxix. 12, 13; xl. 2; lxi. 12; lxxi. 7 it designates the archangels. It is first found in Dan. iv. 13, 17, 23. **6.** Cf. Judges v. 5; Ps. xcvii. 5; Is. lxiv. 1, 3; Mic. i. 4; Judith xvi. 15 (Dln.) Assumpt. Moyseos x. 4. **7.** Dln. thinks that we have in 5–9 a description combining the two great judgments; but everything from verse 4 to end is perfectly applicable to the final judgment. Yet cf. lxxxiii. 7. **8. Will give peace.** See v. 4 note. **The righteous.** This designation is found in all parts of the book: i. 7, 8; v. 6; xxv. 4; xxxix. 4; xliii. 4; xlvii. 1, 2, 4; xlviii. 1, 7, 9; l. 2; liii. 7; lvi. 7; lviii. 3, 5; lx. 2; lxi. 3; lxii. 3; lxxxii. 4; xciv. 3, 11; xcv. 3, 7; xcvi. 1, 8; xcvii. 1, 3, 5; xcviii. 12–14; xcix. 3; c. 5, 7, 10; cii. 4, 10; ciii. 1; civ.

the elect, and grace will be upon them, and they will all belong to God, and it will be well with them, and they will be blessed and the light of God will shine upon them. 9. And lo! He comes with ten thousands of (His) holy ones to execute judgment upon them, and He will destroy the ungodly, and will convict all flesh of all that the sinners and ungodly have wrought and ungodly committed against Him.

II. 1. I observed everything that took place in the heaven, how the luminaries which are in the heaven do not deviate from their orbits, how they all rise and set in order each in its season, and transgress not against their appointed order. 2. Behold ye the earth, and give heed to the things which take place upon it from first to last, how unvaryingly every work of God appears. 3. Behold the summer and the winter, how (in the winter season) the whole earth is full of water, and clouds and dew and rain lie upon it.

III. I observed and saw how (in the winter) all the trees

---

down.' 9. **Will convict all flesh.** **ይዘልፍ**. So G M. Jude 15 ἐλέγξαι. The Giz. Gk. ἐλέγξει. Other MSS. **ይትዋቀስ**=' will plead with all flesh.' See Appendix on this verse.

III. 1. G M read **ኵሉ፡ ዕፀው፡ እፎ** instead of **ከመ፡ ኵሉ፡ ዕፀው፡ እፎ** as Dln.

1, 6, 12, 13. **The light of God will shine upon them.** Cf. xxxviii. 4. **9.** Quoted by St. Jude 14, 15, who in the same passage draws upon v. 4; xxvii. 2; lx. 8. Cf. ci. 3. **Ten thousands of His holy ones.** Cf. Dan. vii. 10. The angels are so called in xii. 2; xiv. 23; xxxix. 5; xlvii. 2; lvii. 2; lx. 4; lxi. 8, 10, 12; lxv. 12; lxix. 13; lxxxi. 5; ciii. 2; cvi. 19, as already in Job v. 1; xv. 15; Zech. xiv. 5; Dan. iv. 13; viii. 13. They are called 'holy angels' in xx. 1–7; xxi. 5, 9; xxii. 3; xxiv. 6; xxvii. 2; xxxii. 6; lxxi. 8; xciii. 2. 'Holy ones of heaven:' ix. 3. For other designations see vi. 2 (note).

II. The author in ii–v. 3 emphasizes the order that prevails in the world of nature as a contrast to the disorder that prevails in the world of man. In Test. Naphth. 3 men are bidden to observe the law of God as the sun, moon, and stars observe the order appointed to them, and the Watchers, who were cursed of God for forsaking their natural order and estate, are held up as a warning. Cf. also Ecclus. xvi. 26–28; Pss. Sol. xviii. 11–14. **2.** The Hebrews divided the year into two seasons, קַיִץ embracing Spring and Summer, and חֹרֶף embracing Autumn and Winter. Gen. viii. 22; Is. xviii. 6; Zech. xiv. 8. Cf. Herzog's *R.E.* vi. 497 'Jar.'

seem as though they had withered and shed all their leaves, except fourteen trees, which do not lose their foliage but retain the old foliage from two to three years till the new comes.

IV. And again I observed the days of summer how the sun is above the earth over against it. And you seek shade and shelter against the heat of the sun, and the earth also burns with glowing heat, and so you cannot tread on the earth, or on a rock by reason of its heat.

V. 1. I observed how the trees cover themselves with green leaves and bear fruit: wherefore give ye heed to everything, and recognise how He who liveth for ever hath made all this for you. 2. How His works are before Him in each succeeding year, and all His works serve Him and alter not but everything is done as God hath ordained. 3. And behold how the seas and the rivers together accomplish their task. 4. But as for you, ye have not continued steadfast, and the law of the Lord have ye not fulfilled but have transgressed it, and have slanderously spoken proud and hard words with your impure mouths against His greatness—O ye hard hearted ye will find no peace. 5. And therefore will ye execrate your days and be bereft of the years of your life: but the years of your destruction will be mul-

---

V. 5. **Be bereft of the years of your life.** ተሀጕሉ may be either 2nd Pers. Pl. Future I. 1 = 'ye will lose, be bereft of' = *ἀποστερηθήσεσθε*, or 3rd Pers. Pl. Present III. 1 = 'They are perishing.' Dln. takes it to be the latter. But the present tense is out of place between two futures. **The years of your destruction.** The words are drawn from the Giz. Gk., having dropped out of the Ethiopic MSS., but the text of G implies them, giving በርገሙት

III. On the fourteen evergreen trees cf. Dln. *in loc.*

V. 4. **The law of the Lord.** Cf. xcix. 2. 'The eternal law.' **Proud and hard words.** Cf. xxvii. 2; ci. 3. From these passages the close of St. Jude 15 is drawn. Cf. Ps. xii. 4; Dan. vii. 8, 11, 20. **Slanderously spoken.** The charge of blasphemy is frequent in xci–civ. Cf. xci. 7, 11; xciv. 9; xcvi. 7; c. 9. **Hard hearted.** Cf. xcviii. 11; c. 8 'obstinate of heart.' **Ye will find no peace.** This phrase occurs in Sects. i–xxxvi. and xci–civ only: i. 8; v. 4; xii. 5; xiii. 1; xvi. 4; xciv. 6; xcviii. 11, 15; xcix. 13;

tiplied in eternal execration and ye will find no mercy. 6. In those days ye shall give your name for an eternal execration unto all the righteous, and they will evermore execrate you as sinners—you together with (all other) sinners. 7. But for the elect there will be light and joy and peace, and they will inherit the earth: but upon you, ye ungodly, there will be execration. 8. Then too will wisdom be bestowed on the elect, and they will all live and never again sin, either through heedlessness or through pride, but they who are wise will be humble nor fall again into sin. 9. And they will not be punished all the days of their life, nor will they die of plagues or visitations of wrath, but they will complete the full number of the days of their life, and their lives will grow old in peace, and the years of their joy will be many, in eternal happiness and peace all the days of their life.

'will be multiplied in eternal execration.' Later scribes, finding no subject for the verb in this clause, omitted the preposition and read ወርገም: hence Dln.'s text, 'eternal execration will be multiplied upon you.' 6. **Ye shall give your name for an eternal execration unto all the righteous**, reading ስመ with G instead of ሰላመ with all other MSS. but M. If we accept the other reading, we are to translate: 'Ye shall give up your peace to become an eternal execration.' The phrase appears to be drawn from Isaiah lxv. 15, 'Ye shall leave your name for a curse unto My chosen,' וְהִנַּחְתֶּם שִׁמְכֶם לִשְׁבוּעָה לִבְחִירַי. The Giz. Gk. supports G.

---

ci. 3; cii. 3; ciii. 8. 7. The temporal blessings promised in the O.T. are here renewed, but on the question of Sheol and the Resurrection the writer has forsaken O.T. ground. 8. **Will wisdom be bestowed on the elect**: see xlii. 1, 2. 9. Cf. Is. lxv. 20, 22; Zech. viii. 4; En. xxv. 4, 5 (note).

VI–XI. The abruptness with which vi–xi are introduced, is quite in keeping with the fragmentary and composite nature of the rest of the Section. As Dln. (Herzog, *R. E.* xii. 352) has already seen, vi. 3–8; viii. 1–3; ix. 7; x. 11 belong to a Semjaza cycle of myths; for in these passages Semjaza is represented as chief and Azazel tenth in command: as also in lxix. 2. Elsewhere in Enoch Azazel is chief and Semjaza is not mentioned. Again x. 1–3 belongs to an Apocalypse of Noah, many fragments of which are found in Enoch. Another fragment of this Apocalypse is preserved by Syncellus in the Greek; but to this there is no corresponding text in the Ethiopic.

VI. 1. And it came to pass when the children of men had multiplied in those days that beautiful and comely daughters were born unto them. 2. And the angels, the sons of the heavens, saw and lusted after them, and spake to one another, 'Come, now let us choose us wives from among the children of men and beget children.' [3. And Semjâzâ who was their leader spake unto them: 'I fear ye will not indeed agree to do this deed and then I alone shall have to pay the penalty of a great sin.' 4. Then answered they all unto

Fragments of the Greek Version of Enoch preserved in the Chronography of G. Syncellus. Ed. by Dindorf, 1829.

Ἐκ τοῦ πρώτου βιβλίου Ἐνὼχ περὶ τῶν ἐγρηγόρων.

G. Syncellus, S. 20–23.

Hen. 6, 1–9, 4.

Καὶ ἐγένετο, ὅτε ἐπληθύνθησαν οἱ υἱοὶ τῶν ἀνθρώπων, ἐγεννήθησαν αὐτοῖς θυγατέρες ὡραῖαι, καὶ ἐπεθύμησαν αὐτὰς οἱ ἐγρήγοροι, καὶ ἀπεπλανήθησαν ὀπίσω αὐτῶν, καὶ εἶπον πρὸς ἀλλήλους, ἐκλεξώμεθα ἑαυτοῖς γυναῖκας ἀπὸ τῶν θυγατέρων τῶν ἀνθρώπων τῆς γῆς. Καὶ εἶπε Σεμιαζᾶς ὁ ἄρχων αὐτῶν πρὸς αὐτούς, φοβοῦμαι μὴ οὐ θελήσητε ποιῆσαι τὸ πρᾶγμα τοῦτο, καὶ ἔσομαι ἐγὼ μόνος ὀφειλέτης ἁμαρτίας μεγάλης. καὶ ἀπεκρίθησαν αὐτῷ

VI. 3. **Pay the penalty of a great sin.** So G M **ፈድየ፡ ለኀጢአት፡ ዐቢይ** and the Giz. and Syn. Gk. *ὀφειλέτης ἁμαρτίας μεγάλης.* Other

---

VI. 2. Sons of the heavens. Cf. xiii. 8; xiv. 3; xxxix. 1. See xv. 1–7. Cf. 'Sons of the holy angels,' lxxi. 1; v. 6 'Descended in the days of Jared.' See Crit. Note. The entire myth of the angels and the daughters of men in Enoch springs originally from Gen. vi. 1–4, where it is said that 'the sons of God came in to the daughters of men.' These words are not to be taken as expressing alliances between the Sethites and the Cainites, but as belonging to a very early myth of Persian origin to the effect that demons had corrupted the earth before the coming of Zoroaster and had allied themselves with women. So Delitzsch, *Neuer Commentar über d. Genesis*, 1887, pp. 146–8. The LXX originally rendered the words 'sons of God' by *ἄγγελοι τοῦ Θεοῦ*, and this rendering is found in Philo, *de Gigantibus*, Eusebius, Augustine, and Ambrose. This view of Gen. vi. 1–4 was held by most of the early fathers. On the myths regarding the intercourse of angels with the daughters of men, see Grünbaum in *ZDMG.* xxxi. 225 ff. (Referred to by Delitzsch.) For statements of later writers either depending directly on this account in Enoch or harmonizing with it, cf. Joseph. *Ant.* i. 3. 1; Philo, *de Gigantibus;* Test. Reuben 5; Napth. 3; Justin Martyr, *Apol.* i. 5; Ps. Clemens, *Hom.* viii. 13; Clem. Alex. *Strom.* v. 1. 10; Tert. *De Virg. Veland.* vii; *Adv. Marc.* v. 18; *De Idol.* ix; Lact. *Instit.*

him and spake: 'Let us all swear an oath, and bind ourselves by mutual imprecations not to abandon this plan but to carry it into execution.' 5. Then sware they all together and bound themselves by mutual imprecations to its fulfilment; and they were in all two hundred. 6. And they descended in the days of Jared on the summit of

πάντες καὶ εἶπον, ὀμόσωμεν ἅπαντες ὅρκῳ καὶ ἀναθεματίσωμεν ἀλλήλους τοῦ μὴ ἀποστρέψαι τὴν γνώμην ταύτην, μέχρις οὗ ἀποτελέσωμεν αὐτήν. τότε πάντες ὤμοσαν ὁμοῦ καὶ ἀνεθεμάτισαν ἀλλήλους. Ἦσαν δὲ οὗτοι διακόσιοι οἱ καταβάντες ἐν ταῖς ἡμέραις Ἰάρεδ εἰς τὴν κορυφὴν τοῦ Ἑρμονιεὶμ ὄρους καὶ ἐκάλεσαν τὸ ὄρος Ἑρμώμ,

---

MSS. 'Pay the penalty of this great sin.' 5. **Bound themselves by mutual imprecations.'** So G M and the Giz. and Syn. Gk. Other MSS. insert 'all.' 'They all bound themselves,' &c. 6. **Descended in the days of Jared.** I have here followed the Greek text *οἱ καταβάντες ἐν ταῖς ἡμέραις Ἰάρεδ εἰς τὴν κορυφὴν τοῦ Ἑρμονιεὶμ ὄρους*. The Ethiopic text reads: 'descended on Ardis which is the summit of Mt. Hermon.' The name Ardis, otherwise unknown, is to be explained with Dln. as a compression of *Ἰάρεδ εἰς*, the translator not having found *ἐν ταῖς ἡμέραις* in his text. Hallévi in the *Journal Asiatique*, Avril-Mai 1867, pp. 356–357, reproduces this verse in Hebrew, whereby we see at a glance, why the angels descended in the days of Jared—from ירד to descend, and why it was that they bound themselves by mutual oaths on Hermon—from חֶרֶם a curse.

וַיֵּרְדוּ בִּימֵי יֶרֶד עַל ראשׁ הַר חֶרְמוֹן וַיִּקְרְאוּ לְהַר חֶרְמוֹן כִּי בוֹ נִשְׁבְּעוּ וְהֶחֱרִימוּ בֵּינֵיהֶם

Cf. Book of Jubilees iv: 'Jared; for in his days the angels of the

---

ii. 15; Commodian. *Instruct.* i. 3. In the *De Civ. Dei* xv. 23, Augustine combats this view, and denies the inspiration of Enoch, which is upheld by Tertullian. **6. Descended in the days of Jared.** See Crit. Note; also cvi. 13. Dln. refers also to Orig. *Comment. in Joann.* tom. viii. p. 132, ed. Huet; Epiph. *adv. Haer.* i. 4, ed. Petav, tom. i. p. 4. The reasons for the descent of the angels in the Book of Jubilees differ from those given in this chapter. In iv and v of that book it is stated that the watchers were sent to the earth by God 'to instruct the children of men to do judgment and uprightness,' and that when so doing they began to lust after the daughters of men. This form of the myth seems to be followed in Test.

Mount Hermon, and they
called it Mount Hermon, because they had sworn and
bound themselves by mutual
imprecations upon it. 7.
And these are the names of their
leaders: Semjâzâ, their leader,
Urâkîbarâmêêl, Kôkabîêl, Tâ-
miêl, Râmuêl, Dânêl, Zaqîlô,
Sarâqujâl, Asâêl, Armârôs,
Batraal, Anânî, Zaqêbê, Sam-
sâvêêl, Sartaêl, Turêl, Jomjâêl,
Arâzjâl. 8. These are their
chiefs of tens, and all the
others were with them.]
VII. 1. And they took unto
themselves wives, and each
chose for himself one, and
they began to go in unto them
and they mixed with them,

*καθότι ὤμοσαν καὶ ἀνεθεμάτισαν
ἀλλήλους ἐν αὐτῷ. καὶ ταῦτα
τὰ ὀνόματα τῶν ἀρχόντων αὐτῶν·
α′ Σεμιαζᾶς ὁ ἄρχων αὐτῶν.
β′ Ἀταρκούφ. γ′ Ἀρακιήλ. δ′
Χωβαβιήλ. ε′ Ὀραμμαμή. ϛ′
Ῥαμιήλ. ζ′ Σαμψίχ. η′ Ζακιήλ.
θ′ Βαλκιήλ. ι′ Ἀζαλζήλ. ια′
Φαρμαρός. ιβ′ Ἀμαριήλ. ιγ′
Ἀναγημάς. ιδ′ Θαυσαήλ. ιε′
Σαμιήλ. ιϛ′ Σαρινᾶς. ιζ′ Εὐμιήλ.
ιη′ Τυριήλ. ιθ′ Ἰουμιήλ. κ′
Σαριήλ. Οὗτοι καὶ οἱ λοιποὶ
πάντες ἐν τῷ χιλιοστῷ ἑκατοστῷ
ἑβδομηκοστῷ ἔτει τοῦ κόσμου
ἔλαβον ἑαυτοῖς γυναῖκας καὶ
ἤρξαντο μιαίνεσθαι ἐν αὐταῖς*

Lord descended on the earth.' **8. These are their chiefs of tens.** So G ሀበይት፡ ዓሥርት፡ ዘእሆሙ and M, but that for the first word it reads ሐበይቶሙ፡ So also the Giz. Gk. *οὗτοί εἰσιν ἀρχαὶ αὐτῶν οἱ δέκα*, which, as M. Bouriant proposes, should be emended into *οὗτοί εἰσιν οἱ δέκαρχοι αὐτῶν.* The Syn. Gk. omits. These twenty dekarchs are over the 200 angels mentioned in verse 5. On the other hand the Giz. Gk. omits the rest of this verse, but the Syn. Gk. gives it. Thus G M point to a text anterior to that of either Greek fragment. All other MSS. but G M give a corrupt reading 'chiefs of the two hundred angels.'

Reuben v. In Enoch the angels are said to have descended through their lust for the daughters of men, and the same reason is given in *Jalkut Schim.* Beresch. 44. See Weber, *Lehren d. Talmud* 244. Against this and other statements of Enoch there is an implicit polemic in the Book of Jubilees. In later tradition (Eisenmenger *Entdeckt. Jud.* ii. 387) the reason that Azazel could not return to heaven was that he had outstayed the limit of time assigned to angelic visitants to earth—seven days. 7. This list contains eighteen names; lxix. 2 twenty-one; the Greek gives twenty. They differ considerably from each other. Dln. makes an elaborate attempt at harmonizing them, pp. 93, 94.

VII. The Ethiopic and Greek vary considerably in this and the following chapter. The notes of time given in

and taught them charms and enchantments, and made them acquainted with the cutting of roots and of woods. 2. And they became pregnant, and they bare great giants, whose height was three thousand ells. 3. And these consumed all the acquisitions of men till men could no longer sustain them. 4. Then the giants turned them against mankind in order to devour them. 5. And they began to sin against birds, and beasts, and reptiles, and fish, and to devour one another's flesh, and drink the blood thereof. 6. Then the earth complained of the unrighteous ones.

VIII. [1. And Azâzêl taught

ἕως τοῦ κατακλυσμοῦ. καὶ ἔτεκον αὐτοῖς γένη τρία· πρῶτον γίγαντας μεγάλους. οἱ δὲ γίγαντες ἐτέκνωσαν Ναφηλείμ, καὶ τοῖς Ναφηλεὶμ ἐγεννήθησαν Ἐλιούδ. Καὶ ἦταν αὐξανόμενοι κατὰ τὴν μεγαλειότητα αὐτῶν, καὶ ἐδίδαξαν ἑαυτοὺς καὶ τὰς γυναῖκας ἑαυτῶν φαρμακείας καὶ ἐπαοιδίας. Πρῶτος Ἀζαὴλ ὁ δέκατος τῶν ἀρχόντων ἐδίδαξε ποιεῖν μαχαίρας καὶ θώρακας καὶ πᾶν σκεῦος πολεμικὸν καὶ τὰ μέταλλα

---

the Greek are no doubt due to later hands. **1. Charms and enchantments.** Cf. Joseph. *Ant.* viii. 2, 5. **2. Bare great giants.** For further references to these cf. Wisd. xiv. 6; Tob. vi. 14; Ecclus. xvi. 7; Bar. iii. 26; 3 Macc. ii. 4; Jubilees v. **Whose height was three thousand ells.** The number three thousand is found in the Giz. Gk. but it is wanting in the Syn. Gk. The three classes of giants mentioned in the Greek—the Great Giants, the Nephalim, and the Eliud—were, we must suppose, originally given in this chapter as they are presupposed in lxxxvi. 4; lxxxviii. 2, and passed from Enoch into Jubilees vii, where they are called Giants, Naphil, and Eljô. **3–6.** These verses occur in a different order in the Greek—at the end of viii. 3 and in a very shortened form. The Greek order seems preferable. **5. Blood.** The eating of blood with the Jews was a great crime, Gen. ix. 4; Acts xv. 20; Book of Jubilees vii, xxi; En. xcviii. 11. **One another's flesh.** This may refer to the destruction of one class of giants by another. Cf. Book of Jubilees vii. The text—cf. the Giz. Gk. ἀλλήλων τὰς σάρκας—does not admit of Dln.'s interpretation.

VIII. 1–3. An interpolation. See p. 61. Azazel in viii. 1 is only the tenth in command, but first in the genuine parts. **1. Azazel.** Cf. Rosenmüller's *Scholia* on Lev. xvi. 8; Herzog's *R. E.* ii. 23–25.

men to make swords and knives and shields, and coats of mail, and made known to them metals and the art of working them, bracelets, and ornaments, and the use of antimony, and the beautifying of the eyebrows, and the most costly and choicest stones and all colouring tinctures, so that the world was changed. 2. And there arose great godlessness and much fornication, and they sinned, and all their ways

τῆς γῆς καὶ τὸ χρυσίον πῶς ἐργάσωνται, καὶ ποιήσωσιν αὐτὰ κόσμια ταῖς γυναιξὶ καὶ τὸν ἄργυρον. ἔδειξε δὲ αὐτοῖς καὶ τὸ στίλβειν καὶ τὸ καλλωπίζειν καὶ τοὺς ἐκλεκτοὺς λίθους καὶ τὰ βαφικά. καὶ ἐποίησαν ἑαυτοῖς οἱ υἱοὶ τῶν ἀνθρώπων καὶ ταῖς θυγατράσιν αὐτῶν, καὶ παρέβησαν καὶ ἐπλάνησαν τοὺς ἁγίους, καὶ ἐγένετο ἀσέβεια πολλὴ ἐπὶ τῆς γῆς. καὶ ἠφάνισαν τὰς ὁδοὺς αὐτῶν. Ἔτι δὲ καὶ ὁ πρώταρχος αὐτῶν Σεμιαζᾶς ἐδίδαξεν εἶναι ὀργὰς κατὰ τοῦ νοός, καὶ ῥίζας βοτανῶν τῆς γῆς. ὁ δὲ ἑνδέκατος Φαρμαρὸς ἐδίδαξε φαρμακείας, ἐπαοιδίας, σοφίας,

---

VIII. 1. **Metals and the art of working them.** So Giz. Gk. τὰ μέταλλα καὶ τὴν ἐργασίαν αὐτῶν. The Ethiopic MSS. give 'what is after (or 'behind') them and the art of working them.' Hence the translator found or mistook μετ' αὐτά for μέταλλα. **The use of antimony.** Dln. translates 'the use of rouge.' But **ኳሐለ** never means to put on rouge, but to use antimony for the eyes. See Lex. Col. 823. Gk. τὸ στίλβειν. **The world was changed.** So G **ተወለጠ**. Dln. gives **ተውላጠ** and translates 'the metals of the earth.'

Metals. Cf. Tertullian, *De Cultu Fem.* i. 2: Metallorum opera nudaverunt. **Antimony.** See Crit. Note. Tertullian borrows from this and the preceding chapter in *De Cultu Fem.* i. 2: Herbarum ingenia traduxerant et incantationum vires provulgaverant et omnem curiositatem usque ad stellarum interpretationem designaverant, proprie et quasi peculiariter feminis instrumentum istud muliebris gloriae contulerunt, lumina lapillorum quibus monilia variantur et circulos ex auro quibus brachia artantur—et illum ipsum nigrum pulverem quo oculorum exordia producuntur: and in *De Cultu Fem.* ii. 10: Quodsi iidem angeli qui et materias ejusmodi et illecebras detexerunt, auri dico et lapidum illustrium, et operas eorum tradiderunt, et jam ipsum calliblepharum—tincturas—docuerunt,—ut Enoch refert . . . . Cf. Test. Reuben 5, which also depends on these chapters in Enoch. **2, 3.** The variations between the Ethiopic and the Syn. Gk. are here numerous. **Astrologers.** Cf. Clem. Alex. *Eclog. Proph.* Dind. iii.

became corrupt. 3. Amêzârâk taught all the enchanters and root-cutters, Armârôs the resolving of enchantments, Baraq'âl (taught) the astrologers, Kôkabêl the signs, and Temêl taught astrology, and Asrâdêl the course of the moon.] 4. And as men perished, they cried, and their voice went up to heaven.

IX. 1. Then Michael, Gabriel, Surjan and Urjan, looked down from heaven and saw the great quantity of blood that had been shed upon the earth, and all the wrong that had been wrought upon the earth. 2. And they spake to one another 'The earth made without inhabitant echoes the voice of their crying up to the gate of heaven.

καὶ ἐπαοιδῶν λυτήρια. ὁ ἔννατος ἐδίδαξεν ἀστροσκοπίαν. ὁ δὲ τέταρτος ἐδίδαξεν ἀστρολογίαν. ὁ δὲ ὄγδοος ἐδίδαξεν ἀεροσκοπίαν. ὁ δὲ τρίτος ἐδίδαξε τὰ σημεῖα τῆς γῆς. ὁ δὲ ἕβδομος ἐδίδαξε τὰ σημεῖα τοῦ ἡλίου. ὁ δὲ εἰκοστὸς ἐδίδαξε τὰ σημεῖα τῆς σελήνης. Πάντες οὗτοι ἤρξαντο ἀνακαλύπτειν τὰ μυστήρια ταῖς γυναιξὶν αὐτῶν καὶ τοῖς τέκνοις αὐτῶν. Μετὰ δὲ ταῦτα ἤρξαντο οἱ γίγαντες κατεσθίειν τὰς σάρκας τῶν ἀνθρώπων· καὶ ἤρξαντο οἱ ἄνθρωποι ἐλαττοῦσθαι ἐπὶ τῆς γῆς. οἱ δὲ λοιποὶ ἐβόησαν εἰς τὸν οὐρανὸν περὶ τῆς κακώσεως αὐτῶν λέγοντες εἰσενεχθῆναι τὸ μνημόσυνον αὐτῶν ἐνώπιον κυρίου. Καὶ ἀκούσαντες οἱ τέσσαρες μεγάλοι ἀρχάγγελοι Μιχαὴλ καὶ Οὐριὴλ καὶ Ῥαφαὴλ καὶ Γαβριὴλ παρέκυψαν ἐπὶ τὴν γῆν ἐκ τῶν ἁγίων τοῦ οὐρανοῦ· καὶ θεασάμενοι αἷμα πολὺ ἐκκεχυμένον ἐπὶ τῆς γῆς καὶ πᾶσαν ἀσέβειαν καὶ ἀνομίαν γενομένην ἐπ' αὐτῆς, εἰσελθόντες εἶπον πρὸς ἀλλήλους ὅτι τὰ πνεύματα καὶ αἱ ψυχαὶ τῶν ἀνθρώπων στενάζου-

3. **The resolving of enchantments.** So G K M ፈቲሕ: all other MSS. give ፈትሕ, which is bad in sense and grammar. The Greek *ἐπαοιδῶν λυτήρια* confirms the reading ፈቲሕ. Dln. gives ፈትሕ in his text, but his German translation is a rendering of ፈቲሕ.

474 *ἤδη δὲ καὶ Ἐνώχ φησιν τοὺς παραβάντας ἀγγέλους διδάξαι τοὺς ἀνθρώπους ἀστρονομίαν καὶ μαντικὴν καὶ τὰς ἄλλας τέχνας.*

IX. Surjan and Urjan are variants of Suriel and Uriel. Suriel is not mentioned again in this book, but is known in later Judaism in Talmud Berachoth, fol. 51. a, as Dln. points out. It is probable, however, that instead of Surjan we should read Raphael in accordance with the Greek. See xl. 2 (note). Michael, Gabriel, Uriel, and Raphael were generally regarded as the four archangels. **2.** This verse is not found in the Greek. **Made without inhabitant:** cf. lxvii. 2; lxxxiv. 5; and Test. Napth. 3

σιν ἐντυγχάνοντα καὶ λέγοντα, ὅτι εἰσαγάγετε τὴν κρίσιν ἡμῶν πρὸς τὸν ὕψιστον, καὶ τὴν ἀπώλειαν ἡμῶν ἐνώπιον τῆς δόξης τῆς μεγαλωσύνης, ἐνώπιον τοῦ κυρίου τῶν κυρίων πάντων τῇ μεγαλωσύνῃ. Καὶ εἶπον τῷ κυρίῳ τῶν αἰώνων, σὺ εἶ ὁ θεὸς τῶν θεῶν καὶ κύριος τῶν κυρίων καὶ ὁ Βασιλεὺς τῶν Βασιλευόντων καὶ θεὸς τῶν αἰώνων, καὶ ὁ θρόνος τῆς δόξης σου εἰς πάσας τὰς γενεὰς τῶν αἰώνων, καὶ τὸ ὄνομά σου ἅγιον καὶ εὐλογημένον εἰς πάντας τοὺς αἰῶνας, καὶ τὰ ἑξῆς. τότε ὁ ὕψιστος ἐκέλευσε τοῖς ἁγίοις ἀρχαγγέλοις, καὶ ἔδησαν τοὺς ἐξάρχους αὐτῶν καὶ ἔβαλον αὐτοὺς εἰς τὴν ἄβυσσον, ἕως τῆς κρίσεως, καὶ τὰ ἑξῆς. Καὶ ταῦτα μὲν ὁ Ἐνὼχ μαρτυρεῖ.

Ἐκ τοῦ λόγου Ἐνώχ.

Τὰ λοιπὰ περὶ ἐγρηγόρων.

(G. Syncellus. S. 42–47.)

Hen. 8, 4–10, 14.

Τότε ἐβόησαν οἱ ἄνθρωποι εἰς τὸν οὐρανὸν λέγοντες, εἰσαγάγετε τὴν κρίσιν ἡμῶν πρὸς τὸν ὕψιστον, καὶ τὴν ἀπώλειαν ἡμῶν ἐνώπιον τῆς δόξης τῆς μεγάλης, ἐνώπιον τοῦ κυρίου τῶν κυρίων πάντων τῇ μεγαλωσύνῃ. Καὶ ἀκούσαντες οἱ τέσσαρες μεγάλοι ἀρχάγγελοι Μιχαὴλ καὶ Οὐριὴλ καὶ Ῥαφαὴλ καὶ Γαβριὴλ παρέκυψαν ἐπὶ τὴν γῆν ἐκ τῶν ἁγίων τοῦ οὐρανοῦ. Καὶ θεασάμενοι αἷμα πολὺ ἐκκεχυμένον ἐπὶ τῆς γῆς καὶ πᾶσαν ἀνομίαν καὶ ἀσέβειαν γινομένην ἐπ' αὐτῆς, εἰσελθόντες εἶπον πρὸς ἀλλήλους, ὅτι τὰ

3. And now to you, ye holy ones of heaven, complain the souls of men, saying, "procure us justice with the Most High."' 4. And they spake to their Lord the King: 'Lord of Lords, God of Gods, King of Kings, the throne of Thy glory (standeth) unto all the generations of the ages, and Thy name holy and glorious unto all the ages: blessed and glorious art Thou! 5. Thou hast made all things and over all things hast Thou dominion: and all things are naked and open in Thy sight, and Thou seest all things and nothing can hide itself from Thee. 6. See then what Azâzêl hath done, how he hath taught all unrighteousness on earth and revealed the secret things of the world which were wrought in the heavens.

πνεύματα καὶ αἱ ψυχαὶ τῶν ἀνθρώπων ἐντυγχάνουσι στενάζοντα καὶ λέγοντα, εἰσαγάγετε τὴν δέησιν ἡμῶν πρὸς τὸν ὕψιστον. Καὶ προσελθόντες οἱ τέσσαρες ἀρχάγγελοι εἶπον τῷ κυρίῳ, σὺ εἶ θεὸς τῶν θεῶν καὶ κύριος τῶν κυρίων καὶ βασιλεὺς τῶν βασιλευόντων καὶ θεὸς τῶν ἀνθρώπων, καὶ ὁ θρόνος τῆς δόξης σου εἰς πάσας τὰς γενεὰς τῶν αἰώνων, καὶ τὸ ὄνομά σου ἅγιον καὶ εὐλογημένον εἰς πάντας τοὺς αἰῶνας· σὺ γὰρ εἶ ὁ ποιήσας τὰ πάντα καὶ πάντων τὴν ἐξουσίαν ἔχων, καὶ πάντα ἐνώπιόν σου φανερὰ καὶ ἀκάλυπτα, καὶ πάντα ὁρᾷς, καὶ οὐκ ἔστιν ὃ κρυβῆναί σε δύναται. ὁρᾷς ὅσα ἐποίησεν Ἀζαήλ, καὶ ὅσα εἰσήνεγκεν, ὅσα ἐδίδαξεν, ἀδικίας καὶ ἁμαρτίας ἐπὶ τῆς γῆς, καὶ πάντα δόλον ἐπὶ τῆς ξηρᾶς. ἐδίδαξε γὰρ τὰ μυστήρια καὶ ἀπεκάλυψε τῷ αἰῶνι τὰ ἐν οὐρανῷ. ἐπιτηδεύουσι δὲ τὰ ἐπιτηδεύματα αὐτοῦ, εἰδέναι τὰ

IX. 4. **Their Lord the King**: so all MSS. but G M, which give 'the Lord of Kings.' **Unto all the ages.** So G M omitting ትውልደ and Greek *εἰς πάντας τοὺς αἰῶνας*. All other MSS. 'unto all the generations of the world.' 6. **Revealed the secret things of the world**

Τάξας τὴν γῆν ἀοίκητον. 3. **Holy ones**: see i. 9 (note). **Most High**: see xcix. 3 (note). 4. The prayer of the angels is fuller in the Syn. Gk., and a still more rhetorical form of it is found in lxxxiv. 2, 3. 6. **All unrighteousness on earth**: cf. vii. 1. **The secret things, &c.** What these are is not told. 7. An interpolation from the same source as vi. 3–8; viii. 1–3; see p. 61. The Syn. Gk. seems to be defective here.

[7. And Semjâzâ to whom Thou hast given authority to bear rule over his associates has made known enchantments.] 8. And they have gone to the daughters of men upon the earth, and have slept with them, with those women, and defiled themselves, and revealed these sins unto them. 9. And the women have borne giants, and the whole earth has thereby been filled with blood and unrighteousness. 10. And now behold, the spirits of the souls which have died, are crying and complaining to the gate of heaven, and their lamentations are ascending:

μυστήρια οἱ υἱοὶ τῶν ἀνθρώπων. τῷ Σεμιαζᾷ τὴν ἐξουσίαν ἔδωκας ἔχειν τῶν σὺν αὐτῷ ἅμα ὄντων, καὶ ἐπορεύθησαν πρὸς τὰς θυγατέρας τῶν ἀνθρώπων τῆς γῆς, καὶ συνεκοιμήθησαν μετ' αὐτῶν, καὶ ἐν ταῖς θηλείαις ἐμιάνθησαν, καὶ ἐδήλωσαν αὐταῖς πάσας τὰς ἁμαρτίας, καὶ ἐδίδαξαν αὐτὰς μίσητρα ποιεῖν, καὶ νῦν ἰδοὺ αἱ θυγατέρες τῶν ἀνθρώπων ἔτεκον ἐξ αὐτῶν υἱοὺς γίγαντας. κίβδηλα ἐπὶ τῆς γῆς τῶν ἀνθρώπων ἐκκέχυται, καὶ ὅλη ἡ γῆ ἐπλήσθη ἀδικίας. Καὶ νῦν ἰδοὺ τὰ πνεύματα τῶν ψυχῶν τῶν ἀποθανόντων ἀνθρώπων ἐντυγχάνουσι, καὶ μέχρι τῶν πυλῶν τοῦ οὐρανοῦ ἀνέβη ὁ στεναγμὸς αὐτῶν, καὶ οὐ δύναται

---

which were wrought in the heavens. So all MSS. and the Giz. Gk. but the Syn. Gk. *ἀπεκάλυψε τῷ αἰῶνι τὰ ἐν οὐρανῷ* gives a better sense. 8. **Upon the earth.** G M give **በዲበ፡ ሰብእ**. This, as the reading of the Giz. and Syn. Gk. *τῆς γῆς* shows, is a corruption of **በዲበ፡ የብስ**. Hence my translation. All other Ethiopic MSS. give wrongly **ኅቡረ** = together. 10. **The spirits of the souls which have died.** Here I have followed the Syn. Gk. *τὰ πνεύματα τῶν ψυχῶν τῶν ἀποθα-*

8, 9. Cf. Justin, *Apol.* ii. 5 *Οἱ δὲ ἄγγελοι—γυναικῶν μίξεσιν ἡττήθησαν καὶ παῖδας ἐτέκνωσαν, οἵ εἰσιν οἱ λεγόμενοι δαίμονες—καὶ εἰς ἀνθρώπους φόνους, πολέμους, μοιχείας—καὶ πᾶσαν κακίαν ἔσπειραν.* 10. **The spirits of the souls, &c.** See Crit. Note. **They cannot escape from, &c.** The Ethiopic is here superior to the Greek. The intercession of the angels on man's behalf which appears in this chapter and is found also in xv. 2; xl. 6; xlvii. 2; xcix. 3, 16; civ. 1, is an O.T. doctrine; cf. Job v. 1; xxxiii. 23; Zech. i. 12. It was evidently a popular doctrine. Cf. Tobit xii. 12 *Ἐγὼ προσήγαγον τὸ μνημόσυνον τῆς προσευχῆς ὑμῶν ἐνώπιον τοῦ ἁγίου* (contrast Acts x. 4); also xii. 15 *ἐγώ εἰμι Ῥαφαὴλ εἷς ἐκ τῶν ἑπτὰ ἁγίων ἀγγέλων οἳ προσαναφέρουσι τὰς προσευχὰς τῶν ἁγίων*: Rev. viii. 3; Test. Levi 3: also 5 *ἐγώ εἰμι ὁ ἄγγελος ὁ παραιτούμενος τὸ γένος Ἰσραήλ.*

and they cannot escape from the unrighteousness which is wrought on the earth. 11. And thou knowest all things before they come to pass, and Thou knowest this thing and every thing affecting them, and yet Thou didst not speak to us. What are we therefore to do in regard to this?'

X. 1. [Then spake the Most High, the Great and Holy One, and sent Arsjalâljûr to the son of Lamech and said to him: 2. 'Tell him in My name "hide thyself!", and reveal to him the end that is approaching: for the whole earth will be destroyed, and a deluge will presently come upon the whole earth, and all that is on it will be de-

ἐξελθεῖν ἀπὸ προσώπου τῶν ἐπὶ τῆς γῆς γινομένων ἀδικημάτων. καὶ σὺ αὐτὰ οἶδας πρὸ τῶν αὐτὰ γενέσθαι καὶ ὁρᾷς αὐτοὺς καὶ ἐᾷς αὐτούς, καὶ οὐδὲν λέγεις. τί δεῖ ποιῆσαι αὐτοὺς περὶ τούτου;

τότε ὁ ὕψιστος εἶπε καὶ ὁ ἅγιος ὁ μέγας ἐλάλησε, καὶ ἔπεμψε τὸν Οὐριὴλ πρὸς τὸν υἱὸν Λάμεχ λέγων, πορεύου πρὸς τὸν Νῶε καὶ εἰπὸν αὐτῷ τῷ ἐμῷ ὀνόματι, κρύψον σεαυτόν, καὶ δήλωσον αὐτῷ τέλος ἐπερχόμενον, ὅτι ἡ γῆ ἀπόλλυται πᾶσα. καὶ εἰπὸν αὐτῷ ὅτι κατακλυσμὸς μέλλει γίνεσθαι πάσης τῆς γῆς, ἀπολέσαι πάντα ἀπὸ

νόντων. The Ethiopic text ነፍሳት፡ እለ፡ ሞቱ = 'the souls which have died' must therefore be emended into መናፍስት፡ ለነፍሳት፡ እለ፡ ሞቱ. We find, moreover, this expression in the correct text of xxii. 3 መናፍስት፡ ለነፍሰሙ፡ ለምዉታን and a similar expression in the correct text of xvi. 1 መናፍስት፡ እምነፍሳት, and the Syn. Gk. *τὰ πνεύματα τὰ ἐκπορευόμενα ἀπὸ τῆς ψυχῆς αὐτῶν*. In ix. 3 read **the spirits of the souls** instead of **the souls**. The Giz. Gk. supports in xvi. 1 and xxii. 3 the readings adopted but agrees with the Ethiopic text in ix. 3, 10.

X. 1-3. These verses belong to an Apocalypse of Noah. **1. The Most High**; see xcix. 3 (note). **The Great and Holy**: see i. 3 (note). **Arsjalâljûr.** For this the Syn. Gk. has simply Uriel, and the Giz. Gk. has Istrael. The name in the text is probably a corruption. **Son of Lamech**, i.e. Noah. If x. 1-3 belonged originally to this section, the writer must have followed the Samaritan reckoning. **Hide thyself**; i.e. in order to receive further disclosures from the angel: cf. xii. 1.

stroyed. 3. And now instruct him that he may escape and his seed may be preserved for all generations.] 4. And again the Lord spake to Rafael: 'Bind Azâzêl hand and foot, and place him in the darkness: make an opening in the desert, which is in Dudâêl, and place him therein. 5. And place upon him rough and jagged rocks, and cover him with darkness, and let him abide there for ever, and cover his face that he may not see the light. 6. And on the great day of judgment he shall be cast into the fire.

προσώπου τῆς γῆς. δίδαξον τὸν δίκαιον τί ποιήσει, τὸν υἱὸν Λάμεχ, καὶ τὴν ψυχὴν αὐτοῦ εἰς ζωὴν συντηρήσει καὶ ἐκφεύξεται δι' αἰῶνος καὶ ἐξ αὐτοῦ φυτευθήσεται φύτευμα καὶ σταθήσεται πάσας τὰς γενεὰς τοῦ αἰῶνος. καὶ τῷ 'Ραφαὴλ εἶπε, πορεύου 'Ραφαήλ, καὶ δῆσον τὸν 'Αζαήλ, χερσὶ καὶ ποσὶ συμπόδισον αὐτόν, καὶ ἔμβαλε αὐτὸν εἰς τὸ σκότος, καὶ ἄνοιξον τὴν ἔρημον τὴν οὖσαν ἐν τῇ ἐρήμῳ Δουδαήλ, καὶ ἐκεῖ πορευθεὶς βάλε αὐτόν· καὶ ὑπόθες αὐτῷ λίθους ὀξεῖς καὶ λίθους τραχεῖς, καὶ ἐπικάλυψον αὐτῷ σκότος, καὶ οἰκησάτω ἐκεῖ εἰς τὸν αἰῶνα, καὶ τὴν ὄψιν αὐτοῦ πώμασον, καὶ φῶς μὴ θεωρείτω. καὶ ἐν τῇ ἡμέρᾳ τῆς κρίσεως ἀπαχθήσεται εἰς τὸν ἐμπυρισμὸν τοῦ πυρός·

X. 3. **For all generations.** So G M reading ለኵሎሙ፡ ትውልድ. Dln. and other MSS. except N give 'for all the earth': cf. the Gk.

---

3. The Syn. Gk. is much fuller. **4–8.** The task deputed to Rufael or Raphael. **4. Azazel** as the chief offender and leader is first punished. The preliminary punishment of Azazel is described in vv. 4, 5: the final one in v. 6. Azazel was conceived as chained in the wilderness into which the scape-goat was led. The Jerusalem Targum (Ps. Jonathan) on Leviticus says that 'the goat was sent to die in a hard and rough place in the wilderness of jagged rocks, i.e. Beth Chaduda.' This Beth Chaduda was three miles, or according to another account, twelve miles from Jerusalem. This is clearly the Dudael mentioned in this verse, and it is thus a definite locality in the neighbourhood of Jerusalem. See *Judische Zeitschrift f. Wissenschaft und Leben* 1864, pp. 196–204. Cf. Lev. xvi. 10, 22. **5. Place upon him.** The Greek gives *ὑπόθες αὐτῷ*, but this is probably a slip for *ἐπίθες αὐτῷ*. **For ever.** Like *εἰς τὸν αἰῶνα*, of which the Ethiopic text is an exact rendering, this phrase has no definite meaning in itself. It may denote according to the context an unending period; or a period of seventy generations, as here; cf. v. 12; or a period of five hundred years, as in v. 10. **6. Great day of judgment**: see xlv. 2 (note). This judgment inaugurates the final punishment of the angels. **The fire**: see

7. And heal the earth which the angels have defiled, and proclaim the healing of the earth, that I will heal the earth, and that all the children of men shall not perish through all the secret things that the watchers have disclosed and have taught their sons. 8. And the whole earth has been defiled through the teaching of the works of Azâzêl: to him ascribe all the sin.' 9. And to Gabriel said God: 'Proceed against the bastards and the reprobates, and against the children of fornication: and destroy the children of fornication, and the children

καὶ ἴασαι τὴν γῆν ἣν ἠφάνισαν οἱ ἐγρήγοροι, καὶ τὴν ἴασιν τῆς πληγῆς δήλωσον, ἵνα ἰάσωνται τὴν πληγήν, καὶ μὴ ἀπόλωνται πάντες οἱ υἱοὶ τῶν ἀνθρώπων, ἐν τῷ μυστηρίῳ ὃ εἶπον οἱ ἐγρήγοροι καὶ ἐδίδαξαν τοὺς υἱοὺς αὐτῶν, καὶ ἠρημώθη πᾶσα ἡ γῆ ἐν τοῖς ἔργοις τῆς διδασκαλίας Ἀζαήλ· καὶ ἐπ' αὐτῇ γράψον πάσας τὰς ἁμαρτίας. καὶ τῷ Γαβριὴλ εἶπε, πορεύου Γαβριὴλ ἐπὶ τοὺς γίγαντας ἐπὶ τοὺς κιβδήλους, ἐπὶ τοὺς υἱοὺς τῆς πορνείας, καὶ ἀπόλεσον τοὺς υἱοὺς τῶν ἐγρηγόρων ἀπὸ τῶν υἱῶν

πάσας τὰς γενεὰς τοῦ αἰῶνος. 7. **Proclaim the healing of the earth, that I will heal the earth.** The Syn. Gk. gives *τὴν ἴασιν τῆς πληγῆς δήλωσον, ἵνα ἰάσωνται τὴν πληγήν.* Thus, as the word rendered 'earth' in the Ethiopic appears as *πληγή* in the Gk., it is most probable that the Hebrew word was תבל which means 'earth' when punctuated תֵּבֵל, a 'pollution' when punctuated תֶּבֶל. **Disclosed.** All MSS. read ቀተሉ 'have slain'; the translator found *ἐπάταξαν* as in the Giz. Gk. which is a corruption of *ἐπέτασαν.* The Syn. Gk. gives *εἶπον.* 8. **To him.** So the Giz. Gk. The Syn. Gk. gives 'to it.' 9. **Bastards.** So also the Giz. Gk. which gives a corrupt trans-

---

xviii. 11; xix; xxi. 7–10. 7. The command given to Raphael is such as his name suggests from רפא 'to heal.' Cf. Tob. iii. 17; xii. 14. 8. Observe how all sin is ascribed to the fallen angels. 9, 10. The destruction of the giants through Gabriel. The account here is followed closely by the Book of Jubilees v. The giants slay each other in the presence of their parents: cf. xiv. 6. The latter are then bound in the abysses of the earth, and their power of hurting the earth is at an end: cf. xiv. 5. But this is not so with the spirits of the giants. They enjoy an impunity in

of the watchers from amongst men: lead them out and send them one against the other that they may destroy each other in battle: for length of days they shall not have. 10. And no request that they (i. e. their fathers) make of thee will be granted unto their fathers on their behalf although they hope to live an eternal life, and that each one of them will live five hundred years. [11. And the Lord said unto Michael: 'Go, announce to Semjâzâ and his associates who have united themselves with women so as to have defiled themselves with them in all their uncleanness.] 12. When all their sons have slain one an-

τῶν ἀνθρώπων. πέμψον αὐτοὺς εἰς ἀλλήλους, ἐξ αὐτῶν εἰς αὐτούς, ἐν πολέμῳ καὶ ἐν ἀπωλείᾳ, καὶ μακρότης ἡμερῶν οὐκ ἔσται αὐτοῖς, καὶ πᾶσα ἐρώτησις οὐκ ἔστι τοῖς πατράσιν αὐτῶν, ὅτι ἐλπίζουσι ζῆσαι ζωὴν αἰώνιον, καὶ ὅτι ζήσεται ἕκαστος αὐτῶν ἔτη πεντακόσια. καὶ τῷ Μιχαὴλ εἶπε, πορεύου Μιχαήλ, δῆσον Σεμιαζᾶν καὶ τοὺς ἄλλους σὺν αὐτῷ, τοὺς συμμιγέντας ταῖς θυγατράσι τῶν ἀνθρώπων τοῦ μιανθῆναι ἐν αὐταῖς ἐν τῇ ἀκαθαρσίᾳ αὐτῶν. καὶ ὅταν κατασφαγῶσιν οἱ υἱοὶ αὐτῶν, καὶ

---

literation of the Hebrew word, i.e. *μαζηρεους*. 10. **No request that they make of thee will be granted unto their fathers.** So G M reading ዘሰ, instead of ኵሎሙ as Dln. So the Syn. Gk.: *πᾶσα ἐρώτησις οὐκ ἔστι τοῖς πατράσιν αὐτῶν*, but M by a slip እስመ፡ ኢይከውን instead of ወኢይከውን, or ወኢይኩን with G. **Although they hope to live an eternal life.** So G K M: እስመ፡ ይሴፈዊ፡ ይሕየዊ፡ ሕይወተ፡ ዘለዓለም. So the Gk.: *ἐλπίζουσι ζῆσαι ζωὴν αἰώνιον*. Other MSS. and Dln. omit the ይሕየዊ 'Though they hope for an eternal life.' 11. **And the Lord said unto Michael: 'Go, announce.'** So G F H L: ይቤሎ፡ እግዚእ፡ ሑር፡ አይድዕ. Other MSS. and Dln. omit ሑር, but wrongly: cf. the Greek *πορεύου*. Instead of announce the

---

wrongdoing till the final judgment: see xv. 11–xvi. **An eternal life,** i. e. five hundred years: see v. 5 (note). Touching the prayer of the angels, cf. xii. 6; xiii. 4–6; xiv. 7. **11.** This verse is an interpolation: see p. 61; vv. 9–16 describe the task assigned to Gabriel. **12. Slain**

other, and they have seen the destruction of their beloved ones, bind them fast under the hills of the earth for seventy generations till the day of their judgment and of their consummation, till the judgment which is for ever and ever is consummated. 13. In those days they will be led off to the abyss of fire: in torment and in prison will they be confined for ever and ever. 14. And whosoever shall be condemned and from thenceforward be destroyed with them, will be bound together with them to the end of all generations.

ἴδωσι τὴν ἀπώλειαν τῶν ἀγαπητῶν αὐτῶν, δῆσον αὐτοὺς ἐπὶ ἑβδομήκοντα γενεὰς εἰς τὰς νάπας τῆς γῆς, μέχρι ἡμέρας κρίσεως αὐτῶν, μέχρι ἡμέρας τελειώσεως τελεσμοῦ, ἕως συντελεσθῇ κρίμα τοῦ αἰῶνος τῶν αἰώνων. τότε ἀπενεχθήσονται εἰς τὸ χάος τοῦ πυρὸς καὶ εἰς τὴν βάσανον καὶ εἰς τὸ δεσμωτήριον τῆς συγκλείσεως τοῦ αἰῶνος. καὶ ὃς ἂν κατακριθῇ καὶ ἀφανισθῇ ἀπὸ τοῦ νῦν μετ' αὐτῶν, δεθήσεται μέχρι τελειώσεως γενεᾶς αὐτῶν.

Syn. Gk. gives δῆσον, but this is an error for δήλωσον. See the Giz. Gk. 14. **And whosoever shall be condemned and from thenceforward be destroyed with them, will be bound together (with them) to the end of all generations.** I have followed the Syn. Gk. The Ethiopic runs: 'And forthwith he will burn and thenceforward suffer destruction with them: they will be bound together to the end of all generations.' The singular in 'he will burn' is meaningless, as we have here only to do with the entire body of watchers. The Syn. Gk. gives at once excellent sense and explains the origin of the Ethiopic corruption: ὃς ἂν κατακριθῇ καὶ ἀφανισθῇ ἀπὸ τοῦ νῦν μετ' αὐτῶν, δεθήσεται μεχρὶ τελειώσεως γενεᾶς αὐτῶν. κατακριθῇ = 'be condemned,' in connexion with the fiery abyss in the preceding line,

---

one another: cf. xii. 6; xiv. 6; Book of Jubilees v. The binding of the angels under the hills seems to be an idea derived from the Greek myths of the Titans. **Seventy generations.** This period has no connexion with the Apoc. of weeks. See Spec. Introd. of xci–civ. With vv. 5, 12 cf. Jude 6. **13. Abyss of fire,** i.e. the same as that mentioned in v. 6; xviii. 11; xix; xxi. 7–10; xc. 24. **14.** See Crit. Note: cf. xix. 2.

15. And destroy all the lustful souls, and the children of the watchers, because they have oppressed mankind. 16. Destroy all oppression from the face of the earth and let every evil work come to an end: and the plant of righteousness and uprightness will appear, labour will prove a blessing: righteousness and uprightness will be established in joy for evermore. 17. And then will all the righteous escape and will live till they beget a thousand children, and all the days of their youth and their old age (lit. sabbath) will they complete in peace. 18. And in those days will the whole earth be tilled in righteousness and will all be planted with trees and be full of blessing. 19. And all desirable trees will be planted on it, and vines will be planted on it: the vine which is planted thereon will yield wine in abundance, and of all the seed which is sown thereon will each measure bear ten thousand, and each measure of olives will yield ten presses of oil. 20. And cleanse thou the earth from all oppression, and from all unrighteousness, and from all sin, and from all godlessness, and from all uncleanness which is wrought upon the earth:

---

could easily be taken by the translator for *κατακαυθῇ* = be burned, and so give rise to the present Ethiopic text. Rightly translated then, the verse refers to the women who are to be destroyed with the fallen watchers. Cf. xix. 2. *κατακαυθῇ* is the reading of the Giz. Gk.

---

15. Destroy, &c. The writer is still describing the duties of Gabriel, i. e. the destruction of the giants and the imprisonment of the fallen watchers. **16. Plant of righteousness,** i. e. Israel. Israel springs from a seed that 'is sown' by God, lxii. 8: hence it is established as 'a plant of the seed for ever,' lxxxiv. 6, is called 'the plant of uprightness,' xciii. 2, 'the plant of righteousness,' xciii. 5, 'the eternal plant of righteousness,' xciii. 10, and finally 'the plant of righteous judgment,' xciii. 5. **17.** The writer has here gone over wholly to a description of the Messianic times. The picture is a very sensuous one. **Their old age**: cf. xxv. 3, 4 (note). **18, 19.** The future is depicted after O. T. prophesy. Cf. Amos ix. 13, 14; Hos. ii. 22, 23; Jer. xxxi. 5; Is. xxv. 6; Ezek. xxviii. 26; xxxiv. 26, 27. **Will each measure bear, &c.**: cf. Is. v. 10, and the chiliastic expectations of Papius in Iren. *adv. Haer.* v. 33. **20.** This verse could be interpreted of the deluge, but it seems better to refer it, as the verses before and after,

destroy them from off the earth. 21. And all the children of men shall become righteous, and all nations shall offer Me adoration and praise, and all will worship Me. 22. And the earth will be cleansed from all corruption, and from all sin, and from all punishment and torment, and I will never again send (them) upon it, from generation to generation, for ever.

XI. 1. And in those days I will open the store chambers of blessing which are in the heaven, so as to send them down upon the earth over the work and labour of the children of men. 2. Peace and justice will be wedded throughout all the days of the world and throughout all the generations of the world.

XII. 1. And before all these things fell out Enoch was hidden, and no one of the children of men knew where he was hidden, and where he abode, and what had become of him. 2. And all his activities had to do with the holy ones and with the watchers in his days. 3. And I Enoch was blessing the great Lord and the king of the world, when lo! the watchers called me—Enoch the scribe—and spake to me. 4. 'Enoch thou scribe of righteousness, go, announce to the watchers of the heaven who have abandoned the high heaven and the holy eternal place, and have defiled themselves with women,

---

to the Messianic kingdom. **21.** The conversion of the Gentiles: cf. xc. 30 (note). **22.** In corrupt MSS. there is a reference to the deluge here.

XI. 1. This chapter concludes an account of the Messianic kingdom. Cf. Deut. xxviii. 12. **2.** Cf. lxxxv. 10; Is. xxxii. 17.

XII–XVI. On these chapters, see Spec. Introd. p. 55. **1. Was hidden,** i. e. in order to receive the following revelation: cf. x. 2. Enoch is still living: his final translation from earth has not yet fallen out; for as a man he writes the petition for the angels, xiii. 6: receives a vision in sleep and is transported in spirit unto heaven, xiv. 2: speaks with a tongue of flesh, xiv. 2: and is terrified, like a mortal man, at the presence of God, xiv. 24. **Was hidden** is the Ethiopic translation of לקח and *μετέθηκεν*: cf. lxxi. 1, 5. **2. Holy ones**: see i. 9 (note). **Watchers**: see i. 5 (note). **3. King of the world**: see i. 3 (note). **The scribe**: cf. xcii. 1. Enoch is further called 'the scribe of righteousness,' xii. 4; xv. 1, because he is himself a righteous man, xv. 1; lxxi. 14–16, and declares the righteous judgment that is coming, xiii. 10; xiv. 1, 3; lxxxi. 6; lxxxii. 1, &c. **4.** Cf.

and have done as the children of men do, and have taken unto themselves wives, and have grossly defiled themselves on the earth. 5. They will have no peace on the earth nor forgiveness of sin: and inasmuch as they delight themselves in their children, 6. the murder of their beloved ones they shall see, and over the destruction of their children will they lament, and will make supplication unto eternity, but mercy and peace will they not attain.'

XIII. 1. And Enoch went and said: 'Azâzêl: thou shalt find no peace: a severe sentence has gone forth against thee —(Rufael) shall put thee in bonds: 2. And alleviation, intercession, and mercy will not be accorded to thee, because of the oppression which thou hast taught, and because of all the works of blasphemy, oppression, and sin which thou hast shown to the children of men.' 3. Then proceeding farther, I spoke to them all together and they were all afraid and were seized with fear and trembling. 4. And they besought me to draw up a petition for them that they might find forgiveness, and to take their petition into the presence of God in heaven. 5. For from thenceforward they could not speak (with Him) nor lift up their eyes to heaven for shame of their sins for which they were punished. 6. Then I composed their petition and the prayer on behalf of their spirit, and for their individual deeds for which they besought forgiveness and forbearance. 7. And I went off and sat down at the waters of Dan, in Dan, to the right (i. e. the south)

XII. 5. **Inasmuch as they, &c.** So G: **ወእስመ፡ ይትፌሥሑ፡ ውሉዶሙ፡ ቀትለ፡ ፍቁራኒሆሙ፡ ይርእዩ**, but with the insertion of **በ** before **ውሉዶሙ** with nine other MSS. Cf. the Giz. Gk. *περὶ ὧν χαίρουσι τῶν υἱῶν αὐτῶν.*

Jude 6. **5. No peace:** cf. v. 4. **6.** Cf. x. 10, 12.

XIII. 1. Azazel addressed in conformity with x. 4. No peace: cf. v. 4. **4, 5.** As the angels could not address God nor lift up their eyes to heaven, Enoch is besought to become their intercessor. It is in keeping with Enoch's literary character that he draws up their petition in writing, and does not present it by word of mouth. **7. Waters of Dan.** This river, called also the little Jordan, Joseph. *Ant.* I. xii. 1, is a tributary of the Jordan. This place, from דין to judge, is chosen

of the west of Hermon, and I read their petition till I fell asleep. 8. And behold a dream visited me and visions fell down upon me, and I saw the vision of a chastisement to the intent that I should recount it to the sons of the heaven and reprimand them. 9. And when I awaked, I came to them, and they were all sitting together weeping with their faces covered at Ublesjâêl, which is between Lebanon and Sênêsêr. 10. And I recounted to them all the visions which I had seen in my sleep, and I began to recount those words of righteousness, and to reprimand the heavenly watchers.

XIV. 1. This book is the word of righteousness and the reprimand of the eternal watchers in accordance with the commandment of the Holy and Great One in that vision. 2. I saw in my sleep what I will now recount with a tongue of flesh and with my breath which the Great One has put into the mouth of men, that they might converse with it, and understand in their heart. 3. As He has created man and given to him the power of understanding the word of wisdom, so hath He created me also and given me the power of reprimanding the watchers, the sons of heaven. 4. 'I wrote out your petition, and in

---

XIII. 9. **They were all sitting.** So all MSS. but G. G reads ይትበሀሉ 'were talking.'

XIV. 4. G inserts after v. 4 ወእምይእዜ፡ ኢትትናገሩ፡ ውስተ፡ ኵሉ መዋዕለ፡ ዓለም፡ ወኰነኔ፡ ፍጽምት፡ ላዕሌክሙ፡ ወኢይከውነክሙ 'And from henceforth their friendship is at an end unto all the days of eternity: and judgment has been finally passed upon you and no

---

because its name is significant of the subject the writer is dealing with, i. e. the judgment of the angels. **8. Sons of the heaven**: see vi. 2 (note). **9. Ublesjâêl and Sênêsêr** are unknown places. **10. Heavenly watchers**: see i. 5 (note). The vision is described in xiv–xvi.

XIV. 1. Eternal watchers, lit. watchers who are from eternity, i. e. in the loose sense in which that word is often used in Enoch. See x. 5 (note). **Holy and Great One**: see i. 3 (note). **2, 3.** As surely as God has created man and given him a tongue for speech and a faculty for understanding, so just as certainly has He appointed Enoch to reprimand the eternal watchers. **Tongue of flesh**: cf. lxxxiv. 1. **The Great One**: cf. ciii. 4; civ. 1. **Sons of heaven**: see vi. 2 (note). **4–7.** The repri-

my vision it appeared thus, that your petition will not be granted throughout all the days of eternity, and that judgment has been finally passed upon you, and no indulgence will be granted to you. 5. And from henceforth you will never again ascend into heaven to all eternity, and on the earth the decree hath gone forth, they shall bind you for all the days of eternity. 6. But previously you will see the destruction of your beloved sons and you will not have them in your keeping, but they will fall before you by the sword. 7. Your petition on their behalf will not be granted, nor that on your own: likewise despite your tears and prayers you will receive nothing whatever contained in the writing which I have written.' 8. And the vision appeared to me thus: behold in the vision clouds invited me and a mist invited me: the course of the stars and the lightnings drove and impelled me, and the winds in the vision gave me wings and drove me. 9. And they lifted me up into heaven and I came till I drew nigh to a wall which is built of crystals and surrounded by a fiery flame: and it began to affright me. 10. And I went into the fiery flame and drew nigh to a

---

indulgence will be granted unto you.' 7. **You will receive nothing whatever.** The Ethiopic, which is a literal rendering of the Giz. Gk. *μὴ λαλοῦντες πᾶν ῥῆμα*, gives no intelligible sense. Hence I have supposed *λαλοῦντες* to be a corruption of *λαχόντες*, and so translated. But the corruption may have originated in the Hebrew through the confusion of קרא and קרה. 8. Instead of ይጸዑቂኒ, G M read ይጸሁቂኒ = 'incited.'

---

mand which Enoch administered to the watchers. **5.** Cf. xiii. 5; also the *Apology* of Athenagoras: *οὗτοι οἱ ἄγγελοι οἱ ἐκπεσόντες τῶν οὐρανῶν... οὐκέτι εἰς τὰ ὑπερουράνια ὑπερκύψαι δυνάμενοι.* **6.** Cf. x. 9. **7.** See Crit. Note. Irenaeus IV. xvi. 2. (Stieren's ed.) refers to this passage: Enoch ... cum esset homo, legatione ad angelos fungebatur et translatus est et conservatur usque nunc testis judicii Dei, quoniam angeli quidam transgressi deciderunt in terram in judicium. **8. Clouds invited me.** This is a peculiar expression and may be due to an error. We should expect some such idea as is found in Ps. xviii. 10, 11; civ. 3. **9–18.** Enoch is carried up into heaven and passes within the outer wall that

large house which was built of crystals: and the walls of that house were like a mosaic crystal floor, and its groundwork was of crystal. 11. Its ceiling was like the path of the stars and lightnings, with fiery cherubim between in a transparent heaven (lit. 'and their heaven was water'). 12. A flaming fire surrounded the walls of the house, and its portal blazed with fire. 13. And I entered into that house, and it was hot as fire and cold as ice: there were no delights of life therein: fear covered me and trembling gat hold upon me. 14. And as I quaked and trembled, I fell upon my face and beheld in a vision. 15. And lo! there was a second house, greater than the former, all the portals of which stood open before me, and it was built of flames of fire. 16. And in every respect it so excelled in splendour and magnificence and extent that I cannot describe to you its splendour and its extent. 17. And its floor was fire, and above it were lightnings and the path of the stars, and its ceiling also was flaming fire. 18. And I looked and saw therein a lofty throne: its appearance was as hoarfrost, its circuit was as a shining sun and the voices of cherubim. 19. And from underneath the great throne came streams of flaming fire so that it was impossible to look thereon. 20. And the Great Glory sat thereon and His raiment shone more brightly than the sun and was whiter than any snow. 21. None of the angels could enter

---

13. **There were no delights of life therein.** So G M ፍግዐ: ሕይወት: also the Giz. Gk. Dln. and F H L O read ፍግዓ: ወሕይወት 'there were no delights and no life therein.' 20. **The Great Glory.** So G and the Giz. Gk. Dln. gives 'He that is great in glory.'

---

surrounds the *πρόναος* or forecourt of the palace of God. **14.** Cf. lx. 3; lxxi. 11; Ezek. i. 28; Dan. viii. 17, 18, &c. **15.** Enoch approaches the palace of God but does not enter, as no mortal may behold God. As the doors are open, he can describe what is within. **18.** In this and the following verses, the writer draws upon Is. vi; Ezek. i, x; Dan. vii. 9, 10. This passage (vv. 18–22) is used by the author of lxxi. 5–8. **A lofty throne**: cf. Ezek. x. 1; Dan. vii. 9. **As hoarfrost**, i. e. dazzling and bright as hoarfrost: cf. Dan. vii. 9 'white as snow.' **19.** Cf. Dan. vii. 10. **20. The Great Glory**: cf. cii. 3. **Whiter than, &c.**: cf. Dan.

and could behold the face of the Honoured and Glorious One and no flesh could behold Him. 22. A flaming fire was round about Him, and a great fire stood before Him, and none of those who were around Him could draw nigh Him: ten thousand times ten thousand were before Him, but He stood in no need of counsel. 23. And the holiness of the holy ones, who were nigh to Him, did not leave by night nor depart from Him. 24. And until then I had had a veil on my face, and I was trembling: then the Lord called me with His own mouth and spake to me: 'Come hither, Enoch, and hear My holy word.' 25. And He made me rise up and approach the door: but I turned my face downwards.

XV. 1. And He answered and spake to me with His voice: 'I have heard, fear not, Enoch, thou righteous man and scribe of righteousness: approach and hear my voice. 2. And go, say to the watchers of heaven, who have sent thee to intercede for them: you should intercede for men, and not men for you: 3. Wherefore have ye left the high, holy, eternal heaven, and lain with women, and defiled yourselves with the daughters of men and taken unto yourselves wives, and done like to the children of earth, and begotten giants

---

22. **A flaming fire.** So A G K M and the Giz. Gk.: Dln. and F H L O 'Fire of flaming fire.' 23. **And the holiness of the holy ones, who were nigh to Him, did not leave by night nor depart from Him.** So G ወቅድሳት፡ ቅዱሳን፡ እለ፡ ይቀርቡ፡ ኀቤሁ፡ ኢይርኅቁ፡ ሌሊተ፡ ወየአትዉ፡ እምኔሁ. Also the Giz. Gk. 24. **Hear.** So the Giz. Gk., but wanting in the Ethiopic MSS.

XV. 1. **I have heard.** So G M ሰማዕኩ. Other MSS. ሰማዕ =

---

vii. 9. **21. The Honoured and Glorious One**: cf. ciii. 1. **22. Could draw nigh**: cf. III Macc. ii. 15: I Tim. vi. 16. **Ten thousand times, &c.** Dan. vii. 10. **23.** Contrast lxxi. 8. **24. My holy word**: see Crit. Note. In xv. 1, I have rendered 'hear my voice' as in the Giz. Gk. The Ethiopic word is the same in both cases and = 'word' or 'voice.' In xci. 1 we should probably translate 'the voice calls me,' rather than 'the word' &c. **25.** Enoch is bidden to draw near the door but not to enter.

XV. 1. Scribe of righteousness: see xii. 3 (note). **2. Intercede**: see ix. 10 (note). **3.** Cf. xii. 4;

(as your) sons. 4. Whilst you were still spiritual, holy, in the enjoyment of eternal life, you have defiled yourselves with women, have begotten (children) with the blood of flesh, and have lusted after the blood of men, and produced flesh and blood, as those produce them who are mortal and shortlived. 5. Therefore have I given them wives also that they might impregnate them, and children be borne by them, that thus nothing might be wanting to them on earth. 6. But you were formerly spiritual, in the enjoyment of eternal immortal life, for all generations of the world. 7. Therefore I have not appointed wives for you; for the spiritual have their dwelling in heaven. 8. And now, the giants, who are produced from the spirits and flesh, will be called evil spirits upon the earth, and on the earth will be their dwelling. 9. Evil spirits proceed

Hen. 15, 8–16, 1.

Καὶ μεθ' ἕτερα· καὶ νῦν οἱ γίγαντες οἱ γεννηθέντες ἀπὸ πνευμάτων καὶ σαρκὸς πνεύματα πονηρὰ ἐπὶ τῆς γῆς καλέσουσιν αὐτούς, ὅτι ἡ κατοίκησις αὐτῶν ἔσται ἐπὶ τῆς γῆς. πνεύματα

'hear.' 5. **That thus, &c.** So G: ከመ፡ ከማሁ፡ ኢይትኀጣእ፡ ግብር፡ በኀበሊሆን። But the last word 'through them' (fem.) I have rendered to them (masc.) as in the Giz. Gk. *ἵνα μὴ ἐκλείπει αὐτοῖς.* Dln. and FHKNO read ከመ፡ ከማሁ፡ ይትገበር፡ ግብር = wie solche Dinge zu geschehen pflegen (Dln.). 8. **From the spirits.** So G እመንፈሳት. So the Gk.: *ἀπὸ πνευμάτων.* Other MSS. and Dln. እምነፍሳት = 'from the body,' but this is clearly

---

Jude 6. 4–7. For man as mortal and dwelling upon the earth wedlock is appointed that so the race may continue to exist: but for the angels who are immortal and dwell in the heaven such commingling is contrary to their nature and involves pollution and guilt. 8, 9. The union of angels and the daughters of men will give birth to a new order of beings, i.e. giants, and from these giants when they die will proceed evil spirits, i.e. demons, and these will have the earth for their habitation. Observe that the evil activities of these demons are not restrained or forbidden as those of their parents, for the latter were thrown into chains immediately on the death of the giants, their children. 8, 9. **From the spirits and flesh**: see Crit. Note. On these verses cf. Justin. *Apol.* xxii, quoted in the note on ix. 8, 9; Tertull. *Apol.* xxii: Quomodo de angelis quibusdam sua sponte corruptis corruptior gens daemonum evaserit.. apud litteras sanctas ordo cognoscitur. In Lact. *Instit.* ii. 15, the demons are regarded purely as

from their bodies; because they are created from above, (and) from the holy watchers is their beginning and primal origin; they will be evil spirits on earth, and evil spirits will they be named. 10. And the spirits of heaven have their dwelling in heaven, but the spirits of the earth which were born upon the earth have on the earth their dwelling. 11. And the spirits of the giants will devour, oppress, destroy, attack, do battle, and cause destruction on the earth, and work affliction: they will take no kind of food, nor will they thirst, and they will be

πονηρὰ ἔσονται, τὰ πνεύματα ἐξεληλυθότα ἀπὸ τοῦ σώματος τῆς σαρκὸς αὐτῶν, διότι ἀπὸ τῶν ἀνθρώπων ἐγένοντο, καὶ ἐκ τῶν ἁγίων τῶν ἐγρηγόρων ἡ ἀρχὴ τῆς κτίσεως αὐτῶν καὶ ἀρχὴ θεμελίου. πνεύματα πονηρὰ ἐπὶ τῆς γῆς ἔσονται, τὰ πνεύματα (al.: *πρῶτα*) *τῶν γιγάντων νεμόμενα, ἀδικοῦντα, ἀφανίζοντα, ἐμπίπτοντα καὶ συμπαλαίοντα καὶ ῥιπτοῦντα ἐπὶ τῆς γῆς καὶ δρόμους ποιοῦντα, καὶ μηδὲν ἐσθίοντα, ἀλλ' ἀσιτοῦντα καὶ φάσματα ποιοῦντα καὶ διψῶντα καὶ προσκόπτοντα.*

---

wrong. 11. **Will devour, oppress, destroy, attack.** So the Syn. Gk.: *νεμόμενα, ἀδικοῦντα, ἀφανίζοντα, ἐμπίπτοντα.* Dln.'s Ethiopic text runs ደመናተ፡ እለ፡ ይገፍዑ፡ ይማስኑ፡ ወይወድቁ, and is thus translated by him: Welche auf die Wolken sich stürzen, werden verderben und herabstürzen, but this is not possible grammatically. Before we compare the two versions we must change ይማስኑ into ያማስኑ in accordance with G and the Gk. *ἀφανίζοντα.* We find there, that ይገፍዑ is the exact equivalent of *ἀδικοῦντα*, ያማስኑ the equivalent of *ἀφανίζοντα*, and ይወድቁ a bad rendering of *ἐμπίπτοντα.* We now come to the main difficulty, ደመናተ፡ እለ as an equivalent of *νεμόμενα.* Dr. Neubauer has suggested to me that the Hebrew may have been ענו i.e. עִנּוּ = 'they oppressed,' of which *νεμόμενα* might stand as a free rendering, and that this ענו may have been confused with ענן 'a cloud' by the Greek translator, whom the Ethiopic followed. The Giz. Gk. supports the corrupt Ethiopic text, and reads *νεφέλας.* **Nor will they thirst.** The Gk.

---

wicked angels. 10. Not found in the Gk. 11 See Crit. Note. An account of the evil activities of the demons.

invisible. 12. And these spirits will rise up against the children of men and against the women, because they have proceeded from them.

XVI. 1. In the days of murder and of destruction and of the death of the giants when the spirits have gone forth from the souls of their flesh, in order to destroy without incurring judgment—thus will they destroy until the day when the great consummation of the great world be consummated over the watchers and the godless.

καὶ ἐξαναστήσονται τὰ πνεύματα ἐπὶ τοὺς υἱοὺς τῶν ἀνθρώπων καὶ τῶν γυναικῶν, ὅτι ἐξ αὐτῶν ἐξεληλύθασι· καὶ ἀπὸ ἡμέρας καιροῦ σφαγῆς καὶ ἀπωλείας καὶ θανάτου τῶν γιγάντων Ναφηλείμ, οἱ ἰσχυροὶ τῆς γῆς, οἱ μεγάλοι ὀνομαστοί, τὰ πνεύματα τὰ ἐκπορευόμενα ἀπὸ τῆς ψυχῆς αὐτῶν, ὡς ἐκ τῆς σαρκὸς ἔσονται, ἀφανίζοντα χωρὶς κρίσεως, οὕτως ἀφανίσουσι μέχρις ἡμέρας τῆς τελειώσεως, ἕως τῆς κρίσεως τῆς μεγάλης, ἐν ᾗ ὁ αἰὼν ὁ μέγας τελεσθήσεται, ἐφ' ἅπαξ ὁμοῦ τελεσθήσεται.

---

is wrong in omitting the negative *διψῶντα.* M is likewise wrong. 12. **Will rise up against.** So M. All other MSS. add a negative: the Gk. confirms M.

XVI. 1. Correct **እምነፍሰት** in Dln.'s text into **እምነፍሳት** with E and N and the Gk. *ἀπὸ τῆς ψυχῆς*, and **ኵነኔ** into **ተፍጻሜት** with A E F G H K L M N O and the Gk. *τελειώσεως*. The text is still very corrupt; but it is not difficult to restore the original with the help of the Book of Jubilees and the Syn. Gk. which runs: *τὰ πνεύματα τὰ ἐκπορευόμενα ἀπὸ τῆς ψυχῆς αὐτῶν, ὡς ἐκ τῆς σαρκὸς ἔσονται, ἀφανίζοντα χωρὶς κρίσεως, οὕτως ἀφανίσουσι μέχρις ἡμέρας τῆς τελειώσεως.* In the Book of Jubilees, ch. x, it is said that the purpose of the demons is **ለአማስኖ፡ ወለአስሕቶ፡ ቅድመ፡ ኵነኔ** = 'to destroy and lead astray until the judgment.' This gives the sense of the Gk. and what should be the sense of the Ethiopic. The text then should read: **እንተ፡ ኀበ፡ ወፅአ፡ መንፈሳት፡ እምነፍሳት፡ ሥጋ ሆሙ፡ ለይኩኑ፡ ዘየማስኑ፡ ዘእንበለ፡ ኵነኔ፡ ከማሁ፡ የማስኑ፡ እስከ፡ ዕለት፡ ተፍጻሜት፡ ዐባይ.** This is the text which we have translated above. For this use of **ለ** in **ለይኩኑ** as an inseparable conjunction of purpose, see Dln.'s

---

XVI. 1. See Crit. Note. The demons will not be punished till the final judgment. This doctrine likewise appears in the Book of Jubilees x, and in the N.T. Cf. Matt. viii. 29, 'Art Thou come hither to torment

The following Fragment is not found in the Ethiopic Version. It probably belongs to the lost Apocalypse of Noah which is interwoven with the book of Enoch.

Καὶ αὖθις· παρὰ δὲ τοῦ ὄρους ἐν ᾧ ὤμοσαν καὶ ἀνεθεμάτισαν πρὸς τὸν πλησίον αὐτῶν, ὅτι εἰς τὸν αἰῶνα οὐ μὴ ἀποστῇ ἀπ' αὐτοῦ ψῦχος καὶ χιὼν καὶ πάχνη καὶ δρόσος οὐ μὴ καταβῇ εἰς αὐτό, εἰ μὴ εἰς κατάραν καταβήσεται ἐπ' αὐτό, μέχρις ἡμέρας κρίσεως τῆς μεγάλης. ἐν τῷ καιρῷ ἐκείνῳ κατακαυθήσεται καὶ ταπεινωθήσεται καὶ ἔσται κατακαιόμενον καὶ τηκόμενον ὡς κηρὸς ἀπὸ πυρός, οὕτως κατακαήσεται περὶ πάντων τῶν ἔργων αὐτοῦ. καὶ νῦν ἐγὼ λέγω ὑμῖν υἱοῖς ἀνθρώπων, ὀργὴ μεγάλη καθ' ὑμῶν, κατὰ τῶν υἱῶν ὑμῶν, καὶ οὐ παύσεται ἡ ὀργὴ αὕτη ἀφ' ὑμῶν, μέχρι καιροῦ σφαγῆς τῶν υἱῶν ὑμῶν. καὶ ἀπολοῦνται οἱ ἀγαπητοὶ ὑμῶν καὶ ἀποθανοῦνται οἱ ἔντιμοι ὑμῶν ἀπὸ πάσης τῆς γῆς, ὅτι πᾶσαι αἱ ἡμέραι τῆς ζωῆς αὐτῶν ἀπὸ τοῦ νῦν οὐ μὴ ἔσονται πλείω τῶν ἑκατὸν εἴκοσιν ἐτῶν. καὶ μὴ δόξητε ἔτι ζῆσαι ἐπὶ πλείονα ἔτη· οὐ γάρ ἐστιν ἐπ' αὐτοῖς πᾶσα ὁδὸς ἐκφεύξεως ἀπὸ τοῦ νῦν διὰ τὴν ὀργήν, ἣν ὠργίσθη ὑμῖν ὁ βασιλεὺς πάντων τῶν αἰώνων· μὴ νομίσητε ὅτι ἐκφεύξεσθε ταῦτα.

Καὶ ταῦτα μὲν ἐκ τοῦ πρώτου βιβλίου 'Ενὼχ *περὶ τῶν ἐγρηγόρων.*

2. And now as to the watchers who have sent thee to intercede for them, who had been aforetime in heaven, (say to them,) 3. "You have been in heaven, and though the hidden things had not yet been revealed to you, you knew worthless mysteries, and these in the hardness of your hearts

---

Lex. Col. 24. The Giz. Gk. supports the view taken above: *ἐκ τῆς ψυχῆς τῆς σαρκὸς αὐτῶν ἔσται*, though it wrongly omits the *ὡς*. Dln.'s text is very corrupt and misleading. **Over the watchers and the godless.** Not in either Greek fragment. 3. **Worthless.** See Appendix. Cf. the Giz. Gk. *τὸ ἐκ τοῦ θεοῦ γεγενημένον.*

---

us *before the time?*' **Consummation:** see xlv. 2 (note). **3.** This statement is the basis of Clem. Alex. *Strom.* ed. Dindorf. iii. 9: *οἱ ἄγγελοι ἐκεῖνοι οἱ τὸν ἄνω κλῆρον εἰληχότες, κατολισθήσαντες εἰς ἡδονάς, ἐξεῖπον τὰ*

you have recounted to the women, and through these mysteries women and men work much evil on earth." 4. Say to them therefore: "You have no peace."'

[XVII. 1. And they took me away to a place where there were forms like flaming fire, and when they wished they appeared as men. 2. And they conducted me to the place of the whirlwind and to a mountain, the point of whose summit reached to heaven. 3. And I saw the places of the luminaries and of the thunder at the ends thereof; in the depths thereof, a fiery bow and arrows and their quiver, and a fiery sword and all the lightnings. 4. And they took me to the water of life, and to the fire of the west,

---

XVII. 2. G reads ወሰዱኒ = they conducted me. Cf. ነሥኡኒ in vv. 1, 4. Other MSS. give ወሰደኒ 'one conducted me.' The Giz. Gk. supports G. 3. **The places of the luminaries.** So M O — መካናተ፡ ብርሃናት, also G መናብርተ፡ ብርሃናት. So also the Giz. Gk. Dln. and F H L N: 'brightly shining places.' **After the places of the luminaries** the Giz. Gk. adds *καὶ τοὺς θησαυροὺς τῶν ἀστέρων*. **At the ends thereof.** See Appendix. **And**

ἀπόρρητα ταῖς γυναιξὶν ὅσα τε εἰς γνῶσιν αὐτῶν ἀφῖκτο. **4. No peace**: see v. 4 (note).

XVII–XIX. These chapters are certainly foreign to the rest of this section. They are full of Greek elements. We have references in xvii. 5, 6 to the Pyriphlegethon, Styx, Acheron and Cocytus: in xvii. 5, 7, 8; xviii. 10, to the Ocean Stream: in xvii. 6, to Hades in the west. Again, xviii. 6–9 is a duplicate account of xxiv. 1–3; xviii. 12–16 a duplicate account of xxi. 1–6, and xix of xxi. 7–10, though in the last case there are important divergencies. Again, xix. 1 contradicts xv. 4–12; for, whereas we have in xix demonic beings before the fall of the angels, in the rest of i–xxxvi the demons are described as the children of the fallen angels.

XVII. 1. Forms like flaming fire, &c. These are some kind of angels: cf. xix. 1. **2. Place of the whirlwind**: cf. Job xxxvii. 9. **A mountain.** It is impossible to determine anything about this mountain. **3. Places of the luminaries.** These may be the 'chambers of the luminaries': cf. xli. 5. **Of the thunder**: cf. xli. 3; xliv; lix; lx. 13–15 and notes. **In the depths thereof**, i. e. of the places of the thunder. **Fiery bow**—the bow with which the lightnings are shot: cf. Ps. vii. 12; Hab. iii. 9; Lam. ii. 4; iii. 12. **Arrows**, i. e. the lightnings: cf. Ps. xviii. 14; lxxvii. 17, 18. **Their quiver**: cf. Lam. iii. 13. **Sword**: cf. Ps. vii. 12; Deut. xxxii. 41. **4. The water of life**: see Crit. Note. Cf. 'the fountain of life,' in

which receives every setting of the sun. 5. And I came to a river of fire, the fire of which flows like water and discharges itself into the great sea towards the west. 6. And I saw all the great rivers and came to a great darkness, and went to the place where all flesh wanders. 7. And I saw the mountains of the darkness of winter and the place whence the waters of the entire deep flow. 8. And I saw the mouths of all the rivers of the earth and the mouth of the deep.

XVIII. 1. And I saw the chambers of all the winds, and I saw how He had furnished with them the whole creation and the firm foundations of the earth. 2. And I saw the cornerstone of the earth, I saw the four winds which bear the earth and the firmament of the heaven. 3. And I saw how the winds stretch out the vaults of heaven and have their station between heaven and earth: these are the pillars of the heaven.

---

a fiery sword. Not in the Giz. Gk. 4. **The water of life.** So the Giz. Gk. All Ethiopic MSS. insert the epithet 'so-called' before **water**, but such a description would be incompatible with the prophetic rôle of the author. 6. After **came** the Giz. Gk. inserts 'to the great river and.' **All flesh.** The Giz. Gk. states exactly the opposite ὅπου πᾶσα σὰρξ οὐ περιπατεῖ. If the Greek is right, we may find a parallel to this statement in xix. 3. If the Ethiopic is right, the place is to be taken as Hades, as in the note. 7. **The mountains of the darkness of winter.** The Giz. Gk. gives 'the wintry winds of the darkness.' We have no means of determining which is right. **The place whence**, not 'den Ort wohin' as Dln. Cf. the Giz. Gk. τὴν ἔκχυσιν.

Ps. xxxvi. 9; Prov. x. 11; xiii. 14; xiv. 27; xvi. 22; Rev. xxii. 17, 'water of life.' **Fire of the west**: see xxiii (notes). **5. River of fire**: the Πυριφλεγέθων. **Great sea**: 'Ωκεανός or the Great Ocean Stream. **6. All the great rivers**: Styx, Acheron and Cocytus. **The place where, &c.**, i. e. Hades. **7. The mountains, &c.**: see Crit. Note. **8. The mouths of all the rivers, &c.**, i. e. Oceanus.

XVIII. 1. Chambers of all the winds: see xli. 4 (note); lx. 11, 12; also xxxiv–xxxvi. **Foundations of the earth.** A frequent phrase in the O.T. Cf. II Sam. xxii. 16; Job xxxviii. 4; Ps. xviii. 15; lxxxii. 5, &c. **2. Cornerstone**: Job xxxviii. 6. **The four winds.** This theory has no root in the O.T. **3. Pillars of the heaven**: the expression is from Job

4. And I saw the winds which turn the heaven, which bring the circumference of the sun and all the stars to their setting. 5. And I saw the winds on the earth, which carry the clouds; and I saw the paths of the angels: I saw at the end of the earth the firmament of the heaven above. 6. And I proceeded towards the south, and there it burns day and night, where there are seven mountains of magnificent stones, three towards the east, and three towards the south: 7. and indeed of those towards the east, one was of coloured stone, and one of pearls, and one of antimony, and those towards the south of red stone. 8. But the middle one reached to heaven like the throne of God, of alabaster, and the summit of the throne was of sapphire. 9. And I saw a flaming fire, which was in all the mountains. 10. And I saw there a place, over against the great earth: there the heavens were gathered together. 11. And I saw a deep abyss, with pillars of heavenly fire and among them I saw pillars of heavenly fire fall which were in number beyond count alike towards the height and towards the depth. 12. And over

---

XVIII. 4. Instead of ያዐርቡ: ለክበበ, G has the strange reading የዐርቡ: ኀዐለ: ኮከበ. 10. **Heavens.** So G M ሰማያተ and the Giz. Gk. Later MSS. ማያተ 'waters.' 11. **I saw a deep abyss.** So G M. Dln. and F H K L N O add 'in the earth.' But this abyss is beyond the earth. The Giz. Gk. supports G M.

---

xxvi. 11. **4. Turn the heaven, &c**: cf. lxxii. 5; lxxiii. 2. **5. Carry the clouds.** An explanation of the difficulties suggested in Job xxxvi. 29; xxxvii. 16. **At the end of the earth the firmament, &c.** The ends of the firmament of heaven rest on the ends of the earth: cf. xxxiii. 2; the vault of heaven is supported by the winds, xviii. 2, 3. **6-9.** This is another version of what is recounted in xxiv. 1–3. These seven mountains lie three in the East and three in the South and the seventh at their point of contact. The description here varies somewhat from that in xxiv. 1–3. These mountains are mentioned in the Book of Jubilees viii. **8. Of sapphire**: cf. Ezek. i. 26. **10.** The same idea as in xviii. 5; xxxiii. 2. **11.** This may be the final place of punishment for the fallen angels. If so, cf. x. 6, 13; xix; xxi. 7–10; xc. 24. **Of heavenly fire**: cf. Gen. xix. 24; Ps. xi. 6; Ezek. xxxviii. 22. **12-16.** This place of punish-

that abyss I saw a place which had no firmament of the heaven above and no foundation of earth beneath it: there was no water upon it and no birds, but it was a waste place. 13. And what I saw there was horrible—seven stars like great burning mountains, and like spirits, which besought me. 14. The angel said: 'This is the place where heaven and earth terminate, it serves for a prison for the stars of heaven and the host of heaven. 15. And the stars which roll over the fire are they which have transgressed the commandment of God before their rising because they did not come forth at the appointed time. 16. And He was wroth with them and bound them till the time when their guilt should be consummated in the year of the mystery.'

XIX. 1. And Uriel said to me 'Here will stand the angels who have connected themselves with women, and their

---

XIX. 1. Dln.'s text is very corrupt. Hence I have transferred the ወ from ብዙኅ to the word before it, in accordance with the Giz. Gk. Again I have read እስከ for እስመ with B C H M N O, and ዐስት, for በዐስት with C G L M N O. Thus we have a literal

---

ment for the disobedient stars is again described in xxi. 1–6. It is already occupied. **13. Seven**: a sacred number in this book. **Mountains.** The stars are larger than they appear. **Like spirits which besought me.** The stars are regarded as conscious beings and accordingly punished for their disobedience. Cf. the ἀστέρες πλανῆται in Jude 13. **16.** The angel knows not when the punishment of these stars will be over, and declares this to be a mystery; yet in xxi. 6 this mystery is disclosed.

XIX. This chapter has been misinterpreted by Dln. We have already seen (p. 87) that xvii–xix are an intrusion in the present text, and the more closely we study this chapter the more certain is this conclusion. In xix. 1 the angels are said to seduce mankind into sacrificing to the demons as gods; but according to x–xvi this is impossible; for the demons are the spirits which have gone forth from the children of these angels, and as the imprisonment of the angels and the destruction of their children were in effect contemporaneous (x. 12), it was impossible for the former to teach men to sacrifice to demons. According to xv. 12–xvi an end was set to the destructive agencies of the fallen angels by their imprisonment, whereas unlimited license was accorded to the demons till the final judgment. We have here, therefore, a different view of the origin of the demon-world. The demons, according to this chapter, are in existence before the fall of the

spirits assuming many different forms have defiled mankind and will lead them astray into sacrificing to demons as gods, (here will they stand,) till the day of the great judgment on which they shall be judged till they are consummated. 2. And with their women also who led astray the angels of heaven it will fare in like manner as with their friends.' 3. And I, Enoch, alone saw the vision, the ends of all things: and no man will see what I have seen as I have seen.]

XX. 1. And these are the names of the holy angels who watch. 2. Uriel, one of the holy angels, the angel over the world and over Tartarus. 3. Rufael, one of the holy angels, the angel of the spirits of men. 4. Raguel, one of

---

translation of the Giz. Gk. 2. The Giz. Gk. differs greatly: *καὶ αἱ γυναῖκες αὐτῶν τῶν παραβάντων ἀγγέλων εἰς σειρῆνας γενήσονται.* 3. **Will see.** So G M, and the Giz. Gk. Dln. and F H O 'has seen.'

XX. 2. **The angel over the world.** So G **ዘለዓለም**, and the Giz. Gk. *ἐπὶ τοῦ κόσμου.* Dln. gives 'over thunder.' **Over Tartarus.** So the Giz. Gk., but all Ethiopic MSS. give 'over

---

angels. 1. **Sacrificing to demons as gods**: cf. Deut. xxxii. 17; Ps. cvi. 37; Bar. iv. 7. This passage and xcix. 7 are probably the source of Tertullian, *De Idol.* iv: Henoch praedicens omnia elementa, omnem mundi censum, quae caelo, quae mari, quae terra continentur, in idolatriam versuros daemonas et spiritus desertorum angelorum, ut pro Deo adversus Deum consecrarentur. **Day of the great judgment**: see xlv. 2 (note). **Are consummated**, or 'are destroyed.' 2. The women will be subjected to the same punishment as the fallen angels: cf. x. 13. 3. **The ends of all things.** Quoted by Clemens Alex. *Eclog. Proph.* (Dind. iii. 456): *ὁ Δανιὴλ λέγει ὁμοδοξῶν τῷ Ἐνὼχ τῷ εἰρηκότι "καὶ εἶδον τὰς ὕλας πάσας,"* and by Origen, *De Princ.* iv. 35: scriptum namque est in eodem libello dicente Enoch 'universas materias perspexi.'

XX. In my Gen. Introd. I have treated this chapter as an interpolation. The comparison, however, of the Giz. Gk. shows that many of the statements discordant with the rest of the section are foreign to the true text. This chapter, therefore, was probably an original part of this section. 1. **Who watch**: see xii. 2 (note). 2. The province assigned to Uriel serves to explain such passages as xxi. 5, 9; xxvii. 2; xxxiii. 3, 4. Cf. his rôle in IV Ezra iv. 1. 3. **Rufael**: see x. 4, 7. The definition here given is vague, but suits admirably in xxii. 3, 6. In xxxii. 6, however, Rufael discharges duties which according to xx. 7 should belong to Gabriel. 4. **Raguel** (from רָעַע 'to chastise' or 'terrify') is the chastiser of the lu-

the holy angels, who takes vengeance on the world and on the luminaries. 5. Michael, one of the holy angels, to wit, he that is set over the best part of mankind, over the people. 6. Saraqâêl, one of the holy angels, who is set over the spirits of the children of men, whose spirits have sinned. 7. Gabriel, one of the holy angels, who is over Paradise and the serpents and the Cherubin.

XXI. 1. And I went round to the place of chaos (lit. 'where nothing was made'). 2. And I saw there something horrible, I saw neither a heaven above nor a firmly founded earth, but a place chaotic and horrible. 3. And here I saw seven stars of the heaven bound together in it, like great mountains and flaming as with fire. 4. On this occasion I said 'For what sin are they bound, and on what account have they been cast in hither?' 5. Then spake Uriel, one of the holy angels, who was with me and was chief over them, and

---

quaking.' The Greek is right; cf. xxi; xxvii. 2. 6. See Appendix. 7. **Paradise and the serpents.** So G and the Giz. Gk. Dln. inverts this order. The serpents may be Seraphim. See Appendix.

XXI. 2. **I saw neither a heaven above.** So G ርኢኩ፡ ወኢሰማየ፡ ለዐለ፡ and the Giz. Gk. *ἑώρακα οὔτε οὐρανὸν ἐπάνω.* Dln. gives 'no high heaven.' **A place chaotic.** So G መካን፡ ዘኮነ፡ ድሉው but that it wrongly omits the negative: cf. the Giz. Gk. *τόπον ἀκατασκεύαστον.* Later MSS. add 'empty' after 'place' against G and the Giz. Gk. 5. **And was chief over them.** So the Giz. Gk., *καὶ αὐτὸς αὐτῶν ἡγεῖτο.* Uriel is over Tartarus, xx. 2. Cf. for

---

minaries and seems to be rightly mentioned in xxiii. 4, according to the most probable text. See Appendix. 5. **Michael** is the guardian angel of Israel: so in Dan. x. 13, 21; xii. 1, and likewise universally: see Weber, *L. d. T.* 165: according to this verse Michael is possibly the right speaker in xxiv–xxvi. 6. **Saraqâêl.** Not found elsewhere. 7. Gabriel should be the speaker in xxxii according to this verse.

XXI. 1–6. This place of punishment of the disobedient stars has been already described in xviii. 6–12. There is no material difference between the two accounts. 1. Origen (*De Princ.* iv. 35) has cited this verse: Ambulavi usque ad imperfectum. 2. **Chaotic**: see Crit. Note.

said: ‘Wherefore dost thou ask, and why dost thou enquire and art curious? 6. These are the stars which have transgressed the commandment of God, and are bound here till ten thousand ages, the number of the days of their guilt, are consummated.’ 7. And from thence I went to another place, which was still more horrible than the former, and I saw a horrible thing: a great fire was there which flamed and blazed, and the place was cleft as far as the abyss, being full of great descending columns of fire: its extent and size I could not see, nor was I able to see its origin. 8. Then I spake ‘How horrible is this place and how hideous to look upon!’ 9. Then Uriel answered me, one of the holy angels who was with me: he answered and spake to me ‘Why do you entertain such fear and alarm at this horrible place and in the presence of this pain?’ 10. And he spake to me ‘This place is the prison of the angels, and here they will be imprisoned for ever.’

XXII. 1. And then I went to another place, and he showed

---

phrase, xxiv. 6. Ethiopic MSS. wrongly ‘and was my chief’ or ‘guide.’ **Why dost thou enquire and art curious?** So G M. Dln. and F H L N O insert ‘why dost thou ask?’ after **why dost thou enquire?** 6. **God.** So G and the Giz. Gk. Dln. gives ‘Most High God.’ 7. **The place was cleft.** So G, reading መተረ instead of Dln.’s corrupt ወሰከ, and the Giz. Gk. διακοπὴν εἶχεν ὁ τόπος. 8. **Hideous to look upon.** So G ሕሡም Other MSS. ሕማም ‘painful to look upon.’

---

6. God. Late MSS. read ‘Most High God,’ but wrongly—see Crit. Note. This title is not found in Enoch though ‘Most High’ is found in all the sections: see xcix. 3 (note). **7-10.** In these verses we have a full description of the final place of punishment for the angels. See xviii. 11; xix.

XXII. This chapter contains a very detailed description of Sheol or Hades. According to this writer Sheol is situated in the far west according to Greek and Egyptian ideas, and in this respect the writer runs counter to the views of the Hebrews who placed Sheol in the underworld. In all the other sections of the book the Hebrew conception prevails. This is the most ancient account of the

me in the west a great high mountain and hard rocks and four beautiful places. 2. And there were there deep and wide (places) perfectly smooth, as smooth as something which rolls, and deep and black to look at. 3. And this time Rufael answered me, one of the holy angels who was with me, and spake to me: 'These hollow places whereon the spirits of the souls of the dead are assembled, have been created to this very end, that all the souls of the children of men should assemble here. 4. These places are appointed as their habitation till the day of their judgment and till their appointed period, and this appointed period is long, till the great judgment comes upon them.' 5. And I saw the spirits of the children of men who were

---

XXII. 2. The Ethiopic here is defective and misleading. See Appendix. 3. **The spirits of the souls of the dead.** So G, reading ለነፍሳቲሆሙ instead of Dln.'s ነፍሳቲሆሙ. H gives the same

---

doctrine of Sheol from the Pharisaic or Chasid standpoint, but clearly this doctrine cannot have leaped into life fullgrown as it appears here, but must already have passed through several stages of development. Hades is no longer here, as in the O.T., a place mainly of a semiconscious non-moral state of existence where the only distinctions that prevailed were social and not moral; but has already become essentially a place of conscious existence, where everything is determined by moral distinctions and moral distinctions alone. See lxiii. 10 for the history of this doctrine. So far as we may infer from i–xxxvi, the doctrine of this chapter must be limited to Israelites and their progenitors from Adam, just as only Israelites are taken account of in Dan. xii. 1. **Four.** There are four divisions in Hades: two for the righteous, vv. 5-9, and two for the wicked, vv. 10–13. **Beautiful.** This epithet has no right here. It represents *καλοί*, a corruption of *κοῖλοι*, and this latter belonged to the next verse. See Appendix. 2. This verse must refer to the places of punishment—'deep and black to look at.' See vv. 10–13. 3. **Rufael.** As Schodde remarks, Rufael has the same rôle in Tobit. **Spirits of the souls of the dead**: see Crit. Note. 3, 4. The object with which Hades was created. 5–7. The first division of Sheol contains those righteous souls which in their life met with persecution and suffered a violent and undeserved death. These cry continually to God for vengeance on those who wronged them. In the time of the author many of the Chasidim must have perished in this way. This idea of the righteous or of the angels crying for vengeance on the wicked is in some form common to all the sections of this book. Cf. ix. 1–3, 10, 11; xxii. 5–8; xlvii. 1, 2; lxxxix. 76; xcvii. 3, 5; xcix. 3, 16; civ. 3. Cf.

dead and their voice penetrated to the heaven and complained. 6. This time I asked the angel Rufael who was with me and spake to him: 'Whose spirit is that one yonder whose voice thus penetrates (to heaven) and complains?' 7. And he answered me and spake thus to me saying: 'This is the spirit which went forth from Abel, whom his brother Cain slew, and he keeps complaining of him till his seed is destroyed from the face of the earth, and his seed disappears from amongst the seed of men.' 8. And therefore at that time I asked regarding him, and regarding the judgment of all, 'Why is one separated from the other?' 9. And he answered me and spake to me: 'These three divisions are made to separate the spirits of the dead. And the souls of the righteous are thus separated (from the rest): there is a spring of water and light above it. 10. Such a (division) likewise has been made for sinners when they die and are buried in the earth without incurring judgment in their lifetime. 11. Here their souls are placed apart in this great pain, till the great day of judgment and punishment and torture of the revilers for ever, and vengeance for their souls, there will they be bound for ever. 12.

---

meaning መናፍስት፡ ነፍሳሙ. Dln. and FKLMN give 'the spirits, the souls of the dead.' The Giz. Gk. supports G. See Crit. Note

---

also Rev. vi. 10; IV Ezra iv. 35; Weber, *L. d. T.* 314. **6, 7.** Abel's soul cries for the destruction of the seed of Cain: cf. Gen. iv. 10. **8.** This verse serves to introduce an account of the three remaining divisions of Sheol. **9.** The second division is for the souls of the righteous who have not as those in the first division met with a violent and undeserved death. These have a spring of water and light. G may be right here: 'a spring of the water of life:' cf. xvii. 4, Crit. Note. **10, 11.** The third division is for those sinners who lived prosperously and escaped punishment in life, and finally attained to honourable burial. According to Hebrew and Greek ideas the privation of funeral rites was a great calamity, and involved, at least according to Greek ideas, inevitable suffering for the departed soul. **11. Great pain**: cf. ciii. 7, 8; Luke xvi. 23–25. **Great day of judgment.** See xcv. 2 (note). **Of the revilers.** This could also be translated 'of the accursed' (lit. on those whom one curses). **For ever.** This means only to the final judgment. **12, 13.** The fourth division is for the sinners who suffered in their life and therefore

And such a division has been made for the souls of those who complain and make known their destruction when they were slain in the days of the sinners. 13. Thus it has been made for the souls of men who were not righteous but sinners, complete in their crimes: they will be with criminals like themselves; but their souls will not be slain on the day of judgment nor will they be raised from thence.' 14. Then I blessed the Lord of glory and said: 'Blessed be my Lord, the Lord of righteousness, who ruleth for ever.'

XXIII. 1. From thence I went to another place towards the west, unto the ends of the earth. 2. And I saw a burning fire which ran without resting and paused not from its course day or night but (ran) regularly. 3. And I

---

on ix. 10. 14. **The Lord of righteousness, who ruleth for ever.** So G M. Dln. and F H L N O give 'The Lord of glory and righteousness who ruleth all things for evermore.'

XXIII. 2. **And paused not.** So Dln. and F H K L M N O and the Giz. Gk. G omits.

---

incur a less penalty in Sheol. 12. **Such a division has been made.** This is the reading of the Giz. Gk. and has good parallels in verses 9, 10. See Appendix. The Ethiopic MSS. insert against the Greek the words 'if it was before eternity.' But this addition is meaningless, and must be corrupt. **Complain, &c.** These sinners demand vengeance on those that did violence to them in life, just as the righteous in the first division demanded justice against those that had destroyed them. **In the days of the sinners**: probably the times of Antiochus Epiphanus. 13. **Their souls will not be slain.** There are degrees of suffering in Sheol. The worst penalty appears to be 'the slaying of the soul,' but even this did not imply annihilation. See cviii. 3 (note); also xcix. 11. **Nor will they be raised.** The sinners in the third division will rise in order to be delivered over to a severer condemnation. The resurrection here implied is of Israel only: so the entire section i–xxxvi would lead us to infer. Otherwise this declaration of a General Resurrection is solitary and unique in pre-Christian Jewish Apocrypha. 14. After each fresh revelation Enoch generally bursts forth into a doxology. Cf. xxv. 7; xxvii. 5; xxxvi. 4; xxxix. 9–12; xlviii. 10; lxxxi. 3; lxxxiii. 11; lxxxiv; xc. 40. These doxologies have as a rule a close connexion in thought with their respective contents. **Lord of glory**: see xxv. 3 (note). **Lord of righteousness**: cf. xc. 40; cvi. 3.

XXIII. 1, 2. Enoch still remains in the West, but proceeds to another quarter of the West where there is a restless river of fire. xvii. 4 appears to deal with the same subject.

asked, saying: 'What is this which rests not?' 4. This time Raguel, one of the holy angels who was with me, answered me and spake to me: 'This burning fire in the direction of the west, the course of which you have seen (is the fire of) all the luminaries of heaven.'

XXIV. 1. From thence I went to another place of the earth, and he showed me a mountain range of fire which flamed day and night. 2. And I approached it and saw seven magnificent mountains each different from the other, and magnificent beautiful stones, magnificent as a whole, of glorious appearance and fair exterior: three towards the east, one founded on the other, and three towards the south, one upon the other, and deep winding ravines, no one of which joined with any other. 3. And the seventh mountain was between these, and in their elevation they all resemble the seats of a throne: and the throne was encircled with fragrant trees. 4. And amongst them was a tree such as I had never yet smelt: neither was any amongst them nor were others like it; it had a fragrance beyond all fragrance: its leaves and blooms and wood wither not for ever: and its fruit is beautiful, and it resembles the dates of a palm. 5. And on this occasion I said: 'Behold this beautiful tree, beautiful to look upon, and its leaves are fair and its fruit very delightful to the eye.'

XXIV. 2. **One founded on the other.** So Dln. and F H K L M O. For ጽኑዓን G N read ጽዑናን = 'mounted or resting upon.' **One upon the other.** So D E F G H K L M N. Dln. with A B C O inserts ወጽኑዓን 'one founded on the other.' The Giz. Gk. supports G.

---

4. The idea, as Dln. suggests, seems to be that the luminaries recruit their wasted fires by passing through this restless stream of fire in the West. The text seems corrupt. See Appendix.

XXIV. 1–3. This mountain range, according to xviii. 6–9, is in the South. On nearer acquaintance Enoch finds it to consist of seven summits, the middle and highest of which is the throne of God. These mountains were composed of precious stones, each of a different one. The throne was girt with fragrant trees, the most desirable of trees. 4. The tree here described, so notable for its fragrance (cf. xxv. 6), is the tree of

6. Then answered Michael, one of the holy and honoured angels who was with me, and was in charge thereof:

XXV. 1. And he spake to me, 'Enoch what dost thou ask as touching the fragrance of this tree and what dost thou seek to know?' 2. Then I, Enoch, answered him and said: 'I should like to know about everything, but especially about this tree.' 3. And he answered me and said: 'This high mountain which thou hast seen, whose summit is like the throne of the Lord, is His throne, where the Holy and Great One, the Lord of Glory, the Eternal King, will sit, when He shall come down to visit the earth with goodness. 4. And no mortal is permitted to touch this tree of delicious fragrance

---

XXV. 4. **Till the great day of judgment, when He shall avenge and bring everything to its consummation for ever; this tree, I say, will (then) be given, &c.** So G: እስከ፡ ዐቢይ፡ ዕለት፡ እንተ፡ ኵሉ፡ እመ፡ ይትበቀል፡ ኵሉ፡ ወይፌጸም፡ እስከ፡ ለዓለም፡ ዝኩ . . . ይትወሀብ. Dln., supported in the main by the other MSS., reads: እስከ፡ እመ፡ ዐቢይ፡ ኵሉ፡ እመ፡ ይትበቀል፡ ኵሉ፡ ወይትፌጸም፡ እስከ፡ ለዓለም፡ ዝኩ . . . ይትወሀብ; which he translates thus: 'Bis um die Zeit des grossen Gerichts: wann Alles gesühnt und vollendet werden wird für die Ewigkeit, wird dieser—'übergeben

---

life, xxv. 4–6 (notes). 6. **Michael,** the patron angel of Israel, is in charge of these special treasures of the Messianic kingdom.

XXV. 3. **This high mountain,** i. e. the middle one of the seven. This mountain, described in xviii. 6–9, xxiv. 1–3, is not to be identified with Sinai, i. 4, for there God descends to judgment. This mountain is God's throne on earth when he comes down to bless the earth. Cf. lxxvii. 1. **Holy and Great One**: see i. 3 (note). **Lord of Glory**: cf. xxii. 14; xxv. 7; xxvii. 3, 5; xxxvi. 4; xl. 3; lxiii. 2; lxxxiii. 8. **Eternal King**: cf. vv. 5, 7; xxvii. 3; only found in i–xxxvi. 4, 5. This tree is the tree of life. By the eating of this tree after the final judgment men are endowed with long life—not eternal life: cf. v. 9; x. 17; xxv. 6. Cf. Apoc. Bar. lxxiii. 2, 3, 6, 7. The writer of i–xxxvi has not risen to the conception of an eternal life of blessedness for the righteous, and so has not advanced a single step beyond the conceptions found in Is. lxv, lxvi. This materialistic conception of the tree of life based on Gen. ii. 9, iii. 22, and here published afresh, gained afterwards a wide currency in Jewish and Christian literature: cf. Rev. ii. 7; xxii. 2, 14; IV Ezra viii. 52. Why this tree should be amongst the mountains in the South does not

till the great day of judgment, when He shall avenge and bring everything to its consummation for ever; this tree, I say, will (then) be given to the righteous and humble. 5. By its fruit life will be given to the elect: it will be transplanted to the north, to the holy place, to the temple of the Lord, the Eternal King. 6. Then will they rejoice with joy and be glad: they will enter the holy habitation: the fragrance thereof will be in their limbs, and they will live a long life on earth, such as thy fathers have lived: and in their days no sorrow or pain or trouble or calamity will affect them.' 7. Then blessed I the Lord of Glory, the Eternal King, because that He hath prepared such (recompense) for the righteous, and hath created it and promised to give it to them.

XXVI. 1. And I went from thence to the middle of the earth, and I saw a blessed and fruitful place, and there were branches there which had taken root and grew out of a dismembered tree. 2. And then I saw a holy mountain, and underneath

---

werden.' 6. **Will enter the holy habitation.** So G: ውስተ፡ ቅዱስ፡ ማኅደር, but defectively, omitting ይበውኡ which later MSS. corrupted into ያበውኡ. Cf. the Giz. Gk. *εἰς τὸ ἅγιον εἰσελεύσονται*. For ጻማ G reads ፃዐር.

XXVI. 1. G omits እምዕፀ: but F H L M N O support Dln.

---

appear. **4. Great day of judgment:** see xlv. 2 (note). **Avenge and bring everything to its consummation:** see Crit. Note. **Righteous:** see i. 8 (note). **Humble:** cf. cviii. 7. **5. Elect:** see i. 3 (note). **To the holy place,** i.e. Jerusalem. We cannot tell whether the author intended here the New Jerusalem, which according to lxxxix. 28, 29 was to be set up by God Himself. It is, at all events, a Jerusalem cleansed from all impurity, and that is probably all that the author meant. **6. The holy habitation:** see Crit. Note. **The fragrance thereof,** i.e. of the tree of life. Cf. xxiv. 4. **No sorrow or pain, &c.:** cf. Is. lxv. 19, 20. **7. For the doxology,** cf. xxii. 14.

XXVI. Enoch visits Jerusalem and its vicinity. **1. The middle of the earth.** The writer regards Jerusalem as the centre of the earth: cf. Ezek. xxxviii. 12; v. 5. In the Book of Jubilees, viii, it is called the navel or *ὀμφαλός* of the earth, just as Delphi was regarded amongst the Greeks. In En. xc. 26 Gehenna is in the middle of the earth. **Blessed and fruitful place:** cf. xxvii. 1; lxxxix. 40; Dan. xi. 16, 41, 45. **A dismembered tree,** i. e. Israel. The branches are the righteous descendants who are to participate in the Messianic kingdom. **2. A holy moun-**

the mountain to the east of it a stream which flowed towards the south. 3. And I saw towards the east another mountain of the same height, and between them a deep and narrow ravine: in it also ran a stream skirting the mountain. 4. And to the west thereof there was another mountain, lower than the former and of small elevation, and underneath it and between them both was a ravine: and other deep and sterile ravines were at the extremities of all three. 5. And all the ravines were deep and narrow (and formed) of hard rock, and trees were planted upon them. 6. And I marvelled at the rocks, and I marvelled at the ravine, yea, I marvelled very much.

XXVII. 1. Then said I: 'For what object is this blessed land, which is entirely filled with trees, and this accursed valley between?' 2. Then Uriel, one of the holy angels who was with me, answered me and spake: 'This accursed valley

---

tain, i.e. Zion. **A stream**, i.e. the brook of Siloah. **3. Another mount**, i.e. the Mount of Olives. **Ravine**, i.e. the valley of the Kedron or of Jehoshaphat. **A stream**, i.e. the brook Kedron. **4. Another mountain**, i.e. the Mount of Offence. **A ravine**, i.e. the valley of Hinnom. **5.** The account is to be relied on. **6.** The valley of Hinnom.

XXVII. 1. This blessed land: see xxvi. 1, note 1. **This accursed valley.** Gehenna was early associated with the worship of Moloch, to whom the Israelites caused their children to pass through the fire. For the repression of their abominations Josiah took the severest measures, II Kings xxiii. 10; II Chron. xxviii. 3, but not with any permanent effect; for we find Jeremiah pronouncing the valley accursed, and declaring that it should henceforth be known as the valley of slaughter: Jer. vii. 31, 32; xix. 2, 6; xxxii. 35. Again, in Is. lxvi. 24 there is a clear reference to the valley of Hinnom as the place where the slain enemies of the Messianic kingdom should suffer by fire, and that in the presence of the righteous. From this point it is not a far cry to the definite conception of Gehenna as it appears in Enoch. Gehenna is in Enoch the place of punishment of the apostate or faithless Jews who suffer in the presence of the righteous; cf. xxvii. 2, 3; xlviii. 9; liv. 1, 2; lxii. 12, 13; xc. 26, 27. Observe that there is a slight modification of the conception in the Similitudes, xlviii. 9 (note). In the N.T. (Matt. v. 29, 30; x. 28; xviii. 9; xxiii. 15, &c.) and in IV Ezra [vi. 1–3] Gehenna is no longer the place of punishment of unrighteous Jews but of the wicked generally. In later Judaism the conception underwent a further change. Gehenna was regarded as the Purgatory of faithless Jews who were afterwards to be admitted into Paradise, but the place of eternal perdition for the Gentiles; cf. Weber, *L. d. T.* 326, 7.

is for those who are accursed for ever: here will all those be gathered together who utter unseemly words with their lips against God, and speak hard things of His Glory; here will they be gathered together, and here is the place of their punishment. 3. And in the last days there will be the spectacle of a righteous judgment upon them, in the presence of the righteous continually for ever: here will those who have found mercy bless the Lord of glory, the Eternal King. 4. And in the days of judgment over the former, they will bless Him for the mercy in accordance with which He has assigned them (their lot).' 5. At that time I also blessed the Lord of Glory and spake to Him and remembered His greatness, as was befitting.

XXVIII. 1. Then I went towards the east, into the midst of the mountain range of the desert, and I saw here nothing save a plain. 2. Nevertheless it was filled with trees of this seed, and water streamed down from above over it. 3. It was manifest that there were many watercourses which flowed as well towards the north as to the west, and here also as everywhere water and dew ascended.

XXIX. 1. And I went to another place, away from the desert, drawing nigh to the east of the mountain range. 2. And then I saw the trees of judgment, particularly such as give

---

XXVII. 3. **Those who have found mercy.** The text gives መሀርያን='the merciful'; but the sense requires the meaning given above. The text may be a corruption of ምሁሩን='those who have found mercy.' The Giz. Gk. gives ἀσεβεῖς, a corruption of εὐσεβεῖς.

---

2. **Utter unseemly words**: see v. 4 (note). 3. **Spectacle**: cf. xlviii. 9; lxii. 12. **Who have found mercy**: see Crit. Note. **Lord of glory**: see xxv. 3. **Eternal King**: see xxv. 3 (note).

XXVIII. 1. Dln. takes the plain here referred to to be that of the Jordan, and the mountain range of the desert to be the rocky region which separates this plain from Jerusalem. According to Ezek. xlvii. 8, this desert should one day be well watered and covered with trees.

XXIX. 1. Enoch goes still further East and comes to the region of fragrant trees. 2. **Trees of judgment**, i. e. trees which will be given to the righteous after the judgment: cf. x. 19; Is. lx. 6; Ps. lxxii. 10. So

forth the fragrance of frankincense and myrrh, and the trees also were similar.

XXX. 1. And above that (even) above these, above the Eastern Mountain and not far distant, I saw another place, valleys (fed) with unfailing streams. 2. And I saw a beautiful tree, which resembles a fragrant tree such as the mastic. 3. And on the sides of those valleys I saw sweet-smelling cinnamon. And passing over these I drew nigh to the east.

XXXI. 1. And I saw other mountains on which there were trees, and there flowed forth from them as it were nectar, and it is named Sarira and Galbanum. 2. And over that mountain I saw another mountain whereon were aloe-trees and those trees were full of a hard substance like almonds. 3. And the taste of that fruit (lit. 'when one took of that fruit') was better than all fragrant odours.

XXXII. 1. And after these fragrant odours, as I looked towards the north, over the mountains, I saw seven mountains full of choice nard and aromatic trees and cinnamon and pepper. 2. And thence I went over the summits of those

---

XXIX. 2. **The trees also were similar.** So G M: **ዕፀውኒ፡ ይትማሰሉ**. Add 'to walnut-trees' from the Giz. Gk. Dln. and F H K L N O give **ዕፀዊ፡ ኢይትማሰሉ**, which Dln. translates 'waren nicht gleich (gewöhnlichen) Bäumen.'

XXX. 2. **Which resembles a fragrant tree such as the mastic.** So G M: **ዘይመስል፡ ዕፀ፡ መዓዛ፡ ከመ፡ እንተ፡ ዘሰኪኖን**. This reading supports the reading of G M in xxix. 2. Cf. xxxii. 4. Dln. and F H L N O give 'the fragrance of which is like the fragrance of mastic.'

XXXI. 1. **There flowed forth from them as it were nectar.** So G: **ወይወፅእ፡ እምኔሆሙ፡ ከመ፡ ኔቅጥር**. Dln. and F H K L N O insert **ማይ፡ ወይወፅእ** 'and there flowed forth water, and there flowed forth from them as it were nectar.' M points to the text of G. The Giz. Gk. supports G.

Dln., but this interpretation seems forced.

XXX. 2. A beautiful tree. What tree he means is uncertain.

XXXI. 1. See Crit. Note.

mountains, far towards the east, and passed above the Erythraean sea and went far from it and passed over the angel Zutêl. 3. And I came into the garden of righteousness and saw beyond those trees many large trees growing there, of goodly fragrance, large, very beautiful and glorious, and the tree of wisdom which imparts great wisdom to those who eat of it. 4. And it is like the Carob tree: its fruit is like the clusters of the vine, very beautiful: the fragrance of the tree goes forth and penetrates afar. 5. And I said: 'This tree is beautiful, and how beautiful and attractive is its look!' 6. And the holy angel Rufael, who was with me, answered me and said: 'This is the tree of wisdom, of which thy old father and thy aged mother, who were before thee, have eaten, and they learnt wisdom and their eyes were opened, and they recognised that they were naked, and they were driven out of the garden.'

XXXIII. 1. From thence I went to the ends of the earth and saw there great beasts, and each differed from the other, and (I saw) birds also differing in appearance and beauty and

---

XXXII. 2. Erythraean sea. The Persian and Indian oceans: cf. lxxvii. 6, 7. **Zutel.** This seems to be the angel who guarded the entrance to Paradise. **3. Garden of righteousness**: cf. lxxvii. 3; also lx. 8, 23; lxi. 12, with notes. In lxxvii. 3 the garden is in the N.E., and the description here would admit of the same locality; in lxx. 3, on the other hand, it is in the N.W. Again, in xxxvii–lxx, as well as in the Noachic fragments, this garden is the abode of the departed righteous; but in i–xxxvi this is not so; for a special division in Sheol is assigned to the souls of the righteous. It would seem therefore that the Garden or Paradise spoken of in xxxvii–lxx is not the earthly Paradise, but the heavenly one, and that it is in fact identical with the division set apart in Sheol for righteous souls. This view is further confirmed by the fact that this Paradise of the righteous is said to lie in the N.W. in lxx. 3, 4—a statement that harmonizes perfectly with the locality assigned to Sheol in xxii. 1, i.e. the West. The earthly Garden of Eden therefore appears to have no further connexion with the destinies of mankind according to the Ethiopic Enoch. **6. Adam and Eve** are here supposed to be still living. Hence, if x. 1 belongs to this section originally, the writer adopted the Samaritan chronology, but if, as we must rather believe, x. 1–3 is an interpolation, then the Hebrew reckoning is here possible. See lxv. 2 (note). Observe that Adam's sin is not regarded as the cause of man's fall and destruction in the deluge.

voice, and they all differed the one from the other. 2. And to the east of these beasts I saw the ends of the earth whereon the heaven rests, and the portals of the heaven were open. 3. And I saw how the stars of heaven come forth, and I counted the portals out of which they proceed, and wrote down all their outlets; of each individual star by itself, according to their number, their names, their connexions, their positions, their times and their months, as the holy angel Uriel who was with me showed me. 4. He showed all things to me and wrote them down for me: also their names he wrote for me, and their laws and their companies.

XXXIV. 1. From thence I went towards the north to the ends of the earth, and there I saw a great and glorious wonder at the ends of the whole earth. 2. Here I saw three open portals of heaven in the heaven: from each of them proceed north winds: when one of these blows there is cold, hail, frost, snow, dew, and rain. 3. And out of one portal it blows for good: but when they blow through the two other portals, it is with violence, and it brings misfortune on the earth, and they blow (at such times) violently.

XXXV. From thence I went towards the west to the ends of the earth, and saw there three open portals such as I saw (afterwards) in the east, the like portals and the like outlets.

XXXVI. 1. From thence I went to the south to the ends

XXXIII. 4. **Their companies.** So G M ማኅበራቲሆሙ. Dln. gives ምግባራቲሆሙ 'their functions.'

XXXIV. 1. **A great and glorious wonder.** So Dln. and all MSS. but G, which reads ምክር = 'device.'

XXXIII. 2. Whereon the heaven rests: see xviii. 5 (note). **3.** The portals of the stars here mentioned are described at length in lxxii–lxxxii. If we are to regard the two accounts as in the main consistent, the portals of the stars are also those of the sun and moon, lxxii. 3.

XXXIV. In this chapter Enoch describes the portals of the north winds as well as the nature of these winds. Cf. lxxvi.

XXXV. Portals of the west winds.

XXXVI. 1. Portals of the south

of the earth, and saw there three open portals of the heaven: thence come the south wind, dew, rain, and wind. 2. From thence I went to the east to the ends of the heaven, and saw here the three eastern portals of heaven open and small portals above them. 3. Through each of these small portals pass the stars of heaven and run their course to the west on the path which is shown to them. 4. And when I saw it I blessed (Him) and thus each time I blessed the Lord of Glory who had made the great and glorious wonders, to show the greatness of His work to the angels and the souls of men, that they might praise His work and all His creation: that they might see the work of His might and praise the great work of His hands and bless Him for ever.

XXXVI. 4. **Might praise His work and all His creation: that they might see.** So G M: ኵሉ፡ ተግባር. Other MSS. and Dln. give 'Might praise His work and that all His creatures might see.'

---

winds. 2. Enoch returns to the East, and here he sees the portals for the winds and the portals for the stars above them.

SECTION II.

(CHAPTERS XXXVII—LXXI.)

THE SIMILITUDES. INTRODUCTION.

A. *Critical Structure.* B. *Relation of* xxxvii–lxxi *to the rest of the book.* C. *Date.* D. *The Problem and its Solution.*

A. Critical Structure. This Section gives on the whole a consistent apocalyptic as distinguished from a prophetic picture of the future, and may be regarded as coming from one and the same hand. It contains, however, numerous and extensive interpolations, i.e. xxxix. 1, 2[a]; xli. 3–8; xliii; xliv; l; liv. 7–lv. 2; lvi. 5–lvii. 3[a]; lix; lx; lxv–lxix. 25; lxxi. These interpolations, with the exception possibly of l; lvi. 5–lvii. 3[a]; lxxi, are drawn from an already existing Apocalypse of Noah and adapted by their editor to their adjoining contexts in Enoch. This he does by borrowing characteristic terms, such as 'Lord of Spirits,' 'Head of Days,' 'Son of Man,' to which, however, either through ignorance or of set intention he generally gives a new connotation: see Notes for details. l; lvi. 5–lvii. 3[a] may be from the same hand, but belong rather to the prophetic than to the Apocalyptic school of thought. lxxi is of the nature of a mosaic and is modelled, as Köstlin saw (*Theol. Jahr.* 1856, p. 378), on ch. xiv, and on various sections of the Similitudes, of which it appears to give a deliberate perversion. See Notes.

B. Relation of xxxvii–lxxi to the rest of the book. As all critics are now agreed that the Similitudes are distinct in origin from the rest of the book, there is no occasion for treating exhaustively the grounds for this conclusion. Accordingly, we shall give here only a few of the chief characteristics which differentiate this Section from all the other Sections of the book. (*a*) **Names of God found only in xxxvii–lxxi.** 'Lord of Spirits' (passim);

'Head of Days' (xlvi. 2); 'Lord of the Mighty' (lxiii. 2); 'Lord of the Rulers' (lxiii. 2); 'Lord of Wisdom' (lxiii. 2). (*b*) **Angelology.** The four chief angels in xxxvii–lxxi are Michael, Rufael, Gabriel, and Fanuel. Fanuel is not mentioned elsewhere in the book, which gives Uriel instead. In xiv. 11 God is surrounded by Cherubim: but in lxi. 10; lxxi. 6, by Cherubim, Seraphim, and Ophanim, angels of power, and angels of dominions. The angel of peace (xl. 8) is also peculiar to the Similitudes. (*c*) **Demonology.** In the other Sections of the book the sins of the angels consisted in their lusting after the daughters of men (vi–viii), but in liv. 6 in their becoming subjects of Satan. In xxxvii–lxx an evil spirit-world is presupposed from the beginning, but not in the rest of the book. Satan and the Satans, xl. 7; liii. 3; liv. 6, are not even mentioned in the other Sections. These have access to heaven, xl. 7, whereas in the other Sections only good angels have access there. The angels of punishment also are found for the first time in xxxvii–lxxi. (*d*) **The Messianic doctrine** in xxxvii–lxx is unique, not only as regards the other Sections of Enoch, but also in Jewish literature as a whole. The Messiah pre-exists xlviii. 2 (note) from the beginning: he sits on the throne of God, xlvii. 3, and possesses universal dominion, lxii. 6; all judgment is committed unto him, lxix. 27, and he slays the wicked by the word of his mouth, lxii. 2. Turning to the other Sections we find that there is no Messiah in i–xxxvi and in xci–civ, while in lxxxiii–xc the Messiah is evidently human and possesses none of the great attributes belonging to the Messiah of the Similitudes. (*e*) **The scene of the Messianic kingdom** in i–xxxvi is Jerusalem and the earth purified from sin; in lxxxiii–xc, a heavenly Jerusalem set up by God Himself; in xci–civ, Jerusalem and the earth as they are; but in xxxvii–lxx, a new heaven and a new earth, xlv. 4, 5 (note). Again, **the duration of the Messianic kingdom** in i–xxxvi is eternal, but the life of its members limited. The duration of the Messianic kingdom in lxxxiii–xc is eternal, and the life of its members eternal (?). The duration of the Messianic kingdom in xci–civ is limited, and the life of its members limited. (In xci–civ the real interest centres, not in the Messianic kingdom, but in the future spiritual life of the righteous.) But the duration of the Messianic kingdom in xxxvii–lxx is eternal, and the life of its members eternal.

C. Date. From a full review of the evidence, which is given and discussed in the notes on xxxviii. 5, it appears that the kings and the mighty so often denounced in the Similitudes are the later Maccabean princes and their Sadducean supporters—the later Maccabean princes, on the one hand, and not the earlier; for the blood of the righteous was not shed as the writer complains (xlvii. 1, 2, 4) before 95 B.C.: the later Maccabean princes, on the other hand, and not the Herodians; for (1) the Sadducees were not supporters of the latter, and (2) Rome was not as yet known to the writer as one of the great world-powers—a fact which necessitates an earlier date than 64 B.C., when Rome interposed authoritatively in the affairs of Judaea. Thus the date of the Similitudes could not have been earlier than 94 B.C. or later than 64 B.C. But it is possible to define the date more precisely. As the Pharisees enjoyed unbroken power and prosperity under Alexandra 79–70 B.C., the Similitudes must be assigned either to the years 94–79 or 70–64. Finally, if we consider that lvi. 5–lvii. 3[a] is an interpolation, and that this passage must have been written and interpolated before 64 B.C., the Similitudes might reasonably be referred to the years 94–79. See also Gen. Introd., p. 30.

D. The Problem and its Solution. Seeing that God is a just God, how comes it that wickedness is throned in high places and that righteousness is oppressed? Is there no end to the prosperity and power of unbelieving rulers, and no recompense of reward for the suffering righteous? The author (in the genuine portions) finds the answer in a comprehensive view of the world's history: only by tracing evil to its source can the present wrongness of things be understood, and only by pursuing the world's history to its final issues can its present inequalities be justified. The author has no interest save for the moral and spiritual worlds, and this is manifest even in the divine names 'Lord of Spirits,' 'Head of Days,' 'Most High.' Whole hierarchies of angelic beings appear in lxi. 10–12. His view is strongly apocalyptic, and follows closely in the wake of Daniel. The origin of Sin is traced one stage further back than in i–xxxvi. The first authors of sin were the Satans, the adversaries of man, xl. 7. The Watchers fell through becoming subject to these, and leading mankind astray, liv. 6. Punishment was at once meted out to the Watchers, and they were confined in a deep abyss, liv. 5, to await the final judgment, liv. 6; lv. 4; lxiv. In the meantime sin flourishes in the world: sinners deny the name of the Lord of Spirits, xxxviii. 2; xli. 2, and of His Anointed, xlviii. 10; the kings and the mighty of the earth trust in their sceptre and glory, lxiii. 7, and oppress the elect of the children of God, lxii. 11. But the prayer of the righteous ascends, and their blood goes up before the Lord of Spirits crying for vengeance, xlvii. 1; and the angels unite in the prayer of the righteous, xlvii. 2. But the oppression of the kings and the mighty will not continue for ever: suddenly the Head of Days will appear and with Him the Son of Man, xlvi. 2, 3, 4; xlviii. 2, to execute judgment upon all alike—on the righteous and wicked, on angel and on man. And to this end there will be a Resurrection of all Israel, li. 1; lxi. 5; the books of the living will be opened, xlvii. 3: all judgment will be committed unto the Son of Man, xli. 9; lxix. 27; the Son of Man will possess universal dominion, lxii. 6, and sit on the throne of his glory, lxii. 3, 5; lxix. 27, 29, which is likewise God's throne, xlvii. 3; li. 3. He will judge the holy angels, lxi. 8, and the fallen angels, lv. 4, the righteous upon earth, lxii. 3, and the sinners, lxii. 2; but particularly those who oppress his saints, the kings and the mighty and those who possess the earth, xlviii. 4–7; liii. 3; lxii. 3, 11. All are judged according to their deeds, for their deeds are weighed in the balance, xli. 1. The fallen angels are cast into a fiery furnace, liv. 6; the kings and the mighty confess their sins, and pray for forgiveness, but in vain, lxiii; and are given into the hands of the righteous, xxxviii. 5; and their destruction will furnish a spectacle to the righteous as they burn and vanish for ever out of sight, xlviii. 9, 10; lxii. 12; to be tortured in Gehenna by the angels of punishment, liii. 3–5; liv. 1, 2. The remaining sinners and godless will be driven from off the face of the earth, xxxviii. 3; xli. 2; xlv. 6. The Son of Man will slay them with the word of his mouth, lxii. 2. Sin and wrongdoing will be banished from the earth, xlix. 2; and heaven and earth will be transformed, xlv. 4, 5; and the righteous and elect will have their mansions therein, xxxix. 6; xli. 2. And the light of the Lord of Spirits will shine upon them, xxxviii. 4; xlviii. 9; they will live in the light of eternal life, lviii. 3. The Elect One will dwell amongst them, xlv. 4; and they will eat and lie down and rise up with him for ever and ever, lxii. 14. They will be clad in garments of life, lxii. 15, 16; and shine as fiery lights, xxxix. 7; and become angels in heaven, li. 4. And they will seek after light and find righteousness and peace with the Lord of Spirits, lviii. 3, 4; and grow in knowledge and righteousness, lviii. 5.

TRANSLATION.

XXXVII. 1. The vision which he saw, the second vision of wisdom—which Enoch the son of Jared, the son of Mahalalel, the son of Cainan, the son of Enos, the son of Seth, the son of Adam saw. 2. And this is the beginning of the words of wisdom which I lifted up my voice to declare and recount to those which dwell on earth: hear, ye men of old time, and see, ye that come after, the holy words which I will speak before the Lord of Spirits. 3. It were better

---

XXXVII. 1. **The vision which he saw**: ራእይ፡ ዘርእየ. These words are omitted in Dln.'s translation. 2. **Lifted up my voice to declare.** አንሣእኩ፡ እትናገር. Dln. gives wrongly 'anhob zu reden,' but the phrase is rightly translated in his Lexicon. ቃለ is to be understood after አንሥእ. The same idiom occurs in xxxvii. 5: lxxxiii. 5: lxxxv. 2. When the writers of Enoch wish to express the idea of beginning to do an action, they use አኀዘ፡ አኀዘ followed by the indicative, as in lxxxvi. 5; lxxxviii. 2, or አኀዘ followed immediately by the subjunctive, lviii. 1. ወጠነ is also used in this sense in this book followed

---

XXXVII. 1. The genealogy with which this section begins agrees with many other characteristics of the Similitudes in marking it out as an independent work. **2. Men of old time.** These would embrace Cainan, Mahalaleel, and Jared, according to the LXX. chronology, which is followed in the Similitudes. See liv. 7 (note); lxx. 4 (note). **Lord of Spirits.** This expression occurs in II Macc. iii. 24 and nowhere else in contemporary or earlier writings that I am aware of. It is found in xxxvii. 4 (twice); xxxviii. 2 (twice), 4, 6; xxxix. 2, 7 (twice), 8, 9 (twice), 12; xl. 1, 2, 4, 5, 6, 7, 10; xli. 2 (twice), 6, 7; xliii. 4 (twice); xlv. 1, 2; xlvi. 3 (twice), 6, 7, 8; xlvii. 1, 2 (twice), 4; xlviii. 2, 3, 5, 7 (twice), 10 (twice); xlix. 2, 4; l. 2, 3 (twice), 5; li. 3; lii. 5, 9; liii. 6; liv. 5, 7; lv. 3, 4; lvii. 3; lviii. 4, 6 (twice); lix. 1, 2; lx. 6, 8, 24, 25 (twice); lxi. 3, 5, 8, 9 (thrice), 11, 13 (twice); lxii. 2, 10, 12, 14, 16 (twice); lxiii. 1, 2 (twice), 7, 12 (twice); lxv. 9, 11; lxvi. 2; lxvii. 8, 9; lxviii. 4 (twice); lxix. 24 (twice), 29; lxx. 1; lxxi. 2, 17. In the text of G, which I have followed, this title occurs in xl. 10 and lxi. 9, where it does not appear in Dln.'s text. In Dln.'s enumeration of the passages in which it occurs, he omits seven by oversight. We find it in all 104 times, and 28 of these at least in the Interpolations. In the genuine portions it stands in the closest connexion with the character of its context: cf. xxxix. 12; xl. 1–10; xlvi. 3–8, &c.: but in the Interpolations this appropriateness is wanting: cf. xli. 6, 7; lix. 1, 2, where

to declare (them) to those men of old time, but even from those that come after we will not withhold the beginning of wisdom. 4. Till the present day the Lord of Spirits has never given such wisdom as I have received according to my insight, according to the good pleasure of the Lord of Spirits by whom the lot of eternal life has been given to me. 5. Three Similitudes were imparted to me, and I lifted up my voice and recounted them to those that dwell on the earth.

XXXVIII. 1. First Similitude. When the congregation of the righteous will appear and sinners are judged for their sins

---

immediately by the subjunctive, እንዘ with the indicative, or ወ and a finite verb. 5. **Lifted up my voice**: see note on v. 2.

---

only things of the natural world are in question: cf. also the other passages. This leads to the conjecture that this title was introduced into these Interpolations when they were incorporated in the Similitudes, with a view to adapting them to their new contexts. 4. **The lot of eternal life**: cf. xl. 9; lviii. 3; lxii. 14. In i–xxxvi the life of the member of the Messianic kingdom is at the best limited in duration, v. 9; x. 17; xxv. 6. In xxxvii–lxix it is eternal: in the Messianic kingdom of the Dream Visions, lxxxiii–lxxxix, its duration is uncertain. The kingdom itself is temporary in xci–civ and the real recompense of the righteous is the eternal life which follows on the close of the Messianic kingdom and the final judgment. 5. **Similitudes.** The Ethiopic word here represents immediately παραβολαί and mediately מְשָׁלִים. מָשָׁל is used pretty much in the same sense here as in Num. xxxii. 7, 18 or Job xxvii. 1, and means merely an elaborate discourse, whether in the form of a vision, a prophecy, or a poem. Its object is generally parenetic. **Those that dwell on the earth.** This phrase (except in xlvi. 7 and lxx. 1, where it is merely geographical) is used in a good ethical sense in the genuine portions of this section. Cf. xxxvii. 2; xl. 6, 7; xlviii. 5. So Rev. xiv. 6. But in the Interpolations it calls up different associations: these are bad in liv. 9; lv. 1; lx. 5; lxv. 6, 12; lxvi. 1; lxvii. 8; and either doubtful or merely geographical in xliii. 4; liii. 1; liv. 6; lv. 2; lxvii. 7; lxix. 1. We should observe that this phrase has an evil significance in Revelation, except in xiv. 8. Cf. iii. 10; vi. 10; viii. 13; xi. 10 (twice); xiii. 8, 14; xvii. 8.

XXXVIII. The time of requital is coming. When the Messiah appears and the light of the Lord of Spirits shines on the face of the righteous and elect, where will be the future habitation of the sinners and godless? 1. **The congregation of the righteous.** This phrase, which is peculiar to the parables, is explained by a comparison of xxxviii. 3; liii. 6; lxii. 8. Cf. Ps. cxlix. 1, 'In the congregation of the saints'; Pss. Sol. xvii. 18. **Driven from the face of the earth.** This form of punishment is frequently

and driven from the face of the earth: 2. And when the Righteous One shall appear before the eyes of the elect righteous whose works are wrought in dependence on the Lord of Spirits, and light will appear to the righteous and the elect who dwell on the earth—where then will be the dwelling of the sinners, and where the resting place of those who have denied the Lord of Spirits? It had been good for them if they had not been born. 3. And when the secrets of the righteous shall be revealed, then will the sinners be judged and the godless driven from the presence of the righteous and elect. 4. And from that time those who possess the earth

---

XXXVIII. 2. **Whose works are wrought in dependence on the Lord of Spirits**: lit. 'hang upon.' The same meaning is to be given to the word ስቁል in xl. 5 and xlvi. 8. In these three instances Dln.'s translation gives to this word the meaning of 'gewogen,' 'weighed': 'whose works are weighed by the Lord of Spirits,' but in his Lexicon he has tacitly withdrawn this interpretation.

---

found. Cf. i. 1; xxxviii. 3; xli. 2; xlv. 2, 6; xlvi. 8; xlviii. 9, 10; liii. 2; lxix. 27. **2. The Righteous One.** The Messiah will not appear till the final judgment. The Messiah is variously named: 'The Righteous and Elect One,' liii. 6; 'The Elect One of righteousness and of faith,' xxxix. 6; 'The Elect One,' xl. 5; xlv. 3; xlix. 2, 4; li. 3, 5; lii. 6, 9; liii. 6; lv. 4; lxi. 5, 8, 10; lxii. 1; 'The Messiah,' xlviii. 10; lii. 4. For other designations, see note on xlvi. 2. Observe that as the members of the kingdom are 'the righteous,' so the Messiah is 'the Righteous One': cf. 'The Elect,' 'The Elect One.' **Elect righteous.** Here only in Enoch. **Denied the Lord of Spirits.** This charge is frequently brought against the sinners: it is in fact 'the head and front of their offending.' Cf. xli. 2; xlv. 2; xlvi. 7; xlviii. 10; lxiii. 7. Cf. St. Jude, 4. They deny likewise the heavenly world, xlv. 1; the Messiah, xlviii. 10; the spirit of God, lxvii. 10; the righteous judgment, lx. 6. The righteous on the other hand believe in the name of the Lord, xliii. 4. Observe that this phrase is taken over into the Interpolations, lxvii. 8, 10. **It had been good for them, &c.** Cf. St. Matt. xxvi. 24. Edersheim, *Life and Times of Jesus the Messiah*, ii. 120, points out that this was a well-known rabbinic expression. **3. When the secrets of the righteous shall be revealed.** The blessings in store for the righteous, the heritage of faith, are still hidden, lviii. 5; but they will one day be revealed. The Messiah himself is hidden with the Lord of Spirits, lxii. 7. **4.** The supremacy and oppression of the earth's rulers and great ones are speedily drawing to a close. This is the constant theme of the Similitudes, xlvi. 4–8; xlviii. 8–10; liii. 5; lxii. 1–12; lxiii, and

will no longer be powerful and exalted, and they will not be able to behold the face of the holy, for the light of the Lord of Spirits is seen on the face of the holy and righteous and elect. 5. Then will the kings and the mighty perish and

---

5. **The kings and the mighty.** So G M.

---

has been taken over into the Interpolations, lxvii. 8–13; and this is one of the leading characteristics which distinguish xxxvii–lxix from xci–civ. With the rulers of the earth as such the latter section has practically no concern. **The holy and righteous and elect.** This designation is found also in xlviii. 1. **The light of the Lord of Spirits is seen on the face of the holy.** This light is at once spiritual and physical: the nearness of God's presence transfigures the countenance and person of His saints. Light in all its forms is the blessing of the kingdom. The righteous will have light, and joy, and peace, v. 7, and the light of God shining upon them, i. 8. In the Similitudes the heaven will be transformed into an eternal light, xlv. 4; and light will appear unto the righteous, xxxviii. 2; and the light of days will abide upon them, l. 1; they will abide in the light of the sun and in the light of eternal life, lviii. 3; their faces will be illuminated with the light of the Lord of Spirits, xxxviii. 4; and they will seek after light and find righteousness, and the light of truth will be mighty for evermore, lviii. 3–6. The idea is still further developed in xci–cviii. The righteous belong to the generation of light, cviii. 11; and will be clad in light, cviii. 12; and will walk in eternal light, xcii. 4; and will be resplendent and shine as the lights of heaven for evermore, cviii. 13; civ. 2. **5. The kings and the mighty**: cf. lxii. 1, 3, 6, 9; lxiii. 1, 2, 12; lxvii. 8, 12. These designations are practically synonymous in the Similitudes. The phrase 'mighty kings,' which appears often in Dln.'s text, is without the support of the best MSS. except in lv. 4, and there I feel we must regard the text as corrupt, and read 'the kings and the mighty.' This better text removes, as we shall find, at least one formidable difficulty in the interpretation. Who then are these kings and mighty ones? The facts taken together point decidedly to unbelieving native rulers and Sadducees. They have denied the Lord and His Anointed, xlviii. 10; and a heavenly world, xlv. 1; they belong to the houses of His congregations—to the Theocratic community, xlvi. 8; but they are an offence thereto, an offence on the removal of which the Theocratic ideal will be realised, liii. 6; they do not acknowledge from whom their power is derived, xlvi. 5; but trust in their riches, xlvi. 7; and place their hope in their sceptre and glory, lxiii. 7; they have made the righteous their servants, xlvi. 7; and outraged God's children, lxii. 11; and shed their blood, xlvii. 1, 2. Accordingly they will have to stand before the Messiah whom they have denied, when He judges the angels, lxi. 8; lv. 4; and the righteous, lxii. 3; and the sinners, lxii. 2; and they will be terrified, lxii. 5; and fall down and worship the Messiah, lxii. 9; and acknowledge the righteousness of their judgment, lxiii. 9; and pray for a respite in order

be given into the hand of the righteous and holy. 6. And thenceforward none will seek for mercy for them with the Lord of Spirits, for their life is at an end.

---

to repent, lxiii. 1; and express their thanksgiving of faith, lxiii. 8; but their prayer will not be heard, and the Lord of Spirits, lxii. 12, and the righteous, xlviii. 9, will execute judgment upon them, and their destruction will form a spectacle over which the righteous will rejoice, lxii. 12; and they will be delivered over to the angels of punishment, lxii. 11; and will descend into the tortures of hell, lxiii. 10. Only one statement seems to point to heathen rulers: i.e. 'their faith is in the gods which they have made with their hands,' xlvi. 7. But this is only a strong expression for the heathen or Sadducean attitude of the Maccabean princes and their supporters, and with it we might aptly compare Pss. Sol. i. 8; viii. 14; xvii. 17, wherein the same persons are charged with surpassing the heathen in idolatries. There is a like exaggeration of the wickedness of the Sadducees in xcix. 7; civ. 9. The kings and the mighty in the text, therefore, are native rulers and Sadducees. We thus agree with Köstlin, *Theol. Jahrb.* 1856, 268 sqq., and Dln., Herzog, *R.E.* xii. 352, in identifying these princes with the last of the decaying Asmonean dynasty. The Herodian dynasty was not supported by the Sadducees, and thus may be left out of consideration. Further, as there are no references to Rome in the Similitudes, it cannot as yet have made its power to be felt in Palestine; and the Similitudes, therefore, must have been written before 64 B.C., when Rome interposed in favour of Aristobulus II. Baldensperger, *Das Selbstbewüsstsein Jesu* (p. 12), indeed, tries to show that there are references to the Roman power; but his main contention, that the falling Asmoneans could hardly be designated as 'mighty kings,' is already answered on critical grounds: the phrase 'mighty kings,' does not belong to the true text. The lower limit is thus 64 B.C., and the higher may be reasonably fixed at 94. The differences between the Maccabees and the Pharisees, which had already grown important under John Hyrcanus with his Sadducean policy, were further developed under Aristobulus I, and in the early years of Alex. Jannaeus were intensified into an irreconcilable antagonism. This antagonism *first* issued in bloodshed about 95 B.C., when 6000 Pharisees were put to death because they insulted Alex. Jannaeus for failing to comply with their views on ritual. This fact explains the writer's demand for vengeance for the murder of the righteous, xlvii. 1, 2, 4. Subsequent years only embittered the strife between the Pharisees and the Asmonean head of the Sadducees, and provoked a civil war in which 50,000 Jews fell. Weary of the struggle, Jannaeus asked the Pharisees to name their conditions of peace: their answer was laconic and irreconcilable, 'Thy death'; but in the subsequent strife they were for the time crushed into impotence. Owing to the multitudes of Pharisees slain by Jannaeus, he came to be called 'the slayer of the pious.' With the accession of Alexandra 79, however, the Pharisees became masters of the nation, and peace prevailed till 70, when again the nation was rent in twain and plunged into devastating and bloody

XXXIX. [1. And it will come to pass in those days that elect and holy children of the high heaven will descend, and their seed will become one with the children of men. 2. In those days Enoch received books of zeal and wrath, and books of disquiet and expulsion] and 'mercy will not be accorded to them' saith the Lord of Spirits. 3. And in those days a cloud and a whirlwind carried me off from the earth, and set me down at the end of the heavens. 4. And here I saw another vision, the mansions of the holy and the resting-places

---

wars, through the fraternal strife of Hyrcanus II and Aristobulus II. To a devout Pharisee, the Maccabees with their Sadducean and Hellenic principles might well appear as enemies of the Theocratic community during the years 94–79 or 70–64. To one or other of these periods, therefore, we assign the composition of the Similitudes. **Will be given into the hand of the righteous.** This phrase would seem to indicate the period of the sword, when the righteous were themselves to slay the wicked. But this would be unsuitable here: the judgment is catastrophic and forensic. The Son of Man is judge, and his judgments are executed by the angels of punishment, xli. 2; lxii. 11. This phrase recurs in xlviii. 9; but there the context requires us to understand the casting of the kings into Gehenna. In l. 2, where we again find this idea unmistakeably, the difficulty is obviated by the fact that l is most probably an interpolation. Either, then, we have here an inconsistent feature introduced by the original writer, or else the phrase is only to be taken in a general sense, as expressing the triumph of the righteous. **Righteous and holy.** This designation of the members of the kingdom is found also in xlviii. 1, 4, 7; li. 2 (lxv. 12). **6. None will seek for mercy.** The season for mercy is past, l. 5. **Their life is at an end**: i.e. their temporal life.

XXXIX. 1, 2ᵃ. This is undoubtedly an interpolation: Dln. tried in his commentary to take this as an account of the descent of the unfallen angels to live with the righteous, but he has since (Herzog, *R. E.*) come to see that it can only refer to the descent of the watchers to unite themselves with the daughters of men, and must therefore be an intrusion here. By omitting it we get a smooth text. **Elect and holy children of the high heaven**: cf. cvi. 13, 'Some from the heights of heaven.' For the epithet 'elect,' cf. I Tim. v. 21 'the elect angels.' Schodde compares Tob. viii. 15. **Enoch received books of zeal, &c.** As we shall find later, sometimes an angel dictates to Enoch, at others the angel himself writes the book and commits it to Enoch. **3. Carried me off.** This seems to be recounted as a real translation of Enoch, as in lii. 1; cf. II Kings ii. 11, and not as a mere incident in a dream, as in xiv. 8, 9. **4. Mansions.** This could be rendered 'dwellings' or 'abiding-places': see xxxix. 7, 8; xli. 2. The vision here (xxxix. 4–12) set forth is prophetic, but there are many difficulties in the interpretation which we can surmount only by bearing in mind that what we have here to deal with is a *vision*

of the righteous. 5. Here mine eyes saw their dwellings with His righteous angels, and their resting-places with the holy, and they petitioned, and interceded and prayed for the children of men, and righteousness flowed before them as water, and mercy like dew upon the earth: thus it is they fare for ever and ever. 6. And in that place mine eyes saw the Elect One of righteousness and of faith, and how righteousness shall prevail in his days, and the righteous and elect shall be without number before him for ever and ever. 7. And I saw his dwelling-place under the wings of the Lord of Spirits, and all the righteous and elect before him are beautifully resplendent as lights of fire, and their mouth is full of blessing, and their lips extol the name of the Lord of Spirits, and righteousness before Him never faileth, and uprightness never

---

XXXIX. 6. **And in that place.** So G: በውእቱ፡ መካን. Dln. reads በውእቱ፡ መዋዕል 'in those days.' **The Elect One of righteousness.** So GM: ኅሩየ፡ ለጽድቅ. Dln. and FHKLO give መካነ፡ ኅሩያን፡ ዘጽድቅ = 'the place of the elect ones of righteousness.' **In his days.** So GM. Dln. and FHKLO give 'in their days.' 7. **His dwelling-place.** So GM ማኅደሮ. Dln. and FHKLNO ማኅደራቲሆሙ = 'their dwelling-places.' The original reading of G is obliterated: a late hand gives ይትኄየሶ. **And uprightness never faileth before Him.**

---

of the future Messianic kingdom, and that we must not press the details; for in this, as in visions frequently, there is no exact observance of the unities of time and place. No one individual period is indicated; for the fact that the Messiah is surrounded by all His righteous and elect ones shows that the history of the world is closed, and the final judgment already passed; yet this is impossible, as the angels are still praying on behalf of men. Nor from this chapter, taken by itself, can we argue as to the locality indicated by the vision. At first sight it seems to be heaven, as the Messiah and the righteous are under the wings of the Lord of Spirits; yet this is impossible, as the history of mankind is not yet consummated, and the Messiah appears only to carry out its consummation. The chief inference that we can legitimately draw is that the Messianic community will one day be composed of both angels and men, under the rule of the Messiah and the immediate protection of the Lord of Spirits. 5. **The water and dew** are here symbolical of abundance. Cf. Is. xi. 9; Amos v. 24. See also ch. xlix. 1; xcvii. 9. 6. **The Elect One of righteousness and of faith**: see note on xxxviii. 2. 7. **Resplendent as lights of fire** =

faileth before Him. 8. Here I wished to dwell and my soul longed for that dwelling-place: here already heretofore had been my portion, for so has it been established concerning me before the Lord of Spirits. 9. And in those days I lauded and extolled the name of the Lord of Spirits with blessings and praises, because He hath destined for me blessing and glory according to the good pleasure of the Lord of Spirits. 10. For a long time my eyes regarded that place and I blessed Him and extolled Him, saying: 'Blessed be and may He be blessed from the beginning for evermore. 11. Before Him there is no ceasing. He knows what the world is before it is created, and generation unto generation that shall arise: 12. Those who sleep not bless Thee: they stand before Thy glory and bless, laud, and extol, saying: "Holy, holy, holy, is the Lord of Spirits: He filleth the earth with spirits."' 13. And here my eyes saw all those who sleep not, how they stand before Him and bless, and say: 'Blessed be Thou and blessed be the name of the Lord for ever and ever.' 14. And my face was changed until I could no longer see.

So C E F G H L M N O. Dln. omits with A B D. 10. **Blessed Him and extolled.** So C E G M. Dln., with A B D, omits 'and extolled Him' **ወሰባሕክዎ**. 14. **Until I could no longer see.** Instead of **እስከ** = 'until,' G reads **እስመ** = 'for.'

'shine as the stars.' **8.** Enoch predestined to a place in the kingdom. Cf. lxxi. 14–17; xc. 31. **9. The good pleasure of the Lord.** In xxxvii. 4, and here, the free grace of God is brought forward, but not exclusively; for, like a true Pharisee, man's part in salvation is emphasised in xxxvii. 4 'according to my insight.' **11. Before Him there is no ceasing.** Past, present, and future are before Him. **12. Those who sleep not**: cf. xxxix. 13; xl. 2; lxi. 12. This designation is taken over into the Interpolations, lxxi. 7. In the note on i. 5 I have identified them with the 'Watchers.' **Holy, holy, holy, is the Lord of Spirits.** The change in the trisagion, Is. vi. 3, is in keeping with the character of the entire section. **13–XL.** Enoch next sees all the chief angels and thousands of thousands of angels who stood before the throne of God, and recounts this, not as a prophetic vision, but as an actual experience. **14.** The change of face here is not to be understood as a transfiguration, as in Ascensio Isaiae vii. 25: Enoch is '*blinded* by excess of light.'

XL. 1. And after that I saw thousands of thousands and ten thousand times ten thousand, a multitude beyond number and reckoning, who stood before the Lord of Spirits. 2. I looked and on the four sides of the Lord of Spirits I saw four presences, different from those that sleep not, and I learnt their names: for the angel that came with me made known to me their names, and showed me all the hidden things. 3. And I heard the voice of those four presences as they gave

---

XL. 1. **Before the Lord of Spirits.** So A D F G M O. Dln. and H L N 'Before the glory of the Lord of Spirits.' 2. **Those that sleep not.** So G **እይነውሙ**. This is better than Dln.'s (also F H L N O) **ይቀውሙ** 'those that stand': cf. xxxix. 13; lxi. 12. Dln.'s **ይቀውሙ** is probably an emendation of M's reading

---

XL. 1. Thousands of thousands and ten thousand times ten thousand. This phrase is taken over exactly into the Interpolations, lx. 1; lxxi. 8, though the phrase was of course a current one, owing to Dan. vii. 10. **2. There are higher angels than those that sleep not:** these are the four angels of the presence—מַלְאֲכֵי הַפָּנִים—so called from Is. lxiii. 9. Their names here are Michael, Rufael, Gabriel, and Fanuel; and the same list is carried over into the Interpolations, lxxi. 9. In later Judaism we find Uriel instead of Fanuel. In ix. 1 the names of the four chiefs are Michael, Gabriel, Surjan, and Urjan (for Surjan, the Greek text gives Raphael). In xx there are six chief angels enumerated: Uriel, Rufael, Raguel, Michael, Saraqael, and Gabriel. Thus, Michael, Rufael, and Gabriel belong in common to xx and xl, but the functions respectively assigned them in these chapters are irreconcilable. In xc. 21 there is a reference to seven chief angels: in lxxxi. 5; xc. 31 three angels are mentioned who were charged with the escort of Enoch: in lxxxvii. 2, 3 we find again four. It would be a mere waste of time to attempt to reconcile the angelology of these various passages. On Angelology see Eisenmenger, *Entdecktes Jud.* ii. 370–468; Herzog, *R. E.* iv. 220–227; but especially Hamburger, *R. E.* i. 305–312: Weber, *Lehren d. Talmud*, 161–168, 242–250. **The angel that came with me.** This angel is mentioned in the same vague manner in xliii. 3; xlvi. 2; lii. 3, 4; lxi. 2, 3; lxiv. 2, but is named the 'angel of peace' in xl. 8; lii. 5; liii. 4; liv. 4; lvi. 2. There is generally a certain fitness in the designation 'angel of peace' in the contexts, where it occurs in contrast to the wicked angels and the angels of punishment. This designation has also been taken over into the Interpolations, lx. 24; and borrowed by the writer of Test. Benj. 6. The origin of the phrase is probably to be traced to Is. xxxiii. 7, as that verse was, according to Jerome, understood of the angels, and מַלְאֲכֵי שָׁלוֹם would in that case = 'angels of peace.' Cf. Rosenmüller's *Scholia* in loc.

glory before the Lord of Glory. 4. The first voice blesses the Lord of Spirits for ever and ever. 5. And the second voice I heard blessing the Elect One and the elect ones who cleave to the Lord of Spirits. 6. And the third voice I heard pray and intercede for those who dwell on the earth and supplicate in the name of the Lord of Spirits. 7. And I heard the fourth voice fending off the Satans and forbidding them to appear before the Lord of Spirits to accuse them who

---

ይነውሙ, which wants the negative. 5. See note on xxxviii. 2.

---

4. The first presence, Michael, has for his task the praise of the Lord of Spirits, as his name indicates, מִיכָאֵל. In verse 9 he is 'the merciful and long suffering.' 5. The second presence is Rufael, who praises the Elect and the elect ones. Conformably to his name (from רפא, to heal) he is appointed to heal the wounds and ills of men (verse 9): cf. Tobit xii. 14 'God sent me (Raphael) *to heal* thee'; and iii. 17 'Raphael was sent to heal them both.' In Rabbinic writings he was the power that presided over medicine: cf. Eisenmeng. *Entd. Jud.* ii. 380. See also x. 7; xx. 3. The Elect One. This designation of the Messiah comes from Is. xlii. 1. Its later use seems to be confined to the Similitudes (see xxxviii. 2) and St. Luke ix. 35, *οὗτός ἐστιν ὁ υἱός μου ὁ ἐκλελεγμένος*='the Elect One' (W and H). This, the correct text, has been preserved in the Ethiopic N. T.: St. Luke xxiii. 35 'the Christ of God the Elect One.' 6. The third presence is Gabriel, whose task is that of intercession on behalf of the inhabiters of the earth. As the hero or strong one of God (גבר and אל) he is naturally set over all the powers (verse 9). Those who dwell, &c.: see xxxvii. 5. 7. The fourth is Fanuel, who is set over the repentance and hope of the inheritors of eternal life (verse 9). He prevents the Satans from appearing before the Lord of Spirits to accuse men. The Satans appear here for the first time in Enoch, xl. 7. They seem to belong to a counter kingdom of evil, ruled by a chief called Satan, liii. 3. They existed as evil agencies before the fall of the watchers; for the guilt of the latter consisted in becoming subject to Satan, liv. 6. This view harmonises exactly with that of Gen. iii. 1 combined with vi. 1–4. These Satans had the right of access into heaven, xl. 7 (cf. Job i. 6; Zech. iii)—a privilege denied to the watchers, xiii. 5; xiv. 5. Their functions were threefold: they tempted to evil, lxix. 4, 6; they accused the dwellers upon earth, xl. 7; they punished the condemned. In this last character they are technically called 'angels of punishment,' liii. 3; lvi. 1; lxii. 11; lxiii. 1; this designation has been taken over into the Interpolations: cf. lxvi. 1 (note). The Talmud (cf. Weber, *L. d. T.* 242–245) does not draw this clear line of demarcation between the Satans and the fallen angels, but rather confuses their attributes just as in ch. lxix. For the close connexion between the Demonology of Enoch and the N. T. see

dwell on the earth. 8. After that I asked the angel of peace who went with me, who showed me everything that is hidden, 'Who are these four presences which I have seen and whose words I have heard and written down?' 9. And he said to me: 'This first is Michael, the merciful and long-suffering: and the second, who is set over all the diseases and the wounds of the children of men, is Rufael: and the third, who is set over all the powers, is Gabriel: and the fourth, who is set over the repentance and hope of those who inherit eternal life, is named Fanuel.' 10. And these are the four angels of the Lord of Spirits and the four voices I heard in those days.

XLI. 1. And after that I saw all the secrets of the heavens, and how the kingdom is divided and how the actions of men

---

8. **Who are, &c.?** Before these words Dln. inserts 'and I said unto him' against G M. 9. **This first is Michael.** So G M. Dln. and F H K L N O read 'this first is the holy Michael.' **The third . . . Gabriel.** So G M. Dln. and F H K L N O 'the holy Gabriel.' **Is named Fanuel.** So G M: **ዘስሙ፡ ፋኑኤል**. Other MSS. 'is Fanuel.' 10. **The Lord of Spirits.** So G M. Dln., with other MSS., 'the Most High God.'

Gen. Introd. (pp. 52–3). **8. Angel of peace**: see note on verse 2.

XLI. 1. The kingdom is divided. What 'the kingdom' means here is doubtful. Dln. takes it to mean the Messianic kingdom; Schodde, the kingdom of this world. Can it refer to the division of heaven into seven parts? **The actions of men are weighed**: cf. lxi. 8. The idea is derived from the O.T., where Job (xxxi. 6) prays to be weighed in an even balance, and the spirits of men are weighed by God, Prov. xvi. 2; xxi. 2; xxiv. 12, and the wicked are found wanting, Ps. lxii. 9; Dan. v. 27; Pss. Sol. v. 6. In Enoch, as in the O.T., this idea is not incompatible with the doctrine of divine grace; but in the Talmud it is absolutely materialised, and man's salvation depends on a literal preponderance of his good deeds over his bad ones: see Weber, *L. d. T.* 269–273. This weighing of man's deeds goes on daily (idem 272). But as the results of such judgments were necessarily unknown, there could not fail to be much uneasiness, and to allay this the doctrine of Abraham's meritorious righteousness was in due time developed, in virtue of which all natural descendants of Abraham through Jacob became entitled to salvation (Weber, 280–285). This doctrine, though as yet unknown in Enoch, was a popular

are weighed upon the balance. 2. There saw I the mansions of the elect and the mansions of the holy, and mine eyes saw there all the sinners being driven from thence which had denied the name of the Lord of Spirits, and being dragged off: and they could not abide there because of the punishment which proceeds from the Lord of Spirits. [3. And there mine eyes saw the secrets of the lightning and of the thunder, and the secrets of the winds, how they are divided to blow over the earth, and the secrets of the clouds and dew: and there I saw from whence they proceed in that place and from whence they saturate the dust of the earth. 4. And there I saw closed chambers out of which the winds are apportioned, and the chamber of the hail and winds, and the chamber of the mist, and the cloud thereof hovers over the earth from before eternity. 5. And I saw the chambers of the sun and moon

---

XLI. 2. Instead of ይስሕብዎሙ G reads ይስሕቡ. The sense practically comes to the same, but G gives a more uniform text. Cf. the co-ordinate verb in the previous line ይሰደዱ. M ይስሐቡ—an easy corruption of G. 3. **The dust of the earth.** G reads ፀቡስ 'the dusty earth.' 4. **The chamber of the hail and winds, and the chamber of the mist.** So G M. Dln. and F H L N give: 'The chamber of the hail and the chamber of the mist and of the clouds.' O combines both readings: 'The chamber of the hail and winds, and the chamber of the mist and clouds.'

---

belief in N. T. times: cf. Matt. iii. 9. **2. The sinners being driven from thence:** see xxxviii. 1. **Denied the name of the Lord of Spirits:** see xxxviii. 2.. **3–8.** These verses are, it is obvious, alien in spirit and position to the context. They belong in character and detail to xliii. 1, 2; xliv; lix; lxix. 13–25: see xliii. They may possibly, as Tideman thinks, belong to the Noah-Apocalypse. **3. The lightning and thunder** are treated of repeatedly: see xvii. 3; xliii. 1–2; xliv; lix; lx. 13–15: cf. Job xxxviii. 24, 25, 35. **The secrets of the winds.** On the manifold functions of the winds in Enoch see xviii. 1–5; xxxiv–vi; lxxvi. **4. The chambers of the winds, mist, cloud, &c.** These conceptions rest on the poetical fancies of Job xxxviii. 22. The writers in Enoch conceive all the natural powers, as thunder and lightning, rain, hail, dew, sun and moon, &c., as dwelling in their respective chambers. **The cloud thereof,** i.e. the cloud of mist. Dln.'s reading (see Crit. Note) is full of difficulty. Have we here a reference to Gen. i. 2? **5.** For the teaching of Enoch on the

whence they proceed and whither they come again, and their glorious return, and how one is superior to the other, and their stately orbit, and how they do not leave their orbit, and they add nothing to their orbit and they take nothing from it, and they keep faith with each other, abiding by the oath. 6. And first the sun goes forth and traverses his path according to the commandment of the Lord of Spirits, and mighty is His name for ever and ever. 7. And after that comes the hidden and the visible path of the moon traversing the orbit of her path in that place by day and by night—the one holding a position opposite to the other before the Lord of Spirits. And they give thanks and praise and rest not; for to them their thanksgiving is rest. 8. For the sun changes oft for a blessing or a curse, and the course of the path of the moon is light to the righteous and darkness to the sinners in the name of the Lord, who made a separation between the light and the darkness, and divided the spirits of

---

5. **Their stately orbit.** Dln. translates 'Ihren festbestimmten Lauf.' But this meaning of ፍኖት is not possible, and is tacitly withdrawn in his Lexicon. **Abiding by the oath.** E G M O give ዘኒዳረ instead of ዘሰበሩ, but the sense does not differ materially. 8. **The sun.** So G. All other MSS. read 'the shining sun.'

---

sun and moon, see lxxii. 5. **Their glorious return**, i.e. from west to east on the other side of the firmament, or, according to lxxii. 5, round by way of the north. The perfect regularity with which the sun and moon traverse their orbits is here emphasised, as in lxxiv. 12 is that of the moon. Yet in lxxx. 4 it is said that the moon will become irregular. We shall find, however, that lxxx is an interpolation. **The oath.** A certain degree of consciousness seems to be attributed to the sun, moon and stars. The sun and moon are subject only to God, xli. 6; they give thanks and praise, and rest not; for to them thanksgiving is rest, xli. 7: cf. lxix. 24. God calls the stars by name and they answer, xliii. 1; they keep faith with each other, xliii. 2; they are weighed, as men, in a righteous balance, xliii. 2; the disobedient stars are punished, xviii. 13. In lxxii–lxxix various functions regarding the division of time are assigned to them. In the Persian religion the stars were regarded as embodied existences divided into troops, each under its own leader, Herzog, *R. E.* xi. 235. This theory would suit lxxxii. 9–20 perfectly. It must be confessed, however, that the conception varies. 7. **Hidden path of the moon**, i.e. when the moon is invisible: see lxxiii–iv. 8. **Divided**

men and strengthens the spirits of the righteous in the name of His righteousness.] 9. For neither angel nor power is able to hinder; for He appoints a judge for them all and he judges them all before Him.

XLII. 1. Wisdom found no place where she might dwell; then a dwelling-place was assigned her in the heavens. 2. Wisdom came to make her dwelling among the children of men and found no dwelling-place: then Wisdom returned to her place and took her seat among the angels. 3. And

---

9. **For neither angel nor power is able to hinder; for He appoints a judge for them all and he, &c.** This is the translation of G, only that I have read መኰንን as መኰንነ; for in this MS. the nominative and accusative are constantly confused. This text gives an excellent sense, and harmonises perfectly with the last words of xli. 2 'because of the punishment which proceeds from the Lord of Spirits.' vv. 3–8 are an interpolation. G differs from the other MSS. and Dln. in reading ኢይክል instead of ኢይክልእ, and ይሬሲ instead of ይሬኢ. The sense of Dln.'s text is poor: 'For an angel hinders not and no power can hinder: but the Judge sees them all and He judges them all before Him.' F H K L M O support Dln. If we do not change መኰንን into መኰንነ, G can be translated 'For the judge has appointed them all.' N reads ይርኢ.

---

the spirits of men. There seems to be an actual predestination here spoken of. This division into children of light and darkness is in the past: the spirits of the righteous are strengthened in the present. 9. See Crit. Note. The judge appointed is the Messiah. This verse is to be read directly after xli. 2: cf. Acts xvii. 31.

XLII. As Dln. and others have already recognised, this chapter is a fragment, and out of connexion with its present context: where in the present book of Enoch it should stand, I do not know. 1, 2. The praise of wisdom was a favourite theme. Wisdom was regarded as having her dwelling-place in heaven, lxxxiv. 3; Job xxviii. 12–14; 20–24; Baruch iii. 29; Ecclus. xxiv. 4; and as coming to earth and desiring to make her abode with men, Prov. i. 20 sqq.; viii sqq.; ix. 1–10; Ecclus. xxiv. 7: but as men refused to receive her, cf. xciv. 5, she returned to heaven. But in the Messianic times she will return, and will be poured out as water in abundance, xlix. 1; and the thirsty will drink to the full of wisdom, xlviii. 1; she will be bestowed on the elect, v. 8; xci. 10: cf. Apoc. Bar. xliv. 14; IV Ezra viii. 52; and the spirit of Wisdom will abide in the Messiah the Elect One, xlix. 3. We are reminded in some measure here of the Prologue of St. John. 3. The different welcome which the wicked

unrighteousness came forth from her chambers: and she found those whom she sought not, and dwelt with them (being welcome to them) as rain in a desert and dew on a thirsty land.

[XLIII. 1. And again I saw lightning and the stars of heaven, and I saw how He called them all by their names and they heard Him. 2. And I saw how they are weighed in a righteous balance according to their proportions of light, the width of their spaces and the day of their appearing, and how their revolution produces lightning: and (I saw) their revolution according to the number of the angels, and how they keep faith with each other. 3. And I asked the angel who went with me and showed me what was hidden, 'What are

---

XLIII. 2. **The day of their appearing, and how their revolution produces lightning.** So G, omitting the ሙብረቅ in Dln. M also omits it, but varies otherwise. Other MSS. give 'The day of their appearing and revolution: how one flash of lightning

---

give to unrighteousness intensifies their guilt in respect to wisdom. They received not wisdom when she came unto them; but they took home unto themselves unrighteousness though she sought them not.

XLIII, XLIV. These chapters belong to the same class of Interpolations as xli. 3–8. The study of the third Similitude, where the Interpolations cannot be mistaken, and of the Similitudes generally, shows that the original writer had no interest in natural phenomena, but that all his attention was directed immediately to the spiritual world, and the great spiritual background and crisis of the world's history. The Interpolations come from minds of a far inferior type; and though of an ethical turn, they are as a rule fantastic and frivolous, and their authors are closely allied to the later Rabbinical writers, but have nothing in common with the great and imaginative thinker who wrote the Similitudes. The original ending of this Similitude is lost; that of the other two is preserved: see lvii. 3; lxix. 29.

XLIII. 1. Called them all by their names: cf. Ps. cxlvii. 4; Is. xl. 26; Bar. iii. 34. **2. Weighed in a righteous balance.** On the conscious existence attributed to the stars, see xli. 5. **3. The angel who went with me and showed me what was hidden:** cf. xlvi. 2. Taken over into the Interpolations, lx. 11. **3, 4.** There is some mysterious connexion between the stars and the holy, whereby the stars represent the names of the holy. Does it mean that the holy will be as numerous as the stars? or as bright as the stars? cf. civ. 2; Dan. xii. 3; Matt. xiii. 43. There was a close connexion between the stars and the angels in the O. T.: cf. Job xxxviii. 7, where the morning

these?' 4. And he said to me, 'the Lord of Spirits hath showed thee their parabolic meaning (lit. 'their parable'): these are the names of the holy who dwell on the earth and believe in the name of the Lord of Spirits for ever and ever.'

XLIV. Also other phenomena I saw in regard to the lightnings: how some of the stars arise and become lightnings and cannot part with their new form.]

XLV. 1. And this is the second Similitude concerning those who deny the name of the dwelling of the holy ones and the Lord of Spirits. 2. They will not ascend into the heaven, and on the earth they will not come: such will be the lot of the sinners who deny the name of the Lord of Spirits, who are thus preserved for the day of suffering and

---

produces another.' 4. **Their parabolic meaning.** Dln. translates 'ein Bild von ihnen.' **The names of the holy.** So G M ለቅዱሳን. Other MSS. 'The names of the righteous.'

XLIV. **How some of the stars arise and become lightnings and cannot part with their new form.** Dln. translates: 'Wie die (i.e. die Blitze) aus den Sternen entstehen und zu Blitzen werden.' But እምከዋክብት is a familiar idiomatic expression for 'some of the stars.' In the above translation we have taken ምስሌሆሙ as if it were ምስሎሙ. Dln. points out that it stands for this form in Exod. xxxiv. 13.

---

stars are undoubtedly angels: cf. also Deut. iv. 19. **4. Believe in the name**: cf. xxxix. 6 'the Elect One ... of *faith*'; lviii. 5 'the inheritance of *faith*'; lxi. 4 'the measures given to *faith*'; lxi. 11 'in the spirit of *faith*.' Contrast the *denial* of sinners, xxxviii. 2.

XLIV. The reference here is to shooting stars, ἀστέρες διαθέοντες: Arist. *Meteor.* i. 4. Lightning in general is produced by the quick movement of the stars, xliii. 2; but some of the stars at times are transformed wholly into lightning.

XLV. 1. It is idle to expect an accurate description of the contents of the Similitude from the opening verse or superscription. We find none such in xxxviii. 1, 2; nor yet in lviii. 1, 2. For a summary of the thought of the Similitudes, see pp. 108–109. **Those who deny the dwelling**: see xxxviii. 2 (note). **2. On the earth they will not come.** The earth will be transformed (v. 5) and be thenceforth the abode of the righteous only. **Deny the name of the Lord of Spirits**: see xxxviii. 2 (note). **Day of suffering and tribulation.** The final judgment is variously named 'that great day,' liv. 6; 'day of judg-

tribulation. 3. On that day Mine Elect One will sit on the throne of glory and make choice amongst their (men's) deeds, and their mansions will be innumerable, and their souls will grow strong within them when they see Mine elect ones and those who have called upon My glorious name. 4. And on

---

XLV. 3. **Mine Elect One.** So G ኅሩይየ. FHLMN and Dln. give 'The Elect One,' as we find in xl. 5; xlix. 2, 4; li. 3, 5; lii. 6, 9; liii. 6. **See Mine elect ones.** So GLN: ርእዮቶሙ፡ ለኅሩያንየ፡ ዘእየ. Dln. and FHMO give 'See Mine Elect One.' **Glorious name.** So GM. Other MSS. and

---

ment,' xxii. 4; c. 4; 'day of judgment and consummation,' x. 12; 'day of the great consummation,' xvi. 1; 'the great judgment,' xix. 1; xxii. 4; 'day of the great judgment,' xix. 1; lxxxiv. 4; xciv. 9; xcviii. 10; xcix. 15; civ. 5; 'great day of judgment' x. 6; xxii. 11; xxv. 4; 'judgment which is for ever,' civ. 5; 'great judgment which is for ever,' xci. 15; 'judgment which is for ever and ever,' x. 12; 'day of tribulation,' i. 1; xcvi. 2; 'day of tribulation and pain,' lv. 3; 'day of tribulation and great shame,' xcviii. 10; 'day of suffering and tribulation,' xlv. 2; lxiii. 8; 'day of affliction,' xlviii. 10; l. 2; 'day of anguish and affliction,' xlviii. 8; 'day of destruction,' xcviii. 10; 'day of slaughter,' xciv. 9; 'day of unceasing bloodshed,' xcix. 6; 'day of darkness,' xciv. 9; 'day of unrighteousness,' xcvii. 1. As the same phrase is applied to quite different events it is necessary to observe that—(1) The Deluge or first world judgment is referred to in x. 4, 5, 12^b; liv. 5, 7–10; xci. 5; xciii. 4. (2) Final world judgment *at the beginning of the Messianic kingdom,* x. 6, 12^c; xvi. 1; xix. 1; xxii. 4, 11; xxv. 4; xlv. 2; liv. 6; lv. 4; xc. 20–27. (3) Judgment of the sword *at the beginning of the Messianic kingdom,* when the righteous slay the wicked, l. 2; xc. 19; xci. 12; xcv. 7; xcvi. 1; xcviii. 12. (4) Final world-judgment *at the close of the Messianic kingdom,* xciv. 9; xcviii. 10; c. 4; ciii. 8; civ. 5. In xlviii. 8–10 there seems to be a combination of (2) and (3), and in xcix. 9, xcix. 15 of (3) and (4). **3. Mine Elect One:** see xl. 5. **On the throne of glory.** The Elect One will sit on the throne of his glory, xlv. 3; lv. 4; lxii. 3, 5: as Son of Man, he will sit on the throne of his glory, lxix. 27, 29; being placed thereon by the Lord of Spirits, lxi. 8; lxii. 2; and his throne is likewise the throne of the Head of Days, xlvii. 3; li. 3. The Elect One sits on his throne to judge; for all judgment has been committed unto him, lxix. 27. **Make choice among their deeds.** This seems to mean 'to separate their good deeds and their evil deeds in order to weigh them in the balance for purposes of judgment.' The step is here distinctly taken towards the later gross conceptions of the Talmud: see xli. 1 (note). **Mansions.** This is not the same word as is used in xxxix. 4; but may be rendered similarly, as it is the Ethiopic rendering of mansio, *μονή*. **4, 5.** After the judgment the Messianic kingdom is established and its scene will be a transformed heaven, xlv. 4;

that day I will cause Mine Elect One to dwell among them, and I will transform the heaven and make it an eternal blessing and light. 5. And I will transform the earth and make it a blessing and cause Mine elect ones to dwell upon it: but the sinners and evil-doers will not set foot thereon. 6. For I have seen and satisfied with peace My righteous ones, and have caused them to dwell before Me: but for the sinners there is judgment impending with Me so that I may destroy them from the face of the earth.

XLVI. 1. And there I saw One who had a head of days, and His head was white like wool, and with Him was another being whose countenance had the appearance of a man and his face was full of graciousness, like one of the holy angels. 2. And I asked the angel who went with me and showed me all the hidden things, concerning that Son of Man, who he

---

Dln. give: 'Holy and glorious name.' 4. **Cause Mine Elect One to dwell among them.** G reads ኣንበሮ፡ በማእከሎሙ፡ ሰኍፋያኒ፡ ዚኣየ which is untranslateable. All other MSS. support the text.

XLVI. 2. **The angel who went with me.** The Ethiopic gives

---

li. 4; and earth xli. 2; xlv. 5: its members will be angels, xxxix. 4 (note), and men; and the Elect One will abide amongst them. This idea of the transformation of the world was derived directly from Is. lxv. 17 and lxvi. 2, and probably originally from Zoroastrianism: see Cheyne's *Origin of the Psalter*, 404, 405. It is found elsewhere in Enoch in lxxii. 1; xci. 16. In Isaiah this idea is only adopted eclectically; for it is incompatible with other facts in the context; i.e. lxv. 20, &c.; but in Enoch it is accepted in its entire significance as logically involving the immortal blessedness of man: cf. Apoc. Bar. xxxii. 6; lvii. 2; IV Ezra [vi. 49].

XLVI. 1. In this and the following chapters Daniel vii has been laid under contribution, and from it have been drawn directly the expressions 'Head of Days,' and 'Son of Man.' The former means in Daniel the Everlasting. It is found in Enoch in xlvi. 2; xlvii. 3; xlviii. 2, and has been carried over into the Interpolations, lv. 1; lx. 2; lxxi. 10, 12, 13, 14. The original writer uses this expression of Daniel with much appropriateness in connexion with the supernatural Son of Man and the question of final judgment; in fact the two expressions are correlative: observe the question, 'Why he went with the Head of Days?' but this technical appropriateness is wanting in the Interpolations. **Another being . . . like one of the holy angels**: cf. 1 Sam. xxix. 9; Acts vi. 15. **2. Son of Man.**

was, and whence he was, and why he went with the Head of Days? 3. And he answered and said unto me 'This is the

---

'one of the angels who went with me.' But, as Volkmar has already recognised, Enoch has only an Angel to guide him in the

---

There are some difficulties connected with this expression in Enoch, as it has there three different Ethiopic renderings, = filius hominis, xlvi. 2, 3, 4; xlviii. 2, filius viri, lxix. 29; lxxi. 14, and filius prolis matris viventium, lxii. 7, 9, 14; lxiii. 11; lxix. 26, 27; lxx. 1; lxxi. 17; and these are the greater as the Ethiopic translator can only have had one and the same phrase before him, i.e. *ὁ υἱὸς τοῦ ἀνθρώπου*. For the LXX. invariably uses *υἱὸς ἀνθρώπου* as a rendering of בן־אדם and בן־אנש, and exact Greek equivalents of the Ethiopic expressions are hardly conceivable. Are we then to suppose that these variations existed in the Hebrew, and accordingly postulate on the part of the Ethiopic translators a direct acquaintance with an Hebrew MS. (similarly, as Nöldeke, *Encyc. Brit.* xxi. 654, in the case of the Ethiopic Bible, postulates the presence of Aramaic teachers in order to explain the fact that certain religious conceptions are there expressed by Aramaic words)? These suppositions are not necessary. There is no strict uniformity of rendering in the Ethiopic Bible. *υἱὸς ἀνθρώπου* is rendered by proles matris viventium in Num. xxiii. 19; Ps. viii. 4; cxliv. 3; cxlvi. 3 (in the last two instances, two distinct Hebrew expressions are used): but by filius prolis matris viventium in Ps. lxxx. 17. This latter rendering is practically the authorised one in the Ethiopic as it is found throughout Ezekiel, in Dan. vii. 13, and universally in the N.T. Again ብእሲ = vir is frequently used where we should expect ሰብእ = homo, and vice versa. Hence filius viri and filius hominis in the Ethiopic text may be synonymous and the variation may be due to the carelessness of the translator. Of such carelessness there are many instances in Enoch. In lxxxix. 1 we find ሰብእ where we should have ብእሲ as it is correctly in vv. 9 and 36. Again in lxxxix. 45 we have twice the rendering 'sheep' where according to the context and the Greek it should be 'lamb.' Accordingly we hold that these variations were confined to the Ethiopic version, and this conclusion is confirmed by the fact that filius viri, lxix. 29, does not imply one born of man without the mediation of a mother as some have supposed; for the same phrase is applied to Enoch in lxxi. 14, and is therefore the equivalent of filius hominis in xlvi. 2, &c. We have above remarked that the expression in the Greek version of Enoch must have been *ὁ υἱὸς τοῦ ἀνθρώπου*, and not *υἱὸς ἀνθρώπου*, for in Enoch it is the distinct designation of the personal Messiah. In xlviii. 10; lii. 4 he is styled the 'Messiah.' For the relation between the title 'Son of Man' in Enoch and in the N.T., see Appendix on 'the Son of Man.' **3.** The Messiah is conceived in the Similitudes as (1) the Judge of the world, (2) the Revealer of all things, (3) the Messianic Champion and Ruler of the righteous. (1) As judge, he possesses (*a*) righteousness, (*b*) wisdom, and (*c*) power (Pss.

Son of Man who hath righteousness, with whom dwelleth righteousness, and who reveals all the treasures of that which is hidden, because the Lord of Spirits hath chosen him, and his lot before the Lord of Spirits hath surpassed everything in uprightness for ever. 4. And this Son of Man whom thou hast seen will arouse the kings and the mighty ones from their couches and the strong from their thrones, and will loosen the reins of the strong and grind to powder the teeth

---

Similitudes. Hence, as in lii. 3, we must read በመልአክ instead of በፀእመላእክት. The error probably arose through the occurrence

---

xlv. 4–8; lxxii; Is. xi. 3–5; Jer. xxiii. 5, 6). (*a*) He is the Righteous One in an extraordinary sense, xxxviii. 2 (see note); liii. 6: he possesses righteousness, and it dwells with him, xlvi. 3, and on the ground of his essential righteousness, xlvi. 3, has he been chosen no less than according to God's good pleasure, xlix. 4. (*b*) Wisdom, which could find no dwelling-place on earth, xlii, dwells in him and the spirit of Him who giveth knowledge, xlix. 3: and the secrets of wisdom stream forth from his mouth, li. 3, and wisdom is poured out like water before him, xlix. 1. (*c*) In him abides the spirit of power, xlix. 3, and he possesses universal dominion, lxii. 6. (2) He is the revealer of all things. His appearance will be the signal for the revelation of good and the unmasking of evil: will bring to light everything that is hidden, alike the invisible world of righteousness and the hidden world of sin, xlvi. 3; xlix. 2, 4: and will recall to life those that have perished on land and sea, and those that are in Sheol and hell, li. 1; lxi. 5. Evil when once unmasked will vanish from his presence, xlix. 2. Hence all judgment has been committed unto him, lxix. 27, and he will sit on the throne of his glory, xlv. 3 (see note), and all men and angels will be judged before him, li. 2; lv. 4; lxi. 8; lxii. 2, 3, and no lying utterance will be possible before him, xlix. 4; lxii. 3, and by the mere word of his mouth will he slay the ungodly, lxii. 2. (3) He is the Messianic champion and ruler of the righteous. He is the stay of the righteous, xlviii. 4, and has already been revealed to them, lxii. 7: he is the avenger of their life, xlviii. 7, the preserver of their inheritance, xlviii. 7: he will vindicate the earth as their possession for ever, li. 5, and establish the community of the righteous in unhindered prosperity, liii. 6; lxii. 8: their faces will shine with joy, li. 5, and they will be vestured with life, lxii. 15, and be resplendent with light, xxxix. 7, and he will abide in closest communion with them for ever, lxii. 14, in the immediate presence of the Lord of Spirits, xxxix. 7, and his glory is for ever and ever, and his might unto all generations, xlix. 2. **Hath chosen him.** Hence he is called 'the Elect One': see xxxviii. 2 (note); xl. 4 (note). **His lot . . . hath surpassed everything in uprightness:** cf. Heb. i. 4. **4–8. Grind to powder.**

of the sinners. 5. And he will put down the kings from their thrones and kingdoms because they do not extol and praise him, nor thankfully acknowledge whence the kingdom was bestowed upon them. 6. And he will put down the countenance of the strong and shame will cover them : darkness will be their dwelling and worms their bed, and they will have no hope of rising from their beds because they do not extol the name of the Lord of Spirits. 7. And these are those who make themselves masters of the stars of heaven, and raise their hands against the Most High, and tread down the earth and dwell upon it, and all their deeds manifest unrighteousness and all their deeds are unrighteousness: their power rests upon their riches, and their faith is in the gods which they have made with their hands, and the name

---

of the latter phrase in the preceding line. 5. **Put down the kings from their thrones and kingdoms.** So all MSS. but G M, which give ይገፈትዮሙ፡ ለነገሥት፡ መናብርቲሆሙ፡ በዲበ፡ መናብርቲሆሙ 'Put down the kings, throne upon throne of them' (?) 7. **All their deeds manifest unrighteousness and all their deeds are unrighteousness : their power, &c.** So G M, omitting the ወ before ይርአዩ with D E F H L, and inserting ወኵሉ after ይርአዩ. Dln. and O give: 'All their deeds are unrighteousness and manifest

---

The phraseology of these verses is largely drawn from the O.T.: cf. vv. 4 and 6 with Is. xiv. 9, 11 ; Pss. iii. 7 ; lviii. 6 ; Lam. iii. 16. We have here a highly figurative description of the Messianic judgment of the mighty ones of the earth. 5. **Put down the kings from their thrones**: cf. Luke i. 52, which seems to depend directly on this verse in Enoch in phrasing and thought. **Nor acknowledge whence the kingdom**: cf. Wisdom vi. 3 ; Rom. xiii. 1. 6. **Worms their bed.** Baldensperger (p. 14) thinks that this expression refers to the disease of which Herod died (B. C. 4). In II Macc. ix. 5, 9 it is said that Antiochus Epiphanes died of this disease. It is rather to be taken as a figurative expression for the destruction awaiting the mighty the oppressors of the righteous : cf. Is. lxvi. 24 ; Judith xvi. 17 ; Ecclus. vii. 17 ; Mark ix. 48. **Worms their bed . . . because they do not extol the name of the Lord**: cf. Acts xii. 23 for a like connexion of thought. 7. **Make themselves masters of the stars.** The stars by a bold figure stand in Enoch for (1) the angels ; (2) the righteous, as in this verse : cf. xliii. 4 ; Dan. viii. 10, 11, 13, 25. **Dwell upon it** (i.e. the earth). When this phrase occurs by itself in the Similitudes it has a good ethical sense. See xxxviii. 2 (note). **Their power rests upon their riches**: cf. Pss. xlix. 6 ; lii. 7 ; En. xciv. 8 (note). **Their**

of the Lord of Spirits have they denied. 8. And they will be driven forth from the houses of His congregations and of the faithful who cleave to the name of the Lord of Spirits.'

XLVII. 1. And in those days the prayer of the righteous and the blood of the righteous will have ascended from the earth before the Lord of Spirits. 2. In those days will the holy ones who dwell above in the heavens unite with one voice and supplicate and intercede and laud and give thanks and bless the name of the Lord of Spirits on account of the blood of the righteous which has been shed, and the prayer of the righteous that it may not be in vain before the Lord of Spirits, that judgment may be done unto them, and that they may not have to suffer for ever. 3. And in those days I saw the Head of Days when He had seated Himself on the throne of His glory, and the books of the living were opened

---

unrighteousness, and their power, &c.' **The Lord of Spirits have they denied.** So G. F H L M N O and Dln. read 'The name of the Lord of Spirits have they denied.' 8. **Will be driven forth from the houses of His congregations.** G M read ይሰድዱ፡ አብያተ 'The houses of His congregations will drive forth.' **Cleave to the name**: see xxxviii. 2 (note).

---

faith is in the gods which they have made . . . and the name of the Lord of Spirits have they denied. This is a strong expression for the idolatrous tendencies of the Sadducean court. For a discussion of the verse, see xxxviii. 5 (note). 8. Cf. liii. 6.

XLVII. 1. On the dethronement and destruction of the mighty follows a description of the judgment. **The blood of the righteous.** 'The righteous' is here a collective in the singular, though, in the preceding phrase, 'the prayer of the righteous,' it is in the plural. Some have thought the singular side by side with the plural must be significant here,—in fact a Christian allusion: but this is not so; the same juxtaposition of cases is found in xlvii. 4; xci. 10 '*the righteous one* will arise from sleep and wisdom . . . will be given unto *them*.' Above all, in the next verse, where the phrase occurs again, we find 'the blood of the righteous ones.' The first of the Maccabees to shed the blood of the righteous was Alex. Jannaeus, 95 B.C. See xxxviii. 5 (note). **2.** On the intercession of the angels see xv. 2 (note). **The prayer of the righteous**: cf. Rev. vi. 10 for exactly the same Judaistic sentiment. See xcvii. 5 (note). **3. Books of the living.** The idea underlying this phrase is to be traced to the O.T. There the book of life (or its equivalents, Exod. xxxii. 32 sq. 'God's book'; Ps. lxix. 28 'book of the living') was a register of the citizens of the Theocratic community. To have

before Him, and His whole host which is in heaven above

---

one's name written in the book of life implied the privilege of participating in the *temporal* blessings of the Theocracy, Is. iv. 3, while to be blotted out of this book, Exod. xxxii. 32; Ps. lxix. 28, meant exclusion therefrom. In the O. T. this expression was originally confined to *temporal* blessings only, but in Dan. xii. 1 it is transformed through the influence of the new conception of the kingdom, and distinctly refers to an immortality of blessedness. It has the same meaning in our text. A further reference to it is to be found in civ. 1. The phrase again appears in the Book of Jubilees xxx in contrast with 'the book of those that shall be destroyed,' but in the O.T. sense. The 'Books of the Saints' in cviii. 3 (ciii. 2?) has practically the same meaning. In the N.T. the phrase is of frequent occurrence, Phil. iv. 3; Rev. iii. 5; xiii. 8; xvii. 8; xx. 12, 15; xxi. 27; xxii. 19, and the idea in Luke x. 20; Heb. xii. 23 'written in heaven.' For later instances of its use see Pastor Hermae, *Vis.* i. 3, 2 (see Harnack in loc.); Sim. ii. 9; Mand. viii. 6; 1 Clem. xlv. 8. There is no idea of absolute predestination involved in this conception. The same thought, i. e. the inscription of the name in the book of life, underlies the words 'the memorial of the righteous will be before the face of the Great One unto all generations,' ciii. 4. Contrast Pss. Sol. xiii. 10, 'the memorial of the wicked shall no more be found.' (2) Books of remembrance of good and evil deeds. For those wherein good deeds were recorded, see Ps. lvi. 8; Mal. iii. 16; Book of Jubilees xxx; wherein evil deeds were recorded, Is. lxv. 6; En. lxxxi. 4; lxxxix. 61–64, 68, 70, 71, 76, 77; xc. 17, 20; xcviii. 7, 8; civ. 7; Apoc. Bar. xxiv. 1; wherein good and evil deeds were recorded, Dan. vii. 10; Rev. xx. 12; Asc. Is. ix. 20. (3) The heavenly tables = πλάκες τοῦ οὐρανοῦ in Test. xii. Patriarch. The conception underlying this phrase is to be traced partly to Ps. cxxxix. 16; Exod. xxv. 9, 40; xxvi. 30, where we find the idea that there exist in heaven divine archetypes of certain things on earth: partly to Dan. x. 21, where a book of God's plans is referred to: but most of all to the growing determinism of thought, for which this phrase stands as a concrete expression. In Apocryphal literature historical events are not depicted according to the manifold variety of life, but are methodically arranged under artificial categories of measure, number, weight, Wisdom xi. 20; IV Ezra iv. 36, 37. The conception is not a hard and fixed one: in Enoch and Test. xii. Patriarch. it wavers between an absolute determinism and prediction pure and simple: whereas in Jubilees, in addition to these significations it implies at times little more than a contemporary heavenly record of events. In Enoch the idea is mainly predestinarian, the 'heavenly tables' record all the deeds of men to the remotest generations, lxxxi. 1, 2; and the entire history of the earth, xciii. 1–3; and all the unrighteousness that will arise, cvi. 19; cvii. 1; as well as all the blessings in store for the righteous, ciii. 2, 3. They are likewise called the Book of the Angels, ciii. 2; for they are designed also for the perusal of the angels, cviii. 7, that they may know the future recompenses of the righteous and the wicked. In Test. xii. Patriarch. Levi 5; Aser 7, the idea is predictive; in Aser 2 it concerns a question of Levitical law. In Jubilees the use

and around Him stood before Him. 4. And the hearts of the holy were filled with joy that the number of righteousness had drawn nigh, and the prayer of the righteous was heard, and the blood of the righteous required before the Lord of Spirits.

XLVIII. 1. And in that place I saw a fountain of righteousness which was inexhaustible: around it were many fountains of wisdom, and all the thirsty drank of them and were filled with wisdom, and had their dwellings with the righteous and holy and elect. 2. And at that hour that

---

XLVII. 4. **Had drawn nigh.** So GM ቀርበ instead of በጽሐ of Dln.

XLVIII. 1. **Which was inexhaustible.** It is not necessary to conjecture with Dln. that ኢይትኄለቍ is a corruption of ኢይትኈልቀ; for the former is the natural rendering of *ἀναρίθμητος*, which in Hellenistic Greek meant variously 'great,' 'strong,' 'immense,'

---

of the phrase is very loose; the heavenly tables are the statute book of the Theocracy, or a mere contemporary record, or else are predictive or determinative. The heavenly tables record: (1) Laws Levitical and criminal, in some instances previously observed in heaven, in others, established for the first time on earth: Feast of weeks, vi; Tabernacles, xvi; Passover, xlix; 'the Festival of the Lord,' xviii; Ceremonial cleanness, iii; Circumcision, l; the Sabbath, xv; tithes, xxxii; marriage of elder daughter, xxviii; destruction of him who gives his daughter to a Gentile, xxx; of the murderer, iv; of the incestuous person, xxxiii (ordained because of Reuben); of the seed of Lot, xvi; of the Philistines, xxiv. (2) Merely a contemporary event: the slaughter of the Shechemites, xxx; the institution of the 'Festival of the Lord,' xviii; the showing of the Seven Tables to Jacob, xxxii; Isaac's blessing of Levi and Judah, xxxi; the naming of Abraham, xix; and of Levi, xxx, as friends of God. (3) Predictions: of the judgment of all creation, v; of the Messianic kingdom, xxiii; of the recording of the faithful as friends of God and the transgressors as haters, xxx. **His whole host.** God, as the Jehovah of Hosts, in His manifestations is generally so accompanied: cf. i. 4, 9; lx. 1, 4; lxxi. 9–14. According to the Similitudes it is the Messiah that judges. **4. The number of righteousness.** Dln. takes this to mean the period determined beforehand for the complete revelation of divine righteousness, i.e. the year of the final judgment. This interpretation is perhaps favoured by ver. 2. On the other hand, would it not be better to take the phrase as meaning that *the number of the elect was almost fulfilled*? cf. Rev. vi. 10, 11.

XLVIII. 1. Place: see xlvi. 1. **Fountains of wisdom**: see xlii. 1, 2 (note). Cf. Is. lv. 1 sqq. **2. At that hour**, i.e. when Enoch was beholding these visions. **That Son of Man was named.** The pre-existence of the Son of Man is plainly taught in the Similitudes. He (not

Son of Man was named in the presence of the Lord of Spirits and his name before the Head of Days. 3. And before the sun and the signs were created, before the stars of the heaven were made his name was named before the Lord of Spirits. 4. He will be a staff to the righteous on which they will support themselves and not fall, and he will be the light of the Gentiles and the hope of those who are troubled of heart. 5. All who dwell on earth will fall down and bow the knee before him and will bless and laud and celebrate with song the Lord of Spirits. 6. And for this reason has he been chosen and hidden before Him before the creation of the world and for evermore. 7. And the wisdom of the Lord of Spirits hath revealed him to the holy

---

'innumerable.' 5. **The Lord of Spirits.** So G: ለእግዚአ፡ መናፍስት. Dln. gives 'the name of the Lord of Spirits.' 6. **And for evermore.** So E G H M N O. L and Dln. add በቅድሜሁ 'And he

---

his name) has been chosen and hidden in God's presence from before creation and unto eternity, xlviii. 3, 6: the Most High has preserved him and revealed him to the elect, xlvi. 1, 2; lxii. 7; his glory is for ever and ever, xlix. 2; and when Enoch was translated, the Son of Man was already abiding with the Lord of Spirits, lxx. 1. This actual pre-existence of the Son of Man is only in keeping with his other supernatural attributes of universal dominion, lxii. 6, and unlimited judicial authority, lxix. 27. That the earlier Rabbis taught only an ideal pre-existence of the Messiah (Weber, *Lehr. d. Talmud*, 339-41) does not in the least make against the idea of an actual pre-existence being found in the Similitudes, as the whole conception of the Son of Man there is unique in Jewish literature. It is moreover found in IV Ezra xii. 32; xiii. 26. Besides, Edersheim, *Life and Times of Jesus*, i. 174-6, maintains that this doctrine is taught in the oldest Rabbinic writings, and Weber (p. 340) concedes its appearance in the later. Cf. Schürer, *Div.* ii. vol. ii. 159-162, who agrees with the view above followed. 3. **The signs.** These are the signs of the Zodiac מַזָּרוֹת, Job xxxviii. 32. See also viii. 3; lxxii. 13, 19. 4. **The light of the Gentiles.** Is. xlii. 6; xlix. 6. The Messiah will become the light of the Gentiles through his future coming and character being made known unto them. Cf. lxii. 7, where he is already revealed to the righteous. 5. **All will bow the knee before him.** Even those who have denied him, lxii. 6, 9, 10; lxiii. See also xc. 33-38. Cf. Phil. ii. 10. 6. **For this reason,** i.e. that given in vv. 4, 5. **Hidden:** cf. IV Ezra xiii. 52. 7. **Revealed him to the holy and righteous,** i.e. through

and righteous for he preserveth the lot of the righteous, because they have hated and despised this world of unrighteousness, and have hated all its works and ways in the name of the Lord of Spirits: for they are saved in his name and he is the avenger of their life. 8. And in those days the kings of the earth, and the strong who possess the earth will be of downcast countenance because of the works of their hands, for on the day of their anguish and affliction their souls will not be saved. 9. And I will give them over into the hands of Mine elect: as straw in fire and as lead in water they will burn before the face of the holy, and sink before the face of the righteous and no trace of them will any more be found. 10. And on the day of their affliction, there

---

will be before Him for evermore.' 7. **He is the avenger of their life.** So all MSS. but G, which reads በፈቃዱ 'According to His good pleasure is their life ordered': lit. 'it happens in regard to their life.' G's reading preserves the parallelism in both form and meaning. 9. **Before the face of the holy.** So G. Other MSS. except M read: 'before the face of the righteous.' **Before the face of the righteous.** So G M. Other MSS. and Dln.

O.T. prophecy. Cf. lxii. 7. **Preserveth the lot of the righteous.** The Messiah is the stay of the righteous and the guardian and surety of the inheritance that awaits them. **Hated and despised this world of unrighteousness**: cf. cviii. 8, 9, 10; Gal. i. 4. **Saved in his name**: cf. 1 Cor. vi. 11 'Justified in the name of,' &c. **Avenger of their life,** i. e. by recompensing the righteous and requiting their foes who should be handed over to the angels of punishment, lxii. 11. **8. Day of their anguish**: see xlv. 2 (note). **8–9.** As the Messiah is the Saviour of the righteous, so is he the destroyer of their oppressors. The souls of the oppressors 'will not be saved': cf. xxxviii. 6. **Give them over into the hands, &c.**: see xxxviii. 5 (note). **As straw in fire.** A common figure in the O.T., Exod. xv. 7 or Is. v. 24; Mal. iv. 1: 'as lead in water,' Exod. xv. 10. **Before the face of the holy.** The reference here is to Gehenna. Cf. xxvii. 2, 3; xc. 26, 27: but in the Similitudes the idea of Gehenna undergoes some transformation. In xxvii. 2, 3; xc. 26, 27, the sufferings of the wicked form an ever-present spectacle to the righteous. Cf. IV Ezra [vi. 1], 'Revelabitur furnus gehennae, et ex adverso ejus iterum paradisus jucunditatum': but in the Similitudes, where heaven and earth are transformed on the advent of the Messiah, this spectacle is only a temporary one, and Gehenna and its victims vanish for ever from the sight of the righteous,

will be rest on the earth: before them they will fall and not rise again: and there will be no one to take them with his hands and raise them: for they have denied the Lord of Spirits and His Anointed. The name of the Lord of Spirits be blessed.

XLIX. 1. For wisdom is poured out like water, and glory faileth not before him for ever and ever. 2. For he is mighty in all the secrets of righteousness, and unrighteousness will disappear as a shadow, and have no continuance, because

---

give: 'before the face of the holy.' 10. **Before them.** So G M በቅድሜሆሙ. Other MSS. 'before him.' **His Anointed. The name of the Lord of Spirits be blessed.** These words are omitted by G through homoioteleuton: found in all other MSS.

XLIX. 1. **Is poured out.** G reads ኽዐመ (sic), which when

---

xlviii. 9; lxii. 12, 13. Cf. Rev. xx. 14. 10. **Rest**: cf. liii. 7. **Will fall and not rise again**: cf. ver. 4 for the opposite: cf. also Ps. xxxvi. 12. **The Lord and His Anointed**: cf. Ps. ii. 2. The term 'Messiah' or 'Anointed One' was applicable to any one specially commissioned by God to a religious or Theocratic function: hence to David and his successors, and even to a Gentile prince—Cyrus (Is. xlv. 1): to the Jewish high-priest—'the anointed priest,' Lev. iv. 3, 5, 16; vi. 22: to the Servant of Jehovah, Is. lxi. 1. In the Psalms the title generally refers to the reigning king or to the Davidic king as such: yet its ideal aspect is never lost sight of. When the historical kingship came to an end, the idea still remained and was kept prominent through the liturgical use of the Psalms. Its imperfect realisation in the kings of the past made Israel look forward to the true Messianic king in whom it should be perfectly embodied. But the term is never used technically in this sense in the O.T. In this technical sense it is first found in the Similitudes, xlviii. 10; lii. 4, and a decade or so later in Pss. Sol. xvii. 36; xviii. 6, 8. For its later occurrence see IV Ezra vii. 29; xii. 32; Apoc. Bar. xxix. 3; xxx. 1; xxxix. 7; xl. 1; lxx. 9; lxxii. 2, and N.T. passim. See Cheyne, *Origin of the Psalter*, 338–39: Art. on the Messiah, *Encyc. Brit.* xvi. 53–56. On the question generally, cf. Herzog, *R. E.* ix. 641–72: Schürer, *Div.* ii. vol. ii. 120–87.

XLIX. That the Messiah will thus deal with the mighty ones of the earth is clear from his nature and attributes. 1. **Wisdom is poured out like water**: cf. Is. xi. 9. Wisdom here = the knowledge and fear of God. Cf. xxxix. 5. **Glory faileth not, &c.** The Messiah is the object of endless glorification. 2. **Mighty in all the secrets of righteousness.** On the revealing and manifesting power of the Messiah see xlvi. 3 (note). **Disappear as a shadow, and have no continuance.** The phraseology is borrowed from Job xiv. 2. The word translated 'continuance' is

the Elect One standeth before the Lord of Spirits, and his glory is for ever and ever, and his might unto all generations. 3. And in him dwells the spirit of wisdom and the spirit of Him who gives knowledge, and the spirit of understanding and of might and the spirit of those who have fallen asleep in righteousness. 4. And he will judge the secret things and no one will be able to utter a lying word before him; for he is the Elect One before the Lord of Spirits according to His good pleasure.

[L. 1. And in those days a change will take place in the

---

taken intransitively is equivalent to Dln.'s reading ተከዐወ. 3. **The spirit of Him who gives knowledge.** Instead of መንፈስ፡ ዘያሌቡ G reads መንፈስ፡ ዘይብሎ = 'The spirit which speaks to him.' 4. **He is the Elect One.** Instead of ኅሩይ G reads ኅሩም 'He is consecrated.'

---

formed from the verb translated 'standeth': 'unrighteousness will have no standing-ground because the Elect One standeth,' &c. **Glory is for ever and ever, &c.**: cf. Is. ix. 6, 7; Mic. v. 2. 3. **Further endowments of the Messiah after Is. xi. 2. The spirit of wisdom**: cf. li. 3. **The spirit of Him who gives knowledge.** This may correspond to 'the spirit of counsel' or to 'the spirit of knowledge' in Is. xi. 2. **The spirit of those who have fallen asleep, &c.** The righteousness which in some measure belonged to all the faithful in the past will in him attain perfect realisation. 4. **Judge the secret things**: cf. v. 2 and xliii. 3 (note). **A lying word.** Falsehood will be impossible in his presence. Cf. lxii. 3; and lxvii. 9, where it is taken over in the Interpolations. The word translated 'lying' denotes 'emptiness': there is no reality corresponding to it. Cf. lx. 6 'take His name *in vain*,' i.e. commit perjury.

For he is the Elect One, &c. For these very purposes has he been chosen: cf. xlviii. 6.

L. This chapter must, I think, be regarded as an interpolation: if it is original, the writer was inconsistent with himself, and the incongruous details were due to literary reminiscence. These details belong to the same sphere of thought as lxxxiii–xc and xci–civ, where the judgment of the sword forms the prelude to the Messianic kingdom which is gradually established and attended by the conversion of the heathen, xc. 30, 33; xci. 14, and ultimately followed by the final judgment. But xxxvii–lxx are strongly apocalyptic in character, and the kingdom is ushered in by the sudden appearing of the Son of Man, who inaugurates his reign by the two tremendous acts of the resurrection and the final judgment. This judgment is summary and forensic, lxii. 2. There is no place of repentance: cf. lxii; lxiii. God's mercy is shown in

lot of the holy and elect ones: and the light of days will abide upon them and glory and honour will turn to the holy. 2. And on the day of affliction, evil will gather over the sinners, but the righteous will be victorious in the name of the Lord of Spirits: and He will cause the Gentiles (lit. 'the others') to witness (this judgment) that they may repent and forego the works of their hands. 3. They will have no honour through the name of the Lord of Spirits, yet through His name will they be saved and the Lord of Spirits will have compassion on them, for His compassion is great. 4. And He is righteous in His judgment, and in the presence of His glory and in His judgment no unrighteousness shall maintain itself: whosoever repents not before Him will perish.

L. 2. **Evil will gather over the sinners.** Instead of ትዘጉቡ፡ እኪት G reads ዘተዘገበ፡ እኩይ and M ዘጉብአ፡ እኩይ. Other MSS. support Dln. **May repent.** ይኔስሑ. G reads ይትኖሥኡ 'may arise.' M N ይትኌስሑ. 3. **Through the name of the Lord of Spirits.** So G M. በስመ instead of በቅድመ of other MSS. and

---

His dealings with the righteous, lxi. 13. All sinners are forthwith driven from off the earth: heaven and earth are transformed and become the habitation of the righteous. Hence there is no room for the period of the sword, or for the progressive conversion of the heathen. The writer has not, any more than Daniel, taken into account the destiny of the latter, save indirectly in teaching a general judgment. These verses, then, are a later addition made with the purpose of filling up a gap in the Similitudes, but in reality they serve only to rend the seamless vesture of their thought and system. 1. The night of oppression will give place to the sunshine of glory and honour for the righteous with the advent of the Messianic kingdom: cf. lviii. 5, 6. Observe that there is no mention of the Messiah in vv. 1–4, nor yet of the kings and mighty ones, both of which facts tend to confirm the conclusion we have above arrived at. **Holy and elect**: cf. lxii. 8. **2.** The period of the sword, when the righteous slay the wicked, is here referred to: cf. xc. 19–34; xci. 12. **Day of affliction**: cf. xlviii. 10; xlv. 2 (note). **Cause the Gentiles . . . that they may repent**: cf. xc. 30, 33, 34; xci. 14. **3. The Gentiles** who repent will be saved as by fire. They will not have the abundant entering in of the Jews. **4, 5.** When the hour of the final judgment arrives, the season of mercy for the Gentiles is past for ever. Note the affinities of thought between l. 3–5 and lx. 5, 25. Cf. IV Ezra vii. 33; Apoc. Bar. lxxxv. 12. Observe that the final judgment here is not at the

5. And from henceforth He will show no mercy to them, saith the Lord of Spirits.]

LI. 1. And in those days will the earth also give back those

Dln.: 'Before the Lord of Spirits.' 5. **He will show no mercy.** This may equally well be translated 'I will show no mercy.'

---

beginning of the Messianic reign, as in the Similitudes, but apparently at its close, as in xci–civ. In IV Ezra and the Apoc. Bar., where the Messianic kingdom is of temporary duration, and brought to a close by the final judgment, a period of repentance is rightly spoken of. Cf. Apoc. Bar. lxxxv. 12; IV Ezra vii. 34.

LI. 1. The resurrection here is a resurrection of all Israel, but not of the Gentiles. li. 1 would indeed seem to point to the latter, and this all the more so as IV Ezra vii. 32 and [vi. 2], which are evidently based on it, and on En. lx. 6, are applied to a general resurrection. But the whole history of Jewish thought points in an opposite direction. As we shall see below, no Jewish book except IV Ezra teaches indubitably the doctrine of a general resurrection; and this may be due to Christian influence, as IV Ezra cannot be earlier than 80 A.D. Individual utterances to the contrary in the Talmud will be noticed below. On the question generally, see Cheyne, *Origin of the Psalter*, 381–452: 'Possible Zoroastrian Influences on the Religion of Israel,' *Expository Times*, 1891, pp. 224–228; 248–253: Eisenmenger, *Entdecktes Judenthum*, ii. 819, 820–949: Weber, *Die Lehren d. Talmud*, 351–4; 371–80: Schulz, *A. T. liche Theologie*, 4te Aufl. 753–68: Herzog, *R. E.* Art. Unsterblichkeit, vol. xvi. 189–195: Hamburger, *R. E.* ii. 98 sqq. (Art. Belebung der Todten): Edersheim, *Life and Times of Jesus*, ii. 397–403: Kahle, *Biblische Eschatologie*, 1870; Stade, *Über d. A. T. lichen Vorstellungen von dem Zustande nach dem Tode*, 1877: Castelli, 'Future Life in Rabbinic Literature,' Art. in *Jewish Quarterly Review*, July, 1889, pp. 314–52: Montefiore, 'Doctrine of Divine Retribution in O. T.,' Oct. 1890, 1–12. The various forms in which the Jewish doctrine of the resurrection appeared are: (1) a resurrection of all Israelites. This doctrine is first taught in Dan. xii. 2; but, though so powerfully attested, it did not become the prevailing belief. It is the accepted faith in En. i–xxxvi (with the exception of one class of sinners in xxii. 13); xxxvii–lxx; lxxxiii–xc; Ps. lxv (title) in Sept.; II Macc. vii. 9, 14, 23, 29, 36; xii. 43, 44 compared with vi. 26; Apoc. Bar. l–li. 6. (2) A resurrection of the righteous Israelites. In post-Exilic Is. xxv. 8; xxvi. 19; Pss. xvi. 10, 11; xvii. 15; xlix. 15, 16; lxxiii. 24–27 (cf. Cheyne, *Origin of the Psalter*, 406–408); Job xiv. 13–15; xix. 26, 27; En. xci–civ; Pss. Sol. iii. 16; xiii. 9; xiv. 7; xv. 15; Apoc. Bar. xxx; Josephus, *Ant.* xviii. 1, 3; *Bell. Jud.* ii. 8, 14. That the resurrection was the sole prerogative of righteous Israelites became the accepted doctrine in Talmudic theology: Weber, *Die Lehren d. Talmud*, 372–3. Individual voices, however, are not wanting who asserted the resurrection of pious Gentiles, Eisenmenger, *Entdecktes Judenthum*, 908, 9: indeed

who are treasured up within it, and Sheol also will give back that which it has received, and hell will give back that which it owes. 2. And he will choose the righteous and holy from among them: for the day of their redemption has drawn nigh. 3. And the Elect One will in those days sit on My throne, and all the secrets of wisdom will stream forth from the counsels of his mouth: for the Lord of Spirits hath given

---

LI. 1. **Those who are treasured up within it, and Sheol also will give back that which it has received.** So G: **እለ፡ ተዘግቡ፡ ውስቴታ፡ ወሲኦል፡ ታገብእ፡ ዘተመጠወት**. The text of G is manifestly better than that of Dln., the parallelism of which is destroyed apparently by the incorporation of marginal glosses. IV Ezra vii. 32 which is evidently modelled on li. 1 confirms text of G. Dln. is supported by F H L N O and gives: 'That which is entrusted to it, and Sheol will give back that which is entrusted to it, which it has received.' M agrees with Dln. but that it omits **ማኅፀንታ** in the first clause and **ታገብእ** in the second. 3. **On My throne.** So G M. Other MSS. and Dln. 'on His throne.'

---

that of all the Gentiles, with some few exceptions, but only to die again, Eisenmenger, 908–10; Weber, 373. We should observe that even imperfect Israelites might attain to the resurrection of life after purgation in Gehenna, Weber, 372. [Observe that in the Didache it is taught as a Christian doctrine that only the righteous are raised, xvi. 7.] (3) A resurrection of all mankind. IV Ezra vii. 32; [vi. 2;] Test. xii. Patriarch. Judae xxv; Benjamin x. In both cases the doctrine is probably due to Christian influences. Concurrently with the above forms of doctrine, other Jews believed only in the immortality of the soul without a resurrection: Wisdom of Sol. iii. 1 sqq.; iv. 7; v. 16; viii. 20, compared with ix. 15; xv. 8; Jubilees xxiv. 1. **Sheol.** This word is here used in its new sense of the Intermediate State. For the history of this word and its various meanings, see lxiii. 10. **Hell,** literally 'destruction,' ἀπώλεια, is the same as 'Abaddon,' Job xxvi. 6: cf. Rev. ix. 11. With the whole verse cf. IV Ezra vii. 32. The resurrection is a resurrection of the body: cf. lxii. 14. So also in i–xxxvi; lxxxiii–xc; in xci–civ it is only a resurrection of the soul and spirit. In this respect the Pss. Sol. probably agree with xci–civ. A resurrection of the body is taught in II Macc.; Apoc. Bar.; IV Ezra. 2. **The day of their redemption has drawn nigh:** cf. Luke xxi. 28. As the Messiah in his judicial capacity discriminates between men's deeds, xlv. 3, so he discriminates between the righteous and the wicked. 3. The Messiah is the embodiment of wisdom, xlix. 3: and in this wisdom shall the members of his kingdom share, xlviii. 1; lxi. 7, 11. Cf. xlii.

it to him and hath glorified him. 4. And in those days will the mountains leap like rams and the hills will skip like lambs satisfied with milk, and they will all become angels in heaven. 5. Their faces will be lighted up with joy because in those days the Elect One has appeared, and the earth will rejoice and the righteous will dwell upon it, and the elect will go to and fro upon it.

LII. 1. And after those days, in that place where I had seen all the visions of that which is hidden—for I had been carried off in a whirlwind and borne towards the West— 2. There mine eyes saw all the hidden things of heaven that shall be, an iron mountain, and one of copper, and one of silver, and

---

LII. 2. **All the hidden things of heaven that shall be.** So G M, omitting the በዲበ፡ ምድር of Dln. and F H L N O. Dln. gives 'The hidden things of the heaven, all things which shall be

---

2 (note). **4. The mountains will leap, &c.**, i. e. with joy: cf. Ps. cxiv. 4, 6. **All become angels in heaven.** This is not to be weakened down into a mere likeness to the angels. At the least it denotes an equality of the righteous with them. In an earlier section, xci–civ, there is the same idea. The righteous will be companions of the heavenly hosts, civ. 6, and rejoice as the angels in heaven, civ. 4. The idea is further developed in Apoc. Bar.; the righteous will be transformed into the glory of the angels, li. 5, and be made like unto them, li. 10, and their surpassing splendour will exceed that of the angels, li. 12. This too is the teaching of the Talmud. **5. The earth rejoices**, for it is transformed, xlv. 5, and has at last become the inheritance of the righteous as anciently promised: cf. Ps. xxxvii. 3, 9, 11, 29, 34.

LII. This obscure chapter seems to symbolize the various future kingdoms of the world, and to be founded on Dan. ii. 31–45. These kingdoms of material force, symbolized by iron and brass and silver and gold and clay, will be as the chaff of summer threshing-floors before the kingdom of the Messiah, Dan. ii. 35: they will be broken to pieces and consumed, Dan. ii. 44. So here the various world powers represented by these mountains of iron and copper and silver and gold, &c., will melt as wax before the fire in the presence of the Messiah, lii. 6, and be destroyed from off the face of the earth, lii. 9, and no earthly might will avail in that day, lii. 7, 8. Observe that the idea of symbolizing the world powers by mountains is drawn from the same section of Daniel. In ii. 35 the Messianic kingdom is symbolized by a mountain. **1. In that place**, i. e. in heaven, where he had seen all the preceding visions. It is idle to attempt to get an exact idea of Enoch's movements. In xxxix. 3 he was carried off by a whirlwind to the ends of heaven: here he is

one of gold, and one of soft metal, and one of lead. 3.
And I asked the angel who went with me, saying, 'What
things are these which I have seen in secret?' 4. And he
said unto me, 'All these things which thou hast seen serve the
dominion of His Anointed that he may be potent and mighty
on the earth.' 5. And that angel of peace answered me
and said, 'Wait a little and there will be revealed to thee
everything that is hidden, which the Lord of Spirits has
established. 6. And those mountains which thine eyes
have seen, the mountain of iron, and of copper, and of silver,
and of gold, and of soft metal, and of lead, all those will
in the presence of the Elect One be as wax before the fire,
and like the water which streams down from above upon
those mountains and will become powerless before his feet.
7. And it will come to pass in those days that none shall
be saved either by gold or by silver, and none shall be able
to escape. 8. And there will be no iron for war nor

---

on the earth.' 5. **Wait a little and there will be revealed to thee everything.** So G M. Other MSS. and Dln. after **Wait a little** insert 'and thou wilt see.' For **ዘተከለ**='which he has established,' G reads **ዘከለለ**='which encompasses the Lord of Spirits.' 6. **Which thine eyes have seen.** So G M: **ዘርእያ፡ አዕይንቲከ**. Other MSS. and Dln. 'which thou hast seen.' 7. **None shall be able to escape.** So G M. Other MSS. and Dln. read 'None shall be able to save himself or escape.' 8. **There**

---

borne to the west. 2. **Soft metal.** The original word denotes an easily melted metal, and may also stand as a general name for tin and lead: cf. lii. 6; lxv. 7, 8; lxvii. 4, 6. 4. These world powers will serve to show forth the might of the Messiah by being destroyed before his face. This, though not the natural sense of the verse, is the only one it can have in this connexion. The natural answer to the question in v. 3 appears in v. 5, and this verse may be a later insertion. 6–9. For the interpretation of these verses see introductory note to this chapter. The writer gives a twofold significance to these metals: that given above and that developed in vv. 7, 8. 6. **As wax before the fire**: cf. i. 6; Ps. xcvii. 5; Micah i. 4. **Like water which streams down from above**: cf. Micah i. 4. **Before his feet**: cf. Micah i. 3. He will tread down the mountains. 7. The phraseology is derived from Zeph. i. 18: cf. Is. xiii. 17. The more precious metals will not redeem from danger and death. 8. The harder

garment for a coat of mail. Bronze will be of no service, and tin will be of no service and will not be esteemed, and lead will not be desired. 9. And all these things will be disowned and destroyed from the surface of the earth when the Elect One will appear before the face of the Lord of Spirits.'

LIII. 1. And there mine eyes saw a valley with open and deep mouths, and all who dwell on the earth and sea and islands will bring to him gifts and presents and tokens of homage, but that deep valley will not become full. 2. For they commit crimes with their hands, and sinners as they are they criminously devour all the acquisitions (of the righteous): accordingly as sinners they will perish before the face of the Lord of Spirits and will be removed from off the face of His earth, continually for ever and ever. 3. For I have seen the angels of punishment abiding (there) and preparing all the

---

will be no iron for war nor garment for a coat of mail. This seems a better rendering than 'Es wird kein Eisen geben für den Krieg noch das Kleid eines Panzers.'—Dln.

LIII. 1. **A valley with open and deep mouths.** So G: ቈላ፡ ርኅው፡ ወዕሙቅ፡ አፈዊሆሙ. Dln. gives 'a deep valley, the mouths of which were open.' 2. **Sinners as they are they criminously devour.** So F H L M N O and Dln. G reads ለኃጥአን፡ ይበልዑ. 3. **Abiding (there) and preparing.** So A E H M O: እንዘ፡ የኀድሩ፡

---

metals will not prove a defence but will disappear before him: cf. Hos. ii. 18; Is. ii. 4; ix. 5; Zech. ix. 10; Ps. xlvi. 9.

LIII. 1. The deep valley here is that of Jehoshaphat, where, according to Joel iii. 2, 12, God was to assemble and judge the Gentiles. The Talmud teaches the same view (Weber, *Die Lehren d. Talmud*, 376). All those who dwell upon earth will bring gifts and presents to the Messiah to win a favourable judgment: but these will be of no avail (cf. lii. 7). The idea of the nations and the rich men of the earth bringing gifts to the Messiah is a favourite one in the Talmud, Weber (368–9). Dln.'s interpretation of the mountains and this valley is unintelligible. **2. Removed from off the face of His earth**: see xxxviii. 1 (note). **3. Angels of punishment**: see xl. 7 (note). These angels apparently prepare the chains and fetters for the kings and the mighty in the valley of Jehoshaphat, where the kings are to be judged. The chains for the fallen angels are forged in Gehenna, liv. 3–5. The kings are then taken and cast into Gehenna,

instruments of Satan. 4. And I asked the angel of peace who went with me, 'These instruments, for whom are they preparing them?' 5. And he said unto me 'They are for the kings and the mighty of the earth, that they may thereby be destroyed. 6. And after this the Righteous and Elect One will cause the house of his congregation to appear: henceforth they will no more be hindered, in the name of the Lord of Spirits. 7. And these mountains will not stand fast as the earth before his righteousness, and the hills will be as a fountain of water, and the righteous will have rest from the oppression of sinners.'

LIV. 1. And I looked and turned to another part of the

ወያስተዳልዉ. So also G, but with verbs in sing. The reading of B C D and also F L N adopted by Dln. 'going and preparing' እንዘ፡ የሐውሩ seems to be an attempted emendation of the text. 5. **They are for the kings.** So G M. Other MSS. and Dln. read 'They are preparing them for the kings.' **The mighty of the earth.** So G. Other MSS. give 'The mighty of this earth.' 6. **Henceforth.** G omits; M supports. 7. **And these mountains will not stand.** So all MSS. but B C which omit the negative. Dln. follows B C. **Before His righteousness.** So G ጽድቅ. Dln. gives ገጹ 'Before His face.' M በከመ፡ ጽድቅ.

---

liv. 2. 6. **House of his congregation**: see xxxviii. 1 (note). The phrase here is in the singular: in liii. 6 it is in the plural. There is apparently no significance in the difference. The houses of his congregations are the synagogues: cf. Ps. lxxiv. 8. 7. **The mountains ... and hills**: see Crit. Note. There is a return here to the figurative language of lii. The mountains and the hills are symbols of the world powers as personated in the kings and the mighty. Before the Messiah's righteousness, the mountains (i.e. the kings) will not be like the earth which abideth for ever, Ps. lxxviii. 69; Eccles. i. 4: and the hills (i.e. the mighty) shall be as a fount of water: cf. lii. 6. The earth's great ones will become strengthless and vanish at the presence of the Messiah.

LIV. In liii the writer described the scene of the judgment and the fetters that were being prepared to bind the kings on their condemnation. Here he speaks of Gehenna into which the kings are cast; they are punished in the sight of the righteous: cf. lxii. 12. The fallen angels are cast into a furnace of fire. The idea of the fallen angels and the kings being judged together is to be traced to Is. xxiv. 21, 22. 1. **To another part of the earth.** The writer now turns from the valley of Jehoshaphat

earth and saw there a deep valley with burning fire. 2. And they brought the kings and the mighty and put them into this deep valley. 3. And then mine eyes saw how they made instruments for them, iron chains of immeasurable weight. 4. And I asked the angel of peace who was with me, saying: 'These chain instruments for whom are they prepared?' 5. And he said unto me: 'These are prepared for the hosts of Azâzêl so that they may take them and cast them into the abyss of complete condemnation, and cover their jaws with rough stones as the Lord of Spirits commanded. 6. Michael, Gabriel, Rufael and Fanuel will take hold of them on that great day and cast them on that day into a burning furnace, that the Lord of Spirits may take vengeance on them for their unrighteousness in becoming subject to Satan and leading astray those who dwell on the earth. [7. And in those days will punishment come from

---

LIV. 2. **Into this deep valley.** So G M ዝኩ. Dln. 'Into the deep valley.' 3. **How they made instruments for them, iron chains.** For ዘመበዐሳቲሆሙ G reads ዘመእዐለቲሆሙ. 5. **Cover their jaws.** So G ይክድኑ in subj. as preceding verb. Other MSS. and Dln. read ይከድኑ 'they will cover.' 6. **Will take hold of them on that great day and cast them on that day into a burning furnace.** For ዕቶን፡ እሳት፡ ዘይነድድ G M read ዕቶን፡ ዘይነድድ and omit 'cast them,' but wrongly, as their reading of ወውስተ instead of በውስተ (Dln.) implies a second verb. For a like possible confusion of በ and ወ see next verse (Crit.

---

on the north-east of Jerusalem to the valley of Hinnom lying to the south of it. **A deep valley**: see xlviii. 9 (note). **3–5.** The pre-Messianic judgment of the watchers in ver. 5 is that described at length in x–xvi. **The abyss of complete condemnation** is not Gehenna but only the preliminary place of punishment: cf. x. 5, 12. We are not told by whom the chains are forged for the fallen angels, nor yet who are the agents who execute the first judgment upon them. **6.** The final judgment on the watchers. **On that great day**: see xlv. 2 (note). Observe that in the Similitudes the guilt of the watchers originated in their becoming subjects of Satan: see xl. 7 (note); Book of Jubilees x. **Burning furnace**: cf. x. 6; xviii. 11; xxi. 7–10; xc. 24, 25. This is to be distinguished from Gehenna. **7–LV. 2.** This digression on the first world-judgment is

the Lord of Spirits, and all the chambers of waters which are above the heavens will be opened and of the fountains which

---

Note). **On them.** G omits. 7. **All the chambers . . . will be opened.** So Dln. and all MSS. but G, which gives ታርኅ: ኵሉ: መዛግብት. **And of the fountains.** For the impossible ወዲበ I read ወእስ. Cf. next clause according to G M ወእስ: እንቅዕት: መትሕት: ምድር. Otherwise for ወዲበ read በዲበ 'in addition to.'

---

a Noachic fragment. A Book of Noah is mentioned in the Book of Jubilees x; xxi. These fragments, xxxix. 1, 2[a]; liv. 7–lv. 2; lx; lxv–lxix. 25, deal mainly with the Deluge. They are to be regarded as interpolations on the following grounds out of many: (1) They always disturb the context in which they occur. (2) They profess to be a revelation of Noah, lx. 7–11, 24, 25; lxv–lxviii. 1. (3) They belong to a much later development of Jewish gnosis or kabbala: cf. liv. 8; lx. 7 sqq.; lxv. 7, 8; lxvii. 6. (4) Such a definite date as is given in lx. 1 is unknown in the Similitudes. (5) The second judgment of the angels is declared an absolute secret in lxviii. 2–5 in contradiction with liv. 4–6; lv. 3, 4. (6) The demonology is different: the Satans and the fallen angels who are carefully distinguished in the Similitudes are confused in the additions, lxix. The chief, moreover, of the fallen angels in the Similitudes is Azazel: in the additions, Semjaza. (7) The interpolator seeks to adapt his additions to their new contexts, and accordingly incorporates in them many terms and phrases from the Similitudes, such as 'Angel of peace,' lx. 24, see xl. 2 (note); 'no lying word can be spoken before Him,' xlix. 4 (note); 'denied the Lord of Spirits,' lxvii. 8, 10, see xxxviii. 2 (note); 'the angel who went with me and showed me what was hidden,' xlvi. 2; lx. 11 (note); *but observe that in such borrowings he misuses technical terms and phrases*, either through ignorance or of set purpose. Cf. 'Lord of Spirits,' see xxxvii. 2 (note); 'Head of Days,' lv. 1, see xlvi. 1 (note); 'Angels of punishment,' xl. 7; lxvi. 1 (note); 'Son of Man,' lx. 10 (note); 'those who dwell on the earth,' liv. 9; xxxvii. 5 (note). (8) The interpolator misunderstands the Similitudes, and combines absolutely alien elements: cf. 'the burning valley in the metal mountains in the west'—an illegitimate combination of lii. 1, 2 and liv. 1. (9) Finally, the Similitudes follow the LXX. chronology: the Interpolations follow the Samaritan. Thus in lxi. 12 Enoch speaks of the elect as being already in Paradise, and in lxx. 4 on his translation he finds his forefathers already there. This could be the case only according to the LXX. reckoning; for according to the Samaritan all his forefathers survived him, and, according to the Hebrew, all except Adam. The Interpolations follow the Samaritan reckoning: see lxv. 2 (note). The object of the interpolator is clear. Although the final world-judgment is treated at length, there are only the briefest references to the first. It was to supply this defect in the Similitudes that an existing Apocalypse of Noah was laid under contribution.

are below the heavens and beneath the earth. 8. And all the waters will be joined with the waters: that which is above the heavens is the masculine and the water which is beneath the earth is the feminine. 9. And all who dwell on the earth will be destroyed and those who dwell under the ends of the heaven. 10. And they will thereby recognise their unrighteousness which they have committed on the earth, and owing to this will they be destroyed.'

LV. 1. And after that the Head of Days repented and said: 'In vain have I destroyed all who dwell on the earth.' 2. And He swore by His great name: 'Henceforth I will not do so (again) to all who dwell on the earth, and I will set a sign in the heavens: this will be a pledge of good faith between Me and them for ever, so long as heaven is above the earth.] 3. And this will be according to My command: when I desire to take hold of them by the hand of the angels on the day of tribulation and pain, before this

---

Dln. emends by reading ዴበዝ. 8. **All the waters will be joined with the waters: that which is above the heavens is the masculine.** So G M, but omitting with B the ዘ which they read before ምስለ. Other MSS. and Dln. give: 'And all the waters will be joined with the waters which are above in the heavens: the water indeed which is above in the heaven is masculine.' 9. G omits **who dwell on the earth, and.** 10. **Owing to this will they be destroyed.** So M በይእቲ and G ይእቲ. Dln.'s MSS. and K L N O ወበእንተዝ—clearly an emendation.

LV. 1. For በከ G reads በከመ. 2. **Will not do so.** G M omits 'so.' 3. **And this will be.** So G M reading ወዝ instead of ወእምዝ = 'after this it will be.' For የኀይር G reads

---

8. **The distinguishing of the waters into masculine and feminine is quite in keeping with the other kabbalistic ideas of these Interpolations:** cf. lx. 7, 8, 16. 9. **All who dwell on the earth:** see xxxvii. 5 (note).

LV. 1. The Head of Days: see xlvi. 1 (note). We have here a good illustration of the method by which the interpolator seeks to assimilate his additions by incorporating technical terms from the main text. **Repented:** cf. Gen. viii. 21. 3. **Here the original text of liv. 6 is resumed. Day of tribulation and pain:** see xlv. 2 (note). **Before this Mine**

I will cause Mine anger and My punishment, Mine anger and My punishment to abide upon them, saith God, the Lord of Spirits. 4. Ye mighty kings who will dwell on the earth, ye shall have to behold Mine Elect, how he sits on the throne of glory and judges Azâzêl, and all his associates, and all his hosts in the name of the Lord of Spirits.'

LVI. 1. And I saw there the hosts of the angel of punishment going with scourges and chains of iron and bronze. 2. And I asked the angel of peace who went with me, and said: 'To whom are these angels with the scourges going?' 3. And he said unto me: 'Each one to his elect and beloved ones that they may be cast into the chasm of the abyss of the valley. 4. And then that valley will be filled with their elect and beloved, and the days of their lives will be at an end, and the days of their being led astray will from that time on no longer be reckoned. [5. And in those

---

ሰንደር (sic), and this I have followed above. 4. **Mighty kings.** See xxxviii. 5 (note). **Throne of glory.** So G M: other MSS. and Dln. 'Throne of My glory.' **All his hosts.** G omits 'his hosts.'

LVI. 1. **With scourges and chains of iron and bronze.** So G ወይእኅዙ፡ መቅሠፍት፡ ወ . . (sic). Other MSS. omit 'scourges and.' 2. **With the scourges.** So G reading መቅሠፍት after እሉ፡ ይእኅዙ. Other MSS. omit 'scourges.' 5.

---

anger, i. e. 'before this manifestation of Mine anger': cf. a similar expression in l. 4. 4. The kings have to witness the judgment passed on the angels: if Azazel and his hosts are judged and condemned by the Messiah, how much more likely will they! The text should almost certainly be 'Ye kings and mighty': see xxxviii. 5 (note); lxii. 6 (Crit. Note).

LVI. 1-4. There is here finally the judgment of the remaining theocratic sinners and their condemnation to Gehenna. It is possible, however, to interpret these verses of the watchers and their children the demons. The term 'beloved' is specially used of the demons in regard to their parents in i-xxxvi: see x. 12; xiv. 6. Moreover, it would be possible to translate, 'the days of their leading astray.' 4. No longer be reckoned, i. e. be at an end. 5-LVII. 3ª. We have here another addition to the text. It depicts the last struggle of the heathen powers against the Messianic kingdom established in Jerusalem. Such a conception is quite in place in lxxxiii-xc, xci-civ, but is irreconcileable with the ruling ideas in xxxvii-lxx. A Messiah who was only a man with his seat at Jerusalem

days will the angels return and hurl themselves upon the East, upon the Parthians and Medes, to stir up the kings and provoke in them a spirit of unrest, and rouse them from their thrones, that they may break forth from their resting-places as lions and as hungry wolves among their flocks. 6. And they will march up to and tread under foot the land of His elect ones, and the land of His elect ones will be before them a threshing-floor and a path. 7. But the

---

Will return. So G ይገብኡ, for ይትጋብኡ of Dln. 'Will gather together.' M supports Dln., but is written over an erasion. **Hurl themselves.** This translation of አርአስቲሆሙ, cf. cviii. 10, seems better than Dln.'s 'Ihre Häupter . . . richten.' For ይወድዩ G reads ይወድቁ. 6. **His elect ones.** So G ዚአሁ. Other

---

might well be conceived of as assailed by the Gentile powers. But this is impossible in the case of a superhuman Messiah, who, possessing universal dominion and attended by legions of angels, holds universal assize, and, supported by the actual presence of the Almighty, destroys all his enemies with the breath of his mouth. Besides, (1) this section forms a harsh break in the context. (2) The Similitudes deal only in general terms: no names are mentioned as here, nor is any definite information given as a means of determining their date or the persons against whom they are directed. (3) And finally the seat of the kingdom on the Advent of the Messiah will not be Jerusalem merely as is here implied, but a transformed heaven and earth. This section though interpolated is important as furnishing a lower limit for the date of the Similitudes. The description is prophetical, and is merely a reproduction of the coming strife of Gog and Magog against Israel. The latter names are replaced by those of the Medes and Parthians, who are the only great world powers from whom the interpolator believes great danger may be apprehended. Syria had ceased to be formidable from 100 B.C. onward, and Rome was practically unknown till 64 B.C. The date therefore of this section must be earlier than 64 B.C. Further, we found (pp. 107–8) on independent grounds that the Similitudes should be referred either to 94-79 or 70–64. If, then, this addition was written and added before 64 B.C., the Similitudes should probably be referred to 94–79 B.C. We ought to have remarked above that lvi. 5–lvii. 3[a] exhibits no sign of having been an independent writing before its appearance in its present context. **5.** In Ezek. xxxviii. 4–7 it is said that God will stir up the Gentiles; but here in keeping with the views of a later time this business is assigned to the angels: cf. Dan. x. 13, 20, 21; xii. 1. **The Parthians and Medes.** These are the chief nations in the league against Israel. **6. The land of His elect ones**, i.e. Palestine. **Threshing-floor**: cf. Is. xxi. 10. 7. But the attack on Jerusalem will fail,

city of My righteous will be a hindrance to their horses, and they will begin to fight amongst themselves, and their right hand will be strong against themselves, and a man will not know his brother, nor a son his father or his mother, till the number of corpses through their slaughter is beyond count, and their punishment be no idle one. 8. And in those days Sheol will open its jaws, and they will be swallowed up therein, and their destruction will be at an end; Sheol will devour the sinners in the presence of the elect.'

LVII. 1. And it came to pass after this that I saw again a host of waggons, whereon men were riding, and they came on the wings of the wind from the East, and from the West to the South. 2. And the noise of their waggons was

---

MSS. and Dln. 'their elect ones.' 7. **A man will not know his brother.** So G M omitting the በካልኡ፡ ወ of Dln. Other MSS. and Dln. give: 'A man will not know his neighbour or his brother.' **Through their slaughter.** G omits: M እምሙ, a corruption. **Is beyond count.** Following Dln.'s suggestion I have emended ይከውን into ኢይከውን. **Their punishment be no idle one.** So G M reading ኢትከውን፡ በከ፡. Dln. gives ወኢይከውን፡ በከ which he translates: 'Das Strafgericht über sie—es wird nicht vergeblich sein.' 8. **They will be swallowed up.** G reads ይሠጠም. **Their destruction will be at an end.** So G ሕጕሎሙ፡ ተኀልቀ. M reads ሕጕሎሙ፡ ተሠጥሙ፡ በሲኦል. Other MSS. and Dln. give: 'Their destruction ... Sheol will devour the sinners, &c.' 'Their destruction' in the text means 'the destruction wrought by them.'

LVII. 1. **Whereon men were riding, and they came on the wings of the wind.** So Dln. and F H N O. For ጸዐኖሙ፡ ወይመጽኡ፡ ዲበ፡ ነፍስ G reads ውስቴታ፡ ወይመጽኡ፡ ዲበ፡ ነፍሳት. So

---

Zech. xii. 2, 3; and civil strife will break out amongst the invading nations, Ezek. xxxviii. 21; Zech. xiv. 13; Hag. ii. 22, and they will involve each other in common destruction: cf. xc. 4; c. 1–3, to which section these ideas rightly belong. 8. On this and the preceding verses, see Crit. Notes. **Sheol will open its jaws**: cf. Num. xvi. 31–3; Is. v. 14. See lxiii. 10 (note).

LVII. On the destruction of the Gentile invaders, the dispersed of Israel return to Jerusalem from the East and from the West: cf. Is. xxvii. 13; xliii. 5, 6; xlix. 12, 22, 23. 1. **Came on the wings of the wind.** A figure expressing the swiftness of

heard, and when this turmoil took place the holy ones from the heaven remarked it, and the pillars of the earth were moved from their place, and (the sound thereof) was heard from the one extremity of heaven to the other in one day. 3. And they will all fall down and worship the Lord of Spirits.] And this is the end of the second similitude.

LVIII. 1. And I began to speak the third similitude concerning the righteous and the elect. 2. Blessed are ye, ye righteous and elect, for glorious will be your lot. 3. And the righteous will be in the light of the sun, and the elect in the light of eternal life: there will be no end to the days of their life, and the days of the holy will be without number. 4. And they will seek the light and find righteousness with the Lord of Spirits: there will be peace to the righteous in the name of the Lord of the world. 5. And after that it

---

M but with the correction of ነኵሰተ into ነኰሰተ. 2. **From the one extremity of heaven to the other.** So G M እምእጽናፈ፡ ሰማይ፡ እስከ፡ አጽናፉ. Other MSS. 'from the extremity of earth to the extremity of heaven.'

LVIII. 1. G omits this verse, but leaves space for it. 4. **In the name of the Lord of the world.** So G በስሙ. Other MSS. and Dln. give በኀበ 'with the Lord of the world.'

---

their return. **2. The pillars of the earth were moved**: cf. Hag. ii. 6, 7; Joel iii. 16.

LVIII. Here begins the third similitude. It is probable that a large part of it has been lost, being displaced to make room for the Noachic fragments. As it stands, it embraces lviii; lxi–lxiv; lxix. 26–29. The introductory words, 'Concerning the righteous and the elect,' in this similitude, as in the other two, are but a very indifferent index to its contents. The similitude as it has reached us, might reasonably be described as 'Concerning the final judgment held by the Son of Man over all created beings, but especially over the great ones of the earth and the final blessedness of the righteous and elect.' **2. Glorious will be your lot.** This lot is preserved for them by the Messiah, xlviii. 7. **3. Light of the sun**: see xxxviii. 4 (note). **Eternal life**: see xxxvii. 4 (note): cf. Dan. xii. 2; Pss. of Sol. iii. 16. **4.** They will through a natural affinity seek after light and righteousness: cf. xxxviii. 4 (note). **Lord of the world.** This title is found again in lxxxi. 10. For similar expressions cf. i. 3; xii. 3; lxxxi. 3; lxxxii. 7; lxxxiv. 2. **5.** They will be bidden to seek and make their own the

will be said to the holy that they should seek in heaven the secrets of righteousness, the heritage of faith; for it has become bright as the sun upon earth, and the darkness is past. 6. And there will be unceasing light and on a reckoning of the days they will not enter; for the former darkness will be destroyed, and the light will be established before the Lord of Spirits, and the light of uprightness will be established for ever before the Lord of Spirits.

[LIX. 1. And in those days mine eyes saw the secrets of the lightnings, and of the luminaries, and the judgments they execute (lit. 'their judgment'); and they lighten for a blessing or a curse as the Lord of Spirits willeth. 2. And then I saw the secrets of the thunder, and how when it resounds above in the heaven, the peal thereof is heard; and they caused me to see the dwelling-places of the earth, and the pealing of the thunder how it ministers unto well-being and blessing, or serves for a curse before the Lord of Spirits. 3. And after that all the secrets of the luminaries and lightnings were shown to me, how they lighten to give blessing and satisfy (the thirsty soil).]

[LX. 1. In the year five hundred, in the seventh month, on

LIX. 1. **Of the luminaries.** So G ብርሃናት and rightly: cf. ver. 3. Dln. gives this word in the acc. and translates: 'die Lichtmassen.' 2. **Before.** So G በቅድሜሁ. Other MSS. 'According to the word of.'

---

hidden recompense of righteousness (cf. xxxviii. 3), the glorious heritage which has been ordained for them in heaven and preserved for them by the Messiah, xlviii. 7. This will not be achieved once and for all; but this will be a progress from light to light and from righteousness to righteousness. **Heritage of faith**: cf. xxxix. 6; lxi. 4, 11. **Bright as the sun, &c.**: cf. 1 John i. 9.

LIX. This chapter is an intrusion, and belongs to the same class as xli. 3-8; xliii; xliv. It is probably drawn from a Noah-Apocalypse. **1.** The statements of the writer rest on Job xxxvi. 31; xxxvii. 5, 13; xxxviii. 24-27. He wishes to bring out the ethical ends of the thunder and the lightning. **For a blessing or a curse**: cf. Job xxxvi. 31; xxxvii. 13. **2.** Cf. lx. 13-15. '**Lord of spirits**' incorporated from the adjoining context. **3.** Job xxxviii. 24-27.

LX. This chapter is one of the Noachic fragments. For the grounds on which these are regarded as interpolations, see liv. 7 (note): also the following notes on lx. 1, 2, 6, 10, 11, &c. **1. The year five hundred.**

the fourteenth day of the month in the life of Enoch. In that similitude I saw how the heaven of heavens quaked with a mighty earthquake, and the host of the Most High, and the angels, a thousand thousands and ten thousand times ten thousand, were thrown into an exceeding great disquiet. 2. And the Head of Days sat on the throne of His glory and the angels and the righteous stood around Him. 3. And a great trembling seized me, and fear took hold of me: my loins became relaxed and my whole being melted away, and I fell upon my face. 4. Then Michael sent another angel from among the holy ones and he raised me up (and)

LX. 2. **The Head of Days sat, &c.** So G M. Other MSS. insert **ሶቤሃ፡ ርኢኩ** 'then I saw the Head of Days sit.' 3. **My loins became relaxed.** So G M. Dln. reads 'my loins bent and were relaxed.' For **ተመስወ** 'melted away' G reads **ወድቀ**: M omits. 4. **Then Michael sent another angel from among the holy ones.** So G M omitting **ቅዱስ** and reading **እምቅዱሳን** instead of **ቅዱሰ፩ እምነ፡ መላእክት፡ ቅዱሳን** in Dln.'s text: 'then the holy Michael sent another holy angel, one of the holy angels.' **And he raised me up.** After these words all MSS. but G M

This date is drawn from Gen. v. 32, and is a date in the life of Noah and not of Enoch as it stands in our text. For Enoch we should read Noah. **In the seventh month, on the fourteenth day of the month.** This according to Levitical law was the eve of the Feast of Tabernacles. **In that similitude.** This phrase marks a clumsy attempt to connect this chapter with the main context, but betrays the hand of the interpolator. A similitude in Enoch's sense is an account of a vision; but the text requires here the word 'vision'; for the writer says, 'I saw the heaven quaking.' **The heaven quaked.** This was a token of the manifestation of divine judgment: cf. i. 6, 7. **Host of the Most High . . . a thousand thousands**: cf. i. 9; xl. 1; lxxi. 8, 13. 2. **Head of Days**: see xlvi. 1 (note); liv. 7 (note). **The angels and the righteous.** According to this we are to regard God as accompanied by angels and *saints*. The righteous here can have no other meaning. Such a conception of the final Messianic judgment is difficult though possible; but in the case of the first judgment (i. e. the Flood) it is not possible except through misconception. Here again the hand of an ignorant interpolator is disclosed. 3. Cf. xiv. 14, 24. **Loins became relaxed.** Ps. lxix. 23; Is. xlv. 1. 4. Cf. Dan. viii. 17; x. 9, 10. **Michael sent another angel.** Michael is the chief archangel: cf. xl. 4, 9. The other angel is appointed to a like duty with the angel of peace in the Similitudes,

my spirit returned; for I had not been able to endure the look of this host, and the commotion and the quaking of the heaven. 5. And Michael said unto me: 'What vision has so disquieted thee? Until this day lasted the day of His mercy; for He was merciful and long-suffering towards those who dwell on the earth. 6. But when the day, and the power, and the punishment, and the judgment have come which the Lord of Spirits has prepared for those who serve not the righteous law and for those who deny the

---

insert 'and when he had raised me up.' 5. **And Michael.** So G M. Other MSS. and Dln. insert ቅዱስ 'the holy Michael.' For similar insertions of this epithet cf. xl. 9 (twice) and lx. 4 (twice). For በእንተ፡ ምንት፡ ራእይ፡ ዘከመዝ፡ ተሀውከ **What vision has so disquieted thee?** G reads ምንት፡ ራእየ፡ ዘከመዝ፡ ተሀውከ. 6. **Who serve not the righteous law.** I have here supposed a loss of the negative before ይሰግዱ. Such an omission is of constant occurrence: cf. in MS. G alone v. 2; lxvii. 8; lxxxix. 3; xcv. 4; c. 11, &c.; Book of Jubilees Dln.'s text chs. xii (twice); xv; xvi. This conjecture is further confirmed by IV Ezra vi. 2: 'Behold and see him, (1) whom ye have denied; (2) whom ye have not served (so Ethiopic version); (3) whose commands ye have despised.' Here clause (2) corresponds to clause (1) in Enoch; clause (1) to clause (2) in Enoch; and clause (3) vaguely to clause (3) in Enoch. See General Introduction (p. 37), where we have shown several points of connexion between Third Vision of IV Ezra and Enoch. Dln.'s text gives 'Those who bow to the righteous judgment'; but to class these with the sceptics and perjurers as alike threatened by the coming judgment is impossible. Hallévi (*Journal Asiat.* 367–9; 1867) first pointed out this difficulty and sought the explanation in the translator's reading לְעוֹבְדֵי מִשְׁפַּט צֶדֶק instead of לְעֹבְרֵי מ״ צ״. Thus we should have 'who have transgressed the righteous law.' In this verse I have followed Hallévi in translating ኵነኔ first as 'law' and then

---

xl. 2, and is actually so named in lx. 24. **5. Merciful and long-suffering:** cf. ver. 25; l. 3, 5; lxi. 13. Cf. 1 Pet. iii. 20; IV Ezra [vi. 47;] vii. 33. **6.** See Crit. Note: cf. IV Ezra [vi. 2]. The Deluge or first world-judgment is here described with features belonging properly to the Messianic judgment of the Similitudes. **The Lord of Spirits:** see xxxviii. 2 (note).

righteous judgment and for those who take His name in vain—that day is prepared, for the elect a covenant, but for sinners an inquisition. 7. And on that day will two monsters be parted, a female monster named Leviathan, to dwell in the depths of the ocean over the fountains of the waters. 8. But the male is called Behemoth, who occupies with his breast a waste wilderness named Dêndâin, on the east of the garden where the elect and righteous dwell, where my grandfather was taken up, the seventh from Adam, the first man whom the Lord of Spirits created.') 9. And I besought that other angel that he should show me the might of those monsters, how they were parted on one day, and the one was placed in the depth of the sea and the other in the mainland of the wilderness. 10. And he spake to

---

as 'judgment,' as מִשְׁפָּט has both meanings. For ይነሥኡ G M read ይነሥእ. 8. For ዴንዳይን G reads ዱዱዳይን.

---

7. This strange fancy about Behemoth and Leviathan which are first mentioned in Job xl, xli, is found by Jewish expounders also in Gen. i. 21; Ps. l. 10; Is. xxvii. 1 (Dln.). For later allusions see IV Ezra vi. 49-52; Apoc. Bar. xxix. 4. Here they are represented as huge monsters created on the fifth day of Creation to be the food of the righteous in Messianic times. This doctrine does not appear in Enoch. For further information see Drummond, *Jewish Messiah*, 352–55; Weber, *Lehren d. Talmud*, 156, 195, 370, 384. The Talmudic view agrees with that of IV Ezra and Apoc. Bar. so far as to make Behemoth food for the righteous. **Fountains of the waters**: cf. Gen. vii. 11; Job xxxviii. 16; En. lxxxix. 7. 8. Dendain from דַּיָּן דִּין, an unknown locality. **On the east of the garden**, i. e. the garden of Eden. The locality of Eden varies in the different sections: in xxxii. 2, 3 it lies in the East: in lxx. 2–4 between the West and North: in lxxvii. 3 in the North. The account as to those who dwell in it varies also. It is apparently empty in Enoch's time in xxxii. 3–6, and the righteous dead are in the West, xxii: it is the abode of the righteous and the elect in Enoch's and Noah's times in lxi. 12; lx. 8, 23: the abode of the earliest fathers in Enoch's time, lxx. 2–4: the abode of Enoch and Elijah in Elijah's time, lxxxix. 52: see lxv. 2 (note). This passage and the LXX. are the oldest testimonies for the translation of Enoch unto Paradise: later this idea made its way into the Latin version of Ecclus. xliv. 16 and the Ethiopic version of Gen. v. 24: eight others shared this honour with Enoch according to the Talmud, Weber, 242. **Seventh from Adam**: cf. xciii. 3; Jude 14; Book of Jubilees vii. 9. **That other**

me: 'Thou son of man, thou dost seek here to know what is hidden.' 11. Then spake unto me the other angel who went with me and showed me what was hidden, what is first and last, in the heaven in the height, and beneath the earth in the depth, and at the ends of the heaven, and on the foundation of the heaven, and in the chambers of the winds: 12. And how the spirits are parted, and how the weighing is done, and how the fountains of the spirits are reckoned each according to the power of the spirit, and the power of the lights of the moon, and how it is a power of righteousness; and how the divisions of the stars according to their

---

11. **Spake unto me.** G reads ይቤሎ 'spake unto him.' **Beneath the earth.** So G M በታሕተ፡ የብስ. Other MSS. and Dln. 'on earth.' **Chambers of the winds.** G gives መዛግብት፡ መንፈሳት. 12. **How the fountains of the spirits are reckoned each according to the power.** So G M ይትኌለቍ፡ አንቅዕት፡ መንፈሳት፡ በበኀይሉ፡ Dln.'s text runs: 'How the fountains and the winds are reckoned according to the power.' I have taken ይትኌለቍ above

---

angel: see vv. 4, 11. **10. Thou son of man.** This use of the phrase after the manner of Ezekiel is found again in lxxi. 14. In both instances it is borrowed like other technical phrases (cf. xxxvii. 2 note; lv. 1, &c.) from the Similitudes and misused as they are. As the main conception of the Son of Man is unmistakeable in the Similitudes, xlvi. 1–3 (notes), this misuse of the phrase is due either to ignorance or to a deliberate perversion of its meaning. The presence of this phrase in the Interpolations is in itself an answer to Drummond's theory that all references to the Son of Man are Christian interpolations. See Gen. Introduction, pp. 15, 16. **11.** We should expect the answer to the question in ver. 9 to follow here, but it is not given till ver. 24, and a long account (11–23) dealing with physical secrets intervenes. Such clumsiness should not cause any surprise in interpolations like the present. **The angel who went with me and showed me, &c.** Borrowed from xlvi. 2; cf. xliii. 3. **Chambers of the winds**: cf. xviii. 1; xli. 4. **12.** Spirits or angels are appointed to control the various phenomena of nature. This is peculiar to these interpolations, as in other parts of the book the powers of nature are either personified or are regarded as conscious intelligences: cf. xviii. 14–16. The view taken by the interpolator is followed by the Book of Jubilees ii, where we find 'angels of the spirit of fire,' 'angels of hail,' 'angels of hoar-frost,' 'angels of thunder,' &c., Rev. vii. 1, 2; xiv. 18 (angel of fire); xix. 17 (angel of the sun); Asc. Is. iv. 18. **How the weighing is done**: cf. xli. 1; xliii. 2; Job xxviii. 25. **Lights of the moon.** Its various

names, and all the divisions are divided. 13. And the thunders according to the places where they fall, and all the divisions which are made among the lightnings that it may lighten, and that their hosts may at once obey. 14. For the thunder has places of rest: there it must wait till it may peal; and the thunder and lightning are inseparable, and, although not one and undivided, they both go together through the spirit and separate not. 15. For when the lightning lightens, the thunder utters its voice, and the spirit enforces a pause during the peal, and divides equally between them; for the treasury of their peals is inexhaustible (lit. 'like the sand'), and each one of them as it peals is held in with a bridle, and turned back by the power of the spirit, and pushed forward according to the number of the quarters of the earth. 16. And the spirit of the sea is masculine and strong, and according to the might of his strength he draws it back with a rein, and in like manner it is driven forward and dispersed amid all the mountains of the earth. 17. And the spirit of the hoar-frost is his own

---

as used impersonally. **All the divisions are divided.** G reads ዙሉ፡ ክፍል፡ ተክፍለ. 14. Dln.'s interpretation of the text is here followed, but it does not seem satisfactory. Hallévi's discussion of this passage (*Journ. Asiat.* 369–72; 1867) is worth consulting. He arrives at the following translation: 'For the thunder has fixed laws in reference to the duration of its peal which is assigned to it: the thunder and the lightning are not separated in a single instance: they both proceed with one accord and separate not. For when the lightning lightens, the thunder utters its voice, and the spirit during its peal makes its arrangements, and divides the time equally between them.' 15. **Each one of them as it peals.** G M omit 'as it peals.' **According to the number of the quarters.** For ብዝኅ G reads ብዝኆ.

---

phases. 13. Cf. Job xxxvii. 1–5. 14. See Crit. Note. 16. The ebb and flow of the sea explained. Dispersed amid all the mountains. With the flow of the sea is connected its subterranean advance into the mountains to nourish the springs. So Dln. 17. Is his own angel,

angel, and the spirit of the hail is a good angel. 18. And the spirit of the snow he has let go, on account of his strength—it has a special spirit, and that which ascends from it is like smoke, and its name is frost. 19. And the spirit of the mist is not united with them in their chambers, but it has a special chamber; for its course is in clearness and in light, and in darkness, and in winter, and in summer, and its chamber is light, and it (i.e. the spirit) is its own angel. 20. And the spirit of the dew has its dwelling at the ends of the heaven and is connected with the chambers of the rain, and its course is in winter and summer; and its clouds and the clouds of the mist are connected, and the one passes over into the other (lit. 'gives to the other'). 21. And when the spirit of the rain goes forth from its chamber, the angels come and open the chamber and lead it out, and (likewise) when it is diffused over the whole earth, and as often as it unites with the water on the earth. 22. For the waters are for those who dwell on the earth; for they are nourishment for the earth from the Most High who is in heaven: therefore there is a measure for the rain and the angels take it in charge. 23. And all these things I saw towards the garden of the righteous. 24. And the angel of peace who was with me spake to me: 'These two monsters are pre-

---

19. **Its chamber is light and it is its own angel.** For ብርሃን፡ ወመልአኩ G M read መልአኩ፡ 'its chamber is an angel.' 21. **And as often as it unites.** Before these words G M make the following addition to Dln.'s text, ይትኃበር፡ ምስለ፡ ማይ፡ ዘዲበ፡ የብስ 'it unites

---

i.e. the hoarfrost has a special angel of its own. **Is a good angel.** Though hail is often hurtful, it is not in charge of a demon but of a good angel. **19. The mist** is to be distinguished from the foregoing phenomena; for it appears in all seasons and by night and day. **20. The dew has its dwelling at the ends of** the heaven: this would agree with xxxiv–xxxvi and lxxv. 5. **21.** As the rain is of such importance alike for the ethical and material well-being of man, Job xxxvii. 12, 13, its spirit is not independent but subordinated to the angels: cf. Job xxviii. 26; xxxviii. 25–28. **23. The garden of the righteous**: see ver. 8 (note).

pared to be fed conformably to the greatness of God, that the punishment of the Lord of Spirits may cause lamentation, and slay the sons with their mothers, and the children with their fathers. 25. When the punishment of the Lord of Spirits shall rest upon them, it will rest in order that the punishment of the Lord of Spirits may not come in vain upon them: afterwards the judgment will take place according to His mercy and His patience.']

LXI. 1. And I saw in those days how long cords were given to those angels, and they took to themselves wings and flew, and they went towards the North. 2. And I asked the angel, saying: 'Why have these angels taken the cords and gone off?' And he said unto me: 'They have gone to

---

with the water on the earth.' 24. **That the punishment of the Lord of Spirits.** So G M. Other MSS. give 'that the punishment of the Lord.' **May cause lamentation and slay the sons.** This rendering rests on an emendation of G's text **ከመ፡ መቅሠፍት፡ ለእግዚእ፡ መንፈሳት፡** (sic) **በኪ፡ ወትቀትል፡ ደቂቀ** into **ከመ፡ መቅሠፍት፡ ለእግዚእ፡ መንፈሳት፡ ታበኪ፡ ወትቀትል፡ ደቂቀ**. Dln. follows B C in inserting **ኢይኩን**, which is wanting in all other MSS. E hazards **ኢይግምጽእ**, borrowing from ver. 25. Dln. gives 'that the punishment of the Lord may not be in vain and the sons will be slain,' &c.

LXI. 1. **Took to themselves wings.** G reads **ክናፍ** instead of **ክንፈ**. 2. **Cords.** So G M. Other MSS. and Dln. give 'long

---

24. See Crit. Note: cf. ver. 7 (note). **25. When the punishment . . . shall rest upon them:** cf. lxii. 12. **Afterwards the judgment will take place according to His mercy.** Gen. viii. 21, 22; En. lx. 5 (note). God's mercy will be manifested after the first judgment, but not till then.

LXI. 1. Here the true text of the Similitudes is resumed, but the opening verses are very difficult. **Those angels.** The angels here referred to may have been definitely named in some preceding part now lost. Dln. takes it as merely a general reference to the angels that have hitherto appeared in the Similitudes. **Wings.** In the O.T. the angels are not represented as winged, unless in its latest books: cf. 1 Chron. xxi. 16. **Towards the North,** i. e. the North-West: cf. lxx. 3. **Paradise is the destination of the angels:** cf. lx. 8 (note). **2.** The cords which the angels take with them are for measuring Paradise. See the reference to this in

measure.' 3. And the angel who went with me said unto me: 'These are bringing to the righteous the measures of the righteous, and the ropes of the righteous, that they may stay themselves on the name of the Lord of Spirits for ever and ever. 4. The elect will begin to dwell with the elect, and those measures will be given to faith and will strengthen righteousness. 5. And these measures will reveal everything that is hidden in the depths of the earth, and those who have been destroyed by the desert, and those who have been devoured by the fish of the sea and by the beasts, that they may return, and stay themselves on the day of the Elect One; for no one will be destroyed before the Lord of Spirits, and none can be destroyed. 6. And all the powers who dwell above in the heaven received

---

cords.' 3. **To the righteous.** So G N ለጻድቃን. Other MSS. omit. 4. **Will strengthen righteousness.** So G M ያፀንዕዋ፡ ለጽድቅ. Other MSS. 'will strengthen the word of righteousness.' 5. **Those who have been devoured by the fish of the sea and by the beasts.** G M read እለ፡ ተበልዑ፡ እመዘገብት፡ ወእለ፡ ተበልዑ፡ እምዓሣ፡ ባሕር. 6. So M ወነሥኡ፡ ትእዛዘ፡ እለ፡ በመልዕልት፡ በሰማይ፡ ዘሎሙ፡ ኃይል፡ ወቃለ፡ ፩፡ ወብርሃነ፡ ፩፡ ከመ፡ እሳት. Also G, but that it inserts ወ before ኃይል and omits ፩ before ከመ፡ Dln. with B C against A D E G M inserts ተውህበ፡ ሎሙ after እሳት; and so we have 'and all who dwell

---

lxx. 3. **3–5. The measures of the righteous,** are according to Dln. the measures wherewith the inheritance of the righteous is measured. But even though these might be a staff whereon the righteous might stay themselves, how could it be said of such 'measures' that they will reveal everything that is hidden, and all that have perished? I cannot give a satisfactory explanation. In some way, however, these 'measures of the righteous' are an ideal representation of the community of the righteous, living and departed, and reveal especially the latter; for it matters not by what death these perished; they are alive unto the Lord of Spirits, and will return and stay themselves on the day of his Elect One: these measures are given to faith and strengthen the righteous. **4. Sinners will be driven from off the face of the earth:** cf. xxxviii. 1 (note). **5.** Only the resurrection of the righteous is here spoken of. In li. 1, 2 there is an account of the resurrection of all Israel: see note. After the resurrection follows the judgment. **6. All who dwell above in the heaven,** i.e. the angels: cf. vv. 10, 12; xlvii. 2. In ix. 3 they are called 'the holy ones of the heaven.' The angels were commanded to sing praises, and

a command, and one voice, and one light like unto fire. 7. And that One above all they blessed, and extolled and lauded with wisdom, and showed themselves wise in utterance and in the spirit of life. 8. And the Lord of Spirits placed the Elect One on the throne of glory, and he will judge all the works of the holy in the heaven, and weigh their deeds in the balance. 9. And when he shall lift his countenance to judge their secret ways according to the word of the name of the Lord of Spirits, and their path according to the way of the righteous judgment of the Lord of Spirits, then will they all with one voice speak and bless, and glorify and extol and laud the name of the Lord of Spirits. 10. And He will call on all the host of the heavens and all the holy ones above,

---

above in the heaven received a command, and one power and one voice and one light like unto fire were given unto them.' 'Power,' 'voice,' and 'light' are in the nom. in Dln.'s text. 8. **On the throne of glory.** So G M. Dln. gives 'on the throne of His glory.' 9. **The Lord of Spirits.** So G M. Other MSS. and Dln. read 'Most High God.' 10, 11. **And He will call on all the host of the heavens . . . and they will raise one voice.** Dln. translates 'and all the host of heaven will cry out,' &c. To arrive at this translation he is obliged to alter ኵሎ in his text twice into ኵሉ, and to give an intransitive meaning to ጸውዐ, which it never seems to have. The reason he gives for such extreme measures is: 'There is no conceivable reason for God calling together the host of heaven, seeing they are already assembled around Him' (p. 194).

---

for that purpose one power and one voice are given to them. 7. **That One,** i. e. the Messiah: cp. ver. 5. So Dln. But this is questionable: the pronoun may just as reasonably be referred to the Lord of Spirits before whom nothing can perish, ver. 5; and it is very doubtful, if it is possible, to translate maqedma qâl, 'before all.' We should perhaps render them 'the first or opening words.' Hence, 'And the opening words (of the angels' song) blessed Him . . . and were wise in utterance.' 8. See xlv. 3 (note): cf. Ps. cx. 1. **The holy in the heaven,** i. e. the angels: cf. lxi. 6 (note). **Weigh their deeds:** see xli. 1 (note). 9. **According to the word of the name of the Lord of Spirits.** This clause is evidently parallel with the next, 'according to the way of the righteous judgment of the Lord of Spirits.' We might therefore translate nagara 'command': 'according to the commands of the name of the Lord of Spirits.'

and the host of God, the Cherubim, Seraphim, and Ophanim, and all the angels of power, and all the angels of principalities, and the Elect One, and the other powers on the earth, over the water, on that day; 11. And they will raise one voice and bless and glorify in the spirit of faith, and in the spirit of wisdom, and of patience, and in the spirit of mercy, and in the spirit of judgment, and of peace, and in the spirit of goodness, and will all say with one voice, "Blessed is He and may the name of the Lord of Spirits be blessed for ever and ever." 12. And all who sleep not above in heaven will bless Him: all the holy ones who are in heaven will bless Him, and all the elect who dwell in the garden of life, and every spirit of light who is able to bless, and glorify, and extol, and hallow Thy blessed name, and all flesh which will beyond measure glorify and bless Thy name for ever and ever.

But ጸውዑ does not mean 'convocare' here, but rather 'invitare ad suscipiendum aliquid.' See his Lexicon, col. 1301. 11. **Glorify.** So G M. Dln. adds 'laud and extol.' 12. **All the holy ones.** So G M. Dln. 'all His holy ones.' For ቅዱሳኑ G reads ቅዱሳን. **Blessed name.** So G M. Other MSS. and Dln. give 'holy.'

---

10. Cherubim, Seraphim, and Ophanim: cf. xiv. 11, 18; xx. 7; lxxi. 7. The Cherubim and Seraphim appear in the O.T. but are carefully distinguished. Schulz, *A. Tliche. Theol.* p. 617, says that in no instance are the Cherubim to be regarded as angels, but as symbolic figures: they form God's chariot, and are the means of revealing or concealing His presence. The Seraphim are beings whose special duty was to serve in God's immediate presence. On the nature of these see also Delitzsch on Is. vi. 2. The Ophanim (i.e. wheels) are derived from Ezek. i. 15. In the Talmud as here they are classed with the Cherubim and Seraphim, Weber, pp. 163, 198, 259. On the angelology of the O.T., see Schulz, *A. Tliche. Theol.* (606-622). **Angels of power and angels of principalities.** These are exactly St. Paul's 'principalities and powers': cf. Rom. viii. 38; Eph. i. 21; Col. i. 16. **The other powers on the earth, &c.**, i.e. the lower angel-powers over nature. **11. In the spirit of faith, &c.** These words express the virtues which animate the angels who give praise. The virtues are seven in number: cf. xlix. 3. **Blessed is He, &c.**: cf. xxxix. 10. **12. All who sleep not**: see i. 5 (note). **Garden of life**: see lx. 8 (note). The LXX. chronology is followed here as in the Similitudes generally: cf. liv. 7 (note). **Spirit of light.** A phrase embracing good spirits, human and angelic. This thought (cf. cviii. 11, 'generation of light') is more fully developed

13. For great is the mercy of the Lord of Spirits, and He is long-suffering, and all His work and all the extent of His work He has revealed to the righteous and elect in the name of the Lord of Spirits.'

LXII. 1. And thus the Lord commanded the kings and the mighty and the exalted, and those who dwell on the earth, and said: 'Open your eyes and lift up your horns if ye are able to recognise the Elect One.' 2. And the Lord of Spirits seated him (i. e. the Messiah) on the throne of His glory and the spirit of righteousness was poured out upon him, and the word of his mouth slew all the sinners, and all the unrighteous were destroyed before his face.

---

13. **All the extent of His work.** So M ኵሉ፡ እምጣኒ፡ ግብሩ and G, but that it omits the pron. suffix. ኵሉ must be changed into ኵሎ. Other MSS. give, 'All His power in all that He has created.'

LXII. 2. **The Lord of Spirits seated him (i. e. the Messiah) on the throne of His glory.** This translation rests on a necessary emendation of the text suggested by Dln.—ወአንበረ instead of ወነበረ. For the following words 'the spirit of righteousness was poured out upon him' cannot be referred to God but only to the Messiah (cf. Isaiah xi. 4), and in verses 3 and 5 the Messiah is represented as sitting on the throne. Dln.'s text gives 'the Lord of Spirits sat on the throne,' &c. **And all the unrighteous were destroyed.** So G, which for ኵሎ reads ኵሎሙ; and

---

in the N.T., 'children of light,' Luke xvi. 8. 13. **Mercy**: see lx. 5 (note).

LXII. Here we have a lengthened account of the judgment, particularly of the kings and of the mighty. This subject has already been handled shortly, xlvi. 4–8; xlviii. 8–10; liii–liv. 3; but here the actual scene is portrayed. The kings and the mighty will be filled with anguish when they behold the Messiah, and will fall down and worship, and pray for mercy at his hands. But their prayers will be of no avail and they will be carried off by the angels of punishment. The blessedness of the lot of the righteous is then dwelt upon in contrast with the fate of the wicked. 1. **The kings and the mighty**: see xxxviii. 5. **Lift up your horns**: cf. Ps. lxxv. 4. **Recognise**, i. e. recognise him to be what he is—the Messiah. The word translated 'recognise' could also be rendered 'comprehend,' 'understand.' 2. **Seated him.** See Crit. Note: cf. Is. xi. 4. **The word of his mouth.** The judgment is forensic. **All the sinners, and all the unrighteous.** Though the writer is chiefly concerned with the judgment of the kings, the condemnation of the sinners

3. And there will stand up in that day all the kings and the mighty, and the exalted, and those who hold the earth, and they will see and recognise him how he sits on the throne of his glory, and righteousness is judged before him and no lying word is spoken before him. 4. Then shall pain come upon them as on a woman in travail, who finds it grievous to bring forth when her son enters the mouth of the womb and she has pain in bringing forth. 5. And one portion of them will look on the other, and they will be terrified, and their countenance will fall, and pain will seize them when they see that Son of Man sitting on the throne of his glory. 6. And the kings and the mighty and all who possess the

---

for ወእምገጸ reads እምገጸ. Dln.'s text gives 'and all the unrighteous and they were destroyed.' M omits the ወ but otherwise agrees with Dln. 3. **Righteousness is judged.** So G M. N O give 'the righteous are judged.' A B C D E F H I L 'the righteous are judged in righteousness.' 5. **That Son of Man.** So G: all later MSS. read 'that Son of the Woman,' -ብእሲት instead of -ብእሲ. Before I had consulted G, I felt convinced that the reading 'Son of the Woman' had arisen through the mistake of an Ethiopic scribe influenced unconsciously through Christian doctrine and possibly through the occurrence of the word a few lines before. For the same corruption see lxix. 29 (Crit. Note). We should observe also that there is only a difference of one letter between the two words. The implication underlying the Similitudes is that the Son of Man is *not* of human descent. It is otherwise with the Messiah of the Dream-vision. 6. **And the kings and the mighty.** So G M. This is the correct text, as we see by comparing lxiii. 2, 12; lxvii. 8. Other MSS. and Dln. give 'the mighty kings'; but this phrase does not occur in Enoch except in lv. 4, if the text there is right.

---

and godless and unrighteous is frequently referred to: cf. xxxviii. 1, 2, 3; xli. 2; xlv. 2, 4, 5, 6; [l. 2;] liii. 2, 7; lxii. 13; lxix. 27. 3. **The fact that even the righteous are judged** opens up a terrible prospect for the kings and the mighty: cf. 1 Pet. iv. 18. **No lying word:** see xlix. 4 (note). 4. Cf. Is. xiii. 8; xxi. 3; xxvi. 17, &c. 5. **One portion of them will look on the other.** This shows that Is. xiii. 8 was in the mind of the writer. **Son of Man.** See Crit. Note and xlvi. 2 (note). 6. **The kings** are now ready to acknowledge and worship the Son of Man, but it is too

earth will glorify and bless and extol him who rules over all, who was hidden. 7. For the Son of Man was hidden before Him and the Most High preserved him in the presence of His might and revealed him to the elect. 8. And the congregation of the holy and elect will be sown, and all the elect will stand before him on that day. 9. And all the kings and the mighty and the exalted and those who rule the earth will fall down on their faces before him and worship and set their hope upon that Son of Man, and will petition him and supplicate for mercy at his hands. 10. Nevertheless that Lord of Spirits will (so) press them that they will hastily go forth from His presence and their faces will be filled with shame, and darkness will be piled upon their faces. 11. And the angels of punishment will take them in charge to execute vengeance on them because they have oppressed His children and His elect. 12. And they will be a spectacle for the righteous and for His elect: they will rejoice over them because the wrath of the Lord of Spirits resteth upon them, and His sword is drunk with their blood

---

7. **Before Him.** So G እምቅዴሙ. Dln. gives 'formerly.' 9. **The kings and the mighty.** So GKM. FILO and Dln. give 'the mighty kings.' 10. **Nevertheless that Lord of Spirits will (so) press them.** So GM. Dln.'s text inserts እንከ 'and accordingly that Lord of Spirits will press them.' 11. **The angels of punishment will take them in charge.** So all MSS. but G, which gives ሜጸጦሙ፡ ለመላእክት፡ ለመቅሠፍት. 12. **His sword.** So GM. FHILO and Dln. give 'the sword of

---

late. **Rules over all**: cf. Dan. vii. 14. **7, 8. Hidden**: cf. xlviii. 6. This word occasions a digression and an explanation. Before he appeared to judge he was preserved by the Lord of Spirits and revealed to the elect through the spirit of prophecy, xlviii. 7. By this means the community of the elect was founded (lit. 'sown'), but was not to behold him till the final judgment. The community that is 'sown' is called the 'plant of righteousness': cf. x. 16 (note). **Congregation**: cf. xxxviii. 1 (note). **9, 10.** The description of the judgment of the kings resumed: they implore mercy, but in vain. **Shame and darkness**: cf. xlvi. 6; IV Ezra vii. 55. **11. Angels of punishment**: see xl. 7 (note). Cf. liii. 3–liv. 2. **12. Spectacle**: see xlviii. 9 (note). **Sword.**

(lit. 'from them'). 13. And the righteous and elect will be saved on that day and will never again from thenceforth see the face of the sinners and unrighteous. 14. And the Lord of Spirits will abide over them, and with that Son of Man will they eat and lie down and rise up for ever and ever. 15. And the righteous and elect will have risen from the earth, and ceased to be of downcast countenance, and will have been clothed with garments of glory. 16. And these shall be your garments, garments of life before the Lord of Spirits; and your garments will not grow old, and your glory will not pass away before the Lord of Spirits.

LXIII. 1. In those days will the mighty and the kings

---

the Lord of Spirits.' 14. **Will they eat.** So G M. F H I L O and Dln. read 'will they abide and eat,' also N (sec. hand). 15, 16. **Clothed with garments of glory. And these shall be your garments, garments of life.** So G M, which read **ለብሱ፡ ልብሰ፡ ስብሐት፡፡ ወውእቱ፡ ይኩን፡ ልብስክሙ፡ ልብሰ፡ ሕይወት**. So also I N, but that they omit **ልብስክሙ**. K reads as Dln.'s text: the other MSS. vary. The concluding words of lxii. 16, 'your garments *will* not *grow old*, and your *glory* will not pass away,' confirm the reading of G M. The fact that all these variations are absent from Dln.'s MSS. points to their being due to a late recension.

LXIII. 1. **The mighty and the kings.** So G M: cf. note on

Used figuratively here: cf. lxiii. 11. **Drunk**: cf. Is. xxxiv. 6. **13. Saved**: cf. xlviii. 7. **14. The kingdom is at last established and God Himself dwells amongst them**: cf. Is. lx. 19, 20; Zeph. iii. 15–17: and the Messiah will dwell with them: cf. xlv. 4; xxxviii. 2. The kingdom lasts for ever. **15.** This verse does not refer to the resurrection but signifies that all the humiliations of the righteous are at an end. **16. Garments of life**: see Crit. Notes on vv. 15, 16. On the garments of the blessed, cf. II Cor. v. 3, 4; Rev. iii. 4, 5, 18; iv. 4; vi. 11; vii. 9, 13, 14; IV Ezra ii. 39, 45; Herm. Sim. viii. 2. See also En. cviii. 12. **Will not grow old**: cf. Deut. viii. 4; xxix. 5.

LXIII. The writer again returns to the kings and the mighty in order to describe their bitter and unavailing repentance. The description is not an amplification of lxii. 5–12, but takes up the history at a later stage after that the kings have appealed in vain to the Messiah and are already in the custody of the angels of punishment. As their appeal to the Messiah has failed, they entreat the angels of punishment, to whom they are delivered, to grant them a respite

who possess the earth implore His angels of punishment to whom they were delivered to grant them a little respite, that they might fall down before the Lord of Spirits, and worship, and confess their sins before Him. 2. And they will bless and glorify the Lord of Spirits, and say: 'Blessed is the Lord of Spirits, the Lord of kings, the Lord of the mighty and the Lord of the rulers, the Lord of glory and the Lord of wisdom, (before whom) every secret is clear. 3. And Thy power is from generation to generation and Thy glory for ever and ever: deep are all Thy secrets and innumerable, and Thy righteousness is beyond reckoning. 4. We have now learnt that we should glorify and bless the Lord of kings and Him who is King over all kings.' 5. And they will say: 'Would that we had rest to glorify and thank Him and confess our faith before His glory! 6. And now we long for a little rest but find it not: we are driven away and obtain it not: light has vanished from before us, and darkness is our dwelling-place for ever and ever; 7. For we have not believed before Him nor glorified the name of the Lord of Spirits, nor glorified our Lord, but our hope was in the sceptre of our kingdom and in our glory. 8. And in the day of our suffering and tribulation He saves us not, and we find no

---

lxii. 6. F I L O and Dln. 'the mighty kings.' H K N omit 'the mighty.' 2. **(Before whom) every secret is clear.** G points to a different meaning ይበርህ፡ በኵሉ፡ ኅቡእ. M gives ይበርህ፡ በኵሉ፡ ኅቡኣት፡ ኃይልከ. 5. **Glorify and thank Him.** So G M. Other MSS. give, 'Glorify, and thank, and bless Him.' **His glory.** G reads 'Thy glory.' 7. **Lord of Spirits.** So G F: H I L N O give 'Lord of kings': M 'Lord of Lords.' **Glorified our Lord.** So G M. Other MSS. 'glorified the Lord for all His

---

to worship the Lord of Spirits and confess their sins before Him. This in fact forms an indirect and last despairing appeal to the Lord of Spirits. At the same time it is a justification of God's justice. For a somewhat similar passage, cf. Wisdom v. 3–8. **2.** Their confession acknowledges all that they formerly denied: cf. xlvi. 5. **3.** Cf. xlix. 2. **6. Darkness is our dwelling-place**: cf. xlvi. 6. **8.** There is no place of repent-

respite wherein to confess our faith that our Lord is true in all His works and in His judgments and His righteousness, and His judgments have no respect of persons. 9. And we shall pass away from before His face on account of our works, and all our sins are reckoned up in righteousness.' 10. Now they will say to them: 'Our souls are satisfied with the mammon of unrighteousness, but this does not prevent us from descending into the flame of the pain of Sheol.'

---

works.' 8. **In His judgments.** So G M. Dln. 'in all His judgments.' 10. **Into the flame.** So all MSS. but G, which

---

ance when the final judgment has come. 10. Riches avail not to their salvation: cf. lii. 7; liii; Ps. xlix. 7-12. **Mammon of unrighteousness**: cf. Luke xvi. 9, 11; Ecclus. v. 8. **Sheol.** This word has borne different meanings at different periods and also different meanings during the same period, owing to the coexistence of different stages in the development of thought. As these different meanings are to be found in Enoch, a short history of the conception will be the best means of explanation. (1) Sheol in the O.T. is the place appointed for all living, Job xxx. 23: from its grasp there is never any possibility of escape, Job vii. 9. It is situated beneath the earth, Num. xvi. 30: it is the land of darkness and confusion, Job x. 21, 22: of destruction, forgetfulness, and silence, Pss. lxxxviii. 12; xciv. 17; cxv. 17. Nevertheless the identity of the individual is in some measure preserved, Is. xiv. 10; Ezek. xxxii. 21; 1 Sam. xxviii. 15 sqq.: but the existence is joyless and has no point of contact with God or human interests, Pss. vi. 5; xxx. 9; Is. xxxviii. 11, 18. In the conception of Sheol there is no moral or religious element involved: no moral distinctions are observed in it: good and bad fare alike. But the family, national and social distinctions of the world above are still reproduced, and men are gathered to their fathers or people, Gen. xxv. 8, 9; xxxv. 29; Ezek. xxxii. 17-32: kings are seated on their thrones even there, Is. xiv. 9, 10; Ezek. xxxii. 21, 24. Thus the O.T. Sheol does not differ essentially from the Homeric Hades, Odyss. xi. 488, 9. This view of Sheol was the orthodox and prevailing one till the second century B. C.: cf. Ecclus. xiv. 16; xvii. 22, 23; xxx. 17; Bar. iii. 11; Tob. iii. 10; xvii. 2; Enoch cii. 11 (i. e. where Sadducees are introduced as speaking). Individual voices indeed had been raised against it in favour of a religious conception of Sheol, and finally through their advocacy this higher conception gradually won its way into acceptance. (2) This second and higher conception of Sheol was the product of the same religious thought that gave birth to the doctrine of the Resurrection—the thought that found the answer to its difficulties by carrying the idea of retribution into the life beyond the grave. The old conception thus underwent a double change. Firstly, it became essentially a place where men were treated ac-

11. And after that their countenance will be filled with darkness before that Son of Man, and they will be banished from his presence and the sword will dwell among them before his face. 12. And thus spake the Lord of Spirits: 'This is the ordinance and judgment of the mighty and the kings and the exalted and those who possess the earth before the Lord of Spirits.'

LXIV. 1. And other forms I saw in that place in secret. 2. I heard the voice of the angel saying: 'These are the angels who descended to the earth, and revealed what was hidden to the children of men and seduced the children of men into committing sin.'

[LXV. 1. And in those days Noah saw the earth that

---

gives ኢምሕሉ. 11. **Darkness.** So G. Dln. adds 'and shame.' 12. For ወከመዝ G reads ከመ.

LXIV. 2. **Descended to the earth.** So G M. Other MSS. 'descended from heaven to the earth.'

LXV. 1. For ኢደነነት G reads ኢጸነነት with the same meaning.

---

cording to their deserts with a division for the righteous, and a division for the wicked. And, secondly, from being the unending abode of the departed, it came to be only an intermediate state: cf. En. xxii; li. 1; cii. 5 (?); Luke xvi. 22 (?). (3) The conception underwent a further change, and no longer signified the intermediate state of the righteous and of the wicked, but came to be used of the abode of the wicked only, either as their preliminary abode, cf. Rev. i. 18; vi. 8; xx. 13, 14, or as their final one, En. lxiii. 10; xcix. 11; ciii. 7. This was probably due to the fact that the Resurrection was limited to the righteous, and thus the souls of the wicked simply remained in Sheol, which thus practically became hell or Gehenna: cf. Pss. Sol. xiv. 6; xv. 11. That this conception of Sheol appeared in isolated cases in the Persian period, see Cheyne, *Origin of the Psalter*, 381-412. Cf. on the question generally, Oehler, *Theol. des A. T.* i. 253-66; Schulz, *A. Tliche. Theol.* 697-708; Schenkel, *Bibel-Lex.* ii. 565-71. In the Talmud Sheol has become synonymous with Gehenna, Weber, *L. d. T.* 326, 7. 11. **With darkness**: cf. xlvi. 6; lxii. 10. **Sword.** Used figuratively here: cf. lxii. 12.

LXIV. A brief digression on the fallen angels whose judgment has already been described in the second similitude, liv. 3 sqq.; lv. 3, 4.

LXV-LXIX. 25. These chapters professedly and in fact belong to a Noah Apocalypse, and have no right to form a part of the text of Enoch. The main reasons for this conclusion are to be found in the note on liv. 7. Like the other Noachic interpolations, this interpolation is of a fragmentary nature: it deals mainly with three

it was sinking down and its destruction was nigh. 2. And he arose from thence and went to the ends of the earth, and cried aloud to his grandfather Enoch; and Noah said three times with vehement utterance, 'Hear me, hear me, hear me.' 3. And I said unto him: 'Tell me what it is that is falling out on the earth that the earth is so fatigued and shaken? May I not perish with it!' 4. And thereupon there was a great commotion on the earth and a voice was heard from heaven, and I fell on my face. 5. And Enoch my grandfather came and stood by me and said unto me: 'Why hast thou cried to me with a cry so vehement and sorrowful? 6. A command has gone forth from the presence of the Lord concerning those who dwell on the earth that their end should be brought about because they know all the secrets of the angels and all the violence of the Satans and all their hidden power and all the power of those who practise sorcery, and the power of witchcraft, and the power of those who make molten images

---

3. **I said unto him.** So G M እቤሎ. Other MSS. 'he said unto him.' 6. **For the whole earth.** These words are in the geni-

---

subjects: (1) lxv. 1–lxvii. 3, the impending Flood and the deliverance of Noah; (2) lxvii. 4–lxix. 1, the punishment of the fallen angels, with a digression on the kings and the mighty; (3) lxix. 2–25, the fall of the angels and the secrets they disclosed.

LXV. 1. Observe that the vision is Noah's. The vision opens here with a subsidence of the earth, as in lx. 1 with a quaking of the heavens. **2. The ends of the earth.** The entrance to heaven is at the ends of the earth. Enoch is still supposed to be alive and to be engaged with the angels: compare this verse with lxviii. 1. Thus it is the Samaritan chronology which is followed here; for according to the LXX. and Hebrew reckonings Enoch was translated many years before Noah was born, whereas the Samaritan makes them contemporaries for 140 years. Thus this vision must be regarded as not later than the 140th year of Noah's life. In lx. 8, 23, on the other hand, a later date is supposed, the 500th year of Noah's life (cf. lx. 1), and Paradise is consistently represented as the abode of Enoch and the elect, as this date is 360 years after Enoch's translation into Paradise. **Grandfather.** In reality great-grandfather: cf. lx. 8. **4. A voice.** This is the command in ver. 6. **Fell on my face.** As in lx. 3. **6. Those who dwell on the earth.** This phrase is borrowed from the Similitudes: cf. xxxviii. 5 (note). **Because they know all the secrets of the angels, &c.:** cf. vii; viii; lxix. **The power of witchcraft:** cf. vii. 1.

for the whole earth: 7. And how silver is produced from the dust of the earth, and how soft metal originates on the earth. 8. For lead and tin are not produced from the earth like the first: it is a fountain which produces them, and an angel stands therein, and that angel is an eminent one.' 9. And after that my grandfather took hold of me with his hand and raised me up, and said unto me: 'Go, for I have asked the Lord of Spirits as touching this commotion on the earth. 10. And He said unto me: "Because of their unrighteousness their judgment has been finally decided and will be executed speedily (lit. 'it will no longer be reckoned before me') because of the months which they have searched out, and through which they know that the earth and those who dwell upon it will be destroyed." 11. And for these

---

tive; but the context requires this rendering. 7. **እስኩ** wanting in G. 8. **An angel stands therein.** So G M, omitting **ዘ** before **ይቀውም**. Other MSS. and Dln. 'There is an angel which stands therein.' **And that angel is an eminent one.** Hallévi (*Journ. Asiat.* 373; 1867) reproduces this in Hebrew ויקדם הוא השר. He supposes ד was read by mistake for ר in יקדם. Hence we get יְקִרֵם Hiph. from קיר with 3rd pl. masc. suffix. Then comparing Jer. vi. 7 he translates, 'the angel who stands therein and makes them to cool is the chief.' But the Hiph. more likely means 'to cause to spring up.' Hence 'the angel who . . . causes them to spring up is the chief.' 9. **With his hand.** So all MSS. but G, which gives 'by my hand.' 10. **Because of the months which they have searched out, and through which they know that, &c.** Hallévi (*Journ. Asiat.* 374–5; 1867) objects that **አውራኅ** signifies months, and never astrology, and that the knowledge of the future could hardly be regarded as criminal by the writers of Enoch, and that the Deluge was generally regarded as a secret: cf. x. 2; lxxxix. 1. He thinks that the corruption arose through reading חרשים (=sorceries, Is. iii. 3) as חדשים = 'months,' and כִּי moreover = ὅτι or γάρ. Hence he would translate, 'Because of the sorceries which they have searched out and know; for the earth,' &c.

Observe that the destruction of the earth is ascribed to the corruption wrought through the angels. 10. See Crit. Note. 11. Enoch here

there will be no place of refuge for ever because they have shown them what was hidden, and (none) for those who are condemned; but as for thee, my son, the Lord of Spirits knows that thou art pure and guiltless of this reproach concerning the secrets. 12. And He has destined thy name to be among the holy, and will preserve thee from those who dwell on the earth, and has destined thy seed in righteousness to kingship and great honours, and from thy seed will proceed a fountain of the righteous and holy without number for ever.'

LXVI. 1. And after that he showed me the angels of punishment who are prepared to come and let loose all the powers of the waters which are beneath in the earth in order to bring judgment and destruction on all who live and dwell on the earth. 2. And the Lord of Spirits gave commandment to the angels who went forth, that they should not raise their hands but should wait; for those angels were over the powers of the waters. 3. And I went away from the presence of Enoch.

LXVII. 1. And in those days the word of God came unto me, and He said unto me: 'Noah, thy lot has come up before Me, a lot without blame, a lot of love and uprightness. 2. And now the angels are making a wooden building, and

---

11. **For those who.** The syntax requires በ to be supplied before እለ, as in በእሉ in preceding line. Dln. wrongly takes እለ to be እሉ, and so translates 'they.' **As for thee.** So G. Dln. inserts a negative.

LXVII. 1. **Noah, thy lot.** So G M. Other MSS. and Dln. 'Noah, behold thy lot.' **A lot without blame.** Wanting in G.

---

addresses Noah. **12.** Noah is to be the founder of a new and righteous generation. **Fountain**: cf. Deut. xxxiii. 28; Ps. lxviii. 26.

LXVI. 1. He, i.e. Enoch. **Angels of punishment.** We have here an illegitimate use of this phrase. These angels have to do solely with the second judgment in the Similitudes, and are employed here only through a misconception as the agents of the Deluge or first judgment, and as angels over the waters: cf. xl. 7 (note); liv. 7. **2. Angels over the powers of the waters**: cf. Rev. xvi. 5.

LXVII. 1. The character of Noah here is based on Gen. vi. 9. **2.** This account differs from lxxxix. 1, where it is said that Noah himself

when they have completed that task, I will place My hand upon it and preserve it, and there will come forth from it a seed of life, and the earth will undergo a change so that it will not remain without inhabitant. 3. And I will make fast thy seed before Me for ever and ever, and I will disperse those who dwell with thee over the face of the earth lest they tempt (thy seed), and (thy seed) will be blessed and will multiply on the earth in the name of the Lord.' 4. And

---

2. **Completed that task.** So G ወዶእ. M ወዶን, which should evidently be read ወዶኡ. This is clearly the right text as against Dln.'s ወፅኡ 'have gone forth to this task.' This latter reading is out of harmony both with the words before and after. For እዐቀበ G reads ዐቀበ. 3. All the best MSS. ACEFGHIKMN read ኢይመክር after ምስሌከ or የብስ. We cannot, therefore, simply omit it as Dln. As it stands, it is unmeaning. It is perhaps best to emend it into ከመ፡ ኢያመክሩ 'lest they should tempt' or 'lead astray,' and render እዘርእሞ 'I will disperse.' Thus we should have a reference to the dispersion of mankind: cf. Gen. xi. Dln.'s text runs, 'and I will spread abroad those

---

makes the ark. **Completed**: see Crit. Note. Dln.'s corrupt reading obliges him to make the angels of punishment build the ark and then go to let loose the waters! It is evidently a class of good angels we have here. **3.** Cf. lxv. 12. **4–LXIX. 1.** This section deals with the punishment of the fallen angels and its significance in regard to the kings and the mighty. It is very confused. Part of the confusion is owing to an original confusion of thought on the part of the writer, and much to the corruptness of the text. The latter is largely obviated by the ascertainment of a better text: see Crit. Notes on vv. 8, 11, 13. As for the former, it has been caused by the writer describing the first judgment in features characteristic of the final, and in identifying localities in the Similitudes which are absolutely distinct: i.e. the burning valley of Gehenna is placed among the metal mountains, lxvii. 4, though it is definitely said to lie in another direction, liv. 1, in the Similitudes. It is obvious, therefore, that no weight is to be attached to phrases denoting locality in this section. **4.** After treating of the judgment of mankind through the Deluge, the writer proceeds to describe the judgment of the angels, who were the real cause of man's corruption. In contradiction with x, the fallen angels are cast into a burning valley—really the Gehenna valley of liv. There is a twofold confusion here. It is not said that the angels in liv. were cast into the valley of Gehenna, but into a 'burning furnace'; and, in the second place, this was the final place of punishment, not the pre-

He will imprison those angels who have shown unrighteousness in that burning valley which my grandfather Enoch had formerly shown to me in the west among the mountains of gold and silver and iron and soft metal and tin. 5. And I saw that valley in which there was a great convulsion and a swelling of the waters. 6. And when all this took place, there was produced from that fiery molten metal and from the convulsion wherewith they were convulsed in that place, a smell of sulphur, and it was connected with those waters, and that valley of the angels who had seduced (mankind) burned continually under the earth there. 7. And through the valleys of that land proceed streams of fire, where those angels are punished who had led astray those who dwell upon the earth. 8. But these waters will in those days serve for the kings and the mighty and the exalted and those who dwell on the earth for the healing of the body, and

---

who dwell with thee over the face of the earth.' 4. **He will imprison.** So F G M. Other MSS. 'they will imprison.' 5. For ተሀውክ G reads ገውክ (sic); M ሀውክ. 6. For ወሀውኩሙ፡ ዘየሀውኩሙ G reads ወየገውኩሙ; M ወክሙ፡ ሀውኩሙ. 8. **For the healing of the body.** So G: and this reading is obviously

---

liminary. But, again, the burning valley is said to be amongst the metal mountains in the west. This, as we have shown above, is a misleading combination of utterly disparate ideas, and should prove a warning against falling into the error of Hilgenfeld and Drummond, and basing conclusions on such equivocal or rather demonstrably groundless statements as appear in this verse. **In the west.** Borrowed from lii. 1, as other phrases from the adjoining context, and with just as little real significance. The phrase is no real note of locality but only another meaningless plagiarism of this interpolator. For others see pp. 15, 16; lx. 10 (note). Hilgenfeld's excursion to Vesuvius in search of a burning valley *in the west* is a bootless and uncalled-for errand. 5, 6. These verses combine features of the Deluge and of volcanic disturbances. The latter are connected with the punishment of the angels. **Burned under the earth there.** Not merely the immediate neighbourhood of the Gehenna valley is here designated, but, as Dln. points out, the adjacent country down to and beyond the Dead Sea. A subterranean fire was believed to exist under the Gehenna valley: cf. xxvii. 1 (note). 8. **In those days.** Those of the writer. **Those waters will serve . . . for the healing of the body.** The hot springs

for the punishment of the spirit, because their spirit is full of lust, that they may be punished in their body; for they have denied the Lord of Spirits and see their punishment daily, and yet believe not in His name. 9. And in proportion as the burning of their bodies becomes severe, a corresponding change will take place in their spirit for ever and ever; for before the Lord of Spirits there will be none to utter a lying word. 10. For the judgment will come upon them, because they believe in the lust of their body and have denied the Spirit of the Lord. 11. And those same waters will undergo a change in those days; for when those angels are punished in these waters, these water-springs will change their temperature,

---

right; for the office of the sulphur springs is medicinal in this world, but punitive in the next. Other MSS. 'for the healing of the soul and body.' **Believe not.** G omits the negative. 9. **A corresponding change will take place.** G reads ከመ፡ ዘበመ፡ ተወለጠ. 11. **Are punished in these waters.** So G M, reading ማያት. Other MSS. 'in those days.' **These water-springs will change their temperature**: lit. 'will be changed as to their temperature.' So G M, reading ይትዌለጡ instead of ይትዌለጥ

---

resulted from the meeting of the water and fire underground by which the angels were punished. As an instance of such a hot spring Dln. mentions Kallirrhoe to the east of the Dead Sea, to which Herod the Great resorted, Jos. *Ant.* xvii. 6. 5; *Bell. Jud.* i. 33. 5. It has been objected that according to the latter passage these waters were sweet and not sulphurous. So far as this objection is valid, it cannot hold against the hot springs of Machaerus, *Bell. Jud.* vii. 6. 3, which were bitter, and in the neighbourhood of which there were sulphur mines. Holtzmann (*Jahrb. f. D. T.* xii. 391) refers to the eruptions of Mount Epomeo in Ischia in 46 and 35 B.C. (quoted by Schodde), but, as we have seen above, there is no need to go to the west for an explanation. **For the punishment of the spirit**, i.e. in the final judgment. **Punished in their body.** In Gehenna they will suffer in the body as well as in the spirit. **Denied the Lord of Spirits**: cf. xxxviii. 2 (note); liv. 7 (note). **See their punishment daily.** The hot springs are a testimony to the present punishment of the angels: a testimony likewise to the punishment that will befall the kings and the mighty. **9.** The punishment will work repentance in the kings, but it will be unavailing. **A lying word**: cf. xlix. 4 (note). **10. Denied the Spirit of the Lord.** This expression is unique in Enoch. **11.** The removal of the angels to another place of punishment is fol-

and when the angels ascend, this water of the springs will change and become cold. 12. And I heard Michael answering and saying: 'This judgment wherewith the angels are judged is a testimony for the kings and the mighty and for those who possess the earth. 13. Because these waters of judgment minister to the healing of the body of the kings and to the lust of their body; therefore they will not see and will not believe that those waters will change and become a fire which burns for ever.'

LXVIII. 1. And after that my grandfather Enoch gave

---

and እለሱ instead of በእለቱ. Other MSS. give 'the temperature of these water-springs will change.' 12. **Michael.** So G M. Other MSS. read 'the holy Michael.' 13. **Minister to the healing of the body of the kings and to the lust of their body; therefore they will not see, &c.** So G M, reading በፈውሰ፡ ሥጋሆሙ፡ በመላእክት፡ ወበተምኔት፡ ሥጋሆሙ, save that I have substituted the word 'kings' for 'angels.' This change is absolutely necessary, as Hallévi (*Journ. Asiat.* 366–7; 1867) has pointed out; for it would be absurd to suppose that the angels were healed by the chemical action of the waters. The mistake arose through the confusion of מַלְאָכִים 'angels' with מְלָכִים 'kings.' Hallévi thinks that 'angels' in verse 11 should similarly be changed into 'kings,' but wrongly. The reading of G is evidently the right one; it is supported throughout by M, and in the first clause 'to the healing of the body' by all MSS. but B C: the text of its second clause 'to the lust of their body' could readily be corrupted into the unintelligible reading of the remaining MSS. 'to the death of their body,' በተውኔት into በሞት through the influence of verses 9 and 10. Dln.'s 'for the healing of the angels' has all MSS. but B C against it: his reading 'for the death of the body' has the support of F H I K L N. His text gives, 'For these waters of judgment minister to the healing of the angels and to the death of their body; but they will not see,' &c.

---

lowed by a cooling of the waters. **13.** See Crit. Note. Dln.'s text is unintelligible, but the text of G as followed above is quite clear.

LXVIII. 1. According to this verse the Similitudes already exist as a complete work in the hands of the interpolator. The meaning of this chapter is difficult to determine. It has probably to do with the Satans or

the signs of all the secrets in a book and the Similitudes which had been given to him, and he put them together for me in the words of the book of the Similitudes.) 2. And in those days Michael answered Rufael and said: 'The power of the spirit transports and provokes me: yet as regards the rigour of the judgment of the secrets, the judgment over the angels, who can endure the rigorous judgment which is passed, before which they melt away?' 3. And Michael answered again and spake to Rufael: 'Who is he whose heart is not softened concerning it, and whose reins are not troubled by this word of judgment that has been passed upon them—upon those whom they have thus led out?' 4. And it came to pass when he stood before the Lord of Spirits, Michael spake thus to Rufael: 'I will not take their part under the eye of the Lord, for the Lord of Spirits is angry with them because they do as if they were like the Lord.

LXVIII. 2. **Michael.** So G M. Dln. 'the holy Michael.' **The power of the spirit transports and provokes me.** Can this mean 'the spirit of God provokes my wrath against the fallen angels'? It would perhaps be better to read ኀይሉ፡ በመንፈስየ: the የ might have fallen out before the initial ይ in ይመስጠኒ. We should thus have: 'the vehemence of my feelings transports me . . . for as regards,' &c. **Is passed.** So G M. Other MSS. and Dln. add 'and abides.' 3. **Michael.** So G M. Dln. 'the holy Michael.' So also in ver. 4; lxix. 14, 15. **Heart is not softened.** G M read እይረብሖ፡ ልቦ. **Word of judgment.** So G reading ቃለ instead of ቃል as in Dln.: 'who is he . . . whose reins are not troubled by this word? A judgment has been passed

---

chiefs of the angels. **2.** The dialogue between Michael and Rufael is designed to set forth the severity of the judgment over the fallen angels. **Judgment of the secrets.** This may mean the judgment on account of the secrets divulged by the angels. **3. Upon those whom they have thus led out.** Dln. thinks this may mean those angels who are conducted from the preliminary to the final place of punishment. It might perhaps be better to translate 'judgment which has been passed upon them because of those whom they have thus led forth.' In this case we should have the judgment of the Satans who are rigorously punished because they seduced the angels into sin. The words 'They do as if they were like the Lord'

5. Therefore all that is hidden will come upon them for ever and ever; for neither angel nor man will have his portion (in it), but alone they undergo their judgment for ever and ever.'

LXIX. 1. And after this judgment they will inspire fear and anger in them because they have shown this to those who dwell on the earth. 2. And behold the names of those angels! and these are their names: the first of them is Semjâzâ, the second Arestîqîfâ, the third Armên, the fourth Kokabâêl, the fifth Tûrêl, the sixth Rûmjâl, the seventh Dânêl, the eighth Nûqâêl, the ninth Barâqêl, the tenth Azâzêl, the eleventh Armers, the twelfth Batarjâl, the thirteenth Basasâêl, the fourteenth Anânêl, the fifteenth Tûrjâl, the sixteenth Sîmâpîsîêl, the seventeenth Jetarêl, the eighteenth Tûmâêl, the nineteenth Tarêl, the twentieth Rûmâêl, the twenty-first Izêzêêl. 3. And these are the chiefs of their angels and the names of their chief ones over a hundred and over fifty and over ten. 4. The name of the first, Jeqûn: that is the one who led astray all the children of the angels,

---

upon them.' 5. **All that is hidden.** So G M. Other MSS. and Dln. 'the judgment that is hidden.'

LXIX. 1. **Inspire fear and anger.** As Dln. remarks, there must be a corruption here. Hallévi (*Journ. Asiat.* p. 383; 1867) thinks **አምዐዐ** is a translation of the Hiphil הִרְגִּיז which means (1) to cause to tremble, (2) to irritate. The Greek translator took the latter meaning, which is unsuitable to the context. Hence translate, 'inspire fear and trembling.' 2. G differs considerably from Dln.'s text in the spelling of the angels' names, but mainly in the matter of vowels. 4. **The angels.** So F G H M.

---

favour this interpretation: cf. Is. xiv. 11-13. 5. In this rigorous punishment in store for them neither angel nor man suffers but those Satans (?) only.

LXIX. 1. See Crit. Note. 2. The list of names here is essentially the same as in vi. 7, but that the thirteenth name is superfluous: see Dln. on vi. 7. In vi. 7 the names are said to be those of the chiefs, but here they are not so described. 4. It is to be observed that in the Similitudes the Satans and the fallen angels are carefully distinguished: the latter fall in the days of Jared according to i-xxxvi and xci-civ. In this chapter, however, the functions of these two classes are confused. It is Azazel in i-xxxvi who is the cause of all the corruption upon earth, and Semjaza

and brought them down to the earth and led them astray through the daughters of men. 5. And the second is called Asbeêl: he imparted to the children of the holy angels the evil counsel and led them astray so that they defiled their bodies with the daughters of men. 6. And the third is called Gâdreêl: he it is who has taught the children of men all the blows of death, and he led astray Eve, and showed to the sons of men the weapons of death and the coat of mail, and the shield, and the sword for battle, and all the weapons of death to the children of men. 7. And from his hand they have proceeded over those who dwell on the earth from that hour for evermore. 8. And the fourth is called Pênêmûe: he taught the children of men the bitter and the sweet, and taught them all the secrets of their wisdom. 9. And he instructed mankind in writing with ink and paper, and thereby many sinned from eternity to eternity and until this day. 10. For it was not intended when man was created (lit. 'men are not created to the end') that he should give confirmation to his good faith with pen and ink in such wise. 11. For man was created exactly like the angels to the intent that he should continue righteous and pure, and death which destroys everything could not have taken hold of him, but through this their knowledge they are perishing and through this power (of knowledge) it (death) is consuming me. 12. And the fifth is called Kasdejâ: he has taught

---

Other MSS. 'the holy angels.' 12. For በምጕቀዐን G reads ወሕፃን,

---

in the interpolated passage vi. 3. Jeqûn = 'the inciter': Asbeêl = 'the deserter from God.' **6.** Gâdreêl is evidently a Satan as he led astray Eve. In viii. 1 the making of weapons of war is ascribed to Azazel. **9, 10.** Though the invention of the art of writing is ascribed to an evil spirit, the writer does not seem to condemn it save in so far as it is used as a safeguard against the bad faith of men. **11.** Man was created exactly like the angels. Man was originally righteous and immortal: cf. Book of Wisdom, i. 13, 14; ii. 23, 24. This is also the doctrine of the Talmud, Weber, *L. d. T.* 208, 214, 239. Man lost his uprightness and immortality through the envy of the devil, Wisdom ii. 24, through the evil knowledge introduced by the Satans or angels, En. lxix. 11, through his own evil act, xcviii. 4. **12.** Cf. Rosenmüller's *Scholia* on Ps. xci. 5, 6,

the children of men all the wicked smitings of spirits and demons, and the smitings of the embryo and the babe, that it may pass away, and the smitings of the soul, the bites of the serpent, and the smitings which befall at noon, the son of the serpent named Tabâ't. 13. And this is the number of Kesbeêl, who showed the head of the oath to the holy ones when he dwelt high above in glory, and its name is Bêqâ. 14. And this (angel) requested Michael to show him the hidden name, that they might mention it in the oath, so that those who revealed all that was hidden to the children of men might quake before that name and oath. 15. And this is the power of that oath, for it is powerful and strong, and he placed this oath Akâe in the hand of Michael. 16. And these are the secrets of this oath, and the heaven was made strong through the oath, and was suspended before the world was created and for ever: 17. And through it the earth was founded upon the water, and from the secret recesses of the mountains come beautiful waters from the creation of the world unto eternity. 18. And through that

---

and this I have followed. 13. **The number of Kesbeêl.** Hallévi (*Journ. Asiat.* p. 383; 1867) suggests that for ኍልቈ there stood פְּקוּדָה which means either 'number' or 'charge.' Hence, 'this is the charge of Kesbeêl,' i. e. to remind the other angels of the oath by which they were bound. 14. **Show him the hidden name.** So G M. Other MSS. give 'show them the hidden name.' After these words Dln. and all MSS. but G M insert 'that thus they might see that hidden name and.' I have followed G. M has a clause peculiar to itself. 16. **Was made strong.** So G ፀንዐ. Dln. reads ጸንዑ 'they were strong . . . and the heaven was suspended.' 17. **Beautiful waters.** So AEFGHIN and practically M. Dln.

---

which according to ancient Jewish interpretation treated of demonic dangers. **The serpent named Tabâ't.** I know nothing about this name. **13.** See Crit. Note: cf. xli. 5. I do not pretend to interpret this and many of the following verses. **16.** **Heaven was suspended**: cf. Job xxvi. 7 for a similar expression regarding the earth. **17.** **Earth was founded upon the water**: cf. Pss. xxiv. 2; cxxxvi. 6. **From the secret recesses of the mountains come beautiful waters**: cf. Ps. civ. 10, 13.

oath the sea was created, and as its foundation He laid for it the sand against the time of (its) anger, and it dare not pass beyond it from the creation of the world unto eternity. 19. And through that oath are the depths made fast, and abide and stir not from their place from eternity to eternity. 20. And through that oath the sun and moon complete their course, and deviate not from the path prescribed to them from eternity to eternity. 21. And through that oath the stars complete their course, and He calls them by their names, and they answer Him from eternity to eternity. 22. And in like manner the spirits of the water, and of the winds, and of all zephyrs, and the paths of all the bands of the spirits. 23. And in it are preserved the voices of the thunder and the light of the lightnings; and in it are preserved the chambers of the hail and of the hoar-frost, and the chambers of the mist and the chambers of the rain and the dew. 24. And all these believe and give thanks before the Lord of Spirits and glorify (Him) with all their power, and their food is nothing save thanksgiving: they thank and glorify and extol the name of the Lord of Spirits for ever and ever. 25. And this oath is mighty over them and through it they are preserved, and their paths are preserved, and their course is not destroyed.] 26. And there was great joy amongst them, and they blessed and glorified and extolled because the name

---

gives 'beautiful waters for the living.' 20. **To eternity**: wanting in G. 22. For **winds** G gives wrongly 'souls,' by a change in one letter. 23. **The voices of the thunder.** So G M. Other MSS., 'the chambers of the voices of the thunder.' 26. **And extolled**:

---

18. **As its foundation He laid for it the sand, &c.**: cf. Jer. v. 22; Job xxvi. 10; Ps. civ. 9, &c. 19. **The depths made fast**: cf. Prov. viii. 28. 21. **Calls them by their names**: cf. xliii. 1 (note). 23. Cf. Crit. Note. **Chambers of the hail, &c.**: cf. lx. 11, 19–21. 24. Cf. xli. 7 for a similar thought. 26–29. These verses form the conclusion of the third similitude. We have again returned to the chief theme of the third similitude. It is not improbable that the interpolator omitted part of this similitude and replaced it with his own additions. 26. **Because the**

of the Son of Man was revealed unto them: 27. And he sat on the throne of his glory, and the sum of judgment was committed unto him, the Son of Man, and he caused the sinners and those who have led the world astray to pass away and be destroyed from off the face of the earth. 28. With chains shall they be bound, and in their assemblage-place of destruction shall they be imprisoned, and all their works vanish from the face of the earth. 29. And from henceforth there will be nothing that is corruptible; for the Son of Man has appeared and sits on the throne of his glory, and all evil will pass away before his face and depart; but the word of the Son of Man will be strong before the Lord of Spirits. This is the third Similitude of Enoch.

LXX. 1. And it came to pass after this that his name was carried aloft during his lifetime to the Son of Man and to the Lord of Spirits from amongst those who dwell on the earth. 2. And he was carried aloft on the chariots of the spirit and

---

wanting in G. 27. For ያማስኑ፡ ኃጥኣነ G wrongly ያማስን. 28. **Imprisoned.** Before ይትዐፀዉ G M insert ዘ. 29. **The word.** For ነገሩ F G I M O and originally N read ይነገሩ; and for ይጸንዕ read ወይጸንዕ. For ብእሲ G reads ብእሲት 'Son of the Woman.'

LXX. 1. **And to the Lord.** So G. Other MSS. omit 'and.'

---

name of the Son of Man was revealed. +This is obscure. Cf. for a different use of the phrase, xlviii. 7; lxii. 7. **27. He,** i. e. the Messiah. **On the throne of his glory:** see xlv. 3 (note). **The sum of judgment,** i. e. all judgment: cf. St. John v. 22, 27. **The sinners.** Though the Similitudes are directed chiefly against the kings and the mighty ones, the author returns repeatedly to the judgment of sinners in general: cf. xxxviii. 1, 2, 3; xli. 2; xlv. 2, 5, 6; [l. 2;] liii. 2, 7; lxii. 2, 13. **From off the face of the earth:** cf. xxxviii. 1 (note). **28.** Cf. liii–vi. **29.** This verse summarises shortly such a chapter as xlix.

LXX. This chapter forms the conclusion as xxxvii forms the introduction of the Similitudes. There is certainly some awkwardness in the author making Enoch describe his own translation; but this in itself forms no valid reason for obelising the chapter, as in every other respect it is quite in keeping with the thought of the Similitudes. **1. His name.** The name here stands for the person. The actual pre-existence of the Son of Man is here supposed: cf. xlviii. 2 (note). **Son of Man:** cf. xlvi. 2 (note). **Those who dwell on the earth:** cf. xxxvii. 5 (note). **2. Chariots of the spirit:** cf. 2 Kings

the name vanished amongst men (lit. 'them'). 3. And from that day I was no longer numbered amongst them, and he set me between the two winds, between the North and the West, where the angels took the cords to measure for me the place for the elect and righteous. 4. And there I saw the first fathers and the righteous who from the beginning dwell in that place.

[LXXI. 1. And it came to pass after this that my spirit

---

3. **Was no longer numbered amongst them.** So G ተሐሰበኩ by a slip for ተሐሰበኩ. This is obviously the right reading, of which ተሰሐብኩ = 'I was drawn or dragged' (so Dln.) is a corruption. I M give the same text as Dln., but by a later hand.

---

ii. 11. This is an account of Enoch's translation: cf. lxxxvii. 3, 4; lxxxix. 52. **3. Numbered**: see Crit. Note. **Between the North and the West.** According to xxxii. 2–6 Paradise lay in the East: according to lxxvii. 3 in the North: see lx. 8 (note). **The cords**: cf. lxi. **4.** Paradise is already peopled with his righteous forefathers. This agrees perfectly with lxi. 12, which speaks of the elect being already in Paradise. Thus in the Similitudes the chronology of the LXX. is followed, whereas in the Interpolations it is the Samaritan reckoning that is adopted. Cp. liv. 7 (note).

LXXI. This chapter is most certainly a later addition. It is alien alike in thought and phraseology to the Similitudes. Outwardly indeed there is a resemblance in phraseology but it is not real, for the technical terms of the Similitudes which are incorporated in this chapter are wrongly used in almost every instance. This chapter was probably added by the same hand that interpolated the Noachic fragments. Some of the grounds for the above conclusion are:—(1) The transcendence of God, of which we have hardly any consciousness in the Similitudes, is here portrayed in the severest manner. The distance between God and even the righteous Enoch in this chapter is immeasurable, whereas in the Similitudes earth and heaven are made one community through the Messiah, and God and the Son of Man dwell with men. (2) The description of the crystal palace of fire, lxxi. 5, 6, is borrowed from xiv. 9–17, but in the hands of the interpolator this account of the theophany becomes an idle transformation scene, a mere tableau vivant—God utters not a word, it is only an angel that addresses Enoch. (3) There is absolutely no evidence to show that the writer of the Similitudes was acquainted with i–xxxvi, though Dln. has thrown out this supposition, Herzog, *R. E.* xii. 351, whereas the dependence of the writer of this chapter on i–xxxvi is demonstrable. (4) Enoch's guide is no longer the angel of peace as in the Similitudes, but Michael, lxxi. 3. (5) The title 'Son of Man' is used in an absolutely different sense in this chapter—exactly indeed as it is in the Noachic fragments: see lx. 10 (note). We may

was hidden and it ascended into the heavens: (there) I saw the sons of the holy angels stepping on flames of fire: their garments were white and their raiment and their faces shone like snow. 2. And I saw two streams of fire, and the light of that fire shone like hyacinth, and I fell on my face before the Lord of Spirits. 3. And the angel Michael, one of the archangels, seized me by my right hand and lifted me up and introduced me to all the secrets of mercy and the secrets of righteousness. 4. And he showed me all the secrets of the ends of the heaven, and all the chambers of all the stars, and of the luminaries, whence they proceed into the presence of the holy ones. 5. And the spirit translated Enoch unto

---

LXXI. 1. **Sons of the holy angels.** So A E F G H I M N. Other MSS. and Dln. 'sons of the angels.' **Their faces shone like snow.** C G O and originally L ብሩሃን. Other MSS. and Dln. 'the light of their faces was like snow.' 5. For መንፈስ:

---

indeed have here a deliberate perversion of this phrase as it appears in the Similitudes: see xlvi. 2, 3 (notes), and this is possible for the following reason. (6) lxxi. 14, 'Thou art the Son of Man who art born unto righteousness and righteousness abides over thee,' is an application to Enoch of the words used of the Son of Man in xlvi. 3. (7) The writer of the Similitudes uses Daniel's phrase, 'Head of Days,' most appositely in connexion with the question of judgment: cf. xlvi. 1 (note). Not so the interpolator; he violates the technical sense of the phrase, and incorporates it merely to give verisimilitude to his additions. (8) lxxi. 17 betrays the hand of an interpolator who either did not know or else ignored the fact that eternal life was the lot of the righteous in the Similitudes: see xxxvii. 4 (note). This verse probably shows the writer's acquaintance with i. 5; x. 17; xxv. 6. (9) Finally, it is quite unfitting that Enoch should have visions such as are recounted in this chapter after his translation into Paradise. 1. The note of time here is meaningless with regard to the Similitudes. **Sons of the holy angels.** This is practically the same phrase as in lxix. 5: cf. lxix. 4 'children of the angels,' and cvi. 5 'children of the angels of heaven.' The expression is to be referred to בְּנֵי אֱלֹהִים, where the Elohim are interpreted as angels. **2. Streams of fire**: cf. xiv. 19; Dan. vii. 10; also ver. 6 of this chapter. These streams really proceed from beneath the throne. **3. Secrets of mercy.** The mercy of God is often referred to in the additions: cf. l. 3–5; lx. 5, 25. **4.** We have seen that it was necessary to regard the verses and chapters dealing with natural phenomena, such as xli. 3–8, xliii, xliv, as intrusions into the text. The reference here to physical secrets connects the writer of this chapter more or less directly with those just mentioned.

the heaven of heavens, and I saw there in the midst of that light a structure built of crystals, and between those crystals flames of living fire. 6. And my spirit saw how a fire girt that house around—on its four sides streams full of living fire, and how they encircled that house. 7. And round about were Seraphim, Cherubim, and Ophanim: these are they who sleep not and guard the throne of His glory. 8. And I saw angels who could not be counted, a thousand thousands, and ten thousand times ten thousand (and they) encircled that house, and Michael and Gabriel and Rufael and Fanuel and the holy angels who are above in the heavens go in and out of that house. 9. And there came forth from that house Michael and Gabriel, Rufael and Fanuel, and many holy angels without number. 10. And with them the Head of Days, His head white and pure as wool and His raiment indescribable. 11. And I fell on my face and my whole body melted away, but my spirit was transfigured; and I cried with a loud voice with the spirit of power and blessed and glorified and extolled. 12. And these blessings which went forth out of my mouth were well pleasing before that Head of Days. 13. And that Head of Days came with Michael and Gabriel, Rufael and Fanuel, and with thousands and ten thousand thousands—angels without number. 14. And he came to me and greeted me with his voice, and said unto me: 'Thou art the son of man who art

---

ሰሂፍኒ G reads መንፈስየ፡ ወሂፍኒ. 14. He. So G M. Other MSS. and Dln. read 'that angel.' Who art born. Dln. wrongly

---

5, 6. Cf. xiv. 9–17. 7. **Cherubim, Seraphim, and Ophanim**: cf. lxi. 10, 12; xxxix. 13; xl. 2. 8. **A thousand thousands, &c.**: cf. xiv. 22; xl. 1. **Go in and out.** This is not so in xiv. 23. **Michaël, Gabriel, &c.**: see xl. 4–7. 10. **The Head of Days**: see (7) of the introductory criticism on this chapter, also xlvi. 1 (note); Dan. vii. 9. 11. **The first** two clauses are practically word for word the same as the last two clauses of lx. 3. **Spirit was transfigured.** Distinguish this from xxxix. 14, and cf. Asc. Is. vii. 25. **Spirit of power**: cf. lxi. 11. 14. **And he**, i. e. 'Michael': see Crit. Note. It is not God Himself who speaks: cf. ver. 15. **Thou art the son of man**: see (5) and (6) of the introductory

born unto righteousness, and righteousness abides over thee and the righteousness of the Head of Days forsakes thee not.'
15. And he said unto me: 'His word for thee is (lit. 'He calls unto thee') peace in the name of the world to come; for from thence proceeds peace since the creation of the world, and so will it be with thee for ever and ever and ever.
16. And all who in the time to come walk in thy ways—thou whom righteousness never forsaketh—their dwelling-places will be with thee and their heritage will be with thee, and they will not be separated from thee for ever and ever and ever.
17. And so there will be length of days with that Son of Man and the righteous will have peace, and the righteous his path of uprightness in the name of the Lord of Spirits for ever and ever.']

'der . . . geboren ist.' **And righteousness**: wanting in G.

---

criticism on this chapter and the references there given. **15. He calls unto thee peace.** Quoted in Test. Dan. 5 βοῶν ὑμῖν εἰρήνην. **The world to come**, i. e. the Olam habba, the Messianic kingdom. **17. Length of days.** See (8) of the introductory criticism on this chapter.

SECTION III.

(CHAPTERS LXXII—LXXXII.)

THE BOOK OF CELESTIAL PHYSICS. INTRODUCTION.

A. *Its Critical Structure and Object.* B. *Its Independence of* i–xxxvi. C. *Its Calendar and the knowledge therein implied.*

A. Critical Structure and Object. Chapter lxxii introduces us to a scientific treatise. In this treatise the writer attempts to bring the many utterances regarding physical phenomena into one system, and puts this forward as the genuine and biblical one as opposed to all other systems. The paramount, and indeed the only aim of this book according to lxxii. 1, is to give the laws of the heavenly bodies, and this object it pursues undeviatingly from its beginning to lxxix. 1, where it is said that the treatise is finished and all the laws of the heavenly bodies set forth. Through all these chapters there is not a single ethical reference. The author has no other interest save a scientific one coloured by Jewish conceptions and beliefs. As a Jew he upholds the accuracy of the moon as a divider of time, lxxiv. 12: 'The moon brings in all the years exactly, so that their position is not prematurely advanced or delayed by a single day unto eternity.' And this order is inflexible: there will be no change in it till the new creation, lxxii. 1. So far, then, we have to deal with a complete and purely scientific treatise, in which there is no breach of uniformity till the new creation. But the moment we have done with lxxix, we pass into a new atmosphere. The whole interest is *ethical and nothing else*: there is, indeed, such a thing as an order of nature, but, owing to the sin of men, this order is more conspicuous in its breach than in its observance, lxxx. 2–8, and even that infallible luminary the moon (lxxiv. 12) becomes a false guide and misleader of men, lxxx. 4.

Chapter lxxx, therefore, is manifestly an addition, made to give an ethical turn to a purely scientific treatise, and so furnish it with some fitness for its present collocation. Before passing on to lxxxi, we may remark that not only does the general tendency of lxxx. 1–6 conflict with the preceding chapters, but the only exact specification ventured on by the interpolator in lxxx. 5 is in glaring contradiction with lxxvi. 13. Yet see notes on lxxx. 5.

Nor, again, can lxxxi belong to this book. Before entering on this question, however, let us consider lxxxii. 1–8, which forms, according to most critics, the close of this treatise, vv. 9–20 being regarded as a Noachic interpolation, but wrongly: see lxxxii. 9 (note). These verses lxxxii. 1–8 manifestly do belong to lxxii–lxxix. The same formula occurs in lxxxii. 1, 'my son Methuselah,' as in lxxvi. 14 and in lxxix. 1 (according to some MSS.). The wisdom dealt with in lxxxii. 1–8 is the same scientific lore as in lxxii–lxxix. And the blessing of the author of lxxxii. 1–8 is for the man who sins not in calculating the seasons, lxxxii. 4.

lxxii–lxxix and lxxxii constitute the original book of Celestial Physics. But, whereas the blessing of the author of lxxii–lxxix, lxxxii is for the man who knows the right reckoning of the years, the blessing of lxxxi. 4 is for the man 'who dies in righteousness, concerning whom no book of unrighteousness is written.' These two blessings, in fact, give the keynote of their respective contents of the book of Celestial Physics and lxxxi, and disclose the motives of their respective authors. This chapter did not, any more than lxxx, belong to this treatise originally. In fact, we find on examination that it is of the nature of a mosaic, and came probably from the editor of the complete Enoch. The phrase 'Those three angels,' in lxxxi. 5, points to some previous statement apparently; but none such is to be found. The words are evidently drawn from lxxxvii. 3, where they occur exactly as here, *but with an explanation.* The heavenly tables in lxxxi. 1, 2 come from xciii. 2, ciii. 2. The expression 'Lord of the world' may be suggested by lxxxii. 7, 'Lord of the whole creation of the world.' The 'books of judgment' in lxxxi. 4 are drawn from lxxxix. 61, 64, &c.

Again, we observe that lxxxi. 5, 6 are written with reference to lxxxii. 1, 2 and xci. 1. This latter verse introduces the section beginning in the *present* form of Enoch with xci. We shall see later that xci does not really form the beginning of the last book of Enoch, but that it has been dislocated from its right position by the author of lxxxi to serve his editorial purposes.

Finally, with regard to lxxxii, it is evident that it does not stand in its original position. The Book of Celestial Physics rightly concludes with lxxix, which closes thus: 'This is the picture and sketch of every luminary as they were shown to me by their leader, the great angel Uriel.' lxxxii must have preceded this chapter originally, and probably immediately. After the long disquisition on the stars in lxxxii, the first words of lxxix would come in most appropriately: 'And now, my son, I have shown thee everything, *and the law of all the stars of the heaven is completed.*' If lxxxii does not precede, these words have practically no justification in lxxii–lxxviii. The final editor of the whole book was fond of such dislocations. There has been a like rearrangement of xci–xciii.

B. Its Independence of i–xxxvi. (1) In i. 2 the revelation of Enoch is not for the present, but for remote generations: in xciii. 10 it is to remain a secret till the seventh week of the world: in civ. 12 it is one day to be disclosed. But in lxxxii. 1 the revelations are entrusted to Methuselah to be transmitted to *the generations of the world.* (2) In xxxiii. 3 Uriel writes down everything for Enoch, but in lxxii. 1, lxxiv. 2, lxxv. 3, lxxix. 2–6 Uriel only shows the celestial phenomena to Enoch, and Enoch himself writes them down, lxxxii. 1. (3) The description of the winds coming from different quarters in xxxiv–xxxvi differs from that in lxxvi. (4) The heavenly bodies are partly conscious in i–xxxvi: cf. xviii. 12–16, xxi. 1–6; but not so in lxxii–lxxxii. (5) The portals of the stars in xxxvi. 2 are described as *small* portals *above* the portals of the winds. As in lxxii–lxxxii these portals are also those of the sun and moon, they can hardly be called 'small,' being each equal to thirty degrees in width. Besides, though described at great length in lxxii–lxxxii, they are never said to be 'above' those of the winds. (6) The river of fire in xxiii, in which the luminaries set and recruit their exhausted fires, has no point of connexion with lxxii–lxxxii. (7) In xxxii. 2, 3 the Garden of Eden lies in the east: in lxxvii. 3 in the north. There is undoubtedly some relationship between the later chapters of i–xxxvi and lxxii–lxxxii; but it is not that of one and undivided authorship.

C. Its Calendar and the knowledge therein implied. The chronological system of this book is most perplexing. It does not in its present form present a consistent whole, and probably never did. We are not to regard it as anything more than the attempt of an individual to establish an essentially Hebrew calendar over against the heathen calendars in vogue around. In itself this calendar cannot be said to have any value. It is useful, however, as giving us some knowledge of the chronological systems more or less known to the Palestinean Jews. For (1) the writer is acquainted with the signs of the zodiac, but carefully refrains from mentioning them, replacing them by his system of portals. (2) He is acquainted with the spring and autumn equinoxes and the summer and winter solstices. (3) He knows apparently the length of the synodic months (cf. lxxviii. 15, 16), which was not published till the time of Gamaliel II, 80–115 A.D. (4) His attempt to reconcile the lunar year and his peculiar year of 364 days by intercalations, in the third, fifth, and eighth years, furnishes strong presumption that he had the Greek eight-year cycle before him, and the presumption becomes a certainty when we consider that, whereas every detail in the Greek cycle is absolutely necessary to the end desired, in the Enochian system, on the other hand, though these details are more or less reproduced, they are absolutely idle, as Enoch's system is really a one-year cycle, and the lunar year is reconciled to his solar year of 364 days by the addition of ten days each year: cf. lxxiv. 13–16. (5) He alludes to the seventy-six years' cycle of Calippus, lxxix. 5 (note).

The writer puts forward a year of 364 days, but this he did only through sheer incapacity for appreciating anything better; for he must have been acquainted with the solar year of 365¼ days. His acquaintance with the Greek cycles shows this. Moreover, in the Slavonic Enoch the year of 365¼ days is distinctly taught. It is surprising also that any writer under cloak of Enoch's name should fix upon a year of 364 days, as Enoch was early regarded as the teacher of the solar year of 365 days, owing to the significant duration of his life. And our surprise is not lessened when we consider that all the surrounding nations and peoples—the Egyptians, Persians, Arabs, Cappadocians, Lycians, Bithynians, the inhabitants of Gaza and Ascalon—observed a year of 365 days. But this year was generally a moveable year of 365 days exactly, and consequently one in which New Year's day ran through all the days of the year in the course of 1461 such years, and the festivals continually changed their season. Now the writer of Enoch recommends his year of 364 days especially on the ground that the position of the years is not prematurely advanced or delayed by a single day, lxxiv. 12. It was, therefore, nothing but his national prejudices, and possibly his stupidity, that prevented him, knowing as he did the Greek systems, from seeing that only a year of 365¼ days could effect such a result. As for Wieseler's theory that the writer held to a year of 364 days with one intercalary day each year, and one every fourth year, there is no evidence for it in the text. The author's reckoning of the year at 364 days may be partly due to his opposition to heathen systems, and partly to the fact that 364 is divisible by seven, and amounts to fifty-two weeks exactly.

TRANSLATION.

LXXII. 1. The Book of the courses of the luminaries of the heaven and the relations of each, according to their classes, their dominion and their seasons, according to their names and places of origin, and according to their months, which the holy angel Uriel, who was with me, who was their leader, showed me; and he showed me all their laws exactly as they are, and how it is with regard to all the years of the world and unto eternity till the new creation is accomplished which dureth till eternity. 2. And this is the first law of the luminaries: the luminary the Sun has its rising in the eastern portals of the heaven, and its setting in the western

---

LXXII. 1. As in the Similitudes, the superscription of this book is far from accurately describing its contents. **Dominion:** cf. lxxv. 3; lxxxii. 8–20. **Names:** cf. lxxviii. 1, 2. **Places of origin.** Probably their places of rising. **The new creation:** cf. xlv. 4; xci. 15, 16; Is. lxv. 17; lxvi. 22; II Peter iii. 13; Rev. xxi. 1. All the laws of the heavenly bodies given in this book are valid till the new creation. **2.** This verse introduces an account of the sun in its progress through the signs of the zodiac and the increase and decrease of the days and nights thereby occasioned. **Portals.** The subject of the portals has already to some extent appeared in xxxiii–xxxvi. But observe that, though portals of the winds and portals of the stars are there described, there is no mention of portals of the sun and moon. According to lxxii–lxxxii, the sun, moon, and stars pass through the same portals: can this hold true of xxxiii–xxxvi, where the portals of the stars are said to be small and situated above the portals of the wind? Moreover, in lxxii. 6 one of the sun's portals is called

portals of the heaven. 3. And I saw six portals out of which the sun rises, and six portals in which the sun sets: the moon also rises and sets through these portals, and the leaders of the stars and those led by them: six in the east and six in the west following each other in accurately corresponding order: also many windows to the right and left of these portals. 4. And first there goes forth the great luminary, named the sun, and his circumference is like the circumference of the heaven, and he is quite filled with illuminating and heating fire. 5. The chariots on which he ascends are driven by the wind, and the sun disappears from the heaven as he sets and returns through the north in order to reach the east, and is so guided that he comes to the appropriate (lit. 'that') portal and shines in the face of the heaven. 6. In this way he rises in the first month in the great portal, and indeed rises through the fourth of those six portals in the east. 7. And in that fourth portal through which the sun rises in the first month are twelve window-openings from which proceeds a flame when they are opened in their season. 8. When the sun rises in the

---

'great.' 3. **Leaders of the stars**: see lxxv. 1 (note). **Windows**: cf. ver. 7; lxxv. 7. **Right and left**, i.e. south and north, according to the familiar Hebrew use. 4. Cf. xli. 5-7, where the conception seems to be different. **His circumference.** The sun is clearly circular: cf. lxxiii. 2; lxxviii. 3; also xviii. 4; lxxviii. 4. It is doubtful whether he is conceived of as a sphere or merely as a disc. I have translated on the latter supposition. 5. The sun, as also the other heavenly bodies, traverses the heaven in a chariot, lxxiii. 2, lxxv. 3, 8, driven by the wind, xviii. 2, lxxiii. 2. **Through the north**: cf. xli. 5. **Is guided.** Possibly by an angel. In the Slavonic Enoch several angels precede the sun on his course. In i-xxxvi the heavenly bodies have a semi-conscious existence; this is not so in lxxii-lxxxii. 6. **In the first month.** The writer begins his description of the sun's course with the first Hebrew month Abib (cf. Exod. xiii. 4), the time of the spring equinox. This month, called generally after the Captivity Nisan (cf. Neh. ii. 1), was the first month of the ecclesiastical year, and corresponds to our April. The civil year began with Tishri, or October. **The great portal.** So called in contradistinction from the 'window-openings' in the next verse. Yet these portals are called 'small' in xxxvi. 2. 7. **Twelve window-openings.** There are twelve such at every portal: cf. lxxii. 3; lxxv. 7. **The flame is the source of heat**: cf. lxxv. 7. 8. The author's system, whereby he seeks to

heaven, he comes forth through that fourth portal thirty mornings in succession and sets directly opposite in the fourth portal in the west of the heaven. 9. And during this period day becomes longer than day and night shorter than night to the thirtieth morning. 10. And on that day the day is two parts longer than the night, and the day amounts exactly to ten parts and the night to eight parts. 11. And

---

LXXII. 10. **Two parts longer than the night.** G adds ተስዓት፡ እዴ, i.e. 'two ninth parts longer than the night.' The

---

replace the heathen conception of the sun's revolution through the signs of the zodiac by a scheme founded as he believes on the O.T., is as follows. There are six portals in the east through which the sun rises in the course of the year, and six in the west in which he sets. The first portal forms the most southern point of the sun's journey, and the sixth portal the most northern. During the first six months, from the shortest day to the longest, the sun advances from the first portal to the sixth, and conversely, from the longest day to the shortest, he returns from the sixth portal to the first. In each portal the sun rises and sets one month in his journey northwards, and likewise rises and sets for one month in each portal on his return journey. Thus arises the division of the year into twelve months. Moreover, during each month on his journey northwards, the day daily grows longer and the night daily shorter, and this is owing to a daily change of position on the part of the sun within each gate. Of these different positions or stations of the sun there are 364. In this way the author seeks to dispense with the signs of the zodiac. The sun's northward journey from the first to the sixth portal corresponds with his course through the signs Capricornus, Aquarius, Pisces, Aries, Taurus, and Gemini; and the sun's return journey from the sixth to the first portal corresponds with his course through Cancer, Leo, Virgo, Libra, Scorpio, and Sagittarius. Though perfectly acquainted with a year of 365¼ days, as we shall see later, the author reckoned it as consisting of 364 days, partly possibly on anti-heathen grounds, and partly for the attractive reason that the sum total is divisible by seven, and thus represents 52 sabbaths of days. The author's solar year of 364 days is made up of eight months of 30 days each, and four months of 31 days each—these latter corresponding with the spring and autumn equinoxes and the summer and winter solstices, or according to the system of our author with the sun's position in the first, third, fourth, and sixth portals. These four months have each 31 days 'on account of the sign,' i.e. that of the equinoxes or the solstices: cf. lxxii. 13, 19. The author's division of the day into eighteen parts is possibly his own device, yet it may rest on traditions derived from northern Asia of the latitude of 49°, as Krieger sup-

the sun rises from that fourth portal, and sets in the fourth, and returns to the fifth portal of the east thirty mornings in succession, and rises from and sets in the fifth portal. 12. Then the day becomes longer by two parts and amounts to eleven parts, and the night becomes shorter and amounts to seven parts. 13. And the sun returns to the east and enters into the sixth portal, and rises and sets in the sixth portal one and thirty mornings in succession on account of its sign. 14. And on that day the day becomes longer than the night, so that it amounts to double the night, i. e. twelve parts, and the night becomes shorter and amounts to six parts. 15. And the sun mounts up to make the day shorter and the night longer, and the sun returns to the east and enters into the sixth portal, and rises from it and sets thirty mornings. 16. And when thirty mornings have elapsed, the day decreases by exactly one part, and amounts to eleven parts, and the night to seven parts. 17. And the sun goes forth from that sixth portal in the west, and goes to the east and rises for thirty mornings in the fifth portal, and sets in the west again in the fifth western portal. 18. On that day the day decreases by two parts and amounts to ten parts and the night to eight parts. 19. And the sun rises from that fifth portal and sets in the fifth portal of the west, and rises for one and thirty mornings in the fourth portal on account of its sign and sets in the west. 20. On that day the day is equalised to the night and becomes of equal length, and the day amounts to nine parts and the night to nine parts. 21. And the sun rises from that portal and

---

night to eight parts. G adds 'exactly,' ጥንቁቀ. 11. **Fifth portal.** G repeats these words wrongly at beginning of next verse. 13. For ዐሐይ፡ በጸብሖ G reads ጸብሖ. **One and thirty.** G reads 'thirty.' 19. **Rises in the fourth portal on account of its sign.** G M read: 'rises in the fourth portal on

---

poses, where the longest day is twice as long as the shortest night, just as our author states it. 13. On account of its sign, i. e. that of the

sets in the west, and returns to the east and rises thirty mornings in the third portal and sets in the west in the third portal. 22. And on that day the night becomes longer than the day, and night becomes longer than night, and day shorter than day till the thirtieth morning, and the night amounts exactly to ten parts and the day to eight parts. 23. And the sun rises from that third portal and sets in the third portal in the west and returns to the east, and for thirty mornings rises in the second portal of the east, and in like manner sets in the second portal in the west of the heaven. 24. And on that day the night amounts to eleven parts and the day to seven parts. 25. And the sun rises on that day from that second portal and sets in the west in the second portal and returns to the east into the first portal for one and thirty mornings, and sets in the west in the first portal. 26. And on that day the night becomes longer and amounts to double the day: the night amounts exactly to twelve parts and the day to six. 27. The sun has (therewith) traversed the divisions of his orbit and turns again on that his orbit and enters that portal thirty mornings and sets also in the west opposite to it. 28. And on that day the night decreases in length by one part, and it amounts to eleven parts and the day to seven parts. 29. And the sun returns and enters into the second portal in the east and returns on that his orbit for thirty mornings, rising and setting. 30. And on that day the night decreases in length, and the night

---

account of its sign . . . in the fourth portal in the east.' 22. **And night becomes longer than night.** So G: ወሌሊት፡ እምሌሊት፡ ትነውኅ. F H I L N O and Dln. give 'till the thirtieth morning.' **Till the thirtieth morning.** So G ጽባሕ. Dln. 'till the thirtieth day.' 25. **In the west in the first portal.** G reads: በይእቲ፡ በአሐቲ፡ ዕለት፡ በምዕራብ፡ ሰማይ. M 'in the west in the sixth portal.' 27. **Enters that portal.** G reads: 'enters all the portals.' 28. **On that day.** F G read: 'on that night.' **By**

---

summer solstice: cf. ver. 19; lxxv. 3; lxxviii. 7. **15. Mounts up or rises up to start on his return journey to the first portal.** **22.** See Crit.

amounts to ten parts and the day to eight. 31. And on that day the sun rises from that second portal, and sets in the west, and returns to the east, and rises in the third portal for one and thirty mornings, and sets in the west of the heaven. 32. On that day the night decreases and amounts to nine parts, and the day to nine parts, and the night is equal to the day, and the year amounts exactly to three hundred and sixty-four days. 33. And the length of the day and of the night, and the shortness of the day and of the night—through the course of the sun these distinctions arise (lit. 'they are separated'). 34. On that account its course by day becomes daily longer, and its course by night nightly shorter. 35. And this is the law and the course of the sun, and his return as often as he returns sixty times and rises, i.e. the great luminary which is named the sun, for ever and ever. 36. And that which thus rises is the great luminary, being so named according to its appearance, according to the command of the Lord. 37. As he rises so he sets and decreases not, and rests not, but runs day and night, and his light is sevenfold brighter than that of the moon; but as regards size they are both equal.

LXXIII. 1. And after this law I saw another law dealing with the smaller luminary, which is called the moon. 2.

---

one part. G reads: ተስዓተ፡ እዴ፡ ዘውእቱ፡ ክፍሉ. 31. **Second portal.** 'Second' wanting in G. 35. **As often as he returns sixty times.** So G, omitting the ይገብእ፡ ስእንተ of Dln.'s text—'As often as he returns: he returns sixty times.' **The great luminary.** So G M. Other MSS. and Dln. 'the great eternal luminary.' 37. **As he rises, &c.** So G M: በከመ፡ ይወፅእ፡ ወከመዝ፡ ይበውእ. **Night.** After this word I omit with G M the phrase 'in the chariot' (Dln.).

Note. 35. **Sixty times.** The sun is one month in each portal on his northward journey, and one month in each portal on his southward: therefore two months in each portal. The author disregards for the time being the extra day in the first, third, fourth, and sixth portals. 37. **Sevenfold brighter**: cf. xci. 16; Is. xxx. 26. **As regards size ... equal.** So Lucretius believed.

LXXIII. This and the following

Her circumference is like the circumference of the heaven, and her chariot in which she rides is driven by the wind and light is given to her in (definite) measure. 3. Her rising and setting changes every month: her days are like the days of the sun, and when her light is uniform (i.e. full) it amounts to the seventh part of the light of the sun. 4. And thus she rises. And her first phase in the east comes forth on the thirtieth morning: on that day she becomes visible, and constitutes for you the first phase of the moon on the thirtieth day together with the sun in the portal where the sun rises. 5. And the one half of her projects by a seventh part, and

---

LXXIII. 4. **Thirtieth morning.** G wrongly gives ፍኖት 'portal.' **Thirtieth day.** So G M. Other MSS. and Dln.

---

chapter treat of the course of the moon. **3. Her rising and setting,** i. e. the place of her rising and setting. **Seventh part of the light of the sun:** cf. lxxii. 37; lxxviii. 4. **4. Her first phase,** lit. 'her beginning.' The moon on the first day of her reappearance is here the new moon in the popular sense, not the new moon strictly so called, which is invisible. **Thirtieth morning,** i. e. of the solar month. **Together with the sun.** The sun and moon are still in the same portal on the first day after conjunction, as each portal embraces an extent of 30 degrees, and the moon advances only 13 degrees daily. **5–8.** The author's account of the phases of the moon is very hard to follow. His scheme seems to be as follows. The lunar month amounts to 30 days and 29 days alternately. It is divided into two parts: during the first part the moon waxes from new moon to full moon in 14 days when the month is 29 days, and in 15 when the month is 30 days. During the second part the moon wanes from full moon till she disappears, always, it would seem, in 15 days. Again, the author divides the moon into 14 parts, and explains the waxing of the moon by the successive lighting up of each one of the 14 parts by the sun, and the waning by the successive withdrawal of light from the 14 parts till it all disappears. But to proceed more exactly, where there are 15 days from new moon to full moon, the author supposes an additional twenty-eighth part; this part only is lighted up on the first day of such a month, whereas one fourteenth part is lighted up each day of the remaining 14 days, till the moon becomes full. The waning which apparently always takes 15 days is the reverse of this process. Again, where there are 14 days from new moon to full moon, the moon has at the end of the first day one fourteenth part + one twenty-eighth part, i. e. three twenty-eighths, and takes an additional fourteenth part of light each of the remaining 13 days. According to the text above followed, vv. 5, 6 suppose the period from new to

her whole circumference is empty, without light, with the exception of one seventh part of her and the fourteenth part of the half of her light. 6. And when she receives one seventh part of the half of her light, her light amounts to one seventh

---

'thirtieth morning.' 5. **With the exception of one seventh part of her and the fourteenth part of the half of her light.** In this translation we have adopted the reading of G with two very slight changes, the insertion of the conjunction ወ and the transposition of the words መንፈቀ፡ እደ. The text of G is: ዘእንበለ፡ ሰብዓት፡ እዴሁ፡ ዐሥርት፡ ራብዕት፡ መንፈቀ፡ እደ፡ ብርሃኑ. This transposition is supported by the fact that Dln.'s MSS. give እደ immediately after the words of number and by the true reading in the next verse—ሰብዓት፡ እደ፡ መንፈቀ 'seventh part of half.' Thus, $\frac{1}{7}$th of it, i.e. of the half moon = $\frac{1}{14}$th of whole moon, and $\frac{1}{14}$th of half moon = $\frac{1}{28}$th of whole moon: thus, $\frac{3}{28}$ths of whole moon are lighted on the first day of new moon, when there are but fourteen days to the full moon. Dln.'s translation of his own text is, 'bis auf einen Siebentheil von seinen vierzehn Lichttheilen:' i.e. 'one seventh part of her fourteen parts of light.' Dln. says this is a clumsy expression, meaning 'one seventh of the half moon, which has seven parts, while the whole moon has fourteen parts.' But it is impossible to get such a meaning out of the German version, and, though the Ethiopic could also be rendered 'amongst her fourteen parts that could be lighted there is no light with the exception of its seventh part,' even so the sense is not good. Dln., which is supported by F H L O, is apparently an emendation of M, ፯ እዴ፡ እም፲ወ፬እዴ፡ ብርሃን, which gives a wrong sense. 6. **And when she receives one seventh part of the half of her light, her light amounts to one seventh part and the half thereof.** So G: ወበዐበት፡ ትነሥእ፡ ሰብዓት፡ እደ፡ መንፈቀ፡ ብርሃኑ፡ ወይከውን፡ ብርሃኑ፡ ሰብዓት፡ እደ፡ አሐቲ፡ ወመንፈቃ.

---

full moon to be 14 days, whereas ver. 7 supposes this period to be 15 days. 5. See Crit. Note. In this verse and the next the fractions are *fractions of half the moon*. 6. Observe when the period from new moon to full moon is 14 days that it is not said that the moon receives one fourteenth part and one twenty-eighth, but only the former: it seems, therefore, that the moon is supposed to have this one twenty-eighth to begin with. It is different in the case of the 15-days' period. On the first day of such a period the moon receives one twenty-eighth part of light: see

part and the half thereof. 7. She sets with the sun, and when the sun rises the moon rises with him and receives the half of one part of light, and in that night in the beginning of her morning [in the beginning of her day] sets with the sun and is invisible that night with the entire fourteen parts and the half of one of them. 8. And she rises on that day with exactly a seventh part and comes forth and recedes from the rising of the sun, and in her remaining days she lightens up the (remaining) thirteen parts.

LXXIV. 1. And I saw another course, and the law pre-

So also M, but that it reads ወ before መንፈቀ. There are here fourteen days to full moon. Other MSS. and Dln. give, 'and when she receives one seventh part and the half of her light, her light amounts to one fourteenth part and the half thereof.' It is to be remarked here that in the first half of this sentence the parts are fractions of the half moon, whereas in the second half the parts are treated as fractions of the whole moon. But, granting this possible, the sense is idle. If A is B, then A is B, is all it states. 7. **In the beginning of her day.** I have bracketed this as a gloss. **With the entire fourteen parts.** M reads, 'with the entire thirteen parts.' 8. **The (remaining) thirteen parts.** So G M N: ቢዶስቱ፡ ወሱባዓቱ፡ እዴ, but G omits the ወ. In the beginning of this verse it is said that the moon rises with exactly a seventh part of half of her light: during the remaining days of her waxing, she lights up the remaining thirteen parts. F H I L O and Dln. give 'the remaining fourteen parts,' but this gives a wrong sense.

---

ver. 7. 7, 8. **Half of one part of light,** i. e. one twenty-eighth. See previous notes, and observe that in this verse the fractions are fractions of the whole moon. These verses suppose the case when there are 15 days from new to full moon. On the first day the moon receives one twenty-eighth part of light, and has advanced to some slight degree out of conjunction, but still practically sets with the sun, and may be said to be invisible. On the second day she receives one fourteenth part of light, and becomes visible to that extent. Thus the one twenty-eighth part is ignored as being practically invisible. During the remaining 13 days the moon receives daily one fourteenth part of light.

LXXIV. In this chapter the writer deals shortly with the waxing and waning of the moon, her monthly change of position with regard to the

scribed to her as she performed her monthly revolution according to that law. 2. And Uriel, the holy angel who is the leader of them all, showed everything to me, and I wrote down their positions as he showed them to me, and I wrote down their months (exactly) as they were and the appearance of their lights till fifteen days are expired. 3. In single seventh parts she waxes till her light is full in the east (lit. 'completes her entire light') and wanes in single seventh parts till she is completely invisible in the west (lit. 'completes her entire darkness'). 4. And in certain months she alters her settings, and in certain months she pursues her own peculiar course. 5. And in two the moon sets with the sun, in those two middle portals the third and the fourth. 6. (That is) for seven days she goes forth and turns about and returns again through the portal where the sun rises; and in that portal her light is full and she recedes from the sun and in eight days enters the sixth portal from which the sun goes forth. 7. And when the sun goes forth from the fourth portal she goes forth seven days, so that she goes forth from the fifth and turns back again in seven days into the fourth portal and her light becomes full, and she recedes and enters into the first

---

LXXIV. 3. G reads: ፩ ለ ፯ ሱብዓት፡ እደ፡ ይፌጽም፡ ኵሉ፡ ብርሃና፡ በሠርቅ፡ በምዕራብ. **Wanes in single seventh parts till she**

---

signs and the sun, and the difference between lunar and solar years. 2. **Of them all**, i. e. the various phases of the moon. **Fifteen days**, i. e. from a conjunction till full moon or from full moon till a conjunction. 3. Cf. lxxiii and lxxviii. 4. **Her own peculiar course**, i. e. a course independent of that of the sun. 5, 6. During two months the moon sets with the sun as new moon and as full moon. When the sun is in Aries and Libra, the new moon and the full moon are in the third and fourth portals. In verse 6 the moon goes forth as it waxes from the third portal through the signs to the first portal in seven days, turns about, and returns to the portal where the sun rises, i. e. the third, in seven or eight days, and there becomes full moon, and proceeds thence through the fourth and fifth to the sixth portal, where she arrives after eight days. Thence the moon returns to the third portal in seven days. 7, 8. The scheme with regard to the fourth portal and the new moon. The moon proceeds to the sixth portal and returns to the fourth in 14 days,

portal in eight days. 8. And she returns again in seven days into the fourth portal from which the sun goes forth. 9. Thus I saw their positions, the sun rising and setting according to the order of their months. 10. And in those days the sun has an overplus of thirty days in five years taken together, and all the days which belong to one of those five full years amount to three hundred and sixty-four days. 11. And the overplus of the sun and of the stars amounts to six days: in five years, six days every year come to thirty days; and the moon falls behind the sun and stars to the number of thirty days. 12. And the moon brings in all the years exactly, so that their position is not prematurely advanced or delayed by a single day unto eternity; but (the moons) complete the changing years with perfect justice in three hundred and sixty-four days. 13. In three years there are one

---

is completely invisible. Wanting in G M. 9. **The sun rising and setting according to the order of their months.** G M read: በከመ፡ ይሠርቁ፡ እሙራት፡ ወየዐርቡ፡ ጸሐይ. 11. **In five years, six days every year.** G reads: ለ ፮ ዓመታት፡ ስሱ. 12. For

---

and thence to the first portal and back in 15 days. 10, 11. The difference between the lunar and the solar year. According to lxxviii. 15, 16, in a lunar year there are six months of 30 days, and six months of 29 days each—in all 354 days. In a solar year there are 12 months of 30 days each and four intercalary days in the equinoxes and solstices—in all 364 days (cf. lxxiv. 10, 12; lxxv. 2). Thus the difference between the lunar and the solar year amounts to 10 days. But in ver. 10^a and 11 no account is taken of the intercalary days in the solar year, so that the solar year is reckoned at 360 days. Thus the difference in this case is six days. **12.** There is manifestly a polemical tone in this verse. The writer asserts the accuracy of the moon as a time-divider against those who put forward the solar year only. The Book of Jubilees vi. protests against the use of the lunar year. **13–16.** We have here clearly a reference to the eight-year cycle or octaeteris. In this cycle an intercalary month of 30 days was inserted in the third, fifth, and eighth years of the cycle in order to reconcile the lunar and solar years, which were reckoned respectively at 354 and 365¼ days. As our author, however, does not reckon the solar year at 365¼ days, but at 364, he proceeds to reconcile this solar year of 364 days with the lunar year of 354. Thus (ver. 13) in three such solar years there are 1092 days; in five, 1820 days; in eight, 2912 days; whereas (ver. 14, 15) in three lunar

thousand and ninety-two days, and in five years eighteen hundred and twenty days, so that in eight years there are two thousand nine hundred and twelve days. 14. In three years there accrue to the moon herself one thousand and sixty-two days, and in five years she falls fifty days behind: i. e. at the close of these an addition is made to the (one thousand and) sixty-two days. 15. And in five years there are seventeen hundred and seventy days, so that the days in eight lunar years amount to two thousand eight hundred and thirty-two. 16. Thus in eight years she falls behind to the amount of eighty days, and the sum total of the days she falls behind in eight years is eighty. 17. And the year is accurately completed in conformity with their stations and the stations of the sun, as they (i. e. the sun and moon)

ይደኅሩ G gives wrongly ይሰሕሩ. 14. **Sixty-two days.** G gives ፳. **An addition is made to the sixty-two days.** G reads 'sixty-two days are added,' omitting ዲበ. 15. Again here G gives unintelligible readings: for **so that the days amount to two thousand eight hundred and thirty-two,** G reads በ፰ መዋዕል፡ ፪ወ፰ወ፰፪ወ፴ወ፪መዋዕል.

---

years there are 1062 days; in five, 1770 days; in eight, 2832 days. Thus there is a difference of 80 days between eight solar years of 364 days and eight lunar years. As all these calculations merely amount to saying that his solar year has 10 days more than the lunar, the writer had obviously the eight-year cycle before him; for only thus can we explain the external resemblance of his system to the Greek cycle: cf. Special Introd. (pp. 189–90). Unless the author had the Greek eight-year cycle before him and wished to give his own work some semblance of likeness thereto, there was no need to go through all these periods of three, five, and eight years; for they do not in fact contribute a single additional fact, but merely say over and over again that the difference between 364 and 354 days is 10 days. **14. In five years she falls fifty days behind.** We should, as Wieseler suggests, read here: 'in three years she falls thirty days behind.' This would give a good sense to the following words: 'at the close of these (i. e. three years) an addition (of 30 days) is made to the (one thousand and) sixty-two days.' That is, the addition of 30 days to the sum of three lunar years makes them equal to three solar years. Dln.'s rendering and explanation of these last words are unsatisfactory: 'Nämlich mit der Summe davon addirt man zu zwei und sechzig Tagen.' **17. With their stations,** i. e. the stations of the moons.

rise from the portals through which it (the sun) rises and sets thirty days.

LXXV. 1. And the leaders of the heads of the thousands, who are placed over the whole creation and over all the stars, have also to do with the four intercalary days, which cannot be separated from their function, according to the reckoning of the year, and those render service on the four days which are not reckoned in the reckoning of the year. 2. And owing to them men go wrong therein, for those luminaries truly render service on the world-stations, one in the first, one in the third, one in the fourth, and one in the sixth portal, and the harmony of the course of the world is brought about through its separate three hundred and sixty-four world-stations. 3. For the signs and the times and the years and the days were shown to me by the angel Uriel, whom the eternal Lord of glory sets over all the luminaries of the heaven, in the heaven and in the world, that they should rule on the surface of the heaven and be seen on the earth, and be leaders for the day and the night, i.e. the sun, moon, and stars, and all the ministering creatures which make their revolution in all the chariots of the heaven. 4. In like manner

---

LXXV. 1. **From their function.** So M: እምነ፡ ምግባሮሙ. Also G, but with sing. suffix. Other MSS. 'from their place.' **Reckoning.** So G M. Other MSS. and Dln. 'entire reckoning.'

LXXV. This chapter deals with the intercalary days, the stars, and the sun. 1. The four intercalary days are under the charge of the highest stars, the leaders of the heads of ten thousands. These are not the chiliarchs, as Dln. supposes (p. 248), but the leaders of the chiliarchs. For further development of this subject see lxxxii. 11, 12. These leaders are not angels, as might be supposed, but simply 'luminaries': cf. ver. 2. **Are not reckoned in the reckoning of the year.** Apparently the year was popularly reckoned at 360 days: cf. lxxxii. 5. 2. Men do not know of these intercalary days, and so reckon wrongly: cf. lxxxii. 4–6. 3. Yet these intercalary days are a reality; for Uriel showed them to Enoch: cf. lxxii. 1. **Signs,** i.e. of the zodiac: cf. lxxii. 13, 19. **Eternal Lord of glory.** Here only: see lxxxiv. 2 (note). **Chariots of the heaven**: cf. lxxii. 5. 4. The variation in the amount of heat given by the sun is explained by twelve openings in the disk of the sun through which heat is given forth in proportion to the number of windows

Uriel showed me in the circumference of the sun's chariot in the heaven twelve door-openings through which the rays of the sun break forth; and from them is warmth diffused over the earth, when they are opened at appointed seasons. 5. [There are also such openings for the winds and the spirit of the dew when they are opened, standing open in the heavens at the ends (thereof).] 6. Twelve portals I saw in the heaven, at the ends of the earth, out of which go forth the sun, moon, and stars, and all the works of heaven in the east and in the west. 7. And many window-openings are to the left and right of them, and one window at its (appointed) season produces warmth, corresponding (as these do) to those doors from which the stars come forth according as He has commanded them, and wherein they set, corresponding to their number. 8. And I saw chariots in the heaven, running in the world, above those portals, in which revolve the stars that never set. 9. And one is larger than all the rest and makes its course through the entire world.

LXXVI. 1. And at the ends of the earth I saw twelve portals opened for all the winds, from which the winds

---

4. **Uriel shewed me.** Wanting in G. **Through which the rays of the sun break forth and.** Wanting in G. 5. **When they are opened, standing open.** So G M N. Other MSS. add 'in their seasons.' G repeats 'when they are opened' at the end of this verse. 8. **Above those portals.** So A E G H I M N. Cf. xiv. 17. Other MSS. and Dln. give: 'above and below those portals.'

LXXVI. 1. **Opened for all the winds.** Hallévi thinks that we

---

opened. 5. The portals of the winds: cf. xxxiii–vi; lxxvi. Dln. thinks this verse is an interpolation on the ground of its inappropriateness here, and of the phrase, 'spirit of the dew,' which connects it with lx. 20. 6, 7. Adjoining each one of these twelve portals of the sun are twelve window-openings to the left and right of them: cf. lxxii. 3, 7. These diffuse warmth over the earth, one being open at a time, and all differing in degree of heating power. 9. **One is larger.** This may be the Great Bear.

LXXVI. This chapter gives a detailed account of the twelve portals of the winds and the nature of the winds which issue therefrom. The short account in xxxiii–xxxvi agrees with it. This disquisition on the nature of the winds has as much relation to reality as that on the year of 364

proceed and blow over the earth. 2. Three of them are opened on the face (i.e. the east) of the heavens, and three in the west, and three on the right (i.e. the south) of the heaven, and three on the left (i.e. the north). 3. And the first three are those towards the east, and three towards the north, and after those on the left three towards the south, and three in the west. 4. Through four of these come winds of blessing and prosperity, and from those eight come hurtful winds: when they are sent, they bring destruction on all the earth and on the water upon it, and on all who dwell thereon, and on everything which is in the water and on the land. 5. And the first wind from those portals, called the east wind, comes forth through the first portal in the east, which inclines towards the south: from it come forth destruction, drought, heat, and rain. 6. And through the second portal in the middle comes a favourable (wind), and from it there come rain and fruitfulness and prosperity and dew; and through the third portal which lies toward the north come cold and drought. 7. And after these come forth the south winds through three portals: in the first place through the first portal of those inclining to the east comes forth a hot wind. 8. And through the middle portal lying next to it there come forth fragrant smells and dew and rain and prosperity and health. 9. And through the third portal lying to the west come forth dew

---

should here render 'open to all the quarters,' see lxxvii. 1, Crit. Note. 3. **After those, &c.** So G: **ቢድኅረ፡ እሉ**, for which Dln.'s MSS. give **ቢድኅር፡ እለ**. Is his rendering possible: Zur Linken entgegengesetzt? 6. **Comes a favourable (wind).** I have emended **ርትዕ፡ ይወጽእ** in Dln.'s text into **ርትዕት፡ ይወጽእ**, as this phrase occurs in lxxvi. 11. We might also translate 'comes in a direct direction,' as in lxxvi. 11.

---

days. 2. This method of designating the four quarters of the earth was usual among the Hebrews: cf. lxxii. 3. 4. Through four of these portals come beneficial winds, i.e. the middle wind of the three in each quarter: the rest are hurtful. 5. The E.S.E. wind. 6. The E. and E.N.E. winds. 7. The S.E.S. wind. 8. The S. wind. 9. The

and rain, locusts and destruction. 10. And after these the north winds: from the seventh portal towards the east come dew and rain, locusts and destruction. 11. And from the middle portal come in a direct direction rain and dew, and health and prosperity; and through the third portal towards the west come cloud and hoar-frost, and snow and rain, and dew and locusts. 12. And after these the west winds: through the first portal adjoining the north come forth dew and rain, and hoar-frost and cold, and snow and frost. 13. And from the middle portal come forth dew and rain, prosperity and blessing; and through the last portal which adjoins the south come forth drought and destruction, conflagration and death. 14. The twelve portals of the four quarters of the heaven are (therewith) completed, and all their laws and all their plagues and all their benefactions have I shown to thee, my son Methuselah.

G I omit this phrase. 10. **North winds.** I have followed Dln. in omitting the words ዘስሙ፡ ባሕር as a gloss. **From the seventh portal towards the east.** After these words the MSS. give the following phrase, ዘታጸንን፡ መንገለ፡ አዜብ, which I have omitted on the following grounds. እንተ፡ ታጸንን means 'inclining to' or 'adjoining,' not 'opposite to.' In lxx. 5 the E.S.E. wind is described as the east wind, እንተ፡ ታጸንን፡ ለአዜብ, 'which adjoins the south.' In lxxvi. 7 the S.E.S. wind is described as the south wind, እንተ፡ ትጸንን፡ ለመንገለ፡ ምሥራቅ, 'which adjoins the east.' In lxxvi. 12 the W.N.W. wind is described as the west wind, እንተ፡ ታጸንን፡ ለመንገለ፡ መስዕ, 'which adjoins the north.' Hence in lxxvi. 10 ዘታጸንን፡ መንገለ፡ አዜብ when spoken of a north wind is absurd. For the same reason we have omitted in our translation the phrase እንተ፡ ታጸንን፡ ለመስዕ in lxxvi. 11, as it would be no less absurd in this context to speak of a north wind as adjoining the north. By the removal of these misapplied phrases the text becomes clear. 11. **Prosperity.** Wanting in G. 12. **Rain.** Wanting in G. 14. **All their benefactions.** F I.

S.W.S. wind. 10. See Crit. Note. The N.E.N. wind. 11. See Crit. Note on preceding verse. The N. and N.W.N. winds. 12. The W.N.W. wind. 13. The W. and W.S.W. winds. 14. **My son Methuselah**: cf. lxxxii. 1.

LXXVII. 1. And the first quarter is called the east, because it is the first: and the second, the south, because the Most High descends there, and there in quite a special sense He who is blessed for ever comes down. 2. And the west is named the waning quarter, because there all the luminaries of the heaven wane and go down. 3. And the fourth quarter, called the north, is divided into three parts: the first of them is for the dwelling of men: the second for the seas of water, with the valleys and forests and rivers, and darkness and clouds; and the third part with the garden of righteousness. 4. I saw seven high mountains, higher than all the mountains

---

G M give 'all benefactions,' ሰላመ፡ ኵሉ. Other MSS. and Dln. 'their benefactions.'

LXXVII. 1–3. As Hallévi (*Journ. Asiat.* 384–5; 1867) remarks, the Greek translator erred in rendering רוּחַ in these verses by 'wind' instead of by 'quarter.' In Ezek. xlii. 20 the LXX. rightly renders it by 'μέρος.' The writer had no intention of teaching the names of the winds. This is clear from his geographical division of the north, and also from his explanation of the Hebrew word דָּרוֹם, which denotes the southern region, and not the south wind. I have therefore translated in ver. 1 'and the first quarter is called the east, and the second the south'; and in ver. 2 'and the west is named the waning quarter'; and in ver. 3 'and the fourth quarter, called the north.' This rendering is absolutely necessary for the sense. 3. **The third part.** G gives, by a slip, 'the

---

LXXVII. 1-3. These verses deal not with the ten winds but with the four quarters: see Crit. Note. The first quarter is the east, i.e. קֶדֶם, because it is in front or the first, קַדְמוֹנִי. The second the south, דָּרוֹם, 'because the Most High descends there' from יָרַד רָם, or because the Most High abides there, דָּר רָם (Dln.): cf. xxv. 3. The west is called the waning quarter, for which probably there stood in the Hebrew אַחֲרוֹן, which the Greek translator rendered by ὑστερῶν. So Dln. The north צָפוֹן is divided into three parts: one for men, the second for waters, cf. צָפָה = an overflowing: for darkness and cloud, from צפן, to render invisible. The third encloses Paradise, from צפן, to reserve. Paradise is the recompense *reserved* for the righteous, Ps. xxxi. 19: cf. Hallévi, *Journal Asiat.* 1867. **The garden of righteousness**: see lx. 8 (note); lxx. 3 (note). **4.** The number seven plays a great rôle in this book, and generally in Jewish writers: cf. xviii. 6; xxiv. 2; xxxii. 1; lxi. 11; lxxii. 37; xci. 16; xciii. 10. **Seven high mountains.** These have nothing to

which are on the earth: thence comes forth hoar-frost, and days, seasons, and years pass away and vanish. 5. I saw seven rivers on the earth larger than all the others: one of them coming from the west pours its waters into the Great Sea. 6. And two of them come from the north to the sea and pour their waters into the Erythraean Sea in the east. 7. And the remaining four come forth on the side of the north to their own sea, (two of them) to the Erythraean Sea, and two flow into the Great Sea there, [according to others into the desert]. 8. Seven great islands I saw in the sea and on the mainland: two on the mainland and five in the Great Sea.

LXXVIII. 1. The names of the sun are the following: the first Orjârês, the second Tômâs. 2. And the moon has four names: the first Asônjâ, the second Eblâ, the third Benâsê,

---

second part.' 5. **Seven rivers.** 'Seven' wanting in G M. 7. **Two flow into the Great Sea.** So H M N O and Dln. G reads 'four flow into the Great Sea.' 8. **Two on the mainland and five in the Great Sea.** So F I L M O and Dln. G reads: ሰብዑ፡ ወእሉ፡ በባሕር፡ ኤርትራ.

---

do with those of xviii. 6; xxiv. 2; xxxii. 1. 5. **One coming from the west.** This must be the Nile as Dln. takes it, but the description 'from the west' if genuine is difficult. **The Great Sea,** i.e. the Mediterranean: cf. Num. xxxiv. 6, 7. 6. The Euphrates and Tigris. **The Erythraean Sea.** A general name for the Arabian, Persian, and Indian seas (Dln.). 7. **The remaining four,** i.e. the Indus, Ganges, Oxus, and Jaxartes (Dln.). **According to others into the desert.** This is manifestly a gloss. Such a second view is impossible in a vision.

LXXVIII, LXXIX. The relations of the sun and moon are again described, as well as the waxing and the waning of the moon. 1. Hallévi points out that the two names of the sun given here correspond to the two seasons of the year in Palestine: cf. iii; iv; lxviii. 15. Orjârês from אוֹר חֶרֶס is the sun when his power is diminished in the winter season; for חרס or חרש = 'potsherd' as well as 'sun.' The second name חַמָּה in our text altered into Tomas by change of ሐ and ተ denotes the sun when the heat is powerful in the summer, from חמם. 2. The four names of the moon are, as Hallévi shows, connected with its various phases. Asônjâ from אִישׁוֹן יָהּ where אִישׁוֹן is a diminutive of אִישׁ and יָהּ merely an intensive termination. This is the name of the moon in connexion with its likeness to the human face: cf. ver. 17. Eblâ, altered from לְבָנָה = the pale star, denotes the moon in her waning period. Benâsê, from בֶּן־כֶּסֶה (i.e. כסה to cover), is an appropriate name of the moon in the

and the fourth Erâe. 3. These are the two large luminaries: their circumference is like the circumference of the heaven, and in size they are both alike. 4. And in the circumference of the sun there is a seventh portion of light wherewith additions are made to the moon, and definite measures are transferred till the seventh portion of the sun is exhausted. 5. And they set and enter the portals of the west, and make their revolution by the north, and come forth through the eastern portals on the face of the heaven. 6. And when the moon rises she is seen in the heaven with the fourteenth part of the light; and in fourteen days she becomes full moon. 7. Also fifteen parts of light are added to her so that on the fifteenth day her light is full, according to the sign of the year, and there arise fifteen parts, and the moon originates in the addition of fourteenth parts (lit. 'through the half of a seventh part'). 8. And in her waning the moon decreases on the first day to fourteen parts of her light, on the second to thirteen, on the third to twelve, on the fourth to eleven, on the fifth to ten, on the sixth to nine, on the seventh to eight, on the eighth to seven, on the ninth to six, on the

---

LXXVIII. 3. **In size they are both alike.** G M read: **አምሳሊ: ክበበሙ: ከመ: ክበበ: ሰማይ: ለክልኤሆሙ: ዕሩየ**, but this addition is only a repetition of the preceding line. 4. **Definite measures.**

---

period of conjunction when she is invisible. Erâe from יָרֵחַ (i.e. from ירה to cast, dart) is suitable as a designation of the waxing or full moon. 3. Cf. lxxii. 4, 37; lxxiii. 2. 4. From lxxii. 37 and lxxiii. 3 we have already learnt that the light of the sun is sevenfold that of the moon: from lxxiii. 2 that light is added to the moon in due measure. Here we are further informed that one seventh of the light of the sun is gradually transferred to the moon, and that this seventh part is wholly transferred when the moon is full. 5. **By the north**: cf. lxxii. 5. 6-17. These verses give a detailed description of the waxing and waning of the moon, of the length of the months, &c. 6. This case where there are fourteen days from new moon to full moon has already been treated of in lxxiii. 5, 6 (notes). 7. This case where there are fifteen days from new moon to full moon has already been discussed: see lxxiii. 7, 8 (note). 8. As the moon wanes, her light decreases each day by one fourteenth part: on the fifteenth day the remainder, i.e. one twenty-eighth,

tenth to five, on the eleventh to four, on the twelfth to three, on the thirteenth to two, on the fourteenth to the half of a seventh of all her light, and all her remaining (light) disappears on the fifteenth. 9. And in certain months the month has twenty-nine days, and once twenty-eight. 10. And Uriel showed me another regulation (which determines) when light is added to the moon on which side it is added to her by the sun. 11. During all the period in which the moon is growing in her light, she is opposite to the sun as she waxes (lit. 'she waxes opposite the sun') till the fourteenth day her light becomes 'full' in the heaven, and when she is illumined throughout, her light is 'full' in the heaven. 12. And on the first day she is called the new moon, for on that day the light rises upon her. 13. And she becomes full moon exactly on the day when the sun sets in the west, and she rises at night from the east, and shines the whole night through till the sun rises over against her and she is seen over against the sun. 14. On the side whence the light of the moon comes forth, there again she wanes till all her light vanishes and the days of the month are at an end, and her circumference is empty, void of light. 15. And three

---

So G M. Other MSS., 'in definite measures it is added.' 8. **Half, &c.** So G : መንፈቀ፡ ወ፯እዴ፡ ዘሰ፡ ብርሃኑ, but that I omit ወ. 9. **Once twenty-eight.** G reads በበ፳ ኣመ፡ ወ፰, and M ወበ፡ ወበ፳፡ ወ፰.

---

vanishes. 9. **Twenty-nine days**: cf. lxxiv. 10–17; lxxviii. 15–17. **Once twenty-eight.** As we learnt from lxxiv. 13–16 that the author was acquainted with the eight-year cycle of the Greeks, so here, as Wieseler has already pointed out, we find a reference to the seventy-six year cycle of Calippus. The cycle of Calippus is really an emended Metonic cycle. According to the cycle of Meton, to which there is no allusion in Enoch, seven lunar months were intercalated in nineteen lunar years, in the third, fifth, eighth, eleventh, thirteenth, sixteenth, nineteenth, and thus the difference between the solar and lunar years at the end of this cycle was about 7½ hours. Calippus, recognising this difference, quadrupled the Metonic cycle and deducted one day from the last month of this period of seventy-six years, and thus this month had only twenty-eight days as in our text. 11. The moon waxes over against the sun on the side turned to the sun, i. e. the western side. 13. This remark is quite true. 15. Each half-year has three months of thirty days and three

months she makes of thirty days at her appointed time, and three months she makes of twenty-nine days each, in which she accomplishes her waning in the first period of time, and in the first portal in one hundred and seventy-seven days. 16. And in the time of her going out she appears for three months (of) thirty days each, and she appears for three months (of) twenty-nine each. 17. At night she appears like a man for twenty days each time, and by day like the heaven, for there is nothing whatever in her save her light.

LXXIX. 1. And now, my son, I have shown thee everything, and the law of all the stars of the heaven is completed. 2. And he showed me all their laws for every day, for every season of bearing rule, for every year, and for its going forth and for the law prescribed in every month and every week: 3. And the waning of the moon which takes place in the sixth portal: i.e. in this sixth portal her light comes to an end, and after that there is the beginning of the

---

15. **Of thirty days at her appointed time.** G reads: በመዋዕሊ፡ ወበአዘመኒ፡ ዚአሃ፡ ሶበ፡ ታኅጸጸት፡ ዚአሁ፡ ይገብር. M resembles G with variations. All other MSS. support Dln. **Twenty-nine days each.** G inserts በከመ before these words.

LXXIX. 1. **My son.** So G M. Other MSS. and Dln., 'my son Methuselah.' **The law of all the stars.** So G M. Other MSS. and Dln., 'all the law of the stars.' 2. **Of bearing rule.** So G: ዘበ፡ ሥልጣን. Dln. reads ዘበዘበ፡ ሥልጣን, which he translates 'für jede Herrschaft.' **For the law prescribed in.** G reads በትእዛዝ፡ ወ. 3. **Comes to an end.** The translator uses this verb ፈጸመ in lxxviii. 11, 13 in the opposite sense, 'to become full moon.' **Beginning of the month.**

---

of twenty-nine. **In the first period of time,** i.e. in the first half-year. The author recognises only two seasons in the year: cf. iii, iv, lxxviii. 1 (note). So often as the moon is in the first portal during the first half-year, she is waning: cf. lxxix. 3, 4. 16. **In the time of her going out,** i.e. in the second half of the year. 17. Cf. ver. 2 (note).

LXXIX. 2. **Every season of bearing rule**: see Crit. Note. 3, 4. As in lxxviii. 15 the writer showed that in the first portal during the first half of the year the moon always waned, so now he shows that in the

month: 4. And the waning which takes place in the first portal, in its season till one hundred and seventy-seven days have elapsed: reckoned according to weeks, twenty-five weeks and two days. 5. She falls behind the sun and in accordance with the order of the stars exactly five days in the course of one period, and when this place which thou seest has been traversed. 6. This is the picture and sketch of every luminary, as they were shown to me by their leader, the great angel Uriel.

[LXXX. 1. And in those days the angel Uriel answered and said to me: 'Behold I have shown thee everything, Enoch, and I have revealed everything to thee that thou shouldest see this sun and this moon, and the leaders of the stars of the heaven and all those who turn them, their tasks and times and departures. 2. And in the days of the sinners the years will be shortened, and their seed will be tardy on their lands and fields, and all things on the earth will alter and not appear in their season: the rain will be kept back and the heaven will withhold it. 3. And in those times the fruits

---

G M N omit 'month' and read ርእስ፡ ታሕጸጺት. 5. **She falls behind.** So G M. N 'and she falls behind.' Other MSS. 'and how she falls behind.'

LXXX. 1. **The angel Uriel.** So G M. Other MSS. 'Uriel.' **I have shown thee.** G reads አርኣየከ. 2. **Will alter.** G M read ይመይጥ. **Will withhold.** G reads ትቀውም.

---

second half of the year the moon always waxes in the first portal. 5. **Exactly five days.** This, according to lxxiv. 10–17, ought to be six days. Wieseler may be right in finding here another reference to the shortening of the last month in the seventy-six year period by one day: see lxxviii. 9 (note).

LXXX. For the reasons for regarding this chapter as an interpolation, see Introd. to this Book of Celestial Physics (pp. 187, 188). In that Introduction we have already remarked, that the moment we have done with lxxix we pass into a world of new conceptions, the whole interest of which is ethical and nothing else. There is absolutely no fixity in natural phenomena: their laws and uniformities are always dependent on the moral action of men: cf. IV Ezra v. 1–13 (quoted by Schodde). This line of thought is quite alien to lxxii–lxxix. 1. **Leaders of the stars**: cf. lxxii. 3; lxxv. 2, 3. **Those who turn them.** These are probably the winds: cf. lxxii. 5; lxxiii. 2. 2. Cf. Jer.

of the earth will be backward and not grow in their season, and the fruits of the trees will be withheld in their season. 4. And the moon will alter her order and not appear at her (appointed) time. 5. And in those days there will be seen in the heaven a great unfruitfulness coming on the outermost chariot to the west, and she (i.e. the moon) will shine more brightly than accords with (her) order of light. 6. And many chiefs of the superior stars will err, and these will alter their orbits and tasks, and will not appear at the seasons prescribed to them. 7. And the whole order of the stars will be concealed from the sinners, and the thoughts of those who dwell on the earth will err concerning them, and they will be estranged from all their ways, and will err and take them to be gods. 8. And evil will be multiplied upon them and punishment will come upon them to destroy everything.']

[LXXXI. 1. And he said unto me: 'O Enoch, observe the writing of the heavenly tablets, and read what is written

---

5. For ሰማይ G reads በሰማይ over an erasion, and for በምዕራብ GM read ለምዕራብ; both of which readings I have accepted. Hallévi tries to show that the text is corrupt here, and that the original reference was to the sun. 8. **To destroy everything.** So GM. Other MSS. 'to destroy them all.'

LXXXI. 1. **Writing of.** G omits; but MN, though also

---

iii. 3; v. 25. 4. Cf. for similar ideas Joel ii. 10; Amos viii. 9; IV Ezra v. 4. 5. If the present text is correct, we may safely regard the words **And in those days ... on the outermost chariot to the west** as an interpolation in this interpolated chapter. If we omit these words the text runs smoothly and intelligibly: 'The moon will alter her order and not appear at her (appointed) time, and will shine more brightly than accords with (her) order of light.' The words were probably added to the text in connexion with some recent event. It is not possible to explain them consistently with the author's scheme. 6. **Chiefs of the superior stars:** cf. ver. 1 (note). 7. **Will be concealed from the sinners:** cf. lxxv. 2; lxxxii. 4–6. **Those who dwell on the earth.** This phrase is used here exactly in the sense in which it appears in the interpolations in the Similitudes: see xxxvii. 5 (note). **Take them to be gods:** cf. Acts vii. 42.

LXXXI. For the reasons for regarding this chapter as an interpolation, see Introd. to this Book of Celestial Physics (p. 188). **1. The heavenly tablets.** For a complete account of this and kindred expres-

thereon, and mark every individual fact.' 2. And I observed everything on the heavenly tablets, and read everything which was written (thereon), and understood everything, and read the book of all the deeds of men and of all the children of flesh that will be upon the earth to the remotest generations. 3. And forthwith after that I blessed the Lord, the King of the glory of the world, in that He has made all the works of the world, and I extolled the Lord because of His patience and blessed Him because of the children of men. 4. And after that I spake: 'Blessed is the man who dies in righteousness and goodness, concerning whom there is no book of unrighteousness written, and (against whom) no day of judgment is found.' 5. And those seven holy ones brought me

---

omitting, imply its presence, and all other MSS. give it. 2. **The book of all the deeds of men.** So M: መጽሐፈ፡ ኵሉ፡ መግበሮሙ፡ ለሰብእ. So G, with one necessary grammatical change. Other MSS.: 'the book and everything which was written therein and all the deeds of men.' **Of all the children of flesh.** So G M, reading ኵሉ instead of ኵሎ. 3. **The King of the glory of the world.** So G M: ንጉሠ፡ ስብሐት፡ ለዓለም. Other MSS. and Dln., ዘለዓለም 'the eternal King of glory.' But some reference to the world in the divine title seems to be required; for God's relation to the world is dwelt on in this verse: 'He has made all the things of the world.' At the close of this chapter He is called 'the Lord of the world.' **Children of men.** So F G I L M O: ውሉደ፡ አዳም. This phrase occurs in Deut. xxxii. 8, and in the Book of Jubilees. Dln.: 'children of the world.' 4. **After that.** So G M ወእምዝ. Other MSS. 'at that hour.' **(Against whom) no day of judgment is found.** So G M: ዕለተ፡ ኵነኔ. Other MSS.: 'against whom no sin is found.' 5. **Seven.** So G M. Dln. gives 'three.' **Brought me.** G M read አቀረቡኒ.

---

sions, see xlvii. 3 (note). 3. Cf. xxii. 14 for a similar expression of praise: see Crit. Note. 4. See Introd. (p. 188) on the contrast between this blessing and that pronounced by the writer of lxxii–lxxix. **Book of unrighteousness**: see xlvii. 3 (note). **No day of judgment is found**: see Crit. Note. If this clause be taken strictly, it is here taught that there is no judgment for the righteous. 5. **Those seven holy ones.** These words have been taken by the interpolator from xc. 21, 22 or xx. Later

and placed me on the earth before the door of my house and spake unto me: 'Declare everything to thy son Methuselah, and show to all thy children that no flesh is righteous in the sight of the Lord, for He is their Creator. 6. One year we will leave thee with thy children, till again a command (comes), that thou mayest teach thy children and record (it) for them, and testify to them (even) to all thy children; and in the second year they will withdraw thee from their midst. 7. Let thy heart be strong, for the good will announce righteousness to the good: with the righteous will they rejoice, and they will offer mutual congratulation. 8. But the sinners will die with the sinners, and the apostate go down with the apostate. 9. And those also who practise righteousness will die on account of the deeds of men, and be gathered together on account of the doings of the godless.' 10. And in those days they ceased to speak to me, and I came to my people, blessing the Lord of the world.]

LXXXII. 1. And now, my son Methuselah, all these things

No flesh. G M omit the negative. 6. **Till again a command (comes).** So G: **እስከ፡ ካዕበ፡ ትእዛዝ**. Other MSS.: **እስከ፡ ካዕበ፡ ትኄዝዝ** 'till thou art strong again.' 7. **With the righteous will they rejoice.** So G M. Other MSS.: 'the righteous will rejoice with the righteous.' 10. **Lord of the world.** So G M. Dln. gives, 'Lord of the worlds.'

MSS. read 'three'—a change which may be due to lxxxvii. 2, 3. **No flesh is righteous, &c.**: cf. Job ix. 2; Ps. xiv. 1. **Creator**: cf. xciv. 10. **6. Till again a command (comes)**: see Crit. Note. These two verses, vv. 5, 6, are inserted to serve as an introduction to xci–civ. **8. The apostate will go down**, i.e. into Gehenna. **9.** The righteous die indeed, yet are they 'gathered' unto the abodes of the blessed. The phrase is borrowed directly from Is. lvii. 1, where the literal translation runs, 'the righteous is gathered out of the way of or because of the evil,' מִפְּנֵי הָרָעָה נֶאֱסַף הַצַּדִּיק: cf. II Kings xxii. 20; Book of Wisdom iv. 7–14. The Hebrew verb is used of being 'gathered to one's fathers,' Num. xx. 26. In Ps. civ. 29 God is said to 'gather' the spirit of animals when they die. **10. Lord of the world**: cf. i. 3; xii. 3; lviii. 4; lxxxi. 3; lxxxii. 7; lxxxiv. 2, 3.

LXXXII. The conclusion of the Book of Celestial Physics. **1.** In xxxiii. 4 Uriel writes down everything for Enoch; but in this book, cf. lxxii. 1; lxxiv. 2; lxxv. 3; lxxix. 2–6; lxxxii. 1, Uriel only shows the

I am recounting and writing down, and I have revealed to thee everything, and given thee books concerning all of them: (so) preserve, my son Methuselah, the books from thy father's hand and commit them to the generations of the world. 2. I have given wisdom to thee and wisdom to thy son, and to thy children that are yet to be, that they may give it to their children, generation unto generation for ever, this wisdom (namely) that passeth their thought. 3. And those who understand it will not sleep, but will listen with the ear that they may learn this wisdom and it will please those that eat (thereof) better than good food. 4. Blessed are all the righteous, blessed are all those who walk in the way of righteousness and sin not, as the sinners, in the reckoning of all their days in which the sun traverses the heaven, entering into and departing from the portals for thirty days at a time, together with the heads of thousands of this order of the stars, together with the four which are added and divided amongst the four portions of the year,

---

LXXXII. 1. **Writing down.** So G M. Other MSS. and Dln. add 'for thee.' **Generations of the world.** G reads: ውሉድ: ዓለም 'children of the world.' 2. **Wisdom to thy son.** So G: ጥበበ: ወልድከ; but ለ must be read before ወልድከ. Dln. gives 'to thy children.' **For ever.** Wanting in G M. 4. **Blessed are all those.** Wanting in G. **Divided.** So G M O ይትሌለዩ. Other

---

hidden things to Enoch, and Enoch writes them down. **Commit them to the generations of the world.** These revelations of Enoch are for all the world from the earliest generations: those in i–xxxvi are only for the far distant generations: cf. i. 2. See Special Introd. (p. 189). It is evidently this passage that Tertullian refers to in *De Cultu Fem.* i. 3: Cum Enoch filio suo Matusalae nihil aliud mandaverit quam ut notitiam eorum posteris suis traderit. **2. Wisdom.** The surpassing wisdom conveyed in these revelations is a frequent theme with the Enoch writers: cf. xxxvii. 4; xcii. 1; xciii. 10–14. **To thee and . . . to thy son**: cf. Ps. lxxviii. 5, 6. As we must infer from these words that Lamech is already born, the writer has followed the Samaritan or Masoretic reckoning: the former would allow of Noah being present. **3. Better than good food**: cf. Ps. xix. 10. **4.** The four intercalary days introduced by four leaders: cf. ver. 11; lxxv. 1, 2. **Heads of thousands**, i. e. the chiliarchs which lead

which lead them in and enter with them four days. 5.
And owing to them men will be at fault and will not reckon
them in the reckoning of the whole course of the world : yea,
men will be at fault, and not recognise them accurately. 6.
For they belong to the reckoning of the year and are truly
recorded (thereon) for ever, one in the first portal and one in
the third, and one in the fourth, and one in the sixth, and the
year is completed in three hundred and sixty-four days. 7.
And the account thereof is accurate and the recorded reckoning thereof exact; for the luminaries, and months, and festivals,
and years, and days, have been shown and revealed to me by
Uriel, to whom in my behoof the Lord of the whole creation
of the world has given command over the host of heaven.
8. And he has power over night and day in the heaven to
cause the light to give light to men—sun, moon, and stars,
and all the powers of the heaven which revolve in their
circular chariots. 9. And these are the orders of the stars,
which set in their places and in their seasons and festivals
and months. 10. And these are the names of those which
lead them, who watch that they enter at their appointed
seasons, who lead them in their places, in their orders, times,
months, periods of dominion, and in their positions. 11.
Their four leaders who divide the four parts of the year enter

MSS. and Dln. 'divide.' 8. **He has power over night and day.** G reads: ሥልጣኒ፡ ቦቱ፡ ሌሊት፡ በመዓልት. **To cause . . . to give light.** G reads ያርእዩ. 10. **Who lead them in their places.** So G M: እለ፡ ይመርሕዎሙ፡ በመካናቲሆሙ. Other MSS.

these days. 5. Cf. lxxv. 2. 6. On the four intercalary days and the portals to which they belong, see lxxv. 7. **Lord of the whole creation of the world.** Here only: cf. lxxxiv. 2. 9–20. Dln. regards these verses as a later addition to the book, but without adequate reason. They are quite in harmony with all that rightly belongs to the Book of Celestial Physics. Moreover, lxxii. 1 promises an account of the stars, and lxxix. 1 declares that the full account has now been given. This would be impossible without lxxxii. 9–20. 11. See Crit. Note. Dln.'s text of this verse, even in the Crit. Note, is practically unintelligible. There is no difficulty in the text of G M which we have followed here. The twelve

first; and after them the twelve leaders of the orders who divide the months; and for the three hundred and sixty days there are the heads over thousands who divide the days; and for the four intercalary days there are the leaders which sunder the four parts of the year. 12. And of those heads over thousands one is added between leader and leader, behind the position, but their leaders make the division. 13. And these are the names of the leaders who divide the four parts of the year which are ordained: Melkeêl, and Helemmêlêk, and Mêlêjal, and Nârêl. 14. And the names of those which they lead: Adnârêl, and Ijasûsâêl, and Ijelûmiêl—these three follow the leaders of the orders and one follows the three leaders of the orders which follow those leaders of positions that divide the four parts of the year. 15. In the beginning of the year Melkejâl rises first and rules, who is named Tamaâni and sun, and all the days of his dominion whilst he bears rule are ninety-one days. 16. And these are the signs of the days which are to be seen on earth in the days of his dominion: sweat, and heat, and anxiety; all the trees bear fruit, and leaves are produced on

---

omit. 11. **Divide the months; and for the three hundred and sixty days there are the heads over thousands who divide the days.** So G M: ይሌልዩዎሙ፡ በአውራኅ፡ ወበ፫፻ወ፷፡ እርእሶት፡ ፲፻. I have here emended ፻ in G into ፲፻ in conformity with M. M, by a slip, gives 300 instead of 360. This text is superior to Dln.'s in sense and clearness. Dln. gives: ይሌልዩዎሙ፡ በአውራኅ፡ ወበዓመት፡ ፫፻ወ፷ወ፬ምስለ፡ እርእሶት፡ ፲፻—welche die Monate u. das Jahr in 364 Tage trennen nebst den Häuptern über Tausend. 12. **Between leader and leader.** So G M. Other MSS., 'between the leader and the led.' 15. **In the beginning of the**

---

leaders of the months divide the months: the chiliarchs divide the 360 days, and the four leaders which divide the year into four parts have charge of the intercalary days. 12. I do not understand this verse. 13. Melkeêl from מַלְכִיאֵל is simply an inversion of Helemmêlêk from אֱלִימֶלֶךְ as Hallévi has shown. Mêlêjal and Nârêl are transliterations of Hebrew names. 14. This verse seems unintelligible. 15–17. The period from spring to summer = 91 days under the dominion of Melkejâl or Melkeêl, 'who is named . . . sun.' How this leader is named 'the sun'

all the trees, and the harvest of wheat, and the rose flowers, and all the flowers bloom in the field, but the trees of the winter season become withered. 17. And these are the names of the leaders subordinated to them: Berkeêl, Zalbesâêl, and another who is added a head, of a thousand called Hêlôjâsêph: and the days of the dominion of this (leader) are at an end. 18. The other leader who is after them is Helemmêlêk, named the shining sun, and all the days of his light are ninety-one days. 19. And these are the signs of the days on the earth: glowing heat and dryness, and the trees bring their fruits to ripeness and ripen and mature all their fruits, and the sheep pair and become pregnant, and all the fruits of the earth are gathered in, and everything that is in the fields, and the wine-press: these things take place in the days of his dominion. 20. These are the names, and the orders, and the leaders of those heads of thousands: Gêdâêl, and Kêêl, and Hêêl, and the name of the head of a thousand which is added to them, Asfâêl; and the days of his dominion are at an end.

---

year. 'Year' wanting in G. 16. **All the flowers bloom.** G reads ዘይወፅእ 'all the flowers which come forth.' M omits 'bloom.' 17. **Head of a thousand.** G reads ርእስ፡ ፲፻. 19. **Signs of the days.** G M read 'days of his sign.' **Ripen and mature all their fruits.** So G M. Other MSS. give, 'to maturity and cause their fruits to become dry.' 20. **The leaders.** So G. Other MSS. 'the subordinate leaders.'

---

does not appear. **16. Rose flowers.** Not known in the O.T., though the word is found in the E. version in Is. xxxv. 1; Song of Solomon ii. 1. The rose is mentioned in Ecclus. xxiv. 14; xxxix. 13; Book of Wisdom ii. 8. But in the first two passages it is probably the oleander that is referred to. **17. The leaders subordinated to them,** i.e. the leaders of the three months. **18–20.** The period from summer to autumn. **20.** This verse is confused. The three names are those of the leaders of the three months. The fourth—Asfâêl from יוספאל 'God aids,' which is merely an inversion of Hêlôjâsêph from אליוסף—is the chiliarch who has to do with the intercalary day under one of the four chief leaders. There is no account of the remaining six months. This may have been omitted by the final redactor.

SECTION IV.

(CHAPTERS LXXXIII–XC.)

THE DREAM-VISIONS. INTRODUCTION.

A. *Critical Structure.* B. *Relation of this Section to* (*a*) i–xxxvi; (*b*) xci–civ. C. *The Date.* D. *The Problem and its Solution.*

A. Critical Structure. There is no difficulty about the critical structure of this section. It is the most complete and self-consistent of all the sections, and has suffered least from the hand of the interpolator. There seems to be only one interpolation, i.e. xc. 15. Of dislocations of the text there are two: lxxxix. 48^b should be read after lxxxix. 49: see lxxxix. 48 Crit. Note; and xc. 19 should be read before xc. 16: see xc. 15 (note).

B. (*a*) **Relation of this Section to i–xxxvi.** This question can only be determined by giving the points of likeness as well as of divergence. The points of likeness or identity in (1) phraseology, and (2) in ideas, are:—

(1) 'Tongue of flesh,' lxxxiv. 1; xiv. 2: 'make the earth without inhabitant,' lxxxiv. 5; ix. 2: 'Holy and Great One,' lxxxiv. 1; x. 1: 'glorious land' (i.e. Jerusalem or Palestine), lxxxix. 40, compared with 'blessed land,' xxvii. 1: 'God of the whole world,' lxxxiv. 2, compared with 'God of the world,' i. 3. The doxology in lxxxiv. 2 appears to be a more rhetorical form of that in ix. 4.

(2) There is, in the main, the same doctrine of the fallen angels: the judgment in both is at the beginning of the Messianic kingdom: Gehenna is found in both, xc. 26; xxvii. 1: the abyss of fire for the fallen angels, xc. 24; xxi. 7–10: the conversion of the Gentiles, xc. 30; x. 21.

There is, practically, nothing that is distinctive in (2)—certainly nothing more than would refer the two sections to the same school of thought. But the evidence of (1) is of a different nature, and points, when combined with the evidence of (2), to a close connexion between the two sections either in identity of authorship, or in the acquaintance of one of the authors with the work of the other. That the latter alternative is the true one, we shall find on the following grounds:—(1) In lxxxiii. 11 the sun comes forth from the 'windows of the east'; this term is never used of the sun in i–xxxvi, nor in lxxii–lxxxii: see lxxxiii. 11 (note). 'Windows' has a different reference altogether: see lxxii. 3 (note). (2) In lxxxiv. 4 'day of the great judgment' = Deluge; in i–xxxvi and xci–civ always = final judgment: see lxxxiv. 4 (note). (3) The account of the descent of the watchers in lxxxvi. 1–3 differs from that in vi. (4) In xc. 21, 22 seven archangels are mentioned; in ix. four—yet see xx. 7, Giz. Gk. (5) In xc. 19 the period of the Sword is an important feature; yet it is not alluded to in i–xxxvi. (6) The throne of judgment is in Palestine in xc. 20–26; on Sinai in i. 4: whereas the throne on which God will sit when He comes to bless His people in xxv. 3 corresponds in locality to the throne of judgment in xc. 20. (7) Appearance of the Messiah emphasised in xc. 37, 38; not alluded to in i–xxxvi. (8) The scene of the kingdom in lxxxiii–xc is the New Jerusalem set up by God Himself; in i–xxxvi it is Jerusalem and the entire earth *unchanged* though purified, x. 18, 20. (9) Life of the members of the Messianic kingdom apparently unending in xc. 33–39; but only finite in v. 9; x. 17; xxv. 6. Life is transfigured by the presence of the Messiah in xc. 38 in the New Jerusalem; but in xxv. 5 by the external eating of the tree of life. (10) The picture on lxxxiii–xc. is developed and spiritual; that in i–xxxvi is naive, primitive, and sensuous. (11) lxxxiii–xc are only visions assigned to Enoch's earlier and unwedded life; i–xxxvi are accounts of actual bodily translations and are assigned to his later life. If these two sections were from the same author and that an ascetic, exactly the converse would have been the case.

On these grounds, therefore, identity of authorship is impossible; but the similiarities in phraseology and idea prove that one of the authors had the work of the other before him. Of the two sections there is no room for doubt that lxxxiii–xc is the later.

(*b*) **Relation of lxxxiii–xc to xci–civ.** See Special Introd. to xci–civ (pp. 262, 263).

C. The Date. The fourth period began about 200 B.C. (see note on xc. 6–17, p. 249), and marks the transition of supremacy over Israel from the Graeco-Egyptians to the Graeco-Syrians, as well as the rise of the Chasids. The Chasids, symbolised by the lambs that are born to the white sheep, xc. 6, are already an organised party in the Maccabean revolt, xc. 6 (note). The lambs that become horned are the Maccabean family, and the great horn is Judas Maccabaeus, xc. 9 (note). As this great horn is still warring at the close of the rule of the twelve shepherds, xc. 16, this section must have been written before the death of Judas, 161 B.C., possibly before his purification of the Temple.

As the fourth period began about 200 B.C., the author of lxxxiii–xc, writing in the lifetime of Judas Maccabaeus, must have expected its close between 140 and 130 B.C.; for, on the analogy of the third period, each shepherd would rule between five and six years. This expectation in connexion with Judas Maccabaeus was not unnatural, as his eldest brother, Simon, did not die till 135 B.C.

D. The Problem and its Solution. This section forms in short compass a philosophy of religion from the Jewish standpoint. It is divided into two visions, the former of which deals with the first world-judgment of the Deluge, and the latter with the entire history of the world till the final judgment. The writer does not attempt to account for the sin that showed itself in the first generation. In his view, it was not the sin of man, but the sin of the angels who fell (in the days of Jared), that corrupted the earth, lxxxiv. 4, lxxxvi–lxxxviii, and brought upon it the first world-judgment.

In the second vision the interest centres mainly on the calamities that befall Israel from the exile onwards. Why has Israel become a by-word among the nations, and the servant of one gentile power after another? Is there no recompense for the righteous nation and the righteous individual? That Israel, indeed, has sinned grievously and deserves to be punished, the author amply acknowledges, but not a punishment so unmeasurably transcending its guilt. But these undue severities have not come upon Israel from God's hand: they are the doing of the seventy shepherds into whose care God committed Israel, lxxxix. 59. These shepherds or angels have proved faithless to their trust, and treacherously destroyed those whom God willed not to destroy; but they have not therein done so with impunity. An account has been taken of all their deeds and of all whom they have wickedly destroyed, lxxxix. 61–64, and for all their victims there is laid up a recompense of reward, xc. 33. Moreover, when the outlook is darkest, and the oppression at its worst, a righteous league will be established in Israel, xc. 6; and in it there will be a family from which will come forth the deliverer of Israel, i.e. Judas Maccabaeus, xc. 9–16. The Syrians and other enemies of Israel will put forth every effort to destroy him, but in vain; for a great sword will be given to him wherewith to destroy his enemies, xc. 19. Then all the hostile Gentiles will assemble for their final struggle against Israel, still led by Judas Maccabaeus, xc. 16; but this, their crowning act of wickedness, will also be the final act in their history and serve as the signal for their immediate judgment. God will appear in person, and the earth open its mouth and swallow them up, xc. 18. The wicked shepherds and the fallen watchers will then be judged, and cast into an abyss of fire, xc. 20–25. With the condemnation of the apostates to Gehenna the great assize will close. Then the New Jerusalem will be set up by God Himself, xc. 28, 29; and the surviving Gentiles will be converted and serve Israel, xc. 30; and all the Jews dispersed abroad will be gathered together, and all the righteous dead will be raised to take part in the kingdom. Then the Messiah will appear amongst them, xc. 37; and all the righteous will be gloriously transformed after his likeness, xc. 38; and God will rejoice over them.

lxxxiii–xc were written by a Chasid in support of the Maccabean movement.

TRANSLATION.

LXXXIII. 1. 'And now, my son Methuselah, I will show thee all my visions which I have seen, recounting (them) before thee. 2. Two visions I saw before I took a wife, and the

---

LXXXIII. 1. **My visions.** So G M. Other MSS. and Dln.

The first Dream-vision, lxxxiii, lxxxiv, deals with the Deluge or first world-judgment.

LXXXIII. 2. Before I took a wife, i.e. before I was sixty-five: cf. Gen. v. 21. The name of this wife was Edna, lxxxv. 3: cf. Book of Jubilees iv. We should observe that lxxxiii–xc are only dreams or dream-visions; whereas in the other sections of the book Enoch has open intercourse with the angels, and is translated bodily and therein admitted to higher privileges than in mere visions. Yet if lxxxiii–xc came from the same hand as the other sections, the converse should have been the case on *ascetic* grounds, and Enoch should have had his bodily translations to heaven and his intercourse with the angels during his unmarried years, and his dream-visions after he had taken a

one was quite unlike the other: on the first occasion when I was learning to write, on the second, before I took thy mother, I saw a terrible vision, and concerning them I prayed to the Lord. 3. I had laid me down in the house of my grandfather Malâlêl, when I saw in a vision how the heaven collapsed and was borne off and fell to the earth. 4. And when it fell to the earth I saw how the earth was swallowed up in a great abyss, and mountains hung suspended on mountains, and hills sank down on hills, and high trees were rent from their stems and hurled down and sunk in the abyss. 5. And thereupon utterance came into my mouth, and I lifted up my voice to cry aloud, and said: "The earth is destroyed." 6. And my grandfather Malâlêl waked me as I lay near him, and said unto me: "Why dost thou cry aloud, my son, and why dost thou thus make lamentation?" 7. Then I recounted to him the whole vision which I had seen, and he said unto me: "What thou hast seen, my son, is terrible, and thy dream-vision is of grave moment as to the sin of all sin of the earth: it must sink into the abyss and be destroyed with a great destruction. 8. And now, my son, arise and make petition to the Lord of glory, since thou art a believer, that a remnant may remain on the earth. 9. My son, all this will come from heaven upon the earth, and there will be violent destruction upon earth." 10. After that I arose and

---

'the visions.' 5. **Lifted up my voice to cry aloud.** See Crit. Note, xxxviii. 2. G reads ተንሣእኩ 'I arose to cry aloud.' 7. **Is of grave moment as to.** So ኀጸበ not = 'betrifft' as in Dln.'s translation: see Lexicon, col. 607. G reads ኃይለ. **Sin of.** So G ኃጢአት, and virtually M. Other MSS. 'secrets of.' 8. **Remain on the earth.** So G M. Other MSS. and Dln. add 'and that He may not destroy the whole earth.'

---

wife. 5. **Came into my mouth,** lit. 'fell into my mouth.' The phrase denotes the spontaneous character of the cry. 7. See Crit. Note. 8. **Lord of glory.** This title is found in xxv. 3, 7; xxvii. 3, 5; xxxvi. 4; xl. 3; lxiii. 2; and 'Eternal Lord of Glory' in lxxv. 3. 9. **From heaven,** i.e. ordained of God.

prayed and implored, and wrote down my prayer for the generations of the world, and I will show everything to thee, my son Methuselah. 11. And when I had gone down and forth and saw the heaven, and saw the sun rising in the east, and the moon setting in the west, and a few stars, and the whole earth, and everything as He had known it in the beginning, then I blessed the Lord of judgment and extolled Him because He made the sun to go forth from the windows of the east, so that he ascends and rises on the face of the heaven, and sets out and traverses the path shown unto him.

LXXXIV. 1. And I uplifted my hands in righteousness and blessed the Holy and Great One, and spoke with the breath of my mouth, and with the tongue of flesh, which God has made for the children of the flesh of men, that they should speak therewith, and He gave them breath and a tongue and a mouth that they should speak therewith:

---

10. **My prayer.** G reads instead: ወሰአልኩ፡ ወጸለይኩ፡ ወ. M: ወሰአልኩ፡ ወጸሎትየ. 11. **And the whole earth.** So CDFGILMO. N and Dln. omit. **And everything as He had known it in the beginning.** Dln. has recognised the ineptness of this reading but has not suggested an emendation. Either, then, read ዘአእመርኩ instead of ዘአእመረ 'and everything as I had known it aforetime;' or, the reading of the MSS. may have been owing, as Professor Margoliouth has suggested to me, to the Greek translator confusing הֵבִין and הֵכִין. In that case we should translate 'and everything as He had established it in the beginning.' **Sets out.** So A B C E F G H M አንሥአ: see Lexicon, col. 637. Other MSS. ተንሥአ = 'sich erhob.'

LXXXIV. 1. **The children of the flesh of men.** So ABCFG HIMN: ውሉደ፡ ሥጋ፡ ሰብእ. L O and Dln. 'children of men.'

---

10. **My prayer.** Found in lxxxiv. 11. See Crit. Note. **Lord of judgment.** Here only. **Windows.** This term never used in i–xxxvi nor in lxxii–lxxxii of the sun. Portal is the word invariably used in connexion with the sun. For the word 'windows,' see lxxii. 3 (note).

LXXXIV. 1. The Holy and Great One: see i. 3 (note). **Tongue**

2. "Blessed be Thou, O Lord, King both great and mighty in Thy greatness, Lord of the whole creation of the heaven, King of Kings and God of the whole world, and Thy power and kingship and greatness abide for ever and for ever and ever, and Thy dominion throughout all generations, and all the heavens are Thy throne for ever, and the whole earth Thy footstool for ever and for ever and ever. 3. For Thou hast created and rulest all things, and hast made all things fast and no manner of wisdom escapes Thee: she departs not from her throne—Thy throne, nor from Thy presence; and Thou knowest and seest and hearest everything, and there is nothing which is hidden from Thee for Thou seest everything. 4. And now the angels of Thy heavens trespass (against Thee) and Thy wrath abideth upon the flesh of men until the day of the great judgment. 5. And now, O God and Lord and Great King, I implore and pray Thee that Thou mayest fulfil my prayer, to leave me a posterity on earth, and not to destroy all the flesh of man and make the earth without inhabitant, so that there should be an eternal destruction. 6. And now, my Lord, destroy from the earth the flesh which

---

3. **Hast made all things fast.** So G: አጸንዐከ፡ ኵሎ, which should be corrected into አጸናዕከ፡ ኵሎ. Dln. gives, 'nothing is too hard for Thee.' **Departs not.** G reads ኢተመይጠከ 'does not turn Thee away'; and M ኢትትመየጠከ.

---

of flesh: see xiv. 2. 2. Cf. ix. 4 sqq. **Lord of the whole creation of the heaven.** Here only: cf. lxxxii. 7; also lviii. 4 (note). **King of Kings.** Also in lx. 4. **God of the whole world.** Here only: cf. 'God of the world,' i. 3 (note). **All the heavens are Thy throne, &c.** From Is. lxvi. 1. 3. **She departs not from her throne—Thy throne**: cf. Book of Wisdom ix. 4, 'Wisdom that sitteth by Thee on Thy throne.' Wisdom is represented in both these passages as the assessor or *πάρεδρος* of God. The idea is to be traced to Prov. viii. 30 in the LXX. version, *ἤμην παρ' αὐτῷ*: cf. Ecclus. i. 1, *μετ' αὐτοῦ ἐστιν εἰς τὸν αἰῶνα.* 4. **Upon the flesh of men**: cf. vv. 1, 5; Job xii. 10. **Day of the great judgment**: see xlv. 2 (note). This phrase can refer here only to the Deluge. In xix. 1 it refers to the final judgment, and so always in xci–civ: cf. xciv. 9; xcviii. 10; xcix. 15; civ. 5. 5. **Great King.** Also in xci. 13. 6.

has aroused Thy wrath, but the flesh of righteousness and uprightness establish as a plant of the seed for ever and hide not Thy face from the prayer of Thy servant, O Lord."

LXXXV. 1. And after this I saw another dream, and I will show all the vision to thee, my son.' 2. And Enoch lifted up his voice and spake unto his son Methuselah: 'To thee, my son, will I speak: hear my words—incline thine ear to the dream-vision of thy father. 3. Before I took thy mother Edna, I saw in a vision of my bed, and behold a bull came forth from the earth, and that bull was white; and after it came forth a heifer, and along with this (latter) came forth two young bulls, one of them black and the other red.

LXXXV. 1. After ኵሎ G adds ሐለመ. 2. **Lifted up his voice.** See Crit. Note on xxxviii. 2. 3. **In a vision of my bed.** So G M. Other MSS. 'in a vision on my bed.' **Came forth two young bulls.** So G N: ወፅኡ፡ ክልኤቱ. Other MSS. give

---

A plant of the seed for ever: see x. 16 (note). This idea was a very favourite one: cf. lxii. 8; xciii. 2, 5, 10.

LXXXV–XC. The second Dream-vision. In this second vision the writer gives a complete history of the world from Adam down to the final judgment and the establishment of the Messianic kingdom. After the example of Daniel men are symbolized by animals. The leaders of the chosen race are represented by domestic animals, the patriarchs by bulls, and the faithful of later times by sheep. This difference is intended to mark the later declension of Israel in faith and righteousness. The Gentiles are symbolized by wild beasts and birds of prey; the fallen watchers by stars; unfallen angels by men. At times the author is obliged to abandon his symbolism, and he is not always consistent in his use of it, as the same symbol varies in meaning. Even the divine name is adapted to the prevailing symbolism. In the main the narrative is based on the O.T., but at times mythical elements from later Jewish exegesis are incorporated.

LXXXV. 2. Cf. Prov. v. 1. **3. Edna**: cf. lxxxiii. 2. **Bull.** The Ethiopic word is lâhm. This word has various meanings in the following chapters. In the sing. it = bull or heifer; in the plur. it = bulls, or cattle, or cows. The context must determine the sense. The author uses also the unequivocal word sôr, which always means a bull. Ta'wa = vitulus or vitula in these chapters. Eve is so designated in this verse, i. e. a heifer, to denote her as a virgin. In ver. 6 she is called 'a cow.' **White** is the colour that symbolizes righteousness throughout this vision: cf. lxxxv. 8; lxxxvii. 2, &c. Cf. Is. i. 18; Ps. li. 7; Rev. vii. 14. **Two young bulls**: see Crit. Note. Cain is black, as this colour symbolizes his sin: Abel is red—the

4. And that black young bull gored the red one and pursued him over the earth, and thereupon I could no longer see that red young bull. 5. But that black young bull grew and a heifer joined him, and I saw that many oxen proceeded from him which resembled and followed him. 6. And that cow, that first one, went from the presence of that first bull in order to seek that red young bull, but found him not, and thereupon raised a great lamentation and (still) kept seeking him. 7. And I looked till that first bull came to her and quieted her, and from that hour onward she cried no more. 8. After that she bore another white bull, and after him she bare many bulls and black cows. 9. And in my sleep I saw that white bull likewise grow and become a great white bull, and from him proceeded many white oxen which resembled him. 10. And they began to beget many white oxen which resembled them, one following the other (in due succession).

LXXXVI. 1. And again I saw with mine eyes as I slept, and I saw the heaven above, and behold a star fell from heaven, and it arose and ate and pastured amongst those oxen. 2. And after that I saw the large and black oxen, and behold

---

ወፅአ፡ ካልእ 'came forth other young bulls.' 5. **But that black.** G omits 'but that.' **Followed him.** G M read 'followed them.' 6. For ሶቤሃ 'thereupon' G reads ኀቤሁ. 8. **Another white bull.** For 'another' G reads ክልኤ 'a pair of white oxen': i.e. Seth and a sister to be his wife.

LXXXVI. 1. **Pastured amongst those oxen.** 2. **And after**

---

colour emblematic of his martyrdom. 4. **Young bull.** So I render ta'wa when it = vitulus, as in vv. 4, 5, 6. 5. **A heifer.** The same word is used of Eve in ver. 3. This heifer is Cain's wife, and according to the Book of Jubilees iv. his sister, by name Avan. **Oxen.** This is the rendering of the plural of lâhm, and includes bulls and cows. 6. **Eve seeks Abel.** 8. **Another white bull,** i. e. Seth, but see Crit. Note. **Black cows.** The adjective 'black' belongs probably to the 'bulls' also. 9. **Bull.** Rendering of sôr: see ver. 3. This bull is Seth. The descendants of Seth are likewise righteous like their progenitor.

LXXXVI. 1. **A star,** i. e. Azazel or Semjaza; for we cannot be sure which of the two forms of the myth is followed here, as it differs from the account given in vi, where all descended together. In the Talmud (Weber, *L. d. T.* 244) these angels descend together. 2. **The result**

they all changed their stalls and pastures and their cattle, and began to live with each other. 3. And again I saw in the vision, and looked towards the heaven, and behold I saw many stars descend and cast themselves down from heaven to that first star, and they became bulls amongst those cattle and (remained) with them, pasturing amongst them. 4. And I looked at them and saw, and behold they all let out their privy members, like horses, and began to cover the cows of the oxen, and they all became pregnant and bare elephants, camels, and asses. 5. And all the oxen feared them and were affrighted at them, and they began to bite with their teeth and to devour, and to gore with their horns. 6. And they began then to devour those oxen; and behold all the children of the earth began to tremble and to quake before them and to flee.

LXXXVII. 1. And again I saw how they began to gore each other and to devour each other, and the earth began to cry aloud. 2. And I again raised mine eyes to heaven, and I saw in the vision, and behold there came forth from heaven

---

that I saw the large and black oxen. For this G reads shortly, 'pastured amongst those large black oxen.' 2. For ወእምዝ፡ ርእኩ M gives ወእሙንቱ፡ ርእኩ፡ እልክቱ. **Began to live with each other.** So G: አኀዙ፡ የሐይዉ፡ ፀምስለ፡ ካልኡ. This alludes to the alliances between the Sethites and Cainites. Other MSS. 'began to lament one with another.' But the time for this had not yet come: it has come in verse 6. 3. **Became bulls amongst those cattle and (remained) with them.** So G M: ማእከለ፡ እልኩ፡ ጣዕዋ፡ እልህምት፡ ኮኑ፡ ወምስሌሆሙ. Other MSS.: 'were amongst those cattle and oxen. There they were with them.' 6. **To flee.** After these words G M add እምኔሆሙ.

---

of the fall of the angels was the intermingling of the Sethites and Cainites. The 'large' oxen are probably the Sethites, and the 'black' the Cainites. Began to live with each other: see Crit. Note. 3. **Fall of the rest of the angels.** 4. **Elephants, camels, and asses.** Symbolizing the three kinds of giants: see vii. 2 (note). 6. **The children of the earth,** i. e. those of purely human descent as opposed to the watchers and their children.

LXXXVII. 1. The conflict of the

beings who were like white men: one of them came forth from that place and three with him. 3. And those three who had last come forth grasped me by my hand and took me up, away from the generations of the earth, and brought me up to a lofty place, and showed me a tower raised high above the earth, and all the hills were lower. 4. And they said unto me: "Remain here till thou seest everything that befalls those elephants and camels and asses, and the stars and the oxen, and all of them."

LXXXVIII. 1. And I saw one of those four who had come forth before, and he seized that first star which had fallen from the heaven and bound it hand and foot and laid it in an abyss: now that abyss was narrow and deep, and horrible and dark. 2. And one of them drew his sword and gave it to those elephants and camels and asses: then they began to smite each other, and the whole earth quaked because of them. 3. And as I was beholding in the vision, lo then one of those four who had come forth cast (them)

LXXXVII. 3. **All the hills were lower.** G reads: ሕጹጽ፡ ኵሉ፡ አህጉር. M: ሕጹጽ፡ ኵሉ፡ አውግር. Other MSS. support Dln. 4. **And the oxen and all of them.** So G M. Other MSS. 'and all the oxen.'

LXXXVIII. 2. **Camels and.** Wanting in G. 3. **One . . .**

---

bulls and giants. **2. Beings who were like white men**, i. e. unfallen angels. As men are represented by animals, the unfallen angels are naturally represented by men. **White**: cf. lxxxv. 3. **One . . . and three with him.** The 'one' is probably Michael. This is the first real occurrence of the 'three angels' in Enoch. It is found again in xc. 31. It is from the present passage that the interpolator of lxxxi borrowed this phrase: cf. lxxxi. 5. **3, 4.** If we are to regard this high tower as Paradise, and it seems we must, as according to the universal tradition of later times Enoch was translated thither, we have in lxxxiii–xc a conception of its locality and inhabitants differing from any that has preceded: see lx. 8 (note).

LXXXVIII. There is a very close connexion between this chapter and x. 4–14, but the variations are numerous enough to preclude any necessity for supposing the same authorship. **1.** Cf. x. 4–8, where Rufael binds Azazel. **2.** In x. 9, 10 Gabriel executes this task. **3.** In x. 12–14 it is really Gabriel who binds and imprisons the fallen watchers, for x. 11 which speaks of Michael is an interpolation. The

down from heaven, and they gathered and took all the great stars whose privy members were like those of horses, and bound them all hand and foot, and laid them in an abyss of the earth.

LXXXIX. 1. And one of those four went to that white bull and instructed him in a secret, as he trembled: he was born a bull and became a man, and built for himself a great vessel and dwelt thereon; and three bulls dwelt with him in that vessel and they were covered in. 2. And again I raised mine eyes toward heaven and saw a lofty roof, with seven water torrents thereon, and those torrents poured much water into an enclosure. 3. And I saw again and behold fountains were opened on the earth in that great enclosure, and that water began to swell and rise upon the earth, and it hid that enclosure from view till the whole surface of it was covered with water. 4. And the water, the darkness, and mist increased upon it; and as I looked at the height of that flood it rose above the height of that enclosure, and streamed over that enclosure, and remained on the earth. 5. And all the cattle of that enclosure were gathered together until I saw how they sank and were swallowed up and perished in

---

cast (them) down from heaven, and they gathered. So G M. Other MSS.: 'One . . . cast (them) down from heaven and gathered.'

LXXXIX. 1. **To that white bull.** So M. All other MSS. 'to those white bulls.' **As he trembled.** G inserts a negative here: 'fearless as he was.' 2. **Poured much water.** G reads ይውሕዝ 'flowed with much water.' 3. **Hid that enclosure from view.** G: አርአየ፡ ለውእቱ፡ ዐጸደ. M: ኢርአየ፡ ለውእቱ፡ አጸደ.

---

implication here, however, is that it is not Gabriel but another of the five who is the agent of judgment. **In an abyss of the earth.** In x. 12 'under the hills.'

LXXXIX. 1–9. The Deluge and the Deliverance of Noah. **1.** Cf. x. 1–3, where Uriel visits Noah for the same end. **To that white bull:** see Crit. Note. In order to build the Ark, Noah is represented as becoming a man. **Three bulls.** Noah's three sons. **Covered in:** cf. Gen. vii. 16; En. lxvii. 2. **2.** As men are symbolized by animals, their place of habitation is naturally called a pen, fold, or enclosure. **Seven:** cf. lxxvii. 4 (note). **3, 4.** The Deluge.

that flood. 6. But that vessel floated on the water, while all the oxen and elephants and camels and asses sank to the bottom together with all the animals, so that I could no longer see them, and they were not able to come out, but perished and sank into the depths. 7. And again I saw in the vision till those water torrents were removed from that high roof, and the chasms of the earth were levelled up and other abysses were opened. 8. Then the water began to run down into these, till the earth became visible; but that vessel settled on the earth and the darkness retired and light appeared. 9. But that white bull which had become a man came out of that vessel, and the three bulls with him, and one of the three was white like to that bull, and one of them was red as blood, and one black; and that white bull

---

6. **Asses sank to the bottom.** We have in ተሰጥሙ: ውስተ: ምድር an idiomatic use of ምድር. See Lexicon, col. 217: practically the same expression recurs in this verse, 'sank into the depths,' ተሰጥሙ: ውስተ: ቀላይ. 'Bottom of the sea' may be expressed either by ምድረ: ባሕር or ቀላየ: ባሕር. Dln.'s rendering 'the asses on the earth sank,' though admissible grammatically, can hardly be right here. 7. **The chasms of the earth were levelled up**: ንቅዐት: ምድር: ዐረየ. Dln. renders: 'Die Quellen der Erde versiegten,' 'the fountains of the earth dried up,' mistaking by a strange oversight ንቅዐት for እንቅዐታት of verse 3. This mistake led him to a forced and unreal rendering of ዐረየ. The writer conceives the flood as having been caused by a cleaving of the depths of the earth. Cf. Gen. vii. 11 ተሠጡ: ኵሉ: ቀላያት, and the staying of the flood as having been due to a closing or levelling up of these clefts or chasms. For this use of ዐረየ, cf. Baruch v. 7, 'the valleys shall be filled up,' ወይዐሪ: ምድር = εἰς ὁμαλισμὸν τῆς γῆς. This idea of closing the abysses was a familiar one: cf. Prayer of Manasses 3, ὁ κλείσας τὴν ἄβυσσον; and Book of Jubilees vi, 'the mouth of the depth of the abyss was closed.' 9. **And one**

---

6. **Sank to the bottom**: see Crit. Note. **With all the animals**, i.e. the real animals. 7. **The chasms of the earth, &c.**: see Crit. Note. 9. **Noah and his three sons. That white bull departed from them,**

departed from them. 10. And they began to bring forth beasts of the field and birds, so that there arose out of them all together a multitude of kinds: lions, tigers, dogs, wolves, hyenas, wild boars, foxes, squirrels, swine, falcons, vultures, kites, eagles, and ravens; and among them was born a white bull. 11. And they began to bite one another; but that white bull which was born amongst them begat a wild ass and a white bull with it, and the wild ass multiplied. 12. But that bull which was born from him begat a black wild boar and a white sheep; and that wild boar begat many boars, but that sheep begat twelve sheep. 13. And when those twelve sheep had grown, they gave up one of them to the asses, and these asses again gave up that sheep to the wolves, and that sheep grew up among the wolves. 14. And the Lord brought the eleven sheep to live with it and to

---

black. Wanting in G M. 10. **Tigers.** G reads ኣንበርት = 'sea monsters,' but this word is frequently confused in MSS. with ኣናምርት = 'tigers.' For ኣጽዐብት G reads ጽበዐት; but no such word exists. For ኣውስት 'vultures' G reads ኣንስርት, which can have the same meaning. 11. For ይትናሰኩ, 'bite each other,' G reads ይትናሰኑ. This form is not found elsewhere. 12. **And that wild boar begat many boars.** Wanting in G I.

---

i. e. Noah died. **10.** The necessities of his subject oblige the author to mar the naturalness of his symbolism. His cattle produce all manner of four-footed beasts and birds of prey. Nearly all these appear later as the enemies of Israel. **A white bull,** i. e. Abraham. **11.** The wild ass is Ishmael, the progenitor of the Arabs or Midianites, who in vv. 13, 16 are called the 'wild asses,' which is on the whole an apt designation: cf. Gen. xvi. 12. The 'white bull' is Isaac. **12. A black wild boar,** i. e. Esau. Later Jewish hatred thus expresses itself in associating Edom with the name of the animal it detested most: cf. vv. 42, 43, 49, 66. In ver. 72 it is used of the Samaritans. **A white sheep,** i. e. Jacob. Israel is specially in the symbolic language of the O.T. the sheep of God's pasture, Pss. lxxiv. 1; lxxix. 13; c. 3; Jer. xxiii. 1, and hence there is a peculiar fitness in representing the individual who first bore the name as a white sheep. The idea of declension in faith (see p. 227) can hardly attach to this instance of its use. **13. One of them,** i. e. Joseph. **The asses,** the Midianites: cf. vv. 11, 16. **The wolves,** i. e. the Egyptians—hence

pasture with it among the wolves; and they multiplied and became many flocks of sheep. 15. And the wolves began to fear them, and they oppressed them till they destroyed their (the sheep's) young, and they cast their young into a river of much water; but those sheep began to cry aloud on account of their young, and to complain unto their Lord. 16. And a sheep which had been saved from the wolves fled and escaped to the wild asses; and I saw the sheep how they lamented and cried and besought their Lord with all their might till that Lord of the sheep descended at the voice of the sheep from a lofty abode, and came to them and pastured them. 17. And He called that sheep which had escaped the wolves, and spake with it concerning the wolves that it should admonish them not to touch the sheep. 18. And the sheep went to the wolves according to the word of the Lord, and another sheep met it and went with it, and the two went and entered together into the assembly of those wolves, and spake with them and admonished them not to touch the sheep from henceforth. 19. Thereupon I saw the wolves and how they oppressed the sheep exceedingly with all their power; and the sheep cried aloud. 20. And their Lord came to the sheep and began to smite those wolves: then the wolves began to make lamentation; but the sheep became quiet and forthwith ceased to cry out. 21. And I saw the sheep till they departed from amongst the wolves; but the eyes of the wolves were blinded, and those

16. **Pastured them.** Cf. ver. 28. Dln. 'nach ihnen sah.' 18. **Met it and went with it, and the two went and entered.** So G, and virtually M. Other MSS. 'met that sheep and went with it and the two entered.' 20. **And their Lord came . . . and began.** G reads 'and their Lord came ... and they began,' እኅዙ: ይዝብጥዎሙ.

forth their standing designation in this vision. 16. **A sheep which had been saved,** i. e. Moses. **Lord of the sheep.** This title is the usual one in this and the following chapters, and occurs about twenty-eight times. 18. **Another sheep,** i. e. Aaron. 20. The plagues of Egypt. 21-

wolves departed in pursuit of the sheep with all their power. 22. And the Lord of the sheep went with them, as their leader, and all His sheep followed Him: His face was dazzling and glorious and terrible to behold. 23. But the wolves began to pursue those sheep till they found them by a sea of water. 24. And this sea was divided, and the water stood on this side and on that before their face, and their Lord who led them placed Himself between them and the wolves. 25. And as those wolves did not yet see the sheep, they proceeded into the midst of that sea, and the wolves pursued the sheep, and those wolves ran after them into that sea. 26. And when they saw the Lord of the sheep, they turned to flee before His face, but that sea gathered itself together, and resumed its own nature suddenly, and the water swelled and rose till it covered those wolves. 27. And I saw till all the wolves which pursued those sheep perished and were drowned. 28. But the sheep escaped from that water and went forth into a wilderness, where there was no water and no grass; and they began to open their eyes and to see; and I saw the Lord of the sheep pasturing them and giving them water and grass, and that sheep going and leading them. 29. And that sheep ascended to the summit of that lofty rock, and the Lord of the sheep sent it to them. 30. And after that I saw the Lord of the sheep standing before them, and His appearance was great and

---

22. **Glorious and terrible to behold.** So G M: ክቡር፡ ወግሩም፡ በርእዩ. Dln. gives, 'His appearance was terrible and glorious.' 24. **And on that.** Wanting in G. 28. **Began to open their eyes and to see.** G reads ይሬእዩ: 'began to open their eyes and they saw.' 30. **Great and terrible.** So G M: ዐቢይ፡ ወግሩም.

---

27. **The Exodus from Egypt.** 28–40. **Journeyings through the wilderness, the giving of the law on Sinai, and the occupation of Palestine.** 28. **Began to open their eyes**, i.e. to recover their spiritual vision and return to God: cf. lxxxix. 32, 33, 41, 44, 54; xc. 6, 9, 10, 26, 35. 29. **Moses' ascent of Sinai and return to Israel at God's command, Exod. xix.**

terrible and majestic, and all those sheep saw Him and were afraid before His face. 31. And they all feared and trembled because of Him, and they cried to that sheep which was with them, which was amongst them: "We are not able to endure the presence of our Lord or to behold Him." 32. And that sheep which led them again ascended to the summit of that rock, but the sheep began to be blinded and to wander from the way which he had showed them, but that sheep wot not thereof. 33. And the Lord of the sheep was wrathful exceedingly against them and that sheep discovered it, and went down from the summit of the rock, and came to the sheep, and found the greatest part of them blinded and fallen away. 34. And when they saw it, they feared and trembled at its presence, and desired to return to their folds. 35. And that sheep took other sheep with it, and came to those sheep which had fallen away, and thereupon began to slay them; and the sheep feared its presence, and (thus) that sheep brought back those sheep that had fallen away, and they returned to their folds. 36. And I saw in this vision till that sheep became a man and built a house for the Lord of the sheep, and placed all the sheep in that house. 37. And

---

Dln.'s MSS. omit 'great and.' 31. Dln. gives 'after that sheep that was with Him to the other sheep which was amongst them.' G reads: ለዝኩ፡ በግዐ፡ ምስሌሆሙ፡ ዘሀሎ፡ ማእከሎሙ, and this we have followed; for Dln.'s MSS. and others give a wrong sense: Moses was not with God when the people appealed to him, Exod. xx. 18 ff.; Deut. v. 19 ff.; but amongst them, and no appeal whatever was made to Aaron. 32. **Again ascended.** ወገብአ ... ወዐርገ: or simply 'returned and ascended.' 33. **Fallen away.** So GM. Other MSS. and Dln. add 'from His path.' 35. **Thereupon.** G reads እንዘ. 36. **In this vision.** So

---

31. That sheep which was with them, i.e. Aaron: see Crit. Note. **32.** Cf. Exod. xxiv. 12 sqq.; xxxii. **34. It**, i.e. Moses. **Return to their folds**, i.e. to abandon their errors. **35.** Cf. Exod. xxxii. 26–29. **36. That sheep**, i.e. Moses becomes a man to build the tabernacle: cf. vv. 1, 9. **Placed all the sheep in that house**, i.e. made the tabernacle the

I saw till this sheep which had met that sheep which led the sheep fell asleep; and I saw till all the great sheep perished and little ones arose in their place, and they came to a pasture, and approached a stream of water.
38. Then that sheep which led them and became a man withdrew from them and fell asleep, and all the sheep sought it and lamented over it with a great lamentation.
39. And I saw till they left off crying for that sheep and crossed that stream of water, and there always arose other sheep as leaders in the place of those which had led them and fallen asleep (lit. 'had fallen asleep and led them').
40. And I saw till the sheep came to a goodly place and a pleasant and glorious land, and I saw till those sheep were satisfied; and that house stood amongst them in the pleasant land.
41. And sometimes their eyes were opened, and sometimes blinded, till another sheep arose and led them and brought them all back, and their eyes were opened.

G M **በዝራእዩ**. Other MSS. and Dln., 'there the vision.' 37. Instead of **ለዝኩ፡ በግዕ** G gives the confused text **ዝኩ፡ ለበግዕ**. **Which led the sheep.** G M read 'which led them.' 41. **And sometimes their eyes were opened.** Wanting in G.

---

centre of their worship. **37.** Death of Aaron and of all the generation that had gone out of Egypt. **Pasture.** The land to the east of Jordan. **A stream.** The Jordan. **38.** Death of Moses: cf. Deut. xxxiv. **39. Other sheep as leaders.** The Judges, including Joshua. **40.** Palestine: cf. xxvi. 1. Observe that the epithet 'glorious' is used in the same connexion by Dan. xi. 16, 41. **41–50.** History of the times of the Judges to the building of the Temple. Of vv. 42–49 there is preserved a valuable fragment of the Greek version. This was published by Mai from a Vatican MS. in the *Patrum Nova Bibliotheca*, t. ii. I have given this fragment for purposes of comparison with the English version of the Ethiopic. The ἐξῆς which occurs between two verses belonging immediately to each other, i. e. 46, 47, and the φησίν inserted in ver. 47 prove that the collector of these Greek excerpts had not the complete Enoch before him, but drew them from an author who had brought together passages from Enoch and annotated them. So Gildemeister, *Zeitschrift D. M. G.*, 1855, pp. 621 sqq. **41.** Periods of religious advance and declension: work of Samuel.

42. And the dogs and the foxes and the wild boars began to devour those sheep till the Lord of the sheep raised up another sheep, a ram from their midst, which led them. 43. And that ram began to butt on either side those dogs, foxes, and wild boars till he had destroyed them all. 44. And the eyes of that sheep were opened and it saw that ram, which was amongst the sheep, forgetting its dignity and beginning to butt those

Greek fragment from Vatican MS., published by Mai, *Patrum Nova Bibliotheca*, t. ii, deciphered by Gildemeister in the *ZDMG*, 1855, pp. 621, 622.

Ἐκ τοῦ τοῦ Ἐνὼχ *βιβλίου χρῆσις.*

Καὶ οἱ *κύνες ἤρξαντο κατεσθίειν τὰ πρόβατα καὶ οἱ ὕες καὶ οἱ ἀλώπεκες κατήσθιον αὐτά, μέχρι οὗ ἤγειρεν ὁ κύριος τῶν προβάτων κριὸν ἕνα ἐκ τῶν προβάτων.* Καὶ *ὁ κριὸς οὗτος ἤρξατο κερατίζειν καὶ ἐπιδιώκειν ἐν τοῖς κέρασιν καὶ ἐνετίνασσεν εἰς τοὺς ἀλώπεκας καὶ μετ' αὐτοὺς εἰς τοὺς ὕας καὶ ἀπώλεσεν ὕας πολλοὺς καὶ μετ' αὐτοὺς . . . τὸ τοὺς κύνας.* Καὶ *τὰ πρόβατα ὧν οἱ ὀφθαλμοὶ ἠνοίγησαν ἐθεάσοντο τὸν κριὸν*

---

42. **Till the Lord of the sheep raised up another sheep.** So G, against all other MSS.: **እስከ፡ አንሥአ፡ ካልአ፡ በግዐ፡ እግዚእ፡ አባግዕ**. The slight error here of **ካልአ፡ በግዐ** for **ካልዐ፡ በግዐ** explains the origin of the later and corrupt reading **ተንሥአ** for **አንሥአ** in an attempt to emend the text. G is confirmed by the Gk. *μέχρι οὗ ἤγειρεν ὁ κύριος τῶν προβάτων κριὸν ἕνα.* Other MSS. give 'till another sheep, the Lord of the sheep, arose.' Dln. in his translation leaves out the words 'Lord of the sheep' as a gloss. The words 'another sheep' are, I believe, a gloss, and we should render 'raised up a ram from

---

42. The dogs and the foxes and the wild boars. The 'dogs' are, according to vv. 46, 47, the Philistines. The 'foxes' are taken by Dln. to be the Amalekites, but this interpretation will not suit ver. 55 where the foxes are still notable foes of Israel close on the time of the Exile, whereas the Amalekites practically disappear from history with the reign of David. We shall most probably be right in taking the 'foxes' to mean the Ammonites. From the earliest times down to the wars of the Maccabees the Ammonites were always the unrelenting foes of Israel. This is the view also of the glosser on the Greek Fragment, vv. 42–49. The 'wild boars' are the Edomites: cf. vv. 12, 43, 49, 66. **Till the Lord of the sheep raised, &c.:** see Crit. Note. **43. Destroyed them all.** The Greek text (*ἀπώλεσεν πολλούς*) is here decidedly better. Saul by no means destroyed them all. **44. The eyes of that sheep were opened.**

sheep and trampling upon them and behaving itself unseemly. 45. And the Lord of the sheep sent the lamb to another lamb and raised it to being a ram and leader of the sheep instead of that ram which had been forgetful of its dignity. 46. And it went to it and spake with it alone, and raised it to being ram, and made it the prince and leader of the sheep; but during all these things those dogs oppressed the sheep. 47. And the first ram pursued that second ram, and that second ram arose and fled before it; and I saw till those dogs pulled down the first

τὸν ἐν τοῖς προβάτοις, ἕως οὗ ἀφῆκεν τὴν ὁδὸν αὐτοῦ καὶ ἤρξατο πορεύεσθαι ἀνοδίᾳ. Καὶ ὁ κύριος τῶν προβάτων ἀπέστειλεν τὸν ἄρνα τοῦτον ἐπὶ ἄρνα ἕτερον τοῦ στῆσαι αὐτὸν εἰς κριὸν ἐν ἀρχῇ τῶν προβάτων ἀντὶ τοῦ κριοῦ τοῦ ἀφέντος τὴν ὁδὸν αὐτοῦ. Καὶ ἐπορεύθη πρὸς αὐτὸν καὶ ἐλάλησεν αὐτῷ σιγῇ κατὰ μόνας καὶ ἤγειρεν αὐτὸν εἰς κριὸν καὶ εἰς ἄρχοντα καὶ εἰς ἡγούμενον τῶν προβάτων καὶ οἱ κύνες ἐπὶ πᾶσι τούτοις ἔθλιβον τὰ πρόβατα. Ἑξῆς δὲ τούτοις γέγραπται ὅτι ὁ κριὸς ὁ πρῶτος τὸν κριὸν τὸν δεύτερον ἐπεδίωκεν καὶ ἔφυγεν ἀπὸ προσώπου αὐτοῦ· εἶτ' ἐθεώρουν, φησίν, τὸν κριὸν τὸν πρῶτον ἕως οὗ ἔπεσεν ἔμπροσ-

---

amongst them.' So Gk. 45. **The lamb to another lamb.** So Gk. All Ethiopic MSS. give 'the sheep to another sheep.' Cf. ver. 48, Crit. Note. **Instead of that ram.** So D, ሐርጊ: በግዕ; and Gk. ἀντὶ τοῦ κριοῦ. Other MSS. 'instead of that sheep.'

This phrase as applied to Samuel here cannot be used in the sense of spiritual awakening and return to God which it has elsewhere in this vision: cf. ver. 28 (note). Here it must mean the prophetic gift of insight as in i. 2. The Greek version certainly escapes this difficulty by applying the phrase in its usual sense to the sheep, and is probably the true text. **45, 46. David anointed king.** Observe that in ver. 45 the Greek used ἄρνα and not πρόβατον for Samuel and for David so long as the latter is not yet king, where the Ethiopic employs the more general term 'sheep.' Observe further that Solomon previous to his coronation, ver. 49, is called 'a little sheep,' i. e. a lamb. I have followed the Greek;

ram. 48. And that second ram arose and led the sheep, and that ram begat many sheep and fell asleep; and a little sheep became ram in its stead and became prince and leader of those sheep. 49. And those sheep grew and multiplied; and all the dogs and foxes and wild boars feared and fled before it,

θεν τῶν κυνῶν. Καὶ *ὁ κριὸς ὁ δεύτερος ἀναπηδήσας ἀφηγήσατο τῶν προβάτων.* Καὶ *τὰ πρόβατα ηὐξήθησαν καὶ ἐπληθύνθησαν· καὶ πάντες οἱ κύνες καὶ οἱ ἀλώπεκες ἔφυγον ἀπ' αὐτοῦ καὶ ἐφοβοῦντο αὐτόν.*

and that ram butted and killed all the wild beasts, and those wild beasts had no longer any power among the sheep and robbed them no more of ought. 50. And that house

---

48. **Arose.** G reads ንሥአ for ተንሥአ, and M ንሥአሙ. **Led the sheep.** So Gk. Ethiopic MSS. give 'led the little sheep.' But the word 'little' should be omitted, as it is wanting in the Gk., and the expression 'little sheep' is pointless here, and found but once before in ver. 37. It crept into the text from the next line. The rest of the verse is also wanting in the Gk., but this is so, only because the fragment ends with ver. 49, at the close of which these words originally stood. Thus they form a natural transition to the account of the temple. A further and stronger reason for their genuineness is the phrase 'a little sheep' applied to Solomon, previous to his becoming king. This phrase has nothing derogatory in it, but can only be a loose rendering of ἀμνός, 'lamb,' applied also to David previous to his being appointed king, see ver. 45. Evidently the Ethiopic translator did not feel the technical use of the word, as he has obliterated it altogether in ver. 45. Thus, as the technical term is not found in the Ethiopic in this connexion, an Ethiopic interpolator could not have produced this manifest, though imperfect

---

see Crit. Notes on ver. 45. **48.** The Greek text gives the true order here: see Crit. Note. The words 'And that ram begat . . . prince and leader of those sheep,' should be placed after ver. 49: see Crit. Note. A little sheep, i.e. lamb: see vv. 45, 46 (note). **49.** This is a description of the reign of David. **50.** That house. As Dln. shows by a comparison of vv. 56, 66 sq., 72 sq. and the passage in Test. Levi x, *ὁ γὰρ οἶκος,*

became great and broad, and a lofty and great tower was built for those sheep: it was built on the house for the Lord of the sheep, and that house was low, but the tower was elevated and lofty, and the Lord of the sheep stood on that tower and a full table was placed before Him. 51. And again I saw those sheep that they again erred and went many ways, and forsook that their house, and the Lord of the sheep called some from amongst them and sent them to the sheep, but the sheep began to slay them. 52. And one of them was saved and was not slain, and it sped away and cried aloud over the sheep; and they wanted to slay it, but the Lord of the sheep saved it from the sheep, and brought it up to me, and caused it to dwell (there). 53. And many other sheep He sent to those sheep to testify and lament over them. 54. And after that I saw that when they forsook the house of the Lord and His tower they fell away entirely, and their eyes were blinded; and I saw the Lord of the sheep how He wrought

---

form of it. 50. **A lofty and great tower was built for those sheep: it was built on the house for the Lord of the sheep.** So G, inserting **ወዐቢይ፡ ተሐንጸ** after **ነዋኅ** and omitting **ዝኩ**. I M N give, 'a lofty tower was built for those sheep on that house and a tower lofty and great was built on that house for the Lord of the sheep.' So also L O, but that they give 'on *the* house for the Lord of the sheep.' F H and Dln., 'a lofty tower was built for those sheep on that house for the Lord of the sheep.' We might also translate 'was built by those sheep for the Lord of the sheep.' 52. **From the sheep.** So G M. Other MSS. and Dln. 'from the hands of the sheep.' 54. **The house of the Lord.** So G M. Other MSS. and Dln. 'the house of the Lord

---

ὃν ἂν ἐκλέξηται κύριος, Ἱερουσαλὴμ κληθήσεται, καθὼς περιέχει βίβλος Ἐνὼχ τοῦ δικαίου, this house is Jerusalem and the tower is the temple. A full table, i.e. offerings and sacrifices. 51–67. Gradual declension of Israel till the destruction of the Temple. 51. Called some . . . and sent them, i.e. the prophets. 52. Escape and translation of Elijah: cf. xciii. 8. 53, 54. The fruitless activity of the prophets, and the complete apostasy of the nation owing to their abandonment of the Temple.

much slaughter amongst them in their individual herds until those sheep invited such slaughter and betrayed His place. 55. And He gave them over into the hands of the lions and tigers and wolves and hyenas, and into the hand of the foxes and to all the wild beasts, and those wild beasts began to tear in pieces those sheep. 56. And I saw that He forsook that their house and their tower, and gave them all into the hand of the lions to tear and devour them, into the hand of all the wild beasts. 57. And I began to cry aloud with all my power and to appeal to the Lord of the sheep, and to represent to Him in regard to the sheep that they were being devoured by all the wild beasts. 58. But He remained unmoved, as He saw it, and rejoiced that they were devoured and swallowed and robbed, and left them to be devoured in the hand of all the beasts. 59. And He called seventy shepherds and put away those sheep that they might pasture

---

of the sheep.' **In their individual herds.** For በበ G M read በ 'in their herds.' **56.** For ይምስጥቆሙ G reads ይምሥቆሙ. 57. **Lord of the sheep.** G M have the strange reading እግዚእ፡ አናብስት 'Lord of the lions.' **All the wild beasts.** G reads 'all of them.' 58. For እሉ፡ ዅሎሙ G reads ዅሉ፡ እሉ. 59. **Seventy.** G M read ሰብዐተ, a mistake for ሰብዓ.

Invited such slaughter and betrayed His place, i.e. called in heathen nations to help them and so betrayed Jerusalem. **55.** The final fortunes of the two kingdoms and the names of their oppressors. **Lions and tigers**, i.e. the Assyrians and Chaldees. In vv. 56, 65 (?) where the lions alone are mentioned, the Chaldees are meant. The 'wolves' are the Egyptians: cf. ver. 13. The 'hyenas' may be the Ethiopians. **56.** This verse describes how God gradually withdrew from the degraded Theocracy and gave Israel defenceless into the hands of its enemies. **To devour.** The prophets use the same figure and phraseology in regard to the destruction of Israel by the heathen: cf. Jer. xii. 9; Is. lvi. 9; Ezek. xxxiv. 5, 8. Barnabas xvi. 4 refers to this verse, see quotation (p. 38). **59. The seventy shepherds.** This is the most vexed question in Enoch. The earliest interpreters took the first thirty-seven shepherds to mean the native kings of Israel and Judah. It was Ewald's merit to point out that this was a conception impossible for a Jew, and that the seventy shepherds must represent so many heathen oppressors of Israel. This interpretation has undergone many forms, but all alike

them, and He spake to the shepherds and their companions: "Let each individual of you pasture the sheep henceforward, and

---

have proved unsatisfactory: cf. Gebhardt's 'Die 70 Hirten des Buches Henoch u. ihre Deutungen' in Merx's *Archiv f. Wissenschaftl. Erforschung*, 1871, pp. 163-246. To Hoffmann, *Schriftbeweis*, i. 422, is due the credit of giving the only possible and satisfactory explanation. This explanation, which has been accepted by Schürer, Drummond, Wieseler, Schodde, Thomson, and Deane, interprets the shepherds as angels and not as men; and that his interpretation is the true one, there is no further room for doubt. For (1) the seventy shepherds exist *contemporaneously*, and are summoned *together* before the Lord of the sheep to receive their commission, lxxxix. 59. This could not be said of either native or Gentile rulers. (2) The shepherds are appointed to protect the sheep, lxxxix. 75, and to allow only a limited portion of them to be destroyed by the Gentiles. This could not be said of heathen rulers. (3) Jews and Gentiles and their kings also are alike symbolized by animals. Hence the shepherds cannot symbolize men. If not men, they are angels. (4) In the earlier history God was the true shepherd of Israel, but on its apostasy He withdrew from it and committed its pasturing to seventy of His angels. With the growing transcendence of God, His place was naturally taken by angels. (5) The angel who records the doings of the seventy shepherds is simply named 'another,' lxxxix. 61, in connexion with them, and so naturally belongs to the same category. (6) In the last judgment they are classed with the fallen angels, xc. 21-25. (7) God speaks directly to the shepherds and not through the medium of angels as elsewhere in the book. The idea of the seventy shepherds is used by the author to explain some pressing difficulties in Israel's history. So long as God was the immediate shepherd of Israel, it was not possible for such calamities to befall it as it experienced from the captivity onwards. Israel, therefore, during the latter period was not shepherded by God but by angels commissioned by Him. But again, though God rightly forsook Israel and committed it to the care of angels, though, further, Israel was rightly punished for its sins, yet the author and the Jews generally believed that they were punished with undue severity, indeed, twofold more grievously than they deserved (Is. xl. 2). How was this to be accounted for? The answer was not far to seek. It was owing to the faithlessness with which the angels discharged their trust. Had they only fulfilled their commission, the Gentiles could not have made havoc of Israel and apostate Jews only could have been cut off. There may be some distant connexion between the seventy angels here and the seventy guardian angels of the Gentile nations: cf. Weber, 165. The theory of the seventy shepherds is a development of the seventy years of Jeremiah, just as the writer of Daniel had seen in Jeremiah's seventy years seventy periods, and the four divisions into which the seventy shepherds fall correspond to the four world empires in Daniel. It is idle, however, to seek for chronological exactness in the four periods into which the writer of Enoch divides all history between the fall of Jerusalem and the Mes-

everything that I shall command you that do ye. 60. And I will deliver them over unto you duly numbered (lit. 'by number') and will tell you which of them are to be destroyed—and those destroy ye." And He gave over unto them those sheep. 61. And He called another and spake unto him: "Observe and mark everything which the shepherds will do to those sheep; for they will destroy more of them than I have commanded them. 62. And every excess and the destruction which will be wrought through the shepherds, record, (namely,) how many they destroy according to My command, and how many according to their own caprice, and record against every individual shepherd all the destruction he effects. 63. And read out before Me by number how many they destroy, and how many they deliver over for destruction, that I may have this as a testimony against them, and know every deed of the shepherds, so that when I give over to them the sheep I may see what they do,

---

62. For ይኅጕልዎሙ G reads ይሓጕሉ. 63. **How many they destroy.** So A D G L M O. Other MSS. and Dln. add 'according to their own caprice.' **They deliver over.** So G M ይሜጥዉ. Dln. ይሜጥዎሙ 'are delivered unto them' (lit. they deliver to them). **That when I give over to them the sheep I may see.** G reads እወጥኖሙ. M እመጥዎሙ፡ ወእመኖሙ. The original reading, therefore, was probably እመጥኖሙ 'that I may comprehend

---

sianic kingdom. These four periods are thus divided: 12 + 23 + 23 + 12. No system whether of Hilgenfeld, Volkmar, or Wieseler, which attributes a like number of years to each shepherd can arrive at any but a forced explanation of these numbers. As Schürer remarks, this division is merely intended to denote two longer periods coming between two shorter. The limits of these periods are on the whole not difficult to determine. The first period begins with the attacks of the heathen powers, and first that of Assyria on Israel, and ends with the return from the captivity under Cyrus. The second extends from Cyrus to the conquests of Alexander, 332 B.C. The third extends from this date to the transference of the supremacy over Israel from the Graeco-Egyptian to the Graeco-Syrian power. The fourth extends from this date, about 200 B.C., to the establishment of the Messianic kingdom. **60. Duly numbered.** The number in each instance to be destroyed was a definite one. **61. Another.** According to xc. 14, 22 this 'another' is an archangel and

whether or not they abide by My command which I have commanded them. 64. But they shall not know it, and thou shalt not declare it to them, nor admonish them, but only record against each individual in each case all the destruction which the shepherds effect and lay it all before Me." 65. And I saw till those shepherds pastured in their season, and they began to slay and to destroy more than they were bidden, and they delivered those sheep into the hand of the lions. 66. And the lions and tigers ate and devoured the greater part of those sheep, and the wild boars ate along with them; and they burned that tower and demolished that house. 67. And I became exceedingly sorrowful over that tower because that house of the sheep was demolished, and afterwards I was unable to see if those sheep entered that house. 68. And the shepherds and their associates delivered over those sheep to all the wild beasts, to devour them, and each one of them received in his time a definite number, and the other wrote of each one of them in a book how many each of them destroyed. 69. And each one slew and destroyed many more than was prescribed; and I began to weep and lament on account of those sheep.

---

and see.' 64. **Thou shalt . . . declare.** G reads ታስተርእዮሙ. 68. **The other.** All MSS. read በካልእ. Either expunge በ as above, or render 'how many each of them destroyed in a different way.' Cf. በ in Asc. Is. v. 14; Mark xv. 38. Or take በ as a corruption of ለ. 69. **Lament.** So G M. Other MSS. add 'exceedingly.'

---

the guardian angel of Israel, and hence, probably, Michael. **64.** No remonstrance against or interference with the shepherds was to be made during their period of dominion, but all their deeds were to be recorded against the final judgment. **65. Into the hand of the lions.** The lions appear to be the Assyrians, and the reign of the shepherds to begin contemporaneously with the final struggles of the northern kingdom; or possibly with a somewhat later date, as the former may come under the account given in vv. 55, 56. **66.** The account in general terms of the destruction of the northern and southern kingdoms by the lions and tigers, i.e. the Assyrians and Chaldeans. **The wild boars**: see ver. 12 (note). Cf. Obad. 10–12; Ezek. xxv. 12; xxxv. 5 sqq.; Is. lxiii. 1–4; Ps. cxxxvii. 7. **That tower, and that house**: see ver. 50

70. And thus in the vision I saw that scribe how he wrote down every one that was destroyed by those shepherds, day by day, and carried this same entire book up to the Lord of the sheep and laid it down and showed (to Him) everything that they had done, and all that each one of them had made away with, and all that they had given over to destruction. 71. And the book was read before the Lord of the sheep, and He took the book from his hand and read it and sealed it and laid it down. 72. And forthwith I saw how the shepherds pastured for twelve hours, and behold three of those sheep turned back and came and entered and began to build up all the ruins of the house; but the wild boars tried to hinder them, but they were not able. 73. And they began again to build as before, and they reared up that tower, and it was named the high tower; and they began again to place a table before the tower, but all the bread on it was polluted

---

71. **The book was read.** G reads መጽሐፈ: ተነበበ. **From his hand.** So G M. Other MSS. 'into His hand.' 72. **Turned back.** G reads ገብኡ. 73. **Began to place a table.** G reads

---

(note). **70.** With the sealing of the book which recorded all the doings of these shepherds it is implied that the first period has come to a close. **72.** At the close of the description of this period, the writer defines its duration exactly as twelve hours long, just as at the close of the third period described in xc. 2–4 he defines its duration in xc. 5. Further, we are to observe that the term 'hour' is to be taken in the same sense as 'time' in xc. 5, since in the fifty-eight times there mentioned, the twelve hours are treated exactly as 'times.' In fact we may feel certain that the variation of expression 'hour' and 'time' originated with the Ethiopic translator as renderings of the same word *ὥρα*. **Three of those sheep.** Two of these were Zerubbabel and Joshua. If the text be correct, I see no objection to finding the third in Ezra or Nehemiah, notwithstanding the interval that separates these from the former. The account of the attempt of the Samaritans to prevent the rebuilding of the temple is as true of the latter as the former, Ezra iv–v; Neh. iv–vi. In later times one of the two was at times mentioned without the other, Ecclus. xlix. 11–13; II Macc. ii. 13. **73, 74. The bread was polluted,** i. e. the offerings were unclean: cf. Mal. i. 7, 'Ye offer polluted bread upon mine altar.' These words furnish no ground for supposing an Essene author of the Dream-visions: they are not stronger than Mal. i, ii, and would only express the ordinary judgment of a fanatical Pharisee such as the writer

and not pure. 74. And besides all (this) the eyes of these sheep were blinded so that they saw not, and the eyes of their shepherds likewise; and they were delivered in large numbers to their shepherds for destruction, and they trampled the sheep with their feet and devoured them. 75. And the Lord of the sheep remained unmoved till all the sheep were dispersed over the field and mingled with them (i.e. the beasts), and they (i.e. the shepherds) did not save them out of the hand of the beasts. 76. And he who wrote the book brought it up, and showed it and read it before the Lord of the sheep, and implored Him on their account, and besought Him, as he showed Him all the doings of those shepherds, and gave testimony before Him against all the shepherds. 77. And he took this book and laid it down beside Him and departed.

XC. 1. And I saw until that in this manner thirty-six

ጸንዙ፡ እንዘ፡ ይትበሩ፡ . . . ማእዶ. 76. **Before the Lord.** So G, በኀበ፡ እግዚእ. Instead of በኀበ Dln. gives ኀበ፡ ቶበዮት, which against the order of the words he is obliged to connect with an earlier verb: 'brought it up to the habitation of the Lord of the sheep.' M ቶበዮት. **Implored Him on their account, and besought Him.** Repeated in G with a slight variation. Other variations in M. **Gave testimony.** G M read ይሰምዩ.

XC. 1. **Thirty-six.** According to MSS. it is doubtful whether

---

of this section on the Persian period—a judgment certainly justified by the few details that survive of that period: see Ewald's *History of Israel*, v. 204–206. The author of the Assumption of Moses—a Zealot writing about the beginning of the Christian era—says that the two tribes grieved on their return 'because they could not offer sacrifices to the God of their fathers,' iv. 8—the author therein implying that the sacrifices of the second temple were no true sacrifices because the nation was under the supremacy of the heathen, and its worship was conducted by an unworthy and heathenised hierarchy. **75.** Israel sinned still further in mingling among the heathen nations. This is the beginning of the 'dispersion.' **77.** Here the second period closes with the fall of the Persian power.

XC. 1. Thirty-six. This must be an error of the MSS. for thirty-five. The Ethiopic is far from being above reproach in this respect. The thirty-five gives the sum of the two periods already dealt with, i.e. 12 + 23, just as in xc. 5 at the close of the third period the three periods are summed

shepherds undertook the pasturing of the sheep, and they severally completed their periods as did the first; and others received them into their hand, to pasture them for their period, each shepherd for his own period. 2. And after that I saw in the vision all the birds of heaven coming, the eagles, the vultures, the kites, the ravens; but the eagles led all the birds; and they began to devour those sheep and to pick out their eyes and to devour their flesh. 3. And the sheep cried out because their flesh was devoured by the birds, and as I looked I lamented in my sleep over that shepherd who pastured the sheep. 4. And I saw until those sheep were devoured by the dogs and eagles and kites, and they left neither flesh nor skin nor sinew remaining on them till only their skeletons stood there: their skeletons too

---

thirty-six or thirty-seven. 3. I looked. So G [illegible]. M gives

---

together, 12 + 23 + 23 = 58. **As the first.** As the twelve had duly completed their times, so likewise did the rest of the thirty-five. **Others received them.** These words mark the transition to the Greek period. This period extends from the time of Alexander, 333, to the establishment of the Messianic kingdom. It falls into two divisions—the first constituted by the Graeco-Egyptian domination over Palestine, 333–200, during which twenty-three shepherds hold sway; and the second constituted by the Graeco-Syrian domination over Palestine from 200 till the establishment of the Messianic kingdom. During the fourth division twelve shepherds bear sway. **2.** The new world-power—that of the Greeks, i.e. Graeco-Egyptian and Graeco-Syrian—is fittingly represented by a different order of the animal kingdom, namely, by birds of prey. The 'eagles' are the Greeks or Macedonians. The 'ravens,' as we see from vv. 8, 9, 12, are the Syrians under the Seleucidae. The 'vultures' and 'kites' must stand for the Egyptians under the Ptolemies. Verses 2–4 deal with the Graeco-Egyptian domination. Yet the 'ravens,' i.e. the Syrians, are mentioned once, and the reason is obvious, for Syrians frequently contested the Egyptian supremacy over Palestine, and in all these struggles Palestine suffered severely. It was as Josephus says, 'like to a ship in a storm which is tossed by the waves on both sides,' *Ant.* xii. 3. 3. **3. That shepherd.** Possibly Ptolemaeus Lagi who captured Jerusalem by deceit and treachery on a sabbath day, *Ant.* xii. 1. 1. **4. The dogs.** According to lxxxix. 42, 46, 47, these are the Philistines: cf. Ecclus. l. 26. **Neither flesh nor skin.** From Mic. iii. 2, 3.

fell to the earth and the sheep became few. 5. And I saw until that twenty-three undertook the pasturing, and they completed in their several periods fifty-eight times. 6. But

---

ርኢኩ. Other MSS. 'I cried.' 5. **Twenty-three.** So G M. Other MSS. add 'shepherds.' **Undertook the pasturing.** G reads

---

5. See ver. 1 (note). **6-17.** The fourth and last period of the heathen supremacy. The beginning of this period synchronises with the transference of the supremacy over Israel from the Graeco-Egyptian to the Graeco-Syrian power about 200 B.C. Though this is not stated in so many words, it is the only legitimate interpretation. For (1) the analogy of the three preceding periods points to this conclusion, as each is marked by a like transference of the supremacy over Israel from one heathen nation to another. (2) Not only does the analogy of the other periods lead to this conclusion, but also every subsequent statement in the text, and with its acceptance the traditional difficulties of interpretation vanish. (3) This period is marked by the rise of the Chasids. As these were already an organised party (see ver. 6 note) before the Maccabean rising, their first appearance must have been much earlier and possibly synchronises with the beginning of this period. (4) There is absolutely no ground in the text for making this period begin with the reign of Antiochus Epiphanes, as all critics have done hitherto. This misconception has naturally made a right interpretation of the subsequent details impossible, and no two critics have been able to agree on their exegesis. **6.** The beginning of this period is marked by the appearance of a new class or party in Israel. These were the Chasids or Asideans who existed as a party for some time before the Maccabean rising. Some have identified the Chasids with the followers of Judas Maccabaeus, and have traced their origin to the efforts of that leader. But the separate mention of the Chasids as distinguished from the immediate followers of Judas, 1 Macc. iii. 13, their leagued organisation already existing before the Maccabean outbreak, as is clear from 1 Macc. ii. 42, iii. 13, and their action generally in support of Judas, but at times actually antagonistic to him, 1 Macc. vii. 13, make it quite manifest that this theory is without foundation. In fact so far from its being true that Judas founded this party, the only available evidence goes to prove that he was originally merely a member of it, as we shall see presently. The Chasids while first appearing as the champions of the law against the Hellenizing Sadducees were really the representatives of advanced forms of doctrine on the Messianic kingdom and the Resurrection. The Chasids possessed all the enthusiasm and religious faith of the nation, and though spiritual children of the Scribes, they drew within their membership the most zealous of the priestly as well as the non-priestly families. Hence our author represents (xc. 9) the Maccabean family as belonging to the Chasids as well as the High-priest Onias III. Within this party, though a diversity of eschatological views was tolerated, the most strict observance of the law was enforced,

behold lambs were borne by those white sheep, and they

ይሬእዩ 6. Behold. So G M ነዮ. Other MSS. ንኡሳንስ 'small.'

---

and with its requirements no political aim was allowed to interfere. On the other hand, any movement that came forward as the champion of the law naturally commanded the adhesion of the Chasids, and so they cast in their lot with the Maccabean party —but that only after much indecision (1 Macc. vii. 13), because the Maccabean movement put them in strife with the high-priest of the time, the legitimate and religious head of the nation. By a member of this party the present Dream-visions were written. This is obvious from the doctrines of the Resurrection, the final judgment, and the kingdom of the Messiah which he teaches, but especially from his severe criticism on the moral and ceremonial irregularities in the services of the second temple (lxxxix. 73). To remedy these abuses and defeat the schemes of Antiochus the Chasids were ready to sacrifice their lives, but all their efforts were directed to one end only —the re-establishment of the Theocracy and the preparation for the Messianic kingdom. To the writer of the Dream-visions all these hopes are bound up together with the success of the Maccabean leader. So long then as the Maccabean family fought for these objects, so long they carried with them the support of the Chasids; but the moment they laid hands on the high-priesthood, from that moment began the alienation of the Chasids, which afterwards developed into a deadly hostility. This hostility of the Pharisees to Hyrcanus is attested by their demand that the latter should resign the high-priesthood (*Ant.* xiii. 10. 5), and the same demand is practically made in the Pss. Sol. xvii. The writer who so severely criticised the temple worship under the *legitimate* line of high-priests could not regard an *illegitimate* holder of that office as the champion of the Theocracy. On this ground, therefore, we hold that chapters lxxxiii–xc must have been written before Jonathan's assumption of the high-priesthood, 153 B.C. This in itself makes it impossible to identify the 'great horn' with Hyrcanus—so Dln., Schürer, and others, or with Alex. Jannaeus—so Hilgenfeld, and we shall find that the natural and unforced interpretation of the text will confirm the conclusion we have thus arrived at. **6, 7. Lambs were borne by those white sheep.** The 'white sheep' are the faithful adherents of the Theocracy: the 'lambs' are the Chasids, a new and distinct party amongst the Jews, as we have above seen. Schürer thinks that it is only 'stubborn prejudice which can prevent any one from seeing that by the symbolism of the lambs the Maccabees are to be understood.' It seems, on the other hand, to be only 'stubborn prejudice' that can hold to such a view if the text is interpreted naturally. By taking the lambs in ver. 6 to symbolize the Chasids, every difficulty is removed. In vv. 6, 7 we have the unavailing appeals of the Chasids to the nation at large: in ver. 8 the destruction of one of them, Onias III, by the Syrians; and in ver. 9 the rise of the Maccabees—the horned or powerful lambs. If with Schürer the lambs in ver. 6 are the Maccabees, what is to be

began to open their eyes and to see, and to cry to the sheep. 7. But the sheep did not cry to them and did not hear what they said to them, but were exceedingly deaf, and their eyes were exceedingly and forcibly blinded. 8. And I saw in the vision how the ravens flew upon those lambs and took one of those lambs, and dashed the sheep in pieces and devoured them. 9. And I saw till horns grew upon those lambs, and the ravens cast down their horns; and I saw till a great horn of one of those sheep branched forth, and their

---

7. **Forcibly.** G M ኃይሉ. 8. **One of those.** G reads እምአሐዱ፡ በግዕ and duplicates this clause. 9. **Of one.** So G ለ ፩. Dln.

---

made of the horned lambs in ver. 9? Moreover, though the lambs or Chasids did appeal in vain to the nation, the Maccabees did not. **8.** The Syrians attack Israel and put Onias III to death, 171 B.C.: see II Macc. iv. 33–35. We are still in the pre-Maccabean period. We should, perhaps, have expected Onias III to be symbolised by a white sheep rather than by a lamb. The writer may have gone back for a moment to the symbolic meaning of this term in lxxxix. 45; but it is more likely that it is used loosely as including Onias among the Chasids. In any case it cannot be interpreted of Jonathan who was chief of the nation, and would have been symbolized by a horned lamb or a ram; nor could it possibly be said, as in ver. 9, that the lambs did not become horned till after the death of Jonathan. **9.** The horned lambs, as we have seen, must be the Maccabees, and in the 'great horn' it is impossible to find any other than Judas Maccabaeus. So Lücke and Schodde; but their interpretation could not be upheld against the objection that the period from Antiochus Epiphanes to Judas Maccabaeus is far too short for the rule of the twelve last shepherds. Schodde indeed tries to show that the 'great horn' comes early in this period, and that it is not the 'great horn' but the Messianic kingdom which forms the *terminus ad quem*. But the text is against him. The 'great horn' is still warring in ver. 16, and the period of the twelve shepherds' rule is closed in ver. 17. But this objection does not hold against the true conception of the period, which dates its beginning about 200 B.C. Thus nearly forty years of this period would have elapsed before the writing of these chapters lxxxiii–xc; for this section must have been written before the death of Judas, 160 B.C. The author, therefore, must have expected the Messianic kingdom to appear within twenty years or more. This would allow sufficient time for the rule of the twelve shepherds, and also admit of the 'great horn' being represented as warring till God interposes in person and establishes the kingdom. The interpretation of Dln., Köstlin, Schürer, and others, which takes the 'great horn' to symbolize John Hyrcanus, does violence to the text, and meets with the insuperable objection

eyes were opened. 10. And it looked at them and their eyes opened, and it cried to the sheep and the rams saw it and all ran to it. 11. And notwithstanding all this, those eagles and vultures and ravens and kites still kept tearing the sheep and swooping down upon them and devouring them: still the sheep took no action, but the rams lamented and cried out. 12. And those ravens fought and battled with it and sought to destroy his horn, but they had no power over it. 13. And I saw them till the shepherds and eagles and those vultures and kites came, and they cried to the ravens that they should break the horn of that ram, and they battled and fought with it, and it battled with them

---

omits ለ. G M add ወርእየ፡ አዕይንቲሆሙ. 10. **It looked at them.** Better take ርእየ as ርዕየ, and translate 'it pastured with them' or 'pastured them.' **It cried.** G I N 'they cried.' 11. **Notwithstanding all this.** Better than Dln.'s 'während alle dem.' **Kites.** Wanting in G. 12. **Fought.** G reads ይትኃየሉ.

---

that thus there would not be even the faintest reference to Judas, the greatest of all the Maccabees. 10. The eyes of the sheep are opened through the efforts of Judas Maccabaeus. **Rams.** So I have rendered dâbêlât here and in the next verse in accordance with Dln.'s latest views: see Lex. col. 1101. The word rendered 'ram' in lxxxix. 42-44 is quite a different one, and has a technical meaning not found in this word. 11, 12. **Eagles and vultures and . . . kites.** In the Syrian armies mercenaries were enrolled from the Greek and other nations: cf. 1 Macc. v. 39; vi. 29. Syria uses every effort against Judas but in vain. 13. It would seem that the use of some of the symbols is not steady. The 'vultures' and the 'kites' in ver. 2 must mean the Graeco-Egyptians; but in this verse and in ver. 11 it is doubtful who are to be understood by these. We have already observed that the writer uses the same brute symbol for different nations, i. e. the wild boars represent the Edomites in lxxxix. 66, but the Samaritans six verses later: see also ver. 16 (note). There may be a fresh change of symbols here, and the vultures and kites may stand for Ammon and Edom: cf. 1 Macc. v. The struggle here depicted is a life and death one, and neither of Hyrcanus' wars against Antiochus Sidetis and Antiochus Cyzicenus can fairly be described as such. The latter, moreover, was conducted by Hyrcanus' sons while Hyrcanus himself was quietly discharging his priestly duties in Jerusalem; while the former occurring during the first year of Hyrcanus could not be referred to in vv. 12, 13, as ver. 11 deals with the first attacks of the

and cried that his succour should come unto him. 14. And I saw till that man who wrote down the names of the shepherds and carried (them) up unto the presence of the Lord of the sheep came, and he helped that ram and showed it everything, that he had come down to help it. [15. And I saw till that Lord of the sheep came to them in wrath, and all who saw Him fled, and all cast themselves into the darkness from before His face.] 16. All the eagles and vultures and ravens and kites assembled together and brought with them all the sheep of the field, and they all came together, and helped each other to break that horn of the ram. 17. And I saw that man who wrote the book according to the com-

---

With it. G reads 'with them.' 14. **Helped.** G adds ወአድኀኖ 'helped and saved.' **He had come down to help it.** So G, reading ለረድኤቶ. Dln. 'that his help had come.' 15. **Cast themselves into the darkness from before His face.** Dln., 'fielen in seinem Schatten vor seinem Angesicht.' 16. **Brought with them all the sheep of the field.** G reads ወጽኡ . . . ሖሩ፡ አባግዕ 'all the sheep . . . went with them.' 17. **Who wrote.** G reads ከመ፡ ይጽሕፍ. **According to the command of the**

---

heathen on the 'great horn.' **Cried that his succour should come unto him:** cf. I Macc. vii. 41, 42; II Macc. xv. 8 sqq. 14. **Ram.** The same word that is used in vv. 10, 11. 15. I feel convinced that this verse is an interpolation, and that ver. 19 should be inserted before ver. 16, as the destruction of the Gentiles in ver. 19 has already been consummated in ver. 18. Ver. 15 seems to be modelled on ver. 18. This twofold appearance of God is uncalled for, and only the second appearance is effectual. The help that is promised in ver. 14 is described in ver. 19 as the sword, which is given to Israel for the destruction of the Gentiles. We should omit ver. 15 and insert ver. 19 before ver. 16 in our interpretation. 19. The period of the sword here has a *national* significance: Israel avenges itself on its heathen oppressors. In xci. 12, on the other hand, the period of the Sword has an *ethical* and vindictive significance: Israel destroys the unrighteous and those who have oppressed it. In this verse we pass over into the future. 16. The first great Messianic victories of Israel are the signal for the final assault of all the Gentiles combined with the apostate Jews (i.e. the sheep of the field) against Israel. Israel is still led by Judas, the great horn. Here, again, there is a loose use of symbols: the eagles, ravens, vultures, and kites represent all the hostile heathen nations in their last Gog and Magog struggle against Israel. 17. The fourth period of twelve shepherds is now at an end, and the period of

mand of the Lord, till he opened that book concerning the destruction which those twelve last shepherds had wrought and showed, that they had destroyed much more than their predecessors, before the Lord of the sheep. 18. And I saw till the Lord of the sheep came unto them and took the staff of His wrath into His hand and smote the earth so that it was rent asunder, and all the beasts and the birds of the heaven fell away from the sheep, and sank in the earth and it closed over them. 19. And I saw till a great sword was given to the sheep and the sheep proceeded against all the beasts of the field to slay them, and all the beasts and the birds of the heaven fled before their face. 20. And I saw till a throne was erected in the pleasant land and the Lord of the sheep sat Himself thereon, and that other took the sealed books and

---

Lord, till he opened that book concerning the destruction. G reads: በቃለ፡ እግዚአብሔር፡ እስመ፡ ተፈትሐ፡ በቃለ፡ እግዚአ፡ በውእቱ፡ ሐጕል። **Destroyed much more than their predecessors, before the Lord of the sheep. And I saw till the Lord of the sheep came unto them.** G makes 'before' an adverb, and reads ወ immediately after it, omitting the ወ before ርኢኩ, thus making 'the Lord of the sheep' subject of the next sentence. Next, for ኀቤሆሙ፡ እግዚእ፡ አባግዐ it reads ኀቤሆሙ፡ ለአባግዐ. Thus it gives, 'destroyed much more than their predecessors formerly. And I saw until the Lord of the sheep came to the sheep.' 18. **Of His wrath.** So B C D F G H I L M N O. A E, which Dln. follows, give 'of wrath.' **It closed over them.** G reads ከደኖሙ፡ ዲቤሆሙ. 19. **All the beasts.** So A E F G H I L M N O. Dln. 'those beasts.' 20. **I saw.** Wanting in G. **Thereon.** G reads ዲቤሆሙ. **That other took the sealed books.** I have emended the text here, reading ካልእ instead of ዝኩ. This seems necessary, as otherwise the writer would say—'the Lord of the sheep opened

---

judgment has arrived. 18. God Himself destroys the last enemies of Israel after the manner of Korah and his followers, Num. xvi. 31 sqq. This is the first act of the final judgment; but the remaining acts are of a forensic nature. 20. The pleasant land: cf. lxxxix. 40, i. e. Palestine. Cf. Dan. xi. 16, 41, 45. God's throne is set up in the immediate neighbourhood of Jerusalem (cf. ver. 26), the books are opened as in Dan. vii. 10: see xlvii. 3 (note). The Messiah does not appear till after the judgment

opened them before the Lord of the sheep. 21. And the Lord called those seven first white ones and commanded that they should bring before Him, beginning with the first star which led the way, all the stars whose privy members were like those of horses, and they brought them all before Him. 22. And He spake to that man who wrote before Him who was one of the seven white ones, and said unto him: "Take those seventy shepherds to whom I delivered the sheep, and who taking them on their own authority slew more than I commanded them." 23. And behold they were all bound, I saw, and they all stood before Him. 24. And the judg-

---

the sealed books before the Lord of the sheep.' Further, the Lord of the sheep does not Himself read the books. Cf. lxxxix. 71, 72, 76, 77; xc. 14, 17. Dln. 'He took all the sealed books.' 21. **Seven.** G ሰቡእ. M has a conflate reading, but supports the text. This verse is most corrupt, and requires emendation. First of all I have accepted Dln.'s correction of **እምነ፡ እለኩ** into **ለኵሉ**. Next, from G we see that confusion is introduced through the repetition of a clause. This repetition is concealed through variations in the later MSS., but it is clear in G. Thus the clause 'the first star which led the way' appears the second time in later MSS. as 'the first star which fell first,' but in G as 'the first star which went before,' i.e. led the way, **ዘወፅአ፡ ቀዳሚ** instead of **ዘወድቀ፡ ቀዲሙ**. I have accordingly omitted this clause on its second occurrence as an interpolation. In the earlier part of the verse I have followed Dln., **ያምጽኡ፡ ቅድሜሁ፡ እምኮከብ** against G **ያምጽኡ፡ ለኮከብ**. 22. **Seven white ones.** 'Seven' wanting in G. Doubtful whether 'six' or 'seven' in M. **Seventy.** Wanting in G. **On their own authority slew more than I commanded them.** G gives unintelligibly **ቀተሉ፡ ብዙኀ፡ ቀተሉ፡ እሉ፡ ወአዘዞሙ**. M **ቀተሉ፡ ብዙኃ፡ እሙንቱ፡ ዘአዘዞሙ**. 23. **ርእኩ፡ ወቆሙ** and the second **ኵሎሙ** are wanting in G, which therefore

---

in lxxxiii–xc. **21. Seven first white ones.** This order of seven archangels is derived from the Zoroastrian Amshaspands. They are spoken of in Tobit xii. 15: cf. Rev. i. 4; iv. 5; viii. 2, 6. See Cheyne, *Origin of the Psalter*, pp. 281, 282, 323–327, 334–337; Schenkel's *Bibel-Lex.* under Engel. **Star:** see lxxxvi–lxxxviii. **22.** The seventy angels who had charge of Israel are judged along with the fallen watchers. **24.**

ment was held first over the stars, and they were judged and found guilty and went to the place of condemnation, and they were cast into an abyss, full of fire and flaming, and full of pillars of fire. 25. And those seventy shepherds were judged and found guilty, and likewise cast into that fiery abyss. 26. And I saw at that time how a like abyss was opened in the midst of the earth, full of fire, and those blinded sheep were brought, and they were all judged and found guilty and cast into that fiery abyss, and they burned: now this abyss was to the right of that house. 27. And I saw those sheep burning and their bones burning. 28. And I stood up to see till He folded up that old house; and all the pillars were taken away, and all the beams and ornaments of the house were folded up with it, and it was taken off and laid in a place in the south of the land. 29. And I saw the Lord of the sheep till he brought a new house greater and loftier than that first, and set it up in the place of the first which had been folded up: all its pillars were new, and its ornaments were new and larger than those of the first one which He had taken away, and the Lord of the sheep was

---

runs, 'and behold they were all bound before Him.' 24. **Flaming, and full of pillars of fire.** G omits ወምሉእ 'flaming with pillars of fire.' 25. **Seventy.** G M ሰብእ. 26. **Full of fire.** G reads ዘምድር instead of ዘምሉዕ. **Fiery abyss.** G L give ዕመቅ. 28. **Folded up**: reading ጠቅም for ጠምየ according to Dln.'s conjecture. M reads ተሰጥመ, N ጠወም. **In a place.** G reads በፀቡተ፡ በመካኒ. 29. **The first one.** So G. Other MSS. 'the first old one.' **The Lord of the sheep was within.**

An abyss full of fire: cf. xviii. 11; xix; xxi. 7–10. **25.** The shepherds are cast into the same abyss: cf. liv. 6 (note). **26.** The apostates are cast into Gehenna. **In the midst of the earth**: cf. xxvi. 1. **To the right of that house**, i.e. to the south of Jerusalem. **27.** The apostates were punished in view of the blessed in Jerusalem: cf. Is. lxvi. 24; En. xlviii. 9 (note). **28, 29.** The removal of the old Jerusalem and the setting up of the New Jerusalem. This expectation is derived from O.T. prophecy: Ezek. xl–xlviii; Is. liv. 11, 12; lx; Hagg. ii. 7–9; Zech. ii. 6–13. The idea of a new Jerusalem coming down from heaven was a familiar one in Jewish Apocalypses: cf. IV Ezra vii. 26; xiii. 36;

within it. 30. And I saw all the sheep which had been left, and all the beasts on the earth, and all the birds of the heaven, falling down and doing homage to those sheep and making petition to and obeying them in every word. 31. And thereafter those three who were clothed in white, who had taken me up before, seized me by my hand, and the hand of that ram seizing hold of me, they took me up and set me down in the midst of those sheep before the judgment took place. 32. And those sheep were all white and their wool was abundant and clean. 33. And all that had been destroyed and dispersed and all the beasts of the field and all the birds of the heaven assembled in that house, and the Lord of the sheep rejoiced with great joy because they were all good and had returned to His house. 34. And I saw till they laid down that sword which had been given to the sheep, and they brought it back into His house, and it was sealed

---

So B E F H M N. G I L O and Dln. 'all the sheep were within.' 30. **Making petition to and obeying them.** G omits 'and obeying them.' 31. **And thereafter those three.** G reads ወእምዝኩ. For እንዘኒ G reads ሕንዚ, and for እበሬትኒ G reads እበርን. 33. **All that had been.** 'That' wanting in G. 34.

Apoc. Bar. xxxii. 2; Rev. xxi. 2, 10. **30. The conversion of the Gentiles**—of those who took no part in the oppression of Israel; for the rest were destroyed in ver. 18—and their spontaneous submission to Israel: cf. Is. xiv. 2; lxvi. 12, 19–21, and parallel passages. Later Judaism almost universally denied even this hope to the Gentiles: cf. Weber, *L. d. T.* 364–369, 376. **31. Those three who were clothed in white**: see lxxxvii. 2, 3. **That ram.** Same word as used in vv. 10, 11. This ram is the sheep saved in lxxxix. 52 from its enemies and brought up to live with Enoch. Paradise is only the temporary abode of Enoch and Elijah. **Before the judgment took place.** These words are most confusing. If they are genuine, it is hard to restore them to their place satisfactorily. **32.** The righteousness of the members of the kingdom is expressed by the whiteness and cleanliness of the wool of the sheep; and the large measure of their righteousness by the abundance of the wool: cf. Is. i. 26; iv. 3; lx. 21. **33.** The righteous dead will rise to share in the kingdom: cf. li. 1 (note). Likewise the dispersed of Israel will be gathered into it: cf. Mic. iv. 6, 7. **Rejoiced**: cf. Is. lxii. 3–5; lxv. 19. **34.** The sword wherewith Israel had crushed its enemies sealed and preserved as a

before the presence of the Lord, and all the sheep were invited into that house, but it held them not. 35. And the eyes of them all were opened to see the good, and there was not one amongst them that did not see. 36. And I saw that that house was large and broad and very full. 37. And I saw that a white bull was born, with large horns, and all the beasts of the field and all the birds of the air feared him and made petition to him all the time. 38. And I saw till all their (different) kinds were transformed, and they all became white oxen; and the first among them became the buffalo, and that

---

Were invited. So G ተጸውዑ. Other MSS. ተዐጽዉ 'they were enclosed.' 35. G reads ወ፩ዘኢይሬኢ፡ በማእከሎሙ. 38. **The first among them became the buffalo**: ቀዳማዊ፡ በማእከሎሙ፡ ኮነ፡ ነገረ. Here as Dln. suggests the Hebrew was רְאֵם. This the Greek translator transliterated into ῥημ, which was in turn taken by the Ethiopic translator for ῥῆμα. Hence the ነገር of the text, and the

---

memorial. **It held them not**: cf. Is. xlix. 19–21; Zech. ii. 4; x. 10. **37. A white bull**, i. e. the Messiah. We have here the Messiah coming forth from the bosom of the community. He is a man only, but yet a glorified man; for he is described as a white bull to mark his superiority to the rest of the community of the righteous who are symbolized by sheep. So far as he is a man only, he may be regarded as the prophetic Messiah as opposed to the apocalyptic of the Similitudes; and yet he is not really the prophetic Messiah; for he has absolutely no function to perform, as he does not appear till the world's history is finally closed. Accordingly his presence here must be accounted for through literary reminiscence, and the Messiah-hope must be regarded as practically dead at this period. The nation, in fact, felt no need of such a personality so long as they had such a chief as Judas. It was very different, however, in the following century, when the fondest enthusiast could no longer look to the Asmoneans, and the helpless degradation of this dynasty forced religious thinkers to give their hopes and aspirations a different direction. Of these, some returned to a fresh study of the O.T. and revived the hopes of the Messianic Son of David as in the Pss. of Solomon (70–40 B.C.): others followed the bold and original thinker who conceived the Messiah as the supernatural Son of Man, who, possessing divine attributes, should give to every man his due and vindicate the entire earth for the possession of the righteous: so in the Similitudes (94–70 B.C.). **38.** All the members of the kingdom are transformed: the white bull (i.e. the Messiah) into a great animal, and the sheep, beasts, and birds into white oxen. Thus mankind is restored to the primitive righteousness of Eden, i.e. Adam was symbolized by a white bull. **The buffalo**: see

buffalo became a great animal, and had great black horns on its head; and the Lord of the sheep rejoiced over them and over all the oxen. 39. And I slept in their midst: then I awoke and saw everything. 40. This is the vision which I saw while I slept, and I awoke and blessed the Lord of righteousness and gave Him glory. 41. Then I fell into a great fit of weeping and my tears stayed not till I could no longer endure it: when I looked, they flowed on account of what I saw; for everything will come and be fulfilled, and all the deeds of men in their order were shown to me. 42. And in that night I remembered my first dream: on its account also I wept and was overcome, because I had seen that vision.'

---

misleading translation 'the first among them was the word.' Some critics have imagined this to be a Christian interpolation referring to the Λόγος, but it is ቃል and never ነገር which is used to translate the word λόγος. The LXX. renders רְאֵם by μονόκερως and Ethiopic by ኣሐዱ: ቀርኑ. **The Lord of the sheep.** G has the peculiar reading መጋዝእ: አባግዕ = 'the fatted sheep.' 41. **After when I looked** G inserts እስመ: እሉ 'till I could no longer endure it, when I looked; for they flowed,' &c.

Crit. Note. Though nothing is said as to the duration of the life of the individual in this section, the implication is that it is eternal. If Enoch and Elijah are transferred to the Messianic kingdom from Paradise, surely it is only reasonable to conclude that the new form of existence is an eternal one; for this new form of existence is more glorious than that enjoyed by Enoch and Elijah in Paradise. In Paradise Elijah was symbolized by a *ram*, but in the Messianic kingdom by a *bull*. 40. Cf. xxii. 14. 41, 42. Enoch weeps because of the woes that threaten mankind in his two visions.

SECTION V.

(CHAPTERS XCI–CIV.)

INTRODUCTION.

A. *Critical Structure.* B. *Relation of* xci–civ *to* (*a*) i–xxxvi; (*b*) lxxxiii–xc. C. *Authorship and Date.* D. *The Problem and its Solution.*

A. Critical Structure. This section may be regarded as complete in the main and self-consistent. It has in some degree suffered at the hands of the final editor of the book, both in the way of direct interpolation and of severe dislocations of the text. The interpolations are—xci. 11; xciii. 11–14; xcvi. 2. The dislocations of the text are a more important feature of the book. They are confined (with the exception of cvi. 17ª, which should be read immediately after cvi. 14) to xci–xciii. All critics are agreed as to the chief of these. xci. 12–17 should undoubtedly be read directly after xciii. In xciii we have an account of the first seven weeks of the ten into which the world's history is divided, and in xci. 12–17 of the last three weeks. But this is far from a full account of the matter. The remaining dislocations only need to be pointed out in order to be acknowledged. On other grounds (pp. 260–263) we find that xci–civ is a book of different authorship to the rest of the sections. Now this being so, this section obviously begins with xcii—'written by Enoch the scribe,' &c. On xcii follows xci. 1–10 as a natural sequel, where Enoch summons his children to receive his parting words. Then comes the Apocalypse of Weeks, xciii. 1–10; xci. 12–17. xci. 18, 19 form a natural transition from xci. 12–17 to xciv. The original order of the text, therefore, was: xcii; xci. 1–10; xciii. 1–10; xci. 12–19; xciv. These dislocations were the work of the editor, who put the different books of Enoch together and added lxxx and lxxxi.

B. (*a*) Relation of xci–civ to i–xxxvi. Do these sections proceed from the same author? or if not, of what nature is the manifest relation between them? Let us proceed to weigh the evidence on the former question. At first sight, the evidence for unity of authorship seems overwhelming. (1) The phrase 'ye will have no peace' is found in xci–civ and in i–xxxvi, and in these sections only—xciv. 6; xcviii. 11, 16; xcix. 13; ci. 3; cii. 3; ciii. 8; i. 8; v. 4; xii. 5; xiii. 1; xvi. 4. 'Plant of righteousness,' xciii. 2, 5, 10; x. 16. (2) Titles of God in common. 'The Holy and Great One,' xcii. 2; xcvii. 6; xcviii. 6; civ. 9; x. 1; xiv. 1; xxv. 3. 'The Great One,' ciii. 4; civ. 1; xiv. 2. 'The Great Glory,' cii. 3; xiv. 20. (3) References in each to the Law, xcix. 2; v. 4: to the eating of blood, xcviii. 11; vii. 5: to the regularity of nature, ci. 1–7; ii. 1–v. 4: to the hardheartedness of men, xcviii. 11; v. 4. (4) No hint of a Messiah in either. (5) The division of human history in the Apocalypse of Weeks into ten weeks, each apparently of seven generations, seems to agree with x. 12, where a period of seventy generations is given. (6) The date of the final judgment over the Watchers in xci. 15 at the close of the tenth week seems to agree with the date assigned to it in x. 12, i.e. at the end of seventy generations. (7) In both the resurrection is taught, xci. 10; xcii. 3; c. 5; xxii. (8) In both the scene of the Messianic kingdom is the earth as it is.

There are thus many points of connexion, but as we proceed we shall see that these are mainly external. The points of divergence, on the other hand, are far more serious because internal. (1) In the first place, the last four points of agreement mentioned above are apparent, but not real. The seventh day of the tenth week in xci. 15 marks *the close of the Messianic kingdom*, which began in the eighth week: whereas the seventy generations in x. 12 terminate with the *establishment of the Messianic kingdom*. Nor do these periods start from the same date: the Apocalypse of Weeks reckons from the creation of Adam: the seventy generations from the judgment of the angels. (2) The final judgment in xci. 15 is held at the close of the Messianic kingdom, but in x. 12, xvi. 1, before its establishment. (3) Whereas the resurrection implied in xxii is only a resuscitation to a *temporary* blessedness, v. 9, x. 17, xxv. 6, the resurrection in xci–civ is not to the temporary Messianic kingdom spoken of in xci. 13, 14, xcvi. 8, but to one of eternal blessedness subsequent to the final judgment. For, from c. 4, 5 we see that the righteous do not rise till God has judged sinners and an end has been made of all sin. Thus the resurrection of the righteous in xci–civ follows the final judgment at the close of the temporary Messianic kingdom in xci–civ. Further evidence to this effect is to be found in xcii. 3, 4, where the righteous are said to 'walk in eternal light': in civ. 6, where they are to become 'companions of the heavenly hosts': in civ. 2, where they are to 'shine as the stars,' and have 'the portals of heaven open to them.' These statements could not possibly apply to the members of the temporary Messianic kingdom. (4) There is only a resurrection of the righteous in xci–civ: cf. xci. 10; xcii. 3; c. 5: whereas in xxii a general resurrection with the exception of one class of sinners is taught. (5) There is no resurrection of the body in xci–civ: there is a resurrection of the body in i–xxxvi. (6) Contrast the spiritual nature of the kingdom in xci–civ with the crass materialism of i–xxxvi, where much of the bliss consists in good eating and drinking and the begetting of large families, and life itself depends on the external eating of the tree of life. (7) Finally, contrast the answers given by i–xxxvi and xci–civ to the question 'why do the righteous suffer?' See pp. 56, 57; 264, 265.

The lines of thought, then, being so divergent in these two sections, there is no conclusion open to us other than that they proceed from different authors; whereas the obvious points of agreement necessitate the assumption that one of the two authors had the work of the other before him, and we need feel no hesitation in concluding that the author of xci–civ had i–xxxvi or some form of this section before him—some form of this section we repeat, for it is at the best fragmentary.

B. (*b*) **Relation of xci–civ to lxxxiii–xc.** There are some points of resemblance between these sections. (1) Elijah's translation referred to, xciii. 8; lxxxix. 52. God rejoices over the destruction of the wicked, xciv. 10; lxxxix. 58. (2) Titles of God in common: 'The Great King,' xci. 13, lxxxiv. 5; 'the Holy and Great One,' xcii. 2 (note), lxxxiv. 1.

But these and other superficial points of resemblance are far outweighed by the divergent lines of thought pursued in the two sections, which render the theory of one and undivided authorship impossible. We should observe then, that—(1) the Messianic kingdom is finite in duration in xci–civ, i.e. from the eighth to the tenth world-week inclusive; whereas in lxxxiii–xc it is eternal. In xci–civ the final judgment takes place at the close of the Messianic kingdom: in lxxxiii–xc it is consummated at the beginning of the Messianic kingdom. (2) There is a resurrection of the righteous only in xci–civ; but in lxxxiii–xc a resurrection of apostate Jews also. (3) The period of the sword is differently dated and conceived in the two sections. In xci–civ it is separated from the final judgment by the whole period of the Messianic kingdom, see xci. 12: in lxxxiii–xc it immediately precedes the final judgment, see xc. 19: in xci–civ it is ethical and vindictive—the destruction of the wicked by the righteous: in lxxxiii–xc it is national and vindictive—the destruction of the hostile Gentiles by the Jews. (4) The building of the Temple precedes the final judgment in xci–civ: in lxxxiii–xc it is subsequent to the final judgment. (5) The scene of the Messianic kingdom in xci–civ is apparently heaven; for in xci. 14–16 the former heaven and earth are destroyed and a new heaven created, but no new earth, and in civ. 2 heaven is thrown open to the righteous.

We must therefore conclude that xci–civ and lxxxiii–xc proceed from different authors, and this conclusion is confirmed when we observe the forcible dislocations that xci–civ have undergone at the hands of the final editor. This section taken in the following order, xcii; xci. 1–10; xciii. 1–10; xci. 12–19; xciv (see p. 260) forms a complete book in itself, and presents a world-view peculiarly its own. Why then was the original order departed from, unless in order to adapt it to a new context? On all sides, then, the conclusion is irresistible that xci–civ once formed an independent writing: that it was afterwards incorporated into a larger work, and underwent its present derangements in the process of incorporation.

C. The Authorship and Date. The author belongs to a clearly defined party. That this party is the Pharisees is obvious; for it is exclusive in an extreme degree, xcvii. 4; it is an upholder of the law against an apostate hellenizing party, xcix. 2, 14; it looks forward to a temporal triumph over its opponents, xci. 12, &c.; it believes in a final judgment and resurrection of the righteous, xci. 10, xcii. 3, and in Sheol as the place of eternal punishment for the wicked, xcix. 11, ciii. 7, 8.

The enemies of this party are rich and trust in their riches, xcvi. 4, xcvii. 8–10, xcviii. 2: they oppress and rob the poor of their wages, xcix. 13: they have forsaken the law, xcix. 2, falsified the O. T. writings, and led men astray through their heathen doctrines, xciv. 5, civ. 10: they are given up to superstition and idolatry, xcix. 7–9: they hold that God does not concern Himself with the doings of men, xcviii. 6, 7, civ. 7, and that life ceases with the grave, cii. 11. As the former party are designated as the 'children of heaven,' ci. 1, these are called the 'children of earth,' c. 6, cii. 3.

The date of this clearly defined and developed opposition of the two parties cannot have been pre-Maccabean, nor yet earlier than the breach between John Hyrcanus and the Pharisees. But a still later date must be assumed according to the literal interpretation of ciii. 14, 15, where the rulers are said to uphold the Sadducean oppressors and to share in the murder of the righteous. This charge is not justified before 95 B.C. As for the later limit, the Herodian princes cannot be the rulers here mentioned, for the Sadducees were irreconcilably opposed to these, as aliens and usurpers. It appears, therefore, that this section should be assigned either to the years 95–79 B.C. or to 70–64 B.C., during which periods the Pharisees were oppressed by both rulers and Sadducees.

If, on the other hand, we might regard the word 'murder' as merely a strong expression for a severe persecution, and the silence elsewhere observed as to the rulers would point to this interpretation, then we should naturally refer this section to the years 134–95 B.C., i. e. after the breach between Hyrcanus and the Pharisees and before the savage destruction of the Pharisees by Jannaeus in 95. If the date of the book is subsequent to 95, the merely passing reference in ciii. 15 to the cruelties of Jannaeus is hardly intelligible. We should expect rather the fierce indignation against 'the kings and the mighty,' which we actually do find in xxxvii–lxx, and which fittingly expresses the feelings of the Pharisees towards Jannaeus, 'the slayer of the pious.' We are inclined therefore to place xci–civ before 95 B.C., and if we may regard c. 2 as an historical reference, these chapters are to be assigned to the years 104–95 B.C.

The author is thus a Pharisee, writing between the years 104 and 95 B.C.

D. The Problem and its Solution. The author of i–xxxvi solves the problem of the righteous suffering by their resuscitation to a temporary blessedness in the Messianic kingdom: the wicked dead who *escaped punishment* in life, xxii. 10, 11, rise also to receive requital for their sin. What becomes of the righteous after their second death is not so much as hinted at in that section.

Thus in this respect the solution of the problem here presented has not advanced a single step beyond that given in Is. lxv and lxvi.

But this solution of the problem must have failed early to give satisfaction. In xci–civ we find another attempt to grapple with this difficulty, and in this an answer immeasurably more profound is achieved. The wicked are seemingly sinning with impunity; yet their evil deeds are recorded every day, civ. 7; and for these they will suffer endless retribution in Sheol, xcix. 11; for Sheol is not a place such as the O. T. writers conceived, but one in which men are requited according to their deserts, cii. 4–civ. 5. From this hell of darkness and flame their souls will never escape, xcviii. 3, 10; civ. 7, 8. But the time is coming when even on earth the wicked will perish and the righteous triumph over them, on the advent of the Messianic kingdom, at the beginning of the eighth world-week, xci. 12; xcv. 7; xcvi. 1; xcviii. 12; xcix. 4, 6. This kingdom will last till the close of the tenth world-week, and during it the righteous will enjoy peace and well-being, and see many good days on earth, xci. 13, 14; xcvi. 8. Then will ensue the final judgment with the destruction of the former heaven and earth, and the creation of a new heaven, xci. 14–16. And the righteous dead, who have been specially guarded by angels all the time hitherto, c. 5, will thereupon be raised, xci. 10, xcii. 3, as spirits only, ciii. 3, 4, and the portals of the new heaven will be opened to them, civ. 2, and they shall joy as the angels, civ. 4, and become companions of the heavenly hosts, civ. 6, and shine as the stars for ever, civ. 2.

TRANSLATION.

XCI. 1. 'And now, my son Methuselah, call to me all thy brothers and gather together to me all the sons of thy mother; for the word calls me and the spirit is poured out upon me that I should show you everything that will befall you for ever.' 2. Thereupon Methuselah went and called

---

XCI. 1. G gives a different order of the words: 'call to me all the sons of thy mother, and gather together to me thy brothers.'

XCI. 1. Enoch calls his sons together. One of the editors of this book has already prepared for the introduction of this section in lxxxi. 5, 6. **All the sons of thy mother.** The names of these sons is given in the Slavonic Enoch. **The word calls me.** This expression must be taken

to him all his brothers and assembled his relatives. 3. And he conversed with all the children of righteousness and spake: 'Hear, ye sons of Enoch, all the words of your father, and hearken befittingly to the voice of my mouth; for I exhort and say unto you, beloved, love uprightness and walk therein. 4. And draw not nigh to uprightness with a double heart, and associate not with those of a double heart; but walk in uprightness and righteousness, and it will guide you on good paths and righteousness will be your companion. 5. For I know that a condition of oppression will increase on the earth and a great chastisement will be executed on the earth, and all unrighteousness will be consummated and be cut off from the roots, and its whole superstructure destroyed. 6. And unrighteousness will again be consummated on the earth, and all the deeds of unrighteousness and of violence and trans-

---

3. **With all the children of righteousness.** So G ውሉደ፡ ጽድቅ. Dln. reads ውሉዱ፡ ጽድቀ 'with all his children concerning righteousness.' **Ye sons of Enoch.** So GM. Other MSS. and Dln. 'my sons.' **Beloved.** So GM. Other MSS. 'my beloved.' 4. **And associate not with those of a double heart.** Wanting in G. **Uprightness and.** So G በርቱዕ፡ ወ. Other MSS. omit and read 'my sons' after 'righteousness.' 6. After ዲበ፡ ምድር G inserts ወትእዘዝ, and FHILMNO ወትትአኃዝ. The former is possibly a corruption of ወትኄይዝ (see lxxxi. 6 Crit. Note) 'will grow strong.' I have however followed the reading of FHILMNO 'will prevail,' omitted in Dln. **And transgression.** From this point the order of G is confused. It omits for the present xci. 7–xcvii. 6^{a} and connects xcvii. 6^{b}–cviii. 10 directly with xci. 6. Then it resumes with the last word of xci. 6 and proceeds without break to xcvii. 6^{a}. With the words 'the Great and Holy One' begins a fresh section, xcvii. 6^{b}–cviii. 10, but from a different MS. than G—a fact which will be confirmed

---

as equivalent to 'the Spirit is poured out upon me.' 3. **Love uprightness, &c.**: cf. xciv. 1. 4. **Draw not nigh to uprightness with a double heart.** This is undoubtedly derived from Ecclus. i. 25, *μὴ προσέλθῃς αὐτῷ* (i.e. *φόβῳ κυρίου*) *ἐν καρδίᾳ δισσῇ*: cf. Ps. xii. 3, לֵב וָלֵב; Jas. i. 8, *δίψυχος*. **Associate not, &c.**: cf. xciv. 2, 3; civ. 6. 5. **The Deluge. Cut off from the roots**: cf. vv. 8, 11. 6. **The growth of wickedness after the Deluge. And transgression**: see Crit. Note. **Prevail**: see Crit. Note.

gression will again prevail. 7. And then when unrighteousness and sin and blasphemy and violence in all kinds of deeds will increase, and apostasy and transgression and uncleanness increase, a great chastisement from heaven will come upon them all, and the holy Lord will come forth with wrath and chastisement to execute judgment on earth. 8. In those days violence will be cut off from its roots and the roots of unrighteousness, together with deceit, and they will be destroyed from under heaven. 9. And all the idols of the heathen will be abandoned: the temples will be burned with fire and they will be removed from the whole earth, and they (i.e. the heathen) will be cast into the judgment of fire and will perish in wrath and in grievous eternal judgment. 10. And the righteous one will arise from sleep and wisdom will arise and be given unto them. [11. And after that the

---

when we deal with that section. Thus, for chapters xcvii. 6b–cviii. 10 we possess two MSS. belonging to the beginning of the sixteenth century. In that section we shall distinguish the two MSS. as G and G[1]. 7. **In all kinds of deeds.** So G M. Other MSS. 'and all kinds of deeds.' **And transgression.** Wanting in G. **From heaven.** Wanting in G. **The holy Lord.** After these words G adds ዲበ: ምድር. 8. For ወእምሥረው: ዐመፃ G reads ወዐመፃ and omits ወይትሐጐሉ against M and all other MSS.: 'in those days violence will be cut off from its roots and unrighteousness together with deceit from under heaven.' 9. For ይትኀጐሉ G reads ይሐጕሉ. 11. For እምሥረው G reads

---

7, 8. This fresh development of wickedness will call forth the final judgment. **Roots of unrighteousness**: cf. vv. 5, 11. **9.** The absolute rejection of the heathen seems to be taught here. This was a prevailing though not the universal belief of later Judaism: see Weber, *L. d. T.* 368. Idolatry is reprobated in xcix. 7–9, 10, as here. **They will be cast into the judgment of fire.** This reprobation of the heathen does not appear to agree with the teaching of ver. 14, where the conversion of the heathen is expected. That verse, however, belongs to the Apocalypse of Weeks which has all the appearance of an earlier fragment incorporated in his work by the original author of xci–civ. **10. The righteous one.** Used collectively as in xcii. 3. In xci–civ only the righteous attain to the Resurrection: see li. 1 (note) for full discussion of the subject. **Wisdom**: see xlii. 1, 2 (note). **11.** As we have already seen (p. 260), xci. 12–

roots of unrighteousness will be cut off and the sinners will be destroyed by the sword (and the roots) will be cut off from blasphemers in every place, and those who devise oppression and those who commit blasphemy will perish by the edge of the sword.] 12. And after that there will be another week, the eighth, that of righteousness, and a sword will be given to it that judgment and righteousness may be executed on those who commit oppression, and sinners will be delivered into the hands of the righteous. 13. And at its close they will acquire houses through their righteousness, and the house of the Great King will be built in glory for ever more. 14. And after that in the ninth week the righteous judgment will

---

እምምርው. **In every place.** 'Place' wanting in G. **Those who devise oppression and those who commit blasphemy.** G reads 'those who devise and those who commit blasphemy.' 13. **The house of the Great King will be built in glory.** So G M በስብሐት. Other MSS. 'a house will be built to the glory of the

---

17 originally stood after xciii. 1–10. As for this verse, we must regard it as an interpolation added by the final editor in order to introduce vv. 12–19 which he had torn from their original context. This verse is wholly out of place here. Judgment has already been consummated, all evil works destroyed, and all the wicked handed over to a judgment of fire (vv. 7–9). In ver. 10 the Resurrection ensues and judgment is now over. But in ver. 11 all this is ignored and a moral chaos is represented as still existing—a moral chaos of exactly the same nature as existed before the judgment of vv. 7–9. Moreover, the period of the Sword—man's part in the final judgment—precedes the Resurrection: cf. xc. 19; xci. 12. The Resurrection follows upon the destruction of all evil and the final judgment, c. 4, 5. Finally, this verse seems modelled partly on vv. 7 and 8, and partly on ver. 12, the expressions about blasphemers being drawn from ver. 7, the phrase 'roots of unrighteousness will be cut off' from ver. 8, and the reference to the Sword from ver. 12. **12–19.** These verses giving an account of the first three weeks of the world's history should be read after xciii. 1–10 (see p. 260), the account of the first seven weeks. **12.** The eighth week sees the establishment of the Messianic kingdom. It likewise forms the first act of the final judgment; for it is the period of the Sword; cf. xc. 19; and the wicked are given into the hands of the righteous; cf. xcv. 7; xcvi. 1; xcviii. 12; xcix. 4, 6; also xxxviii. 5. **13.** On the period of strife will follow that of rest and quiet possession of the earth; cf. Is. lx. 21, 22; lxv. 20–23. **The house of the Great King**: see Crit. Note. This means first of all the Temple, and in the next place Jerusalem. **14.** This verse is difficult. The ninth week, as Dln. supposes, may mean

be revealed to the whole world, and all the works of the godless will vanish from the whole earth, and the world will be written down for destruction, and all mankind will look to the path of uprightness. 15. And after this, in the tenth week in the seventh part, there will be the great eternal judgment, in which He will execute vengeance amongst the angels. 16. And the first heaven will depart and pass away, and a new heaven will appear, and all the powers of the heavens will shine sevenfold for ever. 17. And after that there will be many weeks without number for ever in goodness and righteousness, and sin will no more be mentioned

---

Great King.' 14. **Will be revealed.** G reads ተኅተበ (sic). **All the works of the godless.** G reads 'all the godless.' **The world will be written down for destruction.** G reads ይጽሕፉ፡ በሕጕል፡ ዓለም 'one shall write down the destruction of the world.' 15. **Seventh part.** 'Seventh' wanting in G. **The great eternal judgment, in which He will execute vengeance amongst the angels.** So M, and also G, but that it reads ይበቀል instead of ይትበቀል as M. F H L O and Dln. 'the eternal judgment, which is held over the watchers, and the great eternal heaven which springs from amongst the angels': thus adding ወተተገበር፡ እምትጉሃን፡ ወሰማይ፡ ዘለዓለም. This was probably a marginal gloss. It appears in I N as 'which is held over the watchers of the eternal heaven.' 16. **Will shine sevenfold for ever.** G reads ይበርሁ and omits ለዓለም. 17. **In goodness.** G inserts

---

the period in which true religion will spread over the earth, and the judgment described in ver. 12, and executed by the righteous, will be made known to the neutral Gentile nations with a view to their conversion: cf. l. 2–5; xc. 30, 33, 35. With this view the concluding words of this verse would harmonize well. Yet see ver. 15 (note). **The works of the godless will vanish**: cf. x. 16, 20, 21. **The world will be written down for destruction.** This destination will take effect towards the close of the tenth week. **15.** The tenth week ends with the final judgment on the watchers. As there is no mention of the judgment of the wicked by God in person in this verse, the preceding verse may in some measure refer to it. **The great eternal judgment**: see Crit. Note; also xlv. 2 (note). **16.** Observe that though there will be a new heaven, cf. Is. lxv. 17; lxvi. 22; Ps. cii. 26, there is no mention of a new earth, cf. civ. 2 (note). For the idea of a new creation, cf. xlv. 4; lxxii. 1 (note). **Sevenfold**: cf. Is. xxx. 26; lx. 19, 20. 17. This verse closes the Apocalypse of

for ever. 18. And now I tell you, my sons, and I show you the paths of righteousness and the paths of violence, and I will show them to you again that ye may know what will happen. 19. And now, hearken, my sons, and walk in the paths of righteousness and walk not in paths of violence; for all who walk in the paths of unrighteousness will perish for ever.'

XCII. 1. Written by Enoch the scribe, this complete doctrine of wisdom which deserves the praise of all men and is a judge of the whole earth, for all my children who will dwell on the earth and the future generations who will observe uprightness and peace. 2. Let not your spirit be troubled on account of the times; for the Holy (and) Great One has appointed days for all things. 3. And the righteous one will arise from sleep, will arise and walk in the path of righteousness, and all his path and conversation will be in eternal goodness and grace. 4. He will be

---

before these words ወኵሎሙ 'and all of them in goodness.' 18. **The paths of righteousness.** G reads 'all the paths of righteousness.' **Will show to you.** G reads አርእየክሙ. 19. **Hearken and.** Wanting in G, repeated thrice in M.

XCII. 1. **The scribe, this complete doctrine of wisdom.** G reads: መጽሐፍ፡ ጸሐፈ፡ እንክ፡ ሄኖክ፡ ዘኵሉ፡ ትእምርት፡ ወትምህርት፡ ጥበብ. ወመኰንን. G M omit the ወ. 2. **On account of the times.** G reads በአማን 'indeed,' 'truly.' 3. **For the righteous one will arise from sleep, will arise** G merely gives ይትነሣእ፡ ጥበብ 'wisdom will arise.' M 'righteousness will arise from its

---

Weeks. **18, 19.** These form a most suitable transition from the Apocalypse of Weeks to xciv.

XCII. This chapter forms the real beginning of the independent book composed of chapters xci–civ. The order of the original text was (see p. 260) xcii; xci. 1–10; xciii. 1–10; xci. 12–19; xciv. **1. The scribe:** cf. xii. 3, 4. **Doctrine of wisdom.** This book is mainly practical in character. **A judge of the whole earth.** Wisdom is represented as the πάρεδρος or assessor of God in lxxxiv. 3: see note. **2. The times** are evil; but these too are the ordination of God. **The Holy (and) Great One:** see i. 3 (note). **3. The righteous one.** Used collectively as in xci. 10. **In eternal goodness and**

gracious to the righteous and will give him eternal uprightness, and will give him power, and he will live in goodness and righteousness, and will walk in eternal light. 5. And sin will perish in darkness for ever, and will no more be seen from that day for evermore.

XCIII. 1. And after that Enoch began to recount from the books. 2. And Enoch spake: 'Concerning the children of righteousness and concerning the elect of the world and the plant of uprightness—of these I will speak to you and

---

sleep, will arise.' **4. To the righteous.** G reads ለጽድቅ 'to righteousness.'

XCIII. 1. For ኮነ G reads ወሀበኒ. **2. Plant of uprightness.**

---

grace. These words are further explained in ver. 4. **4. Power.** Uprightness and power will no longer be dissevered. **In eternal light:** see xxxviii. 4 (note). **5.** Cf. x. 16, 20.

XCIII. 1–10. In these verses we have an account of the great events of the world during the first seven weeks of its history. These seven belong to the past, the three last weeks described in xci. 12–17 belong to the future. As this Apocalypse of Weeks comes from a different author and date to the Dream-visions, lxxxiii–xc, we are relieved of the task of harmonizing them, on which many critics have laboured and to no purpose. We are not to regard the ten weeks as being definite and equal periods of 700 years each, as Wieseler, Hoffmann, and others have done; for, not to press the fact that this reckoning would place the book after Christ, the facts recorded as occurring in the individual weeks would not fall within the limits assigned them by this theory. Dln.'s scheme of seventy generations of varying length, seven generations to each week, is still more unsatisfactory. In the first five weeks, seven actual generations are taken for each week; but in the sixth and seventh weeks fourteen or more generations are compressed into the needful seven. Rather we are to regard the ten weeks as periods of varying length, each one of which is marked, especially towards its close, by some great event—the first by the birth of Enoch: the second by the corruption of primitive man and the Flood: the third by the call of Abraham: the fourth by the revelation of the law and the occupation of Palestine: the fifth by the building of the Temple: the sixth by the apostasy of Israel and the destruction of the Temple: the seventh by the publication of Enoch's writings. Cf. also *Le Livre d'Henoch*, par T. G. Peter, Genève, 1890. **1. From the books.** These were either written by Enoch, according to some sections; or by the angel that accompanied him, according to others: cf. xxxiii. 3, 4; xl. 8; lxxiv. 2; lxxxi. 1, 2. In the next verse Enoch appeals to visions, angels, and the heavenly tables, as the source of his revelations. **2.** These disclosures are for the children of righteousness: cf. xcii. 1. **The elect of the world.** This designation of the elect is not found elsewhere in Enoch. **The plant of uprightness:** see x.

announce to you, my sons, I Enoch, according to that which appeared to me in the heavenly vision, and know through the word of the holy angels, and have learnt from the heavenly tables.' 3. And Enoch began to recount from the books and spake: 'I was born the seventh in the first week, while judgment and righteousness still tarried. 4. And after me there will arise in the second week great wickedness, and deceit will spring up; and in it there will be the first end and in it a man will be saved; and after it is ended unrighteousness will grow up and He will make a law for the sinners. 5. And after that in the third week at its close a man will be chosen as the plant of righteous judgment, and after him will come for evermore the plant of righteousness. 6. And after that in the fourth week, at its close, visions of the holy and righteous will be seen, and a law for all future generations and an enclosure will be made for them. 7. And after that in the fifth week, at its close, will the house

---

So G M. Other MSS. 'plant of righteousness and uprightness.' 5. **Plant of righteous judgment.** G adds ዘለዓለም, and omits the rest of the verse. Before ተክለ፡ ጽድቅ M inserts ለ. 6. G reads ጽድቅ፡ ይትሬእዩ 'there will be visions of the holy ones

---

16 (note). **Heavenly tables:** see xlvii. 3 (note) for a complete account of this and similar expressions. **3. Seventh in the first week.** Ewald and Dln. find in this expression the foundation of their theory that the reckoning here is according to generations. But this is to press the words too much. They mean nothing more than 'seventh in his generation,' Book of Jubilees vii, or 'seventh from Adam,' Jude 14. **Still tarried.** The righteous judgment of the Deluge had not yet come. **4. Great wickedness.** According to vi. 6 and cvi. 13 this growth of wickedness should have been assigned to Jared's days, when the fall of the angels took place. This week includes the Deluge and Covenant made with Noah: Gen. viii. 21–ix. 17. The time order in the close of this sentence is not observed. **5.** Abraham and his seed chosen as the race in and through which God would reveal His righteous judgments—'the plant of righteous judgment': cf. ver. 2; x. 16 (note). **6. Visions of the holy, &c.** The divine manifestations in favour of Israel in Egypt. **A law, &c.** The law given on Sinai. This law is of eternal obligation: cf. xcix. 2. **An enclosure.** Dln. thinks this refers to the Tabernacle and the hedging in of the national life by the law. It seems rather to refer to the occupation of Palestine: cf. lxxxix. 2. **7. The Temple.** The Temple will, according to this author, stand 'for

of glory and dominion be built for ever. 8. And after that in the sixth week, all those who live in it will be blinded, and the hearts of all of them will be given over to a wicked forgetfulness of wisdom, and in it a man will ascend; and at its close the house of dominion will be burnt with fire, and the whole race of the elect root will be dispersed. 9. And after that in the seventh week will a generation arise and many will be its deeds, and all its deeds will be apostate. 10. And at its close will the elect of righteousness of the eternal plant of righteousness be elected to receive sevenfold instruction concerning His whole creation. [11. For who

---

and righteousness will appear.' 9. **Generation.** So G M. Other MSS. 'apostate generation.' 10. **The elect of righteousness.** So D G L O. G reads ይትኀረዩ፡ ኅሩያን፡ ጽድቅ. A B C F H I give 'the elect, the righteous.' E N 'the elect and righteous.' **Be elected.** So A (C) E F G H I M N ይትኀረዩ. Dln. with B D gives 'be recompensed.' **Concerning His whole**

---

ever,' though one form of it may give place to another. If this Apocalypse of Weeks was originally an integral part of xci–civ, this 'for ever' means only an indefinitely long time; for though there is an eternal law, there appears to be no Temple after the final judgment, and the risen righteous enjoy a purely spiritual existence like the angels, as in the Book of Jubilees, and possibly in the Pss. of Solomon. **8.** The time of the divided kingdom in Israel, of growing degeneracy and darkness. **A man,** i. e. Elijah: cf. lxxxix. 52. At the close of this week the Temple is destroyed and the nation carried into captivity. **9.** This week embraces the period from the Captivity to the time of the author. It is an apostate period. The same judgment is passed upon it in lxxxix. 73–75. **10.** The writer here refers to his own disclosures which will be made known at the end of the seventh week. It might seem that it would be impossible for any writer to make such extravagant claims for his productions. We find some slight approach to these in Ecclus. xxiv. 28–32, and a perfect parallel in the case of 'Walking' Stewart of the early part of this century. This writer, who was also the greatest traveller of his age, styles one of his productions, 'this unparalleled work of human energy,' and describes himself as possessing a 'unique mind,' and 'unparalleled energies of genius.' Nay, more, he makes the era of 'Intellectual Life or Moral World' to date from the publication of his chief work, and, believing that only future ages would appreciate him, prevailed on his personal friends to bury his books in secure places: see De Quincey's *Essays*, vol. vii. **The elect of righteousness.** The revelations are designed for these, for only these

is there of all the children of men that is able to hear the voice of the Holy One and quakes not (thereat)? And who is there that can think His thoughts? and who is there that can see all the works of heaven? 12. And how should there be one who could behold the heaven and who is there who could understand the things of heaven and see a soul or a spirit and tell thereof, or ascend and see all their ends and conceive them or do like them? 13. And who is there of all men that could know what is the length and the breadth of the earth, and to whom has been shown the measure of all of them? 14. Or is there any one who could discern the length of the heaven and how high it is, and upon what it is founded, and how great is the number of the stars, and where all the luminaries rest?]

XCIV. 1. And now I say unto you, my sons, love right-

---

creation. For ፍጥረት G reads ጥሪት 'concerning His whole possessions.' 12. **Who could behold the heaven and who is there who could understand.** So G M: ዘይክል፡ ነጽሮተ፡ ሰማየ፡ ወመኑ፡ ውእቱ፡ ዘይክል፡ አእምሮ. Other MSS. and Dln. omit 'behold the heaven and who is there who could.' **A soul or a spirit.** So B M: ነፍሰ፡ ወእመ፡ አኮ፡ መንፈሰ, and G gives ነፍሰ and መንፈሰ, and therefore practically supports M. Other MSS. and Dln. give 'His breath or His Spirit.' **Tell.** G gives ገቢረ.

---

will receive them: cf. c. 6; civ. 12, 13. **11–14.** These verses are completely out of place in their present context, as Laurence, Hoffmann, and Schodde have already remarked. They would belong rather to the Book of Celestial Physics, lxxii–lxxix, lxxxii, but are foreign in character to the whole tone of this book, xci–civ, and do not as a matter of fact rightly describe any one of the books of Enoch. **11. The voice of the Holy One**, i.e. the thunder: cf. Job xxxvii. 4, 5; Ps. xxix. **Think His thoughts**: cf. Job v. 9; ix. 10; xxxviii. 33; Pss. xl. 5; xcii. 5; Eccles. xi. 5. **12. A soul or a spirit**: see Crit. Note. This would refer to Enoch's journey through heaven and Hades. **Ascend**: cf. Prov. xxx. 4. **Their ends**, i.e. of the things of heaven. **13.** Cf. Job xxxviii. 4, 5. Not given in Enoch. **14. The length of the heaven, &c.** Jer. xxxi. 37; Job xi. 8. Not given in Enoch. **Founded**: cf. xviii. 2, 3. **Number of the stars.** This is nowhere found in Enoch.

XCIV. This chapter followed immediately on xci. 12–19 in the original text. It introduces the practical part

eousness and walk therein; for the paths of righteousness are worthy of acceptation, but the paths of unrighteousness are suddenly destroyed and vanish. 2. And to certain men of a (future) generation will the paths of violence and of death be revealed, and they will hold themselves afar from them and will not follow them. 3. And now I say unto you, the righteous: Walk not in the path of wickedness, nor on the paths of death, and draw not nigh unto them lest you be destroyed. 4. But seek and choose for yourselves righteousness and a holy life, and walk in the paths of peace that ye may live and prosper. 5. And hold fast my words in the thoughts of your hearts, and suffer them not to be effaced from your hearts; for I know that sinners will tempt men to make wisdom wicked, and no place will be found for her and no manner of temptation will minish. 6. Woe to those who build unrighteousness and oppression and lay deceit as a foundation; for they will be suddenly overthrown and will have no peace. 7. Woe to those that build their houses with sin; for they will be overthrown from their foundation and will fall by the sword; and those who acquire gold and

---

XCIV. 1. **Worthy of acceptation.** G reads ይደሉ፡ ወይትወከፉ. 3. **Path of wickedness.** So G M. Other MSS. add 'and in violence.' 4. **But seek.** G reads ከመ፡ እለ፡ ይፈቅዱ፡ እኩየ, and connects it with the preceding verse, 'as those who seek evil.' **A holy life.** This suits the context better than Dln.'s 'ein wohlfälliges Leben.' **That ye may live and prosper. And hold**

---

of this section. Though written for the righteous, it devotes as much attention to the woes awaiting the sinners. **1. Love righteousness, &c.**: cf. xci. 3. **Worthy of acceptation**: cf. 1 Tim. i. 15. **Paths of unrighteousness are destroyed**: cf. Ps. i. 6. **2.** The revelations through Moses and the Prophets. **Paths of death**: cf. Prov. xiv. 12; Jer. xxi. 8. **3. Draw not nigh**: cf. xci. 4; civ. 6. **5.** We have here a warning against Sadducean or Greek influences. **No place will be found for her**: cf. xlii. **6.** Some of the forms that wickedness will assume in those days. **Build**: cf. xci. 5. **Have no peace.** This recurs in xcviii. 11, 16; xcix. 13; ci. 3; cii. 3; ciii. 8. See also v. 4 (note). **7. Build their houses with sin**: cf. Jer. xxii. 13. **They,**

silver will perish in judgment suddenly. 8. Woe to you ye rich, for ye have trusted in your riches and from your riches ye shall depart, because ye have not remembered the Most High in the days of your riches. 9. Ye have committed blasphemy and unrighteousness and have become ready for the day of slaughter and the day of darkness and the day of the great judgment. 10. Thus I speak and declare unto you that He who has created you will overthrow you and for your fall there will be no compassion, and your Creator will rejoice at your destruction. 11. And your righteous ones in those days will be a cause of shame to the sinners and the godless.

XCV. 1. Oh that mine eyes were a cloud of water that I might weep over you, and shed my tears as a cloud of water; that so I might rest from my trouble of heart! 2. Who has permitted you to practise hate and wickedness? May judgment light upon you, sinners! 3. Fear not the sinners, ye righteous; for again will the Lord deliver them into your hands that ye may execute judgment on them according to

---

fast. G reads: ወትሕየው፡ ወትዴሰው፡ በትእዛዝ. 9. **And the day of darkness.** Wanting in G. 11. **Your righteous ones.** G M read 'Thy righteous ones.'

XCV. 1. **Oh that mine eyes were a cloud of water.** G reads: መኑ፡ ይሁበኒ፡ ማየ፡ ለአዕይንትየ 'Oh that I had water for mine eyes that they might become a cloud of water.' 2. **Who has permitted you to practise hate and wickedness?** G omits ከመ፡ ትገበሩ, and for ይርከብክሙ reads ይረክበክሙ. 3. **Your hands.**

---

i. e. the men who so build. 8. Pss. xlix. 6; lii. 7; Prov. xi. 28; Jer. ix. 23. Cf. also En. xlvi. 7; lxiii. 10; xcvi. 4; xcvii. 8–10. 9. **Through their sin and blasphemy they are now ripe for judgment. Day of slaughter, &c.:** see xlv. 2 (note). 10. **Your Creator will rejoice at your destruction.** This sentiment so opposed to the O.T. (cf. Ezek. xviii. 23, 32; xxxiii. 11) has parallels in lxxxix. 58 and xcvii. 2. 11. **Your righteous ones**, i. e. the righteous among his children's descendants.

XCV. 1. Oh that mine eyes were a cloud of water, &c. From Jer. ix. 1. This verse was probably before the writer of Baruch xxxv. 2: O oculi mei, estote scatebrae. 3. **Yet let not the righteous fear**; for the period of their supremacy is at hand: cf. xci. 12. **Again.** The writer may

your desires. 4. Woe to you who fulminate irreversible anathemas: healing shall therefore be far from you because of your sins. 5. Woe to you who requite your neighbour with evil; for ye will be requited according to your works. 6. Woe to you, lying witnesses, and to those who weigh out injustice, for suddenly will ye perish. 7. Woe to you sinners, for ye persecute the righteous; for ye will be delivered up and persecuted, ye people of injustice, and heavy will their yoke be upon you.

XCVI. 1. Be hopeful, ye righteous; for suddenly will the sinners perish before you, and ye will have lordship over them according to your desires. [2. And in the day of the tribulation of sinners, your children will mount and rise as eagles and higher than the vultures will be your nest, and ye will ascend as squirrels and enter the crevices of the earth, and

---

G reads 'their hands.' 4. **Irreversible anathemas: healing shall therefore be far.** G reads: ግዘታተ፡ ከመ፡ ይትፈትሑ፡ ወፈውስ፡ ከመ፡ ይርኃቅ. M: ግዘታተ፡ ከመ፡ ኢይትፈትሑ፡ ወፈውስ፡ ርኁቅ. 7. **Ye will be delivered up and persecuted, ye people of injustice.** G reads: ትሜጥዉ፡ ወትሰድዱ፡ በዐመፃ 'ye deliver up and persecute with injustice.' For እሰ፡ ዐመፃ M reads እጓንመፃ. For ዘእሆሙ G M read ዘእየ 'its (i. e. injustice) yoke.'

XCVI. 1. **Ye righteous; for suddenly will . . . perish.** Wanting in G. በከመ wanting in G. 2. **And rise.** G reads

---

refer to the Maccabean victories; for these were victories over Sadducean influences. Though the Maccabean princes are now Sadducees themselves, the period of the Sword, the time of the vengeance of the righteous, is coming. 4. Magical practices and incantations are here referred to. 5. **Requited according to your works**: cf. c. 7. 6. **Weigh out injustice**, i. e. are unjust judges. 7. See Crit. Note for a possibly better text.

XCVI. The righteous exhorted to hope in the coming Messianic kingdom, and fresh woes denounced against the sinners. 1. **Lordship**: cf. xci. 12 (note); xcv. 3, 7; xcviii. 12. 2. This verse must be an interpolation: it is silly in itself and interrupts the context. It is the wicked who will flee to hide themselves in secret places, xcvii. 3; c. 4; cii. 1, and not the righteous: the latter will not have to conceal themselves on the day of judgment, civ. 5. **In the day of the tribulation of sinners**, i. e. when the sinners suffer tribulation. **Mount and rise, &c.** From Is. xl. 31. **Higher than the vultures**: cf. Jer. xlix. 16. **Into the crevices**

the clefts of the rock for ever before the unrighteous, and they will sigh and weep because of you as satyrs.] 3. Wherefore fear not, ye that suffer; for healing will be your portion, and a bright light will enlighten you, and you will hear the voice of rest from heaven. 4. Woe unto you, ye sinners, for your riches make you appear like the righteous, but your hearts convict you of being sinners, and this word will be a testimony against you, for a memorial of (your) wickedness. 5. Woe to you who devour the finest of the wheat and drink the power of the source of the fountain, and tread under foot the lowly with your might. 6. Woe to you who drink water at all times; for suddenly will you be requited and will dry up and wither, because ye have forsaken the fountain of life. 7. Woe to you who work unrighteousness and deceit and blasphemy: it will be a memorial against you for evil. 8. Woe to you, ye mighty, who with might oppress the righteous; for the day of your destruction will come. In

---

ይትኀሠኙ. **Will sigh and weep because of you as satyrs.** G reads: ይነሥኡ፡ ቀይሞጸሆሙ፡ ወይበኪ፡ ጼዴናት. 4. **Your riches.** Before these words G inserts እመ. **A memorial of (your) wickedness.** G reads: ተዘካር፡ እኩያን. 8. **Oppress.** G reads ይኩርህዎ.

---

of the earth, &c. These words are taken from Is. ii. 10, 19, 21, and are used there of those who flee through fear from the presence of the Lord. Hence they are most inappropriate in their present connexion. **Before the unrighteous.** These words imply that the righteous go into the clefts of the rocks to escape the unrighteous. **Sigh and weep because of you, &c.** The present text is very doubtful: see Crit. Note. 3. **A bright light**: see xxxviii. 4 (note). 4. **Your riches make you appear like the righteous.** Wealthy sinners could appeal to their riches as a proof of their righteousness; for, according to the O.T. doctrine of retribution, prosperity was a mark of righteousness. **This word**, i. e. that your riches prove you to be righteous. **For a memorial, &c.**: cf. ver. 7. 5. **The finest of the wheat**: Pss. lxxxi. 16; cxlvii. 14. **The power of the source of the fountain.** This must mean the purest water. 6. **Drink water at all times.** If the text is right, this phrase describes the self-indulgent life: the end of such a life will be painful want; for they have forsaken the fountain of true life: cf. Jer. ii. 13; Ps. xxxvi. 9. 7. Cf. xci. 8; xciv. 6, 9. **For a memorial**: cf. ver. 4. 8. **Many and good days.**

those days many and good days will come to the righteous—in the day of your judgment.

XCVII. 1. Believe, ye righteous; for the sinners will come to shame and perish in the day of unrighteousness. 2. It will become known to you that the Most High is mindful of your destruction and the angels of heaven rejoice over your destruction. 3. What will ye do, ye sinners, and whither will ye flee on that day of judgment when ye hear the voice of the prayer of the righteous? 4. And it will not fare with you as with them, ye against whom this word will stand as a testimony: "Ye have been companions of sinners." 5. In those days the prayer of the righteous will reach unto the Lord, and the days of your judgment will overtake you. 6. And all the words of your unrighteousness will be read out before the Great (and) Holy One, and your faces will be covered with shame, and every work which

---

XCVII. 2. **The angels of heaven.** So G M N. Other MSS. omit 'of heaven.' 5. G reads, 'will go forth (ተመጽአ) and reach.' 6. **All the words of your unrighteousness.** G reads: ዙሉ፡ ግመፃ ከሙ. The words **Great (and) Holy One** introduce the repeated section xcvii. 6b–cviii. 10 in G. We shall distinguish the two texts for this section as G and G¹. It will be remarked that the readings of G¹ stand almost midway between G and Dln.'s text. **(And) Holy.** So G G¹ M. Dln. gives 'and Holy.' **Every work which**

The reference here seems to be to the temporary Messianic kingdom in which the righteous who are living at the time will participate.

XCVII. This chapter mainly consists of threatenings against the wicked. **1. In the day of unrighteousness.** A peculiar expression for the day appointed for the judgment of unrighteousness: see xlv. 2 (note). **2.** Cf. xciv. 10 for a similar expression of religious hate contrasted with Luke xv. 10. **3. Whither will ye flee:** cf. cii. 1. **The prayer of the righteous:** cf. ver. 5. **4. This word . . . 'Ye have been companions of sinners.'** xcvi. 4 may be taken in this sense. The Pharisaic duty of separation from the unrighteous could not be more strongly enforced. **5. The prayer of the righteous:** cf. xlvii. 2; xcvii. 3; xcix. 3, 16; civ. 3. This cry of the righteous for vengeance on their persecutors is found in Rev. vi. 10. **6. Will be read out,** i. e. from the books of remembrance of evil deeds: see xlvii. 3 (note). **Great (and) Holy One:** see i. 3 (note); xcii. 2 (note). **Covered with shame:** cf. xlvi. 6;

is grounded in unrighteousness will be rejected. 7. Woe to you, ye sinners, on the mid ocean and the dry land, for their remembrance of you is evil. 8. Woe to you who acquire silver and gold in unrighteousness, yet say: "We have increased in riches: we have possessions; and we have acquired everything we desire. 9. And now let us do that which we purpose; for we have gathered silver and our granaries are full, and plentiful as water are the husbandmen in our houses." 10. And like water your lies will flow away; for riches will not abide with you but will ascend suddenly from you; for ye have acquired it all in unrighteousness and ye will be given over to a great condemnation.

XCVIII. 1. And now I swear to you, to the wise and foolish, for ye will experience much on the earth. 2. For ye men will put on more adornments than a woman and coloured garments more than a virgin: in royalty, and in grandeur, and in power, and in silver, and in gold, and in purple, and in

---

is grounded in unrighteousness will be rejected. G reads የኃደግ፡ ተግባረ፡ ዐመፃ, and G[1] reads ይገደፍ፡ ተግባረ፡ ዘጸንዐ፡ በዓመፃ. Text of other MSS. and Dln. is a free combination of the two, but leaves both in giving a passive 'will be rejected.' 9. **Are full, and plentiful as water are the husbandmen.** G reads: ከመ፡ ማይ፡ ወብዙኃ. This gives a good sense: 'are full as water and many are the husbandmen.' M: ወከመ፡ ማይ፡ ብዙኃት፡ አብያቲነ፡ ሐረስት. All other MSS. support Dln. 10. **Acquired it all.** G omits ኵሎ. G[1] and other MSS. retain it.

XCVIII. 1. **To the wise and foolish.** G and G[1] read ወለአብ ዳን. 2. **In royalty and in grandeur . . . they will be poured**

---

lxii. 10; lxiii. 11. 7. **On the mid ocean and the dry land,** i. e. everywhere. **Remembrance:** cf. c. 10, 11; civ. 8. 8. Cf. xciv. 7, 8 (note); also Ecclus. xi. 17; Luke xii. 19. 10. This verse is a rejoinder to the boasting of the sinners, and plays partly on their words. **Riches will ascend suddenly:** cf. Prov. xxiii. 5.

XCVIII. This chapter introduces a fresh division in xci–civ. This division, xcviii–cii. 3, consists mainly of a denunciation of the sinners, of their errors in life and doctrine, and announces their coming judgment. 1. **I swear to you.** This formula occurs here for the first time but recurs frequently: cf. vv. 4, 6; xcix. 6, &c. **To the wise and foolish.**

splendour, and in food they will be poured out as water. 3. Therefore they will be wanting in knowledge and wisdom, and they will perish thereby together with their possessions and with all their glory and their splendour, and in shame and in slaughter and in great destitution will their spirits be cast into the furnace of fire. 4. I have sworn unto you, ye sinners, as a mountain does not become a slave and will not, nor a hill the handmaid of a woman, even so sin has not been sent upon the earth, but man of himself has created it, and into great condemnation will those fall who commit it. 5. And barrenness has not been given to the woman, but on account of the deeds of her own hands she dies without children. 6. I have sworn unto you, ye sinners, by the Holy and Great One that all your evil deeds are revealed in the heavens, and that none of your deeds of oppression are covered or hidden.

---

out as water. But G omits the በ in every instance, and thus we have, 'royalty and grandeur and power and silver . . . will be poured out as water,' i.e. as plentifully as water, cf. xcvii. 9. G[1] inserts the preposition before the first four, M before the first three, nouns. N inserts it before all. Before 'in royalty' *all MSS.* except G G[1] M read በመንግል, which is not a possible word. This reading is valuable in determining the various worth of the MSS. 4. **I have sworn.** Wanting in G[1]. For ወእመገር G reads መገር 'As a mountain does not become a slave and a hill will not become the handmaid of a woman.' G[1] H I L M N O agree with Dln. 6.

The foolish are addressed in xcviii–cii. 3; the wise in cii. 4–civ. **2. Will be poured out as water.** Their personality giving itself wholly to such external possessions will at last lose itself in them, as water is lost in the earth: cf. Ps. xxii. 14. **3. In great destitution.** In contrast to their wealth in this world. **Their spirits:** cf. ver. 10; ciii. 8. As incorporeal spirits the wicked are cast into hell. This 'furnace of fire' is the final place of punishment. **4.** The writer now proceeds to attack the immoral view that sin is something original and unavoidable. Sin was of man's own devising: see lxix. 11 (note). **5.** And as a consequence of their sin men are punished just because sin is a voluntary thing. The instance in the text is chosen as an illustration of this general law: cf. Hos. ix. 14. **6–8.** The writer next deals with the view that God does not concern Himself with the world or the deeds of men, cf. Job xxii. 13, Ps. lxxiii. 11, and declares that the deeds of men are recorded

7. And do not think in your spirit nor say in your heart that you do not know and that you do not see that every sin is every day recorded in the presence of the Most High. 8. From henceforth ye know that all your oppression wherewith ye oppressed is written down every day till the day of your judgment. 9. Woe to you, ye fools, for through your folly will ye perish: ye have transgressed against the wise, and so good hap will not be your portion. 10. And now, know ye that ye are prepared for the day of destruction: wherefore do not hope to live, ye sinners, but ye shall depart and die; for you know no ransom; for ye are prepared for the day of the great judgment and for the day of tribulation and great shame for your spirit. 11. Woe to you, ye obstinate of heart, who work wickedness and eat blood: whence have ye good things to eat and drink and to be filled? From all the good things which our Lord, the Most High, has placed in abundance on the earth; and ye indeed shall have no peace. 12. Woe to you who love the deeds of unrighteousness: wherefore do you hope for good hap unto yourselves? know that ye shall be delivered into the hands of the righteous, and they will cut

---

Deeds of oppression. G omits 'deeds.' 8. **Is written down.** G reads ይጽሕፍ. **Your judgment.** G 'judgment.' 9. **Transgressed against the wise.** So G and G[1] ትረስዕዎሙ. M ኢተአምርዎሙ. Other MSS. ኢተሰምዕዎሙ 'ye have not hearkened.' 10. **For destruction.** G reads ለዐለ፡ ሐጐልክሙ. 11. **Who work.**

---

every day in heaven. 7. **Recorded:** cf. xcvii. 6; xcviii. 8; c. 10; civ. 7, 8. 8. **From henceforth ye know,** i. e. from the publication of Enoch's book in these later times. 9. This verse introduces a long succession of woes directed against the sinners. 10. **Prepared:** cf. xciv. 9. **Die.** This refers not only to the loss of the life temporal but also of the life eternal. **No ransom:** Ps. xlix. 8, 9. **Day of great judgment, &c.:** see xlv. 2 (note). **For your spirit:** see ver. 3 (note). 11. The denunciation of individual sinners. **Obstinate of heart:** cf. c. 8. **Eat blood:** cf. vii. 5. Not content with enjoying the best of everything that God gives, these sinners eat blood and break the divine law: cf. Book of Jubilees vii, xxi; Acts xv. 29. **Have no peace:** see v. 4 (note). 12. **Delivered into the hands of the righteous:** see xci. 12 (note). 13.

off your necks and slay you, and will have no pity upon you. 13. Woe to you who rejoice in the tribulation of the righteous; for no grave of yours will be seen. 14. Woe to you who set at nought the words of the righteous; for no hope of life will be yours. 15. Woe to you who write down lying and godless words; for they write down their lies that men may hear them and transgress against (their) neighbour. 16. Therefore they will have no peace but will die a sudden death.

XCIX. 1. Woe to them who act godlessly and glory in lying words and extol them: ye will perish and no happy life will be yours. 2. Woe to them who pervert the words of uprightness and transgress the eternal law, and transform themselves into what they were not, i.e. into sinners: they shall be trodden under foot upon the earth. 3. And in

---

G G[1] M give ይገብኡ and ይበልዑ. 13. **No grave of yours will be seen.** So G and G[1] ይትረአይ. Other MSS. 'no grave will be dug for you.' 15. **And transgress against (their) neighbour.** So G[1] M: ወይርስዑ፡ ለባዕድ. G leaves a blank space where the verb should be, but gives ለባዕድ. Other MSS. 'and forget not folly.'

XCIX. 1. **Ye will perish and no happy life be yours.** G reads: ተሐጕልክሙ፡ ሐይወት፡ ሠናይት 'ye will perish as to a happy life.' 2. **Woe to them, &c.** So G G[1] M: አሌ፡ ሎሙ፡ ለእለ፡ ይፄልጥዎሙ. Other MSS. 'woe to you,' &c., but this seems wrong, as verse 1 opens with 'woe to them,' and all the remaining

---

No grave of yours will be seen: see Crit. Note. Cf. Jer. viii. 2; xxii. 19. **14. No hope of life, &c.:** cf. xcvi. 1; xcviii. 10. **15.** Cf. civ. 10. This verse attests the vigorous literary strife existing between the Sadducean or Hellenistic and the Pharisaic party. **Transgress against (their) neighbour:** see Crit. Note. Cf. ver. 9. **16. Have no peace:** see v. 4 (note). **A sudden death:** cf. xciv. 1, 6, 7; xcv. 6; xcvi. 1, 6.

XCIX. 1. In xcviii. 15 the writers of the Hellenistic literature are denounced: here all those who sympathise with or praise them: cf. xciv. 5; xcviii. 15 (note). **Act godlessly.** The Ethiopic could also be rendered 'practise transgression'; for the substantive here is derived from the verb translated 'transgress' in xcviii. 15. **2. Pervert the words of uprightness:** cf. xciv. 5. **The eternal law,** i.e. the Mosaic law: cf. v. 4; xcix. 14. **Transform themselves into what they are not,** i.e. adopt foreign customs and make themselves 'sinners

those days make ready, ye righteous, to raise your prayers as a memorial, and ye will place them as a testimony before the angels in order that they may place the sin of the sinners for a memorial before the Most High. 4. In those days the nations will be stirred up and the families of the nations will arise on the day of destruction. 5. And in those days those who are reduced to want will go forth and mangle their children, and they will cast them away, and there will be miscarriages; and they will cast away their sucklings, and will not return unto them, and will have no pity on their beloved ones. 6. Again I swear to you, sinners, that sin is prepared for a day of unceasing bloodshed. 7. And they will worship stones, and others will make graven images of gold and

---

verbs of verse 2 are in the 3rd pl. 3. G reads, 'the righteous will make ready to raise their prayers,' ይኄሥኡ፡ ጸሎታቲሆሙ. 4. **Will be stirred up.** G gives a false form ተውሀውኩ. **The families of the nations will arise.** G omits 'families.' **Will arise.** G G[1] M read ይነሥኡ, M adding ገጸ. 5. **Those who are reduced to want.** እለ፡ ይጸነሱ. Dln. rendered this in his translation, 'wird die Frucht des Mutterleibes abgehen,' deriving ይጸነሱ from ፀነሰ. But ፀነሰ could not bear this meaning. In his Lexicon, col. 1286, he derives it from ተጸነሰ, ad egestatem redigi. **Cast them away.** So G G[1] M. Other MSS. 'cast

---

of the Gentiles': become apostates. **3. Your prayers**: see xcvii. 5 (note). **Place them . . . before the angels.** This mediatorial function of the angels (cf. ix. 2–11 note) has its root in the O.T., cf. Job v. 1; xxxiii. 23; Zech. i. 12; but has no place in the N.T., except in Rev. viii. 3, 4. **The Most High.** This title is found in all sections of the book. For 'Most High God' see in xxi. 6, Crit. Note. The title 'Most High' appears in ix. 3; x. 1; xlvi. 7; lx. 1, 22; lxii. 7; lxxvii. 1; xciv. 8; xcvii. 2; xcviii. 7, 11; xcix. 3, 10; ci. 1, 6, 9. **4.** In the last times there will be wars and tumults among the nations of the earth. This will be the period of the Sword: cf. xc. 19; xci. 12; xcix. 6. **5.** See Crit. Note. As there will be wars and strifes among nations, so there will be also amongst families: cf. lvi. 7 (note); c. 1. **6–C. 6.** Denunciation of the idolatry and superstition of the wicked. In this denunciation not only the apostates but also the actual heathen are included. **6. Day of unceasing bloodshed,** i.e. the judgment of the sword: see xci. 12 (note); xlv. 2 (note). Quoted by Tertullian, *De Idol.* iv: Juro vobis, peccatores, quod in diem sanguinis perditionis poenitentia parata est. **7. Graven images of gold and** silver and wood and clay, and others will worship impure spirits and demons and all kinds of superstitions not according to knowledge, notwithstanding no manner of help will be found in them. 8. And they will become godless by reason of the foolishness of their hearts, and their eyes will be blinded through the fear of their hearts and through visions in their dreams. 9. Through these they will become godless and fearful, because they work all their works in a lie and they worship a stone: therefore in an instant will they perish. 10. But in those days blessed are all they who accept the words of wisdom, and understand them, and follow out the paths of the Most High, and walk in the path of His righteousness, and become not godless with the godless; for they will be saved. 11. Woe to you who hope for misfortune to your neighbour; for you will be slain in Sheol. 12. Woe to you who make deceitful

---

their children away.' 7. **Impure spirits.** G gives መናፍስት፡ እኩያን 'evil spirits.' M : ነፍሳት፡ እኩያት. **Not according to knowledge.** So G[1] ኢስተምሃር. So Tert. *De Idol.* iv, quoted in Exeget. Note. G ስተምሀር. FHILNO and Dln. በምሕራማት 'in idol temples.' M reads with Dln., but inserts a negative. 10. **Of His righteousness.** So G G[1] M. Other MSS. 'of righteousness.' **With the godless.** Wanting in G. 11. **Hope for misfortune to your neighbour.** So G ትስፈውዋ, i.e. ትሴፈውዋ. Other MSS. ትስፍሕዋ 'who spread evil to your neighbour.' 12. **Woe**

---

silver, . . . and others will worship . . . demons: cf. Rev. ix. 20. **Demons:** cf. xvi. 1; xix. 1. **Not according to knowledge:** see Crit. Note. Observe that this reading is supported by Tertullian, *De Idol.* iv, where he translates this verse: Qui servitis lapidibus, et qui imagines facitis aureas et argenteas et ligneas et lapideas et fictiles, et servitis phantasmatibus et daemoniis et spiritibus infamibus [MSS. give infamis] et omnibus erroribus *non secundum scientiam*, nullum ab iis invenietis auxilium: cf. Book of Jubilees i. 8. The victims of such superstition and idolatry will proceed from bad to worse: cf. Book of Wisdom xiv. 12, 27; Rom. i. 21. **Will become godless:** cf. xciii. 8; xcix. 9. On the relation of dreams to superstition, cf. Ecclus. xxxi. 1–7. 9. **Through these,** i.e. dreams. 10. As sudden destruction will befall the idolaters, ver. 9, so salvation will be the recompense of those who accept the true wisdom. 11. **Hope for misfortune, &c.:** see Crit. Note. **Will be slain:** cf. cviii. 3. This is the extreme penalty of sin: a less severe punishment is eternal condemnation to Sheol, but that not attended by

and false measures, and who tempt (others) on the earth; for they will thereby be utterly consumed. 13. Woe to you who build your houses through the grievous toil of others and their building material is nothing save the bricks and stones of sin; I tell you ye will have no peace. 14. Woe to them who reject the measure and eternal heritage of their fathers and whose souls follow after idols; for they will have no rest. 15. Woe to them who work unrighteousness and aid oppression and slay their neighbours until the day of the great judgment. 16. For He will cast down your glory and bring affliction on your hearts, and will arouse the spirit of His indignation to destroy you all with the sword; and all the righteous and holy will remember your sins.

C. 1. And in those days the fathers together with their sons will be smitten in one place, brothers will fall in death one with another until it streams with their blood like a river. 2. For a man will not withhold his hand from slaying his

---

to you. G gives 'woe to them.' **Measures.** So G G¹ በመስፈርት. M በመቅሠፍት. Other MSS. በመሠረት 'who lay a foundation of sin and deceit.' **Tempt (others).** So G የመክሩ. G¹ reads ያእምሩ. Other MSS. ያመርሩ 'cause bitterness.' 14. **Whose souls follow after idols.** So G M ይተልዉ. G¹ testifies to this text though its present order is confused: ይተልዉ፡ ይኅረ፡ ነፍስ፡ ጣዖት. Other MSS. 'who cause their souls to follow after idols.' 16. **Will bring affliction on your hearts.** Dln.'s rendering is astray here: 'die Bösheit euch ans Herz legen.' **The spirit of His indignation to destroy you.** G¹M read: መዐት፡ ወመንፈስ፡ ይሕጕልክሙ.

C. 1. **Their blood.** G gives 'your blood.' 2. **Withhold**

---

the 'slaying' of the soul: cf. xxii. 13. **Sheol** here means the eternal place of punishment: see lxiii. 10 (note); ciii. 7. **12.** See Crit. Note; Prov. xi. 1; Hos. xii. 7. **13. Build . . . through the grievous toil of others**: cf. Jer. xxii. 13; also En. xciv. 7; xcvii. 8. **14. The measure and eternal heritage**, i. e. the Mosaic land: cf. ver. 2. The apostates as in that verse are here referred to. **Have rest**: see xciv. 6 (note). **15. Day of the great judgment**: see xciv. 9; xcviii. 10; xlv. 2 (note). **16. Remember your sins.** And accordingly pray for your destruction: see xcvii. 5 (note).

C. 1. The thought in xcix. 6 is here expanded. **Streams with their blood**: cf. Is. xxxiv. 3, 7; Ps. lviii.

sons and his sons' sons, and the sinner will not withhold his hand from his honoured brother: from dawn till sunset—they will slay one another. 3. And the horses will walk up to the breast in the blood of sinners, and the chariot will be submerged to its height. 4. And in those days the angels will descend into the secret places and will gather into one place all those who brought down sin, and the Most High will arise on that day of judgment to execute great judgment amongst sinners. 5. And over the righteous and holy he will appoint as guardians holy angels to guard them as the apple of an eye until He has made an end of all wickedness and all sin, and though the righteous sleep a long sleep, they

---

his hand. So G G[1] M. Other MSS. 'withhold in compassion his hand.' G G[1] M give ሰኃጥእ for ወኃጥእ. 3. **To its height.** G reads እስከ፡ እስተ፡ መልዕልት፡ ወ, and G[1] እስከ፡ እስተ፡ መልዕልቷ. 4. **Who brought down sin.** So G G[1] M ያወረደዎ. Other MSS. 'who aided sin.' **Day of judgment.** So G G[1] M: ዕለተ፡ ኵነኔ. Other MSS. 'day.' **Amongst.** So G G[1] M: እማእከሎሙ፡ ለ. Other MSS. 'on all.' 5. **The righteous.** So G. Other MSS. 'all the righteous.' **He has made an end of.** So G G[1] M ይቄይዕ, with the four next words in the acc. Other MSS. 'till all wicked-

---

10. **2. From his honoured brother.** It is very probable that we have here a reference to the murder of Antigonus by his brother Aristobulus I. Josephus (*Ant.* xiii. 11. 1, 2) tells us that Aristobulus specially loved Antigonus, but moved by calumnies put him to death, and afterwards died of remorse for this deed. On the internecine strife that was to initiate the kingdom, cf. lvi. 7; xcix. 5, 6; Zech. xiv. 13; Ezek. xxxviii. 21; Hagg. ii. 22. **3. Up to the breast:** cf. Rev. xiv. 20. **4. Brought down sin:** see Crit. Note. The reference in this verse can only be to the fallen angels who are here described as having 'brought down sin.' These fallen angels were temporarily buried in abysses of the earth, i. e. 'the secret places.' **5.** This verse has always been interpreted of the righteous on earth, but wrongly. The righteous here spoken of are not the living, but are righteous souls in the place of the departed. This place was afterwards called the chambers or promptuaries, as in IV Ezra [vi. 60]: Vident promptuaria animarum aliarum, quae custodiuntur ab angelis in quiete multa; and again in [vi. 68] the souls in their promptuaries requiescunt in quiete multa et ab angelis custodiuntur: cf. also IV Ezra iv. 35; vii. 32; Apoc. Bar. xxx. 2. **The apple of an eye:** cf. Deut. xxxii. 10; Ps. xvii. 8. **The righteous sleep a long sleep.** The

have nought to fear. 6. And the wise amongst men will see the truth, and the children of earth will understand all the words of this book and recognise that their riches will not be able to save them in the overthrow of their sins. 7. Woe to you sinners, when ye afflict the righteous on the day of great trouble and burn them with fire: therefore ye will be requited according to your works. 8. Woe to you, ye obstinate of heart, who watch in order to devise wickedness: therefore fear shall come upon you and there will be none to help you. 9. Woe to you, ye sinners; for on account of the words of your mouth and on account of the deeds of your hands which ye have godlessly wrought, ye will burn in a fire of blazing flame. 10. And now know ye

---

ness and all sin have been made an end of.' 6. **The truth.** GG[1]LMO read እሙነ. 8. **Obstinate of heart.** So GG[1]M: ገዙፋነ፡ ልብ. Other MSS.: ግፍትዓነ፡ ልብ 'ye perverse of heart.' **To help you.** G gives 'to help them.' 9. **Godlessly wrought.** G M

---

writer of xci–civ did not expect the resurrection at the beginning of the temporary Messianic kingdom. The words 'sleep a long sleep' could not be said with reference to this kingdom; for the writer living at the close of the seventh week expects its advent immediately at the beginning of the eighth week. The 'long sleep' extends from his time till the close of the tenth week, when the righteous rise. Again, from vv. 4, 5 we see that the righteous do not rise till God has judged sinners and an end is made of all sin. Thus the resurrection of the righteous in xci–civ follows the final judgment at the close of the Messianic kingdom. 6. Those who are still capable of wisdom will be warned by these revelations of Enoch. Here as in xciii. 10, civ. 12, 13, the writer refers to the appearance of his book. **Children of earth.** This title belongs to the Sadducees, sinners, apostates, paganizers, cii. 3: cf. the Hebrew phrase עַם הָאָרֶץ: the righteous are designated as the 'children of heaven,' ci. 1. **Riches will not be able to save them**: cf. Zeph. i. 18. 7. The righteous underwent such persecution under Antiochus Epiphanes: cf. II Macc. vii, if we may trust the latter. **On the day of great trouble.** These words should probably be read directly after 'woe to you sinners': they would in that case refer to the final judgment: cf. xlv. 2 (note). Otherwise they must be taken of the time of the persecution of the righteous. **Requited according to your works**: cf. xcv. 5. 8. **Obstinate of heart**: cf. xcviii. 11. **Watch**: cf. Is. xxix. 20. 9. The wicked will suffer in the flames of hell for their godless words and deeds. 10. All the

that the angels will seek out your deeds in heaven from the sun and from the moon and from the stars in reference to your sins because ye execute judgment on the righteous upon earth. 11. And He will summon to testify against you cloud and mist and dew and rain; for they will all be withheld by you from descending upon you, and that because of your sins. 12. And now give presents to the rain that it be not withheld from descending upon you, nor yet the dew, when it has received gold and silver from you that it may descend. 13. When the hoar-frost and snow with their chilliness and all the winds of the snow with all their plagues fall upon you, in those days ye will not be able to stand before them.

CI. 1. Observe the heaven, ye children of heaven, and

ረሲዓኒክሙ, and G¹ ረሲዓንክሙ. 10. **Execute judgment on.** G reads ትኩብሩ፤ ኀበ, and G¹ ተገብሩ፡ ምስለ. M: ትገብሩ፡ ምስለ. 11. **Cloud.** So G. Other MSS. 'every cloud.' **From descending.** G reads: ከመ፡ ይረዱ. Other MSS.: ከመ፡ ኢይረዱ. **And that because of your sins.** So G: ወዲበ፡ ኀጢአትክሙ. But the MSS. vary much. G¹ reads: ወይኄልዩ፡ ዲበ፡ ኃጢአትክሙ 'and they will think of your sins.' Dln. gives the same as G¹, with the addition of a negative and ኀበ instead of ዲበ: 'and shall not they think of your sins?' B gives an attractive reading, ኢይሔልዉ 'shall not they keep watch as to your sins?' F H I L M N O same as Dln., except ዲበ for ኀበ. 12. **That it may descend.** So G G¹ I L O. M inserts negative. F H N and Dln. omit entire phrase.

CI. 1. **Ye children.** So G G¹ M. Other MSS. 'all ye children.'

---

heavenly powers which have witnessed the sins of the wicked will testify against them: cf. xcviii. 6–8; also xcvii. 7; civ. 8. In Hab. ii. 11 this testimony is given by the stones and beams of the dwelling of the wicked. **Execute judgment, &c.** Text very uncertain: see Crit. Note. **11.** All the natural powers which minister to the fruitfulness of the earth will testify against sinners, as they have been withholden on account of their sins. This is exactly in keeping with lxxx, one of the chapters interpolated in lxxii–lxxxii: cf. Jer. iii. 3. **12.** Spoken ironically. **13.** Even the lesser punishments of the elements are irresistible.

CI. 1. The same subject pursued; but the writer turns aside for a

every work of the Most High, and fear ye Him and work no evil in His presence. 2. When He closes the windows of heaven and withholds the rain and the dew from descending on the earth on your account, what will ye do then? 3. And when He sends His anger upon you because of all your deeds, ye cannot petition Him; for ye have spoken proud and insolent words against His righteousness: therefore ye will have no peace. 4. And see ye not the sailors of the ships, how their ships are tossed to and fro by the waves and are shaken by the winds and are in sore trouble? 5. And therefore do they fear because all their goodly possessions go into the sea with them, and they are anxious of heart lest the sea should swallow them and they should perish therein. 6. Are not the entire sea, and all its waters, and all its movements the work of the Most High and all its doings and its waters, and has He not confined it throughout by the sand?

Fear ye. G gives ፍናዊሁ 'His ways.' 3. **Because of.** So G M በ. G[1] omits. Other MSS. 'and upon.' 4. **Sailors of the ships.** I have here and in ver. 9 accepted Hallévi's emendation of 'kings of the ships' into 'sailors of the ships.' The false reading arose from a confusion of מַלְּחֵי הָאֳנִיּוֹת with מַלְכֵי הָא״. 5. G G[1] M for ወሠናየ read ሠናይ፡ ወ, and G repeats ምስሌሆሙ—ብሔር through homoioteleuton. 6. **And its waters.** So G G[1] M ወማዩ. E እቀመ. Other MSS. ሐተሞ 'has He not sealed all its doings?' This last, which Dln. follows, is obviously a late conjecture.

---

moment to address the righteous who are here called 'children of heaven,' as elsewhere sinners are called 'children of earth': cf. c. 6; cii. 3. The contemplation of heaven and of nature and of the ends they serve should move them to the fear of God. 2, 3. The writer resumes his address to the wicked and recurs to the subject: cf. c. 11, 12. **Windows of heaven:** Gen. vii. 11. **Proud and insolent words:** v. 4 (note); xxvii. 2. As instances of such insolent speech, cf. xcviii. 7, 8; cii. 6. 4–7. They who go down to the sea in ships are filled with fear at the might of the sea: how much more should not men fear God by whom the sea has been made and of whom it is sore afraid? 4. **Sailors of the ships**; see Crit. Note. For the thought of the verse Ps. cvii. 23–27. 6, 7. The sea can do nothing save according to divine command. **Its doings and its waters**:

7. And at His reproofs it is afraid and dries up and all its fish die and all that is in it; but ye sinners who are on the earth fear Him not. 8. Has He not made the heaven and the earth and all that is therein; and who has given understanding and wisdom to all that move on the earth and to all that move in the sea? 9. Do not the sailors of the ships fear the sea? Yet sinners fear not the Most High.

CII. 1. And in those days when He brings a grievous fire upon you, whither will ye flee and where will ye find deliverance? And when he launches forth His word against you, will you not be affrighted and fear? 2. And all the luminaries will quake with great fear, and all the earth will be affrighted and tremble and be alarmed. 3. And all the angels will execute their commands and will seek to hide themselves from the presence of the Great Glory, and the children of earth will tremble and quake; and as for you, ye sinners, ye are cursed for ever and ye will have no peace. 4. Fear ye not, ye souls of the righteous, and be

---

7. **It is afraid and dries up.** So G[1]M. FHILNO and Dln. 'dries up and is afraid.' G omits 'is afraid.'

CII. 1. **When.** Wanting in G. 3. **The Great Glory.** So G G[1] M: **እቢይ፡ ስብሐት.** Dln. gives 'Him who is great in glory.'

---

see Crit. Note. With this passage cf. Jer. v. 22; Job xxvi. 10: xxxviii. 8–11; Pss. lxxxix. 9; civ. 9; Prov. viii. 29. **8.** God has not only made the sea, but also heaven and earth and all that in them is. He too has given instinct to animals and reason to man. **9.** The whole argument of the chapter summed up in a few pregnant words. **Sailors of the ships**: see Crit. Note on ver. 4.

CII. 1–3. If they now refuse to fear God, the day will come when they will be terrified before the awful day of the Lord—a day so terrible that heaven and earth will be affrighted, and even the holy angels will seek to hide themselves from it. What then will become of sinners? **1. A grievous fire,** i.e. the fire of hell: cf. xcix. 11. **His word,** i.e. word of judgment. **3. The Great Glory**: cf. xiv. 20. **Children of earth**: cf. c. 6; ci. 1 (note). **Have no peace**: cf. xciv. 6 (note). **4–CIV. 9.** The discussion and condemnation of the Sadducean views of the future life. **4, 5.** The righteous are bidden to be of good cheer though their life be such as only sinners deserved, and their latter end be full of grief (vv. 4, 5). **4.**

hopeful ye that die in righteousness. 5. And grieve not if your soul descends in grief into Sheol, and that in your life your body has not fared as your goodness deserved but truly as on a day on which ye became like the sinners, and on a day of cursing and chastisement. 6. And when ye die the sinners speak over you: 'As we die, so die the righteous, and what benefit do they reap from their deeds? 7. Behold, even as we, so do they die in grief and darkness, and what advantage have they over us? from henceforth we are equal. 8. And what will they receive and what will they see for ever? for behold they too have died, and from henceforth for ever they will see no light.' 9. I tell you, ye sinners, ye are content to eat and drink and strip men naked, and rob and sin and acquire wealth and see good days. 10. Have ye seen the righteous how their end falls out? for no manner of violence

---

Children of earth. Wanting in G. 4. **Ye that die.** So C F H I L M N: እለ፡ ምትክሙ. G has ነፍስ፡ እለ፡ ሞቱ, cf. ciii. 3; G[1] እለ፡ ሞቱ. O and Dln., 'hope for the day of your death in righteousness.' 5. **If.** So G and G[1] እመ. Other MSS. 'that,' እስመ. **In grief.** So G G[1] M. Other MSS. 'in great tribulation and wailing and sorrow and grief.' 8. **What will they receive.** G and G[1] read: ምንተ፡ ይትነሥኡ 'how will they arise?' 10.

Die in righteousness: see Crit. Note. **5.** The author, given the standpoint of belief in a blessed future for the righteous, can readily concede that there is often no difference in the outward lot of the righteous and the wicked either in life or death. Such a concession according to the O.T. doctrine of retribution was impossible. **Sheol**: see lxiii. 10 (note). We must apparently assume an aposiopesis at the close of this verse. **Became like the sinners**, i. e. were afflicted just as if ye were sinners. **6–8.** The sinners—the Sadducean opponents—start from the O.T. doctrine of retribution which taught the prosperity of the righteous in this life, and argue that as there is no difference in the lot of the righteous and the wicked in this life—a point just conceded by the author in ver. 5—so there is none in an existence beyond this life: cf. Book of Wisdom ii. 1–5; iii. 2–4; Eccles. ii. 14–16; iii. 19–21, &c. **7. In grief and darkness.** This refers to the O.T. conception of Sheol, lxiii. 10 (note). **9, 10.** The answer of the author. The life of the wicked is fashioned by material and temporal aims only, and so all their desires find satisfaction in this world; but the life of the righteous, as is manifest from first to last, is moulded by spiritual and eternal aims. **How their end**

is found in them till the day of their death. 11. 'Nevertheless they perished, and became as though they had not been, and their souls descended into Sheol in tribulation.'

CIII. 1. Now, therefore, I swear to you, the righteous, by the glory of Him that is great and honoured and mighty in dominion, and by His greatness I swear to you. 2. I know this mystery and have read it in the heavenly tables, and have seen the book of the holy ones and have found written therein and inscribed regarding them: 3. That all goodness and joy and glory are prepared for them and are written down for the spirits of those who have died in righteousness, and that manifold good will be given to you in recompense for your

---

How their end falls out. So G G[1] M, omitting በሰላም. Other MSS. 'how their end is peace.' **Is found.** G reads ተተከሰተ. **In them.** G gives 'in you.'

CIII. 1. **By the glory of Him that is great and honoured.** So G[1]: በስብሐቲ፡ ለዐቢይ፡ ወለክቡር. G gives the same text except that it omits ለ before ዐቢይ. F H I L N O and Dln., 'by His great majesty and glory.' M: በስብሐቲ፡ ዐቢይ፡ ወበክቡር፡ መንግሥቱ. **And mighty in dominion.** So G and G[1]: ዐዚዝ፡ መንግሥት. Dln. 'and by His glorious kingdom.' 3. **Are written down for the spirits of those.** G reads: ተጽሕፈ፡ አስማቲሆሙ 'the names of those . . . are written down.' **Manifold good will be given.**

---

falls out: see Crit. Note. Again, as in ver. 5, the author concedes that there is no outward distinction between the righteous and the wicked in this life, but that there is a religious and ethical distinction. **11.** The wicked rejoin: this difference in character is of no advantage—the same lot awaits good and bad alike.

CIII. 1–4. The author, instead of replying directly to the wicked, turns to the righteous, and solemnly assures them that every good thing is in store for them; for so he has read in the heavenly tables and in the book of the holy ones. Hence they were not to regard the contumely of the wicked. **1.** See Crit. Note. The oath is more solemn here than in xcviii. 1, 4, 6; xcix. 6; civ. 1. **2.** The writer bases his knowledge on the heavenly tables which he has read. **Book of the holy ones,** i. e. of the angels: cf. cviii. 7. See xlvii. 3 (note). Dln. comparing cviii. 3 takes the holy ones here to mean the saints or righteous. **3, 4.** The blessings here depicted will be enjoyed by the righteous, both in Sheol and in the spiritual theocracy established after the final judgment. The words here are vague and might apply to

labours, and that your lot is abundantly beyond the lot of the living. 4. And your spirits—(the spirits) of you who die in righteousness, will live and rejoice and be glad, and their spirits will not perish, but their memorial will be before the face of the Great One unto all the generations of the world: wherefore then fear not their contumely. 5. Woe to you, ye sinners, when ye die in your sins, and those who are like you say regarding you: 'Blessed are they, the sinners: they have seen all their days. 6. And now they have died in prosperity and in riches, and have not seen tribulation or murder in their life; and they have died in honour, and judgment has not been executed on them during their life.' 7. Know ye that their souls will be made to descend into Sheol, and they will become wretched and great will be their tribulation. 8. And into darkness and chains (lit. 'net') and a burning fire, where there is grievous condemnation, will your spirits enter; and there will be grievous condemnation for the generations of the world. Woe to you, for ye will have no

---

So G: ብዙኅ፡ ሠናይ, and M practically. G¹ gives ብዙኃ፡ ወሠናይ. Dln. 'with manifold good is it given.' For ብዙኅ we must read ብዙኃ. **4. And their spirits will not perish.** So G: ወኢትሕጐል፡ መናፍስቲሆሙ; but we must emend ትሕጐል into ይትሐጐል with G¹ M. Other MSS. omit 'will not perish and.' **5. Ye sinners.** G G¹ M curiously read 'ye dead sinners.' **Die in your sins.** G G¹ M read: በብዐል፡ ኃጢአቲክሙ 'die in the riches of your sins.' **Seen all their days.** G adds ሠናየ 'seen good all their days.' 8. **Where there is grievous condemnation.** Dln. renders 'beim grossen Gericht.' **Generations of the world.** So G G¹ M: ትውልደ፡ ዓለም. Other MSS. 'all generations unto eternity.'

---

either. There is apparently only a resurrection of the spirit. 5-8. A different fate awaits the wicked. These have enjoyed all the blessings which according to the O.T. belonged to the righteous. Hence they vaunt themselves on their prosperity and immunity from punishment; but a sure doom awaits them in Sheol—darkness and chains and a burning flame. 7. Sheol: see lxiii. 10 (note). Sheol here is the final place of punishment: cf. the different significations it has in cii. 5, 11. 8. See Crit. Note. Have no peace: see v. 4 (note); xciv. 6 (note). 9-

peace. 9. Say not in regard to the righteous and good who

---

9. From this verse to the end of this chapter the variations are nearly sixty in G alone, but these are mainly between the 1st and 3rd plurals in the verbs and the corresponding suffixes, verbal and substantival. G favours throughout the 3rd pl., whereas G[1] in the main agrees with Dln. in giving the 1st pl. The question now arises on which person, the 1st or 3rd, are we to decide. The evidence of the MSS. would go to prove that *the 3rd person was the original*; for in about fifty instances Dln. gives the 1st person and never the 3rd; G gives the 3rd person in all, except seven instances, confined to vv. 14 and 15. All other MSS. agree with Dln. And the evidence of the context is in the same direction. ciii. 9–15 are pronounced derisively by the sinners of the righteous. For in cii. 6–8, when the sinners declare that the righteous live in trouble and darkness and have no advantage over the wicked beyond the grave, the author (10) in reply points to the nature of their death and the purity of their life. To this the sinners rejoin (11), 'despite all that they go down to Sheol in woe as we.' The author now addresses himself first to the righteous (ciii. 1–4) and then to the sinners. In the case of the latter he gives their glorification of their own life (5, 6) and their depreciation of the life of the righteous (9–15). In these verses the wicked describe the wretchedness and helplessness of the present life of the righteous, just as in cii. 6, 7 they had described the wretchedness of the future of the righteous. The author could not, as Dln. imagines, represent the departed righteous who were in bliss as discouraging the righteous who were still living, and as arraigning, as it were, the justice of God. At the close of these words the author addresses his reply (civ. 1–6) not directly to the sinners who have just spoken but to the righteous, just as in the opening of ciii, and returns to

---

15. These verses are in the mouth of the wicked a sarcastic description of the lot of the righteous: see ciii. 9, Crit. Note. As in vv. 5, 6, the wicked extol the life of the wicked, so here they depreciate the life of the righteous—the *earthly* life, for in cii. 6, 7 they had similarly dealt with the *future* life of the righteous. In these verses the wicked show that in every respect the life of the righteous on earth is a wretched one and contrary to every expectation raised by the O.T.: in fact the righteous suffer all the penalties that were to befall the wicked. 9. In regard

are in life: 'In the days of their life they are worn out with their troublous toil, and have experienced every trouble and met with much evil and suffered from disease, and have been minished and become small in spirit. 10. And they are destroyed, and there has been none to help them (even) in word and have attained to nothing: they are tortured and destroyed, and have not hoped to see life from day to day. 11. And they hoped to be the head and they have become the tail: they toiled laboriously and attained not to the fruit of their toil; and they became the food of sinners, and the unrighteous laid their yoke heavily upon them. 12. And they that hated them and smote them have had dominion over them; and they have bowed their necks to those that hated them and they have had no compassion on them. 13. And they have desired to get away from them that they might escape and be at rest, but have found no place where-

---

the sinners in vv. 7–9. Conclusion. We shall therefore adopt the third person throughout in these verses. Space will not admit of more than a few of the variations being given, and these will not be mere variations of 1st and 3rd persons, but of words. Dln. gives the first person throughout in the case of the righteous. In ciii. 9–15 I have translated the perfects as Greek perfects, and the imperfects as pasts. **In the days of their life they are worn out with their troublous toil.** So G: በመዋዕለ፡ ሕይወቶሙ፡ ጻማ፡ ምሬቶሙ፡ ጸመዉ. Dln. gives, 'in the days of our adversity we were worn out with toil.' G[1]: በመዋዕለ፡ በሬቶሙ፡ ጻማ፡ ጸመወነ. **Suffered from disease.** So G ደዉዩ, which we should emend into ደወዩ. Other MSS. 'were consumed,' ተወጽዑ. 10. **(Even) in word and have attained to nothing.** So G: በነገር፡ ወኢበምንትኒ፡ ኢረከቡ, and also G[1] M, except in the person of the verb. In the translation I have omitted በ in ወኢበምንትኒ with later MSS. Dln. gives, 'with word and deed we were powerless and could attain to nothing.' 11. **Hoped.** So G ይሴፈዉ.

---

to. This can also be translated 'to.' **From disease**: see Crit. Note. Cf. Deut. xxviii. 21, 22. 10. Cf. Deut. xxviii. 29, 66, 67. **Minished and become small, &c.**: cf. Ps. cvii. 39. **Small in spirit.** Not 'humble' but 'poor-spirited' (μικρόψυχος). 11. Cf. Deut. xxviii. 13, 30, 31. 12.

unto they should flee and be safe from them. 14. And they have complained to their rulers in their tribulation and cried out against those who devoured them, but they did not attend to their cries and would not hearken to their voice. 15. And they helped those who robbed and devoured them, and those who made them few; and they concealed their oppression, and they did not remove from them the yoke of those who devoured, and dispersed, and murdered them, and they concealed their murder, and have thought not of the fact that they had lifted up their hands against them.'

CIV. 1. I swear unto you, that in heaven the angels are mindful of you for good before the glory of the Great One:

---

15. The confusion of persons is made worse by G[1] M reading አርዳእክሙዎሙ 'you helped them.' **The yoke of those who.** So G G[1] M: አርዑቶሙ፡ እለ. Dln. reads 'their yoke but.'

CIV. 1. **Unto you.** So G G[1] M. Other MSS. insert 'ye

Cf. Deut. xxviii. 48. **14, 15.** These verses furnish materials towards determining the date of xci–civ. In lxxxiii–xc the rulers are regarded as the divinely appointed leaders of the righteous. In this section, on the other hand, the rulers appear as the aiders and abettors of the enemies of the righteous. These enemies are the Sadducees, sinners, apostates, and paganizers, while the righteous are the Pharisaic party. The issues between these parties as they appear in this book could not have been so clearly defined before the Maccabean times. Nor again could this book have been written before the breach between John Hyrcanus and the Pharisees. But the date must be brought down still further, if we are to explain literally such statements as 'dispersed and murdered them,' and 'their murder,' where the murder of the righteous is meant; for there was no blood spilt between the parties till the reign of Jannaeus, 94 B.C. The later limit is not hard to determine. The close confederacy which here prevails between the Sadducees and the rulers did not exist under the Herodian princes, but only under the later Maccabean princes. Hence this section was written before 64 B.C., and may be assigned either to the years 94–79 B.C. or 70–64 B.C., during which periods the Pharisees were oppressed by the rulers and Sadducees. But the rest of the section is against taking the words 'murder,' &c. literally. We should probably regard them merely as the description of a severe but not murderous persecution: see Special Introd. (pp. 263, 264). **15. Dispersed and murdered them.** These words taken literally would apply well to the actual destruction and dispersion of the Pharisaic families under Jannaeus.

CIV. 1–6. Instead of answering directly the wicked who have thus

your names are written before the glory of the Great One. 2. Be hopeful; for aforetime ye were put to shame through ills and affliction; but soon ye will shine as the stars of heaven, ye will shine and ye will be seen, and the portals of heaven will be opened to you. 3. And persist in your cry for judgment, and it will appear to you; for all your tribulation will be visited on the rulers, and on all their helpers and on those who plundered you. 4. Be hopeful, and cast not away your hope; for ye will have great joy as the angels of heaven. 5. What will ye be obliged to do then? Ye will not have to hide on the day of the great judgment and ye will not be found as sinners, and the eternal judgment will be far from you for all the generations of the world.

---

righteous.' **In heaven.** Wanting in G. 2. **Ye will shine.** This repetition of the verb in G G[1] M wanting in Dln. 5. **What will ye be obliged to do then?** So G G[1] M N and E ምንት. Other MSS. and Dln. እንተ, which is to be translated: 'as for the

---

derisively described the lot of the righteous in this life, the author turns to the righteous and addresses them. This is exactly what he did in the opening of ciii. He returns to the sinners in civ. 7–9. In these verses the author practically concedes that the wicked have rightly described the lot of the righteous in this life; but he holds out a sure hope, a hope however not to be fulfilled in the transitory Messianic kingdom on earth, but to be directed to the blessed future that is awaiting them in heaven: the angels are mindful of them for good even now, and in due time they will become 'companions of the hosts of heaven.' 1. **The angels are mindful of you.** Though apparently forgotten on earth, the righteous are not forgotten before God by the angels. On the intercession of the angels, cf. xv. 2 (note); xl. 5–7; xlvii. 2; lxxxix. 76. **Names are written:** see xlvii. 3 (note). **The Great One:** cf. xiv. 2; ciii. 4. 2. **Shine as the stars:** cf. Dan. xii. 3; IV Ezra [vi. 71]; vii. 55. **Portals of heaven will be opened to you,** i. e. heaven will become their dwelling-place, for they will 'shine as the stars,' 'joy as the angels,' and be 'companions of the hosts of heaven.' The author does not hope for a new earth: cf. xci. 16 (note). 3. Their demand for justice which they make in vain on earth, ciii. 14, 15, will one day be satisfied: wherefore let them continue to make it: cf. xcvii. 3, 5 (note); xcix. 3, 16. **The rulers.** These are brought forward very prominently here: cf. ciii. 14, 15 (note). 4. **As the angels of heaven:** cf. Matt. xxii. 30; Mark xii. 25; also En. civ. 6. 5. See Crit. Note. **Day of the great judgment:** cf. xix. 1; lxxxiv. 4; xciv. 9; xcviii. 10; xcix. 15. **The eternal judgment:** cf. xci. 15, 'great

6. And now fear not, ye righteous, when ye see the sinners growing strong and prospering in their ways and be not like unto them and have no companionship with them, but keep afar from their violence; for ye will become companions of the hosts of heaven. 7. Ye sinners, though ye say, 'Ye cannot ascertain it and all our sins are not written down,' still they will write down all your sins continually every day. 8. And now I show unto you that light and darkness, day and night see all your sins. 9. Be not godless in your hearts, and lie not and alter not the word of uprightness, and do not charge with lying the words of the Holy (and) Great One and glorify not your idols; for all your lying and all your godlessness will prove not to be righteousness but to be great sin. 10. And now I know

---

rôle ye shall have then to play.' 6. **Prospering in their ways.** So G G[1] M በፍኖቶሙ. Other MSS. 'prospering in their lusts.' **Like unto them and.** So G: ከማሆሙ፡ ወ. **Will become.** So G[1] M ሀበውከሙ. Dln.: ሀበውከሙ፡ ትኩኑ 'are destined to become.' G omits verb. 7. G[1]: ኢይጽሕፉ፡ ዘኵሉ፡ ኃጢአትክሙ፡ ይጽሕፉ፡ ሀበዉ. G gives the same sense. 9. **Glorify not your idols.** G reads ተሐሰብዎ, and G[1] ትኅሡብዎ—'take no account of your idols.' All other

---

eternal judgment': also xlv. 2 (note). There appears to be no judgment for the righteous according to this verse. Contrast the teaching of xxxvii–lxx: see lxii. 3. **6. Prospering in their ways**: see Crit. Note. Cf. Jer. xii. 1. The Pharisaic exclusiveness is clearly defined here: cf. xci. 3, 4. Observe that the righteous are not bidden to hope for blessedness on earth through the overthrow of the sinners. No doubt the sinners will be cut off in the period of the Sword, but the author sets little store by the temporary Messianic kingdom thereby established on earth. The hopes of the righteous can be realised in heaven alone. **Companions, &c.**: cf. civ. 2, 4. **7–8.** After showing the blessed destiny of the righteous in the future life, he turns finally to the wicked, and declares that, though they prosper and are strong, and for that reason conceive that no account is taken of their sin, nevertheless all their sins are recorded, and recorded daily. **7. Ascertain,** i.e. our sins. **8.** Even the natural powers will give witness against them: cf. c. 10 (note). **9–13.** From a reproof of the life and the attitude of the wicked towards the O.T. revelation, the author passes on to certain disclosures and directions regarding his own book. **9.** The wicked are admonished not to alter or misinterpret the O.T.: cf. xciv. 5; xcviii. 14; xcix. 2. **Holy (and) Great One**: see i. 3 (note). **Your idols**: cf. xcix. 7–9, 14. **10.** A time will come

this mystery that many sinners will alter and pervert the words of uprightness and will speak wicked words, and lie, and practise great deceits and write books concerning their words. 11. But when they write down truthfully all my words in their languages and do not change or minish ought from my words but write them all down truthfully—all that I first testified concerning them: 12. Then, I know another mystery that books will be given to the righteous and the wise to become a cause of joy and uprightness and much wisdom. 13. And to them will the books be given and they will believe in them and rejoice over them, and then will all the righteous who have learnt therefrom all the paths of uprightness be recompensed.

[CV. 1. 'And in those days,' saith the Lord, 'they shall call

---

MSS. support text. 10. **Will alter and pervert the words of uprightness.** Dln. translates, 'die Worte der Rechtschaffenheit ändern und davon abfallen werden.' It is arbitrary, however, to take የዐልጢ as neuter here. **Practise great deceits.** See Lexicon, col. 1383, 4. Dln. translates, 'grosse Werke schaffen,' but this he withdraws in his Lexicon. **Write books.** G G[1] M give መጽሐፍቲየ. 11. **My words.** G G[1] M give ነገራተ.

---

when the words of revelation will be perverted, and books be written enforcing wicked and heathen doctrine: see Crit. Note. **Practise great deceits:** see Crit. Note. 11. But the writings of Enoch will counteract these heathen teachings, and these writings will be handed down from generation to generation and through various languages, and in the course of transmission be exposed to voluntary and involuntary perversions and changes. The author speaks here from the standpoint of Enoch. **In their languages.** The O.T. was already translated into Greek. It is probable that Aramaic and Greek are the languages here referred to. 12. At last in the course of transmission these books will reach the generation for whom they were designed—a 'righteous and wise' generation, and this generation will be the first to understand their worth. For this idea cf. Dan. xii. 4, 9, 10. 13. The righteous and the wise will recognise and believe in these books: cf. Dan. xii. 10, 'None of the wicked shall understand, but the wise shall understand.' **Recompensed.** The gift of these books with their revelations and wisdom seems to be the recompense of the righteous. This is certainly the view of the writer of cv. 1: cf. xciii. 10; c. 6; civ. 12, 13. Or is it meant that soon after their reception the Messianic kingdom will appear?

CV. This chapter does not seem to

and testify to the children of earth concerning their wisdom: show it unto them; for ye are their guides and a recompense over the whole earth. 2. For I and My Son will unite with them for ever in the paths of uprightness in their lives; and ye will have peace: rejoice, ye children of uprightness. Amen.']

[CVI. 1. And after some days my son Methuselah took a wife for his son Lamech, and she became pregnant by him and bore a son. 2. And his body was white as snow and red as a blooming rose, and the hair of his head and his long locks were white as wool, and his eyes beautiful. And when

---

CV. 2. **Amen.** So G G¹ አሜን. Other MSS. 'in truth,' በአማን.

---

belong to xci–civ. For (1) the phrase 'children of earth,' which in xci–civ is a synonym for the sinners or heathen, has here a good ethical signification: see c. 6 (note); ci. 1 (note). (2) The Messiah is introduced in cv. 2, to whom there is not the faintest allusion throughout xci–civ. (3) The finite duration of the lives of the saints seems to be implied in cv. 2. This is the doctrine in i–xxxvi, but not in xci–civ. (4) The emphasis is laid in cv on the finite life on earth: in xci–civ on the immortal life in heaven. This chapter, like lvi. 5–lvii. 3ᵃ, is a literary revival of O. T. thoughts and ideals. **1. Children of earth.** This phrase has a good signification here; for the books of Enoch, which only 'the righteous and the wise' will receive, are the guides of those designated 'children of earth.' Contrast with this the technical meaning of this phrase in c. 6; cii. 3. **Recompense**: cf. civ. 13. **2. To My Son.** There is no difficulty about the phrase 'My Son' as applied to the Messiah by the Jews: cf. IV Ezra vii. 28, 29; xiv. 9. If the righteous are called 'God's children' in lxii. 11, the Messiah was pre-eminently the Son of God. Moreover, the early Messianic interpretation of Ps. ii would naturally lead to such an expression. In lxii. 14 above we have practically the same thought expressed: cf. John xiv. 23. **In their lives**: see introduction to this chapter. **Ye will have peace.** This was the special blessing of the righteous, as its loss was the curse entailed on the wicked: cf. xciv. 6 (note).

CVI–VII. We have here again a fragment of a Noah Apocalypse. This fragment, as the other fragments of this Apocalypse, uses the Samaritan reckoning: see lxv. 2 (note); lxx. 4 (note). Enoch is still alive and with the angels at the ends of the earth, exactly as it is presupposed in lxv. 2; lxvi. 3, when Noah is born. Only the Samaritan reckoning would admit of this coincidence, as according to it Enoch was only as yet 185 years old. According to the Hebrew text, on the other hand, Noah's birth did not occur till the seventieth year after Enoch's translation, and according to the LXX. not till the 155th year after that event. **2. As wool**:

he opened his eyes, he lighted up the whole house like the sun, and the whole house was very full of light. 3. And when he was taken from the hand of the midwife, he opened his mouth and conversed with the Lord of righteousness. 4. And his father Lamech was afraid of him and fled, and came to his father Methuselah. 5. And he said to him: 'I have begotten a strange son: he is not like man but resembles the children of the angels of heaven; and his nature is different and he is not like us, and his eyes are as the rays of the sun and his countenance is glorious. 6. And it seems to me that he is not sprung from me but from the angels, and I fear that in his days a wonder may be wrought on the earth. 7. And now, my father, I am here to petition thee and implore thee that thou mayest go to Enoch, our father, and learn from him the truth, for his dwelling-place is amongst the angels.' 8. And when Methuselah heard the words of his son, he came to me to the ends of the earth; for he had heard that I was there, and he cried aloud and I heard his voice and came to him. And I said unto him: 'Behold, here am I, my son, for thou hast come to me.' 9. And he answered and said: 'Because of a great cause of anxiety have I come to thee, and because of a disturbing vision have I approached (thee). 10. And now, hear me, my father, hear me: unto Lamech my son there hath been born a son, whose form and nature are not like man's nature, and the colour of his body is whiter than snow and redder than a blooming rose, and the hair of his head is whiter than

---

CVI. 9. **Cause of anxiety.** So G G[1] M ጻሁቅ. Other MSS. ነገር, 'matter.' 10. **Hear me, my father.** So G. Dln. and G[1] give 'my father.' **Colour of his body.** So G: ኅብረ፡ ሥጋሁ. Other

---

cf. xlvi. 1. **3. Conversed with.** According to ver. 11 Noah 'blessed' God. **Lord of righteousness:** cf. xxii. 14; xc. 40. **5. Children of the angels of heaven:** cf. lxix. 4, 5; also lxxi. 1. **7. Amongst the angels,** i. e. at the ends of the earth, as in lxv. 2; lxvi. 3. **9. Cause of anxiety:** see Crit. Note. **10. The colour . . . rose.** Borrowed by *Apoc. Petri: τὰ μὲν γὰρ σώματα αὐτῶν ἦν λευκότερα πάσης χιόνος καὶ*

white wool, and his eyes are like the rays of the sun, and he opened his eyes and thereupon he lighted up the whole house.
11. And when he was taken from the hand of the midwife, he opened his mouth and blessed the Lord of heaven.
12. And Lamech became afraid and fled to me and did not believe that he was sprung from him, but that he was in the likeness of the angels of heaven; and behold I have come to thee that thou mayest make known to me the truth.'
13. And I, Enoch, answered and said: 'The Lord will do a new thing in the earth, and this I have already seen in a vision, and I make it known unto thee that in the generation of my father Jared some from the heights of heaven transgressed the word of the Lord.
14. And behold they committed sin and transgressed the law, and united themselves with women and committed sin with them, and married some of them and have begotten children by them.
15. And there will come a great destruction on the earth, and there will be a deluge and a great destruction for one year.
16. This son who is born unto you will be left on the earth, and his three children will be saved with him; when all mankind

MSS. 'His colour.' 12. **Lamech.** So G. Other MSS. 'his father, Lamech.' 13. **This I have already seen.** ወዳዕኩ፡ ወርኢኩ. By a strange slip Dln. renders, 'diess Weiss ich und habe . . . gesehen.' This, however, is a well-known idiom. G omits ወዳዕኩ፡ ወ. **In the generation of . . . Jared.** G and G[1] read: በትውልዱ፡ በእያሬድ. M: ቤተ፡ ውሉዱ፡ በያሬድ. **Some from the heights of heaven.** So Dln. G G[1]. L M: እመልዕልተ፡ ሰማይ. E H K give መልዕልተ፡ ሰማይ; and N gives መላእክተ፡ ሰማይ. An easy emendation would be እመላእክተ፡ ሰማይ 'some of the angels of heaven.' 15. **On the earth.** G. Other MSS. 'on the whole earth.'

ἐρυθρότερα παντὸς ῥόδου. **Eyes . . . sun:** cf. *Apoc. Petri*: *ἀπὸ τῆς ὄψεως αὐτῶν ἀκτὶν ὡς ἡλίου.* 11. **Lord of heaven.** Here only in Enoch. 13. **Do a new thing.** For this phrase cf. Num. xvi. 30; Is. xliii. 19. **In the generation of . . . Jared:** cf. vi. 6. The sinful generations began with Jared, and according to the Samaritan reckoning, Jared, Methuselah, and Lamech die or are destroyed in the year of the Flood. 14. **The law,** i. e. the law appointed to them as spiritual beings: cf. xv. 15. **One year:** cf. Gen. vii. 11, and viii. 14. 16. See

that are on the earth shall die. 17. The giants are not according to the spirit, but according to the flesh, and there will be a great punishment on the earth and the earth will be cleansed from all impurity. 18. And now make known to thy son Lamech that he who was born was in truth his son, and call his name Noah; for he will be left to you, and he and his children will be saved from the destruction which will come upon the earth on account of all the sin and all the unrighteousness of apostasy which will be consummated on the earth in his days. 19. And after that there will be still more unrighteousness than that which was at first consummated on the earth; for I know the mysteries of the holy ones; for He, the Lord, has showed me and informed me, and I have read in the heavenly tables.'

CVII. 1. And I saw written on them that generation upon generation will transgress, till a generation of righteousness arises, and transgression will be destroyed and sin will pass away from the earth and all manner of good will come upon it. 2. And now, my son, go and make known to thy son

---

16. **That are on the earth shall die.** Here I have omitted with G G[1] the words which come after these in Dln.'s text, 'he and his children will be saved. They will beget on earth.' 18. For ብጽድቅ G G[1] give ጺድቅ. **Unrighteousness of apostasy which will be consummated.** So G[1] እንተ፡ ዐለወት for እንተ፡ ሀለወት of Dln. G reads ዐለውት, and so really supports G[1]. Dln. gives 'unrighteousness which will be consummated.'

CVII. 1. **Till.** G G[1] read እስመ 'that a generation of righteous-

---

Crit. Note. 17. The first half of this verse, ending with the words 'on the earth,' has been transposed through a slip from its right position after ver. 14: in that connexion it should be rendered: 'Giants, who are not according,' &c. Dln.'s incorrect text made any explanation impossible. 18. The name Noah is here derived from נוח in the sense of 'remnant': cf. Ecclus. xliv. 17 where he is described as a *κατάλειμμα*. 19. **The mysteries of the holy ones.** Either the secrets known to the angels, or the secrets relating to the righteous in the future. **Heavenly tables**: see xlvii. 3 (note).

CVII. 1. The fresh growth of sin after the Deluge: its destination and the advent of the Messianic kingdom.

Lamech that this son, which has been born, is in truth his son, and that (this) is no lie. 3. And when Methuselah had heard the words of his father Enoch—for he had shown to him all the secret things—he returned and showed (them) to him and called the name of that son Noah; for he will cause the earth to rejoice in compensation for all destruction.

CVIII. 1. Another book which Enoch wrote for his son Methuselah and for those who will come after him and will keep the law in the last days. 2. Ye who have done good will wait for those days till an end is made of those who work evil, and an end of the might of the transgressors. 3. And wait ye indeed till sin has passed away, for their names will be blotted out of the book of life and out of the books of the holy ones, and their seed will be destroyed for ever, and their

---

ness will arise.' 3. For when G reads ካዕበ 'again.' **Returned and showed (them) to him.** So M: ገብአ፡ ወአርአዮ. G omits. G[1]: ገብሬአ፡ ወአሬአዮ. F H L N O and Dln., 'returned, after having seen him.'

CVIII. 2. **Ye who have done good will wait for.** So G G[1]: እለ፡ ገበርክሙ፡ ሠናየ፡ ትጸንሑ፡ ሰእሉ፡ መዋዕል but that G[1] gives በ for ሰ. F H I L N O and Dln., 'ye who have fulfilled it and are waiting in those.' M, 'ye who have fulfilled it, wait ye for,' ትጸንሑ፡ ሰ. 3. **Out of the book of life and.** So G G[1]: እመጽሐፈ፡ ሕይወት፡ ወ. M, 'out of the book.' Other MSS. omit. **Of the holy ones.** G[1]

---

3. The derivation of Noah given in Gen. v. 29 is here particularly repeated.

CVIII. This final chapter forms an independent addition. Its writer was acquainted with sections i–xxxvi and xci–civ, or at all events with parts of them. But his acquaintance with i–xxxvi is very inaccurate. In vv. 3–6 what was originally the place of punishment for the disobedient stars in chapters xviii and xxi becomes in his hands practically Gehenna. The writer is Essene in tone. Observe the high honour paid to asceticism, the scorn of gold and silver in vv. 8–10, the blessed immortality of the soul, but apparently not of the body, as well as the dualism of light and darkness so prominent in vv. 11–14. cviii is more nearly akin to xci–civ than any other section in the book. The object of this chapter is to encourage the righteous still to hope on despite the long delay of the advent of the kingdom. 1. **Keep the law**, as opposed to 'fall away from the law,' xcix. 2. 2. The faithful are exhorted to further patience. 3. **Blotted out of the book of life**: cf. xlvii. 3 (note). **Books of the holy ones**, i. e. the roll of the

spirits will be slain, and they will cry and make lamentation in a place that is a waste wilderness, and they will burn with fire where there is no earth. 4. And I saw there something like a viewless cloud; for by reason of its depth I could not look thereon, and I saw a flame of fire burning brightly, and there circled (there things) like shining mountains and they swept to and fro. 5. And I asked one of the holy angels who was with me and said: 'What is this shining thing? for it is not a heaven but only the flame of a burning fire, and the voice of crying and weeping and lamentation and strong pain.' 6. And he said unto me: 'This place which thou seest—here are cast the spirits of sinners and blasphemers and of those who work wickedness and of those who pervert every thing that God does through the mouth of the prophets—(even) the things that shall be. 7. For some of them are written and inscribed above in the heaven, in order that the angels may read them and know that which will befall

---

reads ቅዱስ፡ 'of the Holy One,' G ቅዱሳት. **In . . . a waste wilderness.** G gives: በመካነ፡ ደይን፡ ዘኢያስተርኢ. 4. **For by reason of its depth.** G reads: እምብዝኀ፡ ዕመቁ፡ ወ. **A flame of fire.** So G G¹: ላህበ፡ እሳት. Dln. 'the flame of its fire.' 5. **This shining thing.** G reads ዘብሑ = immolatus. 6. **Does.** So G G¹ ገብረ. Other MSS. 'speaks.' **Through the mouth.** G gives በቃለ. 7. **Read them.** G G¹ read ያንብርዎሙ.

---

members of the kingdom: cf. ciii. 2. **Spirits will be slain**: cf. xxii. 13; xcix. 11 (note). Though the extreme penalty of sin, it does not imply annihilation, for the victims of it 'cry and make lamentation.' **In a place, &c.** This chaotic flaming hell beyond the limits of the earth is the place of punishment of the angels in xviii. 12–16; xxi. 1–7. 4. **This hell and its inhabitants further described,** in terms borrowed from xviii. 13; xxi. 3. 5. **One of the holy angels, &c.** This phrase is borrowed from i–xxxvi: cf. xxvii. 2. **Voice, &c.**: cf. xviii. 13. 6. **This hell which is outside the earth is the final place of punishment of sinners and blasphemers and perverters of God's revelation and action through the prophets.** In verses 3–6 the writer of this chapter has confounded places, i. e. Gehenna and the hell of the disobedient stars, that are most carefully distinguished in i–xxxvi, and yet borrowed the phraseology of that section. **Blasphemers**: cf. xci. 7. **The prophets.** Here only mentioned expressly in Enoch. 7. **Written and inscribed.** This refers to the

the sinners, and the spirits of the humble, and of those who afflict their bodies, and are (for that) recompensed by God; and of those who are put to shame by wicked men: 8. Who loved God and loved neither gold nor silver nor any of the goods of the world, but gave over their bodies to torture, 9. and who, since they came into being, longed not after earthly food, but regarded their bodies as a breath that passeth away, and lived accordingly, and were much tried by the Lord, and their spirits were found pure so that they should bless His name. 10. And all the blessings they received I have recounted in the books, and He hath assigned them their recompense because they have been found to be such as loved heaven more than their life in the world, and whilst they were trodden under foot of wicked men and experienced abuse and reviling from them and were put to shame, (nevertheless) blessed Me. 11. And now I will summon the spirits of the good who belong to the generation of light, and I will trans-

---

9. **Their bodies.** So G ነፍስቶሙ. Other MSS. 'themselves.' **Lived accordingly.** Lit. 'observed this.' 10. **He hath assigned them their recompense.** G reads ዓስቦሙ. **Heaven more than their life in the world.** So G ዘበዓለም. G[1] and Dln. give ዘለዓለም 'the eternal heaven more than their life.' But the collocation of the words favours the former. Here ends

---

heavenly tables: cf. xlvii. 3. These records are also called the book of the angels, for their purpose is to acquaint the angels with the future: cf. ciii. 2. See also Asc. Is. vii. 27. 7–9. **The humble.** These are the עֲנִיִּים and עֲנָוִים so often referred to in the Psalms. They constitute the true Israel as opposed to the proud, the selfish, and the paganizers: see Cheyne on Ps. ix. 13. **Those who afflict their bodies, loved neither gold nor silver, longed not after earthly food.** These phrases would apply well to the Essene party: cf. xlviii. 7; cii. 5. These characteristics of the righteous have their counterpart in those of the wicked: cf. xcvi. 5–7; xcvii. 8–10; xcviii. 2. 9. **Regarded their bodies as a breath.** The ascetic scorn of the body is here strongly expressed. The body is left behind in this world and garments of light assumed after death: cf. Asc. Is. iv. 17; En. cviii. 12. 10. Enoch speaks and refers his hearers and readers to his books. **Their life in the world:** see Crit. Note: cf. xlviii. 7. 11. Verses 11 and 12 are represented as being spoken by God. **Generation of light:** cf. lxi. 12 (note); xxxviii. 4 (note).

form those who were born in darkness, who sought not honour in the flesh as their faithfulness deserved. 12. And I will bring forth clad in shining light those who have loved My holy name, and I will seat each on the throne of his honour. 13. And they will be resplendent for times without number; for righteousness is the judgment of God; for to the faithful He will give faithfulness in the habitation of upright paths. 14. And they will see how those who were born in darkness will be cast into darkness, while the righteous will be resplendent. 15. And the sinners will cry aloud and see them as they shine, and they indeed will go where days and seasons are prescribed for them.

---

the repeated section. M has the strange reading: እምንጽሑ፡ ነፍሶሙ፡ ዘሰዓሰሞ. 11. **Sought not honour.** So G: ኢፈቀዱ፡ ክብረ. FHILNO and Dln. 'were not recompensed with honour,' ኢተፈደዩ. M 'were recompensed.' 12. **Clad in shining light.** በብሩህ፡ ብርሃን. Cf. Matt. vii. 15. በአልባስ፡ አባግዕ 'clad in sheep's clothing.' The statement of the next verse, 'they will be resplendent,' calls for this translation. Dln. translates, 'I will bring forth into a brightly shining light.' **The throne of his honour.** So GLMN: መንበረ፡ ክብረ፡ ዚአሁ. Dln. gives 'a throne of honour, of his honour.' 13. **In the habitation of upright paths.** G reads: በማኅደር፡ ወፍኖት፡ ርትዕ 'in a habitation and paths of uprightness.' M 'in a habitation and uprightness.' 14. **Will be cast.** G reads ይትወሰዱ. 15. **As they shine.** For እንዘ፡ ይበርሁ G reads ይወሐውሑ.

Who were born in darkness. Of those who are born in darkness, such as are faithful and seek not honour in the flesh are transformed, but those who remain in their darkness are cast into darkness as their condemnation: cf. ver. 14. **12. Clad in shining light**: see Crit. Note; also lxii. 16 (note); Asc. Is. i. 5; iii. 25; iv. 16, 17; viii. 14, 26; ix. 9, &c. **Throne of his honour**: see Crit. Note. Cf. Matt. xix. 28; Rev. iii. 21; iv. 4; Asc. Is. ix. 10, 18. **13.** Enoch again speaks. **Resplendent, &c.**: cf. xxxix. 7; civ. 2; cviii. 14. **14. Born in darkness**: see ver. 11 (note). **Cast into darkness**: cf. ciii. 8. **15.** Cf. Dan. xii. 2, 3.

APPENDIX A.

EDITIONS AND TRANSLATIONS.

BOURIANT: *Fragments grecs du livre d'Enoch. Mémoires publiés par les Membres de la Mission Archéol. Française*, tom. ix. pp. 91–136.

—— *L'Evangile et l'Apocalypse de Pierre avec le texte grec du livre d'Enoch. Texte publié en fac-simile, par l'héliogravure, d'après les photographies du manuscrit de Gizéh.* Paris, 1893.

MIGNE: *Le livre d'Hénoch* in his *Dictionnaire des Apocryphes*, Paris, 1856, tom. i. pp. 393–514. This French translation is made from Laurence's Ethiopic text.

GOLDSCHMIDT: *Das Buch Henoch aus dem Aethiopischen in die ursprünglich hebräische Abfassungssprache zurückübersetzt; mit einer Einleitung und Noten versehen*, 1892. This retranslation is the work of a very young scholar, and, being so, it is a creditable performance. It labours, however, under many defects. First, it is based on Dln.'s Ethiopic text, which is very corrupt: secondly, the author appears to translate at times not from the Ethiopic as he professes, but directly from Dln.'s German translation, as in xxxvi. 3; xxxvii. 2; lxxxix. 7, &c.: thirdly, he mistranslates occasionally familiar phrases, possibly through carelessness: and finally, he introduces conjectures into the text without any attempted justification in the notes. Notwithstanding, we are grateful to the author for his book, and regard it as full of promise for his future. For my review of this book see *Jewish Quarterly*, Jan. 1893, pp. 327–329.

LODS: *Le Livre d'Hénoch, Fragments grecs, découverts à Akhmîm, publiés avec les variantes du texte éthiopien, traduits et annotés*, Paris, 1892. For some unexplained reason France has not till the present made any original contribution to the study of Enoch, though it has been prolific enough in works of a secondary importance on this subject. But M. Lods has broken through this evil tradition and presented us with a work of first-class importance, a work that is at once learned, scholarly, and judicious. I have been obliged, however, to traverse his main conclusions on the relative values of the Ethiopic version and the Giz. Gk. text; but this is due not to the fault but the misfortune of M. Lods, as he was not acquainted with any better representative of the Ethiopic version than Dln.'s corrupt text. See further, p. 319. On some other occasion I hope to review at some length this attractive and suggestive book.

CRITICAL INQUIRIES.

BISSELL: *The Apocrypha of the Old Testament*, 1880, pp. 665, 666. In this short account of Enoch the usual analysis into Groundwork, Similitudes, and Noachian fragments is accepted.

SCHWALLY: *Das Leben nach dem Tode*, 1892. The traditional division of the book of Enoch into the Groundwork, Similitudes, and Noachic interpolations is here assumed, p. 136. The author, however, is very arbitrary in his interpretation of the text and is often demonstrably wrong; and this is all the more to be regretted as his work is at once original and suggestive. The instances in which the book of Enoch is used or interpreted will be found given at length on p. 200 of Schwally's book.

ZÖCKLER: *Die Apocryphen des Alten Testaments*, 1891, pp. 426–436. Like most writers this author assumes the book of Enoch to consist of a Groundwork of chapters i–xxxvi; lxxii–cv (135–105 B. C.): the Similitudes (of uncertain date):

the Noachic fragments (before the publication of the Book of Jubilees): and cviii of recent origin. Slight Christian additions in the Similitudes are admitted.

BATIFFOL: in the *Dictionnaire de la Bible*, fasc. iii, 1892, pp. 757–759, this writer divides the Book of Enoch into (1) Book of Celestial Physics, xvii–xix; xxi–xxxvi; lxxii–lxxix; lxxxii. (2) Historical Apocalypse, i–xvi; lxxx–lxxxi; lxxxiii–cv (circ. 110 B.C.). (3) Similitudes or Messianic Apocalypse, xxxvii–lxiii; lxix–lxxi (40–44 B.C.). (4) Book of Noah, lxiv–lxviii. It is worthy of notice that this analysis is almost an exact reproduction of Lipsius' article in Smith's *Dict. of Christian Biography*.

DILLMANN: *Sitzungsberichte d. Kgl. Preuss. Akad. d. Wiss. zu Berlin*, 1892, li–liii. pp. 1039–54; 1079–92. This great scholar has here resumed his old Apocalyptic studies, and published an emended edition of the Gizeh MS., with a series of corrections of the Ethiopic text also. That the bulk of these is of great value goes without saying. For some further notice of these papers, see p. 319.

CHARLES: 'The Recent Translations and the Ethiopic Text of the Book of Enoch' (*Jewish Quarterly Review*, Jan. and April, 1893).

APPENDIX B.

'THE SON OF MAN': ITS ORIGIN AND MEANING.

As both the origin and meaning of this title in the New Testament have been very differently understood, it will be necessary to discuss these theories briefly.

(i) It has been taken to mean the Messiah with special reference to its use in Daniel. Hengstenberg, *Christologie*, iii. 91, 1858; Schulze, *Vom Menschensohn und vom Logos*, 1867—'while the concept of the Messiah is contained in the name, the peculiar expression of it in the Danielic sense can never be knowingly left out'; and Meyer, *Comment. on Matt.* viii. 20—'As often as Jesus uses the words "Son of Man," He means nothing else than the Son of Man in the Prophecy of Daniel.'

The Danielic conception has undoubtedly influenced the meaning of this title in the New Testament in certain instances; see S. Matt. xxiv. 30; xxvi. 64; but in the majority of instances it is wholly inapplicable, i. e. when it is used in reference to the homelessness of Christ, S. Matt. viii. 20, or His aversion to asceticism, xi. 18, 19; or His coming not to be ministered unto but to minister, S. Mark x. 45, or His destiny to be rejected of the chief priests and scribes and to be put to death, viii. 31.

(ii) It is taken to mean the ideal man, the typical, representative, unique man. So Schleiermacher, who holds (*Christl. Glaube*, ii. 91) that this title, in our Lord's use of it, implied a consciousness of His complete participation in human nature, as well as of a distinctive difference between Himself and mankind. So Neander, *Leben Jesu*, Eng. Trans. 4th Ed. p. 99, and more or less approximately Tholuck, Olshausen, Reuss, Weisse, Beyschlag, Liddon, Westcott, Stanton.

This supposition cannot be regarded as more successful than the former. It fails to show any fitness in the majority of cases. It is moreover an anachronism in history and thought. No past usage of the term serves even to prepare the way for this alleged meaning; and such a philosophical conception as the ideal man, the personalised moral ideal, was foreign to the consciousness of the Palestinian Judaism of the time. The nearest approach to this idea in the language of that time would be the 'Second Adam.'

(iii) Baur (*Neutest. Theol.* pp. 81–2; *Z. f. W. Theol.* 1860, pp. 274–92) thinks that Jesus chose the expression to designate Himself as a man, not as a man in the ideal sense, but as one who participated in everything that is human, *qui humani nihil a se alienum putat*. But though He thus used it to denote a simple ordinary man in its first acceptation, He afterwards incorporated in it the Danielic conception, as in S. Matt. xxiv. 30, &c. So Schenkel, *Bibel-Lex.* iv. pp. 170–5.

Baur has found but few to follow him. His explanation is the most inadequate that has been offered whether regarded from the standpoint of history or exegesis. His observation, however, that this title had apparently a varying signification is worth noting. This variation is recognised by Weizsäcker, *Ev. Gesch.* 1864, p. 429; *Das Apostol. Zeitalter*, 1890, p. 109. Its explanation is to be found in the complex origin of the phrase.

(iv) Mr. Bartlet ('Christ's use of the term "the Son of Man,"' *The Expositor*, Dec. 1892) takes this title to mean the 'ideal man,' but he gives it a further and more definite content by subsuming under it the conception of the Servant of Jehovah in Isaiah. The actual phrase, he concedes, may have been derived from a current Enochic usage.

Save for the fact that this theory recognises the inclusion in this title of the Old Testament conception of the Servant of Jehovah, it labours under all the difficulties of (ii), and incurs further disabilities of its own. It attributes to Jesus a most capricious and arbitrary method. It supposes Him, first of all, to choose a current Apocalyptic phrase; next to strip it absolutely of its received meaning, and to attach to it a signification in the highest degree questionable for the period and country; and, finally, while rejecting the Old Testament authoritative title of Servant of Jehovah, to subsume its complete connotation under this current Apocalyptic phrase with its new, artificial, and unmediated meaning. That the title, moreover, however transformed, had not parted with its apocalyptic meaning, is proved by S. John v. 22, 27, which are practically a quotation from Enoch lxix. 27.

The above interpretations are all unsatisfactory, and the reason is not far to seek. They are too subjective and one-sided, and they all more or less ignore the historical facts of the age. The true interpretation will, we believe, be found *if we start with the conception as found in Enoch and trace its enlargement and essential transformation in the usage of our Lord. In this transformation it is reconciled to and takes over into itself its apparent antithesis, the conception of the Servant of Jehovah, while it betrays occasional reminiscences of Dan. vii, the ultimate source of this designation.*

First shortly as to the facts of the problem. The expression is found in S. Matthew thirty times, in S. Mark fourteen, in S. Luke twenty-five, in S. John twelve. Outside the Gospels, in Acts vii. 56; Rev. i. 13; xiv. 14. In all these cases we find ὁ υἱὸς τοῦ ἀνθρώπου except in S. John v. 27, and Rev. i. 13, xiv. 14. The two passages in Rev. may be disregarded as they are not real designations of the Messiah. As for S. John v. 27, I can find no satisfactory explanation of the absence of the article.

Our interpretation of this title is as follows:—

(1) Its source in Daniel and its differentiation therefrom. The title 'the Son of Man' in Enoch was undoubtedly derived

from Dan. vii, but a whole world of thought lies between the suggestive words in Daniel and the definite rounded conception as it appears in Enoch. In Daniel the phrase seems merely symbolical of Israel, but in Enoch it denotes a supernatural person. In the former, moreover, the title is indefinite, 'like a Son of Man' as in Rev. i. 13; xiv. 14, but in Enoch it is perfectly definite and distinctive, 'the Son of Man.'

(2) The first occasion of its use. As the Similitudes are pre-Christian, they furnish the first instance in which the definite personal title appears in literature.

(3) Its supernatural import in Enoch. The Son of Man as portrayed in the Similitudes is a supernatural being and not a mere man. He is not even conceived as being of human descent, as the Messiah in En. xc. 37. He sits on God's throne, li. 3, which is likewise His own throne, lxii. 3, 5; lxix. 27, 29; possesses universal dominion, lxii. 6, and all judgment is committed unto Him, xli. 9; lxix. 27.

(4) Its import in the New Testament. This title with its supernatural attributes of superhuman glory, of universal dominion and supreme judicial powers, was adopted by our Lord. The Son of Man has come down from heaven, S. John iii. 13 (cp. En. xlviii. 2, note); He is Lord of the Sabbath, S. Matt. xii. 8; can forgive sins, S. Matt. ix. 6; and all judgment is committed unto Him, S. John v. 22, 27 (cp. En. lxix. 27). But while retaining its supernatural associations, this title underwent transformation in our Lord's use of it, a transformation that all Pharisaic ideas, so far as He adopted them, likewise underwent. And just as His kingdom in general formed a standing protest against the prevailing Messianic ideas of temporal glory and dominion, so the title 'the Son of Man' assumed a deeper spiritual significance; and this change we shall best apprehend if we introduce into the Enoch conception of the Son of Man the Isaiah conception of the Servant of Jehovah. *These two conceptions, though outwardly antithetic, are through the transformation of the former reconciled and fulfilled in a deeper unity—in the New Testament*

Son of Man. This transformation flowed naturally from the object of Jesus' coming, the revelation of the Father. The Father could be revealed not through the self-assertion of the Son, not through His grasping at self-display in the exhibition of superhuman majesty and power, but through His self-emptying, self-renunciation and service (Phil. ii. 6). Whilst therefore in adopting the title 'the Son of Man' from Enoch, Jesus made from the outset supernatural claims, yet these supernatural claims were to be vindicated not after the external Judaistic conceptions of the Book of Enoch, but in a revelation of the Father in a sinless and redemptive life, death, and resurrection. Thus in the life of the actual Son of Man, the Father was revealed in the Son, and supernatural greatness in universal service. He that was greatest was likewise Servant of all. This transformed conception of the Son of Man is thus permeated throughout by the Isaiah conception of the Servant of Jehovah; but though the Enochic conception is fundamentally transformed, the transcendent claims underlying it are not for a moment foregone. *If then we bear in mind the inward synthesis of these two ideals of the past in an ideal, nay in a Personality transcending them both, we shall find little difficulty in understanding the startling contrasts that present themselves in the New Testament in connexion with this designation.* We can understand how on the one hand the Son of Man hath not where to lay His head (S. Matt. viii. 20), and yet be Lord of the Sabbath (S. Matt. xii. 8); how He is to be despised and rejected of the elders and chief priests and scribes and be put to death (S. Luke ix. 22), and yet be the Judge of all mankind (S. John v. 27).

It has been objected that S. Matt. xvi. 13, S. John xii. 34 prove that the Son of Man was not a current designation of the Messiah in the time of Christ; but no such conclusion can be drawn from these passages; for in the older form of the question given in S. Matt. xvi. 13, the words 'the Son of Man' are not found: see S. Mark viii. 27; S.

Luke ix. 18. In S. John xii. 34 it is just the strangeness of this *new* conception of this current phrase of a Messiah who was to suffer death, that makes the people ask, 'Who is this Son of Man? we have heard of the law that the Christ abideth for ever.'

On the other hand, though the phrase was a current one, our Lord's use of it must have been an enigma, not only to the people generally, but also to His immediate disciples, so much so that they shrank from using it; for, as we know, it is used in the Gospels only by our Lord in speaking of Himself.

APPENDIX C.

THE GIZEH GREEK FRAGMENT OF ENOCH.

This important Greek fragment of Enoch was first made accessible to scholars under the editorship of M. Bouriant in October, 1892, though discovered as early as the winter of 1886–87 at Akhmîm by the Mission Archéologique Française at Cairo. The work is done in a scholarly manner, but is not quite free from defects. Some of these have been repaired by Mr. Bensley, who has recently collated the MS. at Gizeh, and from his note in the *Academy* of Feb. 11 six passages omitted through homoioteleuton in M. Bouriant's edition have been restored in the text that follows[1].

Unhappily the greater part of the present edition was already in type before M. Bouriant's work reached me, and I was thus debarred from making extensive changes. Happily, on the other hand, the many new readings I had introduced into the text under the guidance of the MSS. G M were almost in every instance in perfect accord with the new Greek text. By the permission of the Delegates of the Press I was allowed to make such additional changes as would not interfere materially with the type already set up. But excise as I would, I could not at times make sufficient room for the fresh material, and so it occasionally happens that a text is followed in the Translation, the justification of which is given, not in the Crit. Notes which are immediately below, but in the Appendix.

[1] Since the above was written I have received M. Lods' list of corrections from the facsimile of this Greek MS. which is about to be published, and corrected M. Bouriant's text accordingly.

Before I enter on the criticism of the relative merits of the Eth. and Gk. MSS. I wish to call attention to further emendations of the text which are not followed in the Translation, but will be, should the present work reach a second edition. These new renderings will be found in the following Crit. Notes. They are preceded by the readings they are intended to displace and are always printed in *italics*.

In my Introduction (pp. 2–5) I have dealt briefly with the question of the Ethiopic text and the corrupt type of MSS. on which Professor Dillmann's text is based. I called attention to this fact in the *Academy* of Nov. 26, 1892, and as that scholar has since amply admitted this fact (*Sitzungsberichte d. Kgl. Preuss. Akad. d. Wiss. zu Berlin*, 1892, li–liii. pp. 1039–1054, 1079–1092) it is not necessary to pursue this question at any length. In these articles, Dln. enters on the criticism and emendation of the Eth. and Gk. texts, and bases many of his new readings on two new MSS. These MSS., however, appear to fail him in some crucial instances where G M or G are more than satisfactory. I have read these articles with great interest and found that our emendations in the main agree: in a few instances I have adopted his suggestions with due acknowledgements. In many points, however, I have felt obliged to differ, and in many others, on which he has not touched at all, the right solution, I think, is offered in the following pages.

In the revision of this Appendix, I have also had before me the excellent work of M. Lods. This is a most scholarly and suggestive book, but M. Lods has throughout had the great disadvantage of basing his criticism on a corrupt Eth. text, i.e. Dln.'s, and thus more than one-third of his book is already antiquated. Besides, the undeniably inferior character of this Eth. text as against the purer Giz. Gk. text has naturally blinded M. Lods to undoubted excellencies of this corrupt text, and to readings where it is clearly more ancient and correct than the Giz. Gk.

In the *Academy* of Nov. 26 last year, just after the publication of the Giz. MS., I stated shortly the relative positions and values of the Eth. and Gk. texts. As all my subsequent study has only served to confirm these, I will restate them with large additions and supply confirmatory evidence where necessary.

The materials for the textual criticism of Enoch are drawn from three versions or sources—I. Latin, II. Greek, III. Ethiopic. As the first of these is of very minor importance, we will indicate very briefly the contributions made by this source to the restoration of the text, and pass on to the others.

I. The Latin documents are—

iv Ezra [vi. 2] as contributing to the restoration of .	En. lx. 6 (see Crit. Note, p. 154).
vii. 32 as contributing to the restoration of . .	En. li. 1 (see Crit. Note, p. 140).
Tertullian, *De Cultu Fem.* i. 2: Metallorum opera nudaverant	En. viii. 1 (see Crit. Note, p. 66).
De Idol. iv	En. xcix. 7 (see Crit. Note, p. 285).
Latin Fragment of Enoch cvi. 1–18	See, for full treatment, pp. 372–375.
II. S. Jude 14, 15	En. i. 9 (see Crit. Note, p. 327).
Greek Fragment published from Vatican MS. by Mai .	En. lxxxix. 42–49 (see pp. 238–240).
Fragments from Syncellus . .	En. vi. 1–x. 14; xv. 1–xvi. 1 (see pp. 62–75; 83–85).
Gizeh MS.	En. i-xxxii. (see pp. 326–370).

III. The Ethiopic MSS. enumerated on p. 2, which are fairly represented by Dln.'s Ethiopic text as corrected in my Crit. Notes according to G or M or G M, &c. These corrections are close on six hundred. The following criticism is limited to a comparison of the relative merits of the Ethiopic and two Greek versions of chaps. i–xxxii of Enoch.

i. Each of these versions preserves true readings over against corruptions in the other, or in the other two where these exist. So Eth. in vi. 8 (see Crit. Note, p. 64); vii. 1 (see Crit. Note, p. 331); x. 5 (see Crit. Note, p. 337); x. 19 (see Crit. Note, p. 340); xv. 12 (see Crit. Note, p. 350); xvii. 3 (see Crit. Note, p. 352). So Syn. Gk. on vi. 6 (see Crit. Note, p. 63): ix. 10: x. 1 Οὐριήλ (see Crit. Note, p. 336): x. 14 ὃς ἂν . . . κατακριθῇ (Crit. Note, p. 339): xv. 9 τῶν ἀνθρώπων (Crit. Note, p. 349). So Giz. Gk. v. 5 τὰ ἔτη τῆς ἀπωλείας ὑμῶν (see Crit. Note, p. 60): ix. 4 ἅγιον κ. μέγα κ. εὐλόγητον (see Crit. Note, p. 334): xiii. 4 ἀναγνῷ (see Crit. Note, p. 343): xiv. 2 πνεύματι τοῦ στόματός μου (see Crit. Note, p. 344). See also Crit. Notes on xviii. 4; xx. 2, 6, 7. *Observe that Giz. Gk. has no unquestionably true reading over against Eth. and Syn. Gk. combined, whereas Eth. and Syn. Gk. have each many such true and independent readings.*

ii. These versions taken in pairs attest true readings over against corruptions or omissions in the third. So Eth. and Giz. Gk. in vi. 2 καὶ ἐθεάσονται . . . . οὐρανοῦ: vi. 5 (large omission): viii. 1 στίβεις: ix. 7 ἄρχειν: x. 9 μαζηρέους: xv. 10. So Eth. and Syn. Gk. in vi. 1 αὐτοῖς: ix. 4 βασιλευόντων: ix. 8 ἐν ταῖς θηλείαις: x. 9 εἰς ἀλλήλους ἐξ αὐτῶν εἰς αὐτούς: x. 10: xvi. 1 ὡς. So Syn. Gk. and Giz. Gk. in ix. 6: ix. 8 τῆς γῆς (see Crit. Note, p. 70): ix. 10 δύναται: ix. 11 ἐᾷς αὐτούς: x. 7 ἰάσωνται τὴν πληγήν: xv. 11 ἀλλ' ἀσιτοῦντα.

It is thus clear so far that each of these three versions has an independent worth of its own, though apparently the Giz. Gk. is less original than the other two.

iii. We have next to determine the relations of these versions to each other. Even the most superficial study makes it clear that *the Eth. and Giz. Gk. are more closely related than the Eth. and Syn. Gk. or the Giz. Gk. and Syn. Gk.* For evidence that this holds generally we might point to the following passages (see notes): vi. 1, 2, 4; vii. 1; viii. 1, 2, 3; ix. 4, 6, 7, 9, 10, 11; x. 1, 2, 7, 9, 10; xv. 10, 12. But the decisive evidence on this question is found in the fact that the Eth. and Giz. Gk. present the same ungrammatical or corrupt reading in x. 14 κατακαυθῇ against Syn. Gk. κατακριθῇ: xiv. 7 καὶ μὴ λαλοῦντες: xv. 9 ἀνωτέρων against Syn. Gk. ἀνθρώπων: xv. 11 νεφέλας against Syn. Gk. νεμόμενα: xviii. 5 βαστάζοντας ἐν νεφέλῃ for βαστάζοντας νέφελας (?): xxii. 4 ἐποίησαν for ἐποιήθησαν. As no such phenomena are observable in the combinations Eth. + Giz. Gk. and Giz. Gk. + Syn. Gk., it is clear that of the three versions the Eth. and the Giz. Gk. are bound together by a close relationship—in which they stand to each other, either as parent and child, or as children of the same parent. That the former rather than the latter is the case we must infer from the conclusion already arrived at in (i), i.e. that the Giz. Gk. preserves no unquestionably true reading over against the other two versions, whereas the Eth. preserves many such. When I say that the Eth. and the Giz. Gk. stand to each other in the relation of parent and child, I mean, of course, that *the Ethiopic version was made from a text which was the ancestor of that preserved in the Gizeh MS.* This conclusion will receive further confirmation in the sequel.

iv. The relationship existing between the Eth. and the Syn. Gk. can be traced with tolerable certainty from the facts already before us. For, in the first place, not only does the Syn. Gk. preserve many true readings over against corruptions in the Eth. and the Giz. Gk., but it also preserves true readings over against *the same corruptions* in these texts; and, in the next instance, it does not agree in any instance with the Eth. in presenting the same corruption over against the true text in the Giz. Gk. Hence, clearly, it is not derived either from the Giz. Gk. or from the Gk. parent of the Eth. text which we may designate *x*, but stands on a position of equality with *x*. Finally, as there is repeatedly an exact verbal agreement between the Syn. Gk. and the Giz. Gk. which is the descendant of *x*, the Syn. Gk. and *x* proceed from the same original. Further examination shows that *x* preserves a purer form of text than the Syn. Gk. Hence the genealogy of the above documents might be represented as follows:

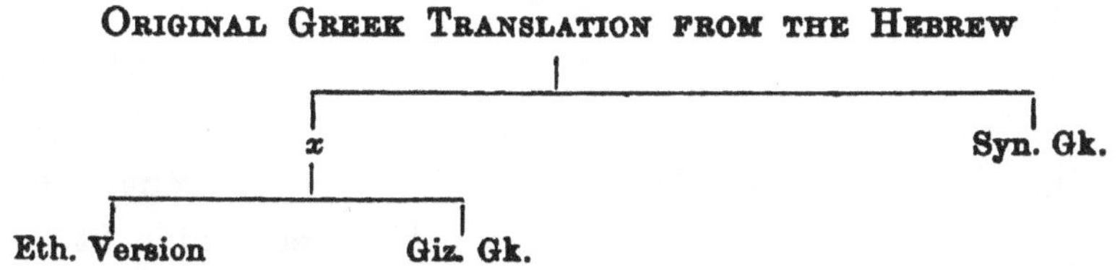

v. We shall now deal shortly with the general character of the Giz. Gk. and the Eth. on the score of *additions*, *omissions*, and *corruptions*.

Whilst the undoubted *additions* in the Eth. are few and trifling in viii. 1; ix. 4; xvi. 1; xx. 6; xxii. 12; xxiv. 2, there is a large list of such in the Giz. Gk.—in i. 3, 5, 6, 8, 9; ii. 2; v. 1, 2, 6, 8; viii. 1; x. 1, 8; xiv. 4, 20; xv. 11; xviii. 15; xxii. 13; xxiv. 3, 4; xxvii. 2.

As to *omissions*, the Eth. is almost certainly guilty in i. 1, 9; v. 4, 5; ix. 6; xiii. 8; xiv. 25; xv. 11; xx. 7; xxii. 2, 5; xxvi. 1: but the list of these in the Giz. Gk. is many times larger in ii. 3; all iii and iv except six words; in vi. 1, 2, 5, 6, 8; ix. 1, 5, 8; x. 10, 16, 19, 21 (?); xii. 3; xiv. 3, 4, 14; xv. 2, 4, 8, 9, 10; xvi. 1; xviii. 3, 11; xix. 1; xxi. 9; xxii. 5, 8; xxiv. 1, 2; xxvii. 1.

As regards *corruptions*, both versions are much at fault, but the Giz. Gk. more so. In the Eth. these corruptions are either native to the Eth. text or are due to the error of the translator or are derived from *x*. There are found in i. 9 ረሰዩ for ረሰዑ; ii. 1, iii. 1 and v. 1 ጠየቁ for ጠይቁ; viii. 1, 3; ix. 1, 4, 8 ሰብእ for የብስ; 11 translator mistaking ἐᾷς αὐτούς for τὰ εἰς αὐτούς: x. 7; xii. 1; xiv. 2, 18, 21, 22, 23, 24; xviii. 4, 7, 9; xix. 2; xx. 2, 6; xxi. 5, 6, 7, 9; xxii. 1, 2, 3, 5, 8, 9; xxiii. 4; xxiv. 2, 3; xxvi. 3, 4; xxvii. 5; xxviii. 1; xxx. 1, 3; xxxi. 2, 3. The corruptions in the Giz. Gk. however, are more numerous and deep-seated: i. 2, 3, 9; v. 1,

5, 6, 8; vi. 8; viii. 3; ix. 4, 6; x. 7, 9 (μαζηρεους a much less correct transliteration than that given by Eth.), 10, 11, 14, 19, 20; xi. 1; xii. 2, 6; xiii. 1, 10; xiv. 2, 6, 8, 13, 15, 18, 19, 23; xv. 8, 9, 12; xvi. 3; xvii. 3, 6, 7; xviii. 3, 4, 5, 11; xx. 4, 5 (?); xxi. 3, 7 (?); xxii. 3, 4, 5, 6, 8, 11, 14; xxiii. 2; xxiv. 3, 4 (?); xxv. 3, 5; xxvi. 2; xxvii. 3; xxviii. 2, 3; xxxi. 2, 3; xxxii. 2, 3.

There is another interesting class of corruptions characteristic of the Giz. Gk. from which the Eth. is comparatively free: i. e. *transpositions of the text*. These are found in i. 2; vi. 8; x. 19; xii. 4; xiii. 1, 10; xiv. 15; xv. 12; xxv. 3, 5; xxxii. 2. In the Eth. in ix. 8; xvii. 4; xix. 1; xxi. 9; xxviii. 3; xxxi. 2.

I have remarked above that the corruptions in the Giz. Gk. are very deep-seated. In fact, without the help of the Eth. it would be impossible to retrieve the original text in such passages as x. 19; xiv. 15; xvii. 3; xxviii. 2, 3 and others. The Eth., on the other hand, is by no means in such an evil strait. Hence the conclusion to which all the preceding facts point is that *the Eth. preserves a more ancient and trustworthy form of text than the Giz. Gk.: that it has fewer additions, fewer omissions, and fewer and less serious corruptions than that text.*

The results at which we have thus arrived are in perfect harmony with the external history of the Giz. Gk. text and the Eth. version. The former cannot be earlier than the eighth century, and may be as late as the twelfth. It is possible, therefore, that it is a descendant of the second or third degree from *x*. This of itself would account for some of the corruptions; but the real explanation of its vicious orthography and syntax and of its very numerous and serious corruptions is that the Book of Enoch was from the fifth century onward practically a proscribed book and under the ban of the Greek and Latin Churches. Accordingly, it was copied without care, and the way was opened for every kind of depravation of the text. The Eth. version (circ. 500 A. D.), on the other hand, was, so far as we know, regarded from the first as a canonical book of the Old Testament in the Ethiopic Church, and thus it was transmitted with the greatest care and accuracy through successive copies till the sixteenth century. After this date the text suffered much from ignorant corrections.

vi. In my Introduction (pp. 21, 22) I have treated the question of a Hebrew original as one now practically settled. In the case of chapters i–xxxii this view is now established beyond the reach of controversy. The translator has transliterated Hebrew words which were not intelligible to him: i.e. in x. 19 *μαζηρεους* = מַמְזֵר; in xviii. 8 *φουκα* = פּוּךְ; in xxviii. 1 and xxix. 1 *μανδοβαρα* and *βαβδηρα* = מִדְבָּר; in x. 19 *βάτους* = בַּת; in xxxi. 1 *σαρραν* = צֳרִי [and *χαλβανη* = חֶלְבְּנָה]; and, strangest of all, in xxvii. 2 *γη* = גֵּיא, where this word has been taken as a proper name, as occasionally in the LXX. (cf. Ezek. xxxix. 15; 1 Sam. xiii. 88).

In the following Critical Notes, Eth. = Ethiopic text of Dln.; Giz. Gk. = text of Gizeh Greek fragment; Syn. Gk. = text of Syncellus' Greek fragments. A, B, C, &c. designate the Ethiopic MSS. described on p. 2. The English renderings intended to replace the corresponding passages in the Translation are always printed in italics. The list of variants given in the notes is not exhaustive, but no single variant of any importance is omitted. Words bracketed ( ) are supplied by me, and that almost universally from the Eth. The source will be found in the Notes. Such words are to be regarded as original constituents of the text. At times such omissions are not supplied but are marked thus .... Words bracketed ⟨ ⟩ may be original, but are without a parallel in the Eth. Words bracketed [ ] are corrupt additions. When the text has called for drastic remedies, attention is drawn to the emendation by a † placed in the margin. Such emendations are made almost universally on the authority of the Eth.

I. 1. Λόγος εὐλογίας Ἐνώχ, καθὼς εὐλόγησεν ἐκλεκτοὺς δικαίους οἵτινες ἔσονται εἰς ἡμέραν ἀνάγκης ἐξᾶραι πάντας τοὺς ἐχθρούς, ⟨καὶ σωθήσονται δίκαιοι⟩.

2. Καὶ ἀναλαβὼν τὴν παραβολὴν αὐτοῦ εἶπεν Ἐνὼχ ἄνθρωπος δίκαιος· Ἔστιν ὅρασις ἐκ θεοῦ αὐτῷ ἀνεῳγμένη, καὶ ἑώρα τὴν
† ὅρασιν τοῦ ἁγίου καὶ τοῦ οὐρανοῦ ἣν ἔδειξάν μοι ἄγγελοι ⟨ἅγιοι⟩ καὶ ἤκουσα [ἀγγέλων ἐγὼ καὶ ὡς ἤκουσα] παρ' αὐτῶν πάντα καὶ ἔγνων ἐγὼ θεωρῶν. καὶ οὐκ εἰς τὴν νῦν γενεὰν ⟨διενοούμην⟩
† ἀλλὰ ἐπὶ πόρρω οὖσαν γενεάν. 3. καὶ περὶ τῶν ἐκλεκτῶν νῦν λέγω καὶ περὶ αὐτῶν ἀνέλαβον τὴν παραβολήν ⟨μου⟩.

Καὶ ἐξελεύσεται ὁ ἅγιός [μου] ὁ μέγας ἐκ τῆς κατοικήσεως αὐτοῦ, καὶ ὁ θεὸς τοῦ αἰῶνος 4. ἐπὶ γῆν πατήσει ἐπὶ τὸ Σινᾶ ὄρος καὶ φανήσεται ἐκ τῆς παρεμβολῆς αὐτοῦ καὶ φανήσεται ἐν τῇ δυνάμει τῆς ἰσχύος αὐτοῦ ἀπὸ τοῦ οὐρανοῦ ⟨τῶν οὐρανῶν⟩.

I. 1. εξαρε 2. Αινωχ — θ̅υ̅ — ην εχων την ορασιν του αγιου και του ουρανου εδειξεν μοι και αγιολογων αγιων — θεορων — ις — επει — εγω αλλω 3. εγλεκτων — θ̅ς̅ 4. επει — επει το σεινα — φαινησεται — παρενβολης

I. 1. After ἐχθρούς Eth. adds καὶ τοὺς ἀσεβεῖς. 2. After አውሥአ add ምሳሌ as in Gk. ἀναλαβὼν τ. παραβολὴν αὐτοῦ. Cf. ver. 4; and for 'answered' read *uttered his parable*. ὅρασις . . . ἀνεῳγμένη. So Eth. M. Lods denies this meaning of Gk., but unreasonably. Cf. Aristot. *de Anima*, iii. 2, Diod. i. 59, for ὅρασις = faculty of seeing. However, Gk. as it stands is in favour of ὅρασις = vision. We have in this verse an example of transposition and corruption which we shall frequently meet with in the sequel: cf. x. 19; xii. 4; xiii. 1, 10; xiv. 15; xv. 12; xxv. 3, 5. First, in ἣν ἔχων τὴν ὅρασιν, ἔχων is a corruption of ἑώρα: ἣν has been removed from its place before ἔδειξεν. Next, the καί before αγιολογων should be written before ἤκουσα. Finally, αγγελων εγω και ως ηκουσα is a false addition. The text thus restored to syntax and meaning = Eth. literally, but that Gk. adds ἅγιοι after ἄγγελοι, and for καὶ τοῦ οὐρανοῦ Eth. reads τοῦ ἐν τοῖς οὐρανοῖς. γενεάν = Eth. ትውልድ, the true text underlying εγω αλλω. 3. See Crit. Note, p. 58. ὁ ἅγιός [μου] ὁ μέγας. Eth. reads καί for μου. 4. ἐπὶ γῆν. Eth. = καὶ ἐκεῖθεν. For ἐκ τῆς παρ. read with Eth. μετὰ τῆς παρ.

5. καὶ φοβηθήσονται πάντες, καὶ [πιστεύσουσιν] οἱ ἐγρήγοροι [καὶ ᾄσουσιν ἀπόκρυφα ἐν πᾶσιν τοῖς ἄκροις τῆς (sic) καὶ] σεισθήσονται [πάντα τὰ ἄκρα τῆς γῆς] καὶ λήμψεται αὐτοὺς τρόμος καὶ φόβος μέγας μέχρι τῶν περάτων τῆς γῆς, 6. καὶ σεισθήσονται ⟨καὶ πεσοῦνται καὶ διαλυθήσονται⟩ ὄρη ὑψηλά, καὶ ταπεινωθήσονται βουνοὶ ὑψηλοὶ [τοῦ διαρρυῆναι ὄρη] καὶ τακήσονται ὡς κηρὸς ἀπὸ προσώπου πυρός [ἐν φλογί]. 7. καὶ διασχισθήσεται ἡ γῆ ⟨σχίσμα ῥαγῶδες⟩, καὶ πάντα ὅσα ἐστὶν ἐπὶ τῆς γῆς ἀπολεῖται καὶ κρίσις ἔσται κατὰ πάντων. 8. καὶ μετὰ τῶν δικαίων τὴν εἰρήνην ποιήσει, καὶ ἐπὶ τοὺς ἐκλεκτοὺς ἔσται συντήρησις [καὶ εἰρήνη] καὶ ἐπ' αὐτοὺς γενή(σε)ται ἔλεος, καὶ ἔσονται πάντες τοῦ θεοῦ, καὶ τὴν εὐδοκίαν δώσει αὐτοῖς καὶ [πάντας] εὐλογήσει [καὶ πάντων ἀντιλήμψεται καὶ βοηθήσει ἡμῖν] καὶ φανήσεται αὐτοῖς φῶς [καὶ ποιήσει ἐπ' αὐτοὺς εἰρήνην]. 9. ὅτι ἔρχεται σὺν τοῖς μυριάσιν [αὐτοῦ καὶ τοῖς] ἁγίοις αὐτοῦ ποιῆσαι κρίσιν κατὰ πάντων, καὶ ἀπολέσει ⟨πάντας⟩ τοὺς ἀσεβεῖς, καὶ (ἐ)λέγξει πᾶσαν σάρκα περὶ πάντων ἔργων ⟨τῆς ἀσεβείας⟩ αὐτῶν ὧν ἠσέβησαν ⟨καὶ σκληρῶν ὧν ἐλάλησαν λόγων καὶ περὶ πάντων ὧν κατελάλησαν⟩ κατ' αὐτοῦ ἁμαρτωλοὶ ἀσεβεῖς.

---

5. ασωσιν — σισθησονται — μεχρει 6. σισθησονται — φλογει 7. ραγαδει — επει — εστε 8. μεγα — δικεων — θ̅υ̅ — ευδοκειαν — αντειλημψεται 9. οτει — αγειοις — λενξει — εσεβησαν — ασεβις

---

5. Full of Christian (?) interpolations. 7. See Crit. Note, p. 58: after πάντων Eth. adds καὶ πάντων τῶν δικαίων. 9. For ὅτι read with Eth. and Jude ἰδού. σὺν τοῖς ... ἁγίοις. An expansion of the original በትእልፊት፡ ቅዱሳኒሁ: Jude ἐν ἁγίαις μυριάσιν αὐτοῦ. For በረሲዓን read ለኵሎሙ፡ ረሲዓን with Giz. Gk. and Jude; and for 'ungodly' read *all the ungodly*. For ἀπολέσει . . . σάρκα Jude reads ἐλέγξαι πάντας τοὺς ἀσεβεῖς. For ኵሉ፡ ዘገብሩ read ኵሉ፡ ግብረ፡ ርስዓኖሙ, πάντων ἔργων τῆς ἀσεβείας αὐτῶν Giz. Gk. and Jude. ረሰዩ is an undoubted corruption of ረስዑ=ἠσέβησαν. Hence my rendering 'ungodly committed.' The last bracketed clause is probably an expansion of καὶ περὶ πάντων τῶν σκληρῶν ὧν ἐλάλησαν. So Jude. Hence after ረስዑ add ወበእንተ፡ ኵሉ፡ ድሩኳት፡ ዘነበቡ. Hence for 'all that the sinners . . . committed' read *all the works of their godlessness which they have ungodly committed and of all the hard*

II. 1. Κατανοήσατε πάντα τὰ ἔργα ἐν τῷ οὐρανῷ πῶς οὐκ ἠλλοίωσαν τὰς ὁδοὺς αὐτῶν, καὶ τοὺς φωστῆρας τοὺς ἐν τῷ οὐρανῷ ὡς τὰ πάντα ἀνατέλλει καὶ δύνει, τεταγμένος ἕκαστος ἐν τῷ τεταγμένῳ καιρῷ ⟨καὶ ταῖς ἑορταῖς αὐτῶν φαίνονται⟩ καὶ οὐ παραβαίνουσιν τὴν ⟨ἰδίαν⟩ τάξιν. 2. ἴδετε τὴν γῆν καὶ διανοήθητε περὶ τῶν ἔργων ἐν αὐτῇ γινομένων ἀπ' ἀρχῆς μέχρι τελειώσεως [εἰσὶν φθαρτά], ὡς οὐκ ἀλλοιοῦνται ⟨οὐδὲν τῶν ἐπὶ γῆς ἀλλὰ⟩ πάντα ἔργα θεοῦ ⟨ὑμῖν⟩ φαίνεται. 3. ἴδετε τὴν θερείαν καὶ τὸν χειμῶνα. III. 1. καταμάθετε καὶ ἴδετε πάντα τὰ δένδρα, V. 1. πῶς τὰ φύλλα χλωρὰ ἐν αὐτοῖς σκέπονται τὰ δένδρα καὶ [πᾶς] ὁ καρπὸς αὐτῶν [εἰς τιμὴν καὶ δόξαν] διανοήθητε, ⟨καὶ γνῶτε⟩ περὶ πάντων ⟨τῶν ἔργων αὐτοῦ⟩, καὶ νοήσατε ὅτι [θεὸς ζῶν] ἐποίησεν αὐτὰ οὕτως καὶ ζῇ εἰς [πάντας] τοὺς αἰῶνας 2. καὶ τὰ ἔργα αὐτοῦ [πάντα ὅσα ἐποίησεν εἰς τοὺς αἰῶνας] ἀπὸ ἐνιαυτοῦ εἰς ἐνιαυτὸν γινόμενα [πάντα οὕτως] καὶ πάντα [ὅσα] ἀποτελοῦσιν

II. 1. κατανοησεται — ηλλυοσαν — τεταγμενο κερω — τες εορτης — φενονται — παραβεννουσιν — ειδειαν 2. ειδετε — διανοηθηται — γεινομενων — μεχρει τελιωσεως — αλλυουνται — επει — θ̄υ — φενεται 3. θεριαν — των χειμωνα

III. 1. καταμαθεται — ιδεται

V. 1. σκεποντα — τειμην — διανοηθηται — γνωται — νοησαται — θ̄ς 2. γεινομενα —

---

things which ungodly sinners have spoken. Eth. wrongly adds *καί* between *ἁμαρτωλοί* and *ἀσεβεῖς*.

II. 1. *κατανοήσατε.* As M. Lods has already observed, ጠየቅ= *κατενόησα* is a corruption of ጠይቁ: cf. also ci. 1. For 'I observed' read *observe ye.* The Eth. translator read *οἱ φωστῆρες οἱ* instead of *καὶ τ. φωστῆρας τ.* *τάξιν.* So G ሥርዓቶሙ. Dln. gives ትእዛዞሙ. 2. For *φαίνεται* the Eth. translator read *φαινόμενα.* 3. Bulk of verse omitted.

III. 1. *καταμάθετε καὶ ἴδετε.* Eth. gives 'I observed and saw': cf. ii. 1. For 'I observed and saw' read *observe ye and see.* Giz. Gk. omits this chapter and the next with the exception of six words.

V. 1. For 'I observed' read *observe ye.* I read *σκέπονται* for *σκέποντα* with Dln. For *ὁ καρπὸς αὐτῶν* Eth. gives *καρποφοροῦσι.* *καὶ ζῇ* spoils the force of the argument. Eth. which reads *ὃς ζῇ* is undoubtedly best. For ዘኵሎሙ we should probably read ከመዝ = *οὕτως.* 2. Eth. preferable: Giz. Gk. very corrupt. *πάντα ὅσα . . . αἰῶνας*

αὐτῷ τὰ ἔργα καὶ οὐκ ἀλλοιοῦνται [αὐτῶν τὰ ἔργα] ἀλλ' ὡσπερεὶ
κατὰ ἐπιταγὴν . . . τὰ πάντα γίνεται. 3. ἴδετε πῶς ἡ θάλασσα
καὶ οἱ ποταμοὶ ὡς ὁμοίως ἀποτελοῦσιν ⟨καὶ οὐκ ἀλλοιοῦσιν αὐτῶν
τὰ ἔργα ἀπὸ τῶν λόγων αὐτοῦ⟩. 4. ὑμεῖς δὲ οὐκ ἐνεμείνατε
οὐδὲ ἐποιήσατε κατὰ τὰς ἐντολὰς αὐτοῦ, ἀλλὰ ἀπέστητε καὶ κατελαλήσατε μεγάλους καὶ σκληροὺς λόγους ἐν στόματι ἀκαθαρσίας
ὑμῶν κατὰ τῆς μεγαλοσύνης αὐτοῦ.

⟨῞Οτι κατελαλήσατε ἐν τοῖς ψεύμασιν ὑμῶν⟩, σκληροκάρδιοι, οὐκ
ἔσται εἰρήνη ὑμῖν. 5. τοίγαρ τὰς ἡμέρας ὑμῶν ὑμεῖς καταράσεσθε
καὶ τὰ ἔτη τῆς ζωῆς ὑμῶν ἀπολεῖτε, καὶ ⟨τὰ ἔτη τῆς ἀπωλείας ὑμῶν⟩ †
πληθυνθήσεται ἐν κατάρᾳ αἰώνων, καὶ οὐκ ἔσται ὑμῖν ἔλεος ⟨καὶ
εἰρήνη⟩. 6. τότε ἔσται τὰ ὀνόματα ὑμῶν εἰς κατάραν αἰώνιον πᾶσιν
τοῖς δικαίοις, καὶ ἐν ὑμῖν καταράσονται πάντες οἱ καταρώμενοι,
καὶ πάντες οἱ ἁμαρτωλοί [καὶ ἀσεβεῖς ἐν ὑμῖν ὀμοῦνται. καὶ πάντες
οἱ (ἀν)αμάρτητοι χαρήσονται, καὶ ἔσται αὐτοῖς λύσις ἁμαρτιῶν καὶ
πᾶν ἔλεος καὶ εἰρήνη καὶ ἐπιείκεια· ἔσται αὐτοῖς σωτηρία, φῶς
ἀγαθόν, καὶ αὐτοὶ κληρονομήσουσιν τὴν γῆν. καὶ πᾶσιν ὑμῖν τοῖς
ἁμαρτωλοῖς οὐχ ὑπάρξει σωτηρία, ἀλλὰ ἐπὶ πάντας ὑμᾶς κατελεύ- †
σεται κατάρα], 7. καὶ τοῖς ἐκλεκτοῖς ἔσται φῶς καὶ χάρις καὶ
εἰρήνη καὶ αὐτοὶ κληρονομήσουσιν τὴν γῆν· ὑμῖν δὲ τοῖς ἀσεβέσιν
ἔσται κατάρα. 8. τότε δοθήσεται τοῖς ἐκλεκτοῖς [φῶς καὶ χάρις,

---

αλλυουνται — επειταγην — γεινεται 3. ειδετε — θαλασα — αλλυουσιν
4. υμις — οκ — ενεμινατε — εποιησαται — απεστηται — κατελαλησαται twice —
στοματει — σκληρωκαρδιοι — εστε ιρηνη 5. υμις κατηρασασθαι — κατα (= καὶ
τὰ ἔτη) — απολιται — αιτη — απολιας — εστε 6. δικεοις — ασεβις — ομουνται —
αμαρτητοι — αμαρτειων — επειεικεια — επει — καταλυσιν καταραν 7. εγλεκτοις
— εστε before καταρ. 8. εγλεκτοις twice —

---

has crept in from preceding verse. ὡσπερεί (? ὥσπερ καί). Eth. καθώς. After ἐπιταγήν add θεοῦ with Eth. 3. ὡς ὁμοίως. Eth. ὁμοῦ. 4. κατὰ τὰς ἐντολὰς αὐτοῦ. Eth. τὴν ἐντολὴν τοῦ κυρίου. 5. I have emended κατὰ τῆς ζωῆς into καὶ τὰ ἔτη τῆς ζωῆς with Eth.: see Crit. Note, p. 60. 6. See Crit. Note, p. 61. πάντες οἱ κατ. . . . ἁμαρτωλοί gives the wrong sense unless we take these words in the vocative, 'all ye blasphemers,' &c. The question here does not concern the cursing of sinners by sinners but the cursing of sinners by the righteous. 7. χάρις. Eth. ፍሥሓ, χαρά. 8. For ወአመ፤ read ወአሜሃ. φῶς . . . ἐκλεκτοῖς repeated from first parts

καὶ αὐτοὶ κληρονομήσουσιν τὴν γῆν. τότε δοθήσεται πᾶσιν τοῖς ἐκλεκτοῖς] σοφία, καὶ πάντες οὗτοι ζήσονται καὶ οὐ μὴ ἁμαρτήσονται ἔτι, οὐ κατ' ἀσέβειαν οὔτε κατὰ ὑπερηφανίαν, ⟨καὶ ἔσται ἐν ἀνθρώπῳ πεφωτισμένῳ φῶς καὶ ἀνθρώπῳ ἐπιστήμονι νόημα.⟩ καὶ οὐ μὴ πλημμελήσουσιν 9. οὐδὲ μὴ ἁμάρτωσιν πάσας τὰς ἡμέρας τῆς ζωῆς αὐτῶν, καὶ οὐ μὴ ἀποθάνωσιν ἐν ὀργῇ θυμοῦ, ἀλλὰ τὸν ἀριθμὸν αὐτῶν ζωῆς ἡμερῶν πληρώσουσιν, καὶ ἡ ζωὴ αὐτῶν αὐξηθήσεται ἐν εἰρήνῃ, καὶ τὰ ἔτη τῆς χαρᾶς αὐτῶν πληθυνθήσεται ἐν ἀγαλλιάσει καὶ εἰρήνῃ αἰῶνος ἐν πάσαις ταῖς ἡμέραις τῆς ζωῆς αὐτῶν.

† (in margin beside "σονται ἔτι, οὐ κατ' ἀσέβειαν …")

VI. 1. Καὶ ἐγένετο, οὗ ἂν ἐπληθύνθησαν οἱ υἱοὶ τῶν ἀνθρώπων, ἐν ἐκείναις ταῖς ἡμέραις ἐγεννήθησαν (αὐτοῖς) θυγατέρες ὡραῖαι καὶ καλαί. 2. καὶ ἐθεάσαντο αὐτὰς οἱ ἄγγελοι υἱοὶ οὐρανοῦ καὶ ἐπεθύμησαν αὐτάς, καὶ εἶπαν πρὸς ἀλλήλους· Δεῦτε ἐκλεξώμεθα ἑαυτοῖς γυναῖκας ἀπὸ . . . τῶν ἀνθρώπων καὶ γεννήσωμεν ἑαυτοῖς τέκνα. 3. καὶ εἶπεν Σεμειαζᾶς πρὸς αὐτούς, ὃς ἦν ἄρχων αὐτῶν· Φοβοῦμαι μὴ οὐ θελήσητε ποιῆσαι τὸ πρᾶγμα τοῦτο, καὶ ἔσομαι ἐγὼ μόνος ὀφειλέτης ἁμαρτίας μεγάλης. 4. ἀπεκρίθησαν οὖν αὐτῷ πάντες· Ὀμόσωμεν ὅρκῳ πάντες καὶ ἀναθεματίσωμεν [πάντες]

σοφιαν — ετει — κατ' αληθειαν — αυπω twice — επειστημονει 9. πασες τες ημερες
VI. 1. υειοι — αυπων — εκεινες τες ημερες — ωρεαι 2. ῢϊοι — εγλεξομεθα — αυπων — γεννησομεν 3. θελησεται — οφειλητης αμαρτειας 4. απεκρειθησαν — αναθεματεισομεν —

---

of vv. 7, 8. κατ' ἀσέβειαν = በረሲዐ. We might also emend κατὰ λήθην. καὶ ἔσται . . . νόημα is more difficult than Eth. and suits the context better: cf. cviii. 13. 9. ἁμάρτωσιν. Inferior in sense to ይትኴነኑ 'will be punished.' ἐν ὀργῇ θυμοῦ. በመቅሠፍት፡ ወኢበመዓት = ἐν ὀργῇ μήτ' ἐν θυμῷ.

VI. 1. ου αν should probably be emended into ὅτε = reading of G, እንዘ. After ἐγεννήθησαν read αὐτοῖς with Eth. and Syn. Gk. καὶ καλαί. So Eth. Syn. Gk. omits. 2. Syn. Gk. against Eth. and Giz. Gk. omits καὶ ἐθεάσαντο . . . οὐρανοῦ and adds οἱ ἐγρήγοροι καὶ ἀπεπλανήθησαν ὀπίσω αὐτῶν after ἐπεθ. αὐτάς. δεῦτε omitted by Syn. Gk. Before τῶν ἀνθρώπων add with Syn. Gk. τῶν θυγατέρων: cf. Eth. እምውሉደ፡ ሰብእ, which we should emend into እምእዋልደ፡ ሰብእ = 'from among the daughters of men.' καὶ γενν. . . . τέκνα. Syn. Gk. omits. 4. After αὐτῷ πάντες Syn. Gk. and Eth. add καὶ εἶπον, but G omits. ἀναθ. πάντες. Eth. and Syn. Gk. omit πάντες.

ἀλλήλους μὴ ἀποστρέψαι τὴν γνώμην ταύτην, μέχρις οὗ ἂν τελέσωμεν αὐτὴν [καὶ ποιήσωμεν] τὸ πρᾶγμα τοῦτο. 5. τότε ὤμοσαν πάντες ὁμοῦ καὶ ἀνεθεμάτισαν ἀλλήλους ἐν αὐτῷ .... 6. ....

7. Καὶ ταῦτα τὰ ὀνόματα τῶν ἀρχόντων αὐτῶν· Σεμιαζᾶ(s)—οὗτος ἦν ἄρχων αὐτῶν—, Ἀραθάκ, Κιμβρᾶ, Σαμμανή, Δανειήλ, Ἀρεαρῶς, Σεμιήλ, Ἰωμειήλ, Χωχαριήλ, Ἐζεκιήλ, Βατριήλ, Σαθιήλ, Ἀτριήλ, Ταμιήλ, Βαρακιήλ, Ἀνανθνᾶ, Θωνιήλ, Ῥαμιήλ, Ἀσεάλ, Ῥακειήλ, Τουριήλ. 8. οὗτοί εἰσιν οἱ δέκαρχοι αὐτῶν (καὶ οἱ λοιποὶ †
πάντες μετ' αὐτῶν).

VII. 1. Καὶ ἔλαβον ἑαυτοῖς γυναῖκας· ἕκαστος αὐτῶν ἐξελέξαντο ἑαυτοῖς γυναῖκας, καὶ ἤρξαντο εἰσπορεύεσθαι πρὸς αὐτὰς καὶ μιαίνεσθαι ἐν αὐταῖς καὶ ἐδίδαξαν αὐτὰς φαρμακείας καὶ ἐπαοιδὰς καὶ ῥιζοτομίας καὶ τὰς βοτάνας ἐδήλωσαν αὐταῖς.

2. Αἱ δὲ ἐν γαστρὶ λαβοῦσαι ἐτέκοσαν γίγαντας μεγάλους

αποστρεψε — ποιησομεν 5. ομοσαν — αναθεματεισαν 7. αρχον — ασεαλρα' κειηλτουριηλ 8. αρχε αυτων οι δεκα.

VII. 1. γυνεκας before και — μειενεσθαι — αυτες twice — ειπαοιδας — ρειζοτομιας 2. εν δε — γαστριν — γειγοντας —

μέχρις ... τοῦτο. Eth. = *καὶ τελέσαι τῆς γνώμης ταύτης τὴν πρᾶξιν.* *καὶ ποιήσ. ... τοῦτο.* Syn. Gk. omits. 5. Before *ἀλλήλους* late Eth. MSS. insert ኵሎሙ 'all,' but G M with Syn. Gk. and Giz. Gk. omit. As ቦቱ = *ἐν αὐτῷ*, for 'to its fulfilment' read *upon it.* Giz. Gk. omits rest of verse and ver. 6. 7. I have followed G in giving Kôkabîêl and Armârôs instead of Akîbêêl and Armers. Read *Ēzēqēēl* instead of Zaqîlô, and *Zaqîlô* instead of Zaqêbê. Eth. and Syn. Gk. agree in main as to the names against Giz. Gk., which is very corrupt. 8. See Crit. Note, p. 64, where I should have added that I had emended the evident corruption ዐሰሬቱ in G into ሀሰሬቱ.

VII. 1. Syn. Gk. adds at beginning of verse *ἐν τῷ χιλιοστῷ ἑκατοστῷ ἑβδομηκοστῷ ἔτει τοῦ κόσμου.* *ἕκαστος αὐτῶν ... γυναῖκας.* Syn. Gk. omits. This clause merely repeats the preceding one. Eth. = *ἐξελέξατο ἕκαστος ἑαυτῷ μίαν* alone preserves the true reading here. *εἰσπορεύεσθαι π. αὐ. καί.* Syn. Gk. omits. *μιαίνεσθαι.* Eth. ተደመሩ 'united.' After *ἐν αὐταῖς* Syn. Gk. makes an important addition, *ἕως ... μεγαλειότητα αὐτῶν*: see p. 65. *αὐτάς.* Syn. Gk. gives *ἑαυτοὺς καὶ τὰς γυναῖκας ἑαυτῶν.* *καὶ ῥιζ. ... αὐταῖς.* Syn. Gk. omits. *τὰς βοτάνας.* Eth. ወዕፀው, 'of trees,' should be read ወዕፀወ, *and trees.* We should expect ወሣዕረ, 'and herbs.' 2. Syn.

ἐκ πηχῶν τρισχιλίων, 3. οἵτινες κατήσθοσαν τοὺς κόπους τῶν ἀνθρώπων· ὡς δὲ οὐκ ἐδυνήθησαν αὐτοῖς οἱ ἄνθρωποι ἐπιχορηγεῖν, 4. οἱ γίγαντες ἐτόλμησαν ἐπ' αὐτοὺς καὶ κατησθίοσαν τοὺς ἀνθρώπους. 5. καὶ ἤρξαντο ἁμαρτάνειν ἐν τοῖς πετεινοῖς καὶ τοῖς θηρίοις καὶ ἑρπετοῖς καὶ τοῖς ἰχθύσιν καὶ ἀλλήλων τὰς σάρκας κατεσθίειν, καὶ τὸ αἷμα ἔπινον. 6. τότε ἡ γῆ ἐνέτυχεν κατὰ τῶν ἀνόμων.

VIII. 1. Ἐδίδαξεν τοὺς ἀνθρώπους Ἀζαὴλ μαχαίρας ποιεῖν καὶ ὅπλα καὶ ἀσπίδας καὶ θώρακας, [διδάγματα ἀγγέλων] καὶ ὑπέδειξεν αὐτοῖς τὰ μέταλλα καὶ τὴν ἐργασίαν αὐτῶν καὶ ψέλια καὶ κόσμους καὶ στίβεις καὶ τὸ καλλιβλέφαρον καὶ παντοίους λίθους ἐκλεκτοὺς καὶ τὰ βαφικά. 2. καὶ ἐγένετο ἀσέβεια

τρισχειλιων 3. οιτεινες κατεσθοσαν — αυτων — αυτοι επειχορηγιν 4. κατεσθιοσαν — αυτους 5. ηριοις — χθυσιν — κατεσθειειν — εμα επινον
VIII. 1. αυτους — μαχερας — ασπειδας — υπεδιξεν — μεγαλα — κοσμος — στειβεις — εγλεκτους 2. ασεβια —

Gk. omits the rest of this chapter. Before ἐκ πηχῶν Eth. inserts ወቆምሙ = καὶ ἡ ἡλικία αὐτῶν. 3. For እሉ read እለ with Giz. Gk. οἵτινες. τοὺς κόπους. Eth. inserts 'all.' ὡς δέ. This may have been ἕως. So Eth. እስከ 'till.' 4. ἐτόλμησαν. Eth. ተመይጡ 'turned.' 5. τὸ αἷμα. Eth. adds እምኔሆ, αὐτῶν.

VIII. 1. τοὺς ἀνθρώπους. So Eth. Syn. Gk. omits. For Ἀζαὴλ Syn. Gk. reads πρῶτος Ἀζαὴλ ὁ δέκατος τῶν ἀρχόντων. ὅπλα. Eth. መጥባሕት = 'knives.' ὅπλα καὶ ἀσπίδας. Syn. Gk. πᾶν σκεῦος πολεμικόν. διδάγματα ἀγγέλων. A gloss; not in Eth. or Syn. Gk. ὑπέδειξεν αὐτοῖς. Syn. Gk. omits. τὰ μέταλλα. See Crit. Note, p. 66. After μέταλλα Syn. Gk. adds τῆς γῆς καὶ τὸ χρυσίον. καὶ τὴν ἐργασίαν αὐτῶν. Hence read with E ወምግባሮሙ. καὶ ψέλια καὶ κόσμους. So Eth. Syn. Gk. καὶ ποιήσωσιν αὐτὰ κόσμια ταῖς γυναιξὶ καὶ τὸν ἄργυρον. καὶ στίβεις. So Eth.: see p. 66. Syn. Gk. ἔδειξε δὲ αὐτοῖς καὶ τὸ στίλβειν. καλλιβλέφαρον. So Eth. እሥነየ: ቀራንብት 'the beautifying of the eyelids.' Syn. Gk. καλλωπίζειν. παντοίους λίθους ἐκλεκτούς. Syn. Gk. τοὺς ἐκλεκτοὺς λίθους. Eth. እብነ: እምኵሉ: እብን: ክቡረ: ወኅሩየ = λίθους τιμιωτάτους καὶ ἐκλεκτοτάτους. τὰ βαφικά. Eth. inserts ኵሉ 'all,' and adds at end of verse 'and the world was changed.' Syn. Gk. adds καὶ ἐποίησαν . . . ἁγίους: see p. 66. 2. ἐγένετο ἀσέβεια πολλή, καὶ

πολλή, καὶ ἐπόρνευσαν καὶ ἀπεπλανήθησαν καὶ ἠφανίσθησαν ἐν πάσαις ταῖς ὁδοῖς αὐτῶν. 3. Σεμιαζᾶς ἐδίδαξεν ἐπα(οι)δὰς καὶ ῥιζοτομίας, Ἀρμαρῶς ἐπαοιδῶν λυτήριον, Ῥακιὴλ ἀστρολογίας, Χωχχιὴλ τὰ σημειωτικά, Σα(θι)ὴλ ἀστεροσκοπίαν, Σεριὴ(λ) σεληναγωγάς.

4. Τῶν οὖν ἀνθρώπων ἀπολλυμένων ἡ βο(ὴ) εἰς οὐρανοὺς ἀνέβη.

IX. 1. Τότε παρ(α)κύψαντες Μιχαὴλ καὶ Οὐριὴλ καὶ Ῥαφαὴλ † καὶ Γαβριή(λ), οὗτοι ἐκ τοῦ οὐρανοῦ ἐθεάσα(ν)το αἷμα πολὺ ἐκχυν-

---

εφανισθησαν 3. αστρωλογιας—σημειωτεικα—αστεροσκοπειαν—σεληνοναγιας
4. τον νουν αντων.
IX. 1. στ . . . ηλ (= Οὐριὴλ ?).

ἐπόρνευσαν. G reads ወኮኑ፡ ረሲዓን፡ ዐቢየ፡ ወብዙኅ፡ ወዘመዉ. Here ዐቢየ፡ ወ is an intrusion. Hence translate on p. 66: *there arose much godlessness and they committed fornication.* Syn. Gk. omits καὶ ἐπορν. καὶ ἀπεπλ. and adds ἐπὶ τῆς γῆς. 3. Syn. Gk. inserts before Σεμιαζᾶς, ἔτι δὲ καὶ ὁ πρώταρχος αὐτῶν. Σεμιαζᾶς = Eth. አሜዜራስ or አሚዚራስ (G). Amizîrâs. This is corrupt. ἐπαοιδὰς καὶ ῥιζοτομίας. Eth. ኵሎ፡ መሰብዐያነ፡ ወመቶርያነ፡ ሥርዋ = πάντας ἐπαοιδοὺς καὶ ῥιζοτόμους. Syn. Gk. εἶναι ὀργὰς κατὰ τοῦ νοός, καὶ ῥίζας βοτανῶν τῆς γῆς. Ἀρμαρῶς = Syn. Gk. Φαρμαρός. Syn. Gk. adds before this ὁ ἐνδέκατος, and after it ἐδίδαξε φαρμακείας ἐπαοιδίας, σοφίας καί. Ῥακιήλ. Eth. በረቅኣል, Baraq'âl. ἀστρολογίας. Eth. = ἀστρολόγους. Χωχχιήλ. Eth. ኮከብኤል, Kôkabêl. σημειωτικά. Syn. Gk. τὰ σημεῖα τῆς γῆς. Σαθιήλ. Eth. ጥምኤል, Temêl. Σεριήλ. Eth. አስራድኤል. σεληναγωγάς (so I have emended σεληνοναγιας) = Eth. ፍኖተ፡ ወርኅ 'the course of the moon.' Syn. Gk. τὰ σημεῖα τῆς σελήνης. Syn. Gk. adds πάντες οὗτοι . . . αὐτῶν: see p. 67.

VIII. 4—IX. 4. For this part there is a doublet given by Syncellus, which we shall designate Syn. Gk.[1] and Syn. Gk.[2].

VIII. 4. At beginning of verse, Syn. Gk.[1] adds μετὰ δὲ ταῦτα ἤρξαντο . . . ἀνθρώπων: see p. 67. After ἀπολλ. Eth. adds ጸርሑ = ἐβόησαν. Syn. Gk. variants very wild. Syn. Gk.[1] καὶ ἤρξαντο . . . ἐνώπιον κυρίου: see p. 67. Syn. Gk.[2] τότε ἐβόησαν . . . τῇ μεγαλοσύνῃ. Yet these may be more correct than the shorter text of Eth. and Giz. Gk., as these repetitions (cf. ix. 2, 3) are natural in Hebrew writing.

IX. 1. For ሱርያን G reads ሱርኤል, an obvious corruption of ኡርኤል. For ወኡርያን, which G omits, read ረፋኤል with Giz. Gk. and Syn. Gk.[1 and 2]. Hence, for 'Surjan and Urjan' read *Uriel and Raphael.* Syn. Gk. καὶ ἀκούσαντες . . . τοῦ οὐρανοῦ (see p. 67)

νόμεν(ον) ἐπὶ τῆς γῆς (καὶ πᾶσαν ἀνομίαν γινομένην ἐπὶ τῆς γῆς). 2. *καὶ εἶπαν πρὸς ἀλλήλους· φωνὴ βοῶν τῶν ἐπὶ τῆς γῆς μέχρι πυλῶν τοῦ οὐρανοῦ.* 3. *ἐντυγχάνουσιν αἱ ψυχαὶ τῶν ἀνθρώπων λεγόντων· Εἰσαγάγετε τὴν κρίσιν ἡμῶν πρὸς τὸν ὕψιστον.*

† 4. *Καὶ εἶπα(ν) τῷ κυρίῳ (τῶν αἰώνων)· Σὺ εἶ κύριος τῶν κυρίων καὶ ὁ θεὸς τῶν θεῶν καὶ βασιλεὺς τῶν βασιλευόντων. ὁ θρόνος τῆς δόξης σου εἰς πάσας τὰς γενεὰς τοῦ αἰῶνος, καὶ τὸ ὄνομά σου τὸ ἅγιον καὶ μέγα καὶ εὐλόγητον εἰς πάντας τοὺς αἰῶνας.*

IX. 1. *εμα — επει* 2. *προ — τω — επει — μεχρι* 3. *αυτων — εισαγαγεται* 4. *κω — κς — θς — αιωνων (= βασιλευόντων)*

= Giz. Gk. *τότε . . . οὐρανοῦ.* Eth. agrees with Giz. Gk. After *γῆς* I have added *καὶ πᾶσαν ἀνομίαν γινομένην ἐπὶ τῆς γῆς* with Eth. ወኵሉ፡ ዐመፃ፡ ዘይትገበር፡ በዲበ፡ ምድር. So also Syn. Gk.[1 and 2] but that before *γινομένην* they add *καὶ ἀσέβειαν.* 2. *καὶ εἶπαν* = Syn. Gk. *εἰσελθόντες εἶπον.* Syn. Gk. omits the rest of verse, and Giz. Gk. is imperfect, and should probably be *φωνὴν βοῶν αὐτῶν γυμνὴ βοᾷ ἡ γῆ*: cf. En. lxvii. 2; lxxxiv. 5. 3. Eth. adds at beginning: ወይእዜ፡ ለክሙ፡ ቅዱሳነ፡ ሰማይ = *καὶ νῦν, πρὸς ὑμᾶς, ὦ ἅγιοι τοῦ οὐρανοῦ. ἐντυγχάνουσιν . . . λεγόντων.* Syn. Gk. *ὅτι τὰ πνεύματα καὶ αἱ ψυχαί* (Syn. Gk.[1]) *στενάζουσιν ἐντυγχάνοντα καὶ λέγοντα* (Syn. Gk.[2]) *ἐντυγχάνουσι στενάζοντα καὶ λέγοντα.* Here *τὰ πν. καὶ αἱ ψ.* or *τὰ πν. τῶν ψυχῶν* is the true text against both Giz. Gk. and Eth.: see Crit. Note on ix. 10, p. 70. *κρίσιν.* So Eth. and Syn. Gk.[1]: Syn. Gk.[2] gives *δέησιν.* After *ὕψιστον* Syn. Gk.[1] adds *καὶ τὴν ἀπώλειαν . . . μεγαλωσύνῃ* (p. 68). 4. After *καί* Syn. Gk.[2] adds *προσελ. οἱ τ. ἀρχ. τῷ κυρίῳ τῶν αἰώνων.* So Syn. Gk.[1] virtually supported by G M ለእግዚአሙ፡ ለንጉሥ = *τῷ κυρίῳ τῶν βασιλευόντων. τῶν αἰώνων*, being early corrupted into *τῶν βασιλευόντων* in the Gk. parent of Eth. text, was omitted later in Giz. MS. Hence for 'their Lord the King' read *the Lord of the ages. σύ.* So Syn. Gk. Eth. እስመ, which as Dln. points out should be አንተ. After *βασιλευόντων* which I have emended from *αἰώνων*, Syn. Gk.[1] adds *καὶ θεὸς τῶν αἰώνων*, and Syn. Gk.[2] *καὶ θεὸς τῶν ἀνθρώπων.* The former reading may have dropped out here both in Eth. and Giz. Gk. *ἅγιον καὶ μέγα καὶ εὐλόγητον εἰς π. τ. αἰῶνας.* Syn. Gk.[1 and 2] omit *καὶ μέγα.* Eth. is here slightly corrupt. In 'blessed and glorious art Thou,' the 'Thou' (አንተ) belongs to the next verse, the 'and glorious' is an intrusion; and the term 'blessed' should be connected with 'name.' Hence for 'Thy name holy . . . art Thou' read *Thy name holy*

5. σὺ ⟨γὰρ⟩ ἐποίησας τὰ πάντα καὶ πᾶσαν τὴν ἐξουσίαν ἔχων, καὶ πάντα ἐνώπιόν σου φανερὰ καὶ ἀκάλυπτα, καὶ πάντα (ὁρᾷς καὶ οὐκ ἔστιν ὃ κρυβῆναί σε δύναται).

6. [Σὺ] ὁρᾷς ἃ ἐποίησεν Ἀζαήλ, ὡς ἐδίδαξεν πάσας τὰς ἀδικίας ἐπὶ τῆς γῆς καὶ ἐδήλωσεν τὰ μυστήρια τοῦ αἰῶνος τὰ ἐν τῷ οὐρανῷ ⟨ἃ⟩ ἐπιτηδεύουσιν γνῶναι ἄνθρωποι, 7. [καὶ] †
Σεμιαζᾶς, ᾧ τὴν ἐξουσίαν ἔδωκας ἄρχειν τῶν σὺν αὐτῷ ἅμα ὄντων, 8. καὶ ἐπορεύθησαν πρὸς τὰς θυγατέρας τῶν ἀνθρώπων τῆς γῆς καὶ συνεκοιμήθησαν αὐταῖς καὶ (ἐν ταῖς θηλείαις) ἐμιάνθησαν καὶ ἐδήλωσαν αὐταῖς πάσας τὰς ἁμαρτίας· 9. καὶ αἱ γυναῖκες

---

5. σοι — εποιησες — ενωπειον 6. ος — αδεικιας επει — επιτεδευουσιν εγνωσαν ανποι 8. ανπων — αυτες before πασας — αμαρτειας 9. ε γυνεκες — τειτανας — αδεικειας

---

and glorious and blessed unto all the ages. So Giz. Gk. Syn. Gk.[1] adds at close τότε ὁ ὕψιστος . . . τῆς κρίσεως: see p. 68. 5. γάρ. Eth. omits. πᾶσαν τὴν ἐξουσίαν. Syn. Gk. πάντων τὴν ἐξουσίαν. So Eth. After καὶ πάντα I have added with Eth. and Syn. Gk. ὁρᾷς . . . δύναται. 6. ὁρᾷς. So Syn. Gk. Eth. ርእኩ, which we should emend into ርኢከ, and for 'see them' read *Thou seest*. After Ἀζαήλ Syn. Gk. adds καὶ ὅσα εἰσήνεγκεν. ὡς. So Eth. Syn. Gk. ὅσα. After ἀδικίας Syn. Gk. adds καὶ ἁμαρτίας, and after γῆς adds καὶ πάντα δόλον ἐπὶ τῆς ξηρᾶς. καὶ ἐδήλωσεν . . . οὐρανῷ. So Eth. Syn. Gk. gives a better sense: ἐδίδαξε γὰρ . . . οὐρανῷ: see Crit. Note, p. 70. ἃ ἐπιτηδεύουσιν γνῶναι ἄνθρωποι. Cf. Syn. Gk. ἐπιτηδεύουσι δὲ . . . ἀνθρώπων: see pp. 69, 70. Eth. አመረ: ሰብአት, corrupt for ተመሀረ: ሰብእ = ἐπιτηδεύουσιν γνῶναι ἄνθρωποι. 7. καί. G and Syn. Gk. omit. The words አመረ: ሰብአት should be connected with preceding verse. Σεμιαζᾶς, ᾧ. Syn. Gk. τῷ Σεμιαζᾷ. ἄρχειν. So Eth. Syn. Gk. ἔχειν. 8. See Crit. Note, p. 70. καὶ ἐμιάνθησαν. Giz. Gk. defective here. After καί Syn. Gk. gives ἐν ταῖς θηλείαις, which is supported by Eth. ምስለ: እልክቱ: አንስት 'with those women,' where, however, the ወ, 'and,' has been wrongly transposed. Hence, for 'have slept . . . themselves' read *have slept with them and defiled themselves with those women.* πάσας. So Syn. Gk. Eth. እሉንተ 'these.' Read with Dln. ኵሎሙ, and for 'these sins' read *all sins*. After ἁμαρτίας Syn. Gk. adds καὶ ἐδίδαξεν αὐτὰς μίσητρα ποιεῖν. 9. After καί Syn. Gk. adds νῦν ἰδού. αἱ γυναῖκες ἐγέννησαν. So Eth. Syn. Gk. αἱ θυγατέρες . . . υἱούς (p. 70).

ἐγέννησαν τιτᾶνας, ὑφ' ὧν ὅλη ἡ γῆ ἐπλήσθη αἵματος καὶ ἀδικίας. 10. καὶ νῦν ἰδοὺ βοῶσιν αἱ ψυχαὶ τῶν τετελευτηκότων καὶ ἐντυγχάνουσιν μέχρι τῶν πυλῶν τοῦ οὐρανοῦ, καὶ ἀνέβη ὁ στεναγμὸς αὐτῶν καὶ οὐ δύναται ἐξελθεῖν ἀπὸ προσώπου τῶν ἐπὶ τῆς γῆς γινομένων ἀνομημάτων. 11. καὶ σὺ πάντα οἶδας πρὸ τοῦ αὐτὰ γενέσθαι. καὶ σὺ ὁρᾷς ταῦτα καὶ ἐᾷς αὐτοὺς καὶ οὐδὲ ἡμῖν λέγεις τί δεῖ ποιεῖν αὐτοὺς περὶ τούτων.

X. 1. Τότε ὕψιστος ⟨εἶπεν⟩ [περὶ τούτων] ὁ μέγας ἅγιος, ⟨καὶ⟩ ἐλάλησεν [καὶ εἶπεν] καὶ ἔπεμψεν 'Ιστραὴλ πρὸς τὸν υἱὸν

10. ειδου βοωσιν — τετηλευτηκοτων — μεχρει — επει — γεινομενων 11. οιδες — αιας — λεγις τει

X. 1. περει

τιτᾶνας. Syn. Gk. γίγαντας. So Eth. Before ὅλη Syn. Gk. adds κίβδηλα . . . ἐκκέχυται καί. αἵματος καί. So Eth. Syn. Gk. omits. 10. βοῶσιν. So Eth. Syn. Gk. omits. αἱ ψυχαί. See Crit. Note, p. 70. Correct ነፍሳት into ነፍሳተ with Gk., and for 'souls which' read *souls of those who*. M. Lods (p. 115) here points out that נֶפֶשׁ simply means 'person.' Thus נַפְשֹׁת מֵת = 'dead persons.' Hence the use of the peculiar expression 'spirits of the souls of those who have died' (see p. 70) to denote the continuance of the life of the spirit after death. δύναται. So Syn. Gk. Eth. supposes δύνανται. M. Lods defends δύναται and urges that the question here concerns the souls of the dead, and not living men, and translates: 'il (leur gémissement) ne peut sortir [de l'entrée des portes du ciel] à cause des iniquités.' But as δύναται ἐξελθεῖν probably represents יְכַל לְצֵאת, it would be better to render '(their lamentations) cannot cease because of,' &c. Hence, for 'they cannot escape from' read *cannot cease because of.* 11. πάντα. So Eth. Syn. Gk. αὐτά. ὁρᾷς. Eth. ተአምር 'thou knowest.' ταῦτα. So Eth. Syn. Gk. αὐτούς. ἐᾷς αὐτούς. So Syn. Gk. Eth. ዘዘኢየሆሙ 'everything affecting them.' Here the translator confused τὰ εἰς αὐτούς with ἐᾷς αὐτούς. Hence, for 'everything affecting them' read *and Thou sufferest them.* ἡμῖν. So Eth. Syn. Gk. omits.

X. 1. Before τότε Eth. adds καί. After ልዑል add ይቤ with Giz. Gk. and Syn. Gk. περὶ τούτων. Eth. and Syn. Gk. omit. καὶ εἶπεν. Eth. and Syn. Gk. omit. 'Ιστραήλ. Eth. አርስያላልዩር, አስርዩ፡ ልዩር (G). Syn. Gk. τὸν Οὐριήλ. After Λέμεχ Eth. reads ወይቤሎ፡ በሎ; but G omits ይቤሎ with Giz. Gk. Hence, omitting ወ, for 'and said . . . in My name' read *tell him in*

Λέμεχ· 2. Εἰπὸν αὐτῷ ἐπὶ τῷ ἐμῷ ὀνόματι· Κρύψον σεαυτόν, καὶ δήλωσον αὐτῷ τέλος ἐπερχόμενον, ὅτι ἡ γῆ ἀπόλλυται πᾶσα καὶ κατακλυσμὸς μέλλει γίνεσθαι πάσης τῆς γῆς καὶ ἀπολέσει πάντα ὅσα ἐστὶν αὐτῇ. 3. καὶ δίδαξον αὐτὸν ὅπως ἐκφύγῃ καὶ μενεῖ τὸ σπέρμα αὐτοῦ εἰς πάσας τὰς γενεὰς τοῦ αἰῶνος.

4. Καὶ τῷ Ῥαφαὴλ εἶπεν· Δῆσον τὸν Ἀζαὴλ ποσὶν καὶ χερσὶν καὶ βάλε αὐτὸν εἰς τὸ σκότος. καὶ ἄνοιξον τὴν ἔρημον τὴν οὖσαν ἐν τῷ Δαδουήλ, κἀκεῖ βάλε αὐτόν, 5. καὶ ὑπόθες αὐτῷ λίθους τραχεῖς καὶ ὀξεῖς καὶ ἐπικάλυψον αὐτῷ τὸ σκότος, καὶ οἰκησάτω ἐκεῖ εἰς τοὺς αἰῶνας, καὶ τὴν ὄψιν αὐτοῦ πώμασον, καὶ φῶς μὴ θεωρείτω. 6. καὶ ἐν τῇ ἡμέρᾳ τῆς μεγάλης τῆς κρίσεως ἀπαχθήσεται εἰς τὸν ἐμπυρισμόν. 7. καὶ ἰαθήσεται ἡ γῆ ἣν ἠφάνισαν οἱ ἄγγελοι, καὶ τὴν ἴασιν τῆς γῆς δήλωσον, ἵνα ἰάσωνται τὴν

---

2. ειπων — επει το — ονοματει — δηλοσον — μελλι γεινεσθαι 4. ανυξον — ηρημων 5. λειθους — οξις — επεικαλυψον — αυτο τω — οικησατο — θεωριτω 6. κρεισεως — ενπυρισμον 7. ειαθησεται — εφανεισαν — ιασονται —

My name. After Λέμεχ Syn. Gk. adds λέγων, π. π. τ. Νῶε. 2. After πᾶσα καί Syn. Gk. adds εἶπον αὐτῷ ὅτι. ὅσα ἐστὶν αὐτῇ. So Eth. Syn. Gk. ἀπὸ προσώπου τῆς γῆς. 3. After καί Eth. adds νῦν. αὐτόν. So Eth. Syn. Gk. τὸν δίκαιον. . . . . Λάμεχ. Syn. Gk. after Λάμεχ adds καὶ τὴν ψυχὴν . . . συντηρήσει. ὅπως ἐκφύγῃ . . . αὐτοῦ. So Eth. Syn. Gk. καὶ ἐκφεύξεται . . . σταθήσεται. 4. After καί Eth. adds πάλιν ὁ κύριος. After εἶπεν Syn. Gk. adds πορεύου Ῥαφαὴλ καί. ποσὶν καὶ χερσίν. Eth. and Syn. Gk. χερσὶν καὶ ποσίν. After χερσίν Syn. Gk. adds συμπόδισον αὐτόν. τῷ Δαδουήλ. Syn. Gk. τῇ ἐρήμῳ Δουδαήλ. After κἀκεῖ Syn. Gk. adds πορευθείς. 5. ὑπόθες. So Syn. Gk. But Eth. supposes (and rightly) ἐπίθες, ደይ፡ ላዕሌሁ. τραχεῖς καὶ ὀξεῖς. So Eth. Syn. Gk. ὀξεῖς κ. τραχεῖς. 6. τῇ ἡμέρᾳ τ. μεγάλης τ. κρίσεως. Syn. Gk. omits τ. μεγάλης. Eth. read τ. μεγάλῃ ἡμέρᾳ τῆς κρίσεως. ἀπαχθήσεται. A technical use. So Syn. Gk. Eth. ይትፈነው is bad: the translator should have used ወሰደ, x. 13. Syn. Gk. adds at end τοῦ πυρός. 7. ἰαθήσεται ἡ γῆ. We should emend this with Eth. and Syn. Gk. into ἴασαι τὴν γῆν. ἄγγελοι. So Eth. Syn. Gk. ἐγρήγοροι. γῆς. So Eth. Syn. Gk. πληγῆς. ἰάσωνται. So Syn. Gk., better than Eth. አሐዩ, ἰάσομαι. Hence

πληγήν, ἵνα μὴ ἀπόλωνται πάντες οἱ υἱοὶ τῶν ἀνθρώπων ἐν τῷ † μυστηρίῳ ὅλῳ ᾧ ἐπέτασαν οἱ ἐγρήγοροι καὶ ἐδί(δα)ξαν τοὺς υἱοὺς αὐτῶν, 8. καὶ ἠρημώθη πᾶσα ἡ γῆ [ἀφανισθεῖσα] ἐν τοῖς ἔργοις τῆς διδασκαλίας 'Αζαήλ· καὶ ἐπ' αὐτῷ γράψον τὰς ἁμαρτίας πάσας.

9. Καὶ τῷ Γαβριὴλ εἶπεν ὁ κύριος· Πορεύου ἐπὶ τοὺς μαζηρέους, ἐπὶ τοὺς κιβδήλους καὶ τοὺς υἱοὺς τῆς πορνείας, καὶ ἀπόλεσον τοὺς υἱοὺς τῶν ἐγρηγόρων ἀπὸ τῶν ἀνθρώπων. πέμψον αὐτοὺς ἐν πολέμῳ ἀπωλείας· μακρότης γὰρ ἡμερῶν οὐκ ἔσται αὐτῶν. 10. καὶ † πᾶσα ὅρεξις (οὐκ) ἔσται τοῖς πατράσιν αὐτῶν [καὶ] περὶ αὐτῶν, ὅτι ἐλπίζουσιν ζῆσαι ζωὴν αἰώνιον καὶ ὅτι ζήσεται ἕκαστος αὐτῶν ἔτη πεντακόσια.

μην απολλωνται — αυτων — επαταξαν (for ἀπέφησαν?) 9. των — κς — επει twice — κειβδελους — αυτων — απωλιας — εστιν 10. εργεσις — αιωνειων

---

read ይሕይው. πληγήν. So Syn. Gk. Eth. = γῆν. I withdraw my suggestion in Crit. Note, p. 73, and accept πληγήν as original. Hence, for 'I will heal the earth' read *so that they may heal the plague*. Before ἵνα Eth. and Syn. Gk. insert καί. τῷ μυστηρίῳ ὅλῳ. I have emended ምሥጢረ፡ ኵሉ, 'the secrets of everything,' into ምሥጢር፡ ኵሉ = τῷ μυστηρίῳ ὅλῳ. Hence my translation. ἐπέτασαν. So M. Bouriant for ἐπάταξαν. Perhaps ἀπέφησαν would be better. Syn. Gk. εἶπον. 8. ἀφανισθεῖσα. Omit with Eth. and Syn. Gk. τοῖς ἔργοις τ. διδασκαλίας. So Syn. Gk. Eth. = τῇ διδασκαλίᾳ τῶν ἔργων. αὐτῷ. Syn. Gk. αὐτῇ. 9. ὁ κύριος. Eth. 'God.' Syn. Gk. omits. After πορεύου Syn. Gk. adds Γαβριήλ. μαζηρέους. This is a corrupt transliteration of מַמְזֵר. Eth. more correctly መንዘራን. Syn. Gk. wrongly γίγαντας. ἐπὶ τ. κιβδήλους. So Syn. Gk. Eth. ወስምቱናን 'and the reprobates.' Before τοὺς υἱοὺς τ. π. Syn. Gk. adds ἐπί. Eth. = καὶ ἐπί. τῆς πορνείας. So Syn. Gk. Hence, for ዘማ, 'of the fornicatress,' should be read ዘሙት, which was first corrupted into ዘማት, pl. of ዘማ. After ἀπόλεσον Eth. adds τοὺς υἱοὺς τῆς πορνείας καί. τῶν ἀνθρώπων. So Eth. Syn. Gk. τῶν υἱῶν τ. α. Before πέμψον Eth. adds ἐξαπόστειλον αὐτοὺς καί. After αὐτούς Giz. Gk. defective: cf. Syn. Gk. and Eth. εἰς ἀλλήλους, ἐξ αὐτῶν εἰς αὐτούς. ἐν πολέμῳ ἀπωλείας. Syn. Gk. ἐν πολ. καὶ ἐν ἀπωλ. Eth. ἐν πολέμῳ ἀπολῶνται. μακρ. γάρ. So Eth. Syn. Gk. καὶ μακρ. αὐτῶν. Syn. Gk. αὐτοῖς. 10. ὅρεξις ἔσται. Syn. Gk. ἐρώτησις οὐκ ἔστι. So Eth.: see p. 74. καὶ περὶ αὐτῶν. Syn. Gk. omits. Eth.

11. Καὶ εἶπεν (τῷ) Μιχαήλ· Πορεύου καὶ δήλωσον Σεμιαζᾷ καὶ τοῖς λοιποῖς τοῖς σὺν αὐτῷ ταῖς γυναιξὶν μιγεῖσι (τοῦ) μιανθῆναι †
ἐν αὐταῖς ἐν τῇ ἀκαθαρσίᾳ αὐτῶν· 12. καὶ ὅταν κατασφαγῶσιν οἱ υἱοὶ αὐτῶν καὶ ἴδωσιν τὴν ἀπώλειαν τῶν ἀγαπητῶν, [καὶ] δῆσον αὐτοὺς ἑβδομήκοντα γενεὰς εἰς τὰς νάπας τῆς γῆς μέχρι ἡμέρας κρίσεως αὐτῶν καὶ συντελεσμοῦ, ἕως τελεσθῇ τὸ κρῖμα τοῦ αἰῶνος τῶν αἰώνων. 13. τότε ἀπαχθήσονται εἰς τὸ χάος τοῦ πυρὸς καὶ εἰς τὴν βάσανον καὶ εἰς τὸ δεσμωτήριον συγκλείσεως αἰῶνος. 14. καὶ ὃς ἂν κατακριθῇ καὶ ἀφανισθῇ ἀπὸ τοῦ νῦν μετ' αὐτῶν †
ὁμοῦ δεθήσονται μέχρι τελειώσεως γενεᾶς.

15. Ἀπόλεσον πάντα τὰ πνεύματα τῶν κιβδήλων καὶ τοὺς υἱοὺς τῶν ἐγρηγόρων διὰ τὸ ἀδικῆσαι τοὺς ἀνθρώπους. 16. καὶ

---

11. *γυνεξιν μειγεντας — αυτες* 12. *ειδωσιν — απολιαν — αυ αυτους = αυτους — μεχρει* 13. *το δεσ το δεσμοτηριον συνκλισεως* 14. *οταν κατακαυσθη — με μετ — τελιωσεως* 15. *πνατα — αυτους*

---

omits *καί*. 11. After *εἶπεν* Eth. adds *ὁ κύριος*. Before Μιχαήλ add *τῷ* with Eth. and Syn. Gk. After *πορεύου* Syn. Gk. adds Μιχαήλ. *καὶ δήλωσον*. So Eth. Syn. Gk. *δῆσον*. *ταῖς γυν. μιγεῖσι*. So Eth.= Syn. Gk. *τοὺς συμμιγέντας ταῖς θυγατράσι τῶν ἀνθρώπων*. Before *μιανθ.* Syn. Gk. adds *τοῦ*. Before *τῇ ἀκαθαρσίᾳ* Eth. adds *πάσῃ*. 12. *καὶ ὅταν*. So Syn. Gk. Eth. omits *καί*. *κατασφαγ*. So Syn. Gk. Eth.= *αὐτοὶ ἑαυτοὺς κατασφάξωσι*. Before *οἱ υἱοί* Eth. adds *πάντες*. After *ἀγαπητῶν* Eth. and Syn. Gk. add *αὐτῶν*. Omit *καί* before *δῆσον* with Eth. and Syn. Gk. After *αὐτούς* add *ἐπί* with Eth. and Syn. Gk. *νάπας*=hills: cf. LXX. Is. xl. 12. So Syn. Gk. and Eth. *καὶ συντελεσμοῦ*. Eth. adds *αὐτῶν*. Syn. Gk. *μεχρὶ ἡμέρας τελειώσεως τελεσμοῦ*. 13. *τότε*. So Syn. Gk. Eth.=*ἐν ἐκείναις ταῖς ἡμέραις*. *ἀπαχθ.* (see x. 6 note). Eth. 'one will lead off.' Syn. Gk. *ἀπενεχθήσονται*. ወ should be added after እሳት with Syn. and Giz. Gk. *συγκλείσεως αἰῶνος*. Syn. Gk. *τῆς σ. τοῦ αἰῶν*. Eth. *συγκλεισθήσονται εἰς τοὺς αἰῶνας τῶν αἰώνων*. በኅበሙ should be struck out. 14. *ὃς ἄν*. So I have emended with Syn. Gk.: see Crit. Note, p. 75. Eth. ሶቤሃ=*τότε*, a wrong vocalisation for ሶቤሁ=*ὅταν*. *κατακριθῇ*. See Crit. Note, pp. 75, 76. *ὁμοῦ*. So Eth. Syn. Gk. omits. *γενεᾶς*. Syn. Gk. adds *αὐτῶν*. Eth. *γενεᾶς γενεᾶς*. 15. Before *ἀπόλ*. Eth. adds *καί*. *πνεύματα τῶν κιβδήλων*. Hence, for ነፍሳት፡ ተውኔት read መናፍስት፡ ምንዛን; and for 'lustful souls' read *spirits of the reprobate* (or *illegitimate*). 16. *καὶ ἀπόλ*. Eth. omits *καί*.

ἀπόλεσον τὴν ἀδικίαν πᾶσαν ἀπὸ τῆς γῆς, καὶ πᾶν ἔργον πονηρίας ἐκλειπέτω. καὶ ἀναφανήτω τὸ φυτὸν τῆς δικαιοσύνης καὶ τῆς ἀληθείας ⟨εἰς τοὺς αἰῶνας⟩ ...... μετὰ χαρᾶς φυτευ(θή)σεται. 17. *καὶ νῦν πάντες οἱ δίκαιοι ἐκφεύξονται, καὶ ἔσονται ζῶντες ἕως γεννήσωσιν χιλιάδας, καὶ πᾶσας τὰς ἡμέρας νεότητος αὐτῶν καὶ τὰ σάββατα αὐτῶν μετὰ εἰρήνης πληρώσουσιν.* 18. *τότε ἐργασθήσεται πᾶσα ἡ γῆ ἐν δικαιοσύνῃ, καὶ καταφυτευθήσεται δένδρον ἐν αὐτῇ, καὶ πλησθήσεται εὐλογίας.* 19. *καὶ πάντα τὰ* † *δένδρα τῆς ἀγαλλιάσεως φυτευθήσεται, καὶ ἔσονται φυτεύοντες ἀμπέλους καὶ ἡ ἄμπελος ἣν ἂν φυτεύσωσιν ποιήσει προχοῦς οἴνου* † *καὶ σπόρου (τοῦ σπαρέντος ἕκαστον μέτρον) ποιήσει χιλιάδας καὶ ἕκαστον μέτρον ἐλαίας ποιήσει ἀνὰ βάτους δέκα.*

20. *Καὶ σὺ καθάρισον τὴν γῆν ἀπὸ πάσης ἀκαθαρσίας καὶ ἀπὸ*

---

16. *δικεοσυνης — αληθιας* 17. *δικεοι — πασαι αι ημερε — ιρηνης* 18. *δικεοσυνη* 19. *γης αγαλιασονται — φυτευοντευοντες — αι — ποιησουσιν προχους οινου χιλιαδες και σπορου ποιησει καθ.*

Eth. omits *εἰς τοὺς αἰῶνας*. After *αἰῶνας* add with Eth. 'labour will prove a blessing: righteousness and uprightness,' omitted through hmt. *φυτευθ.* Eth. ይትከሉ = *φυτεύσουσι*: cf. ver. 19. 17. *ἐκφεύξονται.* So G ይጐይዩ. Dln. ይግነዩ, corrupt. 18. *καταφυτ. δ. ἐν αὐτῇ.* Eth. 'it will all be planted with trees.' 19. *τῆς ἀγαλλ.* This emendation in accordance with Eth. is necessary, as Dln. and Lods have already recognised. After *ἀμπέλους* Eth. adds 'on it.' The emendation of *αι* into *καί* is necessary. Before *φυτεύσ.* Eth. adds 'on it.' For ፍሬ in Dln.'s text read ወይን with G. So Giz. Gk. *οἴνου.* Eth. renders *προχοῦς* freely by በጽጋብ. Gk. is confused and defective; but it agrees word for word with Eth. save that it omits ዘኵሉ፡ ዘርእ፡ ዘይዘርእ፡ ዲቤሃ፡ እሐቲ፡ መስፈርት with the exception of the second word = *σπόρου*. It preserves the verb and acc. of this clause, i.e. *ποιήσει χιλιάδας* = ትገብር፡ እልፈ. *καθ* is a corruption of *καί*. Such disarrangements are frequent: see i. 2 (note). For 'ten thousand' read *thousand*. *προχοῦς* = *ξέστης* (sometimes). *βάτους* is a rendering of בַּת. Hence, instead of 'press' translate *bath* or *vat*. A 'bath' = 8·7 gallons nearly according to Josephus or 4·4 according to Rabbinists. 20. *ἀκαθαρσίας* cannot be right: perhaps *βίας* or

πάσης ἀδικίας καὶ ἀπὸ (πά)σης ἁμαρτίας, καὶ ἀσεβείας, καὶ πάσας τὰς ἀκαθαρσίας τὰς γινομένας ἐπὶ τῆς γῆς ἐξάλειψον. 21. . . . καὶ ἔσονται πάντες λατρεύοντες οἱ λαοὶ καὶ εὐλογοῦντες πάντες ἐμοὶ καὶ προσκυνοῦντες. 22. καὶ καθαρισθήσεται πᾶσα ἡ γῆ ἀπὸ παντὸς μιάσματος καὶ ἀπὸ πάσης ἀκαθαρσίας καὶ ὀργῆς καὶ μάστιγος, καὶ οὐκέτι πέμψω ἐπ' αὐτοὺς εἰς πάσας τὰς γενεὰς τοῦ αἰῶνος. XI. 1. καὶ τότε ἀνοίξω τὰ ταμεῖα τῆς εὐλογίας τὰ ὄντα ἐν τῷ οὐρανῷ, τοῦ κατενεγκεῖν αὐτὰ ἐπὶ τὰ ἔργα, ἐπὶ τὸν κόπον τῶν υἱῶν τῶν ἀνθρώπων. 2. καὶ τότε ἀλήθεια καὶ εἰρήνη κοινωνήσουσιν ὁμοῦ εἰς πάσας τὰς ἡμέρας τοῦ αἰῶνος καὶ εἰς πάσας τὰς γενεὰς τῶν ἀνθρώπων.

XII. 1. Πρὸ τούτων τῶν λόγων ἐλήμφθη Ἐνώχ, καὶ οὐδεὶς τῶν ἀνθρώπων ἔγνω ποῦ ἐλήμφθη καὶ ποῦ ἔστιν καὶ τί ἐγένετο αὐτῷ. 2. καὶ τὰ ἔργα αὐτοῦ μετὰ τῶν ἐγρηγόρων, καὶ μετὰ τῶν ἁγίων δι' ἡμερῶν αὐτοῦ. †

---

20. γειvομενας επει 21. προσκοινουντες 22. ουκετει
XI. 1. ανυξω — ταμια — και κατενενκιν — επει twice — υιον — ανπων
2. αλεθεια — ιρηνη κοινονησουσιν — ανπων
XII. 1. Αινωχ — ουδις — ανπων 2. αυτων — αι ημερε.

βιασμοῦ. Cf. Eth. ገፍዕ 'violence.' Before ἀσεβείας Eth. adds πάσης. After ἐξάλ. Eth. adds ἀπὸ τῆς γῆς. 21. Before καὶ ἔσονται Eth. adds καὶ ἔσονται πάντες οἱ υἱοὶ τῶν ἀνθρώπων δίκαιοι. Perhaps omitted in Gk. through like beginning. πάντες ἐμοὶ καί. Eth. implies κ. π. ε. 22. ἀκαθαρσίας. Eth. ኃጢአት 'sin.' After πέμψω corrupt Eth. MSS. insert አይኅ 'a deluge,' but G omits. For ἐπ' αὐτούς Eth. reads ዲቤሃ 'upon it.' For τοῦ αἰῶνος Eth. reads ወእስከ፡ ለዓለም.

XI. 1. After κατενεγκεῖν Eth. adds ἐπὶ τὴν γῆν. After ἔργα Eth. adds 'and.' 2. καὶ τότε. Eth. omits. ἀλ. καὶ εἰρ. Eth. εἰρ. καὶ ἀλ. τῶν ἀνθρ. Eth. ዓለም 'of the world'—a confusion of αἰώνων and ἀνθρώπων, as M. Lods points out.

XII. 1. Before πρό Eth. adds καί. τούτων τῶν. Eth. ኵሉ 'all,' a corruption of እሉ. Hence, for 'all these things' read *these things*. ἐλήμφθη. Eth. ተከብተ 'was hidden.' This—the usual Eth. rendering of לקח, μετέθηκεν, and ἐλήφθη, in connexion with Enoch—is due to the influence of the Enoch myth. τῶν ἀνθρ. Eth. = τῶν υἱῶν τῶν ἀνθρ. 2. ἐγρηγόρων and ἁγίων in inverse order in Eth. Observe two emendations of Gk. in accordance with

3. Καὶ ⟨ἑστὼς⟩ ἤμην, Ἐνώχ, εὐλογῶν τῷ κυρίῳ τῆς μεγαλοσύνης, τῷ βασιλεῖ τῶν αἰώνων. καὶ ἰδοὺ οἱ ἐγρήγοροι ⟨τοῦ ἁγίου
τοῦ μεγάλου⟩ ἐκάλουν με (Ἐνὼχ τὸν γραμματέα καὶ εἶπεν ἐμοί)·
4. Ἐνὼχ ὁ[ι] γραμματεὺς τῆς δικαιοσύνης, πορεύου καὶ εἰπὲ τοῖς
ἐγρηγόροις τοῦ οὐρανοῦ, οἵτινες, ἀπολιπόντες τὸν οὐρανὸν τὸν
ὑψηλόν, τὸ ἁγίασμα τῆς στάσεως τοῦ αἰῶνος, μετὰ τῶν γυναικῶν
ἐμιάνθησαν καί, ὥσπερ οἱ υἱοὶ τῆς γῆς ποιοῦσιν, οὕτως καὶ αὐτοὶ
† ποιοῦσιν καὶ ἔλαβον ἑαυτοῖς γυναῖκας, καὶ ἀφανισμὸν μέγαν
ἠφανίσαν τὴν γῆν, 5. καὶ οὐκ ἔσται ὑμῖν εἰρήνη οὔτε ἄφεσις.
καὶ περὶ ὧν χαίρουσιν τῶν υἱῶν αὐτῶν, 6. τὸν φόνον τῶν
ἀγαπητῶν αὐτῶν ὄψονται, καὶ ἐπὶ τῇ ἀπωλείᾳ τῶν υἱῶν αὐτῶν
στενάξουσιν, καὶ δεηθήσονται εἰς τὸν αἰῶνα, καὶ οὐκ ἔσται αὐτοῖς
† ἔλεος καὶ εἰρήνη.

† XIII. 1. Ὁ δὲ Ἐνὼχ τῷ Ἀζαὴλ πορευθεὶς εἶπεν· Οὐκ ἔσται

---

3. Αινωχ — κω — βασιλι 4. Αινωχ — δικειοσυνης — ουνου = ουρανου — ουρανων — υψηλων — γυνεκων — γυνεκας αφανισμον μεγαν και ηφανισατε 5. εστε — ιρηνη — αφησις — χερουσιν 6. επει — απολεια — υιον — εστε — εις ελεον και ιρηνην

XIII. 1. ειπεν πορευου — εστε —

Eth. 3. After *καί* Eth. adds 'I' and omits *ἑστώς*. *τῷ κυρίῳ τῆς μεγαλοσύνης.* Eth. ለእግዚእ፡ ዐቢይ 'to the great Lord.' But Gk. is right, and the error lies in the vocalisation. Hence read ለእግዚእ፡ ዕበይ, and translate *to the Lord of greatness.* Before *τῷ βασ.* Eth. adds 'and.' For *τῶν αἰώνων* Eth. reads ዓለም, *τοῦ αἰῶνος.* *τοῦ ἁγ. τοῦ μεγ.* Eth. omits. Gk. omits through like beginning 'Enoch the scribe, and spake to me,' which Eth. preserves. 4. *καὶ εἰπέ.* Eth. አይድዕ = *δήλωσον.* G with Gk. omits ወ before ምቅዋመ. Hence for 'and the holy' read *the holy.* *τὸ ἁγίασμα τ. στάσεως τ. αἰῶνος.* Eth. seems preferable: ምቅዋመ፡ ቅዱስ (or ቅዱሳን)፡ ዘለዓለም. *τῆς γῆς.* Eth. ሰብእ 'of men.' But Gk. is right, as scribes confound የብስ and ሰብእ: cf. ix. 8, Crit. Note, p. 70. Hence, for 'children of men' read *children of earth.* *τὴν γῆν* can stand as a Hebraism with *ἀφ. μέγ. ἠφαν.* Eth. 'on the earth.' 5. For *ὑμῖν* read *αὐτοῖς* with Eth. Before *εἰρήνη* Eth. adds *ἐπὶ τῆς γῆς.* *καὶ περὶ ὧν χαίρουσιν.* See Crit. Note, p. 78. Dln.'s text destroys the sense by inserting a negative. 6. For *εἰς ἔλεον καὶ εἰρήνην* I have read *ἔλεος κ. εἰρήνη* with Eth.

XIII. 1. *Ἀζαήλ.* Eth. Azâzêl. *πορευθεὶς εἶπεν.* Emended in

σοι εἰρήνη· κρῖμα μέγα ἐξῆλθεν κατὰ σοῦ δῆσαί σε, 2. καὶ ἀνοχὴ καὶ ἐρώτησίς σοι οὐκ ἔσται περὶ ὧν ἔδειξας ἀδικημάτων καὶ περὶ πάντων τῶν ἔργων τῶν ἀσεβειῶν καὶ τῆς ἀδικίας καὶ τῆς ἁμαρτίας, ὅσα ὑπέδειξας τοῖς ἀνθρώποις.

3. Τότε πορευθεὶς εἴρηκα πᾶσιν αὐτοῖς. καὶ αὐτοὶ πάντες ἐφοβήθησαν, καὶ ἔλαβεν αὐτοὺς τρόμος καὶ φόβος, 4. καὶ ἠρώτησαν ὅπως γράψω αὐτοῖς ὑπομνήματα ἐρωτήσεως, ἵνα γένηται αὐτοῖς ἄφεσις καὶ ἵνα ἐγὼ ἀναγνῶ αὐτοῖς τὸ ὑπόμνημα τῆς ἐρωτήσεως ἐνώπιον κυρίου τοῦ οὐρανοῦ· 5. ὅτι αὐτοὶ οὐκέτι δύνανται λαλῆσαι οὐδὲ ἐπᾶραι αὐτῶν τοὺς ὀφθαλμοὺς εἰς τὸν οὐρανὸν ἀπὸ αἰσχύνης περὶ ὧν ἡμαρτήκεισαν καὶ κατεκρίθησαν.

6. Τότε ἔγραψα τὸ ὑπόμνημα τῆς ἐρωτήσεως αὐτῶν καὶ τὰς δεήσεις περὶ τῶν πνευμάτων αὐτῶν καὶ περὶ ὧν δέονται ὅπως αὐτῶν γένωνται ἄφεσις καὶ μακρότης. 7. καὶ πορευθεὶς ἐκάθισα ἐπὶ τῶν ὑδάτων Δὰν ἐν ⟨γῇ⟩ Δάν, ἥτις ἐστὶν ἐκ δεξιῶν Ἑρμωνειεὶμ δύσεως. ἀνεγίνωσκον τὸ ὑπόμνημα τῶν δεήσεων αὐτῶν ἕως † ἐκοιμήθην, 8. καὶ ἰδοὺ ὄνειροι ἐπ' ἐμὲ ἦλθον, καὶ ὁράσεις ἐπ' ἐμὲ ἐπέπιπτον, καὶ ἴδον ὁράσεις ὀργῆς, ⟨καὶ ἦλθεν φωνὴ λέγουσα⟩·

ιρηνη κρειμα — δησε 2. εδιξας — ασεβιων — υπεδιξας — $\overline{\text{αντοις}}$ 3. πορευθις 4. γενονται — αναγνοι — $\overline{\text{κυ}}$ 5. δυνονται — οδε επαρε αυτον — εσχυνης 6. δεησις — $\overline{\text{πνατων}}$ 7. πορευθις — ανεγινωσκων — ως 8. ονηροι — ορασις twice — ιδων = ιδον —

accordance with Eth. δῆσαί σε. Eth. '(Rufael) shall bind thee. 2. Omit ወምሕረት with G and Giz. Gk. Hence for 'intercession and mercy' read *intercession*. Strike out ውሉደ with G and Giz. Gk., and for 'the children of men' read *men*. 3. After πᾶσιν Eth. adds 'together.' τρόμος κ. φόβος. Eth. φ. κ. τ. 4. After ἠρώτησαν Eth. adds ἐμέ. ἀναγνῶ. This is better than Eth. እዐርግ, which supposes a reading ἀνάγω. ἐνώπιον. So G ቅድመ: Dln. ኀበ. Hence, for 'take their petition into the' read *read their petition in*. κυρίου. Eth. እግዚአብሔር = θεοῦ. 5. οὐδὲ ἐπᾶραι. Eth. ወኢያንሥኡ. περὶ ὧν ἡμαρ. κ. κατεκ. Eth. እበሳሆሙ፡ ዘተኰነኑ = τῶν ἁμαρτιῶν αὐτῶν διὰ ἃς κατεκρίθησαν. 6. τὰς δεήσεις. So Eth. G አስተብቍዖት. Dln. reads τὰς δεήσεις αὐτῶν. I have omitted the ወ before በእንተ with Giz. Gk. 7. γῇ. Eth. omits. Before ἀνεγ. Eth. adds καί. 8. καὶ ἦλθεν φωνὴ λέγουσα. Eth. omits wrongly: cf. xv. 2. Hence, for 'to the intent . . . recount' read *and a voice*

Εἰπὸν τοῖς υἱοῖς τοῦ οὐρανοῦ τοῦ ἐλέγξαι αὐτούς. 9. καὶ ἔξυπνος γενόμενος ἦλθον πρὸς αὐτούς. καὶ πάντες συνηγμένοι ἐκάθηντο πενθοῦντες [σ]ἐν 'Εβελσατά, ἥτις ἐστὶν ἀνὰ μέσον τοῦ Λιβάνου καὶ Σενισήλ, περικεκαλυμμένοι τὴν ὄψιν, 10. καὶ † ἐνώπιον αὐτῶν ἀνήγγειλα [αὐτοῖς] πάσας τὰς ὁράσεις ἃς εἶδον κατὰ τοὺς ὕπνους. καὶ ἠρξάμην λαλεῖν τοὺς λόγους τῆς δικαιοσύνης, ἐλέγχων τοὺς ἐγρηγόρους τοῦ οὐρανοῦ.

XIV. 1. Βίβλος λόγων δικαιοσύνης καὶ ἐλέγξεως ἐγρηγόρων τῶν ἀπὸ τοῦ αἰῶνος, κατὰ τὴν ἐντολὴν τοῦ ἁγίου τοῦ μεγάλου ἐν ταύτῃ τῇ ὁράσει.

2. 'Εγὼ εἶδον κατὰ τοὺς ὕπνους μου ὃ[ν] νῦν λέγω ἐν γλώσσῃ σαρκίνῃ, ἐν τῷ πνεύματι τοῦ στόματός μου, ὃ ἔδωκεν ὁ μέγας τοῖς † ἀνθρώποις λαλεῖν ἐν αὐτοῖς καὶ νοῆσαι καρδίᾳ, 3. ὡς (ἔκτισε καὶ ἔδωκε τοῖς ἀνθρώποις καὶ ἐμοὶ νοεῖν τοὺς λόγους τῆς γνώσεως

ελενξε 10. ενοπιον αυτων και — ανηνγιλα — ορασις — λαλιν — λογοι — δικεοσυνης — τος = τους before εγρ.

XIV. 1. δικεοσυνης — ελενξεος — ορασι 2. ειδων — ων νυν — σαρκεινη — πνατι — αυτοις λαλιν — νοησει καρδιας 3. οι — εκτεισεν — εδωεν —

---

came to me saying: that I should tell. εἰπόν. Eth. ἵνα εἴπω. τοῦ ἐλέγξαι. Eth. καὶ ἐλέγξω. 9. 'Εβελσατά. Eth. Ublesjâêl. Σενισήλ. Eth. Sênêsêr. 10. κατὰ τοὺς ὕπνους. So G በንዋም. Hence, for 'in my sleep' read *in sleep.* ἐλέγχων. Eth. ወእዘልፍ = καὶ ἐλέγχειν.

XIV. 1. βίβλος λόγων δικαιοσύνης καὶ ἐλέγξεως. Eth. ዝመጽሐፍ፡ ቃለ፡ ጽድቅ፡ ወዘለፋ, οὗτος ὁ βίβλος λόγος δικαιοσύνης καὶ ἔλεγξις. κατὰ τὴν ἐντολήν. Eth. በከመ፡ አዘዘ, καθὼς παρήγγελκε. Before τοῦ μεγ. Eth. adds καί. 2. Before ἐν τῷ πν. Eth. adds καί. ἐν τῷ πνεύματι τοῦ στόματός μου, ὃ ἔδωκεν ὁ μέγας. Eth. ወበመንፈስየ፡ ዘመሀበ፡ ዐቢይ፡ አፉ; transposed and corrupt, but easy to restore by reading አፉ before ዘመሀበ and attaching the suffix to it. Next strike out ወ with D. Thus we have በመንፈሰ፡ አፉየ፡ ዘመሀበ፡ ዐቢይ, a literal rendering of Giz. Gk. and supported by lxxxiv. 1. Hence, for 'and with my breath which the Great One has put into the mouth of men' read *with the breath of my mouth which the Great One has given to men.* ἐν αὐτοῖς. Eth. ቦቱ 'with it.' Better read ቦሙ, *with them.* 3. After ὡς I have restored, with G, the clause (ἔκτισε καὶ ἔδωκε . . . καὶ ἐμέ) lost through hmt. After ለሰብእ add

καὶ ἐμὲ) ἔκτισεν καὶ ἔδωκεν ἐλέγξασθαι ἐγρηγόρους τοὺς υἱοὺς τοῦ † οὐρανοῦ.

4. Ἐγὼ τὴν ἐρώτησιν ὑμῶν [τῶν ἀγγέλων] ἔγραψα, καὶ ἐν τῇ ὁράσει μου τοῦτο ἐδείχθη· καὶ οὔτε ἡ ἐρώτησις ὑμῶν παρεδέχθη . . . . . . 5. ἵνα μηκέτι εἰς τὸν οὐρανὸν ἀναβῆτε ἐπὶ πάντας τοὺς αἰῶνας, καὶ ἐν τοῖς δεσμοῖς τῆς γῆς ἐρρέθη δῆσαι ὑμᾶς εἰς πάσας τὰς γενεὰς τοῦ αἰῶνος, 6. καὶ ἵνα πρὸ τούτων ἴδητε τὴν † ἀπώλειαν τῶν υἱῶν ὑμῶν τῶν ἀγαπητῶν, καὶ ὅτι οὐκ ἔσται ὑμῖν ὄνησις αὐτῶν, ἀλλὰ πεσοῦνται ἐνώπιον ὑμῶν ἐν μαχαίρᾳ. 7. καὶ ἡ ἐρώτησις ὑμῶν περὶ αὐτῶν οὐκ ἔσται οὐδὲ περὶ ὑμῶν. καὶ ὑμεῖς κλαίοντες καὶ δεόμενοι καὶ μὴ λαλοῦντες πᾶν ῥῆμα ἀπὸ τῆς γραφῆς ἧς ἔγραψα.

8. Καὶ ἐμοὶ ἐφ' ὁράσει οὕτως ἐδείχθη· ἰδοὺ νεφέλαι ἐν τῇ ὁράσει ἐκάλουν, καὶ ὁμίχλαι με ἐφώνουν, καὶ διαδρομαὶ τῶν ἀστέρων καὶ διαστραπαί με κατεσπούδαζον καὶ ἐθορύβαζόν με, καὶ ἄνεμοι ἐν τῇ ὁράσει μου ἀνεπτέρωσάν με καὶ ἐπῆράν με ἄνω 9. καὶ εἰσ- † ήνεγκάν με εἰς τὸν οὐρανόν. καὶ εἰσῆλθον μέχρις ἤγγισα τείχους

εκλεξασθαι 4. αγγελων — ορασι — εδιχθη 5. αναβηται 6. περι — ειδητε — απολιαν — εστε — πεσουντε ενωπιων — μαχερα 7. υμις κλεοντες 8. ορασι thrice — εδιχθη — νεφελε — ομοχλε — εφονουν — διαδρομε — διαστραπε — μαι = με — εξεπετασαν 9. εισηνηνκαν — μαι = με — ορανον — τιχους οικοδομης —

ወሊተ with G. Hence, for 'created man and given to him' read *created and given to man and me.* Omit ኒ in ወወሀበኒ with G and Gk. 4. τοῦτο ἐδείχθη. Eth. οὕτως ἐδείχθη. καὶ οὔτε . . . παρεδέχθη. Eth. 'that your petition will not be granted.' After παρεδέχθη several clauses have been lost through hmt., which can be supplied from Eth. 'throughout all the days . . . granted to you.' 5. ἵνα. Eth. καὶ ἀπὸ τοῦ νῦν. ἐν τοῖς δεσμοῖς τῆς γῆς. Eth. ἐν τῇ γῇ. In my Trans. this phrase should be connected with 'shall bind.' γενεάς. Eth. = ἡμέρας. 6. καὶ ἵνα. Eth. καί. πρὸ (a necessary emendation). So Eth. ὄνησις αὐτῶν. Eth. ተሬሲዮሙ 'have them in . . . keeping.' Free, but admissible. 7. See Crit. Note, p. 80. 8. ἐφ' ὁράσει. Eth. ὅρασις. ἐφώνουν. Eth. ይጼውዑኒ. κατεσπ. καὶ ἐθορύβ. Eth. ያጔጕዑኒ፡ ወይጽዕቁኒ 'drove and impelled me.' ἐθορύβαζον is difficult. ἀνεπτέρωσαν. A necessary emendation = Eth. ἄνω appears in Eth. after εἰσήνεγκαν in next verse.

ᾠκοδομημένου ἐν λίθοις χαλάζης καὶ γλώσσαις πυρὸς κύκλῳ αὐτῶν· καὶ ἤρξαντο ἐκφοβεῖν με.

10. Καὶ εἰσῆλθον εἰς τὰς γλώσσας τοῦ πυρός, καὶ ἤγγισα εἰς οἶκον μέγαν ᾠκοδομημένον ἐν λίθοις χαλάζης. καὶ οἱ τοῖχοι τοῦ οἴκου ὡς λιθωπλάκες, καὶ πᾶσαι ἦσαν ἐκ χιόνος, καὶ ἐδάφη χιονικά, 11. καὶ αἱ στέγαι ὡς διαδρομαὶ ἀστέρων καὶ ἀστραπαί. καὶ μεταξὺ αὐτῶν χερουβὶν πύρινα, καὶ ὁ οὐρανὸς αὐτῶν ὕδωρ. 12. καὶ πῦρ φλεγόμενον κύκλῳ τῶν τοίχων, καὶ θύραι πυρὶ καιόμεναι. 13. εἰσῆλθον εἰς τὸν οἶκον ἐκεῖνον θερμὸν ὡς πῦρ καὶ ψυχρὸν ὡς χιών· καὶ
† πᾶσα τρυφὴ ζωῆς οὐκ ἦν ἐν αὐτῷ. φόβος με ἐκάλυψεν καὶ τρόμος με ἔλαβεν, 14. καὶ ἤμην σειόμενος καὶ τρέμων, καὶ ἔπεσον (ἐπὶ πρόσωπόν μου καὶ) ἐθεώρουν ἐν τῇ ὁράσει ⟨μου⟩, 15.
† καὶ ἰδοὺ ἄλλος οἶκος μείζων τούτου καὶ ὅλη ἡ θύρα (αὐτοῦ) ἀνεῳγμένη κατέναντί μου καὶ ᾠκοδομημένος ἐν γλώσσαις πυρός, 16. καὶ ὅλος διαφέρων ἐν δόξῃ καὶ ἐν τιμῇ καὶ ἐν μεγαλοσύνῃ ὥστε μὴ δύνασθαί με ἐξειπεῖν ὑμῖν περὶ τῆς δόξης καὶ περὶ τῆς μεγαλοσύνης αὐτοῦ. 17. τὸ ἔδαφος αὐτοῦ ἦν πυρός, τὸ δὲ ἀνώτερον αὐτοῦ ἦσαν ἀστραπαὶ καὶ διαδρομαὶ ἀστέρων, καὶ ἡ στέγη αὐτοῦ ἦν πῦρ φλέγον.

γλωσσης — εκφοβιν 10. ηνγεισα — οικοδομημενον — χιονεικα 11. αστερον 12. τυχων — κεομενοι 13. οι οικον — τροφη — οκ = ουκ — μαι = με twice 14. εμην σιομενος — τρεμον — εθεορουν — ορασι 15. αλλην θυραν ανεωγμενην κατεναντι μου και ο οικος μειζων τουτου και ολος οικοδομημενος — γλωσσης 16. δειαφερων — τειμη — ωσται — μαι = με 17. ανωτερων

---

9. *γλώσσαις πυρός.* So Eth. Hence I should have translated more literally *tongues of fire* instead of 'a fiery flame.' 10. *πᾶσαι.* We should from Eth. expect *λίθοι.* 13. Before *εἰσῆλθον* and *θερμόν* Eth. adds *καί.* *τρυφή* not *τροφή*, as Dln. and Lods have already recognised. *τρυφὴ ζωῆς.* See Crit. Note, p. 81. 14. *ἤμην.* Eth. omits. After *ἔπεσον* I have added with Eth. *ἐπὶ πρόσωπόν μου καί.* 15. Gk. corrupt. Arranged as given above, it equals Eth. exactly. : cf. x. 19 for a similar dislocation of the text. The Gk. *ὅλη ἡ θύρα* necessitates a change of translation. For 'all the portals of which' read *the entire portal of which.* 17. Before *τὸ ἔδ.* Eth. adds *καί.* *πυρός.* So G ዘእሳት: Dln. እሳት = *πῦρ.* Hence for 'fire' read *of fire.* *ἡ στέγη αὐτοῦ.* Eth. adds 'also.'

18. Ἐθεώρουν δὲ καὶ εἶδον θρόνον ὑψηλόν, καὶ τὸ εἶδος αὐτοῦ ὡς
κρυστάλλινον, καὶ τροχὸς ὡς ἡλίου λάμποντος καὶ ὄψεως χερουβίν. †
19. καὶ ὑποκάτω τοῦ θρόνου ἐξεπορεύοντο ποταμοὶ πυρὸς φλεγο- †
μένου, καὶ οὐκ ἐδυνάσθην ἰδεῖν. 20. καὶ ἡ δόξα ἡ μεγάλη
ἐκάθητο ἐπ' αὐτῷ· τὸ περιβόλαιον αὐτοῦ [ὡς εἶδος] ἡλίου λαμπρό-
τερον καὶ λευκότερον πάσης χιόνος· 21. καὶ οὐκ ἐδύνατο πᾶς
ἄγγελος παρελθεῖν ⟨εἰς τὸν οἶκον τοῦτον⟩ καὶ ἰδεῖν τὸ πρόσωπον
αὐτοῦ διὰ τὸ ἔντιμον καὶ ἔνδοξον. καὶ οὐκ ἐδύνατο πᾶσα σὰρξ
ἰδεῖν αὐτόν. 22. τὸ πῦρ φλεγόμενον κύκλῳ, καὶ πῦρ μέγα παρειστ-
ήκει αὐτῷ, καὶ οὐδεὶς ἐγγίζει αὐτῷ. κύκλῳ μυρίαι μυριάδες ἑστή-
κα(σιν) ἐνώπιον αὐτοῦ, καὶ πᾶς λόγος αὐτοῦ ἔργον, 23. καὶ οἱ
ἅγιοι τῶν ἁγίων οἱ ἐγγίζοντες αὐτῷ οὐκ ἀποχωροῦσιν νυκτὸς οὔτε †
ἀφίστανται αὐτοῦ.

---

18. εθεορουν — ωσυ κρυσταλλινον — οροs 19. φλεγομενοι — ιδιν 20. περιβολεον 21. ειδειν — ιδιν αυτου 22. παριστηκει — ουδις εγγιζι — μυριε 23. αγγελων — ενγιζοντες — αφισταντε

---

18. After ἐθεώρουν Eth. adds ἐν αὐτῷ. ὄψεως. So I have emended οροs. Eth. ቃለ implies ὀπός, 'the voice,' and so points to ὄψεως. Hence, for 'the voices' read *a vision*. 19. Omit ዐቢይ with G and Giz. Gk., and for 'great throne' read *throne*. ἐδυνάσθην. For ኢይክሉ read ኢይክል. Hence, for 'it was impossible' read *I could not*. 21. εἰς τὸν οἶκον τοῦτον. Eth. omits. καὶ ἰδεῖν. So G ወርኢየ. Dln. gives corrupt reading ራእየ. διὰ τὸ ἔντιμον καὶ ἔνδοξον. Eth. ለክቡር፡ ወስቡሕ 'of the Honoured and Glorious One.' But the Eth. is wrong. ለ should be changed into በ with which it is constantly confounded. Thus we get an exact rendering of Gk. Hence, for 'the face of the Honoured and Glorious One' read *His face by reason of the magnificence and glory*. 22. κύκλῳ. Eth. 'around Him.' After αὐτῷ Eth. adds እምእለ 'of those who.' καὶ πᾶς λόγος αὐτοῦ ἔργον. Eth. absolutely dissimilar, but the former is found in the Slavonic Enoch; Eth. may therefore be presumed to be corrupt. For ምክሬ G reads ምክር. Hence Eth. may have been ወዘኮነ፡ ፈቃዱ፡ ውእቱ፡ ምግባር: cf. Pss. xxxiii. 9; cxv. 3 = καὶ πᾶν θέλημα αὐτοῦ ἔργον. 23. οἱ ἅγιοι τῶν ἁγίων. G reads ቅድሳት፡ ቅዱሳን 'the holiness of the holy ones,' and this I have followed in my Trans. Better, however, to read ቅዱሳነ፡ ቅዱሳን, and translate *the holy ones of the holy*, i.e. the archangels. ἁγίων. This is an emendation of ἀγγέλων with Eth.

24. Κἀγὼ ἤμην ἕως τούτου ἐπὶ πρόσωπόν μου βεβλημένος καὶ τρέμων. καὶ ὁ κύριος τῷ στόματι αὐτοῦ ἐκάλεσέν με καὶ εἶπέν μοι· Πρόσελθε ὧδε, Ἑνώχ, καὶ τὸν λόγον μου ἄκουσον. 25. ⟨καὶ προσελθών μοι εἷς τῶν ἁγίων ἤγειρέν με⟩ καὶ ἔστησέν με καὶ προσήγαγέν με μέχρι τῆς θύρας· ἐγὼ δὲ τὸ πρόσωπόν μου κάτω ἔκυφον.

XV. 1. Καὶ ἀποκριθεὶς εἶπέν μοι [ὁ ἄνθρωπος ὁ ἀληθινὸς ἄνθρωπος τῆς ἀληθείας ὁ γραμματεὺς] καὶ τῆς φωνῆς αὐτοῦ ἤκουσα· Μὴ φοβήθῃς Ἐνὼχ ἄνθρωπος ἀληθινὸς καὶ γραμματεὺς τῆς ἀληθείας, πρόσελθε ὧδε καὶ τῆς φωνῆς μου ἄκουσον. 2. πορεύθητι καὶ εἰπὲ (τοῖς ἐγρηγόροις τοῦ οὐρανοῦ) τοῖς πέμψασίν σε (τοῦ περὶ αὐτῶν ἐρωτῆσαι)· ἐρωτῆσαι ὑμᾶς ἔδει περὶ τῶν ἀνθρώπων, καὶ μὴ τοὺς ἀνθρώπους περὶ ὑμῶν. 3. διὰ τί ἀπελίπετε τὸν οὐρανὸν τὸν ὑψηλὸν τὸν ἅγιον τοῦ αἰῶνος, καὶ μετὰ τῶν γυναικῶν ἐκοιμήθητε, καὶ μετὰ τῶν θυγατέρων τῶν ἀνθρώπων ἐμιάνθητε καὶ ἐλάβετε ἑαυτοῖς γυναῖκας (καὶ) ὥσπερ υἱοὶ τῆς γῆς ἐποιήσατε, καὶ ἐγεννήσατε ἑαυτοῖς [τέκνα] υἱοὺς γίγαντας; 4. καὶ ὑμεῖς ἦτε ἅγιοι

---

24. κ̄ς 25. τον αγιον — καγω
XV. 1. αληθεινος 2. ανθρωπω̄ 3. απελειπεται — εκυμηθηται — ελαβεται

See Crit. Note, p. 82. νυκτός. So G. Dln. adds 'and day.' 24. βεβλημένος. Eth. ገልበብ, i.e. περίβλημα, but probably a corruption of ገልቡብ = περιβεβλημένος (?) or περικεκαλυμμένος. As is clear from ver. 25, Enoch is prostrate. βεβλημένος, therefore, is to be accepted. Hence, for 'I had had . . . trembling' read *I had been prostrate on my face and trembling.* ἄκουσον. See Crit. Note, p. 82. For λόγον μου ἄκουσον Eth. has λόγον μου ἅγιον, where ἅγιον is a corruption of ἄκουσον. Hence, for 'hear My holy word' read *hear My word.* 25. καὶ προσελθὼν . . . με may be a gloss.

XV. 1. ὁ ἄνθρωπος . . . ὁ γραμματεύς. An erroneous repetition of later words. Add ወ before በቃሉ with Gk. and connect the words as in Gk. Hence, for 'with His voice: "I have heard, fear not,"' read *and I heard His voice: 'Fear not.'* 2. Before πορεύθ. Eth. adds καί, and omits it after it. After εἰπέ I have added with Eth. τοῖς ἐγρηγόροις τοῦ οὐρανοῦ, and after σε, τοῦ π. αὐ. ἐρωτῆσαι. 3. Before ὥσπερ I have added καί with Eth. ἑαυτοῖς. Eth. omits wrongly. Strike out τέκνα. 4. ἅγιοι καὶ πνεύματα. G preserves this order,

καὶ πνεύμα(τα) ζῶντα αἰώνια· ἐν τῷ αἵματι τῶν γυναικῶν ἐμιάνθητε, καὶ ἐν αἵματι σαρκὸς ἐγεννήσατε, καὶ ἐν αἵματι ἀνθρώπων ἐπεθυμήσατε (καὶ ἐποιήσατε) καθὼς καὶ αὐτοὶ ποιοῦσιν σάρκα καὶ αἷμα, οἵτινες ἀποθνήσκουσιν καὶ ἀπόλλυνται· 5. διὰ τοῦτο ἔδωκα αὐτοῖς θηλείας, ἵνα σπερματίσουσιν εἰς αὐτὰς καὶ τεκνώ- † σουσιν ἐν αὐταῖς τέκνα, οὕτως ἵνα μὴ ἐκλείπει αὐτοῖς πᾶν ἔργον ἐπὶ τῆς γῆς. 6. ὑμεῖς δὲ ὑπήρχετε πνεύμα(τα) ζῶντα αἰώνια καὶ οὐκ ἀποθνήσκοντα εἰς πάσας τὰς γενεὰς τοῦ αἰῶνος. 7. καὶ διὰ τοῦτο οὐκ ἐποίησα ἐν ὑμῖν θηλείας. τὰ πνεύμα(τα) τοῦ οὐρανοῦ ἐν τῷ οὐρανῷ ἡ κατοίκησις αὐτῶν. 8. καὶ νῦν οἱ γίγαντες οἱ γεννηθέντες ἀπὸ τῶν πνευμάτων καὶ σαρκὸς πνεύμα(τα) ἰσχυρὰ (κληθήσονται) ἐπὶ τῆς γῆς, καὶ ἐν τῇ γῇ ἡ κατοίκησις αὐτῶν ἔσται. 9. πνεύμα(τα) πονηρὰ ἐξῆλθον ἀπὸ τοῦ σώματος αὐτῶν, διότι ἀπὸ τῶν ἀνθρώπων ἐγένοντο καὶ ἐκ τῶν ἁγίων ἐγρηγόρων ἡ ἀρχὴ τῆς † κτίσεως αὐτῶν καὶ ἀρχὴ θεμελίου (πνεύματα πονηρὰ ἐπὶ τῆς γῆς

---

4. εμιανθηται — εγενησατε — απολλυντε 5. θηλιας — σπερματιζουσιν — αυτοις
6. υπερχετε υμειν θηλιας 9. εξελθαν — αυτω̄ — ανοτερων —

---

but Dln.'s text inverts. For πνεύματα Eth. read πνευματικοί. ἐν τῷ αἵματι. Eth. ቡጺበ 'with.' Lods takes ቡጺበ as a corruption of በደም = ἐν τῷ αἵματι. Before καθώς I have added with Eth. καὶ ἐποιήσατε. 5. τεκνώσουσιν ἐν αὐταῖς τέκνα. ውሉድ of G supports this. Hence read ይውልዱ, and for 'children . . . borne' read *beget children*. ἵνα μὴ . . . ἔργον. See Crit. Note, p. 83. Correct በኀበሌሆን into ሎሙ. 6. After δέ Eth. adds πρότερον. 7. Before πνεύματα Eth. adds διότι. τὰ πνεύματα τ. οὐρ. መንፈሳውያን, a corruption of መንፈሰ፡ሰማይ. Hence, for 'spiritual' read *spirits of heaven*. 8. ἀπὸ τῶν πνευμάτων. G reads እምንፍስት (so read in Crit. Note, p. 83) = ἀπὸ τῶν ψυχῶν. Better to vocalize thus: እመናፍስት. ἰσχυρά. Probably a scribe's error for σκληρά: see ver. 11. Eth. and Syn. Gk. πονηρά, which is preferable. After ἰσχυρά I have added κληθήσονται with Eth. and Syn. Gk. καὶ ἐν τῇ γῇ. Syn. Gk. ὅτι ἐπὶ τ. γ. 9. Before πνεύματα Eth. adds καί. ἐξῆλθον. So Eth. Syn. Gk. ἔσονται τὰ πνεύματα ἐξεληλυθότα. σώματος αὐτῶν. So Eth. Syn. Gk. σώματος τῆς σαρκὸς αὐτῶν. των ανωτερων. So Eth. This I have, with Syn. Gk., emended into τῶν ἀνθρώπων. Hence, for 'from above' read *from men*. ἐγένοντο. So Syn. Gk. Eth. ተፈጥሩ, which is bad. Better ተወልዱ. ἡ ἀρχὴ τῆς κτίσεως αὐτῶν. So Syn. Gk. Eth. omits τ. κτίσεως. After θεμελίου I have

ἔσονται)· πνεύματα πονηρὰ κληθήσεται. 10. πνεύμα(τα) οὐρανοῦ ἐν τῷ οὐρανῷ ἡ κατοίκησις αὐτῶν ἔσται, καὶ τὰ πνεύματα [ἐπὶ] τῆς γῆς τὰ γεννηθέντα ἐπὶ τῆς γῆς (ἐν τῇ γῇ) ὁ κατοίκησις αὐτῶν ἔσται· 11. καὶ τὰ πνεύματα τῶν γιγάντων νεφέλας ἀδικοῦντα, ἀφανίζοντα καὶ ἐμπίπτοντα καὶ συμπαλαίοντα καὶ συρρίπτοντα ἐπὶ τῆς γῆς † [πνεύματα σκληρὰ γιγάντων], καὶ τρόμους ποιοῦντα καὶ μηδὲν ἐσθίον(τα), ⟨ἀλλ' ἀσιτοῦντα⟩ καὶ διψῶντα καὶ προσκόπτοντα 12. καὶ πνεύμα(τα) ἐξαναστήσει ταῦτα εἰς τοὺς υἱοὺς τῶν ἀνθρώπων † καὶ τὰς γυναῖκας, ὅτι ἐξεληλύθασιν ἀπ' αὐτῶν XVI. 1. ἀπὸ ἡμέρας σφαγῆς καὶ ἀπωλείας καὶ θανάτου (τῶν γιγάντων) ἀφ' ὧν τὰ πνεύματα ἐκπορευόμενα ἐκ τῆς ψυχῆς τῆς σαρκὸς αὐτῶν

κληθησετε 11. ενπιπτοντα — συνπαλεοντα — συνριπτοντα — δρομους — εσθειον = εσθιοντ. — δειψωντα 12. πνευμα και — εξαναστησι — των γυναικων

---

added πνεύματα πονηρὰ ἐπὶ τῆς γῆς ἔσονται, with Syn. Gk. and Eth. Before πνεύματα πον. Eth. adds καί. πνεύμ. πον. κληθήσεται. So Eth. Syn. Gk. omits. 10. Syn. Gk. omits entire verse. Omit ἐπί after πνεύματα with Eth. After γῆς I have added ἐν τῇ γῇ with Eth. ἔσται (at close). Eth. omits. 11. νεφέλας. So Eth.: a manifest corruption. See Crit. Note, p. 84. πνεύματα σκ. γιγ. A gloss. For δρόμους of Giz. and Syn. Gk. I have with Eth. ጕዘዘ read τρόμους. ἀλλ' ἀσιτοῦντα. So Syn. Gk. Eth. omits. After ἀσιτοῦντα Syn. Gk. adds καὶ φάσματα ποιοῦντα. διψῶντα. So Syn. Gk. and M. Other MSS. add a negative, but now I think with Lods and Dln., wrongly. προσκόπτοντα. So Syn. Gk. Eth. ይትዐወቁ. This, as Dln. shows, is a corruption of ይትዐቀፉ = προσκόπτοντα. Hence, for 'they will take no kind of food . . . invisible' read *they will fast and be thirsty and cause offences.* 12. καὶ πνεύματα. I have transposed with Syn. Gk. and Eth. ταῦτα. So Eth. Syn. Gk. omits. For τῶν γυναικῶν (so Syn. Gk.) I have read τὰς γυναῖκας with Eth. After ወፅአ I have added እምኔሆሙ with Giz. and Syn. Gk. ἀπ' αὐτῶν. For እስመ we should read እም as Dln. proposes.

XVI. 1. Before ἀπό Syn. Gk. adds καί. After θανάτου add with Syn. Gk. and Eth. τῶν γιγάντων. After γιγάντων Syn. Gk. adds a gloss Ναφηλείμ . . . ὀνομαστοί. ἀφ' ὧν. Eth. 'whenever.' Syn. Gk. omits. Before ἐκπορ. Syn. Gk. adds τά. ἐκ τῆς ψυχῆς τῆς σαρκὸς αὐτῶν. So Eth. See Crit. Note, p. 85. In Syn. Gk. the text is transposed. ἀπὸ τῆς ψυχῆς αὐτῶν ὡς ἐκ τῆς σαρκός should be read

(ὡς) ἔσονται ἀφανίζοντα χωρὶς κρίσεως οὕτως ἀφανίσουσιν μέχρις ἡμέρας τελειώσεως τῆς κρίσεως τῆς μεγάλης, ἐν ᾗ ὁ αἰὼν ὁ μέγας τελεσθήσεται.

2. Καὶ νῦν ἐγρηγόροις τοῖς πέμψασίν σε ἐρωτῆσαι περὶ αὐτῶν, οἵτινες ἐν οὐρανῷ ἦσαν· 3. ὑμεῖς ἐν τῷ οὐρανῷ ἦτε, καὶ πᾶν μυστήριον [ὃ] οὐκ ἀνεκαλύφθη ὑμῖν καὶ μυστήριον τὸ ἐξουθενημένον † ἔγνωτε, καὶ τοῦτο ἐμηνύσατε ταῖς γυναιξὶν ἐν ταῖς σκληροκαρδίαις ὑμῶν. καὶ ἐν τῷ μυστηρίῳ τούτῳ πληθύνουσιν αἱ θήλειαι καὶ οἱ ἄνθρωποι τὰ κακὰ ἐπὶ τῆς γῆς. 4. εἰπὸν οὖν αὐτοῖς· Οὐκ ἔστιν εἰρήνη.

XVII. 1. Καὶ [παραλαβόντες] με εἴς τινα τόπον ἀπήγαγον, ἐν ᾧ ⟨οἱ ὄντες⟩ ἐκεῖ γίνονται ὡς πῦρ φλέγον καὶ ὅταν θέλωσιν φαίνονται ὡσεὶ ἄνθρωποι.

XVI. 1. εσται αφανειζοντα — αφανησουσιν — τελιωσεως 2. αυτω̄ 3. εκ του θ̄υ γεγενημενον — εμενυσατε — τουτο = τουτω — θηλιαι

XVII. 1. μαι = με — φλεγων

ἀπὸ τῆς ψυχῆς ἐκ (? καὶ) τῆς σαρκὸς αὐτῶν ὡς. After αὐτῶν add ὡς with Syn. Gk. and Eth. ሰ. See my restoration of Eth. text on p. 85, where for ኵሉ read ዘኵሉ, and for last two words read ተፍጻሜት: ዘኵሉ: ዐቢይ with Giz. Gk., and for 'day when the great consummation' read *day of the consummation of the great judgment.* ἐν ᾗ. So Syn. Gk. Hence, with Dln. for እምንበሎም read እንተ: ዓበም. With Giz. and Syn. Gk. strike out እምትጉሃን: ወረሲዓን. Hence, for 'day when . . . godless' read *day of the consummation of the great judgment in which the great age will be consummated.* After τελεσθήσεται Syn. Gk. adds ἐφ' ἅπαξ ὁμοῦ τελεσθήσεται. These words may be original. After ረሲዓን G adds ዘሎ: ይትፌጸም: እምትጉሃን: ወረሲዐን: ዘሎ: እምትጉዓን. 2. After οἵτινες Eth. adds πρότερον. 3. I have omitted ወይእዜ, 'and now,' with Giz. Gk. πᾶν μυστήριον [ὃ] οὐκ ἀνεκαλύφθη ὑμῖν. The sense is contrary to the Enoch tradition. By omitting ὃ we get a text agreeing with Eth., and with the words of Clement ὅσα τε εἰς γνῶσιν αὐτῶν ἀφῖκτο. See p. 86 (note). το εκ του θ̄υ γεγενημενον I have emended into ἐξουθενημένον = Eth. ምኑን. These 'worthless' secrets relate to the various arts of embellishing the human face, working metals, &c.: cf. viii. 1.

XVII. 1. ἀπήγαγον. Eth. ነሥኡ 'took away.' οἱ ὄντες. Eth.

2. Καὶ ἀπήγαγόν με εἰς γνοφώδη τόπον καὶ εἰς ὄρος οὗ ἡ κεφαλὴ ἀφικνεῖτο εἰς τὸν οὐρανόν. 3. καὶ ἴδον τόπον τῶν φωστήρων [καὶ τοὺς θησαυροὺς τῶν ἀστέρων] καὶ τῶν βροντῶν [καὶ] εἰς τὰ
† ἄκρα βάθη ὅπου τόξον πυρὸς καὶ τὰ βέλη καὶ αἱ θῆκαι αὐτῶν . . . καὶ αἱ ἀστραπαὶ πᾶσαι.

4. Καὶ ἀπήγαγόν με μέχρι ὑδάτων ζώντων καὶ μέχρι πυρὸς δύσεως, ὅ ἐστιν [καὶ] παρέχον πάσας τὰς δύσεις τοῦ ἡλίου. 5. καὶ ἦλθον μέχρι ποταμοῦ πυρός, ἐν ᾧ κατατρέχει τὸ πῦρ ὡς ὕδωρ, καὶ ῥέει εἰς θάλασσαν μεγάλην δύσεως. 6. ἴδον τοὺς μεγάλους ποταμού(ς), ⟨καὶ μέχρι τοῦ μεγάλου ποταμοῦ⟩ καὶ μέχρι τοῦ μεγάλου σκότους κατήντησα, καὶ ἀπῆλθον ὅπου πᾶσα σὰρξ [οὐ]
† περιπατεῖ. 7. ἴδον τὰ ὄρη τῶν γνόφων τὰ χειμερινὰ καὶ τὴν

---

2. μαι — ζοφωδε — αφικνυτο 3. θησαυρος — αεροβαθη — τας θηκας — τας αστραπας πασας. 4. μαι = με — παρεχων — δυσις 5. ηλθομεν 6. τους ανεμους — τους χειμερινους

---

omits. 2. γνοφώδη. This is a happy emendation of M. Lods. As γνόφος = 'turbo' as well as 'caligo,' we have the explanation of Eth. 'the place of the whirlwind.' οὗ ἡ κεφαλή. Eth. supposes οὗ ἡ κορυφὴ τῆς κεφαλῆς. 3. τόπον τ. φωστ. See Crit. Note, p. 87. Omit καί before εἰς with Eth. εἰς τὰ ἄκρα βάθη ὅπου. So G: ውስተ፡ እጽናፌ፡ ዐመቅ፡ ኀበ but that I have read እጽናፌ for እጽናፍ፡ ኀበ. For τὰς θήκας and τὰς ἀστραπάς read with Eth. αἱ θῆκαι and αἱ ἀστραπαί. Hence, for 'at the ends . . . fiery bow' read *in the uttermost depths where were the fiery bow,'* &c. After αὐτῶν Eth. adds καὶ μάχαιραν πυρός. 4. After ζώντων Eth. adds a gloss ዘይትነገር 'so-called.' παρέχον. This is right. See p. 363 (notes). Eth. = παραδεχόμενον is wrong. 5. δύσεως. Eth. = πρὸς τὴν δύσιν. 6. Before ἴδον Eth. adds 'and.' Before τούς Eth. adds 'all.' καὶ μέχρι τοῦ μεγάλου ποταμοῦ = the Styx. Eth. omits. Unless we are here dealing with a description of Hades, this clause is an interpolation. But as the whole context points to Hades, the words seem original, and for the same reason we must strike out οὐ after σάρξ with Eth. 7. Before ἴδον Eth. adds 'and.' I have emended τους ανεμους into τὰ ὄρη, as these words seem corrupt, and are without the support of the context or any parallel: cf. lxxvii. 4, where the mountains of the hoar frost are mentioned. Possibly there is also an allusion to Jer. xiii. 16

ἔκχυσιν τῆς ἀβύσσου πάντων ὑδάτων. 8. ἴδον τὸ στόμα τῆς γῆς πάντων τῶν ποταμῶν καὶ τὸ στόμα τῆς ἀβύσσου.

XVIII. 1. Ἴδον τοὺς θησαυροὺς τῶν ἀνέμων πάντων. ἴδον ὅτι ἐν αὐτοῖς ἐκόσμησεν πάσας τὰς κτίσεις, καὶ τὸν θεμέλιον τῆς γῆς, 2. καὶ τὸν λίθον ἴδον τῆς γωνίας τῆς γῆς. ἴδον τοὺς τέσσαρας ἀνέμους τὴν γῆν βαστάζοντας καὶ τὸ στερέωμα τοῦ οὐρανοῦ 3. . . . . . . καὶ αὐτοὶ ἱστᾶσιν μεταξὺ γῆς καὶ οὐρανοῦ (οὗτοί εἰσιν οἱ στῦλοι τοῦ οὐρανοῦ). 4. ἴδον ἀνέμους τῶν οὐρανῶν στρέφοντας καὶ δύοντας τὸν τροχὸν τοῦ ἡλίου καὶ πάντας τοὺς ἀστέρας. †
5. ἴδον τοὺς ἐπὶ τῆς γῆς ἀνέμους βαστάζοντας τὰς νεφέλας· (ἴδον †
τὰς ὁδοὺς τῶν ἀγγέλων·) ἴδον (παρὰ τὰ) πέρατα τῆς γῆς τὸ στήριγμα †
τοῦ οὐρανοῦ ἐπάνω.

6. Παρῆλθον καὶ ἴδον τόπον καιόμενον νυκτὸς καὶ ἡμέρας, ὅπου τὰ ἑπτὰ ὄρη ἀπὸ λίθων πολυτελῶν (τρία) εἰς ἀνατολὰς καὶ τρία εἰς νότον ⟨βάλλοντα⟩. 7. καὶ τὰ μὲν πρὸς ἀνατολὰς ἀπὸ λίθου χρώματος, τὸ δὲ ἦν ἀπὸ λίθου μαργαρίτου, καὶ τὸ ἀπὸ λίθου

XVIII. 2. λιθο̄ — διανευοντας 3. εισταςιν 4. ιδο̄ 5. ἐν νεφελη — στεριγμα 6. κεομενον — πολυτελω̄ — τρις — βαλλο̄τας

הָרֵי נֶשֶׁף 'the mountains of darkness,' which might readily be regarded as mountains of Hades: cf. last clause of ver. 6. 8. Before ἴδον Eth. adds καί.

XVIII. 1. Before ἴδον (1st and 2nd) Eth. adds καί. 2. After γῆς Eth. adds καί. 3. Before καὶ αὐτοί add with Eth. καὶ ἴδον ὡς οἱ ἄνεμοι ἐξέτεινον τὸ ὕψος τοῦ οὐρανοῦ, omitted through hmt. εισταςιν emended in accordance with Eth. γῆς κ. οὐρ. Eth. transposes. After οὐρανοῦ I have added with Eth. οὗτοί . . . οὐρανοῦ. 4. Before ἴδον Eth. adds καί. ἀνέμους τῶν οὐρανῶν στρέφοντας. The Eth. text has been transposed. Hence read ነፋሳት፡ ለሰማይ፡ እለ፡ ይመይጡ, and translate *the winds of the heaven which turn.* δύοντας. So I have emended with Eth. 5. Omit ወ before ርኢኩ in Dln.'s text with G and Giz. Gk. τὰς νεφέλας. This emendation is very doubtful as it has both G and Giz. Gk. against it, i.e. በደመናት = ἐν νεφέλῃ. After νεφέλας add with Eth. ἴδον . . . ἀγγέλων. Before πέρατα I insert παρά τά with Eth. 6. καὶ ἴδον τόπον. Eth. read πρὸς νότον καί. The text has evidently been transposed and corrupted. νυκτὸς κ. ἡμέρας are similarly transposed. βάλλοντα. Eth. omits. 7. λίθου ταθεν.

ταθεν, τὸ δὲ κατὰ νότον ἀπὸ λίθου πυρροῦ· 8. τὸ δὲ μέσον
αὐτῶν ἦν εἰς οὐρανὸν ὥσπερ θρόνος θεοῦ ἀπὸ λίθου φουκά, καὶ ἡ
κορυφὴ τοῦ θρόνου ἀπὸ λίθου σαπφείρου. 9. καὶ πῦρ καιόμενον
ἴδον κα(πέ)κεινα τῶν ὀρέων τούτων. 10. τόπος ἐστίν, πέραν
† τῆς μεγάλης γῆς· ἐκεῖ συντελεσθήσονται οἱ οὐρανοί. 11. καὶ
ἴδον χάσμα μέγα ἐν τοῖς (στύλοις τοῦ πυρὸς τοῦ οὐρανοῦ καὶ ἴδον ἐν
† αὐτοῖς) στύλους τοῦ πυρὸς καταβαίνοντας· καὶ οὐκ ἦν μέτρον οὔτε
εἰς βάθος οὔτε εἰς ὕψος. 12. καὶ ἐπέκεινα τοῦ χάσματος τούτου ἴδον τόπον, ὅπου οὐδὲ στερέωμα οὐρανοῦ ἐπάνω οὔτε γῆ ἡ
τεθεμελιωμένη ὑποκάτω αὐτοῦ οὔτε ὕδωρ ἦν ὑπὸ αὐτῷ οὔτε
πετεινόν, ἀλλὰ τόπος ἦν ἔρημος καὶ φοβερός· 13. ἐκεῖ ἴδον
ἑπτὰ ἀστέρας ὡς ὄρη μεγάλα καιόμενα.

Περὶ ὧν πυνθανομένῳ μοι 14. εἶπεν ὁ ἄγγελος· Οὗτός
ἐστιν ὁ τόπος τὸ τέλος τοῦ οὐρανοῦ καὶ (τῆς) γῆς· δεσμωτήριον

---

8. αυτω̄ — θνος θ̄υ — σαφφιρου 9. κεομενον 10. περας 11. εις τους στυλος (= αὐτοῖς στύλους) 12. γην την τεθεμελιωμενην — αυτο = αυτω 13. κεομενα — π̄υθανομαιον μοι

Eth. እብነ፡ ፈውስ 'antimony' or 'stone of healing.' *ταθεν* is possibly a corruption of *ἀχάτης* = שְׁבוֹ, the agate. Eth. seems to rest on an emendation of *ταθεν* into *ἰάτου* or *ἰατρείας*. 8. *λίθου φουκά.* We have here a transliteration of פּוּךְ: cf. 1 Chron. xxix. 2. 9. *κα(πέ)κεινα.* So M. Lods emends and, so far as I can see, rightly, but he connects them wrongly with the next verse. Eth. ወዘሀሎ፡ ውስተ = *καὶ ὃ ἐστι ἐν* seems wrong. Correct ዙሉ, 'all,' into እሉ, 'those,' with Gk., and for 'which was in all the mountains' read *also beyond those mountains.* As M. Lods observes, the translator does not seem to have understood *ἐπέκεινα*: cp. xviii. 12; xxiv. 2; xxx. 13; xxxi. 2. 10. *τόπος ἐστίν.* Eth. *καὶ ἴδον ἐκεῖ τόπον. οὐρανοί.* See Crit. Note, p. 89. 11. *χάσμα μέγα.* See Crit. Note, p. 89. After *μέγα* I have added with G *στύλοις τοῦ πυρὸς τοῦ οὐρανοῦ καὶ ἴδον ἐν αὐτοῖς*, omitted through like beginning. *εις τους.* A corruption for *ἐν τοῖς.* Omit with G the second ሰማይ, and for 'heavenly fire fall' read *fire fall.* *μέτρον.* Eth. ኍልቍ 'number.' 12. *ἐπέκεινα.* Eth. ዲበ 'over.' See ver. 9 (note). *καὶ φοβερός.* These words are wrongly connected with ver. 13 by Eth. Hence for 'waste . . . horrible' read *waste and horrible place.* 13. *I saw.* For *περὶ ὧν πυνθανομένῳ μοι* Eth. = *καὶ ὡς πνεύματα πυνθανόμενά μου.* 14.

τοῦτο ἐγένετο τοῖς ἄστροις καὶ ταῖς δυνάμεσιν τοῦ οὐρανοῦ. 15. καὶ οἱ ἀστέρες οἱ κυλιόμενοι ἐν τῷ πυρὶ οὗτοί εἰσιν οἱ παραβάντες πρόσταγμα κυρίου ἐν ἀρχῇ τῆς ἀνατολῆς αὐτῶν, [ὅτι τόπος ἔξω τοῦ οὐρανοῦ κενός ἐστιν] ὅτι οὐκ ἐξῆλθον ἐν τοῖς καιροῖς αὐτῶν. 16. καὶ ὠργίσθη αὐτοῖς καὶ ἔδησεν αὐτοὺς μέχρι καιροῦ τελειώσεως [αὐτῶν] ἁμαρτίας αὐτῶν, ἐνιαυτῶν μυρίων. XIX. 1. καὶ εἶπέν μοι Οὐριήλ· Ἐνθάδε οἱ μιγέντες ἄγγελοι ταῖς γυναιξὶν στήσονται· καὶ τὰ πνεύματα αὐτῶν, πολύμορφα γενόμενα, λυμαίνεται τοὺς ἀνθρώπους καὶ πλανήσει αὐτοὺς ἐπιθύειν τοῖς δαιμονίοις (ὡς θεοῖς) μέχρι (τῆς ἡμέρας) τῆς μεγάλης κρίσεως, ἐν ᾗ κριθήσονται εἰς ἀποτελείωσιν. 2. καὶ αἱ γυναῖκες αὐτῶν, τῶν παραβάντων ἀγγέλων, εἰς σειρῆνας γενήσονται.

3. Κἀγὼ Ἐνὼχ ἴδον τὰ θεωρήματα μόνος, τὰ πέρατα πάντων· καὶ οὐ μὴ ἴδῃ οὐδὲ εἷς ἀνθρώπων ὡς ἐγὼ ἴδον.

---

15. *κοιλιομενοι — παραβοντες —* $\overline{κυ}$ 16. *οργισθη — τελιωσεως*
XIX. 1. *λυμενεται — πλανησι — αποτελιωσιν* 2. *σιρηνας* 3. G[2] *ανθρωπον ος ιω ειδον*

After **ከዋክብት**=*ἄστροις* omit **ሰማይ** with G and Giz. Gk. Hence, for 'stars of heaven' read *stars.* 15. For **እምቅድሙ** read **እመቅድሙ**=*ἐν ἀρχῇ*, and for 'before their rising' read *in the beginning of their rising.* *ὅτι τόπος . . . ἐστιν.* A gloss. 16. *ἐνιαυτῶν μυρίων.* Eth. **በዓመት፡ ምሥጢር**=*ἐνιαυτῷ μυστηρίου.* xxi. 6 supports Giz. Gk. Hence, for 'in the year of the mystery' read *ten thousand years.*

XIX. 1. See Crit. Note, p. 90. *καὶ τὰ πν. αὐτῶν, πολύμορφα.* Eth. wrongly transposes the **ወ**, 'and,' and prefixes it to **ብዙኃ**. *λυμαίνεται.* Eth. **አርኩሶሙ**. This is a bad rendering. After *δαιμονίοις* I have added with Eth. *ὡς θεοῖς.* After *μέχρι* I have added *τῆς ἡμέρας* with Eth. *εἰς ἀποτελείωσιν.* Eth.=*μέχρι ἀποτελεσθήσονται.* 2. *τῶν παραβάντων ἀγγέλων.* Eth. corrupt. First, with G strike out **ሰማይ**, 'of heaven,' and read **መላእክት**. For **አስሒቶን** read **ስሒታን**. Thus we have an exact rendering of Gk. *εἰς σειρῆνας.* G **ከመ፡ ሰላማውያት** = *ὡς εἰρηναίαι*, but this clearly has arisen from a misunderstanding of *εἰς σειρῆνας* or from the loss of *σ* in *σειρῆνας*. Hence read the verse thus: *And the women of those angels who went astray will become sirens.* As M. Lods points out, the *σειρήν* and the Lilith or female demon are here probably identified. 3. After *ἴδῃ* G M add **ዘርእኩ**=*ὃ ἴδον.* As M. Lods points

XX. 1. Ἄγγελοι τῶν δυνάμεων. 2. Οὐριὴλ ὁ εἷς τῶν ἁγίων ἀγγέλων ὁ ἐπὶ τοῦ κόσμου καὶ τοῦ ταρτάρου. 3. Ῥαφαὴλ ὁ εἷς τῶν ἁγίων ἀγγέλων ὁ ἐπὶ τῶν πνευμάτων τῶν ἀνθρώπων. 4. Ῥαγουὴλ ὁ εἷς τῶν ἁγίων ἀγγέ-
† λων ὁ ἐκδικῶν τὸν κόσμον τῶν φωστήρων. 5. Μιχαὴλ ὁ εἷς τῶν ἁγίων ἀγγέλων ὁ ἐπὶ τῶν τοῦ λαοῦ ἀγαθῶν τεταγμένος
† [καὶ] ἐπὶ τῷ λαῷ. 6. Σαριὴλ ὁ εἷς τῶν ἁγίων ἀγγέλων ὁ ἐπὶ τῶν πνευμάτων οἵτινες ἐπὶ τῷ πνεύματι ἁμαρτάνουσιν. 7. Γα-

XX. 2. ὁ εἷς τῶν ἁγίων ἀγγέλων ὁ ἐπὶ τοῦ κόσμου καὶ τοῦ ταρτάρου. 3. Ῥαφαὴλ ὁ εἷς τῶν ἁγίων ἀγγέλων ὁ ἐπὶ τῶν πνευμάτων τῶν ἀνθρώπων. 4. Ῥαγουὴλ ὁ εἷς τῶν ἁγίων ἀγγέλων ὁ ἐκδικῶν τὸν κόσμον τῶν φωσ- †
τήρων. 5. Μιχαὴλ ὁ εἷς τῶν ἁγίων ἀγγέλων ὃς ἐπὶ τῶν τοῦ λαοῦ ἀγαθῶν τέτακται [καὶ] ἐπὶ τῷ λαῷ. 6. Σαριὴλ ὁ εἷς τῶν †
ἁγίων ἀγγέλων ὁ ἐπὶ τῶν πνευμάτων οἵτινες ἐπὶ τῷ πνεύματι ἁμαρτάνουσιν. 7. Γαβριὴλ ὁ

XX. 1. τῶ̄ 4. εκδεικων το̄ 5. ο επι τον του — χαω

XX. 2. ος — επει 3. αγγελων — επει — πνυτων — αντων 4. τον — εκεκων 5. μηχαηλ ο εις τον — επει τον του — χαω 6. το αγιον — πνατων οιτεινες επει τω π̄ . . . τι

out, the quotations from Clement and Origen given in my note p. 91, are not derived from this verse.

XX. 1. ἄγγελοι τῶν δυνάμεων. Eth. 'And these are the names of the holy angels who watch.' 2. See Crit. Note, p. 91. 3. ὁ ἐπί. Eth. ዘ, (the angel) 'of.' 4. ἐκδικῶν. So emended in accordance with Eth. See, however, note on xxiii. 4 below. τ. κόσμον τῶν φωστ. Better than Eth. τ. κόσμον καὶ τ. φωστῆρας. Hence for 'world and' read *world of.* 5. Omit καί before ἐπί with Eth. I have emended χαω, which is a *vox nulla*, into λαῷ with Eth. 6. Σαριήλ. Eth. Saraqâêl. τῶν πνευμάτων οἵτινες ἐπὶ τῷ πνεύματι ἁμαρτάνουσιν. Correct and Eth. corrupt, but easy of emendation. First, for መናፍስት read መናፍስት with G, and strike out as a gloss እጓለ፡ እመሕያው. Next, for ዘመናፍስት read ዘበመናፍስት and የኀጥኡ with A B C D E. We have thus an exact rendering of Gk. These angels are possibly the Satans who sinned through pride. The other angels sinned through lust, i.e. through the body. Hence, instead of 'spirits of the children of men whose spirits have sinned' (this rests on an emendation) read *spirits which have sinned in spirit.* 7. See Crit. Note, p. 92. δρακόντων.

βριὴλ ὁ εἷς τῶν ἁγίων ἀγγέλων ὁ[ς] ἐπὶ τοῦ παραδείσου καὶ τῶν δρακόντων καὶ χερουβίν ⟨ἀρχαγγέλων ὀνόματα ἑπτά⟩. XXI. 1. Καὶ ἐφώδευσα ἕως τῆς ἀκατασκευάστου, 2. κἀκεῖ ἐθεασάμην ἔργον φοβερόν· ἑώρακα οὔτε οὐρανὸν ἐπάνω οὔτε γῆν [τεθέαμαι] τεθεμελιωμένην, ἀλλὰ τόπον ἀκατασκεύαστον καὶ φοβερόν· 3. καὶ ἐκεῖ τεθέαμαι ἑπτὰ [τῶν] ἀστέρας τοῦ οὐρανοῦ δεδεμένους [καὶ ἐριμμένους] ἐν

† αὐτῷ (ὁμοῦ) ὁμοίους ὄρεσιν μεγάλοις καὶ ἐν πυρὶ καιομένους. 4. τότε εἶπον· Διὰ ποίαν αἰτίαν ἐπεδέθησαν; καὶ διὰ τί ὧδε ἐρίφησαν; 5. τότε εἶπέν μοι Οὐριήλ, ὁ εἷς τῶν ἁγίων ἀγγέλων ὃς μετ' ἐμοῦ ἦν καὶ αὐτὸς ἡγεῖτο

εἷς τῶν ἁγίων ἀγγέλων ὁ ἐπὶ τοῦ παραδείσου καὶ τῶν δρακόντων καὶ χερουβίν. ⟨Ῥεμειὴλ (ὁ) εἷς τῶν ἁγίων ἀγγέλων ὃν ἔταξεν ὁ θεὸς ἐπὶ τῶν ἀνισταμένων ὀνόματα ζ' ἀρχαγγέλων⟩. XXI. 1. Καὶ ἐφώδευσα μέχρι τῆς ἀκατασκευάστου, 2. καὶ ἐκεῖ ἐθεασάμην ἔργον φοβερόν· ἑώρακα οὔτε οὐρανὸν ἐπάνω οὔτε γῆν τεθεμελιωμένην, ἀλλὰ τόπον ἀκατασκεύαστον καὶ φοβερόν· 3. καὶ ἐκεῖ τεθέαμαι ζ' ἀστέρας τοῦ οὐρανοῦ δεδεμένους [καὶ ἐριμμένους] ἐν αὐτῷ (ὁμοῦ)

ὁμοίους ὄρεσιν μεγάλοις καὶ ἐν †

πυρὶ καιομένους. 4. τότε εἶπον· Διὰ ποίαν αἰτίαν ἐπεδέθησαν καὶ διὰ ποίαν αἰτίαν ἐρίφησαν ὧδε; 5. καὶ εἶπέν μοι Οὐριὴλ ὁ εἷς τῶν ἁγίων ἀγγέλων ὁ μετ' ἐμοῦ ὢν καὶ αὐτὸς αὐτῶν ἡγεῖτο

7. ἀγγελω̃ — παραδισου — δρακοντω̃ — χερουβει

XXI. 3. αστερων — ορασιν — κεομενους 4. επαιδεθησαν

7. τον — παραδισου — τον δρακοντων — θ̅ς — επει

XXI. 1. μεχρει — ακαταταασκευαστου 2. οτε 3. τεθεαμια — ορασει μεγαλη — κεομενους 4. αιτειαν επηδηθησαν 5. τον αγιον — ηγιτο —

These are probably winged serpents or שׂרפים Seraphim mentioned in Is. xiv. 29: xxx. 6 (see Delitzsch *in loc.*). The subject will recur in the Slavonic Enoch. After χερουβίν Eth. omits Ῥεμειὴλ . . . ἑπτα: cf. xc. 21. These clauses seem original.

XXI. 1. ἐφώδευσα. Eth. ዖድኩ = ἐκύκλωσα. 2. ἐπάνω. See Crit. Note, p. 92, where for erroneous ወኪሰማይ read ወኢሰማይ. 3. καὶ ἐριμμένους seems a gloss due to ver. 4. After αὐτῷ add ὁμοῦ with Eth., omitted before ὁμοίους. Strike out ከመ in ወከመ with G and Gk., and for 'flaming as with fire' read *flaming with fire*. 4. αἰτίαν (? for ἁμαρτίαν). Eth. ኃጢአት 'sin': cf. ver. 6. 5. ἡγεῖτο αὐτῶν. Eth. ይመርሀኒ 'he led me' a corruption for

αὐτῶν, καὶ εἶπέν μοι· Ἐνώχ, περὶ τίνος ἐρωτᾷς; ἢ περὶ τίνος τὴν ἀλήθειαν φιλοσπεύδεις; 6. οὗτοί εἰσιν τῶν ἀστέρων τοῦ οὐρανοῦ οἱ παραβάντες τὴν ἐπιταγὴν τοῦ κυρίου καὶ ἐδέθησαν ὧδε μέχρι τοῦ πληρῶσαι μυρία ἔτη, τὸν χρόνον τῶν ἁμαρτημάτων αὐτῶν. 7. κἀκεῖθεν ἐφώδευσα εἰς ἄλλον τόπον τούτου φοβερώτερον, καὶ τεθέαμαι ἔργα φοβερώτερα· πῦρ μέγα ἐκεῖ καιόμενον καὶ φλεγόμενον· καὶ διακοπὴν εἶχεν ὁ τόπος ἕως τῆς ἀβύσσου, † πλήρης στύλων πυρὸς μεγάλων καταφερομένων· οὔτε μέτρον οὔτε πλάτος ἠδυνήθην ἰδεῖν οὐδὲ εἰκάσαι. 8. τότε εἶπον· Ὡς φοβερὸς

καὶ εἶπέν μοι· Ἐνώχ, περὶ τίνος ἐρωτᾷς ἢ περὶ τίνος τὴν ἀλήθειαν φιλοσπεύδεις; 6. οὗτοί εἰσιν τῶν ἀστέρων τοῦ οὐρανοῦ οἱ παραβάντες τὴν ἐπιταγὴν τοῦ κυρίου καὶ ἐδέθησαν ὧδε μέχρι πληρωθῆναι μύρια ἔτη, τὸν χρόνον τῶν ἁμαρτημάτων αὐτῶν. 7. κἀκεῖθεν ἐφώδευσα εἰς ἄλλον τόπον τούτου φοβερώτερον καὶ τεθέαμαι ἔργα φοβερά· πῦρ μέγα ἐκεῖ καιόμενον καὶ φλεγόμενον. καὶ διακοπὴν εἶχεν ὁ τόπος ἕως τῆς ἀβύσσου, πλήρης στύλων πυρὸς μεγάλων καταφερομένων· † οὔτε μέτρον οὔτε μέγεθος ἠδυνήθην ἰδεῖν οὔτε εἰκάσαι. 8. τότε εἶπον· Ὡς φοβερὸς ὁ τόπος

6. κυ̅ 7. κεομενον — στυλλων — μεγαλου καταφαιρομενον 8. ορασι

αληθιαν — φιλοσπευδις 6. κ̅ς̅ — μεχρει 7. τεθεαμε — στυλλων — μεγαλου καταφερομ — ηδυ . . . θην — ειδιν 8. ειπο — φοβηρος —

ይመርሆሙ ‘was chief over them’: cf. xxiv. 6; lxxii. 1; lxxiv. 1. Uriel is over Tartarus, xx. 2. Hence he is in charge of these punished angels. περὶ τίνος τὴν ἀλήθειαν φιλοσπεύδεις; Eth. corrupt. First strike out ወትሴአል with G. We have then በእንተ፡ ምንት፡ ትጤይቅ፡ ወትጸሁቅ. Here ትጤይቅ is manifestly a corruption of ጥይቅ=τὴν ἀλήθειαν. Hence for ‘why dost thou enquire and art curious’ read *why art thou eager after the exact truth?* 6. ἔτη. Eth. ዓለም ‘age,’ clearly a corruption of ዓም ‘a year.’ Hence for ‘ages’ read *years*. τὸν χρόνον. Eth.=ὁ ἀριθμὸς τῶν ἡμερῶν. 7. διακοπὴν εἶχεν ὁ τόπος. See Crit. Note, p. 93. After οὐδέ add with Eth. ἐδυνήθην. In Eth. ስእንኩ፡ ነጽር፡ ዐይኑ, ‘I was not able to see its origin,’ ነጽር is an intrusion and ዐይኑ is a corruption of ዐይኖ=inf. of ዐየነ (=εἰκάζειν in Wisdom ix. 16). Hence for ‘was I able to see its origin’ read *could I conjecture*. 8. δεινός. Hence for ሕማም I have read ሕውም with G. 9. After ἀπεκρίθη μοι I have added

ὁ τόπος καὶ ὡς δεινὸς τῇ ὁράσει.	οὗτος καὶ ὡς δεινὸς τῇ ὁράσει.
9. τότε ἀπεκρί(θη) μοι (Οὐριὴλ) ὁ εἷς τῶν ἁγίων ἀγγέλων ὃς μετ' ἐμοῦ ἦν, καὶ εἶπέν	9. τότε ἀπεκρίθη μοι καὶ εἶπέν

μοι· Ἐνώχ, διὰ τί ἐφοβήθης οὕτως καὶ ἐπτοήθης; καὶ ἀπεκρίθη(ν)· Περὶ τούτου τοῦ φοβεροῦ (τόπου) καὶ περὶ τῆς προσόψεως τῆς δεινῆς. 10. καὶ εἶπεν· Οὗτος ὁ τόπος δεσμωτήριον ἀγγέλων. ὧδε συσχεθήσονται ⟨μέχρι ἑνὸς⟩ εἰς τὸν αἰῶνα.

XXII. 1. Κἀκεῖθεν ἐφώδευσα εἰς ἄλλον τόπον, καὶ ἔδειξέν μοι πρὸς δυσμὰς [ἄλλο] ὄρος μέγα καὶ ὑψηλὸν (καὶ) πέτρας στερεάς. 2. καὶ τέσσαρες τόποι ἐν αὐτῷ κοῖλοι, βάθος (καὶ πλάτος) ἔχοντες καὶ λίαν λεῖοι, ⟨τρεῖς αὐτῶν σκοτεινοί, καὶ εἷς φωτεινός, καὶ πηγὴ ὕδατος ἀνὰ μέσον αὐτοῦ. καὶ εἶπον·⟩ Πῶς λεῖα τὰ κοιλώματα

ω (= ὡς) 9. G[1] ειπ̄ε — G[2] ends with ειπεν — απεκρειθη 10. δεσμωτηριων — συνσχηθησοντε

XXII. 1. εφοδευσα — ειστερεας 2. λειαν λιοι τρεις — εισκοτινοι — φωτινος — λια —

---

with Eth. 'Uriel.' καὶ εἶπεν. Eth. = ἀπεκρίθη μοι καὶ εἶπέν μοι. Here Eth. has transposed the words καὶ ἀπεκρίθην and placed them before καὶ εἶπεν. Hence omit 'answered and,' place the note of interrogation after alarm, and for 'at this horrible . . . pain' read *and I answered: 'Because of this horrible place.'* περὶ τῆς προσόψεως τῆς δεινῆς. Eth. seems corrupt or a mistranslation. ቅድመ፡ ገጹ፡ ለዝ፡ ሕማም. Better render with Gk. *because of this hideous spectacle*, በእንተዝ፡ ገጽ፡ ሕሡም. 10. After εἶπεν Eth. adds μοι. Before ὧδε Eth. adds καί.

XXII. 1. Before πέτρας Eth. adds καί. 2. κοῖλοι. Eth. ሠናያት, 'beautiful,' wrongly reading καλοί. We must further change the punctuation of Eth. text and begin ver. 2 with ወ፬. After βάθος add with Eth. καὶ πλάτος. Omit ወ before በውስቴቱ with Gk. Hence, for 'four beautiful places . . . perfectly smooth,' read *there were in this* (*mountain*) *four hollow places, deep, wide, and very smooth.* After λεῖοι Eth. omits through hmt. τρεῖς αὐτῶν σκοτεινοί, καὶ εἷς φωτεινός, καὶ πηγὴ ὕδατος ἀνὰ μέσον αὐτοῦ. καὶ εἶπον. Hence, insert after 'very smooth' (see note on preceding verse) *Three of these were gloomy and one bright and there was a fountain of water in its midst. And I said.* πῶς λεῖα = Eth. ከመ፡ ልሙጽ. τὰ κοιλώματα ταῦτα. Eth. ዘይትከረከር implies

ταῦτα καὶ ὁλοβαθέα καὶ σκοτεινὰ τῇ ὁράσει. 3. τότε ἀπεκρίθη
Ῥαφαήλ, ὁ εἷς τῶν ἁγίων ἀγγέλων, ὃς μετ' ἐμοῦ ἦν, καὶ εἶπέν μοι·
Οὗτοι οἱ τόποι οἱ κοῖλοι, ἵνα ἐπισυνάγωνται εἰς αὐτοὺς τὰ πνεύματα
† τῶν ψυχῶν τῶν νεκρῶν, εἰς αὐτὸ τοῦτο ἐκτίσθησαν, ὧδε ἐπισυνάγεσθαι πάσας τὰς ψυχὰς τῶν ἀνθρώπων. 4. καὶ οὗτοι οἱ τόποι εἰς
† ἐπισύσχεσι(ν) αὐτῶν ἐποιήθησαν μέχρι τῆς ἡμέρας τῆς κρίσεως αὐτῶν καὶ μέχρι τοῦ διορισμοῦ καὶ διωρισμένου χρόνου ἐν ᾧ ἡ κρίσις ἡ μεγάλη ἔσται ἐν αὐτοῖς.
† 5. Τεθέαμαι (πνεῦμα) ἀνθρώπου νεκροῦ ⟨ἐντυγχάνοντος⟩, καὶ ἡ φωνὴ αὐτοῦ μέχρι τοῦ οὐρανοῦ προέβαινεν, καὶ ἐνετύγχανεν·
† 6. καὶ ἠρώτησα Ῥαφαὴλ τὸν ἄγγελον, ὃς μετ' ἐμοῦ ἦν· καὶ εἶπα
† αὐτῷ· Τοῦτο τὸ πνεῦμα ⟨τὸ ἐντυγχάνον⟩, τίνος ἐστίν, οὗ οὕτως ἡ φωνὴ αὐτοῦ προβαίνει καὶ ἐντυγχάνει ⟨ἕως τοῦ οὐρανοῦ⟩; 7. καὶ ἀπεκρίθη μοι λέγων· Τοῦτο τὸ πνεῦμά ἐστιν τὸ ἐξελθὸν ἀπὸ Ἄβελ, ὃν ἐφόνευσεν Κάειν ὁ ἀδελφός. καὶ ⟨Ἄβελ⟩ ἐντυγχάνει περὶ αὐτοῦ

ολοβαθη — ορασι 3. επισυναγονται — εκρειθησαν — τ̄ω = των 4. επισυνσχεσι — εποιησαν — διορισμενου 5. ανθρωπους νεκρους — προεβενεν 6. ηρωτησεν — δι ο — προβεννι 7. απεκρειθη — εξελθων —

κυκλώματα or κυλίσματα, but κοιλώματα is right: cf. κοῖλοι τόποι in vv. 1, 3. Hence, after 'And I said' (see above) for 'as smooth as something which rolls,' read *How smooth are these hollow places.* ὁλοβαθέα. Eth.=βαθέα. 3. After ἀπεκρίθη Eth. adds μοι. κοῖλοι. Eth. wrongly read καλοί. I have rendered with Gk. τὰ πνεύματα. See Crit. Note, p. 94. εἰς αὐτὸ τοῦτο. So G: ሎቱ፡ ዝቱ. After ψυχάς Eth. adds τῶν υἱῶν. 4. ἐποιήθησαν. Here Eth. and Gk. agree in giving the same corrupt reading ἐποίησαν, ገብሩ. After μέχρι τοῦ διορισμοῦ Eth. adds αὐτῶν. After χρόνου Eth. adds a gloss ውእቱ፡ ዐቢይ. ἐν ᾧ. Eth.= ἕως, but less good. Hence, for 'this appointed period is long, till' read *till the period appointed, in which.* 5. This verse is defective and corrupt in Gk. and Eth. I have adopted M. Lods' emendation in the text. Apparently, we should emend Eth. accordingly, i.e. ርእኩ፡ መንፈሰ፡ ሰብእ፡ ምውት፡ እንዘ፡ ይሰኪ፡ ወቃሉ, *I saw the spirit of a man who was dead complaining and his voice,* &c. 6. For καί Eth. reads 'this time'=τότε. οὗ. A necessary correction of δι ο. 7. After ἀπεκρίθη Eth. adds καὶ εἶπεν. After ἀδελφός Eth. adds αὐτοῦ.

μέχρι τοῦ ἀπολέσθαι τὸ σπέρμα αὐτοῦ ἀπὸ προσώπου τῆς γῆς καὶ †
ἀπὸ τοῦ σπέρματος τῶν ἀνθρώπων ἀφανισθῇ τὸ σπέρμα αὐτοῦ.

8. Τότε ἠρώτησα (περὶ αὐτοῦ καὶ) περὶ τῶν κοιλωμάτων πάντων· †
Διὰ τί ἐχωρίσθησαν ἓν ἀπὸ τοῦ ἑνός; 9. καὶ ἀπεκρίθη μοι
λέγων· Οὗτοι οἱ τρεῖς ἐποιήθησαν χωρίζεσθαι τὰ πνεύματα τῶν
νεκρῶν· καὶ οὕτως (ἐ)χωρίσθη εἰς τὰ πνεύματα τῶν δικαίων, οὗ ἡ πηγὴ
τοῦ ὕδατος (τῆς ζωῆς) ἐν αὐτῷ φωτεινή. 10. καὶ οὕτως ἐκτίσθη †
τοῖς ἁμαρτωλοῖς, ὅταν ἀποθάνωσιν καὶ ταφῶσιν εἰς τὴν γῆν καὶ
κρίσις οὐκ ἐγενήθη ἐπ' αὐτῶν ἐν τῇ ζωῇ αὐτῶν, 11. ὧδε χωρί-
ζεται τὰ πνεύματα αὐτῶν εἰς τὴν μεγάλην βάσανον ταύτην μέχρι
τῆς μεγάλης ἡμέρας τῆς κρίσεως, τῶν μαστίγων καὶ τῶν βασάνων
τῶν κατηραμένων μέχρι αἰῶνος (καὶ) τῆς ἀνταποδόσεως τῶν πνευ- †
μάτων· ἐκεῖ δήσει αὐτοὺς μέχρις αἰῶνος. 12. καὶ οὕτως ἐχωρίσθη
τοῖς πνεύμασιν τῶν ἐντυγχανόντων, οἵτινες ἐμφανίζουσιν περὶ τῆς

απολεσαι 8. κυκλωματων — ην — αιωνος 9. τρις — φωτινη 10. των αμαρ-
τωλω̄ — κρισεις 11. χωρειζεται — αιωνος ην ανταποδωσεις 12. ενφανιζουσιν

ʼΑβελ. Eth. omits. 8. Before τότε Eth. adds 'and therefore.' After ἠρώτησα Gk. wrongly omits περὶ αὐτοῦ καί = በእንቲአሁ: ወ, where αὐτοῦ refers to the division in which Abel was. κοιλωμάτων. So I have emended κυκλωμάτων; for (1) the same corruption is implied by Eth. text in ver. 2; and (2) whereas κυκλωμάτων does not give a good sense, κοιλωμάτων is supported by vv. 1, 2, and 3. See ver. 2 (note). For κοιλωμάτων Eth. followed a corrupt reading κριμάτων. Hence, for 'I asked regarding him and regarding the judgment of all' read *I asked regarding it and regarding all the hollow places.* I have omitted ወኵሉ with G and Gk. 9. For ነፍሰሙ read በመንፈሰሙ = εἰς τὰ πνεύματα. ዘውእቱ is a corruption of ዘውእቱ, ብርሃን of ብሩሃን or ብሩህ = φωτεινή. After τοῦ ὕδατος I have read τῆς ζωῆς with G ማዩ: ሕይወት. Hence, for 'and the souls of the righteous . . . light above it' read *and thus a division is made for the spirits of the righteous in which there is a bright spring of the water of life.* 10. καί. Eth. በከመ. 11. Omit ወ before በዝየ with G and Gk. For ነፍሳቲሆሙ we should read መናፍስቲሆሙ with Gk. τὰ πνεύματα αὐτῶν. Hence, for 'souls' read *spirits* (twice). μέχρι αἰῶνος (καὶ) τῆς ἀνταποδόσεως. So I have emended with Eth. For 'revilers' we may equally well translate *accursed.* 12. I have omitted ወእመሂ: ውእቱ: እምቅድመ: ዓለም as a gloss. Omit ወበ

ἀπωλείας, ὅταν φονευθῶσιν ἐν ταῖς ἡμέραις τῶν ἁμαρτωλῶν. 13. ⟨καὶ⟩ οὕτως ἐκτίσθη τοῖς πνεύμασιν τῶν ἀνθρώπων ὅσοι οὐκ ἔσονται ὅσιοι ἀλλ' ἁμαρτωλοὶ ὅσοι (ὅλοι) ἀσεβεῖς· καὶ μετὰ τῶν ἀνόμων ἔσονται μέτοχοι· τὰ δὲ πνεύματα [ὅτι οἱ ἐνθάδε θλιβέντες ἔλαττον κολάζονται] αὐτῶν οὐ τιμωρηθήσονται ἐν ἡμέρᾳ τῆς κρίσεως οὐδὲ μὴ μετεγερθῶσιν ἐντεῦθεν. 14. τότε ηὐλόγησα τὸν κύριον τῆς δόξης καὶ εἶπα· Εὐλογητὸς εἶ, κύριε, ὁ τῆς δικαιοσύνης κυριεύων τοῦ αἰῶνος.

XXIII. 1. Κἀκεῖθεν ἐφώδευσα εἰς ἄλλον τόπον πρὸς δυσμὰς τῶν περάτων τῆς γῆς· 2. καὶ ἐθεασάμην πῦρ διατρέχον καὶ οὐκ † ἀναπαυόμενον οὐδὲ ἐλλεῖπον τοῦ δρόμου ἡμέρας καὶ νυκτὸς ἀλλὰ διαμένον. 3. καὶ ἠρώτησα λέγων· Τί ἐστιν τὸ μὴ ἔχον ἀνάπαυσιν; 4. τότε ἀπεκρίθη μοι Ῥαγουήλ, ὁ εἷς τῶν ἁγίων ἀγγέλων, ὃς μετ' ἐμοῦ ἦν· Οὗτος ὁ δρόμος τοῦ πυρὸς τὸ πρὸς δυσμὰς πῦρ τὸ ἐκδιῶκόν ἐστιν πάντας τοὺς φωστῆρας τοῦ οὐρανοῦ.

---

13. θλειβεντες — τειμωρηθησονται 14. κ̅ν̅ — κ̅ε̅
XXIII. 2. διατρεχων — αναπεομενον — ενλειπον — αμα 3. εχων
4. εκδιωκων — π̅α̅τας

---

before እለ with G: cf. οἵτινες. 13. Eth. omits καί before οὕτως. For ነፍሳሆሙ, 'souls,' we should read twice in this verse መንፈሳሆሙ = πνεύμασιν, *spirits.* Before ἀσεβεῖς add ὅλοι with Eth. ኃጥኣን. It could easily fall out after ὅσοι. μέτοχοι. Eth. ከማሆሙ = ὁμοῖοι αὐτοῖς or ἑαυτοῖς. ὅτι οἱ ἐνθάδε θλιβέντες ἔλαττον κολάζονται. 'For those who suffer here are punished less.' This is an explanatory marginal gloss thrust into the text. τιμωρηθήσονται. Eth. ትትቀተል 'will be slain.' μετεγερθῶσιν. I. e. 'rise *with*' the rest. Eth. 'rise.' 14. With G I have omitted ወእቱ, ሰብሓት፡ ወ and ዘአ. εἶ. Probably wrong. 3rd pers. used almost universally in the Enochic doxologies: see xxii. 14 (note, p. 96). For κύριε, ὁ τῆς δικαιοσύνης, Eth. read κύριός μου, ὁ κύριος τῆς δικαιοσύνης, which is better.

XXIII. 1. Before τῶν περάτων Eth. adds እስከ = μέχρι. 2. After πῦρ Eth. adds φλεγόμενον. ἀλλά. So emended with Eth. from ἅμα. 4. After ἐμοῦ ἦν Eth. adds καὶ εἶπέν μοι. Rest of verse difficult. First as to the text. Before δρόμος Eth. adds ዘርኢከ = ὃν εἶδες, and omits wrongly τοῦ πυρός after δρόμος. Again, ዘይተዴዴ is obviously a corruption for ዘይሰዴዴ = τὸ ἐκδιῶκον. ἐκδιῶκον

XXIV. 1. (Κἀκεῖθεν ἐφώδευσα εἰς ἄλλον τόπον τῆς γῆς) καὶ ἔδειξέν μοι ὄρη πυρὸς καιόμενα...νυκτός. 2. καὶ ἐπέκεινα αὐτῶν ἐπορεύθην, καὶ ἐθεασάμην ἑπτὰ ὄρη ἔνδοξα, πάντα ἑκάτερα τοῦ ἑκατέρου διαλλάσσοντο, ὧν οἱ λίθοι ἔντιμοι τῇ καλλονῇ· καὶ πάντα ἔντιμα καὶ ἔνδοξα καὶ εὐειδῆ. (τρία ἐπ') ἀνατολὰς ἐστηριγμένα (ἓν) ἐν τῷ ἑνί, καὶ τρία ἐπὶ νότον (ἓν) ἐν τῷ ἑνί. καὶ φάραγγες βαθεῖαι καὶ τραχεῖαι, μία τῇ μιᾷ οὐκ ἐγγίζουσαι. 3. [καὶ τῷ ὄρει] ἕβδομον ὄρος ἀνὰ μέσον τούτων, καὶ ὑπερεῖχεν τῷ ὕψει ὅμοιον καθέδρᾳ θρόνου· καὶ περιεκύκλου δένδρα αὐτὸ εὐώδη. 4. καὶ †

XXIV. 1. εδιξεν — κεομενα 2. επεκεινα — καλλωνη — εστεριγμενα — φαρανγες — τραχιαι — ενγειζουσαι 3. ορι — μεσο̄ — υψι — θρουνου — αυτω ευειδη

cannot mean 'pursues' here, as M. Lods thinks, but 'persecutes,' 'punishes,' or 'avenges.' This would harmonize with xx. 4. But this can hardly be right. The idea of punishing *all* the luminaries is extravagant. It is more probable, therefore, that the author derived Raguel not from רעע, 'to chastise,' but from רעה, 'to feed,' 'nourish,' 'govern.' In this case for Giz. Gk.[1] εκδεικων or Giz. Gk.[2] εκεκων we should read ἐκδιοικοῦν or διοικοῦν, and not ἐκδικῶν. We should then translate *Raguel—who feeds* (or *nourishes*) *the world of the luminaries.* In like manner in this verse we should take ἐκδιῶκον to be an early corruption for ἐκδιοικοῦν or διοικοῦν. Thus Raguel, whose office is to feed the fires of the luminaries, rightly appears here: and the means of so doing is the restless fire of the west: cf. xvii. 4. Hence, for 'This burning fire . . . luminaries of heaven,' read *This course of fire which thou hast seen is the fire towards the west which nourishes all the luminaries of the heaven.*

XXIV. 1. Before καὶ ἔδειξεν I have added with Eth. κἀκεῖθεν . . . τῆς γῆς. Before νυκτός Eth. adds ἡμέρας καί. 2. ἐπέκεινα αὐτῶν ἐπορεύθην. The Eth. translator, not understanding ἐπέκεινα, renders ሖርኩ፡ መንገሌሆሙ = ἐπὶ αὐτῶν ἐπορ. Hence, for 'I approached it' read *I went beyond it.* ὧν οἱ λίθοι. Eth. read καὶ οἱ λίθοι. τῇ καλλονῇ. Eth. read καὶ καλοί. ἔνδοξα. Eth. = ἔνδοξα εἰς τὸ εἶδος αὐτῶν. εὐειδῆ. Eth. = ሠናይ፡ ገጾሙ 'and of fair exterior.' τραχεῖαι. Eth. ጠዋይት = σκολιαί. 3. ὑπερεῖχεν τῷ ὕψει ὅμοιον καθέδρᾳ θρόνου. Eth. corrupt. Emend with Dln. ነዊኆ፡ እምኵሎሙ፡ ይትማሰል. Thus, for 'in their elevation they resemble the seats' read *being higher than all it resembled the seat.* After ὑπερεῖχεν add πάντων

† *ἦν ἐν αὐτοῖς δένδρον ὃ οὐδέποτε ὠσφράνμαι καὶ οὐδὲν ἕτερον αὐτῶν [ηὐφράνθη] καὶ οὐδὲν ἕτερον ὅμοιον αὐτῷ· ὀσμὴν εἶχεν εὐωδεστέραν πάντων ἀρωμάτων· καὶ τὰ φύλλα αὐτοῦ καὶ τὸ ἄνθος καὶ τὸ δένδρον οὐ φθίνει εἰς τὸν αἰῶνα· οἱ δὲ περὶ τὸν καρπὸν ὡσεὶ βότρυες φοινίκων.*

5. Τότε εἶπον· Ὡς καλὸν τὸ δένδρον τοῦτό ἐστιν καὶ εὐῶδες, καὶ ὡραῖα τὰ φύλλα, καὶ τὰ ἄνθη αὐτοῦ ὡραῖα τῇ ὁράσει. 6. τότε ἀπεκρίθη μοι Μιχαήλ, εἷς τῶν ἁγίων ἀγγέλων, ὃς μετ' ἐμοῦ ἦν, καὶ αὐτὸς αὐτῶν ἡγεῖτο, XXV. 1. καὶ εἶπέν μοι· Ἐνώχ, τί ἐρωτᾷς; ⟨καὶ τί ἐθαύμασας⟩ ἐν τῇ ὀσμῇ τοῦ δένδρου; καὶ ⟨διὰ τί⟩ θέλεις τὴν ἀλήθειαν μαθεῖν; 2. τότε ἀπεκρίθη(ν) αὐτῷ· Περὶ πάντων εἰδέναι θέλω, μάλιστα δὲ περὶ τοῦ δένδρου τούτου σφόδρα.

3. Καὶ ἀπεκρίθη λέγων· Τοῦτο τὸ ὄρος τὸ ὑψηλόν, οὗ ἡ κορυφὴ
† ὁμοία θρόνου θεοῦ, καθέδρα ἐστὶν οὗ καθίσει ὁ ἅγιος ὁ μέγας κύριος τῆς δόξης, ὁ βασιλεὺς τοῦ αἰῶνος, ὅταν καταβῇ ἐπισκέψασθαι τὴν γῆν ἐπ' ἀγαθῷ. 4. καὶ τοῦτο τὸ δένδρον εὐωδίας καὶ οὐδεμία σὰρξ ἐξουσίαν ἔχει ἅψασθαι αὐτοῦ μέχρι τῆς μεγάλης κρίσεως,

---

4. *ουδεις ετερος αυτων — ευωδεστερον — φθεινι* 5. *ωρεα — ορασι*
XXV. 2. *απεκρειθη* 3. *θ̅υ̅ — καθειζει — ο μεγας κ̅ς̅ ο αγιος* 4. *ευωδειας —*

---

with Eth. *εὐώδη*. So emended as in Eth. 4. *καὶ οὐδεὶς ἕτερος αὐτῶν ηὐφράνθη*, 'and no one else has enjoyed them.' The reference to the other trees is out of place. Hence, with Eth. omit *ηὐφράνθη*, and for *οὐδεὶς ἕτερος* read *οὐδὲν ἕτερον*. *ὀσμὴν εἶχεν*. Hence, for ዘይምዑዝ read with G ይምዑዝ. *οἱ δὲ περὶ τὸν καρπόν*. Corrupt. Such expressions with masc. or fem. art. are personal, i.e. *οἱ περὶ Ἀρχίαν* = *Ἀρχίας*. Eth. = *ὁ δὲ καρπὸς καλὸς καὶ ὁ καρπός*. 5. Before *τότε* Eth. adds *καί*. *ὡς*. Eth. ነዋ 'behold.' *εὐῶδες*. This seems right: cf. xxv. 1. Eth. supposes *εὐειδές*, but wrongly. Hence, for 'beautiful to look upon' read *and fragrant*. *ἄνθη*. Eth. *καρπός*. 6. Before *τότε* Eth. adds *καί*. After *ἁγίων* Eth. adds *καὶ ἐντίμων*.

XXV. 1. *διὰ τί*. Eth. omits. *θέλεις τὴν ἀλήθειαν* = Eth. ትጤይቅ: cf. xxi. 5. 2. Omit ወ at beginning of verse with G and Gk. After *αὐτῷ* Eth. adds *λέγων*. 3. After *ἀπεκρίθη* Eth. adds *μοι*. After *ὄρος* Eth. adds *ὃ εἶδες*. *καθέδρα*. Eth. adds *αὐτοῦ*. *ὁ ἅγιος . . . κύριος*. I have restored the order as in Eth. *τοῦ αἰῶνος*. Eth. ዘለዓለም = *αἰώνιος*. 4. *τῆς μεγάλης κρίσεως*. See Crit. Note, p. 98.

ἐν ᾗ ἐκδίκησις πάντων κα(ὶ) τελείωσις μέχρις αἰῶνος· τότε δικαίοις †
καὶ ὁσίοις δοθήσεται 5. ὁ καρπὸς αὐτοῦ τοῖς ἐκλεκτοῖς εἰς
ζωήν· καὶ εἰς βορρᾶν μεταφυτευθήσεται ἐν τόπῳ ἁγίῳ, παρὰ τὸν †
οἶκον τοῦ θεοῦ βασιλέως τοῦ αἰῶνος. 6. τότε εὐφρανθήσονται
εὐφραινόμενοι, καὶ χαρήσονται, καὶ εἰς τὸ ἅγιον εἰσελεύσονται·
αἱ ὀσμαὶ αὐτοῦ ἐν τοῖς ὀστέοις αὐτῶν· καὶ ζωὴν πλείονα ζήσονται
ἐπὶ γῆς ἣν ἔζησαν οἱ πατέρες σου· καὶ ἐν ταῖς ἡμέραις αὐτῶν καὶ
βάσανοι καὶ πληγαὶ καὶ μάστιγες οὐχ ἅψονται αὐτῶν. 7. τότε
ηὐλόγησα τὸν θεὸν τῆς δόξης, τὸν βασιλέα τοῦ αἰῶνος, ὃς ἡτοί- †
μασεν ἀνθρώποις τὰ τοιαῦτα δικαίοις καὶ αὐτὰ ἔκτισεν καὶ εἶπεν
δοῦναι αὐτοῖς.

XXVI. 1. Καὶ ἐκεῖθεν ἐφώδευσα εἰς τὸ μέσον τῆς γῆς, καὶ ἴδον
τόπον ηὐλογημένον, ⟨ἐν ᾧ δένδρα⟩ ἔχοντα παραφυάδας μενούσας
καὶ βλαστούσας τοῦ δένδρου ἐκκοπέντος. 2. κἀκεῖ τεθέαμαι
ὄρος ἅγιον, ὑποκάτω τοῦ ὄρους ὕδωρ ἐξ ἀνατολῶν· καὶ τὴν ῥύσιν †
εἶχεν πρὸς νότον. 3. καὶ ἴδον πρὸς ἀνατολὰς ἄλλο ὄρος ὑψηλό-

ει = εν — εκδεικησις 5. εις βοραν και — θ̅υ̅ βασιλευς 6. χαρισονται — εισελευσο̅ται αι οσμε — οσταιοις — μαστειγες 7. ηυλογησαν — θ̅ν̅
XXVI. 2. τεθεαμε — δυσιν

ἐν ᾗ. So M. Lods rightly emends ει η. τότε. Eth. ዝኩ 'this.' The original, therefore, was τότε or τόδε. ὁσίοις. Eth. ትሑታን 'humble.' 5. ὁ καρπὸς . . . ζωήν. Eth. 'by its fruit life will be given to the elect.' καὶ εἰς βορρᾶν. I have thus restored καί to its right position before εἰς. So G : ወመንገለ፡ መስዕ. Further, the μετα in μεταφυτευθ. implies a change of place, 'transplanted to,' and thus requires εἰς βορρᾶν. Gk. corruptly reads εἰς βορὰν καί = 'for food and.' τοῦ αἰῶνος. Eth. ዘለዓለም, αἰώνιος. 6. Eth. omits καί before εἰς. εἰς τ. ἅγ. εἰσελεύσονται. See Crit. Note, p. 99. πλείονα. Eth. ብዙኀ = πολλήν. This is preferable. Before καὶ βάσανοι Eth. adds λύπη. 7. τοῦ αἰῶνος. Eth. = αἰώνιον. ὅς. Eth. እስመ = ὅτι or διότι.

XXVI. 1. After ηὐλογημένον Eth. adds καὶ πίονα. ἐν ᾧ δένδρα. Eth. omits through similarity ዘቦቱ፡ ዕፀው, but to the detriment of the sense. Hence, for 'there were . . . grew' read *there were trees there with branches which kept shooting forth.* 2. Before ὑποκάτω Eth. adds καί. ῥύσιν emended from δύσιν with Eth. 3. For ከመዝ read እምዝ with Gk., and for 'of the same height'

† τερον τούτου, καὶ ἀνὰ μέσον αὐτῶν φάραγγαν βαθεῖαν οὐκ ἔχουσαν πλάτος, καὶ δι' αὐτῆς ὕδωρ πορεύεται ὑποκάτω ὑπὸ τὸ ὄρος— 4. καὶ πρὸς δυσμὰς τούτου ἄλλο ὄρος ταπεινότερον αὐτοῦ καὶ οὐκ ἔχον ὕψος, καὶ φάραγγαν βαθεῖαν καὶ ξηρὰν ἀνὰ μέσον αὐτῶν, καὶ ἄλλην φάραγγαν βαθεῖαν καὶ ξηρὰν ἐπ' ἄκρων τῶν τριῶν ὀρέων. 5. καὶ πᾶσαι φάραγγές εἰσιν βαθεῖαι, ἐκ πέτρας στερεᾶς· καὶ δένδρον ⟨οὐκ⟩ ἐφυτεύετο ἐπ' αὐτάς. 6. . . . καὶ ἐθαύμασα περὶ τῆς φαράγγας καὶ λίαν ἐθαύμασα XXVII. 1. καὶ εἶπον· Διὰ τί ἡ γῆ αὕτη ἡ εὐλογημένη καὶ πᾶσα πλήρης δένδρων, αὕτη δὲ ἡ φάραγξ κεκατηραμένη ἐστί; (τότε ἀπεκρίθη Οὐριήλ, ὁ εἷς τῶν ἁγίων ἀγγέλων, ὃς μετ' ἐμοῦ ἦν, καὶ εἶπεν·) 2. Ἡ γῆ κατάρατος τοῖς κεκαταραμένοις ἐστὶν μέχρι αἰῶνος· ὧδε ἐπισυναχθήσονται πάντες οἵ [κεκατηραμένοι] τινες ἐροῦσιν τῷ στόματι αὐτῶν κατὰ κυρίου φωνὴν ἀπρεπῆ καὶ περὶ τῆς δόξης αὐτοῦ σκληρὰ λαλήσουσιν. ὧδε ἐπισυναχθήσονται καὶ ὧδε ἔσται τὸ οἰκητήριον. 3. ἐπ'
† ἐσχάτοις αἰῶσιν, ἔσονται εἰς ὅρασιν τῆς κρίσεως τῆς ἀληθινῆς

---

3. αυτου 5. ποσε φαραγγες 6. λειαν
XXVII. 1. φαραγξ 2. οικετηριον 3. αισχατοις — εν ταις ημεραις (hence ἔσονται εἰς ὅρασιν) — αληθεινης —

---

read *higher than this.* αὐτῶν emended from αὐτοῦ with Eth. Eth. adds καί after βαθεῖαν. ὑποκάτω ὑπό. Eth. መንገለ. 4. βαθεῖαν καὶ ξηράν. Eth. ታሕቴ 'beneath it.' For ካልኣት . . . ይቡሳት read with Gk. ካልእት፡ ቈላ፡ ዕሙቅት፡ ወይቡስት; and for 'other deep and sterile ravines' read *another deep and sterile ravine.* 5. οὐκ ἐφυτεύετο. G reads ዘይትከል, where the ዘ may be a corruption of እ. 6. Before καὶ ἐθαύμασα Eth. adds καὶ ἐθαύμασα περὶ τῶν πετρῶν, omitted by Gk. through like beginning.

XXVII. 1. καί. Eth. = τότε. After κεκατ. Eth. adds μεταξὺ αὐτῶν. 2. Before ἡ γῆ I have added with Eth. τότε ἀπεκρίθη . . . καὶ εἶπεν. γῆ (Eth. = φάραγξ) to be rendered 'valley,' being a transliteration of גיא, due to misconceiving it as a proper name. It is transliterated as γαί in II Sam. xiii. 18; Ezek. xxxix. 15, &c. κεκατηραμένοι is a gloss; οι and τινες are to be read οἵτινες. For οἰκητήριον we should read κριτήριον with Eth. 3. Omit ወ before በደኃሪ with G and Gk. αἰῶσιν. Eth. መዋዕል 'days.' ἔσονται εἰς ὅρασιν. So I have emended ἐν ταῖς ἡμέραις. *They will be for a spectacle.* Eth. ይከውን፡ ላዕሌሆሙ፡ ትርኢት 'there will be upon them the spectacle.' But most probably we should read ይከውኑ፡ ለሊሆሙ፡ ትርኢተ, *they*

ἐναντίον τῶν δικαίων εἰς τὸν ἅπαντα χρόνον, ὧδε εὐλογήσουσιν οἱ εὐσεβεῖς τὸν κύριον τῆς δόξης, τὸν βασιλέα τοῦ αἰῶνος. 4. ἐν † ταῖς ἡμέραις τῆς κρίσεως αὐτῶν εὐλογήσουσιν (αὐτὸν) ἐν ἐλέει ὡς ἐμέρισεν αὐτοῖς. 5. τότε ηὐλόγησα τὸν κύριον τῆς δόξης καὶ τὴν δόξαν αὐτοῦ ἐδήλωσα καὶ ὕμνησα μεγαλοπρεπῶς.

XXVIII. 1. Καὶ ἐκεῖθεν ἐπορεύθην εἰς τὸ μέσον Μανδοβαρα, καὶ ἴδον αὐτὸ ἔρημον καὶ αὐτὸ μόνον, 2. πλῆρες δένδρων· καὶ ἀπὸ τῶν σπερμάτων ὕδωρ ἀνομβροῦν ἄνωθεν 3. φαινόμενον, † ὡς ὑδραγωγὸς δαψιλὴς ὡς πρὸς βορρᾶν ἐπὶ δυσμῶν πάντοθεν ἀνάγει ὕδωρ καὶ δρόσον.

απᾶτα — ασεβεις — κ̄ν 4. ταις = της 5. κ̄ν
XXVIII. 2. πληρης δενδρον — ανομβρον — ανοθεν 3. φαιρομενο̄

---

themselves will be for a spectacle. εἰς ἅπαντα χρόνον. Eth. = εἰς τὸν αἰῶνα πάσας τὰς ἡμέρας. εὐσεβεῖς corrected from ασεβεις. See Crit. Note, p. 101. τοῦ αἰῶνος. Eth. = αἰώνιον. 5. After τότε Eth. adds καὶ ἐγώ. After ነገርኩ (an imperfect rendering of ἐδήλωσα) add ሰብሐቶ with Gk., and for 'spake to Him' read *set forth His glory.* ὕμνησα. Hence, for ዘከርኩ = ἔμνησα read ዘመርኩ 'I lauded.' μεγαλοπρεπῶς. Eth. በከመ፡ ይደሉ፡ ለዕበዩ is a misleading attempt at a literal translation. Hence for 'remembered . . . befitting' read *lauded Him gloriously.*

XXVIII. 1. After ἐπορεύθην Eth. adds πρὸς ἀνατολάς. Μανδοβαρα. This is a faulty transliteration of מִדְבָּר taken as a proper name. It recurs in still faultier form in xxix. 1, Βαβδηρα. In the LXX. this mistake is also found. See Schleusner on Μαβδαρίτις and Μαδμαρίτις. After μέσον Eth. adds ለደብር 'mountain range.' ἴδον αὐτὸ ἔρημον. Eth. ርእኩ፡ ገደመ፡ ባሕቲቶ. Thus for ἔρημον, an adj., we have 'a desert plain.' καὶ αὐτὸ μόνον. Eth. ወባሕቲቱ corrupt: read ውብሑት 'solitary.' Hence, for 'I saw here nothing save a plain. 2. Nevertheless' read *I saw a desert and solitary plain.* 2. (*but*). 2. πλῆρες δένδρων. So Eth. For 'it was filled with' read *full of.* For καὶ ἀπὸ τῶν σπερμάτων Eth. reads ἀπὸ τοῦ σπέρματος τούτου καὶ ἀνομβροῦν = ይፈለፍል. So I have emended from ἄνομβρον. After ἀνομβροῦν Eth. adds በላዕሉ 'upon it.' 3. φαινόμενον = ይስተርኢ. So I have emended from φαιρομενο̄. ὡς ὑδραγωγὸς δαψιλής. So G: ከመ፡ ሰረበ፡ ውኂዝ፡ ዘይሰርብ. πάντοθεν . . . δρόσον καὶ ἐκεῖθεν. Eth. = καὶ πάντοθεν ἀνάγεται καὶ ἐκεῖθεν ὕδωρ καὶ δρόσος somewhat transposed and corrupt. First restore ወእምህየ to the beginning of

XXIX. 1. Καὶ ἐκεῖθεν ἐπορεύθην εἰς ἄλλον τόπον ἐν τῷ Βαβδηρα, καὶ πρὸς ἀνατολὰς τοῦ ὄρους τούτου ᾠχόμην, 2. καὶ ἴδον κρίσεως δένδρα πνέοντα ἀρωμάτων λιβάνων καὶ σμύρνης· καὶ τὰ δένδρα αὐτῶν ὅμοια καρύαις.

XXX. 1. Καὶ ἐπέκεινα τούτων ᾠχόμην πρὸς ἀνατολὰς μακράν, καὶ ἴδον τόπον ἄλλον μέγαν, φάραγγαν ὕδατος, 2. ἐν ᾧ καὶ δένδρον χρόα ἀρωμάτω(ν) ὁμοίων σχίνῳ. 3. καὶ τὰ παρὰ τὰ χείλη τῶν φαράγγων τούτων ἴδον κιννάμωμον ἀρωμάτων. καὶ ἐπέκεινα τούτων ᾠχόμην πρὸς ἀνατολάς, XXXI. 1. καὶ ἴδον ἄλλα ὄρη, καὶ ἐν αὐτοῖς ἄλση δένδρων, καὶ ἐκπορευόμενον ἐξ αὐτῶν νέκταρ, τὸ καλούμενον σαρραν καὶ χαλβάνη.

2. Καὶ ἐπέκεινα τῶν ὀρέων τούτων ἴδον ἄλλο ὄρος πρὸς ἀνατολὰς

XXIX. 2. ζμυρνα—καροιης XXX. 2. σχινω 3. φαραγγων
XXXI. 1. εκπορευομενων

---

xxix. 1 in place of ወ. Next vocalize የ"፡ ማ"፡ ወጠ" thus የዐርግ፡ ማያ፡ ወጠለ and omit ወ before እምዘ". Hence, for 'there were many . . . xxix. 1 And I went' read *many watercourses which flowed as well towards the north as to the west caused water and dew to ascend on every side.* xxix. 1 *And thence I went.*

XXIX. 1. καὶ ἐκεῖθεν. See preceding note. ἐν τῷ Βαβδηρα. See note on xxviii. 1. Eth. = ἀπὸ τοῦ ἐρήμου. For καί before πρός G reads ዘ 'which.' ᾠχόμην. Eth. ቀረብኩ 'I approached.' 2. Before ἴδον Eth. adds ἐκεῖ. πνέοντα. Eth. ቈስቈስ corrupt. Omit ስ before ሰኂን with G. ὅμοια. See Crit. Note, p. 102. After ይትማሰሉ add ለከርካዕ, i. e. καρύαις with Gk.

XXX. 1. ἐπέκεινα τούτων. Eth. corrupt: ላዕሌሆሙ፡ ላዕለ፡ እላንቱ. The translator also did not understand ἐπέκεινα. See xviii. 9 (note). Hence, for 'above that (even) above these' read *beyond those.* ᾠχόμην πρὸς ἀνατολάς. Eth. corrupt. For ላዕለ፡ ደብረ፡ ጽባሕ read የደኩ፡ ለጽባሕ = ᾠχόμην πρὸς ἀνατολάς. μακράν. Eth. = καὶ οὐ μακράν. μέγαν. Eth. omits. After ὕδατος Eth. adds ከመ፡ ዘኢይትኀጸዕ 'as that which fails not.' 2. ἐν ᾧ καί. Eth. = καὶ ἴδον. χρόα ἀρωμάτων, 'the appearance of fragrant trees.' So G: ዘይመስል፡ ዕፀ፡ መዓዛ. See Crit. Note, p. 102. ὁμοίων σχίνῳ. So G: ከመ፡ እንተ፡ ዘሰኪናን. 3. ἐπέκεινα. Eth. ዲበ 'over.' See xviii. 9 (note). For 'passing over these' read *beyond these.*

XXXI. 1. ἄλση δένδρων. Eth. omits ἄλση. ἐκπορευόμενον. See Crit. Note, p. 102. Before νέκταρ Eth. adds ከመ = ὡς. σαρραν seems to be a transliteration of צְרִי, a kind of balsam. This would suit perfectly here. In the LXX. ῥητίνη = צְרִי. 2. ἐπέκεινα. See

τῶν περάτων τῆς γῆς, καὶ πάντα τὰ δένδρα πλήρη ἐκ στακτῆς ἐν † ὁμοιώματι ἀμυγδάλω(ν)· 3. ὅταν τρίβωσιν αὐτὸ εὐωδέστερον † ὑπὲρ πᾶν ἄρωμα. XXXII. 1. (καὶ μετὰ ταῦτα τὰ ἀρώματα), εἰς βορρᾶν πρὸς ἀνατολὰς τεθέαμαι ἑπτὰ ὄρη πλήρη νάρδου χρηστοῦ καὶ σχίνου καὶ κινναμώμου καὶ πιπέρεως.

2. Καὶ ἐκεῖθεν ἐφώδευσα ἐπὶ τὰς ἀρχὰς πάντων τῶν ὀρέων τούτων, μακρὰν ἀπέχων πρὸς ἀνατολὰς ⟨τῆς γῆς⟩. καὶ διέβην ἐπάνω τῆς ἐρυθρᾶς θαλάσσης, καὶ ᾠχόμην μακρὰν ἀπὸ τούτου καὶ †

---

2. πληρης εξ αυτης — ομοι.ματι 3. διο — ευ.δεστερον — αρωματων

XXXII. 1. τεθεαμε — σχυνου 2. εφοδευσα — επι ακρων και απο τουτου = μακρὰν ἀπὸ τούτου καὶ

---

xviii. 9 (note, p. 354). Eth. 'over,' wrongly. Hence for 'over' read *beyond*. πρὸς ἀνατολὰς . . . ἀμυγδάλων. Here both Gk. and Eth. are corrupt, but the latter less so. First, ἐν ὁμοιώματι ἀμυγδάλων = ዘከመ፡ ከርካዕ. ἐκ στακτῆς. Clearly the original of εξ αυτης was early corrupted into something like εκ στερεας: hence ወጽንዕ, and in its wrong place. Next እሉ is a corruption of ኵሉ = πάντα. Thus so far everything is clear. We have now πρὸς ἀνατολὰς τῶν περάτων τῆς γῆς over against ወውስቴቱ፡ ዕፀው፡ ዘንልቀ. Gk. is not appropriate whereas Eth. is. Eth. = καὶ ἐν αὐτῷ δένδρα ἀλόης. It is needless to pursue the corruption further. Hence, for 'those trees were full of a hard substance' read *all the trees were full of stacte*. 3. ὅταν τρίβωσιν αὐτὸ εὐωδέστερον ὑπὲρ πᾶν ἄρωμα. Eth. ሶበ፡ ይነሥእዎ፡ ለውእቱ፡ ፍሬ፡ ይኄይስ፡ እምኵሉ፡ አፈው 'if they took that fruit, it was better than all fragrant odours.' Gk. here is undoubtedly to be followed. By translating Gk. afresh into Eth. we see at once how the corruption arose. ሶበ፡ ይኄስይዎ፡ ይጼንዎ፡ እምኵሉ፡ አፈው. Then by an error ይኄስይዎ፡ ይጼንዎ got transposed (as constantly happens in these MSS.) and were then emended as in our text ይነሥእዎ፡ ይኄይስ. ለውእቱ፡ ፍሬ is a later explanatory gloss. Hence, for 'And the taste, ... odours' read *When one rubbed it, it smelt sweeter than any fragrant odour*.

XXXII. 1. Before εἰς βορρᾶν I have added with Eth. καί μ. τ. τ. ἀ. omitted through hmt. πρὸς ἀνατολάς. Eth. መልዕልተ፡ አድባር 'over the mountains.' πρὸς ἀνατολάς occurs suspiciously often (see xxxi. 2). σχίνου. 'Mastich.' Eth. ዕፀው፡ መዐዛ, less good. 2. πάντων. Eth. omits. τῆς γῆς. Eth. omits. ᾠχόμην ἐπ' ἀκρῶν καὶ ἀπὸ τούτου. I have emended into ᾠχόμην μακρὰν ἀπὸ τούτου καί = Eth.

διέβην ἐπάνω τοῦ Ζωτιέλ. 3. καὶ ἦλθον πρὸς τὸν παράδεισον τῆς δικαιοσύνης· καὶ ἴδον μακρόθεν τῶν δένδρων τούτων δένδρα † πλείονα καὶ μεγάλα φυόμενα ἐκεῖ μεγάλα σφόδρα καλὰ καὶ ἔνδοξα καὶ μεγαλοπρεπῆ, καὶ τὸ δένδρον τῆς φρονήσεως, οὗ ἐσθίουσιν ⟨ἅγιοι τοῦ καρποῦ αὐτοῦ⟩ καὶ ἐπίστανται φρόνησιν μεγάλην.
4. ⟨ὅμοιον τὸ δένδρον ἐκεῖνο στροβιλέᾳ τὸ ὕψος· τὰ δὲ φύλλα⟩ αὐτοῦ κερατί(ᾳ) ὅμοια· ὁ δὲ καρπὸς αὐτοῦ ὡσεὶ βότρυες ἀμπέλου ἱλαροὶ λίαν· ἡ δὲ ὀσμὴ αὐτοῦ διέτρεχεν πόρρω ἀπὸ τοῦ δένδρου.
5. τότε εἶπον· Ὡς καλὸν τὸ δένδρον καὶ ὡς ἐπίχαρι τῇ ὁράσει.
6. τότε ἀπεκρίθη Ῥαφαήλ, ὁ ἅγιος ἄγγελος ὁ μετ' ἐμοῦ ὤν· Τοῦτο τὸ δένδρον φρονήσεως ἐξ οὗ ἔφαγεν ὁ πατήρ σου.

---

3. ελθων = ηλθον — παραδισον — ιδο̄ — δυω μεν   5. επιχαρη — ορασι.

Here, as frequently, *καί* has been transposed. Before Ζωτιέλ Eth. adds 'angel.' Ζωτιέλ may therefore be merely the name of a place. 3. μακρόθεν τῶν δένδρων τούτων δένδρα πλείονα καὶ μέγαλα = 'from afar trees more numerous than these trees and large.' But G interpreted differently: i.e. ከሐከዊሆሙ፡ ለእሎንቱ፡ ዕፀው፡ ዕፀው፡ ብዙኃን፡ ወዐቢያን = ἐπέκεινα τῶν δένδρων τούτων δένδρα πολλὰ καὶ μέγαλα. I have followed G in my Trans. ከሐከዊሆሙ is from ከሐ or ከሐከ = trans, ultra. φυόμενα = ይበቍሉ I have restored from δυω μεν. There is no question here about two trees. After ἐκεῖ Eth. adds εὐώδη. 4. ἡ δὲ ὀσμὴ αὐτοῦ . . . δένδρου. Eth. = ἡ δὲ ὀσμὴ τοῦ δένδρου ἔβαινεν καὶ διέτρεχεν πόρρω. If we omit የሐውር፡ ወ and for በ read እም, Eth. = Gk. 5. For τότε Eth. reads καί. For ὡς καλὸν τὸ δένδρον Eth. reads καλὸν τὸ δένδρον τοῦτο καὶ ὡς καλόν, 6. For τότε Eth. reads καί. After ὤν Eth. adds καὶ εἶπεν ἐμοί.

APPENDIX D.

ADDITIONAL NOTES ON THE ETHIOPIC TEXT AND TRANSLATION.

XXXVII. 2. For **holy words** G reads 'words of the Holy One.' 3. For እሉ፡ ቀዳሚ read እለ or በእሉ. If the former, take ቀዳሚ as a noun and cf. እለ፡ ዐመፃ, xcv. 7.

XXXVIII. 4. G omits በ before እግዚእ. Hence, for ተርእየ we should probably read አርአየ, and translate *for the Lord of Spirits has caused the light of the face of the holy . . . to appear.* 6. **For them.** So G ሎሙ. Dln. omits.

XXXIX. 1. **High heaven.** So G. Dln. 'high heavens.' 3. **In those days.** So G: በውእቱ፡ መዋእል. Dln. 'at that time.' 4. **The holy.** So G. Dln. 'The righteous.' **The righteous.** So G. Dln. 'the holy.' 5. **His righteous angels.** So G: መላእክቲሁ፡ ጻድቅ. Dln. 'The angels.' 12. After ወይባርኩ I have omitted ከ with G.

XLVIII. 4. I have omitted ለቅዱሳን with G.

LXII. 10. **Darkness will be piled upon their faces.** Perhaps too free. Lit. 'Their faces will be increased with darkness.'

LXIII. 10. **Mammon of unrighteousness** or 'riches of unrighteousness'; for neither here nor in Matt. vi. 24: Luke xvi. 9 does Eth. transliterate *μαμωνᾶς*.

LXXVIII. 4. **Additions are made to the moon.** እምውርኅ. Better perhaps 'to parts of the moon.'

CVII. 3. Before ይስተፌሥሕ G adds ያድኅን፡ ወ = 'will save and.' For 'will cause . . . destruction' better render *will comfort the earth because of the universal destruction* or *after the universal destruction.*

APPENDIX E.

LATIN FRAGMENT OF ENOCH CVI. 1–18.

(*Found in MS. Brit. Mus. Reg. S.* E. XIII. Saec. VIII. ff. 79^b–80.)

THE following Latin fragment has been recently discovered in the British Museum by the Rev. M. R. James, King's College, Cambridge, who is engaged in editing a volume of *Apocrypha Anecdota*. By his kindness I am permitted to add this interesting fragment to my Appendix. According to Mr. James, this fragment is found in an eighth century MS. belonging probably to the Monastery at Rochester. It is without a title. It follows a penitential edict of St. Boniface, while it is preceded by an anonymous tract 'De vindictis peccatorum.'

This MS. is a very imperfect representation of En. cvi. 1–18. It has suffered from additions, omissions, and corruptions, and is very seldom a literal rendering of the original for many words together. Notwithstanding, this fragment *contributes to the formation of a better text of CVI* in not a few instances, as will appear in the notes.

This MS. further *may point to a Latin translation*, or at least to a partially completed Latin translation of Enoch; for (1) occurring in the midst of original Latin treatises it appears to have been found in Latin by the collector and scribe of these treatises. (2) It has suffered much in the course of tradition and may, therefore, go back to a date when the book of Enoch was not reprobated generally, and when a Latin translation would have been acceptable. (3) It does not show signs of being an excerpt from a collection of excerpts, such as we find in the Greek fragment of En. lxxxix. 42–49 (see p. 237, notes); but, standing as it does without any introductory note or explanation, it looks more as if it were drawn directly from at least a larger Latin fragment of Enoch.

I have followed the spelling and punctuation of the MS. as furnished to me by Mr. James. The italics denote expanded contractions.

CVI. 1. Factum est autem [cum ess*et* Lamech annor*um* tricentorum quinquagenta] natus est ei filiu(s) 2. cui oculi sunt sicut radi solis capilli autem ei*us* candi(di)ores in septies niue corpori autem eius ⟨nemo hominum potest intueri⟩ 3. et surexit int*er* man*us* obstetricis suae et adorauit (et)

CVI. 1. The date here is a foolish addition of some copyist. It agrees neither with the Hebrew, Samaritan, nor LXX. chronology, which respectively give 182, 53, 188 years. 2. **Oculi sunt sicut radi solis.** This may safely be regarded as the true text. Cf. Eth. cvi. 10 and the words from the Petrine Apoc., quoted in the note to that verse, p. 303. The corresponding Eth. text. ድምድማሁ፡ ሠናይ (so G G^1 M)፡ አዕይንቲሁ is corrupt—possibly a corruption like ከመ፡ እንሬሁ፡ በፀሓይ፡ አዕይንቲሁ = *ὡς ἀκτῖνες ἡλίου οἱ ὀφθαλμοὶ αὐτοῦ*. Hence, for 'his long locks were white as wool, and his eyes beautiful,' read *were white as wool and his eyes were like the rays of the sun.* In septies or septies, as in ver. 19, is a corruption of capitis. Several words have been lost through hmt.: see ver. 10 (note). **Nemo . . . intueri** may be original = *οὐδεὶς τῶν ἀνθρώπων ἐδυνήθη ἀντιβλέψαι.* Cf. Apoc. Petri f. 19. After these words there is another lacuna. 3. **Et surexit.** For ወሶበ = et cum, read ወሶቤሃ = et tum with G G^1, and translate ተንሥአ not 'was taken,' but *arose* = surrexit. Hence, for 'when he was taken from the hand,' read *thereupon he arose in the hands.* Make the same change in ver. 11. Before et adorauit, Eth. in vv. 3, 11, adds aperuit os suum. Corresponding to adoravit here, there is oravit in ver. 11. For adoravit or oravit,

d*ominum* uiuentem in secula laudauit. 4, 5, 6. et timuit
Lamech ne n*on* ex eo natus e*ss*et nisi n*on*tius d*e*i et uenit ad
patrem suum Mathusalem et narrauit illi om*ni*a 7. dixit
Mathusalem ego autem non possum scire nisi eamus ad
patrem n*ost*r*u*m Enoc 8. q*uu*m autem uidit Enoc filium
suum Mathusalem uenientem ad se [et] ait. quid e*st* quod
uenisti ad me nate 10. dix*it* q*uo*d natus e*st* filio suo
[no*mine*] Lamech cui oculi sunt sicut radi solis capilli[s]
eius candidiores septies niue corpori aut*em* eius ⟨nemo
f. 80 hominum potest intueri⟩ 11. et surexit ‖ inter manus
obstetricis suae ⟨eadem hora qua p*ro*cidit de utero matris
suae⟩ orauit d*ominu*m uiuente*m* in secula ⟨et laudauit⟩

Eth. has ተናገረ = collocutus est. This is wrong, and probably a corruption of ተጋነየ = gratiam petiit, oravit or celebravit. For 'conversed with,' read *prayed to.* **Dominum uiuentem in saecula.** Eth. = Dominum justitiae. The same phrase recurs in ver. 11, where Eth. = Dominum coeli. **Laudauit.** Eth. omits here but gives in ver. 11 ባረከ = benedixit, laudavit. Hence it is probable that Latin is right in both verses and that we should read *prayed to and blessed* in ver. 3 for 'conversed with,' and in ver. 11 for 'blessed.' 4, 5, 6. Very fragmentary but nearly right in sense. **Nontius,** clearly a translation of ἄγγελος, more accurately rendered 'angel' by Eth. **Narrauit illi omnia** summarises vv. 5, 6. 7. For **Mathusalem,** read Mathusalah. **Nisi eamus.** Eth. gives a different sense. After **Enoc** two clauses are omitted. 8. Very fragmentary. See p. 302. **Quid est quod uenisti.** Eth. = quia venisti. Here Eth. is corrupt. The corruption is clear from Gk. which ran *ἰδοὺ ἐγὼ τέκνον μου διὰ τί ἦλθες;* Here Eth. translator read *διότι* instead of *διὰ τί.* Hence, for 'for thou hast come,' read *why hast thou come?* 10. **Capillis . . . corpori**: defective and corrupt. The confusion of order and loss of words seem to have originated in the Latin version. The latter supposes the following transposition: Capilli autem capitis candidiores lana candida, corporis autem ejus color candidior nive. The eye of the copyist straying from candidiores to candidior, he wrote nive instead of lana candida before corporis. After nive there stood originally et rubrior ulla rosa = *ἐρυθρότερος παντὸς ῥόδου.* So Eth. and Apoc. Petri. **Septies,** a corruption of capitis.

12. et timuit Lamech 13. et dixit Enoc | nontiatum *est* mihi ⟨fili⟩ q*uia* [post quingentos annos] 15. mitt*et* d*eus* cataclismu*m* aq*uae* ut deleat omnem creatura*m* [XL.] ostendit oculis no*str*is 16. et erunt illi ·III· filii [et erunt nomina filioru*m* ei*us* · Sem · Cham · Iafeth] 18. et ipse uocabitur Noe [q*ui* *in*t*er*pr*et*atur requies q*uia* requiem prestabit in archam].

---

13. **Nontiatum est mihi.** Eth. = nuntio tibi. 15. **Mittet deus cataclismum aquae.** Eth. = aqua cataclysmi erit. **ut deleat omnem creaturam.** Eth. = et exitium magnum per unum annum erit. **Ostendit oculis nostris.** Eth. = vidi in visione should be read before nontiatum in ver. 13. 18. **Et ipse uocabitur Noe.** Eth. = voca nomen ejus Noe. **Qui . . . requies . . . archam.** Quite an arbitrary departure from Enochic text, partly in dependence on that of the LXX.: i. e. requies recalls the *διαναπαύσει* of that version. Eth. = quia ipse erit vobis reliquiae. Reliquiae = *κατάλειμμα* and follows another meaning of the Hebrew word נוח. See note on cvi. 18, p. 304. Observe that in cvii. 3 the derivation of Noah implied Gen. v. 29 from נחם, is reproduced.

PASSAGES FROM THE SCRIPTURES AND OTHER ANCIENT BOOKS

REFERRED TO IN THIS WORK.

[When the chapter and verse of Enoch are given, the reference will be found in the corresponding critical or exegetical note.]

Jeremiah	Enoch
xix. 2, 6	xxvii. 1
xxi. 8	xciv. 2
xxii. 13	xciv. 7; xcix. 13
xxii. 19	xcviii. 13
xxiii. 1	lxxxix. 12
xxiii. 5, 6	xlvi. 3
xxxi. 5	x. 19
xxxi. 37	xciii. 14
xxxii. 35	xxvii. 1
xlix. 16	xcvi. 2

Lamentations	
ii. 4	xvii. 3
iii. 12	xvii. 3
iii. 13	xvii. 3
iii. 16	xlvi. 4

Ezekiel	
i. 10	xiv. 18
i. 15	lxi. 10
i. 26	xviii. 8
i. 28	xiv. 14
v. 5	xxvi. 1
x. 1	xiv. 18
xviii. 23, 32	xciv. 10
xxv. 12	lxxxix. 66
xxviii. 26	x. 19
xxxii. 17–32	lxiii. 10
xxxii. 21	lxiii. 10
xxxiii. 11	xciv. 10
xxxiv. 5, 8	lxxxix. 56
xxxiv. 26, 27	x. 19
xxxv. 5 sqq.	lxxxix. 66
xxxviii. 4-7	lvi. 5
xxxviii. 12	xxvi. 1
xxxviii. 21	lvi. 7; c. 2
xxxviii. 22	xviii. 11
xl–xlviii.	xc. 29
xlvii. 8	xxviii. 1

Daniel	Enoch.
ii. 31–45	lii.
iv. 13	i. 9
iv. 13, 17, 23	i. 5
v. 27	xli. 1
vii. 8, 11, 20	v. 4.
vii. 9	xiv. 18, 20; lxxi. 10.
vii. 10	i. 9; xiv. 19, 22; xl. 1; xlvii. 3; lxxi. 2; xc. 20
vii. 13	xlvi. 2
vii. 14	lxii. 6
viii. 10, 11, 13, 25	xlvi. 7
viii. 13	i. 9
viii. 17	lx. 4
viii. 17, 18	xiv. 14
x. 9, 10	lx. 4
x. 13, 20, 21	lvi. 5
x. 13, 21	xx. 5
x. 21	xlvii. 3
xi. 16, 41, 45	xxvi. 1; lxxxix. 40; xc. 20
xii. 1	xx. 5; xlvii. 3; lvi. 5
xii. 2	li. 1; lviii. 3
xii. 2, 3	cviii. 15
xii. 3	xliii. 3, 4; civ. 2
xii. 4, 9, 10	civ. 12
xii. 10	civ. 13.

Hosea	
ii. 18	lii. 8
ii. 22, 23	x. 19
ix. 14	xcviii. 5
xii. 7	xcix. 12

Joel	
ii. 10	lxxx. 4
iii. 2, 12	liii. 1
iii. 16	lvii. 2

Amos	Enoch
v. 24	xxxix. 5
viii. 9	lxxx. 4
ix. 13, 14	x. 19

Obadiah	
10–12	lxxxix. 66

Micah	
i. 3	i. 3
i. 3, 4	lii. 6
i. 4	i. 6
iii. 2, 3	xc. 4
iv. 6, 7	xc. 33
v. 2	xlix. 2

Habakkuk	
ii. 11	c. 10
iii. 9	xvii. 3

Zephaniah	
i. 18	lii. 7; c. 6
iii. 15–17	lxii. 14

Haggai	
i. 6, 7	lvii. 2
ii. 7–9	xc. 29
ii. 22	lvi. 7; c. 2.

Zechariah	
i. xii	ix. 10; xcix. 3
ii. 4	xc. 34
ii. 6–13	xc. 29
iii.	xl. 7
viii. 4	v. 9
ix. 10	lii. 8
x. 10	xc. 34
xii. 2, 3	lvi. 7
xiv. 5	i. 9
xiv. 8	ii. 2
xiv. 13	lvi. 7; c. 2

Malachi	
i. 7	lxxxix. 73
iii. 16	xlvii. 3
iv. 1	xlviii. 8

INDEX OF NAMES AND SUBJECTS.

THE END.

www.ingramcontent.com/pod-product-compliance
Lightning Source LLC
Chambersburg PA
CBHW031824090426
42741CB00005B/124